Cultural Dialogue & Misreading

Published by Wild Peony Pty Ltd ACN 002 714 276
PO Box 636 Broadway NSW 2007 Australia
Fax 61 2 9566 1052

International Distribution:
University of Hawaii Press, 2480 Kolowalu Street
Honolulu, Hawaii 96822, USA

Copyright © Wild Peony Pty Ltd & Contributors 1997

First Published 1997

All rights reserved. No part of this publication may be reproduced, stored in a retrieval system or transmitted in any form or by any means electronic, mechanical, photocopying, recording or otherwise, without the prior permission of the publisher.

ISBN 0 9586526 19

Printed in Australia by National Capital Printing, Canberra

CULTURAL DIALOGUE AND MISREADING

Editors
Mabel Lee & Meng Hua

UNIVERSITY OF SYDNEY WORLD LITERATURE SERIES NUMBER 1

wild peony

FOREWORD

More than two hundred academics from China and other parts of the world met in Beijing for the International Conference on Cultural Dialogue and Cultural Misreading, 9–11 October 1995. The Conference, jointly hosted by the Institute of Comparative Literature and Culture of Peking University and the Comparative Literature Association of China, brought together scholars who were united by their strong acknowledgment of the rich diversity of the literatures of the world and their commitment to the investigation of this diversity.

This volume of selected papers in English and French (to be followed by the publication of a more comprehensive volume in Chinese) conveys something of the broad scope of the Conference in terms of participation and content. The papers here include the work of scholars from China, Canada, France, Germany, The Netherlands, USA, Austria, Australia, Denmark, Switzerland, India, Japan, Brazil, Hungary, Greece, Romania and Portugal.

The issues addressed by the Conference have led to the arrangement of the papers into three sections, each offering thought-provoking insights and new perspectives. Part 1: 'Dialogue' explores the territories and limitations of cultural interchange, Part 2: 'Misreading' isolates specific texts for scrutiny to demonstrate how crossing cultural boundaries can often have fascinatingly creative aspects, and Part 3: 'Identity' examines how cultural identity is constructed in literature.

ML
June 1997

Contents

PART ONE: DIALOGUE

3   GERALD GILLESPIE
    The Significance and Limits of Cultural Relativism

11 PAUL CORNEA
    Le Défi Relativiste et la Compréhension de l'Autre

21 AMIYA DEV
    Cultural Relativism and Literary Value

27 MARIO J. VALDÉS
    Eurocentrism and Comparative Literary History

33 DOUWE FOKKEMA
    Western, Eastern and Multicultural Canons of Literature

44 ERSU DING
    The Tale of the Impossible: A Semiotic Critique of Cultural Relativism

49 YUE DAIYUN
    Cultural Relativism and the Principle of Harmony in Difference

55 HAN JIAMING
    Political Criticism in the Postmodern Era

63 GU ZHENGKUN
    Seven Laws Governing the Patterns of Development of Eastern and Western Cultures

67 QIAN ZHONGWEN
    Neo-Rationalism: A Tactic in Cultural Dialogue

70 Z. I. SIAFLEKIS
    Du Dialogue des Oeuvres Littéraires au Dialogue des Cultures

75 RAOUL DAVID FINDEISEN
    Two Aviators: Gabriele d'Annunzio and Xu Zhimo

86 MABEL LEE
    Discourse on Poetics: Paz's *Sunstone* and Yang Lian's *Yi*

100 QIN HAIYING
Réécriture du Mythe: Segalen et *Récit de la Source aux Fleurs de Pêchers*

113 BÉATRICE DIDIER
La Chine d'un Disciple de Voltaire: Senancour

122 WANG YU-GEN
Bi-xing and the Dynamic Interpretive Mode of Chinese Poetics

128 MIHÁLY SZEGEDY-MASZÁK
On the Uses and Limits of Multiculturalism

136 EDUARDO F. COUTINHO
The Effects of Cultural Dialogue on Latin America's World View

143 E. D. BLODGETT
Translation as Dialogue: The Example of Canada

PART TWO: MISREADING

153 JOHN BOENING
Comparative Literature, Incommensurability, and Cultural Misreading

163 WALTER F. VEIT
Misunderstanding as Condition of Intercultural Understanding

175 H. VAN GORP
Dialogism, Literary Genres and Intercultural (Mis)Understanding

183 SHEN DAN
Misreading and Translation

193 ZHANG YINDE
Transposition de l'Onomastique Littéraire

204 MURIEL DETRIE
L'Ecriture Chinoise en Occident: Un Mythe Productif

216 JEAN-MARC MOURA
Dialogue ou Malentendu Culturel? La Chine dans la Littérature Française des Années Cinquante à Soixante-dix: Quelques Aspects

227 JOHN NEUBAUER
Literary 'Misreadings': Brink and Coetzee

237 WANG YIMAN
Misreading at the Meeting of Two Hermeneutics: Ezra Pound's Invention of Chinese Poetry

246 TANAKA TAKAAKI
From Short to Long Forms of Narration: *Genji Monogatari* and Tang *Chuanqi* Tales

252 MANFRED SCHMELING
Kafka en France: La Productivité Littéraire du Malentendu

260 MARIA ALZIRA SEIXO
Malentendu Culturel et Poétique Narrative: Fernão Mendes Pinto et Gaspar da Cruz

267 JEAN BESSIÈRE
Malentendus Romanesques et Données Culturelles: Quelques Exemples Francophones

278 MARGARIDA L. LOSA
Literature and Desire

290 TAO JIE
The (Mis)Reading of Uncle Tom's Cabin

PART THREE: IDENTITY

299 ANTON KAES
Media and Nations: Global Communication and Cultural Identity

304 SVEND ERIK LARSEN
Interplay of Images

313 RIEN T. SEGERS
Cultural Identity: New Perspectives for Literary Study

330 THEO D'HAEN
Transcending Borders: Faulkner and Alternative Identities

338 MENG HUA
Quelques Réflexions sur la Temporalité du Stéréotype

344 HOLGER KLEIN
Laughing at Difference: Maurois, Macdonnell and Mikes on the English

357 SYLVIE ANDRÉ
La Littérature Exotique en France: Un Moment et une Forme du Dialogue des Cultures

367 STEVEN TÖTÖSY DE ZEPETNEK
The Importance of Cultural Dialogue: A Case Study of Ethnic Minority and Cultural Participation in Canada

377 THERESA HYUN
Translation and Cultural Identity: Geographical Images in Early Modern Korean Newspapers and Journals

384 MARÍA ELENA DE VALDÉS
Latin American Testimonial Literature as a Postcolonial Paradigm

390 TANIA FRANCO CARVALHAL
Latin America: Cultural Dialogue from the Periphery

396 WADE KELSON
Primo Levi and the Humaneness of Cultural Understanding

400 STEVEN P. SONDRUP
Hanyu at the Joy Luck Club

409 SONG WEIJIE
Local or Global: Cultural Identity in Multicultural Contexts

415 GUO HONGAN
Le Paradoxe de l'Homme de Lettres

419 CAO SHUNQING
Reconstructing Chinese Literary Discourse

PART ONE

Dialogue

GERALD GILLESPIE

The Significance and Limits of Cultural Relativism

European speculation on relativism can be traced as far back as Plato's comments on Protagoras's views in the *Theaetetus*. But it is legitimate to regard the newer surges of interest in relativism in fields such as epistemology, the sociology of knowledge, and so forth, at least in Occidental countries, as corollary to the process of growing cultural interpenetration and interferences in the age of European colonization and empire. In the late seventeenth century, thus about midway to our own postcolonial situation in terms of Western history, Leibniz predicted that the pattern of world development would bring about an intensifying tendency toward cross-fertilization of cultures and a gradual approximation in vocabulary and structure among major languages. Quantum expansions of the active knowledge-base of humanity available for a global collective, and cultural convergence through the sharing of knowledge, seemed compatible propositions to this great philosopher. Though the underpinning oral literature of prehistory shines through the palimpsestial record, there are only about five millennia of writing accumulated to date. If Leibniz is right in broad terms, we may be at the reaping end of a process whereby the enormous cultural diversity resultant from this rich past will now flow increasingly not only in local channels but into the common global basin. This is the shore on which, for good or ill, through no particular merit of our own except the accident of our time of birth, we all sit as entitled riparians.

The knitting together of peoples in the postcolonial world — a phenomenon which at first was largely trade-driven but is now ever more communications-driven — compels literary theoreticians and critics, as well as social scientists, to face the significance of cultural relativism. In the Renaissance, humanists actively sought to reappropriate the ancient Graeco-Roman and Near Eastern cultural legacies. They could not do so except at the price of forcing a rethinking of Western values — a rethinking that is still vigorously underway and that has acquired further powerful tools through the flourishing of modern science. By the time of the Enlightenment and Romanticism, our specifically European intellectual forebears began proposing ways to appreciate and reappropriate the striking variety of half-submerged, even repressed, European cultural matter (such as folk poetry, forms of religiosity, actual ethnic variety), as well as to appropriate the great cultural wealth of non-European expression. Savants from home bases outside the Euro-American sphere, many of them initially attracted to our field as experts in European studies, began to participate reciprocally in the internationalization of comparative literature. Conjointly, scholars from relatively older nations, from brash new immigrant nations, from emergent nations, from territories being contested culturally, and from territories where nationhood is not a dominant concern helped bring about a post-war awareness of the tasks set for comparatism. Many of today's internationalized breed of comparative literature theoreticians, themselves spread around the world, are suggesting that our field must outgrow its foundational European habits in organizing the study of materials which pertain to the pre-convergence past of the host of literatures which are rooted in their own distinct conditions. One predictable consequence of doing so will be to promote yet another huge reconsideration of Western cultural assumptions, but just as inevitably scholars from non-European environments will be drawn to re-examining the assumptions of their home cultures.

I am not alluding merely to the truism of cultural imperialism, nor to specific hopes of getting beyond more recent or current instances of cultural imperialism. Almost everything that constitutes highly profiled cultural differences is a result of some kind of imperialism. For example, overlapping the period of European overseas expansion, there was the establishment of Mogul dominion in north central India which deeply affected the region's remarkable diversity down to the present, or the Ottoman conquest of the core territories of old Byzantium, and so forth. A cursory review of just two and a half millennia in the history of Britain illustrates this same reality. The indigenous neolithic peoples of the island were overridden by several waves of invading Celts who imposed new languages and customs prior to the adoption of Christianity. Along came the Romans, who remained several centuries into the period of early Christianity, as far north as Hadrian's Wall. Then the Anglo-Saxons and, in due course, also the Norse arrived, extensively dislodging the partly Romanized Celtic culture. The next intruders, whom the meanwhile Christianized Celto-Romano-Anglo-Saxon British faced, were the Norman French whose presence eventually bent the dominant folk idiom into what today we call English. And of course, over further centuries, immigrants within and to the British Isles have spiced the genetic and cultural mix. Because the Scotti had invaded the north of Britain from Ireland in the fifth century AD and the Anglo-Saxons had expanded from the south, the memory of Brythonic greatness receded into Wales, which the Norman-English state eventually absorbed politically, so that today it almost seems counter-intuitive to recall that the greatest medieval Welsh bard, Taliesen, practised amidst Welsh-speaking admirers near Edinburgh and his poems were recited across much of northern England. During the high Middle Ages, the Norman-English paid the Irish back for their intrusion into Scotland by invading Ireland, beginning centuries of British cultural oppression of and symbiosis with the Irish.

In the grander saga of the British Empire, starting in the Elizabethan age, this hybrid people eventually went forth to leave deep marks on vast territories around the globe, such as North America and India, and a cultural contribution that has outlasted the collapse of their world empire. Permit me then to move on from the observation that, unless we personally belong to some small isolated desert or jungle tribe that from time immemorial has never waged war, all of our home cultures can be analysed as some amalgam resultant from earlier or even more recent imperialist moments. The pertinent point here is that, when competent European savants — who were situated historically in newer imperialist waves since the Renaissance — encountered such a dramatic variety of cultural forms around the earth, they could not avoid facing the question of cultural relativism. In its turn, modern comparative literature, moving beyond its already difficult nineteenth-century task of sorting out the cultural tangle of Europe, has arrived at a number of late-twentieth-century approaches for facing the vaster challenge of discriminating the rules and values of a multitude of literary systems of varying size and character.

In effect, the leading general systems theories which have been elaborated in the older home territories of comparative literature in recent decades, such as those by Yuri Lotman, Siegfried Schmidt, and Itamar Even-Zohar, provide ways to address cultural relativism. They do so principally by considering cultures not as closed entities but as metamorphosing, somewhat porous semiotic systems whose repertorial configuration is subject both to internal shiftings and to external interferences. Literature and literary life form one of the master-codings and main channels that may be studied either as a sub-universe with its own repertorial characteristics and dynamics, or in relation to the other codings with which literature relates. This state of awareness is already reflected in Henry Remak's now classic definition of the scope of comparative literature in his essay of 1961. While the degree of familiarity with the particulars of the literary worlds which the individual scholar engages naturally delimits and has an enormous bearing on the efficacy of his or her efforts, the advantage of general systems thinking is that it does not first require that a particular literature or set of literatures serves the individual scholar as the exclusive source of standards on which to base his or her own or to perceive others' truth-claims. Rather it allows the researcher to situate literary works in relation to the significant movements of elements in the repertory of any literature, including phenomena that exhibit intersystemic interferences, such as translation. Each literature offers internal traditions of hermeneutic guidance, and a general systems approach recognizes these hermeneutic principles as cultural facts of content and behaviour in the specific historical flows.

Among obvious examples of the practical consequences for dealing with cultural relativism is the following. A general systems approach could enable a more meticulous formal analysis of the repercussions in literary expression after the introduction of a Western doctrine such as Marxism in China, and cast light on interactions with the Confucian and other important indigenous traditions. Or one could study the European reception of Arabic, Persian, and Indic poetry since the late eighteenth century, distinguish culture-specific differences among the British, French, German, and other poets attracted to these foreign realms, and also common tendencies.

Informative juxtapositions of phenomena in which cultural interferences play a prominent part can be realized without the necessity of presuming the superiority of either the native or the initially foreign repertorial elements as a basis for formulating truth-claims. It seems important to me that, on the international plane, comparatism today can regard ideational contents, even and especially the most fervently held convictions, as repertorial facts. This is a constructive way to advance useful scholarly dialogues on specific topics among the inheritors of such a wildly variegated polylogue as we are caught in under the real conditions of today.

In his 1989 book *Ignorance and Uncertainty: Emerging Paradigms*, Michael Smithson ponders relativism as it has permeated Western philosophy and science of recent decades. He is one of a host of cultural historians who take note of the failure of deterministic models since the Second World War to cope with the overload of disclosed diversity or with the increasing complexity and uncertainty of the artificial common environment which technology and information science have spread over and injected into all older cultural realms. These years since 1945 are precisely the decades of the flourishing of comparative literature, the decades which have brought it into its own crisis of relativism, that is, have brought comparative literature up against its own success as a field attuned to these world developments. It is all well and good to indulge in the paranoiac exercises of so many Western critics who, invoking a classic fallacy, proclaim comparative literature's guilt by association with its own subject-matter. It would be invidious to cite names here. I am sure each of us can instantly think of specific American and European critics who indict comparative literature as a reflection and accomplice of a mindless or diabolically clever cultural imperialism, a global empire which they believe is ever more visible in millions of smaller and larger cultural events and data, for example, in phenomena that exhibit the hybridizations, massive convergences, and the like transformations at work. It is their perfect right to propound such notions, and who of us does not share something of their fear and loathing in the face of many rapid changes which seem to threaten our favourite cultural pleasures and environments? But there are constructive alternatives to such sloganeering. Within the International Comparative Literature Association, this stage of stock-taking is reflected in the desire of influential members to recognize the historical challenge and to transcend any earlier Eurocentric limits of the field by establishing rigorous collaborative programs in intercultural studies of African, Asian, and Pacific literary life. The ICLA Executive Council has voted to create a body of experts to promote exactly such a program.

It is hardly suprising that one of the staunchest advocates of this commitment, former ICLA President Earl Miner, is also one of the theoreticians who have proposed a constructive approach to cultural relativism on the grand scale. I have treated his work entitled *Comparative Poetics: An Intercultural Essay on Theories of Literature* elsewhere but its special pertinence for my topic justifies revisiting its crucial premises in outline. I shall leave it to others to judge case by case the aptness of specific details Miner adduces in illustration from European, East Asian, and South Asian literatures. I shall concern myself here only with the goal he reaches under his final chapter heading, 'Relativism'. This is the main finding that several of the world's greatest literary systems, which are deeply rooted in millennia of practice, do not share the same basic assumptions about literary values. The actual evolutionary pathways these systems have traced have reinforced quite distinct patterns of expectations about genre and promoted striking differences in the cultural habits of response. In some instances, poetic categories important in one system are relegated to a lesser or negligible place in another. Certain categories simply are missing in another system. Each system has also nurtured a correspondingly distinct tradition of poetics and literary history, prior to the diffusion of the newest common habits as brought about by the global convergences I have noted. Therefore, Miner concludes, comparative literature can no longer proceed on the assumption that the ingrained Western habits in analysing language and literature since Aristotle down to Derrida have any efficacious universality. We need to be cautious about the categories spawned by these Western habits and should not presume they are relevant to the living experience of other systems until we have meticulously tested them alongside and against non-European system-specific categories. This means we must expand the critical horizons of comparative literature to incorporate the poetics of non-European civilizations and cultures. By extrapolation, we can predict that experts who follow Miner's principle will also eventually be in a sounder position to elaborate more appropriate categories for analysing those non-European literatures that do not yet boast a long and rich history of repertorial events, and hitherto neglected literatures in languages of minor diffusion. That is, even the newest literatures now emergent should and need not be left out of the picture.

My next remarks may themselves risk appearing to be paradoxical, although I regard them as straightforward. I agree broadly with those who, like Joseph Margolis in his book *The Truth about Relativism*, are dissatisfied with recent theoreticians such as Jean-François Lyotard — theoreticians who express sweeping incredulity toward Western meta-narratives and lump the pursuit of science among such meta-narratives. Such theoreticians, argues Margolis, arrive at an incoherent stand when they presume, on the one hand, 'that we *can dispense with the pursuit of truth*' and yet, on the other hand, seem to suppose that what they themselves say, by way of their theories, 'is true regarding science, knowledge, and philosophy' (1991:196). I shall leave aside here the variety of arguments to cross-purposes by a large contingent sometimes designated as 'deep relativists' (one could start with such names as Michel Foucault and Richard Rorty) and shall foreshorten to my main point, which I deduce from Miner who is silent in this regard in his book. I am not aiming to convince you of the merits of specific arguments against the validity of a relativistic picture of the world in the stricter philosophical sense, such as W. Newton-Smith's demolition of relativist positions on truth-claims in his 1982 paper 'Relativism and the Possibility of Interpretation' and John Ellis's chapter on epistemology and logic in the 1993 book *Language, Thought, and Logic*. What I wish to underscore is that the debate about relativism, as I have touched on it thus far, has become an important strand in the larger repertory of the Western literary system. Therefore we should treat it with due caution, and not rush as interpreters to impose aspects of a Western relativism on the literary productivity of non-Euro-American cultures as if Western relativism possessed a certified universality of relevance or interpretative power. Of course, there are other relativist traditions outside the European varieties, and although I have no competence to describe their attributes they would enjoy the same status as varieties of Western relativism by being repertorial elements in their own contexts.

The accruing evidence of recent decades seems to indicate that the most famous recent relativist doctrines percolating in literary studies have had only a limited heuristic value even when applied to Western writing — they have indeed added a new coloration to criticism and stimulated interesting inquiries, but they have produced a relative paucity of satisfying readings by those who trumpet their alleged virtues. Even more egregious, as John Clark has analysed, has been the failure of a critic such as Edward Said in the books *Orientalism* (1978) and *Culture and Imperialism* (1993), who because of his basic refusal of veridic discourse cannot deal with the evidentiary materials on a level of scholarly expertise such as one expects in competent comparisons of cultures. In addition, no matter how hard some cultural relativists may attempt to assert the primacy of culture-determined variations over the fundamental genetic unity in the brain structure of the human race, they cannot by a mere critical fiat do away with this underlying biological fact. Therefore, until such fields as cognitive psychology thoroughly test out by a comparative methodology the kinds of literary creativity, repertory building and reception which are found in a great variety of cultures, and discover that there is no reliable way to discern the array of perceptual and epistemological processes by which people make and use literature in the several different local contexts, we cannot blithely pin

Euro-American relativist tails onto everybody's donkey. As Steven D. Edwards has suggested in his book *Relativism, Conceptual Schemes, and Categorical Frameworks* (1990), the act of meticulously defining variety seems to rely inherently on an assumption that a search for relevant facts is meaningful; thus 'gaining the plurality of frameworks for the success of relativism is incompatible with what seems a necessary component of any relativist thesis — i.e. relativism of truth' (118).

In brief, discovering the actual variety of the human species reinforces rather than negates the significance of the drive which is summed up in such phrases as the search for truth. The global legacy of science is in no wise rescinded because of cultural differences. To cite an example that is now a commonplace: we can state with confidence that the laws of gravity are not suspended for me and some of my colleagues because they are not Italian like Galileo or English like Newton. Therefore, I would argue that to date no theoretician has convincingly shown that the facts of divergent cultural visions and habits mean that the human species is splitting up into a genus, into several species with markedly different brain functions. Rather, our ability to perceive these facts of diversity indicates that we can devise useful descriptive frameworks in support of constructive discourse.

I hope that in trying to sketch some broad parameters for the manifold topic 'relativism' my remarks have not been so drily general as to suggest that what lurks behind my cautions is some new universalism, that all we need to do is to reject defeatist relativisms and we can then marshall cultural data from anywhere in a triumphal comparatism. Quite to the contrary: my purpose has been to suggest that what we should learn from the observation of the details of actual cultural relativism in real-world conditions is the need for better common descriptive and analytical tools at the international level, respect for the actual variety of cultural life, and the imperative to seek for understanding of each culture's authentic hallmarks. Every act of cultural understanding is in some respect a transgression of limits. No discipline is more reciprocally hermetic for its diverse participants than boundary-crossing comparatism.

Stanford Univeristy

Works Cited

Clark, John 1995 'On Two Books by Edward W. Said' in *Bicitra Seni* (Pinang), no. 2.

Edwards, Steven D. 1990 *Relativism, Conceptual Schemes, and Categorical Frameworks.* Avebury, Aldershot.

Ellis, John M. 1993 *Language, Thought, and Logic.* Northwestern University Press, Evanston, Illinois.

Margolis, Joseph 1991 *The Truth about Relativism.* Basil Blackwell, Oxford.

Miner, Earl 1990 *Comparative Poetics: An Intercultural Essay on Theories of Literature.* Princeton University Press.

Newton-Smith, W. 1982 'Relativism and the Possibility of Interpretation' in *Rationality and Relativism*, Martin Hollis and Steven Lukes (eds). MIT Press: pp. 106–22.

Smithson, Michael 1989 *Ignorance and Uncertainty: Emerging Paradigms.* Springer-Verlag, New York.

PAUL CORNEA

Le Défi Relativiste et la Compréhension de l'Autre

Un des principaux aspects de l'évolution du comparatisme des dernières décennies l'a constitué sans doute son débarrassement progressif des ingrédients 'eurocentriques' et son alignement aux standards d'un universalisme effectif et authentique. Le changement de la science comparatiste a concerné en même temps l''objet' (au début rétréci à l'Europe, ensuite étendu au globe entier), la 'méthode' (le dépassement des rapports binaires, exclusivement factuels à la faveur des approches typologiques, sémiotiques, d'anthropologie culturelle) et la 'vision' (rejet du paternalisme et de l'annexionisme non avoué, acheminement vers dialogue à part entière). Cet important développement a été rendu possible et renforcé par la dynamique même de l'histoire récente. Un événement majeur — *le démantèlement du système colonial* — favorisant l'accès de nombreuses nations à l'indépendance, toutes déployant un grand effort de définition identitaire, a ouvert un immense champ potentiel d'études. D'autre part, un processus qui perdure encore — l'*accélération sans précédent de l'interdépendance économique, technologique, communicationelle* — a multiplié et perfectionné les moyens de transmettre les connaissances, de faire du commerce, de relier dans un seul circuit informatif les coins du monde les plus reculés, ainsi que pour la première fois le concept de *Weltliteratur* dont Goethe avait parlé en 1827 est devenu plausible.

Hors ces facteurs de nature contextuelle, la rénovation et la restructuration du comparatisme, conformément aux exigences d'une modernité toujours plus provocatrice et radicale, a été mise en oeuvre à l'appui d'un courant de pensée que j'appellerais avec une dénomination pas encore suffisamment homologuée, le relativisme culturel. Qu'est-ce que cela signifie c'est D. Fokkema qui nous le dit dans un article perspicace et suggestif, paru en 1984: 'Le relativisme culturel n'est pas une méthode de recherche, encore moins une théorie, il est plutôt une attitude morale' qui influence l'homme de science dans le choix de ses approches et le positionnement de ses points de vue (1984:239). Cette attitude de tolérance envers l'Autre et de prise en compte de ses justifications (même si elles nous contrarient au premier abord) a été largement diffusée par les études anthropologiques et a représenté un grand pas en avant par rapport à l'idée ancienne de la supériorité de la civilisation européenne. Les chercheurs des sociétés primitives sont arrivés au bout de leurs patientes études à une conclusion formulée ainsi par Lévi-Strauss: 'Il faudra admettre que dans la gamme des possibilités ouvertes aux sociétés humaines, chacune a fait un certain choix, et que ces choix sont incomparables entre eux: ils se valent' (1965:346). Ou, en d'autres mots: 'un mode de vie a sa cohérence propre: il n'y pas lieu de le justifier, de le critiquer ou de le réfuter. On peut choisir vivre de cette façon ou différemment; mais en tout cas ce n'est pas le genre de choses qui peut être dit vrai ou faux, juste ou incorrect, authentique ou illusoire' (L. Quéré 1990:110). A mentionner que le relativisme culturel a promu non seulement un esprit de compréhension et d'ouverture face aux sociétés fondées sur d'autres modèles de civilisation, mais aussi une interrogation des européens à l'égard de leur propre légitimité. C'est surtout cette autocritique qui a mené à l'érosion continuelle de leur arrogance de légiférer intellectuellement pour la planète entière.

Tout examen actuel de l'état des choses dans le mouvement comparatiste confirme qu'un long chemin a été parcouru depuis le fameux rapport de Wellek (1958:149–59) qui déplorait 'la motivation fondamentalement patriotique', le refus de dépasser l'étude purement factuelle et l'irreductibilité historiciste du comparatisme néopositiviste (Van Tieghem, J. M. Carré, M. F. Guyard), jusqu'aux appels insistants d'Etiemble 'en faveur d'un humanisme sans frontières' (1988:17).[1] Aujourd'hui, les chercheurs se rencontrent non seulement à Budapest, Munich, Paris, Venise, mais aussi à New York, Montréal, Sao Paolo, Tokyo, Edmonton, Beijing, et les programmes des Congrès s'ouvrent largement vers tous les points cardinaux, sans aucun exclusif, dans une gamme pluraliste de méthodes et approches. Apparemment, le comparatisme est en train de se mondialiser, tandis que l'eurocentrisme est en perte de vitesse, manque de confiance et de consistance; ce n'est plus une alternative défendue.

Une brève citation, extraite d'un article de D. H. Pageaux, me semble clairement illustrer l'effort de surmonter les vieux préjugés et de regarder sans complexes les rapports d'échanges interculturels dans lesquels l'étranger n'est ni un substitut du Soi-même (en pire), ni un toléré, mais purement et simplement un Autre. Pageaux distingue entre 'manie', 'phobie' et 'philie', c'est-à-dire, entre surévaluation de la culture étrangère (menant au snobisme, au pastiche ou au mimétisme vulgaire), xénophobie (haine non-différenciée pour tout ce qui est étranger) et relation dialogique d'égal à égal avec les autres:

> A l'acculturation brutale qui suppose la manie ..., à la mort symbolique de l'Autre qui suppose la phobie ..., la philie tente d'imposer la voie difficile, exigeante qui passe par la reconnaissance de l'Autre; l'Autre vivant aux côtés du Je, ni supérieur,

ni inférieur, ni même différent. ... l'Autre reconnu comme Autre, simplement. (1989:152-3)

Mais si le relativisme culturel en tant qu'attitude interrogative et critique vis-à-vis des fondamentalismes déclarés ou travestis (et l'eurocentrisme se range parmi ces derniers) ouvre de larges perspectives au comparatisme et stimule l'inventivité, sa transformation dans un système rigide, en d'autres mots, son 'institutionnalisation', contient de vrais dangers potentiels. Devenant 'théorie' qui, suivant Jean Lacoste, 'considère que la vérité, les valeurs esthétiques et morales varient selon les individus et les cultures' (1988:200), le relativisme radicalisé jette un défi à toutes les formes d'universalisme — même à la science dans la mesure où la quête de la vérité représente l'essence de sa démarche — mais surtout à l'art et à la morale renvoyés aux limbes de l'arbitraire et du subjectivisme. Pis encore. Poussé à la limite par l'importance attribué au particulier et au local, il se joint souvent au nationalisme. Cette alliance à laquelle nous assistons aujourd'hui dans les anciens pays communistes et au tiers monde est notamment redoutable (et, en même temps, paradoxale, car elle se déploie dans une époque de globalisation de l'économie, de la technologie, des communications, de l'écologie, du style de vie, dans un temps de frontières perméables et diminution présomptive de l'autorité étatique).

Quelques postulats relativistes mis au service du nationalisme sont facilement repérables: la toute puissance contextuelle (qui suppose la modélisation et le conditionnement des individus par les valeurs communautaires: langue, tradition, culture), la méfiance envers l'universalisme (aboutissant à l'exagération du spécifique, à l'isolationisme et à des manifestations de supériorité face aux Autres), l'affirmation du caractère construit et rhétorique de n'importe quelle réalité phénoménale, linguistique ou psychologique (d'où l'effacement de la démarcation entre évidence et opinion, certitude et hypothèse, réalité et fiction).

J'ajoute que ce qui fait problème dans le phénomène nationaliste est son ambiguïté. Au départ il y a un sentiment naturel et bénéfique, le patriotisme, l'amour pour l'endroit où nous sommes nés et où nous vivons, pour les gens qui s'apparentent à nous en langue, coutumes, culture, célébration des même valeurs symboliques. Cependant, à cause de différentes raisons (peur, frustration, rivalité économique, sensibilité blessée, inconfort de l'état adulte etc.) il semble qu'à partir d'un certain moment l'amour pour ses prochains se réfléchisse dans un miroir distorsionné qui change le sourire et la chaleur humaine dans un rictus de haine envers l'étranger et un désir irrationnel de l'abaisser ou de l'anéantir. Ainsi que nous l'avons constaté plus d'une fois, hélas, là où le nationalisme devient politique d'état, il est utilisé en tant que diversion de grande ampleur pour transférer sur l'Autre la responsabilité de la misère économique et du retardement socioculturel. Ethnies habitant le même territoire mais envenimées par le discours nationaliste, autant rhétorique que redevable à certains mythes anciens enfouis au plus profond de la conscience collective, arrivent à se heurter et à s'entre-tuer. Et cela malgré de nombreuses déclarations naïves, annonçant d'ailleurs non sans arguments du point de vue théorique, que la nation est un concept périmé...

Au niveau comparatiste proprement dit, le repli sur sa propre communauté, l'isolation, l'accentuation sans mesure de ce qui est spécifique mettent en question non seulement la chance mais aussi la possibilité même de l'inter-compréhension. Les interrogations s'amoncellent sans fin. Est-il traductible mon idiome dans un autre? Est-ce que les étrangers peuvent nous comprendre du moment que notre manière d'envisager l'univers et de nous le représenter en mots est si caractéristique et distincte? Ne vaut-il pas mieux 'rester chez soi et ignorer les autres que de les connaître trop bien?' (Todorov 1988:92), de refouler les étrangers hors de nos frontières, pour éviter qu'ils nous submergent et nous privent de notre identité culturelle? Faut-il accepter le 'canon' des chefs-d'oeuvre, tel qu'il nous est proposé par les Encyclopédies actuelles et les 'curricula' scolaires, dès lors qu'il ne représente qu'une sélection ouest-européenne et nord-américaine, négligeant les auteurs appartenant aux nations marginalisées et aux minorités? Le fait que le jugement de valeur est subjectif par nature et non-vérifiable par démonstration ne justifie-t-il n'importe qui à dire n'importe quoi?

Ces quelques exemples suffisent à avertir sur les dangers du relativisme extrémiste. Aussi nous font-ils voir combien pressante est le besoin de réagir. Et d'autant plus — je me permets de le rappeler — qu'aujourd'hui, dans les milieux intellectuels libéraux de l'Occident, règne une atmosphère de laxisme moral (il est interdit d'interdire) et une frivole permissivité post-moderne (chaque idée vaut autant qu'une autre). Au baccalauréat français de cette année on a mis la question: 'Peut-on justifier n'importe quoi?' Un enseignant consterné a rapporté dans le *Nouvel Observateur* que neuf candidats sur dix ont essayé d'argumenter que 'tout peut et doit être compris', qu'en admettant la valeur absolue de toute opinion, il faut conclure qu'en dernière instance toutes les opinions deviennent défendables, y compris le génocide ordonné par Hitler, mesure 'correcte de son point de vue'.

Comment corriger les excès du relativisme? C'est un problème complexe et difficile qui dépasse de beaucoup les limites imparties à une communication. Je vais me résumer ici à quelques suggestions et discuter brièvement un seul point qui pourtant intéresse de près le comparatisme: est-ce qu'il est effectivement possible de nous comprendre les uns les autres? Peut-on faire compatibles nos diversités par l'entremise de la traduction?

Je veux préciser tout d'abord qu'il n'est pas question de mettre en doute l'importance de la stratégie de la relativisation — composant fondamental, à mon avis, de la pensée critique. Les interrogations naissent dès qu'on souhaite 'institutionnaliser' cette stratégie. Comme je l'ai déjà remarqué, c'est ce qui va aboutir à un système mécanique, aveugle, qui efface les nuances et abolit les intermédiaires. Or, la positivité du relativisme, s'il y en a, se dissipe quand on raisonne en termes manichéistes, on se prend trop au sérieux et, surtout, on évite de se relativiser soi-même, c'est-à-dire, de négocier, sur certains aspects concrets et circonscrits, avec l'universel.

Parfois, il n'est pas inutile de répéter des banalités. Nous sommes, certes, enracinés dans une histoire, une langue, une culture, mais avant et au-dessus de tout particularisme nous disposons d'une structure commune (biologique, somatique, mentale) qui n'a presque pas varié depuis des millénaires. Chez toutes les sociétés humaines connues, sans distinction de niveau d'évolution, on a identifié des prédispositions vers la connaissance, l'amusement, la croyance, la création artistique, et on s'est trouvé en présence d'une langue dans laquelle les individus ordonnent leurs impressions, classifient le monde et se partagent idées et sentiments. Il y a donc non seulement une base de différenciation mais aussi une autre, plus profonde, renvoyant à l'unité de l'humain. C'est notamment celle-ci qui nous permet, au-delà des frontières qui séparent antiquité, moyen âge et modernité, nations et continents, de nous retrouver dans une communauté semblable de mythes fondateurs et de chefs-d'oeuvre de l'art. On lit des récits ou des poèmes qui nous viennent de loin, de trés loin, intermédiés quelquefois par une double traduction et nous découvrons, à notre étonnement, un horizon thématique qui nous est proche (amour, vengeance, lutte pour le pouvoir, bienfaits et méfaits de la possession, conflit entre individu et société, quête de Dieu) exprimés dans une forme qui continue à résonner dans notre sensibilité. La possibilité (idéale) de l'intercompréhension se fonde sur cette dialectique entre la 'nature humaine' et ses incarnations historiques, entre la projection du général sur le particulier et du particulier sur le général. 'Ce qui est universel', écrit Tzvetan Todorov, 'c'est notre appartenance à la même espèce. C'est peu, mais cela suffit pour fonder nos jugements' (1988:428). Je suis du même avis.

A ces intuitions et à ces expériences on oppose parfois l'analyse déconstructiviste, avec son fameux rejet de la 'métaphysique de la présence' (c'est-à-dire, de l'existence supposée d'un 'signifié transcendental' qui puisse centrer le système linguistique et qui garantisse la détermination du sens). Car si tout est évasif, fallacieux et aléatoire, alors la non-compréhension semble représenter notre destin. Or, voir dans Derrida un protagoniste du 'nihilisme vulgaire', un subtile sophiste qui met la rhétorique au-dessus de la raison, c'est simplifier d'une façon inacceptable une pensée riche, parfois d'une radicalité qui coupe le souffle, mais en dépit de certains détours spéciaux, profondément ancrée dans une grande rigueur argumentative.[2] Récemment, dans une interview accordée à Gerald Graff, Derrida a protesté d'une façon très nette contre l'accusation que son oeuvre aurait encouragé le 'jeu libre' de l'interprétation, qu'il aurait cautionner 'le relativisme et l'anarchie':

> Je n'ai jamais mis radicalement en question des concepts comme la vérité, la référence et la stabilité des contextes interprétatifs, si mettre radicalement en question veut dire contester qu'*il y ait* et *qu'il doive y avoir* de la vérité, de la référence

et des contextes d'interprétation stables. J'ai, ce qui est tout autre chose, posé des questions que j'espère nécessaires au sujet de la possibilité de ces choses, de ces valeurs, de ces normes, de cette stabilité (par essence toujours provisoire et finie). (1990:278)

Il ne reste pas moins vrai que la version derridéenne de la communication s'abrite derrière une 'binarité rigide' qui admet seulement deux paradigmes: ou la réussite exemplaire ou l'échec, l'absolue présence du soi (Dieu, conscience transhistorique), ou le 'jeu libre', indécidable, des significations. John Searle, M. H. Abrams et d'autres encore ont critiqué cette 'dramatisation excessive'. En effet, pourquoi devrait-on réclamer une sorte de 'pureté idéale' de la communication et on jugerait en termes de 'tout ou rien'? Répondant à ces objections Derrida a rappelé qu'un antagonisme du type 'tout ou rien' est impliqué dans n'importe quelle opposition de concepts: 'Quiconque veut parler rigoureusement d'une structure intentionnelle doit prendre en compte le telos de plénitude qui le constitue' (219). Théoriquement, il a raison. Cependant, dans le monde de tous les jours, les concepts servent de repères génériques (*idéal typus*) par rapport auxquels nous pensons les occurrences datées et localisées, les seules que nous rencontrons et auxquelles nous nous heurtons. Sur le terrain de l'empirique, rien n'est 'pur', tout est mélangé, les énoncés et les phénomènes se situent entre 'plus' et 'moins'. La plénitude demeure idéale et inaccessible dans l'intuition immédiate ou comme expérience d'un contenu concret. L'imperfection est inhérente au langage car le signe reste arbitraire (bien que la convention qui relie le 'nom' à la 'chose' soit obligatoire à l'intérieur de chaque communauté linguistique), les contextes varient sans fin et les codes se répartissent et se différencient en fonction des buts poursuivis. Puisqu'une 'garantie transcendentale' du sens nous fait défaut, nous devons nous contenter d'une garantie 'consensuelle', ce qui, en clair, signifie le renoncement au principe de 'tout ou rien'. Nous habitons l'intermédiaire et nous nous débrouillons par 'approximations' plus ou moins ciblées, et par des tentatives répétées de mieux indexer les concepts sur l'infinie variété des 'cas' possibles. Faut-il pleurer sur notre sort et croiser les bras? Faut-il accepter la présence irrévocable des 'malentendus' ou s'essayer à les mettre autant que possible hors d'état de nuire?

Une fois de plus il semble que le bon sens soit du côté de Voltaire: 'Casserez-vous cette jolie statue parce que tout n'y est pas d'or et diamants?' Ajoutons aussi un témoignage contemporain. Sommes-nous réduits, se demandait un jour Leszek Kolakowski, à la suite de Husserl, au dilemme de choisir entre 'un relativisme décourageant et ruineux pour la culture et un dogmatisme transcendental, injustifié, car se fondant sur une décision arbitraire?' Son point de vue: 'Malgré l'impossibilité d'arriver, dans un contexte rationaliste, à une certitude finale, notre culture deviendrait pauvre et misérable sans ceux qui peinent pour atteindre ce but inaccessible et survivrait péniblement si elle était abandonnée aux mains des sceptiques' (1987:85).

Tournons-nous maintenant vers l'acte d'entendement proprement dit qui suppose, au minimum, dans sa forme prototypique, la relation conversative entre deux personnes, le 'dialogue'. Deux philosophes contemporains, H. G. Gadamer et Jürgen Habermas, adversaires en beaucoup de points, se retrouvent toutefois d'accord, chacun à sa manière, pour en souligner l'importance et fixer le statut de cette ancienne forme d'humaniser l'humain et de rechercher la vérité qui, depuis Socrate, ne cesse pas d'inciter les esprits.

Gadamer situe à l'origine de l'entendement une certaine 'entente', dérivée du concept heideggerien de 'l'appartenance à l'être'. Habermas traite cette 'entente' comme une idée régulatrice puisqu'il conteste la convergence des traditions entre locuteurs et dénonce la présence déformatrice de l'idéologie dans le langage de tout un chacun.

Pourtant, dans la description du processus d'inter-compréhension et des conditions requises pour y arriver, les rapprochements des deux auteurs sont parfois frappants. Selon Gadamer (1975:363–6), un 'vrai' dialogue doit déboucher dans ce qu'il appelle une 'fusion d'horizons': chaque interlocuteur va s'efforcer d'avancer vers l'Autre, ainsi qu'en route advienne pas à pas un processus d'intégration des perspectives, une approche plus ample du thème en discussion. L'accord auquel on peut parvenir, mais à la condition expresse de la bonne foi, de l'attention vigilante et de la patience de deux côtés, ne constitue habituellement ni la synthèse critique des points de vue exprimés, ni un consensus de fond, mais une représentation plus claire, plus nuancée, plus précise de la position des deux partenaires.

Habermas dégage de la structure universelle de validité du langage un concept de rationalité, qui n'est pas dépendant d'une culture déterminée (car si la vérité est différente, le 'besoin' de la vérité appartient à tous). Ce concept, défini par l'usage de la critique, dépasse la 'rationalité cognitive-instrumentale' (dont reste lié le nom de Max Weber). Il est appelé 'rationalité communicative' et médiatise le dialogue, en permettant aux interlocuteurs de s'évaluer réciproquement les prétentions respectives à la validité et de les confronter aux points de vue d'un 'Autre généralisé', selon l'expression de Mead. Donc:

> ...il ne s'agit pas de se mettre à la place d'autrui, de revivre ce qu'il éprouve, de reconstituer sa situation ou de déterminer ses états intentionnels; la communication et la compréhension ne sont pas affaire de transmission ou d'appréhension d'états psychologiques mais de jugements sur le bien-fondé des revendications implicites de validité élevées pour les discours et les paroles. Le cadre de ce jugement est une relation dans laquelle des partenaires se rapportent les uns aux autres, non pas dans une posture d'observateurs mais en tant que membres d'une intersubjectivité dans laquelle ils s'orientent en fonction d'exigences de validité à honorer. (1987:424)

Que valent-ils les arguments de Gadamer et de Habermas pour la pratique discursive ordinaire? Nous savons très bien que les dialogues ne sont souvent autre chose que de monologues juxtaposés; que nous prononçons les mêmes mots en les comprenant différemment, que d'innombrables facteurs de perturbation et distorsion limitent ou anéantissent la compréhension mutuelle. Mais s'il est frappant que nos conversations s'interrompent ou finissent souvent par des 'malentendus', il est encore plus frappant que l'entente survient aussi (au moins sous la forme d'un accord sur les points de désaccord). 'Les hommes ont un besoin si profond de se comprendre et une répugnance si grande a y renoncer, en désespoir de cause', constate un observateur lucide, 'que leurs jeux de langage réels ne peuvent être perçus que comme des applications imparfaites d'un jeu de langage idéal en cour de constitution'. Comme tout ce qui s'offre à nos regards, la communication peut être interprétée selon deux perspectives: sceptique et négativiste, d'un côté, constructive et indulgente, de l'autre; de ces perspectives, seulement la dernière est féconde car elle encourage la promotion du dialogue. Et il faut le dire et le répéter inlassablement que, malgré toutes les vicissitudes de la compréhension et en dépit des ruses de la mauvaise foi, il n'y a pas d'alternative au dialogue.

Cependant, le comparatisme impose au dialogue une clause supplémentaire: celle de surmonter la barrière linguistique qui sépare parfois les interlocuteurs. Dès lors que l'humanité est devenue post-Babelienne, bien avant que les sciences inventent leurs alphabets, le problème de faire communiquer les gens parlant des idiomes différents a été ressenti comme une nécessité impérieuse. La pratique de la traduction a une longue histoire, en dépit du scepticisme dont on l'a souvent accablée. Ce scepticisme n'est pas irrationnel: il s'est nourri de la singularité de la vision du monde, caractéristique à chaque langue. Quelque peine que nous prenions, jamais 'bread' ne traduira complètement 'pain'. En anglais, en français, en italien qu'est-ce donc 'Heimat'? Dans un récent article, Yves Chevrel remarquait que beaucoup de recherches dédiées aux traductions 'mettent l'accent sur l'écart entendu comme une déperdition entre l'original et la traduction, contribuant ainsi à renforcer l'opinion qu'un texte traduit n'est qu'un pis aller indigne de toute étude littéraire' (1989:211). Mais l'exagération des traits spécifiques est contre-productive. Le relativisme radical nous contraint de nouveau à un choix du type 'tout ou rien'. Le fait que seulement dans les sciences de la nature les traductions peuvent être 'sans reste', tandis que, par contre, dans les sciences humaines, surtout dans la littérature, elles proposent des versions, plus ou moins ressemblantes, jamais des équivalents absolus, n'a rien de gênant et ne nous autorise aucunement à prononcer un discours rhétorique sur l'incommunicabilité. L'assertion que les nations, les langues, les cultures constituent des univers en soi, discontinus, avec des formes de vie, des critères et des standards si spécifiques qu'elles restent en essence incommensurables, pâtit d'une démesure qui mène à la transformation d'une idée, au départ raisonnable, dans une opinion inadmissible. En fait, le concept de 'différence' est en couple avec celui de 'nature humaine', les deux se supposant réciproquement. D'où la compatibilité de principe de la diversité humaine. 'Ceux qui prétendent que l'expérience de l'autre, individuel ou collectif', écrit Lévi-Strauss, 'est, par essence, incommunicable et qu'il est à jamais impossible, coupable même de vouloir élaborer un langage dans lequel les expériences humaines les plus éloignées dans le temps et dans l'espace deviendront, au moins pour une partie, mutuellement intelligibles, ceux-là ne font rien d'autre que se réfugier dans un nouvel obscurantisme' (dans Todorov 1988:105).

Le traducteur est un personnage central mais, curieusement, sans un statut très honorable, probablement à cause d'un préjugé romantique, encore agissant, au sujet de la préséance accordée à l'"originalité'. Il vérifie dans son labeur la résonance de l'universel dans le particulier et, inversement, le surgissement de ce dernier dans un espace qui, étant vraiment fondamental, nous enveloppe tous. Il nous prête ses yeux et ses oreilles pour voir et entendre ce qui, autrement, nous ignorerions complètement. Par excellence interprétatif, son travail consiste à trouver des équivalences, bien qu'il sâche, par expérience personnelle et compétence, que, *stricto sensu*, il s'agit d'une besogne irréalisable. Il négocie quand même, basculant inlassablement, entre l'original et la version, la totalité et la partie, la 'lettre' et l'esprit', la clarté du concept et la couleur du détail. La balance doit être délicate et nuancée, d'autant plus qu'il n'y a pas de règles bien établies qui puissent l'aider; il peut compter seulement sur son 'esprit de finesse' et sa capacité d'assumer sympathétiquement l'âme de l'Autre. Le pari n'est pas pour la 'fidélité' et contre la 'création' ou inversement mais sur la conjonction des deux dans une proportion que seulement le tact et l'intuition peuvent régir.

Bien sûr, dans l'absolu, 'traduire c'est trahir', mais où le talent, l'imagination et le donné inanalysable de l'empathie se rencontrent, les prétendues 'trahisons' deviennent enrichissantes ('les belles infidèles') à la différence du morne cortège des fidélités stériles. Dans un monde qui se rappelle malheureusement son unité seulement devant les cataclysmes, les menaces écologiques majeures ou devant certaines prédictions apocalyptiques (que deviendront-ils les nationalismes au cas d'une invasion des extra-terrestres?) les traductions constituent des preuves palpables de la possibilité de nous comprendre et de dialoguer convenablement les uns avec les autres. C'est pourquoi j'aime la définition du comparatisme proposée par George Steiner à l'occasion d'un discours prononcé à l'Oxford, le 11 octobre 1994: la littérature comparée 'vise à élucider dans le langage la quiddité, le noyau essentiel d'un sentiment du monde historique et présent (le *Weltsinn* de Husserl), et à clarifier autant que possible entre différentes langues les conditions, les stratégies, les limites de la compréhension et de l'incompréhension réciproques' (1995:388).

Université de Bucarest

Notes

1 Beaucoup de détails sur la 'mondialisation' du comparatisme chez Adrian Marino 1988 *Comparatisme et théorie de la littérature*, PUF: pp. 33–51.

2 Pour la récente tentative de considérer la déconstruction plutôt une correction qu'une alternative à l'herméneutique, voir Christopher Norris 1991 *Deconstruction, Theory and Practice*,

Routledge; et Robert Scholes 1989 *Protocols of Reading*, The University Press, New Haven and London.

Oeuvres Citées

Chevrel, Yves 1989 'Les études de réception' dans *Précis de littérature comparée*, sous la direction de Pierre Brunel et Yves Chevrel. PUF.

Derrida, Jacques 1990 *Limited Inc*. Galilée, Paris.

Etiemble, René 1988 *Ouverture(s) sur un comparatisme planétaire*. Bourgois, Paris

Fokkema, Douwe W. 1984 *Cultural Relativism Reconsidered: Comparative Literature and Intercultural Relations. Douze cas d'interaction culturelle dans l'Europe ancienne et l'Orient proche ou lointain*. UNESCO, Paris.

Gadamer, Hans Georg 1975 *Wahrheit und Methode, 4*. Auf., G. C. B. Mohr, Tübingen.

Habermas, Jürgen 1987 'Explicitations du concept d'activité communicationnelle' dans *Logique des sciences sociale et autres essais*, tr. fr. R. Rochlitz. PUF.

Kolakowski, Leszek 1987 *Husserl and the Search for Certitude*. University of Chicago Press.

Lacoste, Jean 1988 *Le Philosophe au XX-e siècle*. Hatier, Paris.

Lévi-Strauss, Claude 1965 *Tristes tropiques*. Plon, Paris.

—— 1988 'L'Identité' in Tzvetan Todorov 1988.

Pageaux, Daniel Henri 1989 'De l'imagerie culturelle à l'imaginaire' dans *Précis de littérature comparée*, sous la direction de Pierre Brunel et Yves Chevrel. PUF.

Quéré, L. 1990 'Entre relativisme et ethnocentrisme: quelle voies pour les sciences sociales?' dans *Mesure*, 4.

Steiner, George 1995 'Qu'est-ce que la littérature comparée?' dans *Commentaire 2*.

Todorov, Tzvetan 1988 *Nous et les Autres. La réflexion française sur la diversité humaine*. Seuil, Paris.

Wellek, René 1959 'The Crisis of Comparative Literature' dans W. P. Friedrich (ed.) *Proceedings of the Second Congress of Comparative Literature*. University of North Caroline Press.

—— 1971 *Comparative Literature Today. Further Concepts of Criticism*. Yale University Press.

AMIYA DEV

Cultural Relativism and Literary Value

No matter how unlike from one another cultures are and therefore how unequal to one another, they are not incontrovertible fixities. Whether or not they all change in the same direction at the same speed — in other words, whether or not the same determinism is at work in them — they do change. The main point is that in the long run cultures are historical phenomena.

But does cultural relativism recognize that? Its own history is glorious, coming at a time when the universalism of Enlightenment fame was still the order of the day, and countering it by holding that cultures were contained in their own structures and so in no need of a model which was by definition superior. We also know that it was an outcome of field anthropology where the thrust was not on distant theoretical constructions. An anthropologist of that persuasion has done first-hand studies of the tribal population of north-east India, at such depth and with such intensity that by laying down his British antecedents he acquired a *situs* there and is now taken for an exemplum as well as a classic. We can name many more and from many cultures.

From my own country there have been a few of such dedication that to name Malinowski and Margaret Mead alone may smack of intellectual hegemony. Yet an essay of Mead's has stuck in my memory and helped shape my understanding of literary value in relation to culture, an essay on reading Shakespeare with, or rather telling Shakespeare to, a West African tribe. The issue was Hamlet's father's ghost and the small agrarian population of Tiv to whom Ms Mead was telling the tale of Hamlet on a rainy day would not believe in infernal spirits. Coleridge's willing suspension of disbelief or T. S. Eliot's playing along with the belief was not a cultural prescription, in fact could not be, and hence had no relevance to that tribe. It would have been ridiculous for a field anthropologist to tell her audience to suspend willingly their disbelief in such spirits or to play along as if they existed.

This has been crucial to me in questioning the cultural universalist position that literary value is the same everywhere and that what I require as a literary critic is patience in identifying the figure in the carpet.

Few would doubt today that by definition universalism is coercive and contains seeds of cultural imperialism. It is true that we owe this last formulation to Edward Said and perhaps, by way of Said, to Michel Foucault, but its origin surely lay in cultural relativism to which we owe our respect for cultures as such, irrespective of size, shape, colour and creed.

Indeed it is cultural relativism that has given us our sense of cultural equality in the face of the inequalities implied by the universalist rhetoric. The colonialist agenda of education from above and from outside was not unrelated to it, though that history was not perhaps as simple as 'they came — they saw — they conquered'. We know that in the Indian instance proving the thesis that a single shelf of Western classics contained more value than a whole library of Oriental literature and philosophy was not easy sailing and was preceded by a debate in Occidental circles between Westernism and Orientalism as well as by an eagerness on the part of the indigenous elite, not professional orientalists though no less rooted in tradition, to graft Western knowledge within Indian soil. Yet at the core of that complexity was perhaps an acknowledgement, if not a presupposition, that the West was superior to India. There is a piece by one of our major poets, written not in his own language but in English, in which he had acquired an admirable facility, entitled 'The Anglo-Saxon and the Hindu', which seemed to exult in that acknowledgement. Yet he was no Anglophile of the ordinary sort. His 'sigh for Albion's distant shore' was combined with an entreaty to his motherland not ever to forget him if he passes away on his trip overseas. I can multiply such instances to show the complexity of the universalist persuasion of cultural gradation, yet the fact remains that gradation was afoot. Orientalist adulation did not in the long run jar with it, for that adulation was for the past, for the wonder that was India, containing perhaps, if not scorn, some pity for the present. And it is this, if not its letter, its spirit, that cultural relativism came to question.

But did cultural relativism also imply backtracking or stasis? If cultures are individual entities, self-structured and self-contained, beyond comparison with one another in terms of superiority-inferiority, high-low, and therefore beyond gradation, if the very notion of savagery as the antithesis of civilization is questioned, then of course a purity is doubly affirmed, ruling out any possibility of contamination. (Let me confess in passing that my mind is still suffering from such a construction so that every time I utter the word 'culture' the image of a tribal community is called up, perhaps meaning thereby that my relativist deconstruction nearer home is still incomplete.) Yet the question of contamination is a matter of history and to rule it out is to rule out history. Indeed cultural relativism posits an ahistorical *situs* for cultures. But can cultures be ahistorical? There is of course some history within a culture itself, its *sensus communis* moving, no matter how slowly, along a certain path. But there is a second kind of history that relates a culture to another culture in spite of all their individual purity. And this history is so pervasive that few cultures can stay untouched by it. In fact the thesis of cultural isolation necessary for cultural self-sufficiency is untenable in the face of world economic imbalances. If the world were indeed a perfectly chartered federation of cultures, good fences making good neighbours, then isolation would have been a tenable proposition. Every time anthropologists locate a truly isolated culture, it is a matter of cheer to them, yet they know, at least the social historians among them do, that such isolation is now tantamount to reservation. And we will all perhaps agree that reservation is not in the long run a healthy proposition for a culture. In other words, cultures cannot probably be immune to, or afford to be immune to, this other history that paves the way to relations.

Perhaps cultural relativists would agree up to this point. But the main question is not whether cultures are exposed to one another and get interrelated but what happens to them as a result of such interrelations. Do they retain their purity? If the loss were mutual, then it would perhaps have been bearable, though not necessarily justified. If the two interrelating cultures had been equally affected by that event, if the quantum of change taking place in their body were the same, the one moving this way and the other that, then we would have had a kind of anthropological equity.

Yves Chevrel's celebrated analogy of the self thinking of the other as a 'barbarian', of which only what is audible is the phoneme 'ba ba' alone (1989:8), would make sense if it were reciprocated. For a long time the Sanskrit word 'yavana', meaning Ionian (that is, Greek), had a derogatory signification, almost as derogatory as the Greek 'barbaros'. Such instances are often reciprocal. Perhaps such 'image' building is one way of cultures' attempt at protecting their purity against all onslaught from outside. But does it then mean that all cultural dialogue is by definition a cultural misreading? Is that what cultural relativists would say?

The National Book Trust of India, a state-sponsored publishing agency, has popularized a notion of *aadaan-pradaan*, give and take, between Indian letters. That is an ideal of dialogue, *dvi* (two)-logos, if I may coin this *manipravala* or hybrid word, though the ideal is no guarantee for the real. And when we move from intra- to intercultural dialogue the ideal-real tension is likely to increase. The ideal would have *dvi*, while the real favours one — if this is the case then there is no gainsaying the problematic of cultural dialogue. In comparative literary circles we are a bit shy now of the word influence — a hangover, I would say, of cultural relativism — for its obvious high/low implication. But can cultural dialogue be altogether divested of that implication? Do not certain cultures at certain times assume heights and thus put certain other cultures, as it were, to depths — I mean by the very fact of that assumption?

May I submit that there is no dialogue in the full sense of the term, which is, however, not to say that there is only misreading. I will come back to the issue of misreading, but let me first take up the issue of literary value. A simple cultural relativist catechism would deny universality to literary value. However, that presupposes a boundary from within which we do our value reckoning. The ancient Indian *Mahabharata* is *itihasa,* but the *Ramayana* is *kavya* by such reckoning. But if through a cultural dialogue we come to know of the *Iliad* and the *Odyssey* or *Chanson de Roland* and *Nibelungenlied* we may, by a temporary boundary shift, call them both *kavya* or, further, *epic*. Now the question is, is epic a universal category, or is it part of another culture, therefore relativist, but relativist assuming universalist dimensions? The term *epic* has more power today than either *itihasa* or *kavya*: we have given *epic* a kind of universal validity. You ask a student of Sanskrit literature from within the tradition that had produced *Sakuntala* to make an appreciation of that classic, in six out of ten cases he/she may begin by quoting Goethe's *Sakuntala* quatrain whose *situs* was quite different. To be sure Goethe wrote it for fellow Germans or at most for fellow Europeans, not for Indians then or now: then how has it taken on such universal validity? This is an event worthy of deconstruction. Similarly, or more, we are all writing the novel now, though in different cultures the so-called novel of today had different antecedents irrespective of the amount of grafting that went on. The novel has turned out to be a universal category and however much may cultural relativists insist on the difference due to cultural singularities, it has assumed a value of its own. And by virtue of our profession we comparatists are aware of this value — relativism cannot make us desist from that. Perhaps there exists a contradiction between extreme relativism and comparative literature; yet relativism is something that comparative literature cannot do without. Perhaps it is in the dialectic of relativism and functional universalism that comparative literature thrives.

When Goethe praised *Sakuntala* it was an absence that he was celebrating. Maybe in such recognition of absences do we have the roots of exoticism. Interestingly as a category it has been primarily used by Occidentals, though it could have been equally used by Orientals. Said's orientalism has been partly complemented by some occidentalism here and there and I am told that China is engaged in related research. India too has quite a bit of occidentalism, now highlighted by the postmodernist critique of modernism in certain quarters. If orientalism is taken for cultural misreading, a necessary misreading to boot, then occidentalism too may prove to be a misreading. Now, is all cultural dialogue by definition cultural misreading?

Tagore, we are told, was invited to China in 1924 as a representative of the East by a faction of Chinese intellectuals, while another faction bearing the legacy of the May 4th Movement had looked upon him as a vanguard of effective Westernization of Oriental literatures. Tagore himself had thought of China in terms of her ancient relations with India and was caught unawares in the debate around modernization. If he praised the ancient values it was not because he was preaching a pan-Asian ideal of the East, as some scholars might have us believe, for he had on other occasions written against the opium trade.

And when in the late 1930s Japan invaded China, bearing out what he had cautioned Japan against during his visit there in 1916, he came out in open protest. Yet he would always uphold Li Bo against modern Western poetry. Such was the extent of these cultural misreadings in 1924 that Tagore became a controversial guest. And why had a part of modern Japan taken exception to his cautionary words? The so-called Oriental school's eulogy of him helping produce a kind of Tagore boom must have led to a misreading with modern Japanese writers and critics. He was denounced as a representative of a nation in fetters. I am not asking for any hindsight but quoting the case of Tagore as an instance of misreading in both China and Japan. If Tagore had been alive in 1945 then he would have been the first to condemn Hiroshima, and if alive in 1948 would have accorded the heartiest welcome to modern China. In fact with his flowing robe and a no less flowing beard this precursor of modern India was a classic case of misreading in various parts of the world and in one instance his first name, Rabindranath (split into Rabindra Nath in English), was taken for a near anagram of Rabbi Nathan!

Yet it would be presumptuous to claim that cultural dialogue is an absolute alias of cultural misreading. There is no doubt that a dialogue is invested with power, power wielded by the more advanced culture in its relation to the less advanced. Of course the idea of advancement in the case of a culture and of its gradation is basically alien to cultural relativism, but I have made it clear that our cue here is history and not theoretical loyalty. However, with the power thesis granted, it would be foolhardy to believe that there is no resistance to that power, that a less advanced culture laps up without discretion whatever arrives from the more advanced culture. At least in the field of literature there is resistance, even occasional subversion. Nineteenth-century India was a signal instance of this exposure cum dialogue, power investment and resistance. The Indian novel in the different Indian languages was an immediate outcome of this dialogue, pure and unadulterated perhaps in the lay eye, but to the discerning quite acculturated, ruptured by the indigenous narrative tradition. Some work has already been done on this, some more is in the offing. Besides there is no dearth of polemic in the postmodernist program.

Not apropos of postmodernism but apropos of cultural relativism I would like to raise the issue here of cultural fundamentalism. How amenable is it to dialogue? If fundamentalism is not merely to reiterate the fundamentals of a culture to its inmates but to declare to the world outside that one's culture is not only not inferior but superior to another culture, then fundamentalism would be hostile to cultural dialogue. Is the recent rise of fundamentalism to be treated as cultural relativism with a vengeance in a world where cultural dialogue is becoming more and more prevalent, where dialogue itself is being gradually metamorphosed into globalization? Is literary value then going to be split apart, one set being entirely culture specific and therefore varying from culture to culture and the other set being gradually globalized? And are we literary scholars going to be schizophrenic, engaged on the one hand in the study of culture-conscious literatures that revolve round their own axes, and on the other hand in that of literary interrelations that are taking on global proportions?

No, I have no quarrel with cultural relativism as such, but my final allegiance is to history. And history tells me that cultural relativism cannot in the long run protect cultures from dialogue and misreading. Narrating a dialogue cum misreading is not merely to enumerate what went and what came and took what shape; it is to understand the whole process, the power investment, the resilience and the resistance, even subversion. When I look at my own culture which is itself a composite of a number of subcultures (perhaps literary scholars no less than anthropologists will object to this word saying that there are no *sub*cultures, that there are only cultures), I see in it a component of Perso-Arabic origin, outcome surely of a dialogue that took place centuries ago, maybe with some misreading too. At the same time I know that through Persia and Arabia the frame tale probably went all the way from India to Europe. At least that is what Max Mueller told us a century ago and even though the earliest specimen of tale framing had been found in ancient Egypt in an incipient form, no evidence has yet been unearthed to my knowledge to prove the contrary. I am also told that so much material came from ancient India to ancient China in the wake of a Buddhist diaspora that some Indian originals can be only retrieved from their Chinese metamorphoses.

In the classical comparative literary parlance these are also instances of survival, but whether or not we refer back to that we cannot deny the historicity of a dialogue in each case. It is true that polygenesis is a valid category and though borrowed from biology and linguistics it also applies to literary affinities. Under no circumstances can the importance of its functionality be undermined. The historical determinism implied in it is another argument for cultural relativism: no doubt all cultures are structured by their own laws, but all cultures move in the same direction. But historical determinism cannot subsume everyday history where cultural dialogue and misreading are embedded. To say that all cultures are going to go the same way is not to deny the latter. To say, in other words, that literary value systems are independent of one another though laid out in the same mutative pattern is not to deny value shifts through interliterary contacts. And in no way is this acceptance a denial of difference and *situs* — only a purist may demur. But purists are ever flying in the face of history. As a literary scholar committed to my difference and my *situs* I would not like to do that. I would rather be held in a dialectic of difference and its obverse, whether that arises out of a cultural dialogue or a cultural misreading.

Vidyasagar University

Work Cited

Chevrel, Yves 1989 *La Littérature comparée*. Presses Universitaires de France, Paris.

Mario J. Valdés

Eurocentrism and Comparative Literary History

Comparative literary history has been one of the last stands of Eurocentrism in Western Europe and the Americas. It is a name that hides an implicit hierarchy of literary values in a fixed canon of classic authors or great books. It is a small world indeed that passes over most of Africa, the Middle East, all of Asia, and parts of Latin America.

The arguments that are given for this exclusion are the modest ones of colleagues who claim to lack the competence to assess these vast areas of culture and the arrogant claim that Western colleagues should leave these cultures to the natives. My response is direct: if one lacks competence one had better get someone who is competent. If a comparatist does not leave Aristotle to the Greeks or Dante to the Italians, why should she or he leave Basho exclusively to the Japanese?

One of the most remarkable changes in contemporary literary scholarship has been postcolonial theory. In less than a decade it has swept throughout the world to challenge and deconstruct the long-standing Eurocentric bias of humanistic scholarship. The institutionalization of indefensible biases is of course the reason for the almost universal colonial world of ideas we lived in only a few years ago. In Latin America the most pervasive Eurocentric bias was that of Domingo Sarmiento of Argentina, but let me take Hegel's *Philosophy of History* as my example of the articulated sources of Eurocentrism in scholarship.

According to Hegel the only effective relationship between Africans and Europeans was slavery which was on balance more favourable to the Africans since it gave Africans contact with civilization. The people of Mexico and Peru were considered to be impotent culturally and incapable of any spiritual achievement, and China was worn out. Hegel argued that as reason prevailed these backward peoples would be assimilated into the superior European culture with its origins in ancient Greece and its flowering in Western Europe.

Throughout the nineteenth century this Eurocentric racism dominated the humanities under the rubric of science and the purported quest for objective knowledge. Unfortunately, these attitudes are like a virus of the mind and they have extraordinary longevity.

In philosophical terms my thesis is that literature stands at the centre of a linguistic community's identity with the all-important qualifier that language and, therefore, linguistic communities are not self-contained. Historical discourse is a privileged expression of the human capacity to endow the experience of time with meaning, because the immediate referent of this discourse is real, rather than imaginary, events. Historians cannot invent the events of their stories, they must find them. This is so because historical events have already been created by past human agents.

The creation of a historical narrative is an action exactly like that by which historical events are created, but it is in the domain of narration rather than of action. By discerning the plots prefigured in historical actions by the agents that produced them and by configuring them as sequences of events having the coherence of stories, the historian makes history.

The meaning of history resides in the drama of human effort, since it is human effort which endows life with meaning. This universal, human quest for meaning is carried out in the awareness of the corrosive power of time, but it is also made possible and given its distinctly human pathos by this very awareness. In this respect, that manner of being-in-the-world that we call historical is paradoxical and cannot be apprehended by human thought except in the form of an enigma. The historian's task is one of mediation between the events and the story of human agency that gives meaning to these events.

If the historian emplots events into a narrative account, we must now ask which events the literary historian engages in the task of literary history. Can the composition and publication of a book be considered an event, or must we include the reception by the author's contemporaries as part of the event? And, if this be so, how can we account for vastly changing modes of reception of the same work? Can a history of production concomitantly deal with a history of reception?

A postmodern literary history can be neither the cumulative record of everything that has been written nor the compilation of themes and topics that have been emphasized by past historians. Literary history can only be effective in our postmodern world if it continues to search for an understanding of our sense of the past which stands behind the texts we read in the present. There is no doubt that at any given point in history the knowledge of the past is partial and reflective of present perspectives. It is for this reason that every writing of literary history is inadequate to the task of re-enactment, but nevertheless is a necessity for the cultural identity of the society that produces the writing.

A proper historiography of literary history begins with the recognition of the essential problem of description of an event that must be constantly reconstituted. There is no question that the significance of past actions must first be understood in terms of their agents' own values and aesthetic perspectives and not in terms of our very different ones. But on the other hand, to ignore the meanings of our own redescriptions of the events would be to play the fool. There are three preliminary tasks before us: to understand how our narrative form cannot escape our own value spectrum; to abandon the notion of a universal history; and to open up for scrutiny the concept of event itself. The cognitive function of the historian's narrative form is not a neutral compilation of a succession of facts and ascribed purpose and design; it is above all, the making of a whole out of a number of inter-relationships which are not in themselves related by necessity but only for the purpose of exposition. Narrative form is thus an artifice designed to represent a specific explanation for past activity. We would clearly expect that the narrative form of a feminist like Susan Gubar or a Marxist like Fredric Jameson would be the best instrument possible to further their historical ensemble as valid and presenting a general truth-claim. The identification of form with ideology should not be taken as negative. The point to be made is that every telling of a story is partial, limited and directed but it is valid since its telling allows for a debate with other versions. In literary history, the aesthetic perspectives of the past are established from the differences between the notion of reality expressed in the texts and the idea of reality recognized by historians as their own.

Are historian's reconstructions 'what really happened in the past' or are they contemporary constructions on what the past has come to mean in the present? Clearly, there is no agreement on this matter and indeed most literary historians attempt to do both. Through the use of documentary evidence, historians are committed to the reconstruction of what once was and in so doing are also, knowingly or not, making a statement about their own sense of the world. Inasmuch as there is a documentary trace of the past, literary historians attempt their reconstruction as representations of who wrote what and when and may even venture into the question of why. But the problem that makes literary history unique is that standard historiography can only attempt the reconstruction of the author's circumstances. The work of art itself is left on the side as it must be because it is not of the past, but of the present. The texts are read by the historian in the present and at best the texts may yield traces of past readings but they are realized in the present. A literary work took place as an event of writing and production, but this event is no longer; it once was. The traces of the event can lead to an imaginative reenactment of the event but no more. Insofar as literary historians are not content to consider literary works of art only as events of composition, they also actualize a text and comment on this writing of the past from the vantage point of their present. My first point is that literary history not only attempts to realize a reenactment of a past event, it also presents a contemporary reflection of the writing as an aesthetic experience in the present. Literary history treats writing both as document and as experience.

Works of literature are, of course, historical in their composition, but they are also in history as long as there continues to be reception recorded. Certain works of literature are therefore generators of social discourse in the life of a linguistic community, and catalytic agents of change in other communities they reach altered through translation. A history of literature that seeks to grasp together the many versions of the literary work must find new ways of organization.

If the work of literature, its production and reception, in the original language and in translation, is the subject matter of literary history, the literary work must be recast as a historical event, but it is an event that multiplies in time with continuities and discontinuities. Although the production and reception are contemporary at the beginning, they bifurcate soon after, and commentary of reception rapidly exceeds commentary on the work's production. Both change with time; only the composition itself remains stable.

What we have begun to sketch out is not so much a break with literary historians of the past but rather a more structured plan of operation and a rejection of the master narrative. We concur when David Perkins writes:

> A text from the past embodies a lived experience, an aesthetic, a culture that is alien. Of course, it is not completely alien. Continuities and universals in human experience are the themes of antiquarian literary history and humanist criticism. But most literary histories emphasize the difference of the past. (1992:184)

But we cannot agree with the either/or nature of his proposal when a few lines further he writes:

> Here, incidentally, is why literary history cannot surrender the ideal of objective knowledge of the past. Though the ideal cannot be achieved, we must pursue it, for without it the otherness of the past would entirely deliquesce in endless subjective and ideological reappropriation. (185)

Either we strive for objectivity or we risk getting caught in the morass of subjective relativity. Perkins concludes the paragraph with the telling statement: 'A function of literary history is, then, to set the literature of the past at a distance, to make its otherness felt' (185). Indeed, but this function would be better served by a structure of interpretation that opened the past to the multiple varieties of present appropriations without closing the works or their context to a master narrative.

The postmodern model of literary history therefore offers us not only an effective historical instrument but, of major significance for me, it gives us procedures for approaching complex historical conglomerates of comparative literary history. Latin American literatures, the literatures of Central European cultural centres, the literatures of the African cultural diaspora, are such areas of study. Our paradigm calls for the context to be elaborated separately from the narration of events. This is the essence of the Braudel model as we have adapted it to literary history. The social context thus redresses some of the omissions of the past by establishing the basic strata of cultural centres of a society, the social institutions which have been central to the production of literature and also the politics of readership in the community.

There are, of course, numerous ways of narrating the same set of historical markers which have been taken as an event since each historian has to select and sort out the evidence, organize it into a narrative sequence, and give a sense of purpose. The more the series of events takes on importance the more will the historical narratives of these events multiply and differ from each other. In all of these versions, each historian will have implicitly claimed to be presenting 'what really happened in the past'. Each historical narrative has in fact given form and coherence to an assemblage of data. The demand for closure in the historical narrative is a demand for an interpretive statement of purpose behind the event.

Our task is made more complex because we are dealing with multiple social and demographic factors, sometimes of long duration. The historical record as a constituted rendering of the past, in our case the literary past, has come under close scrutiny in the wake of poststructural and postcolonial critiques that point to discontinuities, gaps, ruptures and, above all, exclusions rather than linear development, evolution or continuity. In short, today, the very task of the historian has to be rethought. In Hayden White's words:

> ...a specifically historical inquiry is born less of the necessity to establish that certain events occurred than of the desire to determine what certain events might mean for a given group, society or culture's conception of its present tasks and future prospects. (487)

This shift from validation to signification has also created an impetus to reconceptualize the literary historical process so that it includes the relations between texts and the contexts of production and of reception. The key question of historiography is also the question of literary history: how did a given phenomenon enter the system titled history? The historian, of course, names and constitutes an assemblage of data as an event by selection and narrative positioning. And this constitution of the past is carried out by historians who are as situated in the particularities of time, place, language and gender as were the people who first produced the works being considered. It is in this sense that we recall Nietzsche's words: you can explain the past only by what is most powerful in the present. This observation must not be construed as anti-historical. Quite the opposite purpose will emerge: a hermeneutic re-writing of history.

University of Toronto

Works Cited

Arnold, A. James (ed.) 1994 *A History of Literature in the Caribbean*. John Benjamins, Amsterdam/Philadelphia.

Gerard, Albert (ed.) 1986 *European-Language Writing in Sub-Saharan Africa*, 2 vols. Akademiai Kiado, Budapest.

Hegel, G. W. F. 1956 *The Philosophy of History*, tr. J. Sibree. Dover, New York: pp. 91–9.

Nietszsche, Friedrich 1979 (1872) 'The Philosopher: Reflections on the Struggle Between Art and Knowledge' in *Philosophy and Truth. Selections from Nietzsche's Notebooks of the Early 1870s*, ed., tr. Daniel Breasale. Humanities Press International, New Jersey: pp. 3–58.

Perkins, David 1992 *Is Literary History Possible?* Johns Hopkins University Press.

White, Hayden 1986 'Historical Pluralism' in *Critical Inquiry* 12.3: pp. 484–92.

Douwe Fokkema

Western, Eastern and Multicultural Canons of Literature

Research into the problem of canon formation cannot avoid discussing the psychological and social significance of reading, and since we are focusing on canons of literature, we also cannot avoid examining the concept of literariness. Reading may consist of three stages: the historicist attempt at contextualization; the discovery or attribution of symbolic significance which implies decontextualization; and the presentist attempt at recontextualization, that is, the construction of meaning with reference to the reader's own lifeworld. A literary way of reading will include the second and third stages; emphasis on the first stage will produce a non-literary reading directed at the discovery of scientific, historical, or practical information.

In what ways the text plays a role in not only the respective stages of historicist contextualization, decontextualization and the discovery of literariness but also presentist recontextualization is open to debate. Riffaterre has argued for a fairly large role of the text: 'Literature is the text, and once established, and once the author is gone and can no longer make alterations, the text is ahistorical and its significance lies above all contexts' (in Bernheimer 1995:71). Stanley Fish (1980) has denied any decisive role for textual features (for criticism of this position, see Shen 1988; Fokkema and Ibsch 1995:xv–xvii). The outcome of the debate can be settled only by empirical research. By now there is some empirical evidence (Hoffstaedter 1986; Zwaan 1993; Steen 1994) for assuming that particular readers with some knowledge of literary conventions interpret particular texts as being literary more often than other texts. This does not mean that certain textual features as such trigger the reaction of a literary reading. It means, however, that particular textual features motivate readers to apply their knowledge of literary, generic, and stylistic conventions. The features of the text make a difference, although depending on the cultural and other conditions of particular instances of reading the impact of that difference may vary.

Similarly, we assume that educated readers are able to distinguish high literature from popular literature. In both cases — the distinction between literary and non-literary, high and low — the notion of convention is crucial (Schmidt 1980; for a more elaborate discussion of the aesthetic convention, see Fokkema 1996). Maybe our conventions are infelicitous and perhaps knowledge based on conventions must be suspected, but it remains a fact that many readers can distinguish the literary from the nonliterary and the high from the popular.

At this point the difference between scientific and non-scientific (or pseudoscientific) approaches becomes visible. We can establish by scientific means which texts are read in a literary way by which people, or, more elliptically, which texts are considered to be literary, and I would not immediately give away that kind of research to the social sciences. We need the results of that research in order to get closer to solving the problem of how the literary aesthetic is produced, what its effect on readers is, and how its vitality can be explained. Neither sociology nor psychology has shown much interest in the full complexity of these problems.

It is *impossible*, however, to decide by way of scientific research that the literary is more valuable than the non-literary, or expert literary discourse more important than the popular one. By definition, the correctness of such value judgments cannot be proven by scientific means. But also the moral or common-sense argument in defence of these judgments can hardly be successful in the abstract. It is quite obvious that in many cases (for instance in reports about political developments) non-literary discourse is to be preferred. Fortunately, both political scientists and political commentators express themselves in a discourse that most educated readers will recognize as being different from fiction or poetry. Similarly, it can be established that under certain conditions, for instance among populations with little knowledge of literary conventions, popular literature will have more effect than high literature.

RESEARCH INTO THE COMPOSITION OF CANONS

What does this mean for the problem of canon formation? First, we must emphasize that it will be helpful to know the composition of canons upheld in different parts of the world by different groups of readers. That would be part of our scientific endeavour. Second, as educators or critics we may wish to intervene in the existing canons and, following the advice of the Bernheimer report, to reconceive some of the prevailing canons. Let me first comment on the first issue and conclude with some personal observations on a restructuring of canons in university education, in particular from an international point of view.

A canon can be defined as a selection of well-known texts, which are considered valuable, are used in education, and serve as a framework of reference for literary critics. There is one flaw in this definition and that is its passive construction. No mention is made of the agency which makes the selection and expresses the value judgements, or prescribes the texts as reading matter in the school. The definition leaves the question 'whose canon?' unanswered. Probably this open endedness cannot be avoided, because the question of who maintains which canon is something which in concrete cases must be investigated.

How do we recognize a canon? Jan Gorak has pointed out that it is not easy to determine which texts belong to a particular canon and which not. Critics have often been more explicit about an assumed canon they wished to reject than about a canon they preferred. Gorak notes the 'tendency to narrow the cultural and historical diversity of *canons* into one reactionary *canon*' (1991:248). His own historical research has shown to what extent canons can be different in size, scope (national/international), and rigidity. Indeed, a distinction must be made, as Nemoianu has done, between the canon of the critics (or various groups of critics) and the school canon (the curriculum). The latter can be differentiated again with respect to language and level. The canon of English literature at high school is different from that at the university, and at different universities there may be different school canons or reading lists (Kaat 1987). Gaiser (1983) found striking discrepancies between the 'real' canon of high school students and the 'official' canon of their teachers. Kochan (1990) has collected interesting material about the school canon of literature in German. Perhaps we should also distinguish a canon of literary historians, which generally is more hospitable than that of the critics.

Glen Johnson (1991) has found a way to study the canon of English literature at universities in North America by comparing various editions of anthologies designed for teaching. However, the anthologies offer a rather wide net, which from the publisher's point of view seems the profitable thing to do. Yet, counting names of authors and the number of pages devoted to their work provides a clue which may turn out to be an interesting one, in particular if, in subsequent editions, the attention of the editor has shifted in one way or another. In recent editions of American anthologies, for instance, more women writers can be found. The editorial arguments explaining such shifts can be rather revealing.

Karl Erik Rosengren (1968), whose work is not widely known among literary scholars, developed a method for studying the canons of critics. He suggested counting the number of times particular authors (or texts) have been mentioned in criticism focusing on another author. This method derives from the idea that familiarity with a certain set of writers and texts belongs to the general knowledge of educated people and therefore provides a frame of reference to a critic. Only writers who are well known can be referred to for reasons of comparison or explanation. In this research Rosengren uses the following operational definition of canon: a canon consists of those writers and texts that are frequently mentioned in literary criticism dealing with another author. Although his method of research can be improved by distinguishing between long and short, negative and positive 'mentions', it can be applied quite successfully, including in research on the canons of literary-historical publications.

Instead of taking for granted that Homer, Sophocles, Dante, and Shakespeare belong to *the* canon, as Charles Altieri did (Nemoianu and Royal 1991:2), it is possible now to examine more precisely which authors belong to the canon of a particular critic or group of critics, or to the canon of a particular literary historian or group of literary historians. Moreover, we are able to study fluctuations in the composition of these various canons in the course of time, and we may detect the hurdles which an author (or text) has to take before he or she (or it) is admitted to the rather stable canon of literary historians, who, like the editors of anthologies, prefer to add rather than to delete, expressing their personal emphasis mainly by allotting more or less space.

The results of empirical research, such as that carried out by Johnson and Rosengren, must be interpreted. The question of why there are more women writers in recent editions of American anthologies than in earlier ones is easy to answer. The publication of *The Norton Anthology of Literature by Women* by Gilbert and Gubar (1985) is not difficult to explain either. But the question of why certain authors appear in every new anthology, and remain also frequently referred to by literary critics, is more complicated. Clearly, Christopher Clausen is correct in criticising the view that 'literary works have value and meaning only for the period, culture, class, sex, or ethnic group that produces them' (Nemoianu and Royal 1991:200). This position was not maintained even by Marx or Engels, only by some short-lived radical groups in the history of Marxism. However, what is it that makes people (including Marx) believe that some literary works have lasting value? Perhaps the question should be phrased more correctly as: what is it that makes certain texts have a better chance of surviving than others?

Some scholars will answer that it is a matter of well-organized distribution by publishers or other kinds of institutional support. But if that were the answer, the question is merely deferred, because why should a publisher or academic institution have given its support precisely to this one author, Shakespeare for instance, or Li Bai, or Rabindranath Tagore, or Borges, and not to authors who are by now less popular? If institutional support is given as the main reason for an author's success, the implication is that the work to be supported was selected at random. It is more likely, however, that the distributional and institutional networks have spent their energy on texts by authors who appeared to offer something of value. Publishers and other institutions will have acted on the expectation that with this particular author they would have more success than with another. Therefore, institutional support alone provides no explanation.

Our not so very revolutionary conclusion is that the thematic contents and formal features of a text are a factor determining the chances of survival as well. Christopher Clausen has focused on the thematic elements. His findings are rather tentative and the question why particular texts time and again have been read and commented upon (thus conforming to Kermode's criterion of a canon [1988]) whereas others have not shared this fate, remains one of the most intriguing problems of literary history. Simple answers cannot be expected, since values are contingent, as Herrnstein Smith (1988) has shown. However, that does not mean that within the various cultural traditions they are also arbitrary.

The question of the persistence of certain thematic contents (related to the more private spheres of life: love and death, family relations, the dilemmas of individuals in their confrontation with the outer world) and of certain formal features (a certain complexity of form, resulting from repeated encoding as Lotman [1977] has suggested, including of course the possibility of the zero device or *minus priyom* which is related to the contingent expectations of the readers) remains an important research topic. In order to generate promising hypotheses, however, it will be necessary to have more data.

Relatively much is known about the canons of literature in Europe and the Americas, but we have little knowledge about the composition of canons in other parts of the world, in spite of the great number of publications about postcolonialism and writing in the former Third World. In 1993 I submitted a questionnaire on canon formation to two groups of students at Peking University. In fact, the questionnaire was designed to collect information about the personal literary preferences of these students. The main results may be summarized here.

Thirty-eight students, twenty females and eighteen males, all born in China, completed the questionnaire in two different classroom sessions, twenty-one of them studying English, thirteen Chinese, whereas four did not answer the question about their main field of study. Although there were some first- and second-year students among the group, the majority had studied between three and five years at the university. As to reading, narrative prose (including fiction) was strongly preferred: twenty-six against seven, who preferred poetry, and five who liked to read essays. The (open) question about which novel of traditional Chinese literature was appreciated most yielded the answer *Dream of the Red Chamber* (*Hong lou meng*) thirty times. Only eight respondents preferred another choice: *Romance of the Three Kingdoms* (*San guo yan yi*), or *Water Margin* (*Shui hu zhuan*), or other well-known traditional fiction. The outspoken preference for *Dream of the Red Chamber*, the eighteenth-century family history and tragic love story, is not difficult to explain. I would not be surprised at all if the majority of Western students of Chinese literature would have the same preference. I may recall here that China has a tradition of canon formation that shows at least as much awareness of the process of canonization as the European tradition. For instance Zhi Yu (d. 311), a compiler of an anthology, emphasized the moral, cognitive, and emotive functions of literature in a way that coincides with our emphasis on the significance of literature for the private domains of life, its significance for the relation between the subject and its social and natural environment:

> Literary writings are the means by which one manifests images of superior and inferior, illuminates the order of human relationships, investigates inner principles and exhaustively [expresses] one's nature, in order to examine what is proper to the myriad phenomena. (Quoted by Pauline Yu 1990:175)

Other questions were designed to find out to what extent *foreign* literature was preferred in comparison with traditional *and* modern Chinese literature. Here my findings should be treated with caution as there were many students of English in the group and because some respondents did not complete this (last) question due to lack of time. Nevertheless, the question 'If you now compare your preferred novels and authors, please mention three novels (either Chinese or foreign) in the order of your preference' was answered, even by students of Chinese, by mentioning *War and Peace, The Old Man and the Sea, Sons and Lovers, Wuthering Heights, Remembrance of Things Past* (indeed, French fiction is remembered by English titles and often read in English or Chinese translation), *Jean Christophe* and so on, although again most often *Dream of the Red Chamber* appeared in the first position. There was a notable absence of Japanese novels.

A similar question about poetry brought Li Bai to the first place with eleven mentions in the first position, but the question about the most favoured playwright (either Chinese or foreign) was answered eleven times with Shakespeare in the first position and O'Neill as a second best among the foreign names. Much preferred Chinese playwrights were Guan Hanqing and Tang Xianzu, and from this century, Cao Yu and Lao She.

As far as the preferences for foreign authors is concerned, it should be emphasized that the availability of texts in Peking, preferably in Chinese translation, is a precondition for their being widely mentioned. Therefore, the preferences for foreign writers are bound to be rather conventional. Also the recent showing of films on the campus of Peking University, such as *Tess of the d'Urbervilles, Lady Chatterley's Lover* and *Gone with the Wind,* was reflected in the answers concerning preferred foreign fiction.

Availability is less of a constraint if we consider the preferences for *modern and contemporary* Chinese literature. As to fiction, Shen Congwen (*The Border Town* 1934), Ba Jin (*Family, Spring, Autumn* 1933–40), Lu Xun, Lao She, and Qian Zhongshu (*The Besieged City* 1945) were at the top. A film after the latter novel was shown as a television series, which may have influenced its position. The most favoured modern poets were Xu Zhimo, Dai Wangshu, Ai Qing, Hai Zi, Shu Ting, Feng Zhi, Bei Dao, and Wen Yiduo, some of whom had been published already in the 1930s, whereas others were contemporaries.

The list of preferred modern playwrights is least surprising: Cao Yu was by far the most popular, Lao She occupying the second position, and Tian Han and Xia Yan being mentioned also more than once.

With the expressed popularity of Shen Congwen and Qian Zhongshu as well as Xu Zhimo and Wen Yiduo a link is made with the prerevolutionary past. Strictly speaking, this observation applies also to Ba Jin, Lu Xun, and Lao She whose pre-1949 writings were mentioned, but these writers continued to be widely published and read after the founding of the People's Republic. However, the connection with the pre-revolutionary period is probably not the most important factor determining these preferences. It is the thematic contents and expressed emotions, which were not dealt with in the offical literature of the socialist realist kind during the Great Leap Forward or the Cultural Revolution that makes these works attractive.

My hypothesis is that, however much a text may be interesting from a formal point of view, it will never achieve a high position in the canon unless it is thematically relevant at the same time. As we observed above, this relevance has often to do with the private spheres of life, which are not discussed in other media. The personal canons which can be constructed on the basis of this questionnaire have much to do with the concerns of adolescence: emotional attachments, family relations, individuals in their confrontation with the outer world, and the unknown history of the period before 1949 which was responsible for the later developments. I wish we had longitudinal data about students' preferences so that we might see crucial shifts and perhaps constancies in their personal canons. Our long-term aim, of course, must be to develop a theory that would explain both these constancies and shifts.

CRITICISM OF THE CANON

A concept of literary communication which implies decontextualization and presentist recontextualization has consequences for the canon debate. It appears that the readers' understanding of a text will always deviate from the original context in which it was written. Reading literature is interesting precisely because it allows for metaphorical or symbolic interpretation. It is different from reading expository texts. Even at a time of great political turmoil in China, Lu Xun subscribed to that view: 'In addition to catchwords, slogans, notices, telegrams and notebooks, the revolution needs literature — just because it is literature' (Lu Xun 1928:22).

Riffaterre has argued that the problem of canon formation 'should be the exclusive domain of cultural studies' (Bernheimer 1995:71). Two comments must be made about this position. First we should know whether we have research into the composition of canons in mind (a kind of research that would belong to the cultural sciences) or intervention in the canon debate (that is, cultural criticism). Secondly, as argued above, I do not believe that the formal and thematic qualities — pre-eminently examined by literary scholars — can be neglected in studies of the canon problem.

However, Riffaterre is right in considering that the social context, political concepts, and educational goals cannot be excluded from explaining the composition of a particular canon, or from arguments in favour of changing that canon. If I wish to discuss changes in, let us say, the canon of literature taught in the faculty of Arts, or, more narrowly, the set of texts to be read in comparative literature departments, I must remind myself of the context in which this reading is done and of my educational and, possibly, political goals. Thus, my observations have a personal and not a scientific character and whether they will be shared by others depends on whether one can accept my diagnosis of the social context, my preference for certain goals, and other elements in my argument.

In a world that is threatened by fundamentalism in various appearances, ranging from ethnic cleansing and identity politics to religious persecution and economic and technological ideologies, we need a literature that helps its readers to break through ideological barriers and to unmask fundamentalist beliefs. I assume that complex or 'high' literature is more effective in unsettling ideological dogmas than popular literature, which usually conforms to widely maintained conventions. This depends, of course, partly on the way the various texts of 'high' literature are read, whether, for instance, voices of doubt and contrast are allowed to become part of the reader's interpretation.

Here another aspect of our social context should be mentioned: in a world that favours the commonplace as promulgated by the tabloid press and television, the private spheres of life and individual critical thinking are under considerable pressure. Again it is complex texts, texts with a capacity for eliciting an individual and possibly intellectual response, that should be part of our canon. In modern society the public sphere, which first has undermined family life and communal structures, now also threatens the private. We probably need a kind of literature that discusses problems which are ignored by the other media: moral dilemmas, models of emotional attachment and the experience of death, individual views on the confrontation with the outer world. If we value independent thinking and individual concepts of emotional response, we again must have a preference for complex or 'high' literature, rather than its popular counterpart.

My political convictions include a concept of cosmopolitanism that can compete with identity politics of whatever provenance. The discussion has been carried on now for many years — not only by Scarpetta (1981) and Todorov (1991) but also by Marxist authors — about whether human beings have something in common with each other that distinguishes them from animals. Perhaps that common element is precisely the wish to be different from animals and the reflection on that desire, which, in effect, is a desire not to be completely dependent on natural, biological and other conditions. This desire has resulted in the invention of ethics and human rights. The possibility of a new cosmopolitanism can save us from a proliferation of the culture wars, a term which to our embarrassment is currently used in the United States, for instance in the title of a book by Henry Louis Gates (1992), chair of the department of African-American studies at Harvard University. Gates, however, prefers a peaceful accommodation over a withdrawal into the trenches of cultural identities. He argues that there is no limit to our capacity for learning the conventions of another culture: 'Any human being sufficiently curious and motivated can fully possess another culture, no matter how "alien" it may appear to be' (1992:xv). This coincides with my educational convictions. There are many examples of people who have acquired knowledge of the conventions of another culture and are able to apply them in practice. Think of the many immigrants who have come to North America, or of politicians, such as Jawaharlal Nehru, who was equally at home in Oxford and Cambridge as in his own country. It is a valuable goal for comparative literature departments to foster the idea that conventions of different cultures can be taught and learned, however much some scholars emphasize the fundamental differences between, say, the Chinese and the European tradition, to mention an example of sharp contrast that may serve as a paradigm for other cultural differences. James Liu, one of the most successful mediators between the two cultural traditions, in a posthumous publication, expressed the belief:

...that only by means of juxtapositions of texts from [the] two different traditions can we bring into relief what is truly distinctive in each tradition.... Such juxtaposition will also enable us to become aware of the unspoken presuppositions about the nature of language, poetry, poetics, and interpretation that underlie each tradition, thus paving the way for a genuinely comparative poetics, free from both Eurocentrism or Sinocentrism. (Quoted by Idema 1989:279)

Accepting the fundamental differences between cultural traditions as wide apart as that of China and Europe does not mean that switching from one cultural code to another is impossible. The life and work of James Liu himself have shown that it is not. Such code-switching is not only possible but also highly interesting to those who attempt it. This code-switching does not imply that the codes switched are considered homogeneous or 'pure'. In fact, as Edward Said argues in *Culture and Imperialism*, 'all cultures are involved in one another; none is single and pure, all are hybrid' (1993:xxix). Nevertheless, as hybrids, they are different from each other.

The situation sketched above and the political and educational goals mentioned provide some indications of the axes along which my preferred canon will be composed. That canon will be dynamic; its goal is not to emphasize an — always constructed — identity but to explore possibilities for identification. The search for such a canon is a pre-eminently cultural performance, and the search itself is at least as important as that which will be found. In this context I would subscribe to Walter Mignolo's definition of culture as that which 'guides actions or patterns of behavior, not the accumulated achievements or accomplishments by which "cultures" are often measured and ranked' (1995:179).

My preferred canon, then, will be guided by the possibility of code-switching — the very opposite of identity politics — and focus on contrastive values, on the differences between traditions, on criticism of prevailing ideologies, and on a variety of models of moral behaviour and private life. It will include texts of complex literature from all major cultures of the world, not only contemporary texts but also older ones, on the assumption that it is more rewarding to try to understand difficult texts than to assume to understand simple ones. However, my ways of decontextualization and certainly my attribution of presentist significance (recontextualization) will be different from those of my colleagues, and, therefore, my preferred canon will be different from theirs. As a result, it is useless to provide a list of texts preferred by me, as any final list adopted by a department of comparative literature will always be a product of compromise, dictated by diverse convictions, the specific culture we are living in, and the convenience of the moment (such as the availability of the books).

If I argue for an ideal of cosmopolitanism, it does not mean, of course, that all canons of world literature designed by comparative literature departments should be the same all over the world, but only that each comparative literature department, from its own point of view, establish a reading list (preferably more than one) that should be guided, among other things, by the notion that human nature is one, despite differences of language, nationality, race, religion, gender or culture. It would be most interesting to compare the various Western and Eastern conceptions (of course still partly culture-bound) of such cosmopolitan canons, and to enjoy their differences as well as the aspects they will have in common.

Utrecht University

Works Cited

Bernheimer, Charles (ed.) 1995 *Comparative Literature in the Age of Multiculturalism.* Johns Hopkins University Press.

Fish, Stanley 1980 *Is There a Text in This Class? The Authority of Interpretive Communities.* Harvard University Press.

Fokkema, Douwe 1996 'Comparative Literature and the Problem of Canon Formation' in *Canadian Review of Comparative Literature* 23.1: pp. 1–17.

Fokkema, Douwe and Elrud Ibsch 1995 *Theories of Literature in the Twentieth Century,* 2nd edition, with an extended new preface. C. Hurst, London.

Gaiser, Gottlieb 1983 'Zur Empirisierung des Kanonbegriffs' in *SPIEL 2*: pp. 123–35.

Gates, Henry Louis 1992 *Loose Canons: Notes on the Culture Wars.* Oxford UniversityPress.

Gilbert, Sandra M. and Susan Gubar 1985 *The Norton Anthology of Literature by Women: The Tradition in English.* W. W. Norton, New York.

Gorak, Jan 1991 *The Making of the Modern Canon: Genesis and Crisis of a Literary Idea.* Athlone, London and Atlantic Highlands, New Jersey.

Herrnstein Smith, Barbara 1988 *Contingencies of Value: Alternative Perspectives for Critical Theory*. Harvard University Press.

Hoffstaedter, Petra 1986 *Poëtizität aus der Sicht des Lesers: Eine empirische Untersuchung der Rolle von Text-, Leser- und Kontexteigenschaften bei der poetischen Verarbeitung von Texten*. Buske, Hamburg.

Idema, Wilt 1989 'Some Recent Studies of Chinese Poetics: A Review Article' in *T'oung Pao* 75: pp. 277–88.

Johnson, Glen M. 1991 'The Teaching Anthology and the Canon of American Literature: Some Notes on Theory in Practice' in Nemoianu and Royal: pp. 11–135.

Kaat, Jacques 1987 'The Reception of Dutch Fictional Prose in Great Britain'. Ph.D. thesis, University of Hull.

Kermode, Frank 1988 'Canons' in *Dutch Quarterly Review* 18: pp. 258–70.

Kochan, Detlef C. (ed.) 1990 *Literaturdidaktik — Lektürekanon — Literaturunterricht. Amsterdamer Beiträge zur neueren Germanistik*, vol. 30. GA Rodopi, Amsterdam and Atlanta.

Lotman, Yury M. 1977 *The Structure of the Artistic Text*, tr. Ronald Vroon. Department of Slavic Languages and Literatures, University of Michigan.

Lu Xun 1959 (1928) 'Literature and Revolution: Letter to Dong-fen' in *Selected Works*, vol. 3. Foreign Languages Press, Peking: pp. 20–3.

Mignolo, Walter D. 1995 'Afterword: Human Understanding and (Latin) American Interests — the Politics and Sensibilities of Geocultural Locations' in *Poetics Today* 16: pp. 171–214.

Nemoianu, Virgil and Robert Royal (eds) 1991 T*he Hospitable Canon: Essays on Literary Play, Scholarly Choice, and Popular Pressures*. John Benjamins, Philadelphia and Amsterdam.

Rosengren, Karl Erik 1968 *Sociological Aspects of the Literary System*. Natur och Kultur, Lund.

Said, Edward W. 1993 *Culture and Imperialism*. Chatto and Windus, London.

Scarpetta, Guy 1981 *Éloge du Cosmopolitisme*. Grasset, Paris.

Schmidt, Siegfried J. 1980 *Grundriss der empirischen Literaturwissenschaft, 1: Der gesellschaftliche Handlungsbereich Literatur*. Vieweg, Braunschweig and Wiesbaden.

Shen Dan 1988 'Stylistics, Objectivity, and Convention' in *Poetics* 17: pp. 221–38.

Steen, Gerard 1994 *Understanding Metaphor in Literature: An Empirical Approach*. Longman, London.

Todorov, Tzvetan 1991 'Remarques sur le croisement des cultures' in *Les Morales de l'histoire*. Grasset, Paris: pp. 109–25.

Yu, Pauline 1990 'Poems in Their Place: Collections and Canons in Early Chinese Literature' in *Harvard Journal of Asiatic Studies* 50.1: pp. 163–96.

Zwaan, Rolf A. 1993 *Aspects of Literary Comprehension: A Cognitive Approach*. John Benjamins, Amsterdam and Philadelphia.

Ersu Ding

The Tale of the Impossible: A Semiotic Critique of Cultural Relativism[1]

Michel Foucault begins his *The Order of Things* by citing an interesting text from Jorge Luis Borges which, he says, motivated his writing of the book. In that text, Borges quotes a certain Chinese encyclopedia in which animals are divided into the following categories: (a) belonging to the Emperor, (b) embalmed, (c) tame, (d) sucking pigs, (e) sirens, (f) fabulous, (g) stray dogs, (h) included in the present classification, (i) frenzied, (j) innumerable, (k) drawn with a very fine camelhair brush, (l) *et cetera*, (m) having just broken the water pitcher, (n) that from a long way off look like flies (1970:xv).

In the commentary that immediately follows this exotic quotation, Foucault openly expresses his amusement at the fact that a foreign culture collects under one unified heading what to another are obviously disconnected fragments, but underneath his wonderment over the odd taxonomy lies a self-admitted feeling of despair and pessimism which characterizes much of our contemporary intellectual effort:

> That passage from Borges kept me laughing a long time, though not without a certain uneasiness that I found hard to shake off. Perhaps because there arose in its wake the suspicion that there is a worse kind of disorder than that of the *incongruous*, the linking together of things that are inappropriate; I mean the disorder in which fragments of a large number of possible orders glitter separately in the dimension, without law or geometry, of the *heteroclite*; and that word should be taken in its most literal, etymological sense: in such a state, things are 'laid', 'placed', 'arranged' in sites so very different from one another that it is impossible to find a place of residence for them, to define a *common locus* beneath them all. (xvii-xviii)

In other words, Foucault sees in this encyclopedic entry more than the exotic charm of another thought system. For him, the Chinese way of classifying animals is a forceful demonstration of what he calls 'the limitation of our own, the stark impossibility of thinking that' (xv).

Since its appearance in the above context, the Chinese example (and the idea behind it) has increasingly caught the attention of many cultural critics. The popularity of the story has a lot to do, of course, with Foucault's status and influence as one of the greatest contemporary thinkers, but also because it captures the scepticism of postmodernism. As far as cross-cultural communication is concerned, postmodern theory is characterized by its denial of 'a common locus' between parties involved in continuous intercultural dialogues, so that international or intercultural norms are impossible to achieve.

In my opinion, the reason for such pessimism is less justifiable than it seems. Interesting as it may be, the encyclopedic entry quoted by Borges obviously contradicts our collective experience in cross-cultural exchanges which ought to make us suspicious of the conclusion that Foucault draws from it. We know for a fact that there has been an explosion of bilingual dictionaries in the twentieth century, yet few compilers have expressed the same kind of incompatibility between languages as is suggested by Foucault. As a matter of fact, if we compare entries of, say, an English dictionary and a Chinese dictionary, the semantic explanations there all point to the indication that the two languages register more or less similar features in things and events around us. It is no exaggeration to say that all human beings, whether they are oriental or occidental, have more in common than there are differences between them, especially in terms of basic modes of living, and those common behaviours of humankind can therefore provide a system of reference by means of which they conduct their communicative activities. Even when one language does not have the equivalent of a lexical item in another language, the same meaning can still be expressed using word combinations. This means that, as long as they receive sufficient training in foreign languages, people from different cultures can communicate with one another more or less successfully about the world they live in.

Not surprisingly, when people want to prove that a particular phenomenon in one language cannot be rationally explained in another, they often have to resort to unpublished personal memoirs or travellers' diaries from the past instead of going to direct sources. Ironically, this turns out to be exactly the case with the passage requoted by Foucault. There is an article written by a Chinese scholar which traces the source of the Borges passage as follows:

> The passage Foucault quoted appears originally in Borges' essay on John Wilkins, a seventeenth-century English scholar and Bishop of Chester, whose mind was full of 'happy curiosities' including, among other things, 'the possibility and principles of a world language.' ... Borges greatly admires the courageous, albeit provisional and often thwarted, human effort to penetrate the divine scheme of the universe, and the 'Chinese encyclopedia' represents just that futile yet heroic attempt to probe God's secret. Though he mentions as his source Dr. Franz Kuhn, a German sinologist and translator of Chinese literature, and even gives the title of that 'Chinese

encyclopedia', the so-called Celestial Emporium of Benevolent Knowledge is non-existent except in his own invention. As a matter of fact, it is not at all uncommon of Borges in his writings to mix erudition with imagination, blending real names and titles with imaginary ones. (Zhang Longxi 1988:108-9)

If 'the so-called Celestial Emporium of Benevolent Knowledge is non-existent' and that bizarre classification of animals contained in it is nothing but a German sinologist's imagination, it certainly cannot be used as a valid premise for any cultural theory. The pessimistic view concerning cross-cultural understanding advocated by Foucault should therefore be abandoned as empirically ill-founded.

This is not to say, however, that all cultures and all peoples understand life on this planet in exactly the same way. To deny conceptual differences that exist between cultures is to be blind to the excellent research result of a great portion of linguistic studies of the twentieth century, hence creating a myth of utopia as devastating as Foucault's 'heterotopia'. So the theoretical task that confronts us is to acknowledge cultural differences and justify the possibility of overcoming them at the same time. A great deal of effort has been made in this direction in the past, but without much success. The failure, in my opinion, can be partially attributed to the restriction and limitation of the structuralist interpretation of language that has dominated, and is still dominating, much of our social sciences and humanistic studies. To break the impasse, we need to adopt, or rather revive, a different perspective where language is conceived not as a static structure which articulates our conceptual continuum once and for all but as an ongoing activity through which new meanings are constantly created and accepted by language users.

An early recognition of language as an activity can be found in Anglo-Saxon philosophy of language which extends the object of its investigation from the Saussurean linguistic structure to everyday speech acts. In his posthumous booklet *How to Do Things with Words* (1962), British philosopher John L. Austin argues that, as soon as we abandon our obsession with the abstract systems of lexicon and grammar and expand our analysis to speech acts, the real nature of language as a social practice will come into view. Take the following sentence for example: (1) Basketball is a beautiful sport. In making this statement, the speaker is not only referring to a certain state of affairs that exists in our lifeworld, he is also trying to convince his listener that basketball is pleasant to watch. Thus sentence (1) can be converted into sentence (2) by adding a performative verb: (2) I tell you that basketball is a beautiful sport.

The act of speaking may also bring about some more distant result, depending on specific situations. As a result of hearing the statement, the hearer may very well become a basketball fan thereafter. Thus our example shows that in producing any sentence at all, we accomplish three simultaneous acts: a locutionary act through which we use words to evoke certain states of affairs; an illocutionary act through which we accomplish an action in saying something;

and a perlocutionary act through which we produce an effect upon the hearer by saying something.

The perlocutionary effect of our speech, however, depends on whether both parties involved in the conversation understand a linguistic expression in the same way. If the hearer does not agree with what the speaker is saying, a strategically acting speaker will not succeed in bringing about the desired effect through communicative acts. To ensure a successful coordination of actions, therefore, a speaker has to relate to the world in certain ways that are acceptable to the hearer. In my opinion such a model of communicative action in which both the speaker and the hearer are involved in reaching understanding provides a way out of the dilemma that besets the theory of intercultural communication. On the one hand, it does not rely on the presupposition of a universal norm which is directly contradicted by the factual existence of so many different conceptual systems. On the other hand, it points toward the possibility of intersubjectively establishing a communal consensus. Here is what contemporary German philosopher Habermas has to say on the issue:

> In a distinct analogy to the basic assumption of the semantics of truth conditions, I want now to explain understanding an utterance by knowledge of the conditions under which a hearer may accept it. We understand a speech act when we know what makes it acceptable. From the standpoint of the speaker, the conditions of acceptability are identical to the conditions for his illocutionary success. Acceptability is not defined here in an objectivistic sense, from the perspective of an observer, but in the performative attitude of a participant in communicative action. A speech act may be called 'acceptable' if it satisfies the conditions that are necessary in order that the hearer be allowed to take a 'yes' position on the claim raised by the speaker. These conditions cannot be satisfied one-sidedly, either relative to the speaker or to the hearer. They are rather conditions for the *intersubjective recognition of a linguistic claim which, in a way typical of a given class of speech acts, grounds a specified agreement concerning obligations relevant to the sequel of interaction.* (1984:297-8)

As has been made so clear in the above quotation, language is first and foremost part of social interactions in which the participants negotiate with each other in order to arrive at an agreement that will provide the basis for a consensual coordination of individually pursued plans. When the speaker takes up a position with regard to a certain situation in the lifeworld, she and the hearer enter into an intersubjective relationship that allows her to relate to herself as a participant in an interaction from the perspective of the hearer. In order for her speech act to be accepted by the hearer(s), the speaker has to make the kind of claims whose validity can be redeemed by the hearer from the concrete speech situations. If that fails to happen, either the speaker or the hearer has to modify their initial positions until new meanings are created which are acceptable to both parties.

Although Habermas is talking about the function of human language in general, his theory also applies to the field of cross-cultural communication. No one would deny the fact that we now live in a fast-shrinking world where events in one corner of the global village could seriously affect thousands of inhabitants in another area. The nuclear power plant disaster that happened in Chernobyl on 26 April 1986 is a good case in point. Another example of all nations being closely linked together is the common need for environmental protection, for the extensive destruction of wild forests in one country could lead to disequilibrium in the entire global ecological system. This means that intercultural communication is playing a more and more important role in holding peoples together in their collective fight for survival. Because individual countries are not strong enough to cope with the always threatening conditions of life, they find themselves in need of the cooperation and support of others. Cross-cultural communication, understanding and agreement are the means that make it possible. There is no sense denying that biologically determined factors are also to a certain extent transhistorical and transcultural. It is these shared material conditions of life plus the necessity for international cooperation that provides the grounds for mutual agreement. We do not simply express in language whatever we feel about a situation. It is in the nature of communication that we provide and recognize grounds through which a claim to reason could be redeemed. When another party accepts these conditions as valid, an international norm is then established. Here lies the possibility of successful intercultural communication.

Suzhou University

Note

1 The phrase 'the impossible' is a partial allusion to the Foucaultian aphorism 'the stark impossibility of thinking that'. By calling it 'a tale', I am indicating a different theoretic stand on the issue which is propounded in the main body of the essay. In other words, I hold the opinion that Foucault's or anybody else's pessimistic view about cross-cultural communication is empirically ill-founded. Since the following discussion is conducted from the perspective of contemporary language philosophy, I also call it a semiotic critique of cultural relativism.

Works Cited

Austen, John L. 1962 *How to Do Things with Words*. Oxford University Press.

Foucault, Michel 1970 *The Order of Things*. Random House, New York.

Habermas, Jürgen 1984 *The Theory of Communicative Action*, tr. Thomas McCarthy. Beacon Press, Boston.

Zhang Longxi 1988 'The Myth of the Other: China in the Eyes of the West' in *Critical Inquiry* (Autumn): pp. 108–9.

Yue Daiyun

Cultural Relativism and the Principle of Harmony in Difference

Following the disintegration of the colonial system at the end of the Second World War, Western cultural centrism is in gradual retreat, and a trend towards pluralistic development has emerged in the world's cultures. Developments in world economic trade and the transfer of information have made contact more and more frequent between peoples, nations and regions. Some Western theorists, setting out to protect their own traditional advantages or habits, continue to maintain a doctrine of Western centrism. At the same time, many nationalities which have achieved independence or renaissance, and which cherish feelings for their own culture, have formed a kind of back-to-basics nationalism which tenaciously defends indigenous culture and a traditional conservatism. Some Eastern scholars, in the face of the disasters which have been created by Western culture in the past two centuries, and the oppression they have suffered, have even gone so far as to propose a cultural 'Eastern centrism'. How to dissipate these two contrary currents and prevent them from developing into a large scale confrontation is currently a major problem.

The history of the nineteenth and twentieth centuries proves that using one culture to appropriate or unify another has never really been possible, and the results have been disastrous. Western culture was finally unable to assimilate Eastern culture. Neither was it able to combine cultures to create a new 'world culture'. The reality which faces us is a culturally pluralistic symbiosis. We can only acknowledge this reality. When we do, there is the problem of how different cultures will coexist. As a means of achieving peaceful coexistence, Western scholars have proposed cultural relativism.

Western cultural relativism is clearly a big step forward from Western cultural centrism. It acknowledges that it is reasonable for different cultures to exist, and it opposes judging another culture by one's own standards. It also opposes indiscriminately applying one's own framework to explain the phenomena of other cultures. But cultural relativism has its inherent weaknesses too. For instance, it can lead to exclusivity, to being able to respect only the advantages of one's own culture, or even of safeguarding the recognition of one's own national culture by adopting a closed and isolationist policy, while sacrificing the demands for difference and modernity from a portion of the members. On the other hand, to acknowledge fully cultural relativism it is necessary to accept that cultural phenomena such as fascism or nazism, which have already or may in the future endanger human coexistence, have inherent cultural origins and belong to specific cultures.

It seems that in truly culturally pluralistic societies, while the relativity of cultures must be acknowledged, there still needs to be communication and negotiation between different cultures, through which standards and social consensus are achieved. At the same time, serious regard needs to be given to variation, renewal and progress within national cultures. The principle of Harmony in Difference (*He er bu tong*) in traditional Chinese culture provides us with a positive resource.

The theory of Harmony in Difference comes from a story recorded in the *Zuo Zhuan* more than two thousand years ago. At that time there was an interesting dialogue between Yan Zi, the chief minister of the state of Qi and the Duke of Qi. The Duke of Qi said to Yan Zi, 'Liang Qiuju is the only one of my attendants who is in harmony with me.' Yan Zi said, 'Liang Qiuju only seeks agreement, nothing more. How can you talk of harmony?' The Duke asked, 'Surely harmony and agreement are the same thing?' This elicited a major discourse from Yan Zi, who maintained that:

> Difference was the most basic condition for material composition and development. For example, when cooking food the oil, salt, sauce and vinegar have to be different before they can constitute a cooked dish. Similarly with music, there must be difference between long and short, quick and slow, sad and happy, strong and weak, so that they can come together in concord. What then is the use of someone like Liang Qiuju, if when you say aye he says aye and when you say nay he also says nay?

From that time, Harmony in Difference became one of the core concepts in traditional Chinese culture. Confucius said, 'Gentle people can be in harmony though they differ, while mean people can be in agreement but still not harmonious.' Zheng Zichan said, 'Harmony promotes the birth of things, but sameness is of no use' (*Guo Yu*, 'Zheng Yu'). First of all difference has to be acknowledged, because there can be no development without it, but difference does not mean unrelatedness. There needs to be harmony between all the diverse elements. Harmony is the harmonious and beneficial relationship of material things to each other. New things can only be produced and can only develop if there is harmony. Perhaps by dealing with relationships within a culture or among diverse cultures according to a principle such as Harmony in Difference, some useful conclusions may be reached.

As far as sameness is concerned, we must acknowledge that difference commonly exists, and that within the one culture, an individual has the right to say yes or no; that is, the right to be different from another. We must acknowledge that within a cultural tradition there can also be different traditions. The Confucians, Daoists and Buddhists in China, together with the other popular cultural traditions, intersected and complemented one another. Today's cultural pluralists see cultural singularism as singularity within plurality, acknowledging that not only does difference exist but also that some aspects of different cultures are at times difficult to understand and accept.

The traditional Chinese explanation of Harmony means four things.

Firstly, although things are not the same, they still cannot depart from their relationships with each other and exist in isolation. The literal sense of Harmony means the way in which a lot of different elements coexist in a network of relationships. The relationships between human beings at the basis of the Confucian position, and the relationships between human beings and nature at the basis of the Daoist position both illustrate this.

Secondly, the spirit of Harmony, in seeking to coordinate difference and achieve a new harmonious unity, produces something new, which in turn constitutes new difference with other things. For example, different ingredients go to make up a culinary dish, and that dish in turn, together with several other dishes, goes to make up a banquet. None of the difference is finally lost, but it constitutes a larger, more perfect harmony. It is the same with cultural development. China's Confucians, in seeking to maintain the rituals and music, were in fact trying to preserve social harmony through positive action, whereas the Daoists, in seeking to accord with nature, were trying to maintain social tranquillity (which is also Harmony) through non-action. These were two separate schools of thought at first, but much later, after they had developed for almost a thousand years, a Western Jin philosopher, Guo Xiang, proposed that the Confucians' maintenance of rites and music was in fact in accordance with nature, and that no action was required to make others accept it, and therefore it too was a kind of non-action. That was a statement which both Confucians and Daoists were able to accept, but being no longer totally Confucian or Daoist as before, it had achieved a new Harmony. The highest ideal of traditional Chinese culture, as expressed in the thirtieth chapter of the *Doctrine of the Mean*, is that 'the myriad things of the world develop side by side, yet they do each other no harm', and 'the Ways progress together and are not contrary to each other'.

Thirdly, Harmony subsists chiefly in moderation. In the third century BC a Chinese poet described a beautiful woman in this way: 'Add one inch she would be too tall, take away one inch she would be too short. Apply more powder she would be too pale, apply more rouge she would be too pink' (Deng Tu Zi, 'In Praise of Beauty').

Fourthly, how is moderation to be measured? The Daoists supposed that moderation meant being in accordance with nature. Zhuang Zi pointed out that in nature the sky is above and the earth below, and in each year spring and summer precede and autumn and winter follow. None of these, whether sky or earth, or any of the seasons, can affect each other's order or development either through excess or too little. Thus a sequence of prosperity and decline already exists in nature's way, and in the societies of humanity's way there are common principles which everyone naturally adheres to. Zhuang Zi said that the most complete harmony could be achieved in the world through the 'greater Harmony of all things'; through following natural reason, being moral in action and being in agreement with nature. The concept of moral filial seniority which is at the core of Confucianism emphasizes two-sided standards of behaviour such as a father's kindness and a son's respectfulness, friendship and respect among older and younger brothers, the justice of rulers and loyalty of ministers and so on, striving to find harmony and moderation in relationships between the two. Therefore, in the saying 'Harmony is the most valuable thing in the practice of ritual', ritual means the commonly observed principles and standards which cannot truly come into being unless within the preconditions of harmony and moderation.

It can be seen from the above discussion that the principle of Harmony in Difference makes up for the deficiencies of cultural relativism in some areas. However an important problem still remains to be solved, which is that in dealing with relationships among human beings, certain general principles, approved of by those human beings, must be adhered to before Harmony in Difference can truly come into being. And how are those principles to be arrived at? How can they be made to encroach as little as possible upon the interests of different groups, while allowing as much as possible for the special characteristics of different groups? How can people in different groups be made to acknowledge and voluntarily accept those principles? Neither the Confucians, who consider common principles to derive from the sayings of the Sages, nor the Daoists who consider them to derive from nature, have answered these questions directly.

The German philosopher Jürgen Habermas, taking current Western trends as his point of departure, proposes similar problems and strives to solve them. A central problem which he considers in his recent works is how to find social consensus, to find certain common principles to serve as a moral basis of social cooperation. One of his basic points of departure is that the special characteristics of any people can only find realization through society, but as soon as people become involved in social networks they must submit to the general principles of those networks, causing the special characteristics and wishes of the individual to be suppressed or even alienated. Habermas proposes a Principle of Justice, to protect the equal rights of respect for the individual, and at the same time proposes a Principle of Solidarity, making it the duty of individuals to have fellow feeling and respect for others, continually enlarging the area of tolerance. If the former principle could be said to be about Difference, then the latter is about Harmony. To bring these principles into being, Habermas proposes contact, negotiation and intersubjectivity, among other things, and emphasizes that the principles may come into play at different levels. At a utilitarian level they may be limited to establishing rules for mutual benefit, while at an ethical level they may be used in the common pursuit of a better way of life, or they may even be applied at more abstract levels. All these are of great practical significance in bringing into being the principle of Harmony in Difference, so long pursued in traditional Chinese culture.

Harmony in Difference through contact and negotiation did not begin in modern times, for there have been successful precedents, in several different configurations. In one configuration certain concepts of culture A are not present in culture B, but those concepts are possibly not incompatible with other concepts in culture B. For example, the Indian Buddhist concept of enlightenment did not originally exist in Chinese culture, but by Song and Ming times the various schools of Neo-Confucian metaphysics had accepted it and blended it into their systems, where it promoted new intellectual developments.

Another configuration is where it is found that certain concepts of culture A are in conflict with certain concepts of culture B, but are of great importance for culture B's development, and culture B absorbs and adapts them according to its own needs, so that they become an integral part of its own culture, thereby attaining development. For example, in traditional Chinese culture the common people were merely objects of administrative government, and their only importance was as a means of consolidating the ruler's power. Therefore there were formulas such as 'the people can be made to follow but not to understand', which differed greatly from Western democratic thinking. For Chinese culture to accommodate Western democracy it was neccessary to be critical of some of the concepts existing in the traditional culture, and in this century China's adaptation and absorption of the democratic ideas in Western culture have played a large part in the improvement of China's polity.

There is another configuration where, in the course of cultural contact and negotiation, new concepts are discovered which neither side has possessed before but which are very important, and which are themselves an outcome of the contact and exchange — for example, the principle of pluralistic cultural coexistence as opposed to Western centrism and Asian centrism.

The principle of Harmony in Difference, arrived at through contact and negotiation, can take place at the most basic utilitarian level, for example when two completely different nations are able to achieve Harmony on the point of mutual non-encroachment of territory simply because of mutual interest. Contact and negotiation can also take place at a very abstract level. For example, where Christianity preaches universal love, Buddhism preaches compassion, and Confucianism preaches love extending to all; the connotations of each are quite different, but considered at an abstract level, they all preach love of humanity. Love can thus become a general principle accepted by each different cultural tradition, while at the same time each type of love retains its own particular difference.

In fact it is through the process of continual contact and negotiation leading to new Harmony in Difference that human cultures progress and develop. The British philosopher Bertrand Russell, in a 1922 essay comparing Chinese and Western culture, wrote that exchanges between different cultures in the past have proven many times to be milestones in the development of human civilization. Greece copied from Egypt, and Rome borrowed from Greece. Arabia referred back to the Roman Empire, and Mediaeval Europe in turn imitated Arabia, while Renaissance Europe followed the Byzantine Empire. European culture, in the course of its own development, absorbed all kinds of cultural elements from outside, but not only did it avoid losing its European cultural tradition, it also greatly enriched the content of its own culture. Cultures 'develop side by side, yet do each other no harm' and 'progress together and are not in conflict with each other'. This is how Harmony in Difference is manifested.

However in the past, whether it is the principle of Harmony in Difference or the action of contact and negotiation, all have come about through awareness and self-consciousness. Traditional Chinese culture, in its thousands of years of development, has created very many brilliant and significant intellectual principles which, for social reasons or because they lacked the necessary feasibility, were seldom able to be really put into practice. The principle of Harmony in Difference is among them. Habermas's Universalism, which he makes efforts to construct in his *Discourse Ethics*, accepts pluralism while at the same time insisting on social consensus obtained through negotiation. His ideas concerning the era of postmetaphysical thinking and his deep concern for the fate of humanity, could probably, in concert with the ancient Chinese principle of Harmony in Difference, produce a valuable contribution to the peaceful coexistence and common development of different cultures in the twenty-first century.

Peking University

HAN JIAMING

Political Criticism in the Postmodern Era

In the late 1930s, New Criticism came to dominate literary studies in the USA, a dominance which lasted into the 1960s. New Criticism disregarded material of an author's life and times as external, and the elimination of politics in literary criticism could even be designated as its trademark. In the 1970s and 1980s, when liberal critics reviewed the dated New Criticism, they generally agreed that it was the proper child of the Cold War. When the world was divided into the East and West or Capitalism and Communism, and any political discussion could be labelled as pro-Communist or treason, the best strategy was to avoid politics altogether.

Humanistic criticism is a vague term since it did not exist as a school as in the case of New Criticism. Related to the idea of the humanities, it may be characterized as New Criticism plus some concern with the human factor as its proponents took for granted the basic universality of human nature. As M. H. Abrams wrote:

> ...in discussing a poetic work, Horace takes for granted what I have called the humanistic paradigm, in which a purposive author designs and invests with meanings a literary work that represents human beings and actions and is specifically addressed to the determinate understanding, and the emotional and pleasurable responsiveness, of human readers. And if we look, we find this same paradigm in Aristotle's *Poetics*, in Longinus on the sublime style, and in the classical writers on rhetoric. The changes that occurred in the long history of literary criticism can be mapped largely as changes in focus on one or another of the elements within this overall frame, as the emphasis shifted between the make-up of the environing world; the needs and preferences of readers, the temperament, imagination, and emotional processes of the author; and the internal requirements of the literary work itself as the primary determinants of a literary work. The human world thus served as the setting for just about all critical discourse about literature until some three or four decades ago, when it was displaced by the various theory worlds of

structural and poststructural critics. (1993:12)

Clearly Professor Abrams betrays a strong sense of nostalgia, as if some decades ago everything was fine and suddenly a great chaos occurred. Abrams first presented his theory of literature based on the four basic human elements in 1953 in *The Mirror and the Lamp*, virtually marking the beginning of the era of contemporary theory. For humanistic critics, political criticism again is an anomaly: literature is concerned with universal human experience, not with political propaganda, which, it was believed, would only damage literature. But despite the claim of political immunity, both New Criticism and humanistic criticism actually hold the political norm of modern capitalist society as the basis of their literary judgement. In other words, the claim of an apolitical stance is but an excuse or disguise for upholding the dominant political stance of the day.

The hegemony of New Criticism did not mean that no scholars focused on historical criticism, and their study often involved dealing with politics as an important historical issue. This kind of political study is particularly notable in the study of Renaissance and eighteenth-century English literature, for then many writers wrote for political purposes as can be seen in the cases of Spenser, Milton, Dryden, Swift, Defoe, and Fielding. In such studies, politics often took the narrow meaning, referring to political parties, government change, and specific debates.

There are basically two kinds of critical work here. The first uses literary works to construct an author's politics. Shakespeare and Dr Johnson are usually considered to be less political than, say, Spenser or Swift, but critics have established their politics by studying their literary works. For example, Allan Bloom, a professor of political philosophy, published *Shakespeare's Politics* in 1964 which led to numerous similar studies by later scholars. The literary historian Donald Greene published *The Politics of Samuel Johnson* in 1960 which substantially rejected the view established by the nineteenth-century historian; Macauley, that Johnson was 'ignorant of or indifferent to politics, or alternatively, a blind, bigoted, reactionary "Tory"' (xi).

The second kind uses politics as the background or context for discussing literature, for example, specifying the political context for Dryden's *Absalom and Achitophel* (see Schilling 1961) or examining Book I of *Gulliver's Travels* in relation to early eighteenth-century politics (see Case 1945). This kind of political criticism is still popular and notable studies continue to appear. In *Shakespeare's Political Plays: The History Plays and Roman Plays*, Alexander Leggart concentrates 'on what is political in a more narrow, traditional sense: the ordering and enforcing, the gaining and losing, of public power in the state' (ix). Manuel Schonhorn, in *Defoe's Politics: Parliament, Power, Kingship and 'Robinson Crusoe'* constructs an image of Defoe as a conservative thinker of political power in sharp contrast to the traditional view which sees Defoe as the enlightened liberal apologist for the development of mercantile capitalism. In contrast to Marxist criticism, this kind of political criticism only focuses on the power struggle within the dominating class, making no efforts to expose the class conflicts and deep social problems underneath. Such studies are important for understanding the authors or for interpreting specific works but, like New Criticism and humanistic criticism, traditional political criticism does not touch on actual social political life, and conforms to the dominant social order.

❖

If traditional political criticism is detached from actual political life or conforms to the dominant social order, contemporary political criticism usually highlights its oppositional political agenda, dealing with all kinds of oppositional relationships concerning gender, class, race, sexuality or sexual orientation. From the 1940s and 1950s, when every critic tried to avoid politics, to the 1980s and 1990s when everyone talks about politics and everything becomes political, the causes are very complicated.

First, the Cold War ended. Second, the 1960s witnessed the rapid development of anti-war demonstrations, Black Rights movements, sex liberation, and feminism, especially on university campuses; by the early 1980s, the student activists of the 1960s had become established as professors on campus, with the right and power to propagate their ideas. This was at the time when the Reagan-Bush conservative administration was in power in the United States, the Soviet Union was undergoing great changes that led to its collapse, and socialism-oriented political revolution was experiencing great setbacks. All this promoted the development of academic politics. Thirdly, considering literary studies, structuralism and deconstruction still followed the text-centred bias characteristic of New Criticism; the issues of gender, race, class, sexuality or sexual orientation that had won great popularity since the 1960s were not dealt with properly in literary studies. As a result, pure theory was losing its hold on scholars. About the same time, the importation of Western Marxism, feminism, and Lacanian psychoanalysis suited the atmosphere and helped people to reconsider politics and its position in literary studies (see Cohen 1987).

Political criticism now probably includes at least the following: feminism, Marxism, postcolonial studies, and psychoanalysis. Correspondingly gender, class, race, and sexuality or sexual orientation are focal points. For critics related to these schools, politics is anything concerned with 'oppression' or 'opposition', be it racial, sexual, or class. Traditional party politics has retreated to the background or become but one kind of politics. New historicism seems to be the combination of all these, and its special concern, if it has one, may be identified as power. New historicist critics offer a kind of political criticism that emphasizes political containment: subversion is always contained and neutralized by the dominant ideology. As a result, rather than polarizing oppositional struggle, these critics focus on exploring the power structure in which different ideas go through a process of exchange and negotiation, and they often reinforce the dominant power which contains the oppositional forces. Because of this, radical critics often distance themselves from new historicism. Thus, even at the time of its early development, Felicity Nussbaum and Laura Brown wrote in their introductory essay to *The New Eighteenth Century*:

> Perhaps one danger in the 'rise' of new historicism in America lies in its potential establishment as a new orthodoxy, particularly if it comes to be perceived as a flight from the theoretical possibilities of other poststructuralist movements such as deconstruction, or as an alternative to the more explicit political commitments of Marxism, feminism, and antiracist, postcolonial critiques. (1987:20)

Unlike new historicism that seems to embrace everything, feminism, postcolonial studies, psychoanalysis and Marxism have more explicit political concerns. Feminists not only attempt to expose the explicit and implicit phenomena of gender discrimination in literary texts but also try to eliminate it in actual social life. It is generally agreed among contemporary critics that in the last twenty years feminism perhaps has had greater influence on social and political life than any other school of criticism. Postcolonialism or postcolonial studies is a more complicated term, for it could mean either anti-colonialism, or a new kind of colonialism that followed the global completion of decolonization in the last few decades. Because most of the scholars engaged in postcolonial studies are Third-World scholars teaching in First-World countries (especially the USA), or descendants of immigrants or black slaves, postcolonial studies also has a strong political agenda. Psychoanalysis seems to have split into two groups: the first has identified with feminism to form what some critics have called 'a marriage of strange bedfellows' because Freud had first developed his theory with a male bias; and the other group has joined gay and lesbian studies, but this may also be related to feminism since radical feminists believe that only lesbians are true feminists (see Gaines 1995). Marxist criticism has been gaining ground in English and American universities with Terry Eagleton and Fredric Jameson as the leaders on either side of the Atlantic. Their studies tend to be all-inclusive with a strong traditional Marxist concern over the issue of class and have become part of contemporary cultural studies.

In American criticism now, we might distinguish three parties: the traditional humanistic critics who are still arguing that the value of literature lies in its universal human concerns; the poststructuralists or deconstructionists who study literature mainly to dismantle the text and aggrandize their theory; and the political critics who aim at fighting for the oppressed in the academy. Generally speaking the humanistic critics tend to be aloof to the contemporary explosion of political criticism. De Man once imagined a picture of literary studies with deconstruction as the hegemonic power, but that vision is long gone, and de Man himself has experienced a posthumous trial by history when his war journals were discovered in 1987. Although some deconstructionists are still trying to deconstruct the printed text to aggrandize the imagined theory, many of them have already made signal movement towards the all-embracing trend of cultural studies. Judging at least from the amount of articulation, political critics clearly hold the day. If you open any critical journal, or a catalogue of any press notable for publishing literary studies, such terms as 'gender, race, politics, body, slavery, sexuality' are among the most frequently used in titles, which tells us something about the critics' central concerns.

Political criticism is controversial. Its supporters are unquestionably numerous, but opponents are not rare, and many are raising serious challenges. First, pan-political criticism itself is questionable. As Leggart remarks: 'if everything is political then nothing is, for the word has lost its edge' (1988:ix). One clear result of pan-political criticism is that the issue of class — the central concern in Marxist theory — has been pushed to the margins. More opponents to political criticism are arguing that, if you want to change the world, create an uprising or revolution, which is certainly much more effective to social change than discussing the politics of literature to graduate students in prestigious universities. If you hate American politics or are critical of its system, why are you still making money in this system instead of freeing yourself from it? What's the use of pointing out that women have been mistreated in literature since everyone knows that? Do the Third-World scholars who trade in postcolonial discourse help their compatriots in any way? Whatever one may say about such attacks against politically conscious scholars, there is one significant problem with the scholars' political claim: they fail to articulate clearly how their critical work serves their political purpose.

Tobin Siebers argues that despite its explicit claim for political criticism, new historicism is not essentially different from New Criticism and deconstruction: they all are based on the skepticism lying behind the Cold War psyche. New Criticism suspected authorial intention and effect on the reader, so they raised the banners of 'intentional fallacy' and 'affective fallacy'; deconstruction suspected logocentrism, so they advocated 'indeterminacy'; new historicists suspect the distinction between 'text' and 'context', so they indulge in searching for anecdotes in historical archives. Siebers is not blindly against skepticism which may lead people to question the dominant order, but, he argues, if one suspects everything and abandons value judgement, such skepticism may cause treacherous results:

> The skeptical project dreams of mastery by opposing itself to 'false' groundings and constructions of thought.... It makes a virtue of thinking otherwise without thinking about the directions in which it may lead. Often, this project does arrive at a genuinely critical understanding of the dogmatic aspects of the categories and institutions by which the history of ethics and politics has proceeded, and herein lies its great value. But, just as often, it ends in the irony of saying one thing and meaning something else, where the 'something else' recovers not the skeptical insights of thinking otherwise or an immaculate and radical alterity but the categories, conventions, and traditions against which skeptics desire so ardently to oppose themselves. (1993:28)

In other words, skeptical strategy does not lead anywhere but only makes one indulge in one's own self:

> Critics are grinding out essays on race, gender, and class. The academic publishing world is in a fever. These books and essays all have political agendas, but rarely does the writer have the nerve to spell out the issues and make proposals. Instead, we find an idle and illusory political rhetoric that encourages abstraction and self-congratulation rather than action. (154)

❖

Siebers is concerned about how to push political criticism forward to make it useful politics. As if to answer Siebers' demand, in her latest book *Ends of Empire: Women and Ideology in Early Eighteenth-Century English Literature*, published in the same year as Siebers', Laura Brown presents an explicit political message:

> I want to reorient the project of eighteenth-century literary studies toward an integrated account of categories of oppression so that the examination of this field can promote the ends of a feminist, anti-imperialist, anti-racist, libertarian politics. ... Ideology critique becomes a means of recovering past progressive positions, and also a basis for supporting radical change in our own period by making the literature of those in power politically usable to those in opposition. (1993:11)

Brown's book examines what lies at the margin of the power structure. She moves around the world to discuss Surinam slaves, African natives, and colonized and poverty-stricken Irish people. In this political reading of early eighteenth-century English literature, political struggle in England itself does not take an eminent position; on the other hand, slaves, African natives, Amazons, and the portrayal of fetishized or corrupt women in satiric and aesthetic literature become the central figures. The marginal comes to the centre and offers a new perspective to view the power structure at the centre.

Brown studies the literary work not to tell the reader what it means but to show the complicated relationships involved in it. The strength of her study owes much to her insight that:

> ...the figure of the woman seems to present two different faces in the literary culture examined here. First, through an association with trade, commodification, and consumption generated by the economic devaluation of women's labor, woman takes a central position in the representation of such fundamental dimensions of cultural experience as character, identity, and value.... The second major function of the figure of the woman arises from the connection between gender and difference — the radical heterogeneity of sexual, racial, or class dissimilarities. (18–9)

The interaction of the two functions makes woman the central figure in the development of mercantile capitalist ideology closely related to issues of commodification, sexuality, slavery, and colonialism. 'These conjunctures ...

provide a concrete staging of the ways in which apparently divergent critical perspectives might be integrated' (21). For example, in her discussion of Swift's misogynist poetry, Brown notes that Swift attacks women as essentially corrupt. In his Irish tracts he blames women's desire for luxury and ornament for destroying the country and to save the country women must dress in native linen rather than relying on foreign trade. The attack on female luxury leads to a critique of mercantile capitalism and colonialism; Swift the misogynist is found to be one of the earliest and strongest champions against colonialism. In other words, Brown reads something positive in the apparently negative portrayal of the figure of woman in Swift's work.

As a radical critic committed to both feminism and Marxism, Brown is concerned about the practical use of criticism. She writes:

> Feminists might find insights into the multiple forces that maintain female subordination today in these descriptions of the complex role of the female figure in the eighteenth century. Activists working for cultural diversity might be able to find modern connections among seemingly disparate positions through analogies to the mutually dependent situations of women, slaves, blacks, colonizers, and colonized defined in these readings. More generally, a radical intelligentsia might be able to use an account of imperialist ideology in this period to analyze modern crises, or to delegitimize some of the dominant institutions of modern society. (11–12)

Whether we agree with Brown or not, her presentation of the practical use of political criticism is valuable.

If Brown's proposal for the political use of criticism goes further than a simple skeptical analysis, Siebers offers another way out after criticizing contemporary criticism at length. He writes, 'We are bound in this age of suspicion to be skeptical.... But we must place our natural skepticism in the service of something and not allow it to be directed to ends willy-nilly by the force of our exhaustion.' How to avoid this pitfall? For one thing, 'Literary criticism needs to take account of what politics really is, which means, first of all, that we need to understand that politics takes place in the world'. Furthermore:

> Criticism needs to include within its province once more life-affirming principles in addition to the ascetic and skeptical ones that it has come to embrace. Pleasure, beauty, knowledge, and the world (both as nature and human experience) should have a place in the language of criticism.... [Literary criticism] should uphold a reverence for our inner lives. We have learned that the self is not a self-contained, autonomous power. Now we need to understand that the interdependence of human beings that constitutes our subjectivity does not preclude the possibility of agency, private feelings, and an inner life. (156–7)

It is clear that Siebers here is offering a kind of compromise between the assumptions of postmodern skeptical criticism and traditional humanistic beliefs. In the era of suspicion we are justified in being skeptical of Siebers' proposal, but it at least indicates that skepticism cannot be the only way ahead, for pure skepticism will lead to nihilism and we cannot bear that. In fact, as human history has proved again and again, the world proceeds through the process of continual compromise or negotiation between the new and the old, and the development of literary theory or cultural studies is not and cannot be an exception.

Peking University

Works Cited

Abrams, M. H. 1993 'What Is a Humanistic Criticism' in *The Bookpress*, Cornell University Press, vol. 3, no. 4: p. 1, pp. 6–7, pp. 12–4.

Bloom, Allan 1964 *Shakespeare's Politics*. Basic Books, New York.

Brown, Laura 1993 *Ends of Empire: Women and Ideology in Early Eighteenth-Century English Literature*. Cornell University Press.

Case, Arthur E. 1945 *Four Essays on 'Gulliver's Travels'*. Princeton University Press.

Cohen, Walter 1987 'Political Criticism of Shakespeare' in *Shakespeare Reproduced: The Text in History and Ideology*, ed. Jean E. Howard and Marion F. O'Connor. Methuen, New York: pp. 18–46.

Gaines, Jane 1995 'Feminist Heterosexuality and Its Politically Incorrect Pleasure' in *Critical Inquiry* 21: pp. 382–410.

Greene, Donald J. 1990 *The Politics of Samuel Johnson*, 2nd ed. with a new Introduction. University of Georgia Press.

Leggart, Alexander 1988 *Shakespeare's Political Drama: The History Plays and the Roman Plays*. Routledge, New York.

Nussbaum, Felicity and Laura Brown 1987 'Revising Critical Practices: An Introductory Essay' in *The New 18th Century: Theory, Politics, English Literature*, ed. Nussbaum & Brown. Methuen, New York: pp. 1–22.

Schilling, Bernard N. 1961 *Dryden and the Conservative Myth: A Reading of 'Absalom and Achitophel'*. Yale University Press.

Schonhorn, Manuel 1993 *Defoe's Politics: Parliament, Power, Kingship and 'Robinson Crusoe'*. Cambridge University Press.

Siebers, Tobin 1993 *Cold War Criticism and the Politics of Skepticism*. Oxford University Press.

GU ZHENGKUN

Seven Laws Governing the Patterns of Development of Eastern and Western Cultures

Viewed from a macroscopic perspective, human cultures are monistic; from a microcosmic perspective, however, the multiplicity of human cultures suggests pluralism. Today, when human cultures are developed to a very high degree, overemphasizing their monistic elements will result in cultural nihilism that tends to repress the multiple potentialities of human cultural development. Overemphasizing cultural pluralism, on the other hand, incurs a danger of giving rise to cultural chauvinism.

This view of cultures in general also holds true for the relationship between Western and Eastern cultures. Briefly speaking, I think there are seven laws governing the patterns of Western and Eastern cultures. The following is a brief introduction to these seven laws.

1. THE LAW OF CULTURAL COMMONALITY

Cultures have a common root — human desires. The fact that all cultures are created by human beings justifies the belief that cultures on earth must be of one common nature, that is, the nature of mankind. All cultures are born of an interaction between the objective world and three innate human desires: the desire for food, for sex and for power. Moreover, human beings on earth have to live and develop in a pattern fashioned by the conditions that the earth has to offer.

The root (the common nature), however, can be also understood as a unity of two roots: the Yin root (spiritual) stemming from the three desires and the Yang root (substantial) stemming from the objective world. Cultures are flowers based on this graft. That is why, on many occasions, one finds that the root of Western culture is in a way that of Eastern culture, and vice versa. And logically and naturally, one can see in certain historical phases, the spirit of

Western culture somehow substantialized in some form of Eastern culture and vice versa.

2. THE LAW OF CULTURAL INTERSTRUCTURING

Two cultures are like two persons of different manners and values; once they discover the opposite, they intentionally or unconsciously try to influence it. Each side attempts to reform, fashion or regulate the other side. They are doing so because they both firmly believe they are doing the right thing; because they sincerely believe they are saving their opponents. For instance, Christianity in the West and Buddhism in the East have been doing things this way earnestly for thousands of years, as have other so-called doctrines or ideas clothed in -isms. For the past three hundred years, Eastern cultures and Western cultures have been yoked in this way.

It is in the process of cultural interstructuring that both Eastern and Western cultures find their own unique nature, values and potentialities, as well as their particular position and significance in the great Yin-Yang cycle of West-East cultures.

One of the issues of vital importance, at least for the Chinese scholar, is to consider to what extent the process of interstructuring between Western and Eastern cultures can be properly developed, since the process has its limitations. The process of interstructuring usually comes to a standstill at a point where a certain degree of compromise is reached, for West-East cultures are of opposed polarity as far as their orientation of development is concerned.

3. THE LAW OF CULTURAL COMPLEMENTARITY

The totality and perfection of global cultures is found in the complementarity of Eastern and Western cultures. It naturally follows that Eastern cultures or Western cultures, when judged alone, are imperfect because the environments, the climate, the race, the languages, the time, the resources available and many other factors are quite different. Fortunately, Eastern and Western cultures are so organically formed into a whole that where the Eastern culture presents as a disadvantage it is often balanced by an advantage in the Western culture, or, where the Western culture is weak, the Eastern culture is often proved to be strong. When a culture is ill, its remedy should be found in another culture. Or in other words, Western culture is a doctor for Eastern culture, and vice versa. When we refuse a culture, we are refusing to be cured of our illness.

One misunderstanding that some scholars often commit is to believe that cultural advantages can be simply moved from one culture into the other. In my opinion, advantages are of a different nature and two categories: spiritual and physical. Scientific and technological advantages, for instance, are of the physical sort, while literary and artistic advantages the spiritual sort. Physical advantages can be easily borrowed or imitated while spiritual advantages are often difficult (sometimes simply impossible) to move from one culture into another. Computer software can be imported from abroad and used only if the physical conditions (such as computers) and related operational commands are provided. But literary or cultural values are different in that they call for related psychological conditions such as similar cultural background and aesthetic taste (habit) on the part of the user. The physical is movable while the psychological usually is not. To cultivate a shared aesthetic tendency we must sharpen our sensibility to particular values of a particular culture, to the plurality and complementarity of both Eastern and Western cultures.

4. THE LAW OF CULTURAL CONFLICT

On one hand, contemporary human beings are now well equipped to perceive the following truth: modern cultural development calls for a challenging intensity of opposition so that the creative spirit can be aroused to the utmost degree. On the other hand, we perceive more clearly that, when a culture tends to suppress or eradicate what is called a heathen culture, it is just weakening its own potentialities of development.

The inevitability of cultural conflict or cultural misreading does not warrant the inevitability of a war or fierce strife; human beings now learn more and more how to tolerate rather than to struggle against each other. Apparently we need a sort of appropriateness of opposition, that is just strong enough to stimulate the steady development of culture and just weak enough to avoid the possible destruction of any other culture.

5. THE LAW OF CULTURAL MUTUAL MANIFESTATION

Only by comparing with and contrasting to its own opposite can a culture really understand and manifest its own virtues. In other words, the advantages or merits of a culture are shown by the very existence of its opposite culture. For instance, the healthy side of the belief typical of Eastern culture that nature and humanity have coexisted in harmonious union is made strongly felt only when Western science has made Westerners keenly aware of the suffering from a painful separation of humanity from nature. Similarly, modern Western culture backed up by science can well boast that it is analytical and precise only when it is in sharp contrast to the Eastern culture that appears comprehensively obscure and over-synthetic.

6. THE LAW OF CULTURAL MUTUAL VERIFICATION

The rationality of many aspects of a culture is often verified with the aid of borrowing many sides of its opposite culture. Many propositions raised in ancient Eastern culture have been finally proved or verified by Western science. For instance, many concepts of Buddhism, the *Book of Changes* and the *Book of Lao Tzu* have been verified by modern science in the West. In general, although both Eastern and Western cultures are characterized by rational and irrational elements, it is safe to say that the rational side of Eastern culture is less apparent than that of Western culture; or, in other words, without the development of modern science in the West, many profound ideas of ancient culture in the East cannot be understood and verified. Similarly, without the wisdom and pioneering efforts of Eastern ancients, the modern culture of the West will incur the danger of going astray. Eastern culture is a mirror of Western culture, and vice versa. To make myself understood, I'd like to offer a clumsy metaphor that Eastern culture is a proposition as well as conclusion, while Western culture is an argument (evidences and process of demonstration). It seems that the supreme truth of God can be obtained only in the perfect combination of Eastern and Western cultures.

7. THE LAW OF THE YIN-YANG CYCLE OF CULTURAL DEVELOPMENT

Following the rule that all things must develop in the opposite direction when they reach the extreme, both Eastern and Western cultures in many ways will sooner or later develop in opposite patterns. Scholars of the twentieth century need not feel puzzled that Eastern culture becomes more and more Westernized while Western culture becomes more and more Easternized. This can be obviously seen in the development of modern poetry and art.

Generally speaking, the Yin-tendency in Eastern culture is stronger than that of Western culture while the Yang-tendency in Western culture is stronger than that of Eastern culture.

Before the sixteenth century, the main trend of world culture was Yin represented by the cultures of ancient Egypt, Babylon, India and China, with the exception of the Greek and Roman cultures. Then the tide turned. The Yang cultures represented by Western countries rose into prominence. During recent years, modern science has been developing at an amazing speed and Western culture has reached its peak of development at the end of twentieth century. Following the same law as I have mentioned above, a great yet gradual change may take place in the global culture frame. As many believe, the twenty-first century might witness a rise of Eastern culture. Again, it may not be superfluous for me to emphasize that the rise of one culture need not accompany a decline of another, because the predicting power that modern people possess enables them to regulate or adjust to a certain extent their own course of cultural evolution. Moreover, the rise of a seemingly-new culture often is only the rise of a variation of its former model.

Peking University

QIAN ZHONGWEN

Neo-Rationalism: A Tactic in Cultural Dialogue

The twentieth century is an age of artistic and literary innovation. While some of these innovations have diversified and extended literature, other new literary schools have gone to extremes since the late 1950s by regarding the operations of the words as the final artistic ends, triggering a total negation of artistic and literary meanings and the gradual erosion of humanistic spirit.

The diminishing and debasement of literature concurs with existential frustrations and crises of twentieth-century human beings. Catastrophes and social upheavals have deprived human beings of their beliefs and ideals. Under the weight of enormous universal existential crises, some intellectuals in the field of the humanities have sought to find a new perspective to reinterpret existence, tradition, culture and the meaning of art. This new humanistic perspective can also be called neo-rationalism.

Neo-rationalism upholds a new kind of humanistic spirit aimed at enriching human spirituality. The humanistic spirit is an ideal, a relationship network and a criterion for guiding existence, actions and lifestyles. The humanistic spirit craves for and reaffirms the meaning and value of human existence. Humanistic spirit, a common core of civilization, has universal significance in that its basic constituents include a sense of shame, sympathy, pity, passion, conscience, honesty and justice. Secondly, humanistic spirit is a historical phenomenon while patriotism means a love for one's country and its cultural heritage, it contains different connotations in different historical periods. Thirdly, humanistic spirit has an intensely idealistic character. In the Chinese cultural tradition humanistic spirit pays great attention to human relationships and idealistic qualities such as self-discipline, self-reliance, self-respect and social commitment. On the other hand, Western humanism focuses on individuality by emphasizing each individual's right to freedom, equality, knowledge and truth.

In China the new humanistic spirit needs not only to inherit valuable parts from traditional Chinese humanism but also to absorb, to some extent, the elements of value from Western humanism, so that it will foster healthy growth both in the individual and in the individual's relationships with society. One of the objectives of art and literature is to uphold the new humanistic spirit to prevent the debasement of meaning and value.

Equipped with the new humanistic spirit, neo-rationalism aims at combatting spiritual mediocrity and degradation and tries to promote positive human qualities. Critical judgement and awareness on the part of humanistic intellectuals need to be strengthened. The new literary schools appearing in the past decades, influenced by language philosophy and linguistic philosophy, focus their attention on language and form by responding with the noisy call for a return to literature proper. Indeed, literature returns to itself when language has been changed and the artistic form has been renovated. But the text loses its appeal for the reading public when it only narrates itself instead of public concerns, anxieties and worries. Consequently, when a text uses 'narrative tactics' appreciated only by a narrow circle of fellow writers and is meaningless to the reading public, the writer's subjectivity becomes twisted and eventually his or her humanistic spirit is eroded.

Some contemporary writers who discard the modernist artistic aim create a worship of the language signifier by resorting to 'discourse expansion'. Originally, the separation and application of the signifier has served as a catalyst for language renovations. But some writers take the abuse of language signifiers as their final aim, resulting in randomness in expressions, sentences and narrative forms. The features of these kinds of texts are summarized by Hassan as indeterminacy, selflessness, superficiality, inexpressiveness, mixed imitation and innerness (1993:156), that is, 'the mind's ability to summarize itself by symbols' (Shklovsky 1983:91). The subject is destroyed, the object is illusory and meaning and value are altogether deconstructed.

Neo-rationalism pays great attention to aesthetics, but not to 'pure aesthetics' which is both limited in its significance and value and sometimes even becomes a language game. Neo-rationalism draws much from tradition which is the chain of cultures, arts and minds. Today humanity and morals have been debased somewhat in China because in the past several decades tradition was rendered worthless. In European and American cultures, almost every new radical school declares its independence by claiming its depature from tradition. It is true that these schools, including deconstructionism, made significant breakthroughs in breaking away from traditions containing certain weaknesses after a long history of development. However, repeated departures from tradition usually give people a sense of rootlessness. Such a sense of rootlessness may drive people to spiritual crisis and spiritual nothingness. In the view of Eastern scholars, the spiritual crisis in the West is largely connected to the West's nihilistic attitude towards tradition. Tradition can be defined as the kind of past which directs and generates the future. Although it contains many old things, they are things of enduring force and vitality because they are deeply rooted in the national culture. To negate these old things, therefore, is to place oneself in a groundless position. In the humanities, we cannot help but inherit tradition, and transform it creatively into a new tradition which will provide us with new theories and insights.

Neo-rationalism also advocates 'dialogism' in cross-cultural communications. Due to cultural differences, cross-cultural communications between the East and the West may give rise to cultural conflicts. Viewed positively, such conflicts can serve as catalysts for assimilation and enrichment, resulting in cultural reinvigoration and reconstruction. Large-scale cultural conflicts give rise to cultural shocks which fill the local culture with a thirst for foreign cultures, leading to their assimilation and integration, or even to a large-scale cultural reconstruction. In my view, purely cultural conflicts cannot trigger war as predicted by Huntington: Chinese culture is a rationalistic culture which observes the doctrine of the harmonious mean. How can wars occur if cultural communications between the East and the West set as their aim only the communication of cultures? The true hegemonic nature of wars such as the Crusades and the Opium War has been further disguised by being called 'cultural conflicts'.

Neo-rationalism aims at cultural synthesis at a higher level. Although in the future art and literature will highlight the uniqueness of each nation, synthesis cannot be avoided as new things are drawn from other nations. Such a synthesis or integration will not lead culture to uniformity, because unlike scientific and technical synthesis, cultural synthesis or integration can always only be partial.

To summarize, neo-rationalism aims to explore the meaning of human existence, culture and the arts, and to reconstruct the value and spirit of culture and the arts in an anti-cultural and anti-artistic world. Neo-rationalism seeks to rebuild a human spirituality. It seems absurd to remark that human existence is meaningless when people are still suffering in an age of material prosperity produced by developments in science and technology. Exploration into the value and spirit of the arts and culture may be quixotic, but it is still necessary.

Chinese Academy of Social Sciences

Works Cited

Hassan, Ihab 1993 *The Postmodern Turn,* tr. Liu Xiangyu. Time Daily Press, Taipei.
Huntington 1993 'The Clash of Civilizations' in *Foreign Affairs* vol. 72, no. 3: pp. 22–49.
Shklovsky, V. 1983 *Selected Works* vol. 2. Literature Press, Moscow.

Z. I. SIAFLEKIS

Du Dialogue des Oeuvres Littéraires au Dialogue des Cultures

On sait depuis Bakhtine que l'orientation dialogique caractérise tout discours, y compris celui de l'oeuvre littéraire: d'abord par rapport à la littérature nationale dont l'oeuvre est issue, et, ensuite, par rapport à l'ensemble des cultures auxquelles elle peut être destinée. Or, la mise en mouvement de cette relation est conditionnée par certains éléments dont le rôle reste capital: la spécificité de la culture nationale; la place de l'écrivain; le rôle du lecteur; le niveau de réceptivité du texte littéraire. Ce sont également ces facteurs-là qui peuvent favoriser une lecture idéologique du texte littéraire.

C'est dans cette optique que nous allons essayer d'analyser quelques condition préalables à l'élaboration d'un discours interculturel, dans lequel le texte littéraire devrait être le point de départ et le terme du processus.

L'objet de cette analyse sera un texte de Nicos Kazantzakis publié vers la fin des années 30, dans lequel on pourra discerner les différents niveaux de réception d'une culture étrangère et la mise en mouvement de son interprétation par le biais de la culture d'origine de l'auteur. En effet, lorsque Nicos Kazantzakis publie en 1938 les mémoires de son *Voyage en Chine*, effectué trois ans au paravant, offre au lecteur grec un cadre narratif qui réunit, de par sa nature, les conditions préalables à l'élaboraton d'un modèle de dialogue interculturel. Ce récit de voyage ne transmet pas seulement l'image, plus au moins exacte, d'un peuple à une autre, mais il a apparemment l'ambition d'être l'élément décisif à un processus de rapprochement et de dialogue entre les deux cultures.

Kazantzakis organise son récit sur la base des expériences vécues durant son voyage. Le texte se compose, d'une part, de transmission de faits réels et, d'autre part, de commentaires. Les circonstances du voyage, ses rencontres avec des gens importants de l'époque (des littéraires et des politiques), occupent évidemment la plus grande part du récit. La description de l'environnement naturel, son rôle dans la vie des Chinois, les références à Bouddha, aux superstitions populaires sont des éléments principaux d'une narration dont le but est, d'une part, d'explorer, dans la mesure du possible, l'espace étendu de la culture chinoise, et, d'autre part, de créer les conditions préalables à la transmission au lecteur grec, d'un univers quasi inconnu.

C'est dans cette optique qu'il faut placer et évaluer le travail de Kazantzakis. Dépositaire d'une culture millénaire, l'auteur grec s'ouvre à un monde peu familier avec lui, étant lui-même son propre lecteur et visant à mettre en mouvement le processus de dialogue entre les deux cultures. Rappelons qu'auparavant Kazantzakis avait voyagé au Japon, en Espagne et en Russie. Là aussi il avait essayé de s'approprier les éléments nécessaires à l'élaboration d'un langage interculturel, dans lequel la culture grecque serait le point de départ, et jouerait éventuellement le rôle de médiateur entre l'Orient et l'Occident.

Le *Voyage en Chine* est un texte dont la structure repose d'une part sur le vécu et d'autre part sur tout ce qui a été mémorisé par l'auteur. Cette distinction structurale correspond également à une division du temps de la narration. C'est ainsi que le temps du récit couvre l'espace narratif dans lequel la narration place tous les événements relatifs au voyage, alors que les anachronies, faites tout au long du récit, ont trait à un ensemble d'informations, d'opinions personelles, de commentaires concernant le passé littéraire. Leur place dans la narration est stratégique puisque ce sont ces éléments qui conditionnent la production du sens et orientent le lecteur vers les choix ésthétiques et culturels de l'écrivain.

Ces deux niveaux de narration correspondent aussi à une division plus profonde qui s'établit entre la culture de l'Occident et celle de l'Orient. Kazantzakis reste sans faille tout au long du récit un lecteur à la fois sévère et condescendant de la culture chinoise. Mais c'est surtout grâce à cette division temporelle de la narration que l'auteur grec réussit à mettre en mouvement le processus de dialogue entre les deux cultures.

En effet les anachronies constituent un espace narratif dont le trait caractéristique est un nombre de références à des auteurs tels qu'Homère, Socrate, François Villon, Cervantès, Shakespeare et à des oeuvres réspectives. La combinaison des deux niveaux de narration, c'est-à-dire du présent et du passé, donne naissance à la mise en mouvement d'une relation organique entre les deux cultures.

C'est ainsi qu'il est question de 'Circé jaune', de Confucius, de Socrate, des ballades de Villon, des images de Don Quichotte au milieu des plaines chinoises et des images poétiques du poète chinois du dixième siècle, Chou-Kung-tou. Ce qui est étonnant dans ce récit, c'est la facilité de la combinaison des éléments appartenant à des traditions culturelles différentes. Kazantzakis utilise sans aucun doute la culture occidentale comme un instrument de réception et d'interprétation de la culture chinoise. Les multiples références à la philosophie chinoise montrent incontestablement ses propres choix spirituels mais elles soulignent, en même temps, le fond de sa démarche. Or cette jonction si nécessaire et séduisante à la fois se fait par le biais de la littérature et spécialement des oeuvres littéraires. Kazantzakis se montre ici non seulement un connaisseur profond de la littérature occidentale mais surtout un lecteur idéal, capable de mettre en mouvement l'interaction entre deux oeuvres, et, de là, entre deux cultures. Le présent de la Chine ne peut être interpréter que par le biais du passé occidental. Bien entendu il s'agit d'un pari difficile que Kazantzakis tient, quand même tout au long de son récit, grâce précisément à la structure de celui-ci qui constitue une forme objective de la culture, appelant à l'amorce d'un processus de communication interculturelle.

D'ailleurs, comme le dit Bakhtine, 'les traditions littéraires et culturelles (y compris les plus anciennes) se préservent et vivent non pas dans la mémoire subjective de l'individu, ni dans une "psyche" collective, mais dans les formes objectives de la culture elle-même; en ce sens elles sont intersubjectives et interindividuelles... c'est par là qu'elles interviennent dans les oeuvres littéraires' (Todorov 1981:131).

Le récit de Kazantzakis s'adresse en premier lieu à la littérature néo-hellénique dont il fait partie. L'image de la Chine transmise ainsi s'insère d'abord dans la culture grecque. La spécificité de cette culture, son rôle, ses activités et ses aspirations sont parmi les facteurs qui conditionnent la réception de la culture chinoise. La place de l'écrivain lui-même dans sa culture natale est également un facteur décisif dans le processus de rapprochement des deux traditions culturelles. La fonction de lecteur d'une culture étrangère que l'auteur Kazantzakis revêt donne une dimension dynamique dans le processus dialogique. Par ailleurs le niveau de réceptivité du texte est conditionné précisément par cette double fonction de son production. C'est un texte à la fois explicatif et descriptif d'une réalité lointaine et peu connue de la culture néohellénique.

Il va de soi qu'une fois traduit le texte de Kazantzakis est ouvert sur une grande partie du public européen et dans ce cas les relations décrites auparavant devraient être placées dans des contextes différents. Mais la fonction initiale, celle du principe dialogique, reste inchangée.

Ce récit de voyage, modeste dans son expression mais riche en idées, offre au lecteur contemporain un modèle de réception d'une réalité culturelle étrangère dont la diachronie reste sa caractéristique essentielle. Sans être un texte de fiction il utilise les produits fictionnels et les mélange à une perception subjective d'une réalité extérieure. Cependant la place de la fiction et son rôle dans le récit est de la plus grande importance, car c'est grâce à elle que le lecteur arrive à former une idée de la réalité chinoise des années trente.

J'ai dit plus haut que le lecteur grec est le premier qui est concerné par ce récit. Cela veut dire qu'il doit recevoir le texte de Kazantzakis en fonction de son savoir, de son expérience esthétique antérieure et surtout en fonction du niveau de sa propre réceptivité. Il pourra ensuite l'insérer dans sa constellation mentale et lui donner une ou des significations possibles. Ce processus mène inévitablement à une mise en dialogue des deux cultures. Mais outre la culture grecque c'est surtout la culture européenne qui est visée. Kazantzakis l'entend bien lorsqu'il utilise avec une grande aisance une partie de son patrimoine littéraire.

Mais la possibilité d'un dialogue entre les cultures repose sur la nature du texte. Le récit de voyage est un genre spécifique qui favorise à la fois le développement des idées personnelles de l'auteur et la transmission à un peuple d'une culture étrangère. Dans ces conditions le rôle de l'auteur et celui du lecteur s'intervertissent en créant une forme d'interaction interne au récit. En effet le destinataire du texte pourra se mettre soit à la place de l'auteur soit à celle du lecteur suivant le cours de la narration, le mode de transmission de la réalité extérieure et les références littéraires.

Ce type de récit, considéré comme littéraire, doit prouver à chaque instant sa propre littérarité, étant donné qu'il ne s'agit pas d'une fiction. Or la littérarité surgit d'une part du mode de narration et d'autre part des références littéraires, c'est-à-dire de la gestion narrative d'un matériel esthétique appartenant à une grande tradition culturelle. Au fond, la révélation de la littérarité du récit est le facteur décisif à l'adhésion du lecteur à la narration proposée par l'auteur. Les qualités esthétiques du texte doivent être en accord avec les aspirations analogues du lecteur. L'image de la Chine transmise au lecteur grec au moyen d'une narration réaliste, truffée de références au patrimoine culturel européen, est une démarche complexe mais efficace: Kazantzakis achève, de manière pratique, ses propres recherches philosophiques en offrant à ses lecteurs un texte où les idées philosophiques sont investies dans une réalité sociale concrète.

Espace, voyage, idées d'une part, histoire, société, culture de l'autre. Le dialogue des cultures repose avant tout sur le dialogue des oeuvres littéraires, produits individuels, à portée générale. Le discours littéraire rencontre le discours d'autrui et met en mouvement l'interaction, condition préalable à la communication. Le récit de voyage, par la complexité de sa nature, contient le dialogisme intérieur entre oeuvres littéraires et le met en fonction à tous les niveaux de la narration. C'est aussi un discours sur le discours littéraire, une signification proposée au lecteur dont la portée dépassera les limites strictes du littéraire.

Il s'agit d'un discours individuel qui porte sur le général en visant la durée historique. Entre Socrate et Confucius se tisseront des liens d'analogie et le lecteur admirera les parallélismes entre les deux philosophes. Le discours de Kazantzakis se nourrit du présent mais survit grâce au passé. Le rôle précisément du lecteur dans ce type de récit a une double fonction: d'une part suivre les traces de la narration en compagnie de l'auteur; et d'autre part, faire son propre trajet à travers les oeuvres mentionnées. C'est là le processus d'interaction qu'il entame et le début des significations qu'il donnera au récit.

C'est dans ces conditions que la notion d'histoire littéraire pourra acquérir une dimension dynamique. Mise en dialogue des chefs-d'oeuvre des différentes cultures, à travers un genre littéraire, tel que le récit de voyage, englobant les diverses expériences esthétiques de l'auteur et du lecteur, pluralité des discours, voilà les principaux éléments d'un langage interculturel dans lequel le texte littéraire reste au centre du processus.

Aristotle University of Thessalonika

Oeuvres Citées

Genette, Gérard 1972 *Figures III*. Seuil, Paris.

Janiaud-Lust, Colette 1970 *Nicos Kazantzakis, sa vie, son oeuvre*. Maspero, Paris.

Jauss, H. R. 1978 *Pour une esthétique de la réception*, tr. Claude Maillard. Gallimard, Paris.

Kazantzakis, Nicos 1969 *Voyage au Japon et en Chine*. Ed. Hélène Kazantzakis, Athènes.

Poulakidas, Andreas K. 1988 'Kazantzakis as Traveller and Storyteller: His Settings' in *Proceedings of the XIIth Congress of the International Comparative Literature Association: Space and Boundaries,* vol. 2, ed. Roger Bauer & Douwe Fokkema. Iudicium, Munich.

Schaeffer, J. M. 1989 *Qu'est-ce qu'un genre littéraire*. Seuil, Paris.

Todorov, Tzvetan 1981 *Mikhail Bakhtine le principe dialogique*. Seuil, Paris.

Raoul David Findeisen

Two Aviators: Gabriele D'Annunzio and Xu Zhimo

To the memory of Harvey Anselm (d. 1995), engineer of aeronautics

> *But the aircraft is an ideal, the aircraft is communism, our final aim, forward to the aircraft.*
> Valeria Narbikova (b. 1963)

Our fascination with flight has long been embodied in a great variety of traditional myths. In China flying generally meant going to a place where human mortality does not reach, but where worldly rules are otherwise valid. Mythical flights in the Chinese tradition are frequently related to means of acquiring immortality, especially when celestial journeys are connected to the use and abuse of drugs.[1] The sky therefore appears as an imaginative extension of earth. So, tradition has it, four millennia ago, Chang'e flew to the moon after she had taken an immortality drug. The poet Qu Yuan (fourth–third centuries BC), the first ever to emerge from anonymity, described how he...

> *...caused my phoenixes to mount on their pinions*
> *And fly ever onward by night and by day.*
> *The whirlwinds gathered and came out to meet me,*
> *Leading clouds and rainbows, to give me welcome.*
> (In Hawkes 1959:29)

Not so Icarus. In the Greek myth, whereas his father Daedalus is shown as a representative of solid and careful craft, in other words, of traditional (worldly) values, Icarus conquers a completely different world, beyond human social rules. Both Daedalus and Icarus search for a means of elevating themselves physically, the former contributing technical means he keeps under control rationally, the latter contributing the aim of transgressing them. In Chinese antiquity in another aviation-related tradition the philosopher Mo Di (circa fourth century BC) and his contemporary Lu Ban are reported to have contented themselves with constructing wooden birds that could fly — a comparatively playful form of flying where the initiators remain on the ground.

Two opposed attitudes in Chinese and Western mythology may be hypothetically fixed. Whereas in China myths of flying are directed towards worldly ends, Western tradition tends to put forth another world which could be reached by flying. Obstacles to celestial flights in the Chinese tradition emerge from existential categories such as mortality, or human emotions such as envy, whereas in the Icarus myth an opposition is presupposed between rational and transgressive imagination.

To have the technical means available to ascend from the earth is an aspiration for literature as well. Among the various attempts to find a satisfying definition for modernism, some are immediately linked to aviation. Gottfried Benn (1951) has suggested that the year 1909 marks the very beginning of modernism when aviation, six years after the Wright brothers, developed rapidly and was omnipresent in the media and demonstrated in mass events. It was the year when one of the so-called 'meetings' (whence the expression spread into all European languages) took place in Brescia, immortalized by Kafka's report written in 1909 for a Prague newspaper.[2] It is from this year on that aviation made its great entry into literature with for example *Hans Himmelhoch* (John Fly-in-the-Skies, 1909) by the Swiss author Jakob Schaffner (1875–1944).[3] In the same year, Filippo Tommaso Marinetti wrote his *Manifesto of Futurism*.

Two years before this turning-point, the writer Lu Xun (1881–1936), who is generally venerated as 'father of modern Chinese literature', had started to use pen-names related to aviation. In 1907 he wrote on Western Romanticist poetry under the name Lingfei ('let fly!') and stressed its destructive impact, using the Buddhist label of *māra* (Chinese *moluo* 'the demonic'). In a similar drive towards destruction, Marinetti had called for museums and libraries to be burned so that the new could be set up. One year later, in 1908, Lu Xun signed by the name of Xunxing ('moving upwards') when he vigorously criticized the then already obviously one-sided trend to modernize China's material culture.[4] One of his sources had been the Old Testament where the prophet Jeremiah is elevated and shown the whole country, yet Lu Xun also explicitly refers to Nietzsche and quotes him with the sentence, 'I *flew* too far into the future' (Nietzsche 1969:142, quoted in Lu Xun 1981, 1:49 emphasis added). Nietzsche in his usage of the ambivalent metaphor may be duly regarded as precursor of both types of aviation: the Promethean aspect of revolt against gravity, as embodied in the whole set of traditional values, and of the imaginative prophetic force.

In China, the first plane took off on 5 May 1911 — five months before the Wuchang Uprising that initiated the fall of the last imperial dynasty — when the French pioneer René Vallon gave a demonstration above the race-course of Shanghai's International Sport Club. As it happened quite frequently in those times, the plane crashed and the pilot died with a crowd of 10,000 watching. One year before, Feng Ru (1883–1912) had won a prize in a USA contest but he also died in a crash when back in China. Regular passenger services were established by the end of the 1920s when the Chinese-American 'China Aviation Company' was founded, yet domestic mail had already been carried by air from the mid-1920s.[5]

In the early 1930s aviation became immensely popular for painful reasons. Japanese troops had attacked Shanghai with air raids. The Government then propagated again the slogan 'saving the country by aviation' (*hangkong jiuguo*), once coined by Sun Yixian ('Sun Yat-sen', 1886–1925), a slogan which would attract bitter comment from the writer and satirist Lu Xun who wrote, 'it is as if suddenly all had become patriots'.

❖

Two recent poets who were obsessed with flying are Gabriele D'Annunzio (1863–1938) and Xu Zhimo (1897–1931). The Italian, who was a pilot during the First World War, prided himself on his 'dangerous life' (*vita sfarzosa*) in the Nietzschean sense, but died in a room of his sumptuous villa, the 'Vittoriale', whereas Xu Zhimo died in a plane crash the first time he ever went into an aircraft. The two are linked since the latter translated parts of the former's play *Città morta* (1898) into Chinese.

D'Annunzio's poetry was widely read and enormously successful. At least twice during his lifetime he virtually created a tide of *dannunzianismo*. When Italian authorities sought him for tax fraud, he could afford to escape to France where he started to write plays, among other things. His love affairs were famous, namely the one with the great actress Eleonora Duse (1858–1924). It was she who inspired him to go on writing plays. He was convinced that she was the only one who was able to stage his female characters appropriately.

In *Città morta* (1898) the poet Alessandro working on a tragedy entitled 'Victory of Man' (*La vittoria dell'uomo*) is married to the blind woman Anna, yet he loves the poor maid Bianca Maria. Bianca's brother Leonardo desires his sister in incestuous passion and kills her out of jealously and in order to destroy the object of his desire. This drama with all its pathetic ingredients is staged on the Greek island of Argos, close to the ruins of Mykene — whence the title 'Dead City'.

D'Annunzio was among the active participants of the Brescia meeting. Soon afterwards he wrote a four-part novel *Forse che sì, forse che no* (1910) in which one of the protagonists is an aviator who dies in a crash. This novel was to become his greatest prose success and it was almost immediately translated into most major European languages.

Xu Zhimo also belonged to the privileged. Son of a banker, the young talent (of a traditional *caizi* type) became a personal protégé of the powerful reformer and brilliant journalist Liang Qichao (1873–1929) after his brother-in-law Zhang Junmai (1887–1969), a philosopher also known under his Westernized name, Carsun Chang, had acted as a go-between. Xu was sent to the USA and Britain to study political economy. His poetry, first published in various journals, gained wide recognition, to the extent that one of his poems was soon set to music. Xu Zhimo reached a peak of popularity especially after he had served as an interpreter to the Bengali poet Rabîndranâth Tagore (1861–1941) on his journey through China. 'It was hard not to love him', as one contemporary remarked of Xu Zhimo.

❖

Probably the first Chinese ever to write on D'Annunzio was the prolific novelist, influential critic and late Minister of Culture Mao Dun (1896–1981). Although after the Second World War the European fame of D'Annunzio had already started to decline, in the aftermath of the cultural reform movement of May Fourth China was in a feverish search for models in all domains of social life, not least in literature. Mao Dun's article, published 75 years ago, closely followed the critical presentation by Arthur Symons (1865-1945) whose *The Symbolist Movement in Literature* (1899) was the bible of Western literature for a whole generation of Chinese authors and critics (McDougall 1971:66–8). Right at the beginning, Mao Dun stresses the fact that D'Annunzio is both an aviator and a poet whose 'position in Italian literary history — this is certainly not exaggerated — can only be compared to Dante' (1920:62).

Doubtless among the earliest translations of D'Annunzio into Chinese was a story with the title 'Silver Spoon' (1922, 2:16), which was actually a version of 'La fine di Candia' from 1885, afterwards included in *San Pantaleone* (1886) and modified in *Novelle della Pescara* (1902). This piece of prose belongs to D'Annunzio's early period *ante Dusam* — if the expression is allowed — in which he developed his *verismo* style, with realistic descriptions and a psychology of 'ordinary people'. D'Annunzio relied heavily on authors such as Giovanni Verga (1840–1922) and Maupassant (1850–93). In the case of 'La fine di Candia' he drew from the model of 'La ficelle' by Maupassant (in *Miss Harriet* 1884), then scarcely known in Italy. He simply transposed the story from Maupassant's Brittany into his own native land around Pescara.[6] To those stories, Mao Dun's description was apt, but not for his later theatrical and other works that were going to fascinate Xu Zhimo.

However, having lived abroad for many years Xu Zhimo was not aware he already had some Chinese precursors when he read and admired D'Annunzio in Symons' translation for the first time in 1922. He wanted to translate into Chinese all three plays he had read (also *La Gioconda* 1899, and *Francesca da Rimini* 1902) and 'bring them back as a present from abroad'. Yet in fact he only translated parts of *Città morta*.

In 1922, Xu Zhimo met the future writer and architect Lin Huiyin (1904–55). She was travelling in Europe with her father at the time and became Xu's object of desire, yet she was already promised to his mentor's son Liang Sicheng (1901–72).[7] In 1925, Xu was in Europe again since public rumours of his emotional commitment to the married opera singer and actress Lu Xiaoman (1902–65) had forced him to quit his university teaching job in Peking. It was in Florence that he took up work again on his translation started in Cambridge three years before, adding to it a series of articles on D'Annunzio.[8] When in Italy, Xu Zhimo tried to arrange a meeting with D'Annunzio who had recently settled down on the shores of the Lake of Garda, but failed — probably to his advantage, since it was the year of closest flirtations between D'Annunzio and Mussolini, who had taken power in 1922 (Xu Zhimo 1991 [henceforth XQ], 5:503).

These articles (in which he plays down his previous enthusiasm) first discuss D'Annuzio's relationship to Italy and its literature and politics, and then his early poetry, his novels and his plays (Lu 1981:261–90).[9] In this context, *L'innocente* (1892) is also introduced and even translated in selected sections which, by virtue of D'Annunzio's cascades of metaphors, offer a fine opportunity for Xu Zhimo to show his talent in creating rows of binomical compounds formed from classical Chinese (281–3). Significantly, the aviation novel *Forse che sì, forse che no* goes unmentioned on this occasion.

In 1928, Xu Zhimo wrote the play *Bian Kungang* together with Lu Xiaoman who had finally become his wife. The play clearly draws inspiration from D'Annunzio's *Città morta*.[10] It is situated in a similarly symbolic landscape, in 'a village near Yungang in Shanxi province', a place famous for its hundreds of Buddha statues carved into the rocks of caves. Hence the Chinese Buddhist past of the Northern Wei dynasty (fifth century) is equated with D'Annunzio's mythical Greece. Moreover, the protagonist's name also refers to another important mythical place in Chinese history: it means 'ridges of the Kunlun Mountains' — traditionally the residence of the 'Royal Lady of the West' (*Xiwangmu*), the very person who had handed the drug of immortality to Chang'e (Williams 1932:226–8). In *Bian Kungang* the protagonist is also an artist, a respected sculptor who diligently adds to the Buddha statues and, in accordance with traditional ideas of morality, only after years of widowerhood gives in to his mother's urging and marries again, for his son's sake. His new wife cannot bear Bian's way of continuously idealizing his dead wife's eyes — for which he loves his son most — and she starts a love affair with a peddlar from the village. The lovers conspire against the son Aming and blind him. Aming then tries to kill his stepmother's lover but fails and is, in his turn, beaten to death. The bloody tragedy had already been predicted by a blind wandering musician who, when asked when the arid region would enjoy rain again, had sung: 'It will rain, it will rain, floods of blood.' The beggar-musician who arrives at the scene of the murder sings one of Xu Zhimo's most famous poems as a farewell to the child:

I am a cloud in the Sky,
By chance casting a shadow on the ripples of your heart.
...
You and I met on the sea at night;
You had your direction, I had mine.
    You may remember,
    Better you forget.[11]

Since the child Aming, after being blinded and before dying, enters into closer and closer relationship with the musician and proves particularly gifted in music, the whole play may also be read as a *memento mori* for Desheng ('Peter'), Xu Zhimo's son with his first wife Zhang Youyi (1900–?) who died as a child in Berlin in 1925. His father had never seen him and had pondered in a commemorative essay that Peter might have become a Chinese Mozart.[12]

In the blind musician we find also a figure with prophetic qualities, clearly derived from the model of Tiresias who, for D'Annunzio, had formed an archetype for the sacred function of the artist as a priest. As soon as he is blinded, Bian Kungang's son also develops such an ability which is prominently expressed in music. It is precisely the ability for presentiment that qualifies as a poet, according to Xu Zhimo's view. This ability is transposed by D'Annunzio to the fact of being an aviator.

In *La Gioconda*, one of the other plays by D'Annunzio that had attracted special attention from Xu Zhimo, the artist-protagonist is even a sculptor, like Lu Xiaoman's and Xu Zhimo's *Bian Kungang*. As in *Bian Kungang*, this sculptor Lucio Settala is oscillating between two women: his wife Silvia representing pure love and his model Gioconda to whom he is devoted in a fulfilling passion. He tried to escape the conflict by attempting suicide. As in *Bian Kungang*, an isolated physical quality of one of the two women is the object of the artist's obsession: the eyes of Bian Kungang's deceased wife, as he sees them incarnated in his son, play the same role as *leitmotif* as the hands of Silvia do for Lucio Settala in this play. In *Bian Kungang*, the boy Aming's eyes are blinded, whereas in *La Gioconda*, the hands of the sculptor's wife, Silvia, are smashed. The sculptor's jealous model pulls a statue down onto them when she hears that, after his attempted suicide, he had promised his wife to end his passionate relationship with the model. Hence motifs from at least two plays by D'Annunzio are merged in the collective work by Xu Zhimo and Lu Xiaoman, both from *Città morta* and *La Gioconda*.

How persistent was Xu's commitment to 'Sicheng' (both D'Annunzio's play and maybe symbolically his rival Liang *Sicheng*) is most clearly testified to by a piece of prose also named 'Dead City' and classified by himself as *xiaoshuo* ('fictional prose'). It was written in December 1927, probably just before he joined his wife Lu Xiaoman to produce *Bian Kungang*, yet was only published in 1929. The story carries the subtitle 'An Evening in Beijing' and hence rhetorically echoes his volume of poetry 'A Night in Florence' (*Feilengcui de yi ye*) published that same year. It is part of a cycle that attempts the portrayal of inner landscapes which can duly be regarded as symbolist, first from the four seasons, then in scenes from big cities, Beijing, Paris, Singapore and Hong Kong. In this 'Dead City', the protagonist Lianfeng ('honest maple', or 'office-holder', by way of the homophone 'seal' for *feng*) is standing amidst the noise and late afternoon traffic near the Qianmen gate. In this urban landscape, things become animate, laugh and even have a 'melancholy' (*youyu*) of their own (XQ 1991, 2:57). After wandering through the narrow *hutong* lanes, Lianfeng finds himself in a Foreigners' Cemetery. He wipes off the snow from one gravestone and reads that a certain 'Fraulein Eliza Berkson' — who died at age twenty-two — is buried there.[13] Lianfeng imagines how this dead woman could have saved him and his potential for love and now defines 'flying as dissolution into ashes' (XQ 2:63).

The cemetery's old guardian, asked whether he liked the city, answers: 'Beijing is like a dead city.... If you cannot make your living, you just love death' (XQ 2:65). Hence the story resembles D'Annunzio's early *verismo* style with lyrical passages describing the socially underprivileged, as well as the technique of using a given environment as pretext, yet the narrative structure essentially differs from D'Annunzio's and tends to transcend those same lyrical elements.

Still during Xu's lifetime, *Città morta* was translated once again, but this time in a complete version and together with an introduction to Sophocles' *Antigone,* thus elucidating part of its background. The translation was made by Xiang Peiliang (1905–61) who belonged to a group of young extravagant romantic artists. The members of this group were much closer to the aestheticist heroism of D'Annunzio and had legitimately been characterized by Lu Xun as 'regarding themselves as [Nietzschean] overmen' (Lu 1981, 6:251). Yet interestingly enough, since Xiang was also a dramatist and director himself, he added a text 'On Eleonara Duse's Art' to his translation. Xu Zhimo meanwhile had not been passive and, as the editor of the collection 'New Literature', did not fail to pay special attention to D'Annunzio: *L'innocente* and *Il trionfo della morte* were published during his editorship, just a few months before Xu Zhimo's death.[14]

❖

In D'Annunzio, man ultimately reveals his heroism when dying. The Nietzschean superman concept, vividly absorbed by D'Annunzio, is pushed forward and superman is not just a creator but creator even of his own death, which is literally staged. Again we find a four-part story where the death of the overman hero Giulio is described as follows: 'L'occipite aderiva alla massa del motore per modo, che i sette cilindri irti d'alette gli facevano una sorta die aggiera spaventosa, lorda di terra e d'erba sanguigne' (1981:112; The occiput was affixed to the motorblock in such a way that the seven cylinders bristling with fins gave him a kind of radiant crown, heavy with earth and blood-stained grass).

Xu Zhimo, on the other hand, has a wholly romantic notion of death in which such a solitary hero with an anonymous crowd (the readership) watching him is virtually inconceivable. Flying and aviation are by no means linked to his idea of death in which the dead are even rather reanimated in order to form a living company for the poet — as can be seen in his various visits to cemeteries where he finds models for the right way to live rather than for the heroic way to die.[15] His is the 'dialogical death' of the romanticists.

Xu Zhimo's poetics of flying are best summarized in an essay 'Wanting to Fly', written in 1926, where he explicitly refers to Icarus as the very first hero in the history of flying:

> Flying. Humans originally all could fly. Angels have wings and fly. Originally we had wings and were able to fly. When we first arrive, it is by flying, and when we have accomplished our task, we leave flying.... But most humans have forgotten about flying. Some have just too short feathers on their wings and therefore are unable to take off.... Some happen to have their wings cut and hence just spring dancing above ground. (XQ 3:198)

Unlike D'Annunzio's physical flying into new worlds, flying here is a metaphor for lost emotional innocence and imagination: 'Poetry is leaving the world on wings; flying, that is overcoming all.... Civilization is both a history of constructing wings and obstructing the [original] ability of flying' (XQ 3:198).

Hence, the final crash in such a conception means the ultimalte fulfilment of emotions: the romantic love death he highly praised in many poems, and is not D'Annunzio's solitary heroic sacrifice which has its ends in itself. It metaphorises the search for a better life and not the destructive and nihilistic striving that stresses fame after death. One of Xu Zhimo's poems shows clearly which position flying takes in this context:

Now that I
Really, really can die. I want you to
Hold me until I pass away,
Until my eyes can open no more,
Until I fly, fly, fly into the outer space.
                    (In Birch 1961:289)

In this respect the conversation Xu Zhimo reportedly had with Han Xiangmei, wife of Zhang Xinha, the night before he died is quite revealing:

> '*Suppose something happens tomorrow*, Zhimo!' Xu Zhimo became pale and smilingly asked: 'Are you afraid I am going to die?'— 'Zhimo, don't be silly! [...] Is the pilot Chinese or a foreigner?' — 'I don't know! I don't care, *I always wanted to fly*. I think the sky is bright and smooth, very adapted to travel by air.' — 'Did Xiaoman say anything when you told her you would go by plane?' — 'Xiaoman said if I died on the plane, she would become a *merry widow*.' — Then Yang Xingfu [another friend in Nanjing] said, '*All widows are merry*.' (XQ 5:588, italics indicate English in original)

❖

Though staging great passions and very probably co-inspired by D'Annunzio, *Bian Kungang* still maintains an ideal of balance which is much closer to Greek antiquity than D'Annunzio's two works,[16] *Forse che sì, forse che no* and *Città morta*. The outburst of emotions in Xu Zhimo's play is not heroicized, but is both fateful and fatal. This shows in the prophetic characters and, more generally speaking, in the role that Xu Zhimo attributes to art.

It should be noted in this context that the image of Icarus has undergone fundamental shifts within the European context as well. For the Romantics, Icarus was a perfect allegory of Art and the role of the artist, whereas in Modernism the physical ascension by technical means began to play an important role, namely in Futurism. Thus the mastering of those means becomes the source of heroism and topic of the artistic works.[17]

University of Zurich

Notes

1 Cf. R. Wagner: 'Lebensstil und Drogen im chinesischen Mittelalter' in *T'oung Pao* 59 (1973), pp. 80–178.

2 Cf. the inspiring discussion of aviation in Western literatures by F. P. Ingold: *Literatur und Aviatik. Europäische Flugdichtung*, Basel: Birkhäuser 1978, esp. pp. 10–52.

3 Cf. H. Bänziger: *Heimat und Fremde. Ein Kapitel 'Tragische Literaturgeschichte' in der Schweiz*, Bern: Franke 1958, pp. 21–62.

4 The articles in Lu Xun 1981 are 'Po esheng lun' (8:23–38), 'Moluo shili shuo' and 'Wenhua pianzhi lun' (1:44–115). The first two are translated by J. Kowallis respectively as 'Towards a Refutation of the Voices of Evil', in *Renditions* no. 26 (autumn 1986), pp. 108-19, and as 'On the Power of Mara Poetry' in *Warriors of the Spirit: Mara and Other Turn-of-the-Century Wenyan Essays by Lu Xun* (forthcoming). For Italian excerpts see *Lu Xun: Poesie e scritti sulla posia*, ed. A. Bujatti, Roma: Istituto della Enciclopedia Italiana 1981 (Bibliotheca Biographica. Sezione artistica-letteraria), pp. 95–116. Cf. M. Gálik, 'Studies in Modern Chinese Intellectual History: Young Lu Xun (1902–9)', in *Asian and African Studies* 21 (1985), esp. pp. 43–5.

5 On the history and the historiography of Chinese aviation see B. Wiethoff, in: *Bochumer Jahrbuch zur Ostasienforschung* 6 (1983), pp. 8–97 and esp. his 'Luftfahrt-Historiographie in der VR China. Topoibestand und Traditionssynthese chinesischer Luftfahrt-Geschichte in der Zeitschrift 'Luftfahrt-Wissen' (Hangkong zhishi 1958–82)', ibid. 8 (1985), pp. 1–112.

6 Cf. F. Roncorni 1983 'Gabriele d'Annunzio: profilo storico-critico', in *Prose*, Garzanti, Milano:

LXXIV-LXXXII.

7 The Memorial for the Revolutionary Heroes on Tian'anmen Square is their work, as well as the design of the national emblem on Chinese passports, either on the cover or within the visa stamp. On the couple's achievements in architecture see Fairbank 1994 esp. pp. 39–98.

8 The translation was published as 'Sicheng' in nos 122 and 123 of *Chenbao fukan* in July 1925; repr. in XQ 2:570–97. In his article on D'Annunzio's plays, Xu also translated the closing scene (in XQ 4:289–90). Note the homophony of 'Dead City' and the first name of his competitor for Lin Huiyin's love in 1922 when Xu first took up his translation.

9 The texts were first published in several instalments between 8 May and 5 July 1925, in the two different supplements to the *Chenbao* (Morning Post) daily in Peking.

10 The play is even translated into Italian as 'Bian Kungang: Tragedia cinese di ispirazione dannunziana', tr. M. N. Rossi 1991 in *Culture. Annali dell'Istituto di Lingue della Facoltà di Scienze Politiche dell'Università degli Studi di Milano* 5: 87–148, unfortunately with several misleading translation and transcription errors. I am indebted to Professor Stefania Stafutti (Torino) who kindly provided me with this semi-official publication.

11 XQ 1:100 and 2:568; quoted from the translation as 'A Chance Encounter' by M. Yeh (1992:8).

12 See 'Wo de Bide' (My Peter), in XQ 3:217.

13 The calculation made by the protagonist '28 minus 6 is 22' as well as the narrator's assertion that she died 'three years ago' suggests the young woman lived 1906-28 and that the event is in the future (1931); or, seeing the date of writing in late 1927, that she is even still living (XQ 2:60).

14 *Xisheng* (Sacrifice), tr. Cha Shiyuan; and *Si de shengli*, tr. Wu Chunwu, both 1931, Zhonghua shuju, Shanghai. There were four more translations of *Trionfo della morte*, all published before 1937, one among them abridged (cf. *Minguo shiqi zong shumu: Waiguo wenxue* [General List of Books Published During the Republican Period: Foreign Literatures], ed. Tian Dawei et al. 1987, Wenxian chubanshe, Beijing, p. 318).

15 See his 'Ou you manlu' (Casual Notes from a Journey to Europe), where he ponders on Japanese, Russian, French, British, and Italian graveyards he visitied in 1924 and 1925 (XQ 3:245-88).

16 See Xu's article 'Life and Art' (in English), in *Xu Zhimo quanji bubian* (Amendments and Additions to Complete Works), 4 vols, eds Lu Yaodong, Wu Hongcong and Hu Congjing, Shanghai: Shanghai shudian 1994, 3:433–59.

17 The 'Icarus syndrome' labelling the 'ascensionist personality' (Henry A. Murray) invoked by Leo Ou-fan Lee has, as a matter of fact, merged both tendencies in constructing Icarean images and therefore is by no means an inalterable category adapted to analyse Xu Zhimo's work, but rather should be seen as a contribution to the history of the concept.

Works Cited

Benn, Gottfried 1977 (1951) 'Probleme der Lyrik' in *Essays: Reden, Vorträge*. Klett-Cotta, Stuttgart.

Birch, C. 1961 'English and Chinese Metres in Hsü Chih-mo' in *Asia Major* NS 8, 2.

D'Annunzio, Gabriele 1981 *Forse che sì, forse che no*. Mondadori, Milano.

—— 1922 'Yinchi' in *Zi luolan ji*, 2 vols, tr. and ed. Zhou Shoujuan. Dadong shuju, Shanghai.

—— 1995 *Novelle*, ed. D. Redaelli. Ganzanti, Milano.

Fairbank, Wilma 1994 *Liang and Lin: Partners in Exploring China's Architectural Past*. University of Pennsylvania Press.

Hawkes, D. 1959 *Ch'u Tz'u. The Songs of the South*. Clarendon Press, Oxford.

Lee, Leo Ou-fan 1973 *The Romantic Generation of Modern Chinese Writers*. Harvard University Press.

Lu Xun 1981 *Lu Xun quanji* (Complete Works), 16 vols. Renmin Wenxue Chubanshe, Beijing.

Mao Dun 1920 'Yidali xiandai di yi wenxuejia Dengnanzhe' (D'Annunzio, First-Rate Writer of Modern Italy) in *Dongfang zazhi* (Eastern Miscellany) 17, 19 (10 October): p. 62.

McDougall, Bonnie 1971 *The Introduction of Western Literary Theories into Modern China*. The Centre for East Asian Cultural Studies, Tokyo.

Narbikova, Valeria 1995 (1994) *Flüstergeräusch*, tr. A. Nitschke. Suhrkamp, Frankfurt.

Nietzsche, Friedrich 1969 (1883–5) *Thus Spoke Zarathustra*, tr. R. J. Hollingdale. Penguin, Harmondsworth.

Williams, C. A. S. 1932 *Outlines of Chinese Symbolism and Art Motives*. Kelly & Walsh, Shanghai.

Xu Zhimo (XQ) 1991 *Xu Zhimo quanji* (Complete Works), 5 vols, eds Zhao Xiaqiu and Zeng Qingrui. Guangxi minzu chubanshe, Nanning.

Yeh, Michelle 1992 *Anthology of Modern Chinese Poetry*. Yale University Press.

MABEL LEE

Discourse on Poetics: Paz's *Sunstone* and Yang Lian's *Yi*

This study seeks to explore a small area of the innumerable and diverse interliterary processes occurring in present times by looking specifically at Chinese literary and philosophical influences on the poetics of Octavio Paz and the extent of Paz's influence on the poetics of a younger contemporary, the Chinese poet Yang Lian. A study such as this necessarily highlights the crucial role of the literary translator: Paz had access to Chinese literature and philosophy through English and French translations and Yang Lian had access to Paz's writings through Chinese translations of the Spanish originals (or more likely of their English translations). For my reading of Paz I am indebted to English translations.[1]

Paz's poetic vision contains more facets than can easily be summarized but his basic understanding of humanity has strong affinities with the traditional Chinese concept of oneness, of the unity of heaven and man. The broad scope of his study and reflection on humanity and civilization (manifested in his numerous essays and in his poetry) points to an understanding of humanity in which human differences are deleted. Paz's understanding closely approximates Yang Lian's which is derived primarily from the study of Chinese literature, history and philosophy.

Paz observes that in the modern age humanity's separation from nature has transformed into confrontation and conflict, and that man has separated from man:

> Within each civilization, more differences emerge: the language that enables us to communicate with one another also encloses us in an invisible web of sounds and meanings, so that each nation is imprisoned by its language, a language further fragmented by historical eras, by social classes, by generations. As for the intercourse among individuals belonging to the same community, each one is hemmed in by his own self-concern. (1992:153–4)[2]

It was in the extreme alienation of the individual from human characteristics of his or her own self imposed by the Cultural Revolution in China that Yang Lian grew up. Ironically the 'great design' of the Cultural Revolution purported to eliminate differences by remaking Chinese humanity. Political leaders of the time progressively implemented programs for destroying memory, that is the individual's and society's past and present history and the artefacts which would serve as reminders. In the post-Mao period many young Chinese began to question the meaning of human existence, to try to understand the events of their recent past and to understand themselves: their basic human instincts, self and knowledge. Such questions led them to the study of Chinese history dating back to early records of primitive man, of the literature of China's past (pre-dating the Cultural Revolution), and of the lives of minority groups whose belief systems seemed not to have been eroded to the same degree as that of the Han Chinese. This search is reflected in the literature.

Of the poetry to emerge after the Cultural Revolution Yang Lian's is most clearly steeped in the traditional concept of oneness and the unity of heaven and man. The title of his major work to date is the symbol 🝧 to which he has given the pronunciation 'yi' to simultaneously connote 'oneness, unity', the *Book of Changes* (*Yijing*), and poetry.[3] The visual image symbolizes the unity of heaven and man. The sixty-four poems (and prose-poems) of *Yi* contained within four books were written over the five year period 1985–9 and together constitute a single poem. Poetic creation for Yang Lian is a conscious striving to delve deep into the self, distancing the self of the poet from the name and the face which differentiates the individual from others. This image recurs frequently in the later poems of *Yi* and figures prominently in the short 'Mask' poems of *Masks and Crocodile* which were written while he was revising his final draft of *Yi*, and reflecting on poetry and poetic creation:

The epitaph is the last mask removed
people who have discarded their faces
finally recognize one another

begin to speak the same language
when ears rot off
the sea   boring though skulls is louder and clearer
                                                              ('Mask 21')

You look at masks in the house by the sea
as sunlight on the water floods in
under each face are countless faces

speaking together   rippling
looks drown you

flowing away you see that all creation is you
('Mask 30')

In 1978 Yang Lian (b. 1955) learnt of the Democracy Movement in Beijing and rushed back from his travels in the south-west of China to join in the movement. Prior to that his only association with poetry was traditional Chinese poetry. It was with a sense of exhilaration that he encountered the new poetry of the *Jintian/Today* poets in Beijing: Bei Dao, Mang Ke, Gu Cheng, Shu Ting and Jiang He. He trashed his total output of several hundred classical poems and began to read and to write what he called 'modernist' poems (Lee 1990:10).

The *Jintian/Today* poets had grown to prominence through their central role in the student democracy movement. Alongside their political struggle for freedom of expression, they were united also by their common cause: to break from the literary straitjacket prescribed by the Cultural Revolution and to redefine literature. A major means to achieving this goal was the reading of Western 'modernist' literature which, rigorously banned for several decades, 'slipped in' alongside books on science and technology as China opened to foreign countries in the late 1970s as a result of Deng Xiaoping's modernization program (see Goodman 1981 and Pollard 1985). The young *Jintian/Today* poets consciously modelled their writings on modern Western literature as well as modern Chinese literature pre-dating the establishment of the People's Republic of China in 1949. There was a general perception that a 'modernist' literature was emerging.

By August 1979 Yang Lian was writing 'modernist' poetry, some of which was published in *Jintian/Today* a few months before it was closed down by the authorities. The poets re-grouped to publish *Source Materials of the Today Literature Research Society* but ceased publication after the third issue.[4] However, the liberalization of the early 1980s was laced with intermittent clampdowns. The *Jintian/Today* poets disbanded but, in the initial stages of China's new modern literature, they played a dynamic role in re-establishing the principles of free expression of the self in literary creation and the evaluation of Chinese literature as a part of the literature of the world. During the 1980s a significant number of the original group had opportunities to travel abroad; some have remained abroad and now form the backbone of the re-established *Jintian/Today* magazine which is currently published and distributed by Oxford University Press in Hong Kong.

From 1978 Yang Lian began to read vast numbers of handwritten translations of modern Western literature which were circulated amongst like-minded youth who had no interest in reading what was being published by the official presses. However, a huge publication industry of foreign literature in the original and in translation gradually began to flourish. Paz was amongst the foreign authors Yang Lian recalled having read in the early 1980s. Others were T. S.

Eliot, Dante Alighieri, George Orwell, Dylan Thomas, William Blake, Ezra Pound, Saul Bellow, Walt Whitman, William Golding, Thomas Hardy, W. B. Yeats, James Joyce, Franz Kafka, Friedrich Nietzsche, Marcel Proust, Samuel Beckett, Eugene Ionesco, Baudelaire, Vladmir Mayakovsky, Boris Pasternak, Solzhenitsyn, Fyodor Dostoevsky, Milan Kundera, Czeslaw Milosz, Tagore and Gabriel Garcia Marquez (cf. Golden and Minford 1990). Describing his intensive reading of world literature in those times, Yang Lian states that he 'devoured' these works and that the writers he admired most were Dante, Beckett, Eliot, Yeats and Pound; his reading of foreign works dwindled after 1986 as he became totally engrossed with completing *Yi* (see Lee 1990:16–17).

Yang Lian's first encounter with Paz was around 1983 when Chinese translations of a few of Paz's poems began to circulate in stencilled copies among students and writers in Beijing.[5] In the following sections it will be shown that a central part of Paz's understanding of humanity which informs his poetics derives from traditional Chinese sources. This, together with the wide reading of modern world literature by Chinese writers from the late 1970s, accounts for the 'conjunctions'[6] linking Paz's poetics with that of Chinese writers such as Yang Lian. In the context of Western literature, Paz has argued that the term 'influences' was not exact and that it would be better to consider Western literature as a composite whole comprised of styles and trends and that these are invariably 'translinguistic' (1992:160). It is along these lines of thinking that the present study has been conceived: the discourse in poetics between Paz and Yang Lian proposed in the title here is an abstract construct. It attempts to isolate aspects of Paz's poetics which might explain resonances to be found in Yang Lian's poetics.

❖

1990 Nobel Poet Laureate, Octavio Paz (b. 1914), has an acute awareness of how poets of the present and past — in those languages directly accessible to him or through translation — have shaped his own poetics. Many of his essays are devoted to his associations through literature with writers of the past and present. The essays contained in *On Poets and Others,* for example, write of Robert Frost, Walt Whitman, William Carlos Williams, Jean-Paul Sartre, Baudelaire, André Breton, Henri Michaux, Dostoyevski, Solzhenitsyn, José Ortega y Gasset, Luis Buñuel and Luis Cernuda.

However the influences of 'the other' on Paz are substantially broader than those indicated in the essays of *On Poets and Others*. In *One Word to the Other,* Paz's expanded and revised commentary[7] to the first of three public readings given in Mexico City in 1979 on the occasion of the publication of his *Poems 1935–1975* (1978), he summarizes past influences, acknowledging in detail the various literary and philosophical influences on his thinking and poetry. Relevant to the present study, Paz elucidates the impact of his intensified readings in Chinese literature and philosophy from 1962, when he abandoned himself 'to an interior murmur' and began to read Japanese and later Chinese poetry as 'an unconscious attempt to build a dam against the surrealist overflow'. He was drawn in particular to their economy of form where 'minimal and precise constructions made from a few syllables were capable of containing a universe'. With help from Eikichi Hayashiya, Paz translated Basho's 'Oku no Hosomichi'. With help from Wai-Lim Yip and others and using 'various versions and phonetic transcriptions', he translated some poems by Wang Wei, Tu Fu [Du Fu], Su Tung-p'o [Su Dongpo] and others. For Paz these translations were — as were his other translations — 'homages'; each is 'a fragile monument' to the memory of a poet who has enlightened or enchanted him (1992b:32–4).

Paz's act of translating these Chinese poets heightened his sensitivity for Daoist philosophy.[8] Daoism had inspired these and many other Chinese poets for generations and many classical masterpieces may be considered condensations of that philosophy. The 'ghosts' who are amongst the many influences on Paz's poetry therefore also include the Chinese poets whom he read in translation.

❖

Yang Lian refers to *Yi* as 'his biography'. However, there are marked changes in his later works and he does not ever revert to the various poetic forms contained in that work. Like Paz, Yang Lian is aware of ghosts in his poetry, although his ghosts are not confined to the poets who have been influences, as is clearly the case with Paz. In fact he does not anywhere acknowledge literary influences in the way that Paz does. The cosmic substance Yang Lian attributes to his poetry would presumably preclude specific reference to any literary influences. Consider these two extracts from 'Thunder 7' of 'The Descent', the fourth book of *Yi* which he equates with Dante's return to the pure world from Hell and Zarathustra's descent from the mountain (see Lee 1993:96). Yang Lian's ghosts are of the substance of the cosmos; his poetry is not of his making but that of the totality of ghosts from the cosmos. He is 'Forever excavating the darkness behind the eyes' until 'Eyes so desolate see mankind as before stark naked'. His poetry is a striving for 'God-like infiniteness':

As before naked   As before reading
A book which only death can tell us can never be understood
Real death   Like the great land
    Sinks into my depths writes my skin
    Sinks into a stare   Omnisciently designating names

...

All life is a poem
Wailing with grief at the destruction and laughing in the midst of
destruction
I am a precipitation of the myriad things and the myriad things
descend into me

Yang Lian states that *Yi* is his biography: it is in fact his poetic autobiography up to his completion of that single long poem. The work was essentially completed by the time he left China in 1988. He has now spent several years abroad and has found spiritual companions among the poets of various cultures and languages. While the priestly tenor and the poetic forms employed — vestiges of his training in classical Chinese poetry[9] — are now a part of the history of Yang Lian, the basic philosophical underpinnings of his poetics remain the same today.[9]

❖

Paz sees translation and creation as twin processes with constant interaction between the two: literary intercrossings take place as imitation and as translation (see Lee 1996a). European poetry is best viewed as a chronicle of the convergences of the various traditions in Western poetry which include the Japanese *haiku* and Chinese poetry. He describes styles as translinguistic, which means they 'are coalescent and pass from one language to another':

> ...the works each rooted in its own verbal soil, are unique ... unique, but not isolated: each is born and lives in relation to other works composed in different languages. Thus the plurality of languages and the singularity of the works produce neither complete diversity and disorder, but quite the opposite: a world of interrelationships made of harmonies, unions and digressions. (1992a:160)

For Paz literary creation is a constant search for perfect linguistic expression and this justifies his rewriting his own poetry. As ghosts have written his poems Paz argues that he is entitled to revise them and that in doing so he is following the examples of poets he admires, such as Wordsworth, Mallarmé, Yeats, Juan Ramon Jiminez and Jorges Luis Borges. He resoundingly states: 'What counts isn't the poet but the poem.... The poem exists at the expense of the poet.' The poet who writes the poem is not the same person who goes under that name. The real person possesses a physical, social and psychic consistency and has a body and a face and responds to a name whereas the poet is 'not a real person' but 'a fiction, a figure of speech' (1992b:17).

In the process of poetic creation Paz therefore clearly discerns three disparate entities: the person with a name and a face, the poet, and the poem:

> To write poems is to balance, like a tightrope walker on a loose rope, between fiction and reality, the mask and the face. The poet must sacrifice his real face in order

to make his mask more alive and believable: at the same time he must take care that his mask is not immobilized but rather that it have mobility — and more: the vivacity — of his face. (18–9)

The mask is also a central image in Yang Lian's interpretation of the creative act. However, whereas Paz equates the living mask with the poet, Yang Lian equates the mask to the face with a name. For Yang Lian, the face with a name in socialized humanity is a mask which separates individuals. Poetic creation is a struggle to distance oneself from the mask with its accretions of dehumanizing socialized existence and to reach the self which is a part of the cosmos. This struggle leads Yang Lian to Death as the great equalizer of humanity and results in the recurrent, almost obsessive image of skeletons, bones, and skulls throughout his poetry.

Although Paz and Yang Lian use the metaphor of the mask in diametrically different ways to explain the creative act, for both of them the poet and the poem are disparate and autonomous. This may be seen for example in Yang Lian's 'The Book of Exile':

You are not here   Marks of this pen
Just written are swept off by a wild wind
Emptiness like a dead bird soars across your face
Funereal moon is a broken hand
Turning back your days
Back to the page when you do not exist
In writing   You
Bask in your deletion

Like another's voice
Bits of bone are spat carelessly in a corner
Hollow sound of water brushing water
Carelessly enters breathing
Enters a pear and ceases to look at others
Skulls all over the ground are you
In words and lines you grow old in a night
Your poetry invisibly traversing the world
(Yang 1990: in lieu of preface)

In Paz's understanding, what induces poetic creation? In the Author's Notes to *A Tree Within* he states his commitment to Goethe's maxim: 'all poems are occasional, the products of circumstance.' In 'Translation: Literature and Letters', while discussing the processes of literary translation, Paz gives one of his most lucid and concrete metaphors for the creation of poetry, focusing on the poet's use of language to express reality: 'The poet, immersed in the movement of language, in constant verbal preoccupation, chooses a few words — or is chosen by them. As he combines them, he constructs his poem: a verbal object made of irreplaceable and immovable characters.' The poem is 'language congealed yet living' (1992a:159).

However for Paz the autonomous reality which the poem constitutes is governed by form. He is opposed to the automatic writing and 'dictation by the unconscious' of the surrealist poets, even though he feels moral and spiritual affinity with these poets. 'Freedom is the existential, vital element but subject to one condition: that of art, that of poetry.' He does not subscribe to the idea that poetry 'is born of spontaneity or dream, neither is it a child of a lucid consciousness'. Instead he sees it as a struggle and sometimes an embrace between the two. It is the opposition between the two which 'secretly animates any poetic act: the conditional freedom of the work. That freedom is achieved not outside form but within it and by means of it' (1992b:38–9).

For Paz, then, poems are autonomous realities. The poet is immersed in the movement or flow of language and 'chooses a few words — or is chosen by them', a notion also graphically represented in Yang Lian's 'Crocodile' poems, where he likens the agony and ecstasy of poetic creation to crocodiles tearing at the physical self and deleting the self in the process:

The crocodile's nostrils shut like a word
ignoring you
floating and sinking on the page of blank paper

despairing you call for help
and with long submerged words
sink into crocodile waters
                            ('Crocodile 7')

One word considers you at length
more silently
than a lurking crocodile

throat soft and warm
this black tunnel
sees you deleted from the world
                            ('Crocodile 16')

While Paz is acutely aware of the poet 'ghosts' who wrote his own poems, he is perhaps less aware of how his own poetry has created 'ghosts' in modern Chinese poetry in precisely the same way. As mentioned above, Paz was being read in China from about 1983 from hand-copied translations which were circulated amongst students. During 1985 and 1986 his poetry appeared in Chinese language publications and several volumes of his works including

Sunstone were published during 1989–91.[10] Paz is listed amongst the sponsors of the early editions of *Jintian/Today* literary journal which was re-established in 1990 in Sweden by the diaspora Chinese community of writers. By the late 1980s Paz would certainly have been aware that his writings were being widely read in Chinese.[11]

❖

My reading of Paz's 'Translation: Literature and Letters' in 1994 led me to an intensive reading of Paz's writings.[12] I was startled by the resonances of Paz within Yang Lian's poetry and poetic vision to such an extent that I tried to solicit details from Yang Lian about his reading of Paz. However, Paz's long poem *Sunstone* (1957) was the only one of Paz's works that Yang Lian mentions. He seems reluctant to say when he read *Sunstone*: either he read an unpublished manuscript (as *Sunstone* was not published in Chinese until after Yang Lian had completed *Yi* to travel abroad in 1988) or a published version recently. My impression is that he has only read a limited amount of Paz's works.

While Paz writes a great deal on the writers who have had an influence on him, Yang Lian and other Chinese writers of his generation seem somewhat reluctant to identify writers who have shaped and directed their writing. No doubt this is partly due to the fact that modern Chinese writings during the 1980s have often suffered from harsh critics: their works were criticized by the authorities as 'modernist' (and therefore subversive), and on the other hand labelled by some Western sinologists as 'derivative' and inferior to the Western works they allegedly imitated.[13] However, in the 1990s there has been considerable integration in the publishing worlds of the PRC, Taiwan and Hong Kong. The publication of Western literature in Chinese translation is continuing to expand and to supply a readership (including Chinese writers) which extends to all parts of the world; Chinese literature is now beginning to emerge from different cultural milieux and will in future provide interesting material for studies on inter-cultural literary processes.

Sunstone (*Piedre de Sol* 1957) is but one of Paz's many great works in a writing career which spans some forty years. By comparison Yang Lian's writing career has a short history of fifteen years. However, Yang Lian is dedicated to poetry and (like other Chinese writers of his generation) he is highly motivated to catch up on a lost half-century of development during which writers consciously or unconsciously distorted literature for patriotic goals or else were intimidated by the authorities to write according to specified guidelines (see Lee 1996b). Since leaving China in 1988, Yang Lian has continued to write; a large number of his poems have been published in English, French, German, Swedish and Italian translations. *Yi*, which he began to write in China in 1985 and finalized for publication in New Zealand in 1989, was first published in

China in 1991 (Yang and Yu) and reprinted in Taipei (Yang 1994). Paz's *Sunstone* and Yang Lian's *Yi* have both been inspired by ancient calendars which provided in both cases symbolic and concrete confirmation for their thinking about cyclical time in human history.

The New Directions edition of *Sunstone/Piedra de Sol* (New York 1987) as a separate volume, with Eliot Weinberger's translation, contains illustrations of the ancient Mexican calendar which forms the conceptual framework of *Sunstone*. Paz states that the representations 'were probably drawn by native informants in the sixteenth and early seventeenth century'; Spanish captions were later added and the calendars were drawn and redrawn. The versions used in the book are based on Mariano Fernandez de Echeverria y Veytia's *Los canderios mexicanos*, reprinted in 1907 by the National Museum, which Paz states are but 'one set of the many variants of no surviving original' (1987:59 note). The Mexican signs corresponding to Day 4 Olin (Movement) and Day 4 Ehecatl (Wind) appear at the beginning and end of the poem. There are 584 lines to the poem excluding the final six as these are identical to the first six and are therefore not counted. In fact the poem does not end but returns to its beginning. The six lines in question set the theme of cyclical time of the poem — in structure, in form, in sensuality (movement and wind) and in content:

a crystal willow, a poplar of water,
a tall fountain and the wind arches over,
a tree deep-rooted yet dancing still,
a course of a river that turns, moves on,
doubles back, and comes full circle,
forever arriving:

The framework of the ancient Mexican calendar is inherent in the 584 lines of the poem as these:

> ...equal the synodical revolution of the planet Venus, which is 584 days. The ancient Mexicans began their count of the Venusian cycle (and of the other visible planets) with Day 4 Olin; Day 4 Ehecatyl, 584 days later marked the conjunction of Venus and the Sun, the end of one cycle and the beginning of another.
>
> The planet Venus appears twice each day, as the morning star (Phosphorus) and the evening star (Hesperus). This duality (Lucifer and Vesper) has inspired every civilization whose people have taken Venus as a symbol, a sign or an incarnation of the essential duality of the universe. (57)

In Yang Lian's case it was a stone engraving of a Southern Song dynasty astronomical chart which propelled him in January 1985 to write in a single sitting the three long prose-poems of *Shizhe* (*The Departed* 1989) and when he had completed them he knew that he could no longer delay the writing of *Yi*. The following paragraph comes from his essay 'Guan yu *Yi*' (About *Yi*) written in mid-1990. In these are reverberations of many of Paz's thoughts on poetry and the writing of poetry:

> *Yi* is not a word; it is a diagram or just a sign. This book of long poems was without a name; like an unborn child its life belonged to the darkness of the cosmos, yet its constant pulsating struck at me, and prodded me to forewarn me of its existence.[14]

In 1982 Yang Lian conceived the idea of writing a book of long poems which 'would totally recreate the world through a series of changes in the language'. It would be based on the perceptions of a poet of modern times and yet at the same time would also be linked to the spirit and marrow of Chinese tradition; it would be a book of poems in which the Chinese cultural tradition would be reborn through the poet. From that time on, he wrote, 'each volume of my works was a subconscious pursuit of it, an imitation of it, turning into something like it, but never it; they were like so many first drafts still needing revision and waiting to be finalized.' It was as if *Yi* 'invisibly looked on'.

In traditional Chinese culture human beings were subservient to heaven. In *Yi* there is a significant change. Humanity penetrates heaven, is a part of heaven: both man and heaven exist simultaneously. As man changes, heaven changes: as man increases his experience of self, he will at the same time experience a richer world. The unity of heaven and man therefore constitutes perpetually 'changing unities' in the world perceived by the self.

The framework of *Yi* is the *Book of Changes* which, with its trigrams formed from Yin (female) and Yang (male) and the hexagrams formed from the trigrams, were simple depictions of the environment inhabited by the Chinese people of ancient times, its changes and humankind's increasingly complex observations of these. For Yang Lian the 'changes' are free and unrestricted and refer to direct perceptions:

> Heaven, earth, mountain, marsh, water, fire, thunder, wind do not specifically symbolize anything yet together constitute and symbolize everything. They neither belong simply to antiquity which documented them nor to the present which has rediscovered them. They are the products of human hands, spatial demarcations of knowledge. At the same time they constitute a miniature of nature which changes with time and changes with man.... The spirit of poetry is similar to the 'changes': its objective is not to explain, its objective is solely its existence.

Yang Lian explains that the four books of *Yi* form an interconnected whole. Each book has its own structure, language and content and these too are interrelated, and deepen in layers, as concentric circles of ideas:

> The poet's perceptions unfold on different levels but have the same centre: man's existence. Man plunges into the abyss of existence, continues to plunge deeper, and in the process discovers a 'more profound' language for dialogue with the world. Or, one might say, by sinking deeper and deeper into oneself, man instead envelops the world. This is the path to what is 'beneath the phenomenal, ie the metaphysical'. It may be compared with Dante's descent to the pure world from Hell or Nietzsche's Zarathustra going down from the mountain.

The sixty-four poems of *Yi* are divided into four books, each containing sixteen poems. 'The Untrammelled Man Speaks' confronts nature; 'In Symmetry With Death' confronts history; 'Living in Seclusion' confronts the self; and 'The Descent' is man's transcendence. The four books of *Yi* may be summarized in these terms: external transcendence; external hardship; internal hardship; internal transcendence. The structure and language of each book express a unique spiritual quality: the untrammelled gush of 'Qi', the solidity of 'Earth', the flooding of 'Water' and the brilliance of 'Fire'.

❖

Both Paz and Yang Lian are highly experimental in their use of poetic forms and styles. In the creative act they are conscious of pitting themsleves against language to explore various means to express more fully the poetic self, a self which is at the same time a part of humanity and of the cosmos. Their shared sense of cyclical time and return to the beginning has concrete symbolization in their reference to ancient calendars. While Yang Lian, speaks of poetry as linguistic representations of the direct perceptions of the poet, Paz refers to the same act as the translation of reality.

University of Sydney

Notes

1 References to Paz's writings in this paper are to English language editions, although titles and dates of the original works are also indicated; translations from Chinese texts are mine.
2 Original text *Traduccion: Literatura y Literalidad*, 1971, Tusquests, Barcelona.
3 Through the rhyme with the ancient pronunciation of *shi*, that is, 'poetry'.
4 See early accounts such as 'Modernism and Tradition: A Symposium' (1983); Wai-lim Yip (1985); William Tay (1985); and Pan Yuan and Pan Jie (1985).
5 I am grateful to Tang Xiaodu of Beijing University for his investigations and personal comments on the early translation and publication of Paz in China.
6 Paz argues that the rejection of the human body has brought about differing cultural manifestations, see Paz 1990a; original Spanish text *Conjunciones y Disyunciones (*1969 Editorial Joaquin Moritz, S. A.).
7 Original Spanish version *De una palabra a otra* (1985 Editorial Seix Barral, S. A.). This work is a concise but comprehensive summary of the various influences on his poetry and poetics.
8 Paz is fascinated by human beings and how they deal or have dealt with reality; one of these means is through the creative act. His reading of the literatures of various cultures have been accompanied by his reading of their histories and philosophies.
9 For details of Yang Lian's early association with classical Chinese poetry, see Lee 1990.11–2.
10 Ten poems by Paz were included in *Lading Meizhou qingshi xuan* (Selection of Latin American Love Poems; 1985, Jiangsu renmin chubanshe) and selections of his poems were published in the influential journals, *Shijie wenxue* (World Literature) and *Waiguo wenxue* (Foreign Literature) during 1986. An interview by Jiang Zhifang was published in the

monthly *Waiguo wenxue* 1 (1989), p. 49.

11 The original *Jintian/Today* was established by the group of mainly Beijing poets, Bei Dao, Mang Ke, Gu Cheng and others in 1978; their poetry inspired and supported the Democracy Wall movement 1978–9. Patton (1995) and Van Crevel (1996) contain detailed documentation of the history of *Jintian/Today* as well as extensive bibliographies of both primary and secondary sources.

12 I am indebted to Michael Loosli whose knowledge of Paz's writings was invaluable in the early stages of my study of Paz.

13 Rey Chow (1993) stridently attacks some of the critics of China's modern literature as 'Orientalist'.

14 This essay does not appear in *Taiyang yu ren* (Yang and Yu 1991) although comments by Zhou Shi in the volume contain much of the information from it, presumably from earlier notes or correspondences with Yang Lian. It is however included in the Taipei edition. Parts of this essay have been summarized in Lee 1993a and 1993b.

Works Cited

Chow, Rey 1993 *Writing Diaspora: Tactics of Intervention in Contemporary Cultural Studies*. Indiana University Press.

Goldblatt, Howard (ed.) 1990 *Worlds Apart: Recent Chinese Writings and its Audiences*. M. E. Sharpe, Armonk.

Golden, Sean and John Minford 1990 'Yang Lian and Chinese Tradition' in Goldblatt: pp. 119–37.

Goodman, David S. G. 1981 *Beijing Street Voices: The Poetry and Politics of China's Democracy Movement*. Marion Boyars, London.

Kinkley, Jeffrey 1985 *After Mao: Chinese Literature and Society, 1978–1981*. The Council on East Asian Studies, Harvard University.

Lee, Mabel 1990 'The Philosophy of the Self and Yang Lian' in Yang Lian 1990: pp. 9–36.

—— 1993a 'Before Tradition: *The Book of Changes*, Yang Lian's *Yi* and the Affirmation of the Self Through Poetry' in eds Mabel Lee and A. D. Syrokomla-Stefanowska *Modernization of the Chinese Past*. Wild Peony, Sydney: pp. 94–106.

—— 1993b 'Man Confronts History: Six Poems from Yang Lian's "In Symmetry with Death"' in *Ulitarra* 3: pp. 57–66.

—— 1996a (in print) 'Octavio Paz on Literary Translation and Yang Lian's Poems on Poetry' in *Canadian Review of Comparative Literature*.

—— 1996b (in print) 'Personal Freedom in Twentieth Century China: Reclaiming the Self in Yang Lian's *Yi* and Gao Xingjian's *Lingshan*' in eds Mabel Lee and Michael Wilding *History, Literature and Society: Essays in Honour of S. N. Mukherjee*. Sydney Association for Studies in Society and Culture, Sydney.

'Modernism and Tradition: A Symposium' 1983 in *Renditions* 19 & 20: pp. 41–80.

Pan, Yuan and Pan Jie 1985 'The Non-Official Magazine *Today* and the Younger Generation's Ideals for a New Literature' in Kinkley: pp. 193–219.

Patton, Simon 1995 'The Poetics of *Wubuwei*: Two Texts by Gu Cheng', PhD thesis University of Melbourne.

Paz, Octavio 1987 'Sunstone/Piedre de Sol', tr. Eliot Weinberger, in *The Collected Poems of Octavio Paz, 1957-1987*. New Directions, New York.

—— 1988 *A Tree Within*, tr. Eliot Weinberger. New Directions, New York.

—— 1990a *Conjunctions and Disjunctions*, tr. Helen Lane. Arcade Publishing, New York.

—— 1990b *On Poets and Others*, tr. Michael Schmidt. Arcade Publishing, New York.

—— 1991 *Sunstone/Piedre de Sol*, tr. Eliot Weinberger. New Directions, New York.

—— 1992a 'Translation: Literature and Letters', tr. Irene del Corral in Rainer Schulte and John Biguenet (eds), *Theories of Translation: An Anthology of Essays from Dryden to Derrida*. The University of Chicago Press: pp. 153–4.

—— 1992b *One Word To The Other*, tr. Amelia Simpson. Latitudes Press, Mansfield.

Pollard, D. E. 1985 'The Controversy Over Modernism, 1979–84' in *China Quarterly* 104, pp. 641–56.

Tay, William 1985 '"Obscure Poetry": A Controversy in Post-Mao-China' in Kinkley: pp. 133–57.

Yang, Lian 1989 *Huang*. Renmin Wenxue Chubanshe, Beijing.

—— 1990 *Masks and Crocodile*, tr. Mabel Lee. Wild Peony, Sydney.

—— 1994a *Guihua*. Lianjing wenxue, Taipei.

—— 1994b 'Dahai tingzhi zhi chu' (Where the Sea Stands Still) tr. Mabel Lee in ed. Leonard Schwartz 'The Contemporary Instance: A Selection of New Chinese Poems' in *Talisman* 12: pp. 182–90.

—— 1994c *Yi*. Xiandaishishe, Taipei.

—— and Yu Feng 1991 *Taiyang yu ren*. Hunan wenyi chubanshe, Changsha.

Yip, Wai-lim 1985 'Crisis Poetry: An Introduction to Yang Lian, Jiang He and Misty Poetry' in *Renditions* 23: pp. 120–30

Van Crevel, Maghiel 1996 *Language Shattered*. Research School CNWS, Leiden.

QIN HAIYING

Réécriture du Mythe: Segalen et *Récit de la Source aux Fleurs de Pêchers*

'Les mythes ne sont guère plus que des mots tout assemblés, et qui ne valent que si on les disloque pour en tirer de nouveaux heurts ou de nouveaux accords' (Manceron 1985:58). C'est au sujet de son projet de drame *Orphée-roi* que Segalen a écrit ces lignes juste avant son grand départ pour la Chine. Cette assertion qui situe explicitement le problème du mythe sur le terrain de l'écriture et de la réécriture se prête parfaitement à l'ensemble de son oeuvre 'chinoise'. En effet, si on prend 'mythe' dans un sens très large et qu'on considère la Chine comme une énorme matière mythique, on pourra voir dans la plupart de ses textes inspirés par la Chine la dislocation systématique des mythes chinois qui se manifeste concrètement par la transposition des textes littéraires consacrées — poèmes, légendes, récits mythiques, sentences morales, expressions rituelles, images figées. Les nouveaux heurts ou les nouveaux accords issus de ce 'transfert' sont d'autant plus significatifs qu'ils affectent deux cultures éloignées et deux mondes à bien des égards différents — 'Empire de Chine' et 'Empire du soi-même' (108).

De cette réécriture du mythe chez Segalen, nous examinons ici un exemple peu étudié jusqu'ici, tiré d'un épisode de son oeuvre *Equipée*. A la lumière d'une lecture intertextuelle et comparée, cet épisode nous apparaît comme un palimpeste qui cache un texte-source très célèbre de la littérature chinoise : *Récit de la Source aux Fleurs de Pêchers* (Tao Hua Yuan Ji) écrit par Tao Yuanming (365–427), poète de la dynastie des Jin qui a exercé une influence considérable sur les écrivains des époques postérieures et qui est toujours très aimé par les intellectuels chinois d'aujourd'hui.

C'est après avoir assisté à bien des malheurs sociaux et après avoir mené une longue vie de retraite en paysan simple et sobre, qui lui apporte un grand apaisement dans l'âme, que Tao Yuanming a composé, à l'âge de 58 ans, le

Récit de la Source aux Fleurs de Pêchers, une des pièces en prose les plus connues de son oeuvre. Ce récit raconte comment un pêcheur avait découvert, à la source d'un cours d'eau bordé d'un bois de pêchers en fleurs, un petit pays isolé et pittoresque où les gens d'une autre époque vivaient dans la paix et la prospérité, à l'abri des avatars du monde extérieur.

Ce récit peut être considéré comme un 'mythe' dans plusieurs sens du terme. D'abord, par sa source d'inspiration, il est lié à un mythe proprement dit (c'est-à-dire une histoire primordiale transmise par la tradition), celui du *Shanhai Jing, Livre canonique des montagnes et des mers*, le plus ancien livre de géographie de Chine et aussi le plus ancien recueil de mythes chinois. Les recherches biographiques nous apprennent que Tao Yuanming s'était beaucoup nourri de ce livre pour écrire ses propres poèmes (cf. 1992:290, 246). Son *Récit de la Source aux Fleurs de Pêchers* (suivi d'un poème en guise de commentaire) était inspiré, entre d'autres anecdotes de son temps, d'un des contes de ce recueil qui brosse le tableau enchanté d'un 'Pays des Zhi' où les habitants vivaient dans une extrême félicité: toutes sortes de céréales y poussent naturellement, les animaux de toute espèce y vivent en harmonie, les oiseaux et phénix y chantent et dansent librement.[1] Ce lieu fabuleux contraste avec la dure réalité historique dans laquelle se trouvait Tao Yuanming: effondrement de la Dynastie des Jin sous le coup des usurpateurs Song, corruption de la Cour, souffrances du peuple tourmenté par les guerres et écrasés par le poids des charges. Pour traduire sa déception devant le réel et son aspiration à un monde harmonieux, libre et prospère comme dans le mythe antique, il imagine alors son propre lieu de bonheur à travers l'apologue de la *Source aux Fleurs de Pêchers*. Dans le poème en annexe qui commente le récit, il parle de la retraite des Sages face à la tyrannie, célèbre la vie simple et autarcique dans la campagne reculée où chacun cultive la terre et bénéficie de toute la récolte sans subir les impôts royaux. C'est donc une allégorie reflétant indirectement les problèmes sociaux de l'époque.

Ensuite, par son caractère euphorique et fictif, ce texte est en lui-même un 'mythe', au sens de rêverie fantaisiste, mirage embellissant, représentation idéalisante sans fondement réel, puisque la dite Source aux Fleurs de Pêchers ne se trouve nulle part dans la réalité (malgré le grand nombre de toponymes chinois qui lui sont similaires et malgré la tentative des historiens littéraires de l'identifier à tel ou tel district chinois).[2] Nous savons que, dans la tradition occidentale, cette catégorie de mythes, quand elle véhicule un idéal politique et institutionnel sous les traits d'un Etat imaginaire, prend plus précisément le nom d''utopie' (non-lieu) et devient presque un genre littéraire depuis le livre de Thomas More. Comme mythe et comme genre littéraire, 'l'utopie est la construction verbale d'une communauté quasi-humaine particulière, où les institutions socio-politiques, les normes et les relations individuelles sont organisées selon un principe plus parfait que dans la société de l'auteur' (Angenot 1979:217). Dans ce sens, le récit de Tao Yuanming est bien un mythe utopique à la chinoise, puisqu'il offre aussi de la société une image idéale fortement marquée par la pensée taoïste de Laozi qui prêche le principe du 'petit Etat peu peuplé' sans communication avec le monde extérieur, gouverné par la politique de non-gouvernement et de laisser-aller. C'est souvent dans ce sens moral et socio-politique que la critique littéraire moderne interprète ce texte, le considérant comme 'première utopie de la littérature chinoise'.

Enfin, et c'est pour nous l'aspect le plus important de ce récit qui implique le problème de la réécriture, par sa fortune postérieure au cours de plus de mille ans d'histoire littéraire chinoise, le *Récit de la Source aux Fleurs de Pêchers* joue pleinement le rôle catalyseur de 'mythe littéraire'. Selon Pierre Albouy, un mythe littéraire est un thème littéraire impliqué dans un récit hérité, susceptible d'être ressuscité par différents auteurs qui le traitent et le modifient avec une grande liberté en l'investissant de significations nouvelles tout en gardant sa structure fondamentale (cf. Albouy 1969:9–10). Ainsi des générations de poètes et de littérateurs chinois, notamment ceux des Tang et des Song, n'ont cessé de reprendre ce récit sous des titres tels que *Voyage à la Source aux Fleurs de Pêchers* ou *Peinture de la Source aux Fleurs de Pêchers*. Chaque époque a son usage et sa version de ce mythe. Sous les Song par exemple, il est lié à la vogue taoïste de l'ermitage et de la quête de l'immortalité à travers un voyage initiatique.[3] En d'autres temps et d'une manière générale, il est interprété soit comme expression d'une vision plutôt pessimiste du monde qu'adoptent beaucoup de lettrés chinois dans les moments malheureux de leur existence ou de leur époque (déception vis-à-vis du pouvoir, résignation en temps de troubles ou sous l'occupation d'une race étrangère, échec aux examens mandarinaux, impossibilité de réaliser leurs ambitions sociales et de contribuer au salut du peuple), soit comme leçon de sagesse de vie teintée d'épicurisme à l'antipode d'une philosophie d'action (repli sur soi, désengagement politique, plaidoyer pour le retour à la spontanéité naturelle et à la vie paysanne, aspiration à la liberté individuelle, à la pureté de l'âme et à une société aux moeurs épurés et simples). A travers des siècles de palingénésie, ce mythe littéraire finit par se cristalliser en une seule image lexicalisée — 'source aux fleurs de pêchers en dehors du monde', synonyme de paradis terrestre, jardin d'Eden, Eldorado, en un mot, version chinoise du mythe de l'Age d'or.

❖

C'est un tel mythe lourd de connotations historiques et morales chinoises que Segalen semble réécrire dans son livre *Equipée*, récit de voyage basé sur ses expériences de mission archéologique en Chine. Cette oeuvre en prose est structurée dans l'ensemble comme un itinéraire 'réel', rythmé par les étapes successives qui sont autant de chapitres. Le chapitre qui laisse lire en filigrane le mythe de la *Source aux Fleurs de Pêchers* fait partie de la vingtième 'étape' du voyage, étape assez 'déroutante', puisqu'en plein voyage 'au pays du réel', le Je, narrateur et voyageur français, se détourne de sa route normale et fait une fugue vers l'impossible, dans la direction d'un village inexistant. Et c'est là que commence l'analogie structurelle et thématique avec la *Source aux Fleurs de Pêchers*. Pour un lecteur doué d'un minimum de mémoire littéraire chinoise, cette analogie est trop frappante pour passer inaperçue. Elle nous incite à 'gratter' le texte-palimpseste de Segalen en regard de son modèle chinois, à faire une lecture intertextuelle pour observer le processus précis de la réécriture et pour arriver à des constatations générales sur la différence de sens obtenue par cette transposition.

Pour la commodité de l'exposé, nous procédons d'abord à une mise en parallèle des séquences analogiques des deux textes dans leur ordre narratif originel. A chaque séquence nous donnerons un titre commun. Pour le texte de Segalen, seuls seront cités les passages qui intéressent directement notre comparaison (cf. Segalen 1983:96–102). Quant au récit de Tao Yuanming, il sera reproduit intégralement selon la version de Margouliès (1948:119–20)[1]:

1. Le personnage s'engage sur un chemin inconnu et rencontre un bois.

Source aux Fleurs de Pêchers:

> Sous la dynastie des Tsin, un homme de Wou-Ling, pêcheur de son métier, s'est égaré en suivant un cours d'eau et ne savait plus combien de chemin il avait fait. Il rencontra soudain une forêt de pêchers en fleurs qui s'élevait sur les deux rives à plusieurs centaines de pas, sans qu'il y ait un seul arbre d'une espèce différente. Les herbes épanouies étaient belles et parfumées, les fleurs tombées jonchaient le sol.
>
> Le pêcheur, ayant admiré ce spectacle, se remit en route, voulant aller jusqu'au bout de la forêt. Celle-ci se terminait à la source même du cours d'eau; il trouva une montagne. Dans la montagne, il y avait un petit orifice par lequel il lui sembla voir de la lumière. Alors, quittant sa barque, il entra dans cette caverne. Au début, elle était très étroite, permettant à peine le passage d'un homme.

Equipée:

> Je suivrai donc l'autre, la route vers l'impossible, la route impériale, la route aux chemins du passé....
>
> Brusquement la voici perdue sous une futaie où elle se prolonge cependant, d'où l'on ne peut plus enfin regarder en arrière. D'où l'on ne peut plus voir d'où l'on vient....
>
> La route qui menait ici est étouffée, est perdue, est mangée de plantes et de mousses ... il faut bien marcher quand même, aveuglé, marchant de ses mains puisque les pieds trébuchent....

2. Découverte d'un nouvel espace et d'un groupe d'hommes.

Source aux Fleurs de Pêchers:

> Mais, lorsqu'il eut fait quelques dizaines de pas, il arriva soudain à un espace découvert et clair.

La terre était plate, la plaine s'étendait au loin, on voyait de belles maisons. Il y a avait là des champs bien cultivés et de jolis étangs, des groupes de mûriers et de bambous. Des sentiers s'entrecroisaient, on entendait de tous côtés chanter des coqs et aboyer des chiens. Mais les vêtements des hommes et femmes qui allaient et venaient, labouraient ou travaillaient, étaient tous comme ceux d'étrangers. Depuis les vieillards aux cheveux jaunis jusqu'aux enfants ébouriffés, tous avaient l'air paisible et satisfait.

Equipée:

Et me voici, débouché, étonné de lumière et du nouvel espace, dans un très nouveau, très haut et très cerné canton du monde. Une vaste cuve baignée d'air, d'un ciel neuf et pleine jusqu'aux bords de calmes cultures. Des chiens familiers aboient. Des fumées montent dans le soir. Les montagnes, très hautes à l'entour, non pas implacables, mais douces, font de ceci un canton évidemment isolé, évidemment inconnu du monde puisque mes gens et les habitants d'en bas l'ignoraient. — Je songe ironiquement combien cet improviste village presque imaginaire est cerné, entouré, et réalise le voeu littéral du Vieux Philosophe: 'Que d'un village à l'autre ne s'entendent les abois des chiens... ni les appels chantants des coqs.'

3. L'accueil du nouvel arrivant par les gens du village.

Source aux Fleurs de Pêchers:

Lorsqu'ils eurent aperçu le pêcheur, tout le monde fut stupéfait. On lui demanda d'où il venait et il leur raconta tout. Alors on l'invita à entrer dans une maison, on lui offrit du vin, on tua une poule pour le régaler. Lorsque dans le village on eut appris qu'un homme était arrivé, tout le monde est venu lui parler et l'interroger.

Equipée:

Et voici en effet, à ma rencontre, un troupeau de vieillards, jacasseurs, lents et doux: je vais leur demander accueil, je vais leur témoigner mon gré de ce qu'ils existent bien réellement là où mes gens avaient affirmé leur vacuité néante, leur absence....

Mais je reste devant eux, étonné.... Ils n'ont pas en effet de tresses mandchoues, contemporaines..., ils ont la coiffure enchignonnée du vieux Ming et les longs vêtements que peignent les porcelaines.

4. Le personnage se renseigne sur l'histoire de ces habitants qui vivent en décalage par rapport à leur époque.

Source aux Fleurs de Pêchers:

Pour ce qui est d'eux-mêmes, ils ont expliqué que leurs aïeux, fuyant les troubles du temps, emmenant femmes, enfants et voisins, étaient tous venus se réfugier dans ce coin perdu et jamais plus n'en sont ressortis. Aussi n'avaient-ils aucun rapport avec les gens du dehors.

Equipée:

Ces gens seraient donc d'un autre âge ... seraient-ils d'avant la conquête tartare? Ils auraient alors près de trois cents ans de recul....

Je m'enquiers du nom du village. C'est précisément le doublet antique des marchands d'en bas.

C'est le Trou de Sel Noir, cette sous-préfecture évasive que les Annales déclarent abolie depuis l'antiquité....

Je n'ose pas interroger plus loin. Mais je pressens tout d'un coup comme un éclair que ce sont là peut-être les descendants du puissant général fidèle, Wou San-K'ouei, qui, vaincus par les conquérants tartares aux longs cheveux tressés, vinrent se réfugier ici, et se faisant, pour vivre, oublier, derrière le rideau des montagnes, ont peut-être oublié leurs temps.... Peut-être. Ne pouvant se hasarder ailleurs, ils se cantonnent ici.

5. Les habitants réfugiés se renseignent sur ce qui se passe en dehors de leur monde clos.

Source aux Fleurs de Pêchers:

Ils demandèrent au pêcheur quelle dynastie régnait maintenant en Chine; ils n'avaient même pas entendu parler de celle des Han, sans parler des suivantes.

Le pêcheur leur raconta en détail tout ce qu'il savait; tous l'écoutèrent en soupirant. Puis les autres habitants l'ont invité chez eux l'un après l'autre, et tous lui offraient à boire et à manger.

Equipée:

En effet, ils me questionnent. 'Où en est la grande affaire des Grands Ming, la dynastie? La légalité, la filiation.... Quel est le nom dicible du Fils du Ciel vivant aujourd'hui dans la Capitale du nord?...'

Je ne puis évidemment pas répondre. Les Grands Ming sont périmés et abolis autant que leur ville depuis trois cents ans. Je ne puis les déconcerter à ce point.... Leur dire que les Nomades du nord se sont assis sur Péking est une injure qu'ils ne croiraient pas possible....

6. Le personnage quitte le village.

Source aux Fleurs de Pêchers:

Après y être resté quelques jours, le pêcheur prit congé pour partir. Alors ces hommes de l'intérieur de la montagne le prièrent de ne pas parler d'eux aux autres. Une fois sorti, il retrouva sa barque et prit à nouveau le chemin parcouru en prenant bien soin d'en marquer tous les endroits. Arrivé à la ville, il alla trouver le préfet et lui exposa tout cela. Le préfet envoya aussitôt des hommes reconnaître la route. Ils ont cherché les marques laissées, mais se sont aussitôt égarés et n'ont plus réussi à retrouver le bon chemin.

Equipée:

Je me retire. Je m'en vais à reculons, loin de leur vie trop prolongée. Je n'éclaircirai point leur droit administratif à la vie ... je ne trahirai pas présomptueusement le passé qui a miraculeusement réussi à vivre....

...Je ne porterai point sur la carte précise, au milieu de mots topographiques, l'existence dans l'espace de ce lieu paradoxal, imaginaire peut-être, et qu'on ne retrouvera point officiellement après moi.

7. 'Dénouement' des deux récits.

Source aux Fleurs de Pêchers:
> Lieou Tseu-ki, de Nan-yang, un lettré de grand mérite, ayant entendu parler de cette histoire, voulut avec enthousiasme s'y rendre en personne. Mais ses recherches n'ont pas abouti. Bientôt après il tomba malade et mourut et depuis il n'y a eu plus personne qui se soit mis en quête de cette source.

Equipée:
> Ceci est un rêve de marche, un rêve de route, un sommeil sur deux pieds balancés, ivres de fatigue, à la tombée de l'étape....

❖

La confrontation textuelle permet de voir que les deux récits sont construits selon un même schéma structurel: *un étranger découvre, au terme d'un cheminement rempli d'obstacles (voyage initiatique), un lieu de bonheur inconnu où des gens vivent en décalage par rapport à leur temps.* L'*étranger* est, chez Tao Yuanming, le pêcheur égaré qui rencontre par hasard un bois de pêchers en fleurs, chez Segalen, le 'Je'— voyageur occidental (donc doublement étranger) qui choisit délibérément sa 'route aux chemins du passé'. Le *cheminement pénible* et initiatique est représenté chez l'un par la caverne étroite de la montagne, chez l'autre, par une futaie sombre et une route 'mangée de mousse'. La *découverte* se produit dans les deux cas de façon inattendue, au sein d'un espace cerné et pittoresque. Le *lieu du bonheur* s'appelle d'un côté 'Source aux Fleurs de Pêchers', de l'autre 'Trou de Sel Noir'. Le *décalage temporel* consiste en un anachronisme dynastique de cinq cents ans chez le poète chinois, de trois cents ans chez le poète français. C'est ce même schéma structurel et fonctionnel qui donne au lecteur une première impression de lire du Tao Yuanming.

Mais on ne tarde pas à remarquer que, sur fond de cette structure commune, le texte de Segalen présente bien des éléments visiblement différents du texte-source. Ces éléments différents, qui ont pour effet de gommer le texte-source, résultent précisément d'une opération de réécriture: transformations spatio-temporelles, changements du mode de narration (de la troisième personne à la première personne), amplifications par addition d'un long préambule spéculatif et des détails descriptifs (qui fait que l'épisode en question est quatre ou cinq fois plus long que le récit de Tao Yuanming), modification de ton, insertion de nouveaux éléments (citation, référence historique), introduction de nouveaux thèmes (notamment celui de l'exotisme à l'envers et du conflit entre le Réel et l'Imaginaire). On peut dire que le texte de Segalen respecte la 'syntaxe' du récit de Tao Yuanming en y permutant de nouveaux syntagmes et en la prenant souvent à contre-pied, donnant ainsi un effet de symétrie inversée ou de reproduction en négatif (comme en photographie).

La transformation la plus massive que nous pouvons observer est évidemment celle de l'espace et du temps. Grâce au changement spatio-temporel, la nouvelle version du mythe se donne d'emblée comme une 'autre histoire'.

D'abord, pour ce qui est de l'espace, Segalen transpose l''u-topia' de Tao Yuanming dans un lieu 'fantôme', encore plus imprécis, puisqu'il s'agit d'une ville antique abolie 'sans nulle localisation logique'. On sait seulement qu'il se trouve aussi dans un endroit isolé du monde et entouré de montagnes. Le nom de la 'Source aux Fleurs de Pêchers' est de ce fait entièrement effacé, et disparaît en même temps l'image-cliché contenue dans ce toponyme. A sa place, on trouve un nouveau nom de lieu et une nouvelle image: 'Trou de Sel Noir'. D'ailleurs ce n'est pas le seul toponyme évoqué dans le texte, car à ce village du passé correspond un doublet —'Puits de Sel Blanc' désignant 'le gros village marchand' qui vit au présent (dans le récit). Cette opposition entre deux villages en contraste 'noir' et 'blanc' n'existe pas dans le texte de Tao Yuanming; elle est un élément ajouté par Segalen. Sa signification est à chercher dans la problématique générale d'*Equipée*. Comme le narrateur nous en avertit dès le début du livre, 'cette Equipée dans le Réel' n'a d'autre but que de confronter sur le terrain, sous un climat différent et parmi une race différente, le Réel et l'Imaginaire, le concret et l'idée, le mont et la métaphore, l'acte et le rêve, pour savoir lequel des deux triomphe. Elle n'a d'autre plaisir que de vivre le choc de ces deux mondes opposés pour pouvoir sentir le Divers comme moment mystérieux. Dans ce cas, les deux villages sont manifestement les images mêmes du Réel et de l'Imaginaire en conflit.

Concernant l'opposition entre ces deux villages 'noir' et 'blanc', il est intéressant d'évoquer le fameux symbole taoïste du mouvement de l'Univers, symbole longuement commenté dans *Equipée* même:

> L'enroulement réciproque des deux virgules du Tao, l'une blanche, l'autre noire, égales, symétriques, sans que l'une l'emporte jamais sur l'autre.... La traduction commune en est 'Yin et Yang' Femelle et Mâle ... et cette opposition et cette pénétration qui ... engendrèrent le monde, sont également capables de contenir tout ce qu'on veut. (1983:50)

Le principe de l'unité des contraires et du relativisme universel contenu dans ce vieux symbole chinois, Segalen l'étend sur son propre domaine symbolique: comme le Yin et le Yang, le Réel et l'Imaginaire sont dans un rapport d'implication réciproque, d'interpénétration constante. Le fait que le village antique (village Yin, noir et mort) surgit anachroniquement en présence du village réel (village Yang, blanc et vivant) laisse justement entrevoir le moment mystérieux d'un choc entre le Réel et l'Imaginaire.

Quant au problème du temps, le changement le plus vertigineux est le décalage chronologique raconté dans les deux récits: les textes parlent de la discordance entre l'époque où vit le personnage principal (pêcheur de Wuling ou voyageur français) et l'époque où se croyaient vivre les habitants du village 'surpris' par lui. Ce qui est compliqué par la réécriture, c'est que le décalage historique lui-même se trouve déplacé comme 'en bloc' dans un autre temps: dans le récit de Tao Yuanming, le pêcheur vivait sous la dynastie des Jin (Tsin, 317–420) et il a découvert dans le village perdu des descendants des Qin (Ts'in, 221–206 avant Jésus-Christ) qui ignoraient même l'avènement de la dynastie des Han (206 avant Jésus-Christ–220); chez Segalen, le 'Je' voyageait au début du vingtième siècle sous la dernière dynastie chinoise, les Qing (Ts'ing, les Mandchous, 1644–1911) et il a rencontré dans cette sous-préfecture déclarée 'abolie' des villageois vivant encore à l'heure et à la manière des grands Ming, dynastie qui précède les Mandchous (d'où l'absence des longues tresses chez ces habitants). Les gens de la Source aux Fleurs de Pêchers s'étaient cachés dans la montagne pour fuir le pouvoir tyrannique de l'empereur des Qin, alors que les habitants du 'Trou de Sel Noir' sont supposés être descendants du célèbre général Wou San-k'ouei,[5] lesquels voulaient fuir les conquérants tartares. Segalen transpose donc le récit de Tao Yuanming dans son propre temps et remplace un anachronisme par un autre en y ajoutant un élément réel de l'histoire chinoise.

A côté de ces transpositions diégétiques, d'autres transpositions plus ponctuelles concourent aussi au renouvellement de la signification du mythe chinois. Elles procèdent le plus souvent par inversion, distorsion ou renversement des éléments thématiques du texte-source.

Dès la première séquence par exemple, nous nous heurtons à une grosse différence relative au thème du 'bois', signe précurseur de la découverte: chez Tao Yuanming, c'est le bois fleuri qui séduit le pêcheur et l'amène, après l'obstacle de la caverne, au nouveau pays enchanté, alors que chez Segalen, il n'est pas question de caverne, l'obstacle vient du bois lui-même qui n'est pas du tout fleuri, mais délaissé et morne (il n'y a pas de source d'eau, ni de fleurs de pêchers), et c'est simplement par amour du passé que le voyageur défie le chemin 'impossible'.

Dans la séquence 2, les récits décrivent l'atmosphère bucolique du nouveau pays par un même détail qui pourrait sembler anodin: abois des chiens et chants des coqs. C'est en fait une image-cliché qui renvoie à une expression très connue du grand maître taoïste Laozi (littéralement 'Vieux Philosophe'), expression que le récit de Tao Yuanming utilise de façon implicite et que le récit de Segalen cite littéralement: '(Je) réalise le voeu littéral du Vieux Philosophe: "Que d'un village à l'autre ne s'entendent les abois des chiens... ni les appels chantants des coqs".' Dans le contexte culturel chinois, cette formule évoque l'idéal politique du 'petit Etat peu peuplé' et signifie par extension une vie simple et cloîtrée. Le texte originel de Laozi est le suivant: 'Je les tiendrais tellement isolés, séquestrés, que les petits pays voisins fussent-ils si proches que les coqs et les chiens puissent s'entendre, mes sujets mourraient de vieillesse avant d'avoir eu aucun rapport avec ces voisins' (cf. Wieger 1906:124–5). La citation dans *Equipée* n'est donc qu'une fausse citation qui feint d'être vraie par l'emploi des guillemets: elle est faussée par une particule négative ('ne') qui donne un ton ironique à cette nouvelle version du mythe.

La fin du récit de Segalen prend encore le contre-pied de l'apologue de Tao Yuanming: à son retour, le pêcheur de Wuling 'dénonce' à la préfecture le village caché (mais qu'on n'aura jamais réussi à retrouver), alors que le voyageur français d'*Equipée*, fidèle aux habitants du village fantôme, garde pour lui leur secret afin de préserver le passé contre le présent décevant. Par cette fidélité au passé s'estompe le thème chinois de refuge politique et se dégage une idée force de Segalen: exotisme du temps. Pour celui-ci, le passé est 'exotisme historique', le futur, 'exotisme imaginaire', mais 'l'exotisme du présent n'existe par définition pas' (1986:34). Ce 'Trou de Sel Noir' est donc le lieu de rencontre entre exotisme historique et exotisme imaginaire. Il se dresse face au 'Puits de Sel Blanc' comme une différence substantielle et savoureuse (comme le sel justement).[6]

Pour tirer toutes les conséquences de la réécriture du mythe chinois par Segalen, il faut encore tenir compte du fait que l'épisode que nous venons d'analyser n'est pas un récit indépendant comme le texte de Tao Yuanming, mais fait partie d'un journal de route à caractère autobiographique. Ce n'est qu'à la fin de la vingtième étape que le narrateur-voyageur nous apprend que la découverte du village antique n'est qu'une 'vision' du marcheur fatigué par la route. C'est donc un récit de rêve éveillé. Son insertion dans le récit de voyage s'apparente au fondu-enchaîné du montage cinématographique: en l'espace de deux phrases et à l'aide de points de suspension, l'évocation du voyage réel se brouille peu à peu pour laisser 'monter' le rêve, rêvé d'après le vieux rêve chinois de la Source aux Fleurs de Pêchers. Par ce trucage de récit qui fond dans un tout, le réel et l'imaginaire, la vue et la vision, Segalen n'a pas seulement bouleversé la logique de la vraisemblance du conte de Tao Yuanming, mais il a aussi fait éclater en quelque sorte l'illusion du récit utopique occidental (qui est toujours rapporté comme une histoire vraie): le narrateur-voyageur d'*Equipée*, seul témoin de l'Ailleurs, ne tient pas du tout à garantir l'authenticité de son propre témoignage. Au contraire il insécurise le lecteur par le brusque recul final qui annule tout ce qui vient d'être raconté: 'Ceci est un rêve de marche ... à la tombée de l'étape.' Le mythe se démystifie, l'utopie' est rendue à son sens propre et plat de 'non-lieu', ou plutôt comme 'ce qui n'a pas eu lieu'. Ici nous observons une tendance caractéristique d'*Equipée*: si Segalen se fait le chantre de l'Imaginaire et du 'Désir-Imaginant' dans *Stèles* et *Peintures*, il sait aussi ici tempérer l'Imaginaire pour le compte du 'gros' Réel. Par l'insertion de ce rêve dans le journal de route, il réussit merveilleusement le jeu égal, symétrique et réciproque du Réel et de l'Imaginaire.

Par ces transpositions de divers ordres, Segalen donne du mythe de la Source aux Fleurs de Pêchers une version originale et moderne, celle d'un poète occidental du vingtième siècle qui se préoccupe avant tout du problème esthétique et philosophique de la différence, du conflit et de l'alternance entre le même et l'autre.

Ces réflexions abstraites ne sont évidemment pas celles qui présidaient à la création du *Récit de la Source aux Fleurs de Pêchers*. La distance spatio-temporelle et la différence culturelle et existentielle sont trop grandes entre les deux auteurs pour qu'ils se servent du même mythe dans les mêmes intentions. Comme nous l'avons dit plus haut, le problème d'engagement et de désengagement politique est un des aspects les plus importants de l'oeuvre et de la vie de Tao Yuanming. Son récit est le reflet d'un conflit moral et porte la marque de son temps, tandis que la réécriture de Segalen débouche plutôt sur une allégorie spéculative et atemporelle qui illustre un conflit métaphysique. Ce qui permet le passage d'un récit à l'autre, c'est avant tout la signification la plus générale de ce mythe: conflit entre le réel et l'idéal. Ce réel et cet idéal se situent chez le poète chinois sur un plan moral et politique, chez le poète français sur un plan philosophique et abstrait, puisque l'idéal dans *Equipée* ne se réfère pas à une conception politique précise, mais retrouve son sens intellectuel d''idée' (selon Segalen, c'est tout ce qui se produit dans l'esprit et tout ce qui s'oppose à l'acte) et équivaut à la notion philosophique de l'Imaginaire.

❖

Tout au long de cette étude, une question épineuse nous guette: Segalen a-t-il lu ou non le *Récit de la Source aux Fleurs de Pêchers*? S'est-il jamais réclamé de Tao Yuanming? Si l'hypothèse de l'emprunt peut être prouvée biographiquement, notre étude sera non seulement justifiée par le rapport intertextuel, mais aussi légitimée par le rapport de fait.

Il faut dire que la réponse n'était pas évidente au départ.[7] On sait que les manuscrits de Segalen, parsemés de caractères chinois (qu'il supprimera dans la version définitive), fournissent souvent des indications directes et des pistes de recherche pour les sources livresques chinoises dont ses textes français s'inspirent. Pourtant, à notre connaissance, aucune note manuscrite d'*Equipée* n'a mentionné cet emprunt au *Récit de la Source aux Fleurs de Pêchers*, et Segalen n'a nulle part parlé de Tao Yuanming. Dans ce cas, aussi frappante que soit l'analogie des deux textes, on ne peut que s'exclamer d'admiration pour cette très heureuse coïncidence des deux textes, qui montre une fois de plus que la quête d'un Ailleurs heureux et parfait est vraiment une des constantes, un des 'lieux communs' de la littérature universelle et de l'esprit humain.

Or, cette hypothèse de l'emprunt semble maintenant confirmée par une trouvaille que nous avons faite lors d'un dernier séjour à Paris. En consultant à la Bibliothèque Nationale les manuscrits de Segalen, nous avons découvert une page manuscrite de *Peintures* (et non d'*Equipée*) au verso de laquelle Segalen avait copié au crayon et en caractères chinois de petits fragments du *Récit de la Source aux Fleurs de Pêchers*. Il est difficile d'expliquer pourquoi ces fragments se trouvaient là,[8] et à partir de quelle édition il les avait copiés, mais c'est là au moins une preuve, biographique et graphique, que Segalen avait réellement connu dans le texte originel le récit de Tao Yuanming et que le rapprochement entre les deux textes est positivement fondé.

Notons enfin qu'Eliane Formentelli, dans un article très éclairant sur la source d'inspiration de ce vingtième épisode d'*Equipée*, a mentionné 'un vieux mythe chinois du temps passé' dédoublé d'un rouleau de peinture au titre de 'ma peinture T'ao houa' que Segalen avait possédé et qui faisait partie de la collection du fils du poète (collection perdue dans un incendie à Saïgon, cf. Formentelli 1979:64). Bien que le nom de Tao Yuanming n'y soit pas prononcé, il y a lieu de penser que ce 'vieux mythe chinois' renvoie à celui de la Source aux Fleurs de Pêchers et que cette peinture 'T'ao houa' (transcription phonétique du mot chinois 'Fleurs de Pêchers') est relative au même mythe (on sait que ce mythe littéraire devient aussi un thème fréquent des peintres chinois). Ainsi, en dehors d'un emprunt livresque, Segalen avait très probablement une autre source d'inspiration, picturale, de ce rêve de route dans *Equipée*.

Université de Wuhan

Notes

1 Cf. 1985 *Shanhai Jing Jiao Yi,* Shanghai Guji Chubanshe: p. 259.

2 Le fait est que, dans le symbolisme chinois, la fleur de pêcher, comme le fruit de pêcher, est chargée d'une forte connotation mythique liée aux thèmes de longévité, immortalité, jeunesse, beauté féminine. Elle est une image poétique usée jusqu'à la corde sous le pinceau des poètes chinois.

3 A propos des différentes versions que des poètes des Song ont données de l'Histoire de la Source aux Fleurs de Pêchers, cf. Qian Zhongshu 1987 'Introduction à la poésie des Song' dans *Cinq essais de Poétique*, traduit du chinois par Nicolas Chapuis, Editions Christian Bourgois: p.p. 158–60.

4 Cette traduction beaucoup plus tardive par rapport à l'oeuvre de Segalen est la seule que nous avons sous la main pour entamer cette comparaison textuelle.

5 Wu Sangui (Wou San-K'ouei, 1612–78), général chinois qui eut l'imprudence de laisser pénétrer dans la capitale, Pékin, les Mandchous qui finiront par monter sur le trône et fonderont la dynastie des Qing (Ts'ing). Il fut obligé de se réfugier dans le Yunnan et y mourut.

6 Nous n'avons pas pu commenter l'image du sel contenue dans les deux noms de village inventés sans doute par Segalen. Ces deux noms 'trou de sel' et 'puits de sel' sonnent comme deux toponymes banals en Chine et donnent au récit 'sa couleur locale', très campagnarde. Paradoxalement l'image du sel n'est pas fréquente dans la littérature chinoise, elle n'est pas un cliché poétique comme la fleur de pêcher. Par contre elle porte un symbolisme très fort en Occident (sel: un feu délivré des eaux de la mer, à la fois quintessence et opposition).

7 Une partie de la présente étude remonte à notre thèse de doctorat soutenue il y a dix ans (*Empire de Chine, Empire de Signes, l'oeuvre poétique de Victor Segalen,* Université de Toulouse-le Mirail, 1986), dans laquelle, nous avons laissé en suspens cette hypothèse de l'emprunt, à défaut d'autres preuves que celle du texte même.

8 Apparemment ces caractères n'ont pas la même fonction que ceux qu'on trouve tracés dans les manuscrits de Stèles qui sont toujours liés au texte français en train de s'écrire. Segalen probablement s'était servi du dos d'une feuille manuscrite de *Peintures* pour faire des exercices d'écri-

ture le temps d'une pause de travail, car les phrases qu'il copie ne sont pas continues, il recopie plusieurs fois un même caractère, ou un même groupe de caractères, juste pour perfectionner ses traits droits et obliques. Et on sait que la composition de *Peintures* et celle d'*Equipée* sont contemporaines aux environs de 1914–5.

Oeuvres Citées

Albouy, Pierre 1969 *Mythes et mythologies dans la littérature française*. Armand Colin, Paris.

Angenot, Marc 1979 *Glossaire pratique de la critique contemporaine*. Editions Hurtubise HMH, Québec.

Formentelli, Eliane 1979 'La marche du cavalier' dans *Regard, espaces, signes*. L'Asiathèque, Paris.

Manceron, Gilles (ed.) 1985 *Victor Segalen Henri Manceron, Trahison fidèle, correspondance*. Seuil, Paris.

Margouliès, Georges 1948 *Anthologie raisonnée de la littérature chinoise*. Payot, Paris.

Segalen, Victor 1983 *Equipée*. Gallimard, Paris.

——— 1986 *Essai sur l'Exotisme*. L. G. F., Paris.

Tao Yuanming 1992 *Oeuvres complètes* (Tao Yuanming Ji Quanyi). Editions du Peuple de la Province du Guizhou.

Wieger, P. 1906 *Textes philosophiques*. Imprimerie de la Mission Catholique.

BÉATRICE DIDIER

La Chine d'un Disciple de Voltaire: Senancour

De tous les écrivains de la première génération romantique, Senancour (1770–1846) est certainement celui qui a subi le plus profondément la marque de l'esprit des Lumières que jamais il ne renia. Il est aussi celui chez qui la Chine tient la place la plus grande. La concordance de cette double spécificité n'est pas due au hasard. On peut certes relever des références à la Chine chez Chateaubriand et chez Mme de Staël, ses exacts contemporains: Mme de Staël dans *De l'Allemagne* (IV:195–6) évoque avec admiration ce pays de rois astronomes et sages. On pourrait trouver une présence de la Chine plus grande chez Fabre d'Olivet et surtout chez Quinet. Cependant R. Etiemble marque justement avec cette première génération romantique la fin de l'"Europe chinoise': 'Qu'à la fin du dix huitième siècle l'Europe chinoise perd beaucoup de son prestige, je viens à point nommé d'en trouver une preuve résolument péremptoire en relisant ... le tome premier des *Mémoires d'Outre-Tombe*' (1989, t. II:381). La cause de ce déclin de l'"Europe chinoise', R. Etiemble la voit d'abord dans la condamnation par le Pape de la Compagnie de Jésus et de son action en Chine. A quoi viendront s'ajouter l'affaire de l'ambassade Macartney, et plus tard, la guerre de l'Opium. Senancour donc peut appparaître comme un intéressant survivant de l'époque des Lumières, sur le chapitre de la Chine comme dans d'autres domaines. Il prolonge l'Europe chinoise au dix-neuvième siècle.

Comme les Philosophes, ses modèles, il ne connaît la Chine que par des sources livresques, et qui sont à peu de choses près les mêmes que celles d'un Voltaire, non sans bénéficier cependant des parutions plus récentes, car, à l'affût de renseignements sur la Chine, il ne cesse de se documenter et de noter tout ce qui tombe sous ses mains. Ses lectures sur la Chine remontent certainement très haut dans son existence. Il fut un lecteur précoce, avide de récits de voyages. Nous pouvons avoir une idée assez précise de ses lectures, grâce à un énorme cahier que j'ai découvert et en partie publié, les *Annotations encyclopédiques* qui sont un recueil de notes commencées en 1795, et complétées durant toute sa vie. Classées par sujet et par ordre alphabétique, elles sont relativement faciles à consulter, même si certains articles sont fort embrouillés. Tel est bien le cas de l'article 'Chine', et l'on verra dans le caractère touffu de cet ensemble, le signe justement de l'intérêt porté par Senancour à la question: il rajoute sans cesse. Il cite l'*Histoire philosophique* de l'abbé Raynal, renvoie à une note, malheureusement perdue ('Chine Warburton' qui, je suppose, portait surtout sur l'écriture chinoise) renvoie aussi à l'*Encyclopédie* et à l'article de Diderot. Il ajoute encore:

> *Voyage de la Chine*, Hütner.
> *Histoire chinoise de la Chine*. V. *Mercure*, 12 juin 1813.
> *Nouvelle histoire de la Chine*. V. *Diable boiteux*, 2 février 1824.
> Voyage de Macartney.
> *De la philosophie des chinois* par Diderot.
> *Histoire chinoise* par M. Le Clerc.
> *Langue chinoise*, v.p. 96 et s. *Mercure* avril 1814.

Ces 'Annotations encyclopédiques' sont suivies d'une précieuse liste des livres lus, par ordre chronologique, avec souvent des indications de dates. Parmi les titres qui peuvent nous intéresser: *Zoroastre, Confucius et Mahomet* par Pastoret; *La Bibliothèque orientale* de d'Herbelot, *Yu le grand et Confucius*, hist. chinoise par M. Le Clerc, *Le Monde primitif* de Court de Gébelin; *Lettres sur l'origine des Sciences et sur celle des peuples de l'Asie* adressées à M. de Voltaire par M. Bailly 'consulté à Senlis, juillet 1797'. La *Législation orientale* d'Anquetil-Duperron a été consultée aussi lors de ce séjour à Senlis, période de grand abandon, mais aussi de grand travail. On relève encore: *Abrégé de l'histoire générale des Voyages* de La Harpe, *Histoire du Japon* de Kaempfer, *Histoire de la Chine* par le jésuite Mailla, *Le Chou-King*, un des livres sacrés des Chinois (par M. de Guignes, 1770); Julius von Klaproth, *Mémoires relatifs à l'Asie* (1826-8), H. Ellis, *Voyage en Chine ou journal de la dernière ambassade anglaise à Pékin* (1818). On s'étonne de ne pas trouver le classique Du Halde, qu'évidemment Senancour connaît bien, mais on remarquera aussi l'existence en fin de liste d'ouvrages récents. De même le *Résumé de l'Histoire de la Chine* renvoie à un journal anglais de 1824 (2ème éd.:361).

Cet intérêt constant et même croissant pour la Chine se manifeste davantage encore par l'oeuvre même de Senancour. Présente dans presque tous ses textes, la Chine cependant bénéficie d'un traitement de plus en plus favorable. Ainsi dans *Sur les Générations actuelles*, oeuvre d'extrême jeunesse, elle ne figurait guère que pour augmenter la liste des absurdités dont l'humanité s'est rendue coupable. Les *Rêveries*, dans leur première édition, traitaient bien légèrement la morale chinoise de 'savante et maniérée' (Droz 1939, I:150), et l'on s'étonne de ne pas voir Confucius dans une liste de sages que donne ce texte (I:184–5). La Chine est pratiquement absente de l'ouvrage le plus célèbre de Senancour: *Oberman* (1804). Mais il opère un net virage avec les *Observations sur le Génie du Christianisme*, ouvrage de polémique, publié contre Chateaubriand, avec un certain retard. C'est en effet, dans ce contexte de polémique religieuse, bien conforme à l'esprit des Lumières, que l'exemple de la Chine est invoqué: 'On a présenté effectivement qu'il n'y avait rien de nouveau dans les dogmes, dans les institutions, dans la philosophie du christianisme. On a prétendu que, sous un autre nom, l'intérieur de l'Asie avait aussi son christianisme' (1816:25). Il semble que Senancour ait manifesté un vif intérêt pour la Chine, essentiellement dans ces années 1816–25 qui correspondent chez lui à la fois à une vive hostilité devant le catholicisme de la Restauration ultra, mais aussi à un désir d'approfondissement de ses connaissances et de sa réflexion religieuses. Les deux textes fondamentaux pour notre étude appartiennent à cette période: il s'agit du *Résumé de l'Histoire de la Chine* qui paraît chez Lecointe et Durey en 1824 et connaît une réédition en 1825, ce qui est le signe d'un succès assez exceptionnel chez Senancour. Le *Résumé de l'histoire des traditions morales et religieuses*, dont toute une partie est consacrée à la Chine, lui aussi va connaître deux éditions (1825 et 1827) et, de plus, un procès, car Senancour y avait traité Jésus de 'jeune sage'.

Outre ces deux massifs importants, on retrouve la Chine un peu partout dans les textes de Senancour de cette époque-là, le *Petit vocabulaire de simple vérité* qui ne paraîtra qu'en 1833, mais a probablement été écrit plus tôt, procède par maximes inspirées de la sagesse chinoise. Dès 1825 un article du *Mercure* qui annonce très nettement un passage du *Petit vocabulaire*, loue un sage chinois dans un 'Chant du laboureur' (t. X:95–6). La même année dans le *Mercure*, Senancour donne un texte: 'Des chansons populaires chez quelques orientaux', occasion de revenir à ses chers Chinois. Un article sur Clémence Robert l'amène à critiquer notre ignorance de la Chine. En 1821, des articles dans l'*Abeille* sont également remplis de références à la Chine. Comptes rendus, textes d'imagination: tout est alors prétexte pour parler de la Chine (pour un relevé plus systématique cf. B. Le Gall-Didier, *L'Imaginaire chez Senancour*, t. I:538–9; t. II:226–7)

❖

La Chine. Mais quelle Chine? Celle des Philosophes, certes, mais avec des tonalités nouvelles parfois. Il pourra sembler intéressant d'analyser cette reprise et ce renouvellement d'une thématique riche en elle même, quoiqu'étant évidemment bien loin de recouvrir la diversité de la Chine réelle.

La Restauration n'est pas parvenue à rétablir l'Ancien Régime, même si le procès des *Traditions morales* nous ramène aux plus beaux jours de la censure royale. Les formes de la lutte idéologique ont évolué. Mais le triomphe des

Lumières n'est pas encore certain; il est toujours menacé dans cette vaste opération de marche arrière que tente la monarchie. On ne s'étonnera donc pas de voir dans ces années 1820 réapparaître sous la plume de Senancour un certain nombre de thèmes que Voltaire avait utilisés dans son combat. Et d'abord celui de la chronologie chinoise opposée à la chronologie biblique. Cette question était ressentie comme très importante, dans la mesure où elle mettait aussi en cause le monogénisme de l'humanité et le récit de la création selon la Bible. Elle ne pouvait donc être contournée, et Senancour l'aborde dès l'introduction du *Résumé de l'histoire de la Chine*: 'Il était d'usage ici de chercher dans la terre de Mesraïm l'origine de tout ce qu'on ne pouvait pas attribuer aux enfants d'Abraham; des érudits tracèrent donc la route des premiers Chinois sortant de l'Egypte'. Cette hypothèse est inconciliable 'avec les documents les plus positifs de l'histoire orientale' (2ème éd.:10). Le parallèle entre l'univers biblique et l'univers chinois soustend toute cette introduction, et cela pour la plus grande gloire de la Chine. 'Vers l'Euphrate on paraît avoir connu des lois peu différentes; mais la Chaldée fut le jouet des conquérans. La situation de la Chine était plus heureuse' (13–14). C'est là un thème que Voltaire avait amplement exploité: le peuple hébreu a été perpétuellement asservi par ses voisins. Autre pointe contre la tradition chrétienne, lorsque Senancour évoque le 'livre de la loi' où le souverain 'sans y lire le contraire de ce qui s'y trouve, convient qu'il fut dicté par des mortels' (14). Double attaque, puisque les Tables de la Loi sont censées avoir été dictées par Dieu à Moïse, et que la Bible a donné lieu à de multiples interprétations contradictoires que Voltaire s'est plu à ridiculiser, en particulier dans le *Dictionnaire philosophique*. Antiquité de la Chine et sûreté des documents, tels sont deux leitmotiv de l'*Histoire de la Chine*:

> Nous touchons à peine au règne de Sésostris, moins certain que ceux de Chun, de Yao, de Hoang-ti, et déjà le grand empire a obtenu assez de prépondérance dans l'Asie orientale pour que, l'an 1635 avant l'ère vulgaire, la cour de Tai-vou réunisse les envoyés de seize princes des contrées voisines. (48)

Autre point névralgique dans la polémique, le rôle des missionnaires. Senancour ne pratique pas l'ironie cinglante d'un Voltaire; néanmoins, en demi-teinte, apparaît très nettement la reprise des arguments essentiels contre les missionnaires. De quoi se mêlent les Européens? La réaction de Kang-hi devant le légat de Clément XI n'est-elle pas légitime? 'Peut-être trouve-t-il mauvais qu'on examine chez les Européens si on autorisera ou si on proscrira sa croyance ... peut-être aussi est-il difficile d'expliquer à un Mandchou ce que c'est qu'un légat *a latere*' (309).

La conversion des Chinois repose sur des équivoques savamment entretenues par les jésuites. L'Empereur avait écrit à un jésuite dont les travaux scientifiques (relevé du plan de la grande muraille) lui avaient semblé sérieux:

> ...'je suis convaincu de votre droiture, au point de dire hautement qu'on doit vous

croire.' Le P. d'Entrecolles avoue que plusieurs Chinois durent à cette équivoque leur conversion au christianisme; voilà un de ces moyens un peu indirects que la grâce ne dédaigne pas toujours. (310-1)

Ce dernier trait est bien digne de Voltaire! Si les religieux furent chassés de Chine, c'est qu'ils apportaient la superstition et des troubles politiques, et non par une intolérance religieuse étrangère aux Chinois. Voici la réponse qu'en 1721 l'empereur aurait chargé le légat de rapporter au Pape:

> Cette espèce de décret ne regarde que de vils Européens; comment y déciderait-on quelque chose sur la grande doctrine des Chinois, dont ces gens d'Europe n'entendent même pas la langue? Il paraît assez par cet acte qu'il y a beaucoup de ressemblance entre leur secte et les impiétés des lamas et des Tao-sse, qui ont avec eux des disputes si violentes. Il faut donc défendre à ces nouveaux lamas de débiter leurs fables; c'est le moyen de prévenir des événements fâcheux. (314-5)

Les discours prêtés aux Chinois pour expliquer l'expulsion des missionnaires font penser non seulement à Voltaire mais aussi à Diderot et au *Supplément du Voyage de Bougainville*: 'Que diriez-vous si j'envoyais dans votre pays une troupe de lamas?'(324).

Senancour ne s'est pas privé non plus des plaisirs de ce jeu qui consiste à utiliser les mots chinois pour désigner l'univers chrétien, jeu dont les Philosophes avaient bien exploité les possibilités. Pour ne donner qu'un exemple parmi beaucoup d'autres possibles, dans les *Rêveries* (1833), les termes de 'lamas' et de 'ho-changs' désignent les prêtres catholiques dans leur aspect le plus rétrograde (253-4). Contradiction dans la représentation de la Chine? Pas absolument, car Senancour comme Voltaire prend soin de distinguer la philosophie chinoise véritable des superstitions populaires. Chez presque tous les peuples, écrit Voltaire dans le *Dictionnaire*, 'il y avait la théologie sacrée et l'erreur populaire'. L'article 'Catéchisme chinois' insiste aussi sur cette distinction nécessaire.

❖

Elément du combat philosophique, la Chine est le lieu d'une idéalisation, et là aussi Senancour suit son maître Voltaire dont il connaît bien l'oeuvre, et dont il n'hésite pas à rappeler également le théâtre. Ainsi lorsqu'il évoque dans le *Résumé de l'histoire de la Chine* l'aventure de Li-ouang et de son fils sauvé grâce à Chao-kong, il note: 'Ainsi la fable dramatique de l'Orphelin de la Chine a eu pour fondement une tradition qui datait de près de vingt-six siècles' (56, n.). Madame Meng Hua a bien analysé ce que la pièce de Voltaire devait au théâtre chinois.

La Chine de Senancour, comme celle de Voltaire, est la véritable patrie du déisme et de la vertu. Des principes moraux simples, universellement admis, sont la base de cette religion qui est surtout une morale, et le déisme des Lumières tend effectivement à être surtout une morale qui s'accorde facilement avec le confucianisme, comme Mme Meng Hua l'a brillammment montré à propos de Voltaire. La Chine est donc le lieu idéal où les projette ce rêve d'une religion sans dogme, sans rites, sans fanatisme. Alors que les Philosophes se sont insurgés énergiquement contre la collusion du religieux et du politique en France, ils l'admettent volontiers en Chine, et pour une raison que Senancour explique très clairement. La réunion du pouvoir religieux et du pouvoir politique en la personne de l'empereur de Chine 'n'a point les inconvénients de la théocratie dans un pays où la base des institutions est morale, et non dogmatique. La politique y est religieuse comme la politique doit l'être: la Divinité n'y intervient pas dans les choses humaines selon l'ordre temporel.' Pays de tolérance religieuse également: 'les divers cultes sont librement admis dans l'empire lorsqu'ils n'excitent pas de troubles' (329). Voltaire lui aussi avait exalté la tolérance chinoise.

De la morale confucéenne, Senancour retient essentiellement deux traits fondamentaux, et d'abord le respect des vieillards, et l'importance de la piété filiale. Le mépris avec lequel les vieillards sont souvent traités en Europe l'a toujours scandalisé, et il le dénonçait déjà dans *Les libres Méditations*. Sur ce point encore, il existe un lien profond entre morale familiale et politique: 'Comme (les Chinois) comprennent sous ce nom [de piété filiale] l'affection d'un père envers ses fils, ils y rattachent tous les principes de gouvernement' (94). L'humilité et le pardon des offenses sont également les piliers de cette morale, ce qui est l'occasion pour Senancour de lancer une pointe contre le christianisme et contre sa prétention à avoir établi une morale nouvelle:

> Cela n'a pas empêché des docteurs de l'Occident de prétendre qu'une morale particulière leur avait été donnée pour les distinguer du reste du monde, et que l'humilité ainsi que le sincère pardon des offenses étaient au nombre de ces préceptes nouveaux. (*Résumé des Traditions*:109, n.)

Senancour, pas plus que Voltaire, ne manque alors d'exalter également le paganisme gréco-romain qui lui aussi avait su cultiver ces vertus prétendûment chrétiennes.

L'histoire de la Chine est pour Senancour l'occasion d'une réflexion sur la Révolution qui appartient bien à sa génération, cette génération qui a eu vingt ans en 1789. On sait combien elle a médité sur cet événement si surprenant pour ceux qui avaient connu l'apparente stabilité de l'Ancien Régime. Le jeune Chateaubriand intitule son premier ouvrage, *Essai sur les Révolutions*. La pensée sur la Révolution est alors largement tributaire d'une conception cyclique de l'histoire qui prend le mot de 'révolution' dans son sens astronomique, de retour régulier d'un astre. Comment expliquer que, du moins d'après Senancour, il n'y ait pas eu de révolution en Chine comparable à celle de 1789? La réflexion s'alimente d'événements à la fois français et chinois que Voltaire n'a pu connaître, ainsi de ces agitations des 'illuminés de la céleste raison' des années 1813. Evidemment la désignation même de ces mécontents les rapproche de ceux qui ont fait la Révolution française en s'inspirant des principes de la Raison. Nouveaux troubles en Chine en 1824 — que tirer de ces faits pour l'avenir?

> La Chine n'a éprouvé jusqu'à présent que les premiers symptômes d'une de ces révolutions utiles à la fois et redoutables qui, d'âge en âge, changeront les dispositions des races, aussi nécessairement que le renouvellement des individus. La constance, qui semble particulière à quelques nations, annonce seulement l'inégale durée de ces périodes. (*Histoire de la Chine*, 362)

Le système cyclique des révolutions serait donc universel, mais la révolution de l'astre 'Chine' serait plus lente que celle des astres européens. Que risque-t-il de se passer si les idées et les techniques industrielles européennes parviennent en Chine? 'L'empreinte inconsidérée de nos fantaisies sur toute la surface du globe exigerait peut-être un nouveau cataclysme avant l'époque marquée dans le mouvement des cieux' (362). L'influence de l'Europe risquerait donc de précipiter d'une façon dangereuse une révolution qui en Chine aurait dû se produire, selon l'ordre naturel, beaucoup plus tard. La vision volontiers apocalyptique de l'Histoire qu'affectionne Senancour trouve donc avec l'exemple de la Chine l'occasion d'une méditation assez originale sur un avenir possible du continent asiatique.

Moins neuve peut-être, en tout cas héritière de toute une réflexion du siècle des Lumières, mais toujours riche en prolongements dans le monde imaginaire, sont les considérations sur la langue chinoise:[1]

> La langue (de la Chine) est la seule langue vivante qu'on puisse regarder comme une conception primitive, comme un libre essai des peuples qui, en toutes choses, ne savent plus aujourd'hui que se copier mutuellement, et peut-être même n'auront plus d'autre parti à prendre que de réformer ce qu'ils imiteront. (*Résumé des Traditions*, 87)

La langue chinoise est 'féconde, très différente de toute autre' (*Histoire de la Chine*, 363). Mais ce qui a frappé Senancour, comme tous les européens, c'est le système d'écriture. La langue chinoise serait:

> ...l'ancienne langue hiéroglyphique dont les clefs, ou caractères fondamentaux, en grand nombre, au lieu d'être simplifiés ensuite, comme dans les alphabets que la moyenne antiquité nous a transmis, au lieu de s'unir pour former des mots, restent détachés et subissent par conséquent des modifications innombrables. Il en résulte une langue énergique, mais difficile à écrire, difficile à apprendre, et à laquelle la parole n'a pu se conformer: perpétuel obstacle d'où provient, sans doute, l'espèce d'uniformité des opérations de l'esprit chez un peuple qui en général ne paraît pas manquer d'aptitude. Les Chinois ont conservé l'usage, vraisemblablement primitif, d'écrire par colonnes, et de droite à gauche. (363, n.)

Senancour n'a peut-être pas compris quelle force de cohésion l'uniformité de l'écriture donnait à la Chine, mais on voit que ses remarques sur l'écriture et la langue chinoise se situent dans un courant de réflexion sur les hiéroglyphes dont on connaît la richesse, aussi bien en Angleterre, chez Warburton, que par la *Lettre sur les sourds et muets* de Diderot. Senancour reprend aussi un topos de la linguistique des Lumières, celui du langage primitif, parole et chant à la fois que Rousseau avait brillamment développé dans l'*Essai sur l'origine des langues* qui fut d'abord conçu comme un Essai sur l'origine de la musique:

> Autrefois les termes trop indécis du langage s'éloignaient peu du vague de la musique; on pouvait donc la regarder comme une langue universelle, moins ignorée des peuplades grossières, et des animaux eux-mêmes, que les paroles séparées du chant. (*Résumé des Traditions*:102–3)

Cette langue-musique de la Chine primitive serait donc une langue universelle qui, comme dans les rêves de l'illuministe Blake, contemporain de Senancour, scellerait une alliance entre tous les êtres vivants sur terre.

Cette musique chinoise — inutile de souligner que Senancour la connaît mal — lui semble plus parfaite que l'européenne, parce qu'elle serait monodique procédant à l'unisson ou l'octave, et l'on retrouve là un topos de la querelle des Bouffons dans cette condamnation de l'harmonie savante:

> La musique orientale diffère beaucoup de celle qui a prévalu en Europe. Au sentiment des Asiatiques, la savante harmonie des compositeurs du nord n'a rien que de factice et de bizarre; c'est du bruit avec des variantes adroites peut-être mais puériles. (*Résumé des Traditions*:104)

Résurgence d'une attaque contre Rameau? Cependant, en ces premières années du dix-neuvième siècle, l'ire des anti-harmonistes s'est déplacée vers la musique allemande, et les réactions que l'on oppose à l'introduction de Mozart et de Beethoven en France répètent les arguments utilisés contre Rameau: trop d'harmonie, une harmonie trop savante. C'est probablement à quoi fait allusion dans ce texte de Senancour les 'compositeurs du Nord'.

L'harmonie de la musique chinoise serait d'un autre ordre; elle ne serait pas produite par une savante science des accords et du contrepoint, mais par la valeur morale de la musique, et dans son lien avec l'équilibre des astres et des nombres et par conséquent avec l'harmonie de l'univers. On ne s'étonnera pas de trouver alors sous sa plume un parallèle avec la conception de la musique chez Pythagore. On sait en effet l'importance du néo-pythagorisme en Europe au début du dix-neuvième siècle dont Fabre d'Olivet offre un témoignage particulièrement frappant.[2] 'Les disciples d'Orphée et de Pythagore exigeaient que la musique inspirât des vertus, et conduisît au repos de l'âme. Le but principal était le même dans les premiers siècles de la Chine' (*Résumé des Traditions*: 104).

Cette valeur morale de la musique chinoise a donc particulièrement attiré Senancour. Autour du thème musical se réunissent en faisceau les principaux aspects du mythe chinois chez cet écrivain: pureté morale, simplicité de la religion et des principes politiques, unité de la musique et de la parole.

Décidément, et même si Senancour n'a garde d'oublier dans son *Résumé de l'Histoire de la Chine* qu'au cours des siècles, il y eut quelques entorses à ces beaux principes, l'Europe chinoise en ce début du dix-neuvième siècle, fleurit encore, et enrichie de fleurs nouvelles, chez ce disciple des Lumières.

Ecole Normale Supérieure, Paris

Notes

1 On se reportera à D. Droixhe 1978 *La linguistique à l'appel de l'Histoire (1600–1800)*, Droz, Paris.
2 Cf. à ce sujet la belle thèse de L.Cellier 1953 *Fabre d'Olivet, contribution à l'étude des aspects religieux du romantisme,* Nizet, Paris.

Oeuvres Citées

Senancour 1825 *Résumé de l'Histoire de la Chine*, 2ème éd. Lecointe et Durey, Paris.

—— 1827 *Résumé de l'Histoire des traditions morales et religieuses*, 2ème éd. Lecointe et Durey, Paris.

WANG YU-GEN

Bi-xing and the Dynamic Interpretive Mode of Chinese Poetics

Hermeneutics can be roughly defined as the science or art of understanding and interpreting the meaning of a text. Interpretation is not, of course, an activity invented by twentieth-century literary theorists. The interpretations of the meaning of a text has always been the central activity of the humanities and social sciences. The word 'meaning' has very complicated meanings, but generally speaking it manifests a relationship: a single object cannot produce meaning. Meaning is produced only when one object confronts another. Meaning is produced in a network of 'relations'. 'Understanding' also manifests a relationship: the relationship between the understanding subject and the understood object. The hermeneutic phenomenon is ontologically constitutive of human life, hermeneutics has implications that are truly universal. How does the process of interpretation, or the process of the production of the meaning of a text, take place? Are there limits to what can be interpreted in a text? Is there any objective criterion for judging the validity of an interpretation? There are certainly various ways to approach these questions. A formalist theory, for example, may claim that what determines our interpretations of a text is the text itself, the words on the page, while an intentional theory may argue that what determines interpretation is not the text but the author's intention, intention behind or between the words of the text.

Nineteenth-century hermeneuticists tried to relate the text to its historical conditions, considering the reconstruction of the author's mind as the only goal of interpretation. Such attention to the author's historicity neglects that of the interpreter. Since modern hermeneuticists such as Heidegger and Gadamer have recognized the general historicity or temporality of interpretation, problems of interpretation can be investigated from new perspectives. Gadamer indicates that the interpretation of a text is a conversation between the text and the interpreter. In the process of questioning and answering, giving and taking, the act of interpretation evidently takes into account all the elements concerned and every act of reading is a difficult interaction between the competence of the reader and the kind of competence that a given text postulates.

This paper does not deal with these problems themselves, but tries to view them from a particular perspective: that of traditional Chinese poetics. The concept of *bi-xing*, a core concept of Chinese poetics, is our starting point.

❖

Bi-xing is composed of two interrelated elements: *bi*, to compare, and *xing*, to evoke or stir. The terms can be traced back to the earliest Chinese literary anthology, *The Book of Songs*. Scholars in the Han dynasty (206 BC to 220 AD) first interpreted them. According to Zhen Zhong, one of the famous exegetes of the Han dynasty, *bi* means to compare A to B, while *xing* means to evoke B with A (in Zheng Xuan 1979:796). Generally speaking, no rigorous definitions ever existed, for both lack a clear-cut demarcation and are open to rich possibilities. Comparatively speaking, scholars in the past have shared common interpretations of *bi*, but the debate about the interpretation of *xing* has lasted over 2,000 years.

Whether they are independent concepts or belong to the same category has always been a controversial issue. Some scholars pay much attention to the relationship between *bi* and *xing*, considering that they belong to the same category. For instance, in his annotations to the poem 'Li Sao' by Qu Yuan of the Warring Kingdoms period (475 BC to 221 BC), Wang Yi equated *xing* with *pi*, the equivalent of *bi*. On the other hand, some exegetes emphasized the difference between *bi* and *xing*. If one searches for an outside object that can express feelings, that is what is meant by *bi*; in a word, feelings rely on the object. If one catches sight of an object that evokes feelings, that is what is meant by *xing*. (See Guo Shaoyu and Wang Wensheng 1978:51.)

In my view, to distinguish *bi* from *xing* cannot result in a satisfactory interpretation of these two concepts. For example, Zhu Xi, the Confucian exegete of the Song dynasty, endeavoured to distinguish *bi* from *xing* theoretically, but the interpretations remain as blurred as ever (see Zhu Ziqing 1980:235). *Bi* and *xing* were initially regarded as specific rhetorical strategies for the interpretation of *The Book of Songs*, then defined as poetic devices of representation in general, and finally distilled into a basic mode of aesthetic perception and poetic thinking.

In the 'Great Preface' to *The Book of Songs*, *bi* and *xing* are named as two of the 'six principles'. When extracted from the specific context of the interpretation of *The Book of Songs*, *bi* and *xing* have been acknowledged as unique devices of poetic representation. Many modern theorists tend to ascribe the rich, implicit and profound characteristics and flavours of Chinese poetry to the adoption of distinctive poetic devices such as *bi* and *xing*. According to Zhao Peilin (1987), for example, it is with the advent and prevalence of *xing* that Chinese poetry finally finds a useful way to express itself. With the rise of *xing*, Chinese poets are able accurately to convey their feelings with natural scenery and finally to accomplish a unification between their inner feelings and the outer world in their creative writings. Therefore, he argues, the poetic device *xing* embodies the essential artistic principles of classical Chinese poetry and serves as one of its most outstanding aesthetic features. Nowadays, scholars increasingly assert that *bi* and *xing* represent an essential mode of thinking. For instance, in *The Cultural Interpretation of The Book of Songs*, Ye Shuxian advocates that *xing* is more a mode of thinking and argumentation than a mere rhetorical device. In an article entitled 'On the Linguistic Structure of *Fu-bi-xing*', Zhou Yingxiong considers *xing* to be a key to the study of classical Chinese poetry, for *xing* implies the poet's basic philosophy of life. In his view, through the study of classical Chinese poetry based on the analysis of *xing*, it is possible to render a more accurate definition of the essential features of Chinese poetics.

A clear-cut difference between *bi* and *xing* will not be made here. Instead, I would like to view *bi-xing* as a conceptual unity, with the two elements so interrelated that both can be viewed as part of a theoretical entity. Compare *bi-xing* with I. A. Richards' 'tenor' and 'vehicle'. As Joel Weinsheimer argues in *Philosophical Hermeneutics and Literary Theory*, the relationship between a text and its interpretation is like that between tenor and vehicle (1991:81–2) and in the same way, poetic meaning is produced through the interaction of *bi* and *xing*. Or, in another context, *bi-xing* may be compared to Roman Jakobsen's metaphor and metonymy.

However, such an oversimplified association between Chinese and Western poetic terms may lead to misunderstandings. Jakobsen's terms are deeply rooted in the structuralist idea of 'binary opposition' and he neglects, intentionally or not, the interrelationship between the two concepts.

Since Aristotle, 'metaphor has been categorized in rhetorical terms. However, contemporary studies of metaphor have penetrated into the realms of philosophy and poetics. Gadamer (1989) maintains that language is essentially metaphorical, and Derrida (1974) also argues that philosophical discourse is essentially metaphorical. In general, the concept of metaphor — more accurately metaphoricity — includes that of metonymy and has come to be understood as a term that has gained prevalence in rhetoric, poetics and philosophy. In this sense, the Chinese poetic term can be understood as meaning metaphor.

❖

Through *bi-xing*, Chinese poetics has developed a distinctive mode of aesthetic perception, characterized by the argument that the perceiver's point of view should not be fixed to one point; it should be mobile, and free to move between the perceiver and the perceived. The process of aesthetic perception is therefore not static but open-ended and dynamic. With this aesthetic assumption, Chinese hermeneutics has constructed its unique system of textual interpretation, insisting that the process of interpreting a literary text is a reciprocal interaction between the interpreter and the text.

This dynamic mode of text interpretation is accomplished by means of *qu-lei*, meaning to discern and abstract the relationship or similarity between different things. Some scholars maintain that *qu-lei* is one of the major features of Chinese logical thinking. According to the 'Appendices' of *The Book of Changes*, the binary category of *yin-yang* and the hexagrams are all abstracted by means of *qu-lei*, through which the inherent interrelationship between the inner feelings of the interpreting subject and the interpreted objects in the outer world, and the similarities and contiguities among various things and phenomena in nature can be understood.

Qu-lei is associated with the concept of *qu-xiang*, or image-establishing. This is theoretically premised by the Confucian belief that 'words cannot exhaust meaning', expressed first in *The Book of Changes*. Words express what is in the mind, but at the same time camouflage and fragment it. To avoid this, *The Book of Changes* proposes the concept of *xiang* as a medium between words and meaning, and *qu-xiang* as the best solution to the contradiction between words and meaning. *Xiang* is neither the particular thing (though it may be perceived as imminent in particular things) nor the idea of a thing, but rather a sensuous schematization of the normative thing.

The process of meaning production rooted in *qu-xiang* is motivated and accomplished by the innermost tension between the two interrelated elements in it. Chinese critics believe that one should try to use the simplest signifier to exhaust the most diverse feelings in the mind. As Sun Liankui argues, 'one word induces a thousand meaningful things while a thousand meaningful things can be deduced from a single word' (in Sun Changxi 1962:27).

Such interaction between deduction and induction can help put two irrelevant semantic fields together, and, when they meet, there is new meaning and a new relationship through *qu-xiang* on the conceptual basis of *bi-xing*. In this sense, Gadamer associates metaphor with the motivation to 'think more', especially 'the freedom (of language) to form an infinite number of concepts and to penetrate what is meant ever more deeply' (1989:428).

Though *bi-xing*, like metaphor, is based on similarity and contiguity between two semantic fields, the premise of meaning production is their difference. In other words, the innermost tension between similarity and difference leads to a meaning integration on the basis of the association between the known and the unknown, the visible and the invisible, in which the process of meaning originates. In Gadamer's terms, this is like the 'fusion of horizons'.

Such tension also functions as the strategy for textual interpretation in Chinese literary criticism which aims to achieve various meaning possibilities beyond the text itself. The strategy and process of textual interpretation in Chinese literary criticism can be roughly described as follows: first, based on the text and the reader's own experience, the reader teases out the explicit meaning of the text itself; then, the reader relates this to the historical and cultural context of both the text and the reader; and, finally, the reader extracts the implicit meaning from beyond and within the text. It is these implicit meanings — 'meaning beyond the text' (*wen-wai-zhi-zhi*), 'image beyond image' (*xiang-wai-zhi-xiang*), 'scene beyond scene' (*jing-wai-zhi-jing*) — that Chinese poetic interpretation aims at. According to the Song dynasty scholar, Mei Yaochen, to express the inexpressible with simple new words is the most admirable ability a poet has. 'The very best thing,' he says, 'is to have new thoughts and well-crafted diction, to achieve what no-one has ever said before' (quoted by Ouyang Xiu in Owen 1992:375). As the Qing dynasty critic, Ye Xie, puts it:

> Where poetry is at its most perfect, its subtlety lies in a boundless reserve of the implicit and in the thought reaching what is faint and indistinct; what is implicit in poetry lies between what can be said and what cannot be said; what it refers to lies at the conjunction between the explicable and the inexplicable; the words seem to be about one thing, while the meaning lies in something else. (Quoted in Owen 1992:529.)

This is not only the case with lyrical writings, but also with narrative. As the Tang dynasty (618–907) historian, Liu Zhiji, advocated, a good narrative also should have rich implicit meaning possibilities beyond the words themselves.

It is necessary to note that the implicit meaning possibilities beyond the text are not without limitation; any interpretation should be based on the text itself and certain common interpretative conventions. There is a harmonious balance between the inner and outer meanings of a text which controls the whole process of text interpretation and meaning production. A good case in point is the Song dynasty scholar Lu Benzhong's concept of *huo-fa*, or 'harmonious balance'. He defines it as being able 'to transcend accepted conventions and at the same time not to violate them' (in Guo Shaoyu 1979:367). Ye Xie, however, understands *huo-fa* as 'animate rules', in contrast to *si-fa* (dead rules), and maintains that the animate rules are volatile and intangible (1980:343–6).

In conclusion, the concept of *bi-xing* leads to the discussion of interrelationship between the mind and the outside world, between subjective feelings and objective reality. By means of *bi-xing*, we associate the known with the unknown, the speakable with the unspeakable, the definite words with indefinite implications, in order to achieve a harmonious balance. Theoretically speaking, the harmonious balance between the mind and the outside world can help exhaust the rich meaning possibilities of text interpretation. Therefore, *bi-xing* can be viewed as the conceptual basis and starting point for the dynamic interpretive mode of Chinese poetics.

Peking University

Works Cited

Derrida, Jacques 1974 'White Mythology: Metaphor in the Text of Philosophy' in *New Literary History* 6: pp. 5–74.

Gadamer, Hans-Georg 1989 *Truth and Method*, tr. Joel Weinsheimer and Donald G. Marshall. Seabury Press, New York.

Guo Shaoyu (ed.) 1979 *Zhongguo lidai wenlun xuan* (An Anthology of Chinese Discussions of Literature through the Ages). Shanghai guji chubanshe.

—— and Wang Wensheng 1978 'Lun Bi-xing' (On *Bi-xing*) in *Wenxue pinglun* (Literary Review) no. 4.

Owen, Stephen 1992 *Readings in Chinese Literary Thought*. Harvard University Press.

Sun Changxi et al (eds) 1962 *Sikong Tu jieshuo er zhong* (Two Explanations of Sikong Tu's 'Twenty-four Categories' of Poetry). Shandong renmin chubanshe, Jinan.

Weinsheimer 1991 *Philosophical Hermeneutics and Literary Theory*. Yale University Press.

Ye Shuxian 1994 *Shijing de wenhua chanshi* (The Cultural Interpretation of *The Book of Songs*). Hubei renmin chubanshe, Wuhan.

Ye Xie 1980 'Yuan-shi' (On the Origins of Poetry) in Guo Shaoyu (ed.) *Zhongguo lidai wenlun xuan*, vol. 3.

Zhao Peilin 1987 *'Xing' de yuanqi: lishi jidian yu shige yishu* (The Origin of *Xing*: Historical Turning Points and the Art of Poetry). Zhongguo shehui kexue chubanshe.

Zheng Xuan 1979 *Zhouli zhushu* in Ruan Yuan (ed.) *Shisanjing zhushu* (Thirteen Classics with Annotations). Zhonghua shuju, Beijing.

Zhu Ziqing 1980 'Shi-yan-zhi bian' (An Analysis of the Notion that Poetry Articulates the Mind's Intent) in *Zhu Ziqing gudian wenxue lunji* (Zhu Ziquing's Writings on Classical Chinese Literature) vol. 1. Shanghai guji chubanshe.

Zhou Yingxiong 1983 'Fu-bi-xing de yuyan jiegou' (The Linguistic Structure of *fu-bi-xing*) in *Jiegou zhuyi yu Zhongguo wenxue* (Structuralism and Chinese Literature). Dongda tushu gongsi, Taipei.

Mihály Szegedy-Maszák

On the Uses and Limits of Multiculturalism

One of the ambiguities of the eighteenth century is that it was the period in which Europe reached maturity in historical understanding and turned to mononationalism in culture. The complex relations between these two facts proved to have far-reaching consequences for later developments. Jean-Jacques Rousseau and others insisted that the role to be played by cultural products was 'de renforcer le caractère national'(1960:137), and Herder gave special emphasis to the binary opposition between organic and imitative culture. Historians, philosophers and writers inspired by their ideas compared the fate of a nation to a teleological process. Having the confidence that a certain pattern could be discerned in national development, they told a highly constructed story in the form of an edifying tale, explaining the essence of a national literature by a hypostatized national psychology.

As I have argued elsewhere, in the present age the Romantic concept of national character can no longer be regarded as a narrative paradigm in what is loosely called the Western world.[1] It has become customary to speak of multiculturalism and global citizenship. In 1967 Heidegger characterized modern art in the following way: 'Ihre Werke entspringen nicht mehr den prägenden Grenzen einer Welt des Volkhaften und Nationalen. Sie gehören in die Universalität der Weltzivilisation' (1983:140). Yet the emergence of new cultures in Africa, Asia or Canada, as well as the cult of a search for roots and the rise of ethnic history in the United States, suggest that it may be too early to speak of globalization. Furthermore, as a result of the collapse of the Warsaw Pact and the decline of the international Communist movement, more national cultures seem to be active in Europe today than ever before. In view of this, it seems preferable to accept a third option, different from both a nostalgic return to a Humboldtian view of culture as expression of national identity and a utopic form of universalism. Such an intermediate and rather self-contradictory position was taken by Jacques Derrida when he gave the following definition at a conference on European identity: 'l'histoire d'une culture suppose sans doute un cap identifiable, un telos vers lequel le mouvement, la mémoire et la promesse, l'identité, fût-ce comme différence à soi, rêve de se rassembler' (1991:22–3).

How can we arrive at a legitimate evaluation of different cultures? In a postcolonial age this seems to be a very difficult question. On the one hand, the strict hierarchy inherited from a Eurocentric past has to be avoided; on the other hand, it is hardly deniable that cultural movements tend to establish centres of their own. It would be futile to deny that most of the initiatives associated with the Enlightenment originated in Britain, France, and Germany, just as most people would admit that between the middle of the eighteenth century and the 1820s the best music was composed by Gluck, Joseph Haydn, Wolfgang Amadeus Mozart, Beethoven, and Franz Schubert. Yet the opposition between centre and periphery may imply a strictly linear view of history and even a kind of cultural imperialism. The importance of a nineteenth- or twentieth-century painting is often judged in terms of a teleological process leading from Classicism to Romanticism, Impressionism, Postimpressionism, Avantgardism, and Postmodernism. Multiculturalism may offer an alternative that would make it possible to see different traditions. From such a perspective doubts could be raised about the legitimacy of the overwhelming consensus that between 1870 and 1940 it was Paris and after 1940 New York that were at the centre in the visual arts.

In any case, it is difficult to speak from a centre about peripheral cultures. To what extent can it be taken for granted that the substance of generic or historical concepts is the same when applied to cultures other than those in which their definition had been originally developed? Is it justifiable, for instance, to speak about elegies in old Chinese literature?[2] Does it help any reader understand the works of Hungarian poet, Endre Ady, if he is called a Symbolist, and is it possible to speak of Postmodernism in countries that have not experienced the advantages and distadvantages of a consumer society? The danger is that the hermeneutic process is stopped too early and too easily when the unfamiliar is quickly reduced to the familiar. The so-called minor cultures are often treated as imperfect replicas, their history is viewed in terms of derivativeness and *décalage*, displacement in time and space.

It seems somewhat problematic to deduce conceptually progress or delay or to define the contemporaneity of the non-contemporaneous unless you can locate a centre with absolute certainty. The assumption that a culture is either central or marginal is closely related to the Classicist legacy in which the manners of the court are opposed to those of the provinces. It is by no means obvious that this ideal can be used in the interpretation of the cultures of the last two centuries. If the impersonal and agnostic Mallarmé is considered to be the crucial figure of Symbolism, it may seem doubtful whether a writer who used not only discursive prose but also verse as an instrument of political message can be associated with this movement. When a Hungarian is asked about Symbolism in his literature, he may try to 'sell' Ady as a representative of that movement and thereby avoid the nominalist-realist debate, but the question remains unanswered whether the concept of Symbolism, closely tied to a rejection of both self-expression and didacticism, is helpful for the understanding of Ady's egotistical sublime, political Messianism, or Calvinism. The interpretation may be so reductive that it can hardly be called a form of historical understanding. In a similar way, it is possible to have reservations about the legitimacy of calling writing which affirms Christian values Postmodern.

The dilemma of cosmopolitanism vs provincialism, the tension between the legacies of universalism and relativism, cannot be regarded as outmoded. Colonialism has taught us that if the distance between two cultures is too great, no merging of horizons seems possible. As Goethe wrote to Herder in 1796: 'Die Fremde hat ein fremdes Leben, und wir können es uns nicht zu eigen machen, wenn es uns gleich als Gästen gefällt' (cited in Wierlacher 1990:59).

The historical nature of understanding is closely related to the intertextual nature of meaning and may be the reason why the dialogue of cultures is not a matter of good intentions. You cannot enter a tradition, you have to stand in it. 'Traditions ist nichts, was Einer lernen kann, ist nichts ein Faden, den aufnehmen kann, wenn es ihm gefällt; so wenig, wie es möglich ist, sich die eigenen Ahnen auszusuchen'(1984:76). *Bel canto* singing is incompatible with Wagnerian style. There are limits to multicultural understanding ('Rezepzionsschwelle'), just as there are different degrees of translatability, depending on the distance between the source and the target language.

Displaced natives and refugees are always exposed to multicultural influence. A special category is represented by expatriates who decide to leave a homeland which they regard as provincial. In the late nineteenth and early twentieth centuries Americans from Henry James and Edith Wharton to Gertrude Stein, Ezra Pound, and T. S. Eliot settled in Europe, because they missed high culture in the New World. Painters and sculptors moved to Paris because they viewed it as the place where visual artists were validated, certified, accredited. In many of these cases the interaction of different cultures led to greater complexity of meaning. Yet it would be a mistake to ignore the risks of *dépaysement*. The French poems of T. S. Eliot are generally considered to be mediocre, the films Fritz Lang made in America are inferior to those he directed in Germany, the later works of Stravinsky are less innovative than the three ballets of his early 'Russian' period, and a decline of integrity has been ascribed to the last compositions of Bartók. When Pierre Boulez detected 'un piétinement' and 'trop de clichés dans l'écriture et la construction,' in such a work as the *Concerto for Orchestra* (first performed in Boston in December

1944), he suggested that the composer's attempt to meet the demands of the American public proved to be self-destructive (1966:304).

It is easier to condemn ethnocentrism and cultural imperialism than to have a more than superficial knowledge of other cultures. While no legitimate interpretation of literature can be given by scholars whose reading is limited to texts in one language, some works of verbal art — especially those in which ambiguity and polyvalence can be traced back to the signifier, or in which connotations are based on etymology — can be understood only in the original by those who have a full command of the language in a very broad sense, including the history of the language. Interpretive communities and practices cannot exist without an intimate knowledge of certain conventions. The relative absence of great orchestral conductors in the late twentieth century, for example, may suggest that interpretive traditions built up gradually by several generations may die out if radical changes occur in the cultural climate.

Awareness of the limitations to knowing other cultures may lead scholars to the belief that historically relevant interpretations only of mother tongue literature may be written. It is only in such cases that a true reading occurs or takes place — in the sense the words 'Es ereignet sich aber das Wahre,' taken from Hölderlin's late hymn 'Mnemosyne', have been applied to interpretation.[3]

One of the advantages of multiculturalism is that it points to the provincial nature of monolithic concepts of *Weltgeschichte*. The works György Lukács wrote in his middle period, between the two World Wars, his frequent use of the labels *progressive* and *reactionary*, might serve as a warning that *Weltgeschichte* may involve a uniform idea of teleology that makes cultural dialogue impossible and may give rise to totalitarian consequences. The interpretation of Epochenschwelle as developed by Hans Blumenberg, Reinhart Koselleck, and Hans Robert Jauß is incomparably more sophisticated, but even this concept implies a universalism that may relegate some cultures to the periphery. Nor can I accept the argument made by some of the critics of these universalist ideas. I would say tentatively and with great respect for those who use the term that it is somewhat misleading to speak of Eurocentrism. While it is important to remember that European imperialism has certainly distorted the understanding of mankind's legacy, it is a dangerous temptation to ignore the cultural diversity of Europe.

In the first half of the twentieth century two types of intellectuals introduced the concept of multiculturalism. Some ventured into this field out of intellectual curiosity (Western specialists of Oriental languages are obvious examples), others were forced to insist on the dialogue of different cultures by the vagaries of fate or the tragedies of history. Paul Celan, a Jewish poet born in Bukovina, decided to write in the language of the people whose politicians had sent him to a death camp, yet he combined the language of Hölderlin, Nietzsche, and Heidegger with Hebrew and Yiddish. A similar dialogism is exemplified by the activity of Vladimir Nabokov. In the 1920s he started his career as an avant-garde novelist and poet in exile. Because of the limited chances of a writer with a small public consisting of Russian émigrés, he had to switch to the English language in middle age, during the Second World War. The next decade brought him international success, and by the 1960s his works became regarded as an epitome of multiculturalism. *Speak, Memory* (1966) and *Ada* (1969) were written about pre-revolutionary Russia in English by a writer living in Switzerland. In 1967 he gave the following answer to the question as to whether he had any conspicuous flaw as a writer:

> The absence of a natural vocabulary.... Of the two instruments in my possession, one — my native tongue — I can no longer use, and this is not only because I lack a Russian audience, but also because the excitement of verbal adventure in the Russian medium had faded away gradually after I turned to English in 1940. My English, this second instrument I have always had, is however a stiffish, artificial thing, which may be all right for describing a sunset or an insect, but which cannot conceal poverty of syntax and paucity of domestic diction when I need the shortest road between warehouse and shop. An old Rolls Royce is not always preferable to a plain jeep. (1967:110)

Of course, I would accept the view that comparative literature has legitimacy only if there are degrees of translatability. It is more possible to read *Bleak House* in translation than *Atemkristall*, a sequence of short and cryptic lyrics by Celan. However tempting the universalism of some Enlightenment thinkers, the Romantics may remind us that literary works are language-dependent. In the early twentieth century there were avant-garde journals in most parts of Europe and in America which aimed at the creation of an international literary climate. My guess is that the illusion of Valéry Larbaud, Ivan Goll, and Lajos Kassák has been lost by now. While in music and possibly even in the visual arts it is easier to speak of an international canon, in literature there are no institutions that are comparable to concert halls or museums. There exists a public which can equally appreciate the works of Hokusai and Giovanni di Paolo, Lassus and Cage, but it would be difficult to find many readers with a historical understanding of the poetry of both Tu Fu and Shakespeare. I admire and enjoy *The Dream of the Red Chamber* more than many European or American novels, but I cannot claim to be able to develop a historical interpretation of this work.

The self-contradiction in Derrida's definition — culture as identity and *différance* — suggests that history is knowledge of alien experience, yet it is also constituted by memory. 'Zuletzt kann niemand aus den Dingen, die Bücher eingerechnet, mehr heraushören, als er bereits weiss,' wrote Nietzsche (1969:297–8), and one of the possible implications of his remark is that if the distance between the text and the reader is too great, no continuity, ellipsis, or disruption of tradition can be felt and no historical understanding seems possible. It may be easier to learn about the place of a text in history than to acquire a sense of history in that text. 'Durch sein Gedicht stiftet der Dichter

Gedächtnis,' says Gadamer (1986:131). The historical nature of understanding is closely related to the intertextual character of meaning and may be the main reason why there are limits to the fruitfulness of creative misinterpretation. When reading in Hungarian, I can have an awareness of intertextuality that is natural, almost instinctive, whereas if I read Celan, my memories of Hölderlin and Rilke will depend on my studies which relate to ideas about the text rather than to the text itself. When I peruse Keats or Ashbery, Milton and Stevens are not in my ear, so I am at a disadvantage in comparison with a native speaker who has a kind of organic contact with texts in that language and therefore it is less difficult for him/her to sense the contest that takes place between texts in English. If you know more, you can afford to be more flexible, relaxed, and spontaneous in your reading, whereas if you know less, your response might be somewhat stiff and unoriginal. It is not difficult to see a failure of historical understanding in the way the verse of Poe was read by Baudelaire, Mallarmé, and Valéry. Historically relevant interpretations have to be based on a sense of continuity and discontinuity in the history of a semiotic system, some assessment of the relation between precursor and ephebe.

It is one thing to assert that 'il n'y a pas de hors texte' (Derrida 1967:227), because the inner/outer dichotomy has to be deconstructed, and quite a different one to question the existence of traditions of interpretation. The third *Brandenburg Concerto* as conducted by Furtwängler is interesting yet somewhat misleading, because Furtwängler ignored the basic rules of Baroque music making. His excuse was that the institutions of music making had changed so radically in the nineteenth century that it seemed impossible to recreate eighteenth-century conditions in the twentieth. While the Romantic interpretive tradition made his reading of Bach at least partly justifiable, it would be difficult to make such historical claim for Glenn Gould's recording of Beethoven's Opus 57, which may shed more light on the Canadian pianist's idiosyncratic ideas on artistic flaws in the works composed by Beethoven in his middle period than on the *Appassionata* sonata. In his interpretation preserved in a 1967 CBS recording, the first movement ('Allegro assai') lasts 14 minutes and 57 seconds, in sharp contrast to the versions by Arthur Schnabel and Edwin Fischer, recorded for His Master's Voice in 1933 and 1935, in which the same movement lasts 8 minutes and 56 seconds and 8 minutes and 35 seconds respectively. An excessively slow performance of an allegro movement composed in the classical sonata form may be compared to a 'Nachdichtung' that is too free to be accepted as a translation. No hermeneutic dialogue is developed, no 'Horizontverschmelzung' occurs, and the primacy of self-understanding leads to arbitrary interpretation. Such cases may remind us that it is easier to insist on multiculturalism than to do justice to its requirements, since understanding is mediation rather than self-expression or contemplation.

If cultural relativism has some legitimacy in music, it plays an even more crucial role in the historical understanding of literature. Reading in one's mother tongue necessitates interpretive stategies different from those followed when reading in a foreign language or in translation. The international status and accessibility of a language undoubtedly affects the reception of literary works. English, French, German, Russian, Chinese, and Spanish are taught as second or 'foreign' languages. This makes it easier to view the literature in these languages from the outside. In the case of Albanian, Estonian, or Mongolian it would be difficult to speak of the outsider's perspective since the community of readers with Albanian, Estonian, or Mongolian as a second language must be rather small. Intercultural hermeneutics is a fascinating field, but in some cases it seems more possible than in others. The range of reading positions in the case of an Estonian poem is so narrow in comparison with a novel originally written in English that the interpretive strategies might be radically different in the two cases and it is virtually impossible to use the methods of *Wirkungsgeschichte* or *Rezeptionsästhetik* in the first case.

The world is extremely fragmented and yet the canons, highly institutionalized and based on accessibility, are very rigid. In view of the increasing globalization and standardization — what some call Americanization — all countries have to address two issues. Since the humanities will no longer be centred in the study of national cultures, all the institutions of secondary and higher education need to be restructured. The rise of comparative studies will ask not only for a rearrangement of departments but also for publications which can meet the new demands. To make some progress, it would be advisable to deconstruct the opposition between Western and non-Western cultures and examine the distinction between 'great' and 'small' literatures. If it is true that Western poetics is mimetic, whereas the conception of literature characteristic of East Asia is 'affective-expressive' (Miner 1990:19), the task of comparative scholars is to attempt reinterpretations of both cultures from a double perspective. The evaluation of individual literatures involves even more difficult problems, including the relations between aesthetic value and accessibility, so-called high and popular culture. In any case, without a radical opening up of the international canon comparative literature research cannot justify its legitimacy in the future. Multiculturalism will change both research and teaching in ways that are hardly predictable at the present moment. One of the far-reaching consequences will be a rethinking of history, together with an undermining and possible restructuring of cultural legacy.

Eötvös Loránd University

Notes

1 'The Idea of National Character: A Romantic Heritage' in Peter Borner (ed.) 1986 *Concepts of National Identity: An Interdisciplinary Dialogue*. Nomos, Baden-Baden: pp. 45–61.
2 Ferenc Tôkei 1959 *A kinai elégia születése: K'ü Jüan és kora*. Akadémiai Kiadó, Budapest; in French translation 1968 *Naissance de l'élégie chinoise*. Gallimard, Paris.

3 Paul de Man 1989 'Foreword to Carol Jacobs, The Dissimulating Harmony' (1978) in *Critical Writings, 1953-1978*. University of Minnesota Press: p. 221.

Works Cited

Boulez, Pierre 1966 'Béla Bartok' in *Relevés d'apprenti*. Seuil, Paris.

Derrida, Jacques 1967 *De la grammatologie*. Minuit, Paris.

—— 1991 *L'autre cap, suivi de La démocratie ajournée*. Minuit, Paris.

Gadamer, Hans-Georg 1986 *Wahrheit und Methode: Grundzüge einer philosophischen Hermeneutik*. C. C. Mohr (Paul Siebeck), Tübingen.

—— 1986 *Wer bin Ich and wer bist Du? Ein Kommentar zu Paul Celans Gedichtfolge 'Atemkristall'*. Suhrkamp, Frankfurt am Main.

Heidegger, Martin 1983 'Die Herkunft der Kunst und die Bestimmung des Denkens' in *Denkerfahrungen 1910–1976*. Vittorio Klostermann, Frankfurt am Main.

Miner, Earl 1990 *Comparative Poetics: An Intercultural Essay on Theories of Literature*. Princeton University Press.

Nabokov, Vladimir 1967 'An Interview' in *The Paris Review*, no. 41, summer-fall.

Nietzsche, Friedrich 1969 *Ecce homo*. Walter de Gruyter and Co., Berlin.

Rousseau, Jean-Jacques 1960 *Lettre à M. D'Alembert*. Garnier, Paris.

Wierlacher, Alois 1990 'Mit fremden Augen oder: Fremdheit als Ferment: Überlegungen zur Begründung einer interkulturellen Hermeneutik deutscher Literatur' in Dietrich Krusche & Alois Wierlacher (Hrsg.), *Hermeneutik der Fremde*. Iudicium, München.

Wittgenstein, Ludwin 1984 *Culture and Value* (Vermischte Bemerkungen). University of Chicago Press.

EDUARDO F. COUTINHO

The Effects of Cultural Dialogue on Latin America's World View

Any critical review of the historical development of comparative literature leads immediately to an awareness that, from the 1970s to the present day, the subject has undergone considerable change. Without fear of reductionism, this may be summed up as the passage from a cohesive, unanimous discourse to a pluralistic, decentred one, historically situated and conscious of the differences which identify each literary corpus involved in the comparative process. Although this change originated within the great axis of comparative studies composed of Western Europe and North America, and may be owed largely to the vogue for literary theory during that period, and particularly to the importance taken on by such currents as deconstructionism, New History, and so-called cultural and postcolonial studies, its corollary was the dislocation of the subject's focus of operation to poles hitherto considered marginal, such as Asia (China and India), Africa, and Latin America. It is this verifiable transformation within the heart of traditional comparativism, above all with respect to the Latin American context, which shall be the object of our investigation.

Initially marked by a historicist perspective based on scientific-causalist principles stemming from the historical moment and context in which it was formed, and later on by a predominantly formalist outlook (which, however, coexisted with dissonant voices of significant relevance), comparative literature reached its first century of existence amid intense debate, albeit sustained by certain solid pillars of distinctly ethnocentric colouring. Among these pillars, which remained almost unshaken until the 1970s, it is impossible not to recognize a claim to universality, for which the cosmopolitanism of comparative studies was often mistaken, present in its earliest manifestations, and the apolitical discourse preached above all others by the so-called 'American School' which dominated the field in the middle of the twentieth century. The former expresses itself through a hope that, despite the literary phenomenon's diversity and multiplicity, it is possible to constitute a unified discourse on the subject, as well as the hope that literature may be a sort of ennobling force of humanity which transcends all barriers. The latter may be condensed in affirmations that comparative literature is the study of literature independent of linguistic, ethnic or political frontiers, and should therefore remain unaffected by (among others) economic, social and political circumstances.

Although these two types of discourse present superficial variations, they contain a strong common denominator — the hegemonic character of their construction — and it was upon this fundamental fact that a good deal of criticism toward traditional comparativism was based. In the name of a pseudo-democracy of letters, which proposed a general history of literature or a universal poetics, thus developing a common instrument with which to approach the literary phenomenon regardless of specific circumstances, what comparativists (of predominantly Euro-North American origin) did was to extend to other literatures those parameters instituted from reflections about the European literary canon. The inevitable result of all this was the overestimation of a given system and the identification of this system — the European — with the universal one. Similarly, the idea that literature ought to be approached from an apolitical perspective, a notion we currently understand to be impossible, only served to camouflage the reaffirmation of one system's supremacy.

The challenge to this universalizing posture and the demythification of the proposal of apoliticization, which became a keynote of comparative literature during the 1970s, had different effects on the hegemonic centres and on the focal points of comparative studies which might be considered peripheral, but a similar phenomenon could be verified in both contexts: the increasingly greater approximation of comparativism to issues of national and cultural identity. On the Western European/North American axis, the essential concerns were displaced onto ethnic or sexual minority groups, whose voices were heard with increasing strength, seeking public discussion for alternative forms of expression. Elsewhere in the world there were claims for a displacement of the gaze, so that one might focus upon literary questions from one's own *locus*. Preoccupation with literary historiography, theory and criticism remained relevant in both of the aforementioned contexts, but it came to be directly associated with everyday political praxis. Theoretical discussions about the search for universals ceased to have meaning and were replaced by localized questions, which began to dominate the subject's agenda: problems such as the relationships between local and imported traditions, the political implications of cultural influence, and the need for a revision of both the literary canon and the criteria for periodization.

This decentring which took place within the scope of comparative studies, now much more attuned to contextualized issues, greatly expanded the international and interdisciplinary character of comparative literature, which came to embrace a complex network of cultural relationships. The literary work or series could no longer be approached from an exclusively aesthetic perspective; as cultural products it was necessary to take into account their relationship with other fields of knowledge. Beyond this, elements which until then had functioned as safe references in comparative studies, such as the concepts of nation and language, fell to earth, and the traditionally established dichotomy between National and comparative literature was seriously upset. The linear perspective of historicism gave way to a multiple, mobile vision, able to account for specific differences, for disjunctive forms of representation which signify a people, a nation, or a culture, and it became imperative that literary series or sets be seen from a plural perspective, which would consider such aspects. Categories such as Chicano literature, Afro-American literature or feminist literature came to integrate the spectrum of comparative studies, and blocks such as Oriental, African, or Latin American literature instituted by hegemonic centres were revealed to be fragile constructs, acquiring new features which changed in accordance with the gaze that informed it.

The shift of the gaze which took place at the core of comparativism, resulting from an awareness of the ethnocentric character which had dominated it in previous phases, bestowed new life upon the subject. The result was great effervescence in precisely those places that were marginally situated and that had now become fundamental sites in the international debate. In these places, where there is no sense of incompatibility between national literatures and comparative literature, the Eurocentric model which had stood as reference until then, has been increasingly questioned, and traditional paradigms have given way to rich and flexible alternative constructions, whose main preoccupation resides in articulating the perception of local cultural products in relation to the products of other cultures, especially those with which the former had maintained ties of subordination. When critics such as Edward Said and Homi Bhabha challenge the systematic process of 'inventing' other cultures, the repercussions are tremendous, giving rise to claims for the constitution of a literary history based on local tradition, whose recovery had become indispensable in places such as India, Africa, and Latin America. The political element of comparativism is now not only consciously assumed, but even emphasized, and an imperative need arises for a review of the literary canon.

Central to comparative literature's current situation, the 'question of the canon', as it has been designated, constitutes one of the most vital instances of the struggle against Eurocentrism currently being fought in the academic milieu. To discuss the canon amounts to little more than an attemp to curb a value system instituted by the ruling groups which have legitimized private decisions with a globalizing discourse. Courses on the 'great books', for example, so frequently offered in comparative literature, have almost always been restricted to the canon of Western tradition (in reality, to the tradition of a few powerful European countries that maintain cultural politics of a hegemonic stamp), and have always been based on premises which either completely ignore all production outside of a certain restricted geographical radius, or touched only tangentially upon such production and included one or another of its manifestations as a sort of concession. Reactions to this stance have arisen in many forms, with different shadings which depend upon their origins. In central countries, it is obviously the so-called 'minority groups' who once again ask the main questions and, in peripheral contexts, the question has become a constant one, sometimes situated on the front lines of the process of cultural decolonization.

Large, complex and varied, the question of the literary canon exceeds our objectives in the present paper, as it could not be treated with the necessary care. But it should be mentioned that the question extends from the exclusion of the vigorous literary production of minority groups in the hegemonic centres and the stifling of a significant literary tradition in recently colonized countries such as India, all the way to problems of the specificity or non-specificity of the literary element, standards for an aesthetic evaluation, and the establishment of frontiers between constructs such as national literatures and comparative literature. With the deconstruction of the pillars upon which traditional literary studies once stood and the lack of definition which established itself between referential limits, the traditional canon or canons no longer possess a foundational base, thus affecting the entire structure of literary historiography, theory, and criticism. How to construct canons, on a national or international level, which account for differences voiced by each group or nation (if we are to understand this term in its widest sense, as used by authors such as Homi Bhabha), and how to attribute to these new constructs a sufficiently flexible character which would allow them constant reformulations, are questions being raised today about such rapidly shifting ground. One might also inquire as to the possibility of instituting canons with margins of flexibility, which would not inevitably crystallize and become new impositions. Would they still be canons?

Comparativism would appear to leave such questions nearly always unanswered, especially after the development of so-called postcolonial and cultural studies, which attacked the field's ethnocentrism with a vehemence hitherto unseen. Criticism of this element, expressed by means of a supposedly liberal discourse, which at bottom concealed its authoritarian and totalizing content, had already started during the time of Wellek and Etiemble and, if we observe the spectrum of comparative literature, we shall see that, during its evolution, it always flourished with great variety. In most cases, however, this criticism manifested itself by means of a binary opposition, which paradoxically continued to hold the European element as its reference. Aware of the fact that it is no longer a question of a simple inversion of models nor of the substitution of what had been considered central by its peripheral antithesis, current comparativists who question the hegemony of the colonizing cultures abandon the dichotomic paradigm and engage in an exploration of the multiple paths which have been opened up as a result of the contact between colonizer and colonized. Consequently, they see themselves before a hermetic, albeit useful, labyrinth, generated by the de-hierarchization of those elements involved in the comparative process, and their greatest task lies precisely within this open construction, this voyage of discovery devoid of definite markers.

Profoundly marked by a process of colonization, which is still alive today from both a cultural and an economic standpoint, literary studies in Latin America were always undertaken after the European manner, and a brief glance at questions of literary historiography, theory and criticism shall suffice as evidence of this. In the case of historiography, one need only remember that literary periodization has always taken European (and, more recently, also North American) literary movements as their reference, and regarded the Latin American ones as mere extensions or adaptations of the former. In the case of theory, we need only mention the dominant practice of importing currents from the European intellectual milieu, which acquired a dogmatic character and were indiscriminately applied to Latin America's literary reality, without ever taking into consideration the historical and cultural differences which distinguished the two contexts. And, finally, in the field of criticism mention should be made of parameters for evaluation, which have always been based on the so-called 'great books' of Western (read 'European') tradition, and considered ours as minor manifestations, imperfect copies of the instituted models. The literary canon or canons of the many Latin American countries were made up of criteria stipulated by the dominant sectors of society which reproduced the European gaze — at first, in colonial times, the Iberian gaze, and later, after political independence, the gaze of other countries, especially France.

Although, as a response to its own colonial condition, Latin America had already developed during this time a strong tradition of search for identity, as much in literature as in essay writing, comparativism produced on the continent generally remained tied to the French model of sources and influences or the North American formalist perspective, both of which gave them a sterile quality and ratified their situation as dependent. However, with the changes made from the 1970s to the present date, it appears to have been reborn from the ashes, and is today one of the centres of greatest effervescence in Latin American studies. Associating itself with the search for identity, no longer seen from an ontological perspective, but rather as a construction open to questioning and renewal, comparative literature in Latin America seems to have firmly taken on the need to focus on literary production from its own perspective, based on the reality of this continent, and has been seeking true dialogue on an international level. Thus, questions such as those of the canon and literary history have acquired a new countenance and theoretical and critical models have been relativized, giving way to a more effective reflection.

The restructuring of the canon or canons of the various Latin American literatures has been the object of intense activity on the Latin American academic scene, with a growing demand for the inclusion of a number of registers hitherto marginalized by official discourse: still-living indigenous tongues such as quichua and guarani, *créole* production in the French Caribbean world, the so-called popular forms of the Mexican *corrido* or the Brazilian *cordel*, and oral or compiled tradition such as that of the Maya Indian myths. It has also been argued that work by the Hispanic minorities of the United States (Chicano, Puerto Rican, and Cuban), the Québecois French, and the voices of the 'power minorities' within the continent itself (such as feminist groups which have played a prominent part in the process of the critical re-reading of Latin American culture) cannot be ignored. In the same way, the need for a new literary historiography, exempt from traditional distortions, in which the concept of 'great literature', or even 'literature' *tout court*, would be problematized, is ever more pressing, along with the urgent need for the development of theoretical reflection which might have the continent's literary corpus as a starting point or reference.

All of these topics, which examine Latin American differences, reveal the inadequacy of transferring paradigms from one culture into another. The very idea of 'national literature', conceived within the European academic environment and based on notions of unity and homogeneity, cannot be applied without problems to the hybrid reality of the Latin American continent where Indian nations such as the Aymara, for example, are divided by arbitrarily instituted political frontiers. Any monolithic conception of Latin American culture is currently being questioned and frequently substituted by alternative proposals which seek to account for its hybrid nature. Such proposals, diversified and subject to constant critical scrutiny, indicate the many directions being taken by comparativism on the continent, in perfect consonance with the subject's general tendencies and primarily observable in other contexts previously considered peripheral. Comparative literature today, especially in these places, is a wide and mobile field, with countless possibilities for exploration. It has gone beyond the totalizing hopes of its earlier stages, and is on the rise as a transcultural dialogue based on the acceptance of differences.

Universidade Federal do Rio Janeiro

Works Cited

Ahmad, Aijaz 1992 *Classes in Nations, Theory, Literature*. Verso, London.

Amin, Samir 1989 *Eurocentrism,* tr. Russell Moore. Monthly Review Press, New York.

Bassnett, Susan 1993 *Comparative Literature: A Critical Introduction*. Blackwell, Oxford.

Beverly, John and José Oviedo (eds) 1993 *The Postmodernism Debate in Latin America.* A Special Issue of *Boundary 2*. vol. 20, no. 3., Duke University Press.

Bhabha, Homi (ed.) 1990 *Nation and Narration*. Routledge, London.

Chanady, Amaryll (ed.) 1994 *Latin American Identity and Constructions of Difference*. University of Minnesota Press.

Costa Lima, Luiz 1991 *Pensando nos trópicos*. Rocco, Rio de Janeiro.

Guillén, Claudio 1985 *Lo uno y lo diverso: introducción a la literatura comparada*. Ed. Crítica, Barcelona.

Koelb, Clayton and Susan Noakes (eds) 1988 *The Comparative Perspective on Literature: Approaches to Theory and Practice*. Cornell University Press.

Lauter, Paul 1991 *Canons and Contexts*. Oxford University Press.

Pizarro, Ana (ed.) 1985 *La literatura latinoamericana como proceso*. Centro Editor de América Latina, Buenos Aires.

Rama, Angel 1982 *Transculturación narrativa en América Latina*. Siglo XXI, México.

Said, Edward 1993 *Culture and Imperialism*. Vintage Books, New York.

Todorov, Tzvetan 1982 *La conquête de l'Amérique: la question de l'autre*. Seuil, Paris.

Tomlison, John 1991 *Cultural Imperialism: a Critical Introduction*. John Hopkins University Press.

Williams, Patrick and Laura Chrisman 1994 *Colonial Discourse and Post-Colonial Theory: A Reader*. Columbia University Press.

Yúdice, George, Jean Franco and Angel Flores (eds) 1992 *On Edge: The Crisis of Contemporary Latin American Culture*. University of Minnesota Press.

E. D. BLODGETT

Translation as Dialogue: The Example of Canada

Inasmuch as Canada is officially a bilingual state, it means that all documents of a national character, such as laws and federal policy documents, must be made public in both languages. Such a state of affairs has various consequences for the cultures so affected. I want to address some of these consequences with a view to indicating what the conditions for dialogue are, at least between francophone and anglophone Canada, and what some of the shapes of the dialogues can be. By way of introduction, I will comment upon the political conditions and then I will raise aspects of more familiar kinds of cultural reception and response.

From the perspective of a monolingual state, such a point of departure may seem unnecessary. In Canada, not to speak of Belgium or India, the question of language and its use through translation is of such significance as to be part of the debate on whether the country survives in its current shape or not. This only means that Canada's constitutional problems of the last thirty years are a belated response to what Benedict Anderson has referred to as 'the philological revolution' (1983:75) of the nineteenth century in Europe. Contrary to Anderson's otherwise valid assertion that '[i]n the Americas there was almost perfect isomorphism between the stretch of the various empires and that of their vernaculars' (77), Canada has participated in its way in this revolution for the past century and a half. The debate, which is now at the centre of public policy issues, depends upon how bilingualism is to be understood and acted upon. The sensitive character of the debate is of interest because it has created certain attitudes which affect translation practice.

Although the dominant federal attitude in Canada until the 1960s was the liberal view that English is the language of commercial opportunity in North America, its ability to impose that position has been continuously opposed by

Quebec nationalistic arguments. Thus despite legislation passed in 1841 to make English the national language, the governor-general already in 1849 gave his Speech from the Throne in English and French.¹ Although modified by provincial legislation in respect of education in the course of time, the policy in practice did not become an issue until the expansion of the civil service following the Second World War. 'Because the language of work became an important criterion for employment, and one subject to political pressure', Ramsey Cook writes (1986:156), legislation to prevent cultural glossophagia — 'the consumption of the minority by the dominant language' — was subsequently enacted and later repeated in the Charter of Rights and Freedoms.

Far from solving a problem, the legislation appeared to exacerbate it. Because all federal laws are prepared in English initially and subsequently translated into French, not only the policy but its servant — the act of translation — perpetuate what may be perceived as a condition of civil inequality. As one commentator has observed, '[l]a traduction, dans un sens symbolique, me semble être au coeur de la problématique dès le débout du régime britannique' (Ben-Z. Shek 1977:111). This is because '[l]a traduction à sens unique a reproduit les rapports réels dominants-dominés de la conjoncture militaire, en premier lieu, puis et par conséquent, politique et économique' (111). As the author goes on to argue, efforts on the part of Quebec to enact a monolingual language policy, that is, glossophagia in reverse, is symbolically a necessary response that would overcome the hierarchical relationship that obtains between the two languages. From this perspective, the bilingual policy is paradoxically both necessity and anathema. Nor has the effort to enact monolingual policies in Quebec done more than indicate that if language is the articulation of culture, then mutual glossophagia must in some way be prevented.

Prevention takes place under conditions that inhibit hierarchical relations and modify the communication situation from a vertical to a horizontal axis. It follows, then, that in Canada translation is not a value-neutral activity nor would any theory be that was based upon it. As Pierre Cardinal has succinctly observed, '"[l]'institution traduction" joue un rôle éminement politique dans la vie du Canada' (1978:146). One consequence is that a preferred translation model would be a dialogic model. Since the burden of this paper consists in describing and defining what I mean by such an expression, let us consider first those models with which it may appear to have certain affinities.

With its notion of reciprocity, Steiner's model of 'the hermeneutic motion', which has found an occasional echo in Canadian discussions (Jones 1977:70 *et passim)*, hints, at least, at dialogue. Nevertheless, the metaphors of appropriation with which it is invested, despite Steiner's qualifications, deeply limit its usefulness. The four moments of the translator's act are initiated by a sense of trust. This is followed by 'an incursive and extractive' gesture of aggression (297), that is, '[t]he translator invades, extracts and brings home' (298). Next, the translator embodies, and, finally, the translation as hermeneutic act compensates: 'If it is to be authentic, it must mediate into exchange and restored parity' (300). Without referring to all the terms that infiltrate his discussion, it is clear that translation is akin to violation, transgression and rape. It concludes, however, in 'restored parity', which may also be construed as a compensation of the source-text as victim. It may be that, as a history of translation that has often been no more than appropriation, Steiner's description has a certain validity. But the price of parity is too high to be helpful in Canada.

Steiner anticipates Bassnett-McGuire's interest in what she frequently refers to as the dialectic process of translation (1980:36). The attraction of the dialectical in Canada is that it allows for two possibilities: the preservation of distinct autonomy and the exercise of mutual subjectivity. Furthermore, because of the necessary, intimate relation the translator must have with the text in process of being realized, the subject is also engaged in its own realization, which possesses an aspect of mutual subjectivity. As D. J. Jones remarked, '[i]f we translate Quebec poetry so that Quebeckers may exist, we do so as well so that we may exist. Any genuine intercourse is reciprocal, reinforcing our existence, providing a heightened and more articulate sense of our identity — of oneself and the other' (1977:80). Barbara Godard suggests the extent to which subjectivity is at risk: 'dans l'échange interculturel qui est l'interprétation ou la traduction, le "je" est mis en question au même titre que "l'autre"' (1982:154). In such a context, it should be evident that the losses that translation may cause are not simply those of meaning, unless meaning were to include both textual and psycho-sociological meaning. And surely it should, especially when a text and a translator are complementary signs of cultures in such highly charged semantic relationships as those are in Canada. What happens, however, if the relationship is construed as dialectical?

Fredric Jameson defines dialectical thinking as 'a moment in which thought rectifies itself, in which the mind, suddenly drawing back and including itself in its new and widened apprehension, doubly restores and regrounds its earlier notions in a new glimpse of reality' (1971:372). It is 'not only thought to the second power, thought about pre-existing thought, but also the latter's fulfilment, its realization and abolition' (341). Although Marxists find it possible to look upon thought as somehow either impersonal or a common property, the translator, I think, should hesitate to do so. The translator's thoughts address a specific text, often the work of a living, specific author, whose work frequently is the articulation of a specific culture. Is, after all, 'the latter's fulfilment, its realization and abolition' a desirable goal? We may achieve 'solutions on a higher level' (307), but to do so we construct hierarchies that tend to efface what might be called representative subjectivities. A dialogue, however, in which both speakers possess a mutual disposition of power has other modalities.

The classical example in Canada of dialogic translation is recorded in *Dialogue sur la traduction* by two of Canada's more respected poets, Anne

Hébert and F. R. Scott. Referring in a letter to the dialogue they were able to conduct on her poetry, Hébert perceives that through translation 'le poème pressé de tous côtés livre son coeur le plus secret aux prestiges d'une langue étrangère' (1970:49). As a consequence, poetry is 'équipée à mesure pour une seconde vie fidèle à son sens originel, mais recréée selon le génie propre à une autre langue' (49). While this may suggest a dialectical movement of death and rebirth, it is more likely a double life in both senses of the term, and it is achieved through dialogue, which she understands as 'tout un jeu de balance excessivement subtil et important' (49).

Scott and Hébert belong to an older generation of poets and translators whose first fidelity was toward finding some primary meaning as represented by the source-text. The contemporary project, while different in attitude and performance, is still dialogic, but emphasizes more the ludic character of dialogue, that allows for unexpected turns and discoveries beyond the reach of the rigours of dialectic. Here the example of feminist discussions of translation is instructive because it plays upon the political sense of translation along a vertical axis. As a consequence, it recognizes the agency of the translator. It does so not by searching for a meaning which is assumed to reside in the source-text, but to problematize a number of concepts which most theories of translation depend upon; for example, meaning, mimesis, the literal, equivalence. It does so by means of play, by privileging the ludic character of translation, and by insisting that translation is analogous to femininity by being 'a provisional performance, not an essence' (111).

According to Godard, the feminist translator problematizes meaning through semantic shift of attention from the signified to the signifier, in other words, 'a shift from the object of interpretation to a concern with the implications of that interpretation' (112). The point of such a gesture is to subvert any sort of fixed identity, implied by both the signified and metaphor, and to move at ease among signifiers and metonymies by means of a 'ludic repetition or supplement that exposes the operations of representation as the production of value within an economy of meaning configured by a specific set of overlapping signifiers' (111). Although such a project constitutes deliberate 'misreading' or, if the pun is excused, 'msreading', by which the 'I' becomes a signifier among others in the play of language, it does not necessarily constitute a complete distortion of the source-text, but rather a reconfiguration of it demanded by the highly polysemous character of much feminist writing. Translating in such a fashion is not an idiosyncratic mode of behaviour on the part of the translator but, in fact, is a response to the promptings of the source-text that 'follows the lead of the feminist writers she translates' (von Flotow 1991:74).

One of the more astounding examples of the process of translation has been thematized in Nicole Brossard's text, *Le Désert mauve*. The title serves as both the title of the book and the title of the narrative the book contains and translates. Part of the elaborate game of the book as a whole is that both narrative and translation are in French. While there are minor deviations between the source-text and target-text, they are not sufficient to constitute significant rewriting, except for the transposition of writing about the murderer in the narrative to his being captured later in photographs. But because the text as a whole foregrounds the act of translation, it urges the reader to concentrate upon the central sections between text and translation entitled 'Un livre à traduire', which comprises the notes of the translator. The title projects the task into the future, transposing the reality of the text into the virtuality of its being translated, suggesting that translation as a process exists somewhere between the past of the source-text and the future of the target-text. It therefore privileges the transitory character of translation. It is also the moment in which the translator becomes engaged with the implications of the text to be translated.

The book to be translated is understood as various moments of insight which are organized around meditations upon the translator as subject, notes on places, things and characters, re-examinations of various scenes in the narrative, an interview that includes a murdered character, notes on key terms, and finally a return to the narrator as subject. The whole is designed to emphasize that both text and translator are part of the translation process and, consequently, to imply that the translator is also a text preparing herself for the task of writing herself into the other's text. This, I take it, is what Godard means when she observes that to translate Brossard 'oblige le traducteur ... à participer dans une cocréation avec elle ... de trouver cet "autre" en moi-même' (1982:155). The method for doing so is clearly dialogic insofar as the translator, always presented in the third person in contrast to the first-person narrator of her text to translate, appears as always prepared to be the other in the texts she prepares, especially those that engage the characters in conversations that the source-text either omits or has no knowledge of. All the scenes she prepares are dialogues that manifest the refractory power of talk to seize upon the unexpected and change topics at will, unconcerned with the oppositions of dialectic. The conversations, then, repeat in surprising ways the sometimes didactic manner of the narrator in the text to be translated, whose adolescence is often revealed in her preemptory pronouncements on the cosmos. Unwaveringly postmodern, the narrator's assertions make it clear that signifiers appeal only to other signifiers in such a way as to make a referentiality outside language impossible to locate. Thus reality becomes for the narrator 'un devenir espacé dans le mémoire' (37). The signifier *réalité* becomes a cue for the translator to disseminate its meanings:

> La réalité est ce que nous retrouvons par un incalculable retour des choses imagées, comme un sens familier dispose bien distinctement dans nos vies. Mais à tout cela il y a certainement, pensons-nous, un autre sens, une autre version puisque nous en rêvons comme d'une musique d'accompagnement, une voix centrée capable de nous livrer un passage, une petite ouverture. (156)

Reality in the text, one might say, is the virtual. It is capable of conferring upon the translator not only a passage of music, but also, if we elide momentarily the indefinite article in the concluding infinitive phrase, allowing one simply to pass, to go through, which is precisely what the translator desires to do as both subject and text. Thus, in the penultimate note before translating, we read: 'D'une langue à l'autre, il y aurait du sens, juste distribution, contour et rencontre du moi.... [The translator] savait que le temps est maintenant venu de glisser anonyme et entière entre les pages' (177). The full paradox of the translator is here: although anonymous, she is credited as the translator, and so she remains, as a subject, 'entière'. In doing so she is made to slide, as if she were a signifier herself, from one tongue or language to another.

As part of the effort of drawing the threads of this paper together, let me remark first that the translation process in Canada's literature requires a discussion both of the practice and its effect upon subject positions. While it could be argued that the subject position of the translator in Brossard's text is split and, therefore, an echo of a frequently constructed subject position in women's writing, one might readily reply that border-figures such as this are not uncommon in contemporary Canadian fiction. It is a stance shared by both Canadian and Québécois writers of both genders and reflects in a variety of ways the sense of divided as well as shared realities. The translator is the emblematic figure of such a situation, and, as such, becomes more than simply a receiver and respondent in a communication situation. The translator may be said to enact translation as dialogue, as the example of Brossard indicates. In the middle, she is the site of the dialogue.

Because of the political character of translation in Canada, such a 'translator' as Jacques Brault prefers to imagine himself 'sur le seuil invisible d'un entre-deux' and like Brossard's translator both 'me niant et m'affirmant' (1975:14–15). He prefers to make use of a '[l]angue suspendue entre deux certitudes maintenant problématiques, langue qui reconnaît alors sa difficulté d'être' (15). As Laurent Mailhot has commented, translating in this way never quite arrives or finishes its task (1978:47). Although this appears to echo Scott's despair at never being able to get Hébert exactly as he might (1970:56–7), it comes closer to Godard's remarks on translation as an extension of signifiers that metonymically continue a text without necessarily becoming its mimesis. This is a model of translation, then, that like a conversation can always start again in a different place, the responses taking the shape of allusions capable of modification, mimicking at a distance the turns of Canada's own unfinished dialogue with itself.

Do such dialogues issue necessarily from misunderstanding? The question implies that there is something to be understood in the same way by both parties, something like a fixed source-text or some 'invariant semantic core' (Popovic 1976:11). If, however, it were understood in the same way, dialogue would be barely possible. The 'text to be translated', to borrow Brossard's term, is the continuation of a ludic operation that would issue, at least provisionally, in what Brault has called a 'tierce réalité, la seule désormais viable' (1975:34).

University of Alberta

Note

1 This review of language policy is based on Ramsey Cook's excellent chapter, 'Language Policy and the Glossophagic State' (1986:150–8).

Works Cited

Anderson, Benedict 1991 (1983) *Imagined Communities*. Verso, London and New York.

Bassnett-McGuire, Susan 1980 *Translation Studies*. Methuen, London and New York.

Blodgett, E. D. 1991 'Towards a Model of Literary Translation in Canada' in *TTR IV*, 2: pp. 189–206.

Brault, Jacques 1975 *Poèmes des quatre côtés*. Editions du Noroît, Chambly.

Brossard, Nicole 1987 *Le Désert mauve*. Editions de l'Hexagon, Montréal.

Cardinal, Pierre 1978 'Regard critique sur la traduction au Canada' in *Meta* 23, ii: pp. 141–7.

Cook, Ramsay 1986 *Canada, Québec and the Uses of Nationalism*. McClelland & Stewart, Toronto.

Godard, Barbara 1982 '"Je est un autre": Nicole Brossard au Canada anglais' in *Traces: Ecriture de Nicole Brossard, La nouvelle Barre du jour*: pp. 150–5.

—— 1991 'Translating (With) the Speculum' in *TTR IV*, 2: pp. 85–121.

Hébert, Anne and Frank Scott 1970 *Dialogue sur la traduction*. HMH, Montréal.

Jameson, Fredric 1971 *Marxism and Form*. Princeton University Press.

Jones, D. G. 1977 'Grounds for Translation' in *Ellipse* 21: pp. 58–91.

Mailhot, Laurent 1978 'Traduction et "nontraduction": l'épeuve du voisin étranger dans la littérature québécoise' in *L'Alternité dans la littérature québécoise*. CLUEB, Bologna.

Popovic, Anton 1976 *Dictionary for the Analysis of Literary Translation*. Department of Comparative Literature, Edmonton, AB.

Shek, Ben-Z. 1977 'Quelques réflexions sur la traduction dans le contexte socio-culturel canado-québécois' in *Ellipse* 21: pp. 111–7.

Steiner, George 1975 *After Babel: Aspects of Language and Literature*. Oxford University Press.

Von Flotow, Luise 1991 'Feminist Translation: Contexts, Practices and Theories' in *TTR IV*, 2: pp. 69–84.

PART TWO

Misreading

JOHN BOENING

Comparative Literature, Incommensurability, and Cultural Misreading

As technology, trade and travel shrink the globe and the cultures of the world come into ever greater and more intimate contact, one should think there would be a proportionally greater exchange of information and ideas across national and cultural boundaries, and especially an increase in cultural understanding and dialogue. But as anyone who travels widely realizes, and as we as comparatists, with our multilingual, multitextual background and perspective, realize perhaps more acutely than most, this exchange operates on at least two levels, with very different results. On the one hand, there is indeed an enormous worldwide trade in commercial and mass-market culture. On the other hand, this globalization of commercial culture has not brought with it a concurrent globalization of intellectual culture. The cultures of the world are still in many ways as opaque to one another, or as misread by one another, as they have been for centuries.

One reason for this is that while contemporary commercial culture is dominated by visual and musical forms, intellectual, or 'literary', culture ('textual culture' might be a better phrase) axiomatically relies on verbal forms, on texts (be they oral, written, printed or even electronic). Textual culture is still ultimately linguistic, is still kept from successfully crossing international and intercultural boundaries by the reality that most people in the world remain limited to spoken and written comprehension of some few languages and by the corollary reality that translation, when it has in fact occurred, has often been at best a mixed blessing, a clothing of one culture's ideas in the garb of another, with the chances for an even greater misreading often increased, rather than diminished, by the product. If being able to understand another culture means being able to understand, or being able to read and fully comprehend the texts in which it makes itself manifest, then the cultures of the world, we are forced to admit, seem condemned to remain mutually incommensurable. The implications for international intellectual exchange and dialogue seem disheartening indeed.

Before we bemoan this state of affairs, however, we ought to ask whether or not it would be desirable — even if it were possible — for cultures to be completely transparent to one another. The poet Paul Valéry, in a celebrated after-dinner talk at a banquet of the international P.E.N. Club in 1925,[1] spoke to this very issue, when he observed, in a toast to the extraordinarily multilingual group assembled before him, that such a meeting as the one he was addressing was itself a paradox:

> Literature is the art of language. It is an art concerned with the means of mutual comprehension.... One can understand that mathematicians, economists, or manufacturers of all races should with advantage gather together, since they are dedicated to those studies or hold those interests whose aims are one and identical. But writers!... Men whose business is based directly on their native tongue, *whose art, as a result, consists in developing what most clearly — and perhaps most cruelly — separates one people from another people!*... What means the reunion of those who, in every nation, necessarily labor to maintain, strengthen, and perfect just those most palpable obstacles, those most remarkable and precise differences, which isolate the nation from all other? How is this meeting possible?

It is possible, Valéry goes on to suggest, precisely because the very elements which remain untranslatable between cultures, the very incommensurability of cultures, is precisely what makes them fascinated by and finally attracted to one another. To solve the paradox, Valéry says, 'one must invoke the miraculous. I mean, of course, the miracle of love':

> The different literatures are amorous of each other. And this miracle was not a recent one. Virgil yearned toward Homer. And what have we French *not* loved? Italy, in Ronsard's day, Spain in Corneille's, England in Voltaire's, Germany and the ... [Orient] with the Romantics, America with Baudelaire, and always, from century to century, like mistresses enjoyed with more constancy, Greece and Rome.

❖

Much has been written in the last few years about the ultimate 'incommensurability' of the world's cultures, on the one hand, and the 'universalizing', or 'totalizing' power of intellectual discourse — all discourse, really — on the other. The world scene has been cast as a stage upon which a giant battle is allegedly being fought between the 'globalizing' tendency of Euro-American culture, by virtue of its powerful and privileged discourse, and the world of cultural 'difference' and complexity which seems in danger of displacement, appropriation, or even erasure — a battle, in short, about whose discourse defines the terms or establishes the code.

The discipline in which this notion of a cultural battleground is most prominent and in which it plays an almost foundational role is the field of post-colonial studies, a specialty which came into existence in the 1980s and which has gathered momentum ever since.[2] Indeed, the emergence of colonial (or post-colonial) studies from the status of a marginal subdiscipline into one of the most visible academic enterprises of our time, at least in the Anglophone world, has already been prominently remarked in leading journals and in surveys of the state of scholarship in the humanities. In the last few years alone it has advanced in leaps and bounds, drawing on work in critical theory and cultural studies. Recently, for example, we have seen the appearance of two anthologies in the field: Columbia University Press's *Colonial Discourse and Post-Colonial Theory: A Reader* (edited by Patrick Williams and Laura Chrisman) and Routledge's *Post Colonial Studies Reader* (edited by Bill Ashcroft, Gareth Griffiths and Helen Tiffin), as well as special issues of the journals *PMLA*, *Critical Inquiry*, *Diacritics* and *Nineteenth-Century Studies*, the last suggestively entitled 'Colonialisms'.[3]

One indicator of just how established ('establishment'?) post-colonial studies have now become in England and North America, is that the field has recently been made a target for the critical slingshot of *Lingua Franca*, that scorekeeping chronicle of the trends and fashions of North American academic life. The David chosen by *LF* to bring this newly-grown Goliath down to earth is Russell Jacoby, and his piece is entitled 'Marginal Returns: The Trouble With Post-Colonial Theory' (1995:30–7). While Jacoby's principal critique of post-colonial scholarship concerns its institutional standing and contentions — that it claims to be marginal when it is actually mainstream — what Jacoby has to say on that matter is of less interest to our present subject than the two features of the post-colonial enterprise which Jacoby correctly identifies and foregrounds in the process of making his argument.

One such feature is the primacy of language and discourse. Jacoby writes, 'The first sentence of [Franz] Fanon's book *Black Skins, White Masks* reads 'I ascribe a basic importance to the phenomenon of language'; it is through language, he went on to say, that '"the Other" is created'. Jacoby then draws a genealogical connection from Fanon and Michel Foucault, the two theorists whose work undergirds the field, to Edward Said, whose *Orientalism* was a major attempt to advance the connection between discourse, representation and power. Jacoby notes (1995:31) that 'post-colonial theorists ... in an earlier incarnation were known as post-colonial *discourse* [my italics] theorists' who raised 'a series of vexing issues concerning "representation", "subjectivity", and "agency"', which, Jacoby contends, find their culmination in the titles of such key essays as Gayatry Spivak's 'Can the Subaltern Speak' (first published in 1988; reprinted in the 1994 Columbia anthology) and books such as the now-famous collection, *The Empire Writes Back: Theory and Practice in Post-*

Colonial Literatures (1989, edited by the same team which has since produced the new Routledge reader).

The second feature of post-colonial studies identified and foregrounded by Jacoby is what he calls its 'cult of difference and complexity, another consequence of Foucault and deconstructionism'. The post-colonialist theorists 'rightfully object to generalizations that have been used to dominate and deprecate', Jacoby writes, 'For instance, they excoriate the idea that European literature is the benchmark of the true and the beautiful.' But they go too far when they hold that:

> ...general concepts and categories themselves are suspect. The editors of Routledge's *Post-Colonial Studies Reader* devote a section to the danger of 'universality'. They explain that 'the concept of universalism' — here is that word — 'marginalizes and excludes the distinctive characteristic, the difference, of post-colonial societies.' They state that 'the assumption of universality is the fundamental feature of the construction of colonial power'. Conclusion: the myth of universality is thus a primary strategy of imperial control. (1995:35)

❖

To those of us who have made our vocation the nurturing of international ties and the promotion of intercultural dialogue and understanding, the message which thus seems to be emerging from post-colonial studies, as the field is currently conceived and grounded, is ultimately disturbing as well as dispiriting. To quote Homi Bhabha, who has become perhaps its leading theorist, in an essay setting forth the goals and designs of the post-colonial project: 'The incommensurability of cultural values and priorities that the post-colonial critic represents cannot be accommodated within theories of relativism or pluralism' (1992:439). 'The post-colonial perspective', Bhabha contends, 'forces us to rethink the profound limitations of a consensual and "liberal" sense of cultural community' (441).[4]

But cannot one be a proponent of international intellectual dialogue and partnership without being an agent of a great evil called 'universalism' which will ultimately destroy or eradicate all the world's diversity? One promising way of thinking about this question is indirectly suggested by Anthony Pagden in an exceptionally stimulating recent study entitled *European Encounters with the New World: From the Renaissance to Romanticism*. Pagden works in the area where cultural studies and the new historicism come together, and his title has echoes of Tzvetan Todorov's *La conquête de l'Amerique: La question de l'autre*. Pagden's concern, it turns out, is also with alterity, with the construction of the Other, but whereas Todorov's focus is on discovery and first encounters, Pagden is more interested in discovery's aftermath.

In the culminating chapters of his book, Pagden takes as his focus the place of Denis Diderot in the discourse on colonialism. According to Pagden, Diderot was concerned that:

> ...the discovery, settlement and colonization of America threatened the possibility of further imaginative response to difference, threatened to reduce us all to the citizens of a single invariable culture. Colonization ... could, [of course] with time, patience and sufficient force, make the incommensurable commensurable. But it could only ever do this by lessening, and finally, perhaps, even eliminating the gap which lay between ourselves and the 'other', by making the other entirely like us. (1993:167–8)

This concern, Pagden asserts, is what connects the French encyclopedist to his German contemporary, Johann Gottfried Herder (and Pagden's is the first major work of scholarship in English to do justice to Herder's interest in the question of colonialism). On this issue, Pagden contends, the views of these two eighteenth-century figures, who are usually seen as representing almost opposite sides of the Enlightenment, are complementary. He writes: 'It might seem odd to link Diderot the cosmopolitan to Herder, the supposed father of German nationalism.' But 'for Herder, as for Diderot, colonialism is an evil because it reduces, or threatens to reduce through human, and thus artificial, means, the number of political variants that exist in the world. This is an evil because plurality is part of the way the world is constituted' (173).[5]

Thus colonial empires, to both Diderot and Herder, are 'unworkable, monstrous and unnatural societies', as destructive to the imperial powers, spiritually and materially, as they are to their dominions (168). In this sense:

> ...the discovery of America, 'the most significant event for the human species in general and for the peoples of Europe in particular', would seem to have been an unmitigated disaster. In 1782, however [the Abbe Guillaume-Thomas de] Raynal suggested to the Académie de Lyon that they offer a prize for the best essay in answer to the question of what had been the advantages, and what the disadvantages, to Europe of the discovery. On the face of it, the 1780 edition of his own *Histoire* would seem to have demonstrated overwhelmingly that it had been a disadvantage. Yet for both Raynal and Diderot, and for most of those ... who wrote essays for the prize, there was another side to the story, one which made travel into a virtue, and which might yet for all the miseries it had inflicted upon man transform the history of European colonisation: this was commerce. (169–70)

Pagden reminds us that Diderot believed that commerce had gone a long way towards the peaceful erosion of the older 'prejudices' which had traditionally separated the various races of men. Already, he believed, 'the fanaticism of religion and the spirit of conquest, those two causes of disturbance in the world, are not what they were'. But this was due to commerce, not colonization. *Le doux commerce*, in Montesquieu's famous phrase, was responsible for 'making men gentle' since it involved far more than the mere exchange of necessities. 'Ever since the days of Aquinas', Pagden contends, 'the exchange of goods and the acquisition of the knowledge and understanding of a common humanity had shared a single vocabulary...

Commercium has always been more than mere trade' (170).

To Diderot, in Pagden's thinking, the counterweight to a colonial paradigm of hegemony and domination was a paradigm of multilateral exchange and interchange, in his case of goods and services. But why, we might ask, shouldn't or couldn't the same paradigm apply in the situation we find ourselves confronting today — a paradigm in which the spread of international, intercultural contacts and the multilateral exchange of texts and ideas serves as a counterweight to the truly universalizing, totalizing effects of mass commercial culture, the real scourge of difference and diversity?

As comparatists, we have long believed it could and should apply. Our discipline may have been founded in the heyday of nationalism and empire, and may have been coloured in its early years by the Eurocentric perspective of its chief practitioners, but it has emerged, especially in the years since 1945, as one of the few scholarly disciplines which has attempted to internationalize its institutions and its perspective. We have begun, though perhaps in fits and starts and not always as successfully as we yet hope, to build a disciplinary structure in which the participants can relate intersubjectively, even, to use an overused term, dialogically. At our last two congresses in Tokyo and Edmonton, with so many participants from outside the Euro-American sphere, we even had a lively discussion of 'Occidentalism'.[6]

Edward Said, who one wishes had been present to hear those discussions, holds a much less benign view of comparative literature, his own discipline. In his well-known critique of our field in *Culture and Imperialism*, he claims that:

> ...it is evident that when most European thinkers were celebrating humanity or culture they were principally celebrating ideas and values they ascribed to their own national culture, or to Europe as distinct from the Orient, Africa or even the Americas. Even the comparatists trained in the dignified tradition that produced Curtius and Auerbach [who was Said's own teacher!] showed little interest in Asian, African or Latin American texts.... But the field was epistemologically organized as a sort of hierarchy, with Europe and its Latin Christian literatures as its center and top.

He accuses the discipline, in other words, of touting ideals but violating them in practice. Without simply admitting that comparative literature, like all disciplines, was of course constrained by the ideological and institutional realities from which it emerged, he ridicules the idealistic words of those who, like Edward Woodberry, the holder of the first North American Chair of Comparative Literature (at Columbia, where Said teaches!), spoke of the discipline's potential role in fostering 'a bright new world, a new age, a world citizenship', or of 'the intercommunication, the commingling of nations, the unity of mankind'.. To Said, the student of *realpolitik*, of worldly power and its abuses, such sentiments seem to have a Pollyanna-ish quality. He says it 'uncomplicatedly and naively resonates with the influence of Croce and DeSanctis, and also with the earlier ideas of Wilhelm von Humboldt'. And then — without evidence, or citation — Said leaps to the conclusion that 'academic work in Comparative Literature' implies 'the notion that Europe and the United States together were the center of the world, not simply by virtue of their political positions, but also because their literatures were the ones most worth studying' (45–7).

Within the space of four pages, Said goes even further, contending that:

> Without significant exception the universalizing discourses of modern Europe and the United States assume the silence, willing or otherwise, of the non-European world. There is incorporation; there is inclusion; there is direct rule; there is coercion. But there is only infrequently an acknowledgement that the colonized [that is, 'all other'] people should be heard from, their ideas known.

The international colloquium of which we are a part speaks volumes to the excesses of such generalizations. As does the work of comparative literature as a discipline. We know that we have much yet to do to expand our reach and compass. But we have come farther than most other disciplines in listening to — and attending to — as many of the world's cultural voices as we can. Current work in post-colonial studies, by contrast, is almost exclusively being pursued in Anglophone or Francophone cultures and draws both its rhetoric and its principal intellectual nourishment and valorization from the theoretical and philosophical traditions of England and the European continent.[7] Despite its origins and early history, comparative literature has now moved beyond those cultural and geographical limits, as it has always, at least ideally, sought to do. In their insistence that the path to the Other, culturally speaking, is through language, comparatists have also long recognized that the more intimately one comes to know the language of the Other, the more one has to acknowledge the Other's ultimate incommensurability.

Paul Valéry concluded his after-dinner speech by proposing a toast:

> However perfectly we know a foreign language, however deeply we penetrate into the intimacy of a people that is not our people, I think it impossible to flatter ourselves that we understand its language and literary works as a native of that country may. There is always some fraction of meaning, some delicate or faraway echo that escapes us; we can never be sure of full and unquestioned possession.... Between these literatures, as they embrace, there remains always some inviolable tissue. It may be worn extremely thin, reduced to the utmost fineness; it can never be broken.... [The intercourse] of these impenetrable literatures is no less fruitful for that. On the contrary, it is more fruitful than if we understood each other perfectly. Creative misunderstanding is at work, and the result is an endless progeny of unforeseen values.

Whatever else one makes of the unabashedly erotic metaphor Valéry here unfolds, the suggestion is that the possibilities — Homi Bhabha's pessimism notwithstanding — for fruitful cultural interaction, and consequently for moving toward a global sense of cultural community, are enhanced rather than diminished by an acknowledgement of difference and impenetrability. If the spread of international cultural and intellectual exchange has indeed heightened, rather than diminished, our awareness of what may well be ultimate difference, need not be a cause for despair at all. Quite the contrary. History, and the history of colonialism in particular, has taught us that most efforts to make the Other commensurable have usually been efforts to make it 'one's own'. Seen in this light, textual culture, in its inherent heterogeneity and polyphony, can be seen to operate as a counterweight to the homogenizing, leveling tendencies of mass commercial culture. To the extent that the project of comparative literature as an international academic discipline is to honor this textual culture and to acknowledge — indeed to insist on — rather than deny, its inherent diversity, this project deserves to be applauded rather than disparaged, especially by all those who are concerned that we not perpetuate, into the twenty-first century — and perhaps even ironically under the banner of post-colonial studies — the very homogenizing, universalizing discourse we pretend to abjure.

University of Toledo

Notes

1 'Discours au PEN Club' a toast at a banquet in Paris, 1925. First appeared in *Les nouvelles littéraires* June 6, 1925; reprinted in Valéry, *Oeuvres*, Volume E (1935). My English text is Denise Folliot's translation, given the title 'An After-Dinner Speech' in Paul Valéry, *The Art of Poetry*, *Collected Works of Paul Valéry*, vol. 7. Princeton University Press, 1958, pp. 275–8.

2 Its coming out, as it were, was the 1984 University of Essex symposium on 'Europe and its Others'.

3 Also suggestively titled was Bruce Robbins' 1992 review essay in *Victorian Studies*: 'Colonial Discourse: A Paradigm and its Discontents'.

4 Not every postcolonial critic sees the issue that way. The Routledge *Post-Colonial Studies Reader*, for example, contains a polemic by Aijaz Ahmad entitled 'Jameson's Rhetoric of Otherness and the "National Allegory"', which takes issue with Fredric Jameson's contention that, as Ahmad formulates it, 'one cannot proceed from the premise of a real unity of the world without falling back into some general liberal and humanistic universalism.' Ahmad is disappointed that Jameson, whose Marxist stance he has long admired, does not recognize that 'what gives the world its unity ... is not a humanist ideology but a ferocious struggle between capital and labour....' What makes Ahmad's disagreement with Jameson (which originally appeared in the journal *Social Text* in 1987, responding to a Jameson piece in an earlier issue) interesting to us now is perhaps less the particulars of his argument about class struggle than his readiness to admit that it is fully possible to accept — indeed embrace — the idea of global unity without necessarily being a partisan of some kind of discredited ideology, 'liberal-humanist' or otherwise.

5 Herder's place in the history of discourse on colonialism and the relevance of his ideas to the current discourse on the Other has yet to be fully acknowledged in England and America. Astonishingly, there is still no comprehensive translation of Herder's works available in English. Nor has there been much dialogue between scholars of literature and those in such fields as anthropology or the history of exploration who have long recognized Herder's key contribution. See, for example, Gerald Broce, 'Herder and Ethnography', *Journal of the History of the Behavioral Sciences*, 22 (April 1986), pp. 150-70, and Urs Bitterli's *Cultures in Conflict: Encounters between European and Non-European Cultures*, 1492–1800, tr. R. Robertson

(Stanford University Press, 1989). Perhaps the fact that so many scholars in the humanities have become interested in the work of anthropologists like Clifford Geertz will help to stimulate more cross-disciplinary discussion.

6 It is significant that two books with this main title have just been published (both, coincidentally, at Oxford, though with two different presses): James Carrier's edited collection *Occidentalism: Images of the West*, and Xiaomei Chen's *Occidentalism: A Theory of Counter-Discourse in Post-Mao China*.

7 It is also less of a conversation — much less dialogic — than it ought to be. For example, a volume which has just appeared, *After Colonialism: Imperial Histories and Postcolonial Displacements*, brings together, among other contributions, an essay by Said ('Secular Interpretation, the Geographical Element, and the Methodology of Imperialism') which had already become part of his *Culture and Imperialism*, and an essay by Pagden ('The Effacement of Difference: Colonialism and the Origins of Nationalism in Diderot and Herder') which has since become a part of his *European Encounters with the New World*. Both were originally contributions to a series of seminars and colloquia on colonialism and related topics held at Princeton in the years 1990–1992. And yet they hardly inform one another. Said's work here and elsewhere, for example, like so much influential work on post-colonial subjects, seems to operate with certain fixed points — and spheres — of reference, linguistic as well as cultural, points of reference which may not be common to other fields or, ironically, to scholars working out of other — that is, different — intellectual traditions. It should come as no surprise to learn, as we have at this colloquium, that scholars in many parts of the globe — East Asia, for example — may in fact consider post-colonial studies to be one of the more Eurocentric, or at least one of the more geoculturally parochial, of contemporary academic and scholarly enterprises.

Works Cited

Ahmad, Aijaz 1987 'Jameson's Rhetoric of Otherness and the "National Allegory"' in *Social Text* 17: pp. 3–25.

Ashcroft, Bill, Gareth Griffiths and Helen Tiffen 1989 *The Empire Writes Back: Theory and Practice in Post-Colonial Literatures*. Routledge, London.

—— 1994 *Post-Colonial Studies Reader*. Routledge, London.

Bhabha, Homi K. 1992 'Postcolonial Criticism' in *Redrawing the Boundaries: The Transformation of English and American Literary Studies*. MLA, New York: pp. 437–65.

Bitterli, Urs 1989 *Cultures in Conflict: Encounters Between European and Non-European Cultures, 1492–1800*, tr. R. Robertson. Stanford University Press.

Broce, Gerald 1986 'Herder and Ethnography' in *Journal of the History of the Behavioral Sciences* 22: pp. 150–70.

Carrier, James G. (ed.) 1995 *Ocidentalism: Images of the West*. Clarendon Press, Oxford.

Chen Xiaomei 1995 *Occidentalism: A Theory of Counter-Discourse in Post-Mao China*. Oxford University Press.

Jacoby, Russell 1995 'Marginal Returns: The Trouble with Post-Colonial Theory' in *Lingua Franca* 5, No. 6: pp. 30–7.

Pagden, Anthony 1993 *European Encounters with the New World: From Renaissance to Romanticism*. Yale University Press.

Prakash, Gyan (ed.) 1995 *After Colonialism: Imperial Histories and Postcolonial Displacements*. Princeton University Press.

Robbins, Bruce 1992 'Colonial Discourse: A Paradigm and its Discontents' in *Victorian Studies* 35: pp. 209–14.

Said, Edward 1979 *Orientalism*. Vintage, New York.

—— 1993 *Culture and Imperialism*. Knopf, New York.

Todorov, Tzvetan 1982 *La conquête de l'Amérique: La question de l'autre*. Seuil, Paris.

Williams, Patrick and Laura Chrisman 1994 *Colonial Discourse and Post-Colonial Theory: A Reader*. Columbia University Press.

Valéry, Paul 1958 (1925) 'An After-Dinner Speech', tr. Denise Folliot in Jackson Matthews (ed.) *The Art of Poetry*, vol. 7 of *Collected Works of Paul Valéry*. Princeton University Press.

WALTER F. VEIT

Misunderstanding as Condition of Intercultural Understanding

THE QUESTION

> *Delicatus ille est adhuc cui patria dulcis est, fortis autem cui omne*
> *solum patria est, perfectus vero cui mundus totus exilium est ...*

Can we understand other cultures at all? This question has been answered negatively just as frequently as positively. Given the eruptions of conflict between nations, doubts and frustration persist. In fact, these doubts are so strong that the very possibility is negated. It is therefore necessary to investigate the cognitive foundations of both literary and ethnographical or cultural studies since both are wedged within the dialectic of the foreign and the familiar in their efforts not only to know the other but also to make meaning of it.

I propose to establish the function of misunderstanding as necessary in order to achieve understanding in the study of relationships between cultures. I will then present some cases of cultural misunderstandings in eighteenth-century European writings, particularly in Georg Forster's *Voyage Round the World*, and discuss their necessity and productivity in an intercultural dialogue. This discussion will remind us of the dialectical relationship between the understanding of the self and the other as the foundation of all interculturality. An epistemological analysis of the textual interpretation will, then, look at the philosophical analyses of understanding in Wilhelm Dilthey, Martin Heidegger and Hans-Georg Gadamer. It will also draw attention to theories which take human existence to be dialogical.

It is reported that the indigenous Australians seemed to have noticed the big ship of James Cook approaching their coast only when captain and crew rowed the small boat ashore. And when the indigenes saw the white faces of Cook's party they took them to be returning ancestral spirits. Total non-comprehension is followed by misunderstanding. It is not suggested here that they could not see the tall ship but, rather, that what they saw had no meaning for them.

Keeping in mind that understanding, in a first approach, is the purpose of dialogue; we need to investigate the process of gaining understanding. What we call misunderstanding seems to be only a slight variation of not understanding at all. But is it? What if misunderstanding has a special function in the process of communication which, if Habermas is right, belongs to the three anthropological givens of humanity: work, communication and domination? What if misunderstanding is the first step in overcoming non-communication? The problem is obviously of fundamental importance to every human being, be they politician in search for peace among nations, scholars and scientists in general, or to cultural studies and comparative literature in particular which deal with communication of a special kind.

In a preliminary analysis we could point out that this process of communication, this dialogue between people, directly or indirectly, seems to involve an understanding self and an other which may be understood or perhaps misunderstood. Sometimes the self is also described as the familiar, the other as the foreign.

THE EVIDENCE

I would like to analyse the problem more closely with the help of an example taken from Georg Forster's account of his *Voyage Round the World* with Captain Cook (1772–5). Forster writes that on Saturday 21 August 1773, a party from the *Resolution* takes a walk on a lesser peninsula of O-Taheitee, meeting with and being entertained by very friendly natives:

> We walked up along its banks [of a brook] to a perpendicular rock, fringed with various tufted shrubberies, from whence it fell in a crystalline column, and was collected at the bottom into a smooth limpid pond, surrounded with many species of odoriferous flowers. This spot, where we had a prospect of the plain below us, and of the sea beyond it, was one of the most beautiful I had ever seen, and could not fail of bringing to remembrance the most fanciful descriptions of poets, which it eclipsed in beauty. In the shade of trees, whose branches hung over the water, we enjoyed a pleasant gale, which softened the heat of the day, and amidst the solemn uniform noise of the waterfall, which was but seldom interrupted by the whistling of birds, we sat down to describe our new acquisitions. (1986:174)

Even if Forster, in order to set the scene at the beginning of the chapter, had not quoted some famous lines from Book VI of Virgil's *Aeneid*, we would still recognize the poetic language of Arcadia, containing everything the *topos* of the *locus amoenus* requires. However, the enjoyment is not to last:

> Our walk continued along the shore beyond another marai, much like the first, to a neat house, where a very fat man, who seemed to be the chief of the district, was lolling on his wooden pillow ... a woman who sat down near him, crammed down

his throat by handfuls the remains of a large baked fish, and several bread-fruits, which he swallowed with a voracious appetite. His countenance was the picture of phlegmatic insensibility, and seemed to witness that all his thoughts centred in the care of his paunch.... The great degree of satisfaction which we had enjoyed on our different walks in this island, and particularly the pleasure of this day's excursion, was diminished by the appearance and behaviour of the chief, and the reflection which naturally arose from thence. We had flattered ourselves with the pleasing fancy of having found at least one little spot of the world, where a whole nation, without being lawless barbarians, aimed at a certain frugal equality in their way of living, and whose hours of enjoyment were justly proportioned to those of labour and rest. Our disappointment was therefore very great, when we saw a luxurious individual spending his life in the most sluggish inactivity, and without one benefit to society, like the privileged parasites of more civilized climates, fattening on the superfluous produce of the soil, of which he robbed the labouring multitude. His indolence, in some degree, resembled that which is frequent in India and the adjacent kingdoms of the East, and deserved every mark of indignation which Sir John Mandeville expressed in his Asiatic travels. That worthy knight, who, top-ful of chivalry, and the valourous spirit of his time, devoted his life to constant activity, was highly incensed at the sight of a monster of laziness, who passed his days 'withouten doynge of ony dedes of armes', and lived 'everemore thus in ese, as a swyn that is fedde in sty, or to ben made fat'.

In a footnote to this text Forster quotes at length the passage from the *Voyages and Travaylles of Sir John Maundevile, Knight [which Treateth of the Way to Hierusalem & of Marvayles of Inde, with other Ilaunds and Countryes]* which was published in English in London in 1500, and supposed to be a translation of Jean de Mandeville's *Voyages d'outre mer*, written around 1357 and printed for the first time in 1480. As we know today, the book was an early literary hoax, a compilation of texts of other authors. At the time and right up to Forster, it was a great and unchallenged success dominating the Western perception of the Near and Far East.

Forster's description still bristles with indignation when remembering the fat man of O-Taheitee. Although he should have been instructed by Descartes' suggestion that by travelling 'we may be enabled to form a more correct judgement regarding our own, and be prevented from thinking that everything contrary to our customs is ridiculous and irrational as is the custom of those who have not seen anything', Georg Forster is clearly unable to overcome his aversion which seems to be based on an unreflected pre-judgement offering a paradigmatic case of cultural misunderstanding. For a misunderstanding it is. The commentary points out that 'corpulence was the prerogative, sign of dignity and ideal of beauty of members of the [Tahitian] nobility. In order to comply with this ideal a methodical fattening treatment had to be undertaken' (1986, IV:329). How does the misunderstanding arise? What are the elements of this pre-judgement? The description juxtaposes the experience of the 'fat man' as an alien, disillusioning reality to an economic, social and political ideal in the spirit and tradition of the European Enlightenment. Although Forster acknowledges as a 'pleasing fancy' his perception of a civilization of 'frugal equality' in which all levels in Tahitian society enjoy equally work and leisure, he continues to describe the scene in terms of the critique levelled by the Enlightenment against the social reality in Europe itself. He sees already a destruction of a seemingly existing paradise by a division of classes into a 'labouring multitude' and 'privileged parasites' who exist 'without any benefit to society'. It is obvious that Forster understands the experience in terms of the completely opposite values of the European Enlightenment.

However, this misunderstanding is initiated by a further misunderstanding on a deeper level: it is based on a literary hoax, Sir John Mandeville's imaginary voyage to India which gave rise to the view of a luxurious, debauched Orient which has dominated the European imagination for centuries. It became the complete counterpart to an ascetic spirituality Europe was supposed to represent or, at least, aspire to. The cognitive process is obvious: the quotation of and the comparison with an image of the Orient well known in Europe makes it possible to convey not only an image of the Tahitian experience but also the resentment of the observer. On a different occasion (Veit 1979) I have analysed the function of these quotations for the description and understanding of the foreign and the new. As it turns out, comparison is the only way in which the new and foreign can be approached. Thus the understanding must of necessity be related to something thought of as familiar. Before we talk of misunderstanding we could say: understanding must, at least initially, be of something else than that which is observed. The added twist in Forster's account is, of course, that the pre-judgement is based on another misunderstanding. It seems, however, that only in this fashion can a dialogue be initiated. Without the image and critique of the debauched Orient in mind, the 'fat man' might not have rated a mention.

On a third and even deeper level, invective and critique are not directed here as in other places of the travelogue only on the surface against the unfamiliar customs of the islanders or the Indians and Chinese. Rather, they are directed against the familiar self, 'the privileged parasites of more civilized climates', in other words, the social condition in Europe itself. One could argue that the whole purpose of the voyage was the search for the Antipodes, and the purpose of Forster's description that of a search for the counterpart of Europe, an earthly paradise. The misunderstanding is given a function of its own. It is turned into cultural criticism which, in other places, uncovers the dialectic of Enlightenment in no uncertain terms albeit *avant la lettre*. It becomes plain that Forster's effort toward understanding Pacific cultures is completely directed by a Eurocentric perspective and, in more than one respect, a Eurocentric interest.

The analysis has not yet arrived at its final target. It has become clear that the misunderstanding has its roots in the very process of understanding the other, so that we can say that misunderstanding is primarily and essentially 'understanding differently'. It appears, too, that the misunderstanding has opened the dialogue with the misunderstood other. Although the incident reported by Forster is not returned to nor its understanding revised, there is some indication that Forster was aware of the pitfalls of describing the alien. His preface to the *Voyage* must be read as an outline and justification of his research methodology. But the dialogue has only started in his description, it does not end there. In fact, it is continued in the commentaries of the editors of the critical edition and, come to think of it, in this very paper. We become aware that Forster's dialogue with the unfamiliar and new is the location and origin of his and our understanding and, with it, of his and our misunderstanding.

THE THEORY

This brief analysis could be repeated with numerous examples from the *Voyage* which turns out to be not only one of the most important travelogues of the eighteenth century and hardly surpassed since in the genre, but also the best source for epistemological considerations. The results of our interpretation so far allow us to look at its position in the development of epistemology after Kant. On the one hand, Forster appears to be the ideal Enlightenment scientist who strives for objectivity; his text, on the other hand, offers enough hints towards his awareness of the importance of the cognitive subject and the productivity — not necessarily in the right direction — of its perspectives. After discussing the difficulties in overcoming fabulous assertions and the problem that the establishment of facts does not increase knowledge, he continues:

> Besides this, two travellers seldom saw the same object in the same manner, and each reported the fact differently, according to his sensations, and his peculiar mode of thinking. It was therefore necessary to be acquainted with the observer, before any use could be made of his observations. The traveller was no longer to trust chance for a variety of occurrences, but to make use of his first discovery, as the thread of Ariadne, by the help of which he might guide his steps through the labyrinth of human knowledge. It was therefore requisite that he should have penetration sufficient to combine different facts, and to form general views from thence, which might in some measure guide him to new discoveries, and point out the proper objects of farther investigation. This was the idea with which I embarked on the late voyage round the world, and agreeably to which I have collected materials for the present publication, as far as the time, my situation and abilities, would permit. I have always endeavoured in this narrative to connect the ideas arising from different occurrences, in order, if possible, to throw more light upon the nature of the human mind, and to lift the soul into that exalted station, from whence the extensive view must 'justify the ways of God to man.' Whether I have succeeded or failed in the attempt, remains to be decided; but the rectitude of the intention cannot, I trust, be misconstrued. I have sometimes obeyed the powerful dictates of my heart, and given voice to my feelings; for, as I do not pretend to be free from the weaknesses common to my fellow-creatures, it was necessary for every reader to know the colour of the glass through which I looked. Of this at least I am certain, that a gloomy livid tinge hath never clouded my sight. Accustomed to look on all the

various tribes of men, as entitled to an equal share of my good will, and conscious, at the same time, of the rights which I possess in common with every individual among them, I have endeavoured to make my remarks with a retrospect to our general improvement and welfare; and neither attachment nor aversion to particular nations have influenced my praise or censure. (1986, I:13–14)

This is the closest Georg Forster comes to formulating his hermeneutics of the foreign and familiar. It is obvious that there is no longer a trust in the certainty of personal observation and the veracity of descriptions, both of which are stressed by the instructions given by the Royal Society of London to travellers into unexplored parts of the globe (cf. Sprat 1959). It is a vast extension of the consciousness of the conditions of knowing and understanding. It is indicative of the beginning of modern hermeneutics in the writings of Schleiermacher in the eighteenth century, followed by Wilhelm Dilthey[2] in the nineteenth, and Martin Heidegger and Hans-Georg Gadamer in the twentieth.

The doctrine of the Enlightenment which elevates doubt to a universal methodology for the understanding of texts and other cultural phenomena is still visible in Schleiermacher's statement: 'Rigorous practice starts with the assumption that misunderstanding arises by itself and that understanding has to be intended and sought at every point' (1974:82). It is well known that Dilthey refined Schleiermacher's methodology through psychology, returning in a certain sense to Terence's claim in his comedy *Heautontimorumenos* (The Self-tormentor) to understanding human affairs because 'I am a human being and nothing human is foreign to me' ('Homo sum; humani nil a me alienum puto' [I,1:25]). But a rigorous methodology is necessary to come to an intersubjectively valid understanding. The process of understanding, presented in the figure of the circle, has in it a promise of completion at which point a perfect understanding will be reached. Hermeneutics is revolutionized when Martin Heidegger asserts in his ontological analysis of understanding that Dilthey's methodological circle of understanding is not a vicious circle to be avoided at all cost but, in fact, an existential circle that we need to get into if we want to understand at all. Moreover, understanding is essential to human existence. It is not a question of whether we can or cannot use our ability to understand; as human beings we always already understand (Heidegger 1962:31–4). This understanding embraces those with whom we are, the others, because human existence, *Dasein*, is a Being-with. Therefore Heidegger can argue:

> Being-with is such that the disclosedness of the Dasein-with of Others belongs to it; this means that because Dasein's Being is Being-with, its understanding of Being already implies the understanding of Others. This understanding, like any understanding, is not an acquaintance derived from knowledge about them, but a primordially existential kind of Being, which, more than anything else, makes such knowledge and acquaintance possible. Knowing oneself [*Sichkennen*] is grounded in Being-with, which understands primordially. (160–1)

The being-with others is primordially disclosed in human action and, particularly important for us, in language. Whatever we do, whatever we say, our acting and speaking presupposes the other. This presupposition does not prevent misunderstanding, it makes it first of all possible. It also makes misunderstanding rather likely since all understanding is perspectivistic, that is, directed by my perception of the past, my present interest and my anticipation of the future. But it is in misunderstanding the other that the other is recognized as the other which does not want to be mistaken for a familiar being. Expressed differently, in the process of cognition, misunderstanding constitutes and understands the other as foreign, unfamiliar, new. With respect to foreign cultures, understanding has two fundamental aspects: the desire to understand the foreign other, to appropriate and integrate it into the familiar; and, at the same time, the need to preserve the foreign as foreign. But within this juxtaposition the familiar is also and first of all established as the self and understood as the familiar. In the dialectic of appropriation and rejection we find the birthplace of self-consciousness and, at the same time, the locus of misunderstanding. All misunderstanding of the other in the cultural area is the necessary corollary of the understanding of the self.

The chance of bringing the misunderstanding to an understanding, without mistaking the other for the self, lies precisely in the dialogic structure of human existence, in the fact that every self constitutes itself in juxtaposition to every other on the wide fields of human action and human speech. Building on this position, Hans-Georg Gadamer shows that in the dialogue of self and other, of the familiar and the foreign, misunderstanding is overcome only and in the same degree and to the same extent as the self comes to an understanding of its own being. In Gadamer's own words: 'Self-understanding always occurs through understanding something other than the self, and includes the unity and integrity of the other' (1992:295).

Gadamer can draw a conclusion from this existential circle that all 'hermeneutic work is based on a polarity of familiarity and strangeness' (295). In fact in the context of a discussion of the claim already found in Schleiermacher and others that the interpreter will understand the meaning of a text better than the author, he can claim that 'not just occasionally but always, the meaning of a text goes beyond its author' and that understanding is, indeed, not a matter of better or lesser understanding, but that 'It is enough to say that we understand in a *different way, if we understand at all*' (296–7).

In consequence, we need to realize that on the epistemological level understanding is precisely *understanding differently* — or first of all and in common parlance, misunderstanding. Put differently: understanding can only happen if and when the foreign is understood as the other and not misunderstood as the familiar. There is a tension between the otherness and strangeness of a text and what it wants to tell us, and its familiarity due to the language in which it addresses us. '*The true locus of hermeneutics is this in-between*' (295) which is located in language.

Forster's text demonstrates the epistemological situation very clearly: because the situation of the 'fat man' is experienced as a familiar phenomenon (already known from literature) we recognize in the text an attempt at an appropriation of and a refusal of dialogue with the other. The appropriation is made possible by a pre-judgement: in the first instance that there is nothing unfamiliar in the observation, and thereafter that the experience is pre-judged by a comparison with another observation in literature and, lest we forget, Forster's personal experience and judgement of the European social situation. The imagery of a 'parasite' shows its cognitive strength as a convincing topos such that it does not even allow for an objection. Thus any dialogue is refused.

It is worth recognizing here that it is the scientific ethos which is driving Forster's description. Using the method of comparing and contrasting the phenomenon of the 'fat man' to reports of similar phenomena found in authoritative travel reports he tries to secure 'objectivity', that is, to describe the phenomenon 'itself', to penetrate to its characteristics, the *Eigentliche* in the literal sense of the word. But this method of securing the object is precisely the method of avoidance of dialogue and must necessarily lead to misunderstanding. Any scientific methodology can only verify the inherent expectation, it cannot deal with the truth of the other.

I do not have to mention that hermeneutic principles such as 'productivity of pre-judgement and fore-knowledge', 'horizon of expectation', 'effective history', and 'productivity of temporal distance', can easily be developed from this basis. However, the crucial position of language which is obviously the key to hermeneutics is too broad a field to be discussed here.

Other writers concerned with the problem of the foreign and misunderstanding have followed Gadamer's lead. In his recent book *The Sting of the Foreign* (1990), Bernhard Waldenfels investigates the phenomenology of borderline situations in discussing the problem of the self and the foreign under headings such as 'dialogue and discourse', 'experience of the foreign between appropriation and expropriation' and 'beyond the subject principle'. He comes to conclusions which are very similar to those of Gadamer. He states that 'the familiar and the foreign originate at the same time and change at the same time' (65) and, agreeing with Merleau-Ponty, that 'it is necessary to learn how we regard as foreign that which is our own, and as our own that which was foreign to us' (9). But on the more practical level of the much discussed phenomenon of ethnocentricity, he seems to support our interpretation of Forster's text.

Ethnocentricity, which has been and still is much discussed in anthropology and ethnology, must be seen as a phenomenon of misunderstanding in which the misunderstanding of the foreign turns into an understanding of the familiar and an affirmation of the self as the correct, the good and the civilized, while the foreign is mostly depicted as the wild, uncivilized and, even, evil. The topoi of the 'noble savage' in good, and of 'Asian luxuriousness' and 'Asian despotism' in bad, are well-known examples. But significantly, such a turn has its particular uses: it constitutes the other either as a good or bad example for the self. This boomerang-function of human interest seems to be especially the function of cultural misunderstanding with reference to experiences which are negatively perceived. They generate cautionary tales. However, whenever the experience is positive, its use is to criticize the self for not achieving such a positive situation. In both cases the familiar norms prevail. These norms prevail, too, in a situation where the effort to understand the foreign turns into a *dépossession*, into an expropriation of the self in favour of the foreign. Here, as Waldenfels points out, egocentrism is removed and the foreign and unfamiliar takes the place of what is our own and characteristic. He argues that:

> A European buddhist remains a European who has converted to buddhism. In so far as the foreign is seen and valued *only* in contrast to what is our own, ethnocentricity remains unbroken even if it comes only in the harmless form of chinoiseries. (63)

It remains to be discussed, however, whether such a disowning of the self in favour of the foreign (the 'noble savage' for example), where the foreign takes the place of the familiar, is in fact a surrender to the foreign. The foreign cannot but be appropriated on the terms of the self. It seems, therefore, more likely that the norms of the self prevail, and a dialogue is again rejected.

An example is provided by the effort of Australian governments to foster stronger links with Asia, to promote *Asia-literacy*, even *Asianization*. All this occurs within an intense debate about the self of Australia, whether it is Asian (because of its location), or European (because of the origin and language of the majority of its inhabitants). The critique of Lee Kuan Yew, the elder statesman of Singapore, of the position taken by Australia makes the view of the other pretty clear. It is seen again as an appropriation of the other, not a dialogue of equals.

Although mentioned only once, Gadamer's findings with respect to the foreign and the familiar are corroborated in Bernard McGrane's analysis of the pre-judgement in anthropology in his book *Beyond Anthropology: Society and the Other* (1989). His statements sound very familiar when he investigates the theoretical stances involved in the apperception of the other in three historical periods (the Renaissance, the Enlightenment and the nineteenth century): 'A culture which "discovers" that which is alien to itself also thereby fundamentally reveals that which it is to himself' (ix). And most significantly:

> In the early twentieth century, finally, the authoritative paradigm for interpreting and explaining the difference of the Other undergoes a mutation once again and now for us, 'Culture' accounts for the difference of the Other. We think under the hegemony of the anthropological response to the alienness of the Other; we are, today, contained within an anthropological concept of the Other. Anthropology has become our modern way of seeing the Other as, both fundamentally and merely, culturally different. (ix)

McGrane considers at length the implications of the self-understanding of anthropologists as *scientists*, armed with methodologies which allow them to be *objective*, that is, to distance themselves from the culture they research. But precisely this distancing became methodologically unacceptable and was to be replaced by the famous *participant observation*:

> This pretheoretical legitimizing framework, however, preserves-while-denying the same historical power relations toward the alien Other insofar as 'participant observation' is really interested in observing rather than participating; i.e., it is analytically really about observation rather than participation; it is epistemologically committed to the sovereignty of observation and its monologue *about* the Other rather than the democracy of genuine participation and its dialogue *with* the Other. (124)

For the sake of Aristotelian science anthropology has rejected the participatory Socratic dialogue which entails 'the ability to be in ignorance' (126). Therefore:

> ...atrophy of dialogue is, thus, *condition* of our contemporary anthropological discipline. Anthropological 'scientific method' is the decay of dialogue, the sustained, cultivated, and epistemologically enforced atrophy of dialogue.

McGrane refers also to a number of other anthropologists and ethnologists, students of culture, such as Johannes Fabian (1983) and Tzvetan Todorov (1965) who have come to similar conclusions. A parallel debate is continuing in German ethnography and cultural anthropology, involving scholars such as Wolfdietrich Schmied-Kowarzik (1980), Justin Stagl (1980, 1981), Peter Koepping (1980) and Hans Peter Duerr (1978, 1980). On the other hand, there is, surprisingly, very little mention of the problem in *Neue Anthropologie* (1973) a standard work edited by Hans-Georg Gadamer and Paul Vogler; surprising all the more as the discussion of our problem has become very intense indeed. This is amply demonstrated in the volume *Kulturthema Fremdheit* (1993), in which Alois Wierlacher has edited a great number of essays in which the topoi and areas of argumentation in research into the cultural phenomenology of the foreign are investigated. Nothing less than a critical *xenology* within the cultural sciences is intended. The urgency of the research is highlighted by reference to the nascent or militant racial, religious and cultural intolerance in Europe. Here as elsewhere the fundamental conflict manifests itself, the conflict between the universalist notion of human rights which was developed mostly during the Enlightenment and the modern anthropological view of the other, that is, as different but equal.

But it surprises again that the cognitive foundation for the proposed xenology, arising as it does from and in the context of earlier work by many in the area of intercultural studies,[3] is — judging by its extensive but strangely provincial bibliography — built on the work of Alfred Schütz (1974, 1944) and Helmuth Plessner (1983) and does not engage in a serious philosophical debate with Gadamer.

For our purposes, the whole problematic is brought again — and already for some time — into focus in Walter Schulz's discussion (1972: particularly 531–41) of Gadamer's analysis of historicity as a dialogue with the past in literature, with the radical other which nevertheless determines and addresses us as tradition. In Schulz's words, the effective history is substantively an all-embracing working out of truth in the dialogue with the other. If we can accept this existential position for our dialogue with the past, we are equally asked to accept the dialogue with the culturally foreign and the new as the over-arching existential situation for the understanding of the self. In the ontological understanding, the familiar is existentially bound to the foreign as all misunderstanding is bound to understanding, or as life is bound to death. It is out of this ontological situation that the cognitive function which I have tried to analyse can arise.

Monash University

Notes

1 This is the background to the quote from Hugo of St. Victor's *Didascalia*. Bernard McGrane's (1989:129) translation and use of the quote in his Conclusion is an amusing incident of misunderstanding, that is, avoidance of dialogue and a telling example of Gadamer's *Wirkungsgeschichte*: 'The man who finds his country sweet is only a raw beginner; the man for whom each country is as his own is already strong; but only the man for whom the whole word is as a foreign country is perfect (Eric Auerbach).'

2 Dilthey's influence is clearly visible in Adolf Bastian's instructions to researchers travelling abroad in his 'Allgemeine Begriffe der Ethnologie' in Georg von Neumayer (ed.) 1888 *Anleitung zu wissenschaftlichen Beobachtungen auf Reisen* 2, Aufl. 2 vols, Berlin, II, 236: 'When dealing with the natives of a foreign country, the first task for the traveller remains to maintain an objective point of view of observation in order to (— while disregarding as far as possible subjectively familiar prejudices —) to make his own the way of thinking of those who enter with him into an exchange of thoughts (— on his part to follow with his way of thinking their way and to think himself into it —) and in such manner to understand the often strictly logical reasoning in its concatenation of its connection, in spite of seeming non-reason.'

3 A. Wierlacher (ed.) 1987 *Perspektiven und Verfahren interkultureller Germanistik*, Iudicium, München; B. Thum and G-L. Fink (eds) 1993 *Praxis interkultureller Germanistik. Forschung – Bildung – Politik,* iudicium, München; J. Rehbein (ed.) 1985 *Interkulturelle Kommunikation,* Narr, Tübingen; D. Krusche 1985 *Literatur und Fremde. Zur Hermeneutik kulturräumlicher Distanz*, Iudicium, München.

Works Cited

Duerr, H. P. (ed.) 1981 *Der Wissenschaftler und das Irrationale,* 2 vols. Syndikat, Frankfurt.

Fabian, J. 1983 *Time and the Other: How Anthropology Makes its Object*. Columbia University Press.

Forster, G. A. 1986 *A Voyage Round the World (1772–1775)*, 4 vols, Sämtliche Schriften, Tagebücher, Briefe. Akademie-Verlag, Berlin.

Gadamer, H.-G. 1992 *Truth and Method*, 2nd rev. ed., tr. J. Weinsheimer and D. G. Marshall. Crossroad, New York.

—— and P. Vogler (eds) 1973 *Neue Anthropologie*, 7 vols. Dtv-Thieme, München-Stuttgart.

Heidegger, M. 1962 *Being and Time*, tr. and ed. J. Macquarrie and E. Robinson. Blackwell, Oxford.

Koepping, Kl.-P. 1980 'Probleme der Ethik der Ethnographie in Theorie und Methode' in Schmied-Kowarzik: pp. 93–105.

McGrane, Bernard 1989 *Beyond Anthropology: Society and the Other.* Columbia University Press.

Plessner, H. 1983 'Mit anderen Augen' in *Gesammelte Schriften*, vol. 8. Suhrkamp, Frankfurt.

Schleiermacher, Fr. D. E. 1974 *Hermeneutik*, ed. H. Kimmerle. Carl Winter, Heidelberg.

Schmied-Kowarzik, W. and J. Stagl 1980 *Grundfragen der Ethnologie: Beiträge zur gegenwärtigen Theorie-Diskussion.* Riemer, Berlin

Schulz, W. 1972 *Philosophie in der veränderten Welt.* Neske, Pfullingen.

Schütz, A. 1974 (1932) 'Grundzüge einer Theorie des Fremdverstehens' in *Der sinnhafte Aufbau der sozialen Welt: Eine Einleitung in die verstehende Soziologie.* Suhrkamp, Frankfurt.

Sprat, Th. 1959 (1667) *History of the Royal Society of London for the Improving of Natural Knowledge,* eds J. A. Cope and H. W. Jones. Washington University Studies, St Louis.

Stagl, J. 1981 'Die Beschreibung des Fremden in der Wissenschaft' in H. P. Duerr (ed.): vol. 1, pp. 273–95.

Veit, W. 1979 'Intellectual Tradition and Pacific Discoveries — The Function of Quotations in Georg Forster's *Voyage Round the World*' in *Captain James Cook — Image and Impact. South Seas Discoveries and the World of Letters. Vol. 2 The Pacific Syndrome: Conditions and Consequences,* ed. W. Veit. The Hawthorn Press, Melbourne: pp. 95–117.

Waldenfels, B. 1990 *Der Stachel des Fremden.* Suhrkamp, Frankfurt.

Wierlacher, A. (ed.) 1987 *Perspektiven und Verfahren interkultureller Germanistik.* Iudicium, München.

H. VAN GORP

Dialogism, Literary Genres and Intercultural (Mis)Understanding

I would like to discuss here Bakhtin's concept of dialogism in relation to the notions of speech genres and intercultural (mis)understanding. My point (hypothesis) is that misunderstanding seems inherent to the diachronical and intercultural transfer of literary genres, because of the 'loss' of their original 'Sitz im Leben'. In Bakhtin's words: the life of literary genres necessarily implies a sort of 'monologization' or 'neutralization'. I will try to illustrate this (hypo)thesis with examples out of the history of the modern novel in sixteenth- to eighteenth-century Western Europe. Finally, I will make some critical remarks on Bakhtin's concept of monologization.

BAKHTIN'S CONCEPT OF SPEECH GENRES
Our starting point is some passages from Bakhtin's essay on 'Speech genres' in which he tries to explain the major aspects of the genre concept, namely: the dialogic principle (implication of the addressee, responsiveness, achievement); the pre-existence of the genre (it exists before the particular use of it); and the coexistence of first and second speech genres. Together with the notion of 'chronotope', that is, the historical situation (time and space to which any genre refers and of which it gives a world view), these three aspects form the essence, so to speak, of the concept of speech genre according to Bakhtin.

The dialogic principle. The concept of speech genre is imbued with the Bakhtinian brand par excellence — 'dialogism'. Speech genres are conceived of as speech acts that presuppose a speaker and an addressee, as well as a concrete historical and ideological situation. In other words, all cultural texts are situated in such a context, so that speech utterances draw effects of meaning from the multiple and variable competing discourses or speech practices which coexist in a society at a given moment (Zavala 1990:77–8). As Bakhtin notes in a reflection on the human sciences:

> Le texte ne vit qu'en contact avec un autre texte (contexte). Ce n'est qu'en leur point de contact que la lumière jaillit, qui éclaire à l'arrière et à l'avant, faisant que le texte participe d'un dialogue ... Dès que nous faisons du dialogue un texte compact, en d'autres termes, dès que nous effaçons la distinction des voix, ... le sens profond ... disparâit. (1984:384–5)

In order to interpret a speech genre it is thus necessary to take into account the following data: who speaks? to whom does one speak? in which particular situation? What is mostly forgotten is: at which question (even not expressed) does the speaker or writer give or fail to give an answer, and for whom and for which reason?

The pre-existence of speech genres. Speech genres, moreover, already exist as a sort of 'language system'. In other words, one does not invent a genre, but one 'sub-scribes' oneself in an already existing type of discourse. The generic patterns in which we put our words are, generally speaking, more flexible and more free than language forms. They vary according to the circumstances, the social position and the personal relation of the interlocutors. A number of speech genres manifest themselves as fairly stable and even prescriptive, so that the personal intention of the individual speaker is limited to the boundaries of the genre concerned; only minor nuances in the expression are allowed. Other genres are more free, so that there is plenty of room, within the given boundaries, for a creative restructuration. A generic competence makes it possible for speakers/writers to realize their discursive intention.

The co-existence of primary and secondary speech genres. In the global field of 'relatively stable types' of utterances (1986:60), Bakhtin makes an important distinction between primary (or simple) and secondary (or more complex) speech genres. Primary genres are specific forms of individual and spontaneous discourse, characterized by its alternation of interlocutors. The most typical examples are the everyday dialogue, the report (question-answer; order-execution) and the correspondence by letters. Secondary genres are more complex, arising in a comparatively higher developed and organized cultural, primarily written, communication. Bakhtin mentions novels, dramas, all kinds of scientific research, major genres of commentary and so forth (1986:62). These secondary genres absorb and digest various primary genres, which will lose their immediate relation to actual reality. For example, rejoinders of everyday dialogue or letters found in a novel get a new existence in the novel as a whole. This 'localization' in a higher order of cultural exchange tends to a sort of 'monologization'. As Bakhtin notes:

> Le processus d'oubli progressif des auteurs — dépositaires du mot d'autrui. Le mot d'autrui devient anonyme, familier (sous une forme retravaillée, bien entendu); la conscience se monologise. On oublie complètement le rapport dialogique originel au mot d'autrui.... La conscience créatrice, en cours de monologisation, se complète de mots anonymes.... Après quoi, la conscience monologisée ... s'insère dans un dialogue nouveau (avec, désormais, de nouvelles voix d'autrui, extérieures). (1984:386)

Bakhtin underlines the necessity for literary genres to constantly feed on primary genres in order to revitalize themselves.

LITERARY GENRES AND INTERCULTURAL UNDERSTANDING

Against the background of the above, I would like to stress that the historical and intertextual situation in which specific secondary genres, narrative genres for example, have emerged, is equally important for understanding the 'generic' utterance. As Bakhtin rightly puts it, every utterance must be regarded primarily as a response to preceding utterances of the given sphere. Each utterance refutes, affirms, supplements, and relies on the others, presupposes them to be known, and somehow takes them into account (1986:91). If this is the case for primary genres, it certainly applies also, and even in a stronger way, to secondary ones.

Indeed, it is generally accepted that literary genres function in literary history as sort of problem-solving models (Wesseling 1991:18). They suggest specific solutions — whether consciously or not — to problems of form and content. The form problem concerns all sorts of topoi, stylistic devices, and strategies intended to instruct, entertain or persuade the reader. In order to achieve this, authors normally use and select appropriate primary forms next to successful secondary forms. As far as the content is concerned, specific contemporary problems of the time are often focused on or referred to. For the reader these literary genres constitute sets of expectations which steer the reading process. Generic repertoires may thus be regarded as bodies of shared knowledge in a certain historical and cultural context (19). These repertoires can be explicitly codified in various kinds of metatexts, such as poetic treatises, prefaces and reviews, but they are, anyhow, always implicitly present in the creative works themselves, that is, in their specific plots, characters, setting and worldview, since a genre, as any speech act, is an answer to or argument against other utterances on the same topic or in the same tradition. This fact, precisely, makes readers aware of a genre. Bakhtin speaks in this respect of utterances 'filled with dialogic overtones' (1986:92), which must be taken into account in order to fully understand the style (and thus the full meaning) of the utterance in question. The same is true for literary genres. Any literary work, when it is studied in greater depth under the concrete conditions of cultural communication, reveals to us many partially or completely concealed utterances of others with varying degrees of foreigness. Various viewpoints, worldviews, and trends cross, converge, and diverge in it. The subject of authors' communication inevitably becomes the arena where their opinions meet those of others. When writing, they always take into account the apperceptive background of the addressees' perception of their work: the extent to which the latter are familiar with the situation, whether they have special knowledge of the given cultural area of communication, their views and convictions, 'prejudices', sympathies and antipathies — all this will determine the active responsive understanding of the work (1986:94).

From such a genre concept it appears that the knowledge of the dialogic overtones and various voices implicitly present in a text (intertextuality) are necessary for fully understanding it in its actual intention. But this knowledge gradually diminishes during the post-processing activity from primary to secondary speech genres and, further on, to imitations, adaptations and translations. This is the well-known phenomenon of monologization and redialogization occurring in the life and evolution of literary genres. I would like to illustrate some of these cultural shifts (caused by, and in their turn leading to, 'other' cultural understandings of prototypical representatives of a genre) with examples from three narrative text types that knew a great success in seventeenth- and eighteenth-century Western Europe — the travel story, the picaresque novel and the Gothic novel. They form, at the same time, 'typical' examples of three kinds of 'transfer'.

Monologization in the travel story. The travel story is a secondary genre, based upon and integrating primary speech genres such as the logbook, the description and epistolary forms. These primary genres presume a certain objectivity such as an answer to precise questions or a piece of information about new events. In the case of a voyage of discovery, they include, moreover, specific documents like geographic maps, which by their nature ask for a spatial and 'objective' approach. By using and integrating these simple speech genres, the travel story tries to represent and model a foreign world. Although the primary speech genres lose their direct relation to their 'Sitz im Leben', their influence remains: they are, so to speak, 'romanticized' in a higher type of discourse within the cultural exchange, by individual authors with their own intentions.

This kind of monologization explains at the same time the ambivalence of the travel story between objectivity and subjectivity, which may lead to different interpretations. Anyway, written from the point of view of a non-participating 'third person', the mentioned primary speech utterances are stripped of their original plurality of equally authoritative ideological positions and of their multi-voiced context, in favour of an exotopic story — a monological discourse about (not by) the others (Zavala 1990: 84).

The dilution of the picaresque novel. My second example concerns the transfer, not from primary to secondary speech genres, but from a prototype of a narrative genre to all kinds of imitations, adaptions and translations. The picaresque novel, which relies itself on primary forms such as the (auto)biography, the confession, the portrayal of character-types and the battle of wits, found its 'Sitz im Leben' in sixteenth- to seventeenth-century Spain. The prototypical representatives that gave birth to the genre of the 'novela picaresca' (Lazarillo, Guzman, Buscon) show, in spite of major differences, a number of formal and thematic characteristics. As far as the plot is concerned the typical picaresque novel presents an episodic storyline, in which events are largely determined by chance. The motifs which steer the plot are mostly of a materialistic nature, although they also touch on the Spanish concept of 'honour' — and that is very important as socio-cultural background. They are held together by the central theme of disillusion (*desengaño*). As for the relation between the picaro and the world around him/her, the narrator-protagonist is a lonely figure, a man or woman of poor origin, badly treated even by his/her social equals, and generally leading a somewhat shady existence. The world that confronts the picaro is peopled by a series of stereotyped lords and masters (gallery of character-types) and by representatives of all walks of life. The relation between the picaro and his antagonists, often marked by dishonesty on both sides (cf. battle of wits) embodies the central theme of disillusionment and underlines a highly critical view of society typical of the picaresque novel. These summarily sketched characteristics are common to a large number of novels published in Spain between 1600 and 1645, following on the spectacular success of Mateo Aleman's *La vida de Guzman de Alfarache* (1599–1604). It was his novel that led to renewed interest in the anonymous *La vida de Lazarillo de Tormes* of 1554, which may be regarded as the prototype of the genre.

What did happen to the genre in its 'postprocessing' during the seventeenth and the first half of the eighteenth century? Because of the success of the genre, many authors felt attracted to write, imitate or translate similar works (genre awareness). The monologization phenomenon is for that matter typical for adaptation and translation processes: the 'dual' aspect of most literary (secondary) texts — that is, the tension between its denotative meaning and its connotative context — is often, for clarity's sake, strongly simplified, so that the stratified actual meaning of the original is lost. As far as the picaresque is concerned, this monologizing process developed in two directions. On the one hand there appeared a number of so-called picaresque novels that stressed the adventurous character of the plot at the expense of the original Spanish thematics (*honra*). The result was a tradition of hybrid picaresque adventure stories, especially in France (De Geneste's *L'Avanturier Buscon* of 1633; Scarron's *Le Roman Comique* of 1651) and England, culminating in Lesage's *Gil Blas de Santillane* (1715–32) and Smollet's *Roderick Random* (1748). On the other hand the confessional element, clearly present in *Guzman*, led to a tradition, especially in Germany, in which picaresque and didactic elements combined in a sort of *Bildungsroman* (Grimmelshausen's *Simplicissimus*). These two forms of 'monologization' or 'over-interpretation' are clearly influenced by cultural (national) traditions: the initial structure and thematics are adapted to the current norms of the literary system of the time and the country. One could thus say that the evolution of the genre is a clear manifestation of one-sided (mis)understandings and interpretations of the prototypical examples, furthered by socio-cultural factors (van Gorp 1985).

The Gothic novel and cultural diversities. The example of the success of the Gothic novel is still more significant as far as cultural diversities are concerned. This appears very clearly from the many reactions and post-processing activities of the time in all kinds of metatexts (literary criticism, translations, drama versions, abridgements, parodies). As a first stage in the evolution of the historical novel during the late eighteenth and the early nineteenth century, the genre manifested itself as an appropriate vehicle in that respect, for it enabled authors and readers to compare the present with the past and 'own' with 'other'.

As a literary genre the Gothic novel can very precisely be situated in the history of West European literatures. It started with the publication of Horace Walpole's *The Castle of Otranto* (1764), but became only a real 'genre' in the 1790s with the enormous success of Radcliffe's novels (especially *The Mysteries of Udolpho* in 1794 and *The Italian* in 1797) and *The Monk* (1796) by Matthew Gregory Lewis. The 'English' character is, at least in the beginning, undeniable. As Maurice Lévy puts it in the conclusion of an article bearing the significant title 'Le roman Gothique, genre anglais', 'l'essentiel de ce qui fut le gothique a sa source dans une histoire, une culture, une tradition qui sont d'abord celles du peuple anglais dans la seconde moitié du 18e siècle' (1984:13). For that matter, that is why French literary critics preferred to use the term 'roman anglais' instead of 'roman gothique' or 'roman noir'! But saying that the Gothic novel is in the first instance an English genre does not mean at all that its plot is situated in England. On the contrary, the success of the Gothic novel in England depended for a large part on its 'foreign', not to say 'exotic', setting. The Gothic novel is a typically English view on remote Roman-Catholic countries in the south of Europe (south of France, Spain, and especially Italy). This stereotyped view is clearly referred to in a notice introducing some translated 'extraits' of Radcliffe's *The Italian* in the 'Bibliothèque Britannique' of 1797. It reacts against the prejudices that existed against Italy: 'ce titre semble donner pour le type du caractère national, celui du scélérat profond qu'elle [Radcliffe] a mis en scène; et il y a toujours de l'injustice et de l'indécence dans ces proscriptions générales d'un peuple.' With reference to a number of imitations and translations, specific cultural diversities between the English, French, and German literary systems manifest themselves in literary criticism. Nearly at the same time 'nationalized' types of Gothic novel writing arise in France and Germany (*romans noirs*, *Ritter-*, *Räuber- und Schauerromane*), often characterized by further 'trivialization' (a frequent variant of monologization). A thorough study of the major shifts in such imitations, adaptations and translations would reveal a lot about explicit or implicit cultural diversities which led to misunderstandings of the original works.

SOME CONCLUDING REMARKS
Following these examples of so-called monologization procedures in the post-processing of primary and secondary speech genres, some critical remarks on Bakhtin's interesting ideas seem necessary. Indeed, it looks rather paradoxical that, for example, the transfer from primary to secondary utterances is reduced to such a monologization process. Bakhtin is right in saying that the initial 'Sitz im Leben' with all the voices involved is taken up by an individual author (a third person) who dominates the whole story. On the other hand, this stylization can be called an essential aspect of what we expect 'literary' texts to be, so that they can function in all sorts of contexts (decontextualization process). Bakhtin is aware of this fact. An artistic creation implies, so to speak, an exotopic point of view, by which a person (the author) encloses and consequently makes meaningful the other. The monologization is the price one has to pay for another dialogism, which is to say the never-ending interpretation and re-dialogization or re-contextualization by successive readers in their sociocultural contexts as new addressees of the monologized work.

In that perspective Bakhtin's opposition between dialogism and monologism must not just be referred to different kinds of primary and secondary texts, but also, and in my view chiefly, to different kinds of intertextual configurations and evolving writing and reading practices. This implies that the same text(s) might function dialogically in certain historical junctures, and relatively monologically in others; and that they might sometimes function centrifugally, and at other times be mobilized for projects of centralization or consolidation (N. Glazener); that they might function now as innovating and then as conservative ones (even Zohar). It is a pity that Bakhtin apparently has overlooked in this sphere the impact of those reading practices, influenced by political, ideological, and psychological factors, and at the same time by cultural institutions, especially since different understandings and misunderstandings of literary texts are often caused by a conjunction of (some of) these factors.

Katholieke Universiteit Leuven

Works Cited

Bakhtin, M. M. 1986 *Speech Genres & Other Late Essays*, eds C. Emerson and M. Holquist. University of Texas: especially pp. 60–102.

Bakhtine, M. 1984 *Esthétique de la création verbale*. Gallimard, Paris.

Even-Zohar, I. 1990 *Polysystem Studies*. Special volume of *Poetics Today*, 11, 1 (spring).

Glazener, N. 1993 'Planned Obsolescence: The Institutions of Reception that Produced the (Realist) Novel in the U.S.' Paper delivered at the Sixth International Mikhail Bakhtin Conference, Cocoyoc, Mexico.

Gorp, H. van 1981 'Traductions et évolution d'un genre littéraire: Le Roman picaresque en Europe au 17e et 18e siècles' in *Poetics Today*, 2, 4 (summer/autumn): pp. 209–19.

Lévy, M. 1984 'Le Roman gothique, genre anglais' in *Le Roman Gothique*, special issue of *Europe*: pp. 5–13.

Wesseling, E. 1991 *Writing History as a Prophet*. John Benjamins, Amsterdam and Philadelphia.

Zavala, I. M. 1990 'Bakhtin and Otherness: Social Heterogeneity' in *Critical Studies*, 2, 1/2: pp. 77–89.

SHEN DAN

Misreading and Translation

INTRODUCTION
Traditionally, academic discussion of 'translation' is usually restricted to interlingual transference. In his influential article 'On Linguistic Aspects of Translation', however, Roman Jakobson puts interlingual translation on a par with intralingual and intersemiotic translation by proposing the following tripartite distinction:

(1) Intralingual translation or *rewording* is an interpretation of verbal signs by means of other signs of the same language.

(2) Interlingual translation or *translation proper* is an interpretation of verbal signs by means of signs of some other language.

(3) Intersemiotic translation or *transmutation* is an interpretation of verbal signs by means of signs of nonverbal sign systems. (1959:233)

What we have here are three different kinds of sign interpretation. That any kind of sign interpretation is translation is an idea emphasized by the American semiotician Charles C. Peirce, an idea Jakobson seems to applaud without reservation (1977:1029; see Gorlée 1994:152-6). Although Jakobson's tripartite distinction appears to be all-embracing, it fails to accommodate, among others, one particular kind of sign interpretation which has gained great importance in the present globalization of comparative literature, namely, critical introduction or exposition of foreign literary theories or ideas. The present study is mainly concerned with misreading occurring in this kind of translation.

INTERLINGUAL EXPOSITION AS A KIND OF TRANSLATION
Interlingual exposition as a kind of translation, while sharing essential similarity with Jakobson's 'translation proper', differs from the latter in more than one aspect. As a rule, 'translation proper' involves a dual incidence of interpretation: (1) the translator's hermeneutic reading of the original text; and (2) his or her heuristic interpretation in the actual transfer of the text (that is, its

interpreted version) from the source language into the target language (see Gorlée 1994:68–9). As for interlingual exposition, it also involves a dual incidence of interpretation: (1) the translator's hermeneutic reading of the original theory; and (2) his or her critical exposition of the theory in the target language. But insofar as the first interpretive process is concerned, interlingual exposition as a kind of translation differs from translation proper in that it may involve more than one original text or analytical model centring on the same theoretical problem. Because of this, misreading may occur as a result of the translator's failure to realize the essential differences among the texts or analytical models under discussion. In terms of the second incidence of interpretation, interlingual exposition also differs significantly from translation proper in that it often constitutes a process of synthesizing, editing, expanding, and reformulating the source theory. As the translator here is, generally speaking, free to offer his or her own version of the theory with his or her own choice of words (except for the necessity to translate strictly certain terms or concepts), linguistic differences, which constantly pose a problem in translation proper, often do not come into play in this kind of translation. So our focus is shifted accordingly from the correspondence in words between the source language text and the target language text to the accuracy of the translator's representation of the essence of the original theory.

MIXING UP DIFFERENT ANALYTICAL MODELS
Of the various kinds of misreading taking place in interlingual exposition, we shall first look at misreading caused by the translator's indiscriminate treatment of essentially different analytical models. The case chosen for exemplification is an article by Wang Liyun and Zhang Wenhao, titled 'Free Indirect Speech in Fiction' ('Ziyou jianjie yinyu zai xiaoshuozhongde yunyong'). Free Indirect Speech (or Thought), a mode of presentation also referred to as 'free indirect style', 'free indirect discourse', 'independent form of indirect discourse', 'narrated monologue' and so on, has been frequently employed in Western fiction since the nineteenth century and in Chinese fiction since the New Cultural Movement (around the May 4th Movement in 1919). It has attracted a huge amount of critical discussion in the West from the 1960s, but hardly received any attention in China until quite recently. The article in question, published in 1989 in *Foreign Language Teaching and Research*, is an edited and expanded version in Chinese of the discussions made by some English and American linguists or critics.

In Anglo-American discussions of Free Indirect Speech (or Thought), there is an opposition between two critical stances. One may be called the 'dual voice' position, a position based on the communication model and characterized by its acknowledgment of two speech situations: (1) the primary speech situation, in which the authorial or dramatized narrator reports the character's speech or thought to the narratee or reader; and (2) the reported or embedded speech situation, in which the character thinks or talks to his/her addressee. Because of the presence of the two speech situations, there are two spatio-temporal reference points: one is the *here/now* of the narrator's reporting act, and the other the *here/now* of the reported character's speech. The character's present is always the narrator's past, and the character's 'here' the narrator's 'there', since to the narrator, the character's speech act is a past happening. Compare the following modes:

Direct Speech: He said, 'I'll come back here tomorrow.'
Indirect Speech: He said that he would *return there the following day.*
Free Indirect Speech: He would *come back here tomorrow.*

In Free Indirect Speech, since the character's speech act retains its independent status (instead of being subordinated to the narrator's reporting clause as in Indirect Speech), the character's subjectivity can in varying degrees be preserved. So in reporting the character's 'I'll come back here tomorrow', the narrator, while shifting its tense into the past and the 'I' into 'he', preserves the original spatio-temporal references indicating the character's *here/now*. As a result, we have the interesting phenomenon of the character's *here/now* being coexistent with the shifted past tense and third person pronoun.

This dual-voice position is rejected by Banfield (see also Hamburger), who contends that the narrator exists only in first-person narration, and that in third-person narration the assumption that there is an authorial narrator narrating the tale to the reader does not hold. Such a text, that is to say, ought to be regarded as speakerless or autonomous, with its past tense indicating writtenness rather than temporality attributable to a narrator situated outside the narrated story. To avoid confusion with the dual-voice model, Banfield uses the epithet 'represented speech and thought' instead of 'free indirect speech' and so on, with the term 'represented' emphasizing the point that the character's speech or thought is shown by the text rather than reported by a narrator's separate voice.

While the dual-voice position is shared by almost all Anglo-American linguists and critics, Banfield's mono-voice model has remained isolated, subjected to a series of criticisms (see, for instance, Cohn, McHale, Ron, and Adamson). It goes beyond the concern of the present paper to evaluate the validity of Banfield's model. Suffice it to say that the two models are fundamentally different from each other.

In the Chinese article, the two models are seriously mixed up. The article is mainly based on the relevant discussion in *Style in Fiction* by Leech and Short and that in *Unspeakable Sentences* by Banfield, the former representing the dual-voice model and the latter the mono-voice model. The article draws alternately on the two books, among others, without taking into account that they in effect embody two incompatible positions. Starting with a classification made by Leech and Short and with the epithet 'free indirect speech' consistently employed, the article is committed to a model containing two voices: that of the reporting author and that of the reported character. (It may be noted that in China the author is still quite 'alive' and many people tend to stick to the notion of the author rather than the narrator.) In this dual-voice framework, there is found 'hidden' here and there Banfield's mono-voice viewpoint.

At the beginning of the first section following an introduction, the article defines the main semantic feature of Free Indirect Speech as the author's silence, a point illustrated by examples such as:

> (He told the Kramers that their attitude toward Saul Bird was disgusting.) They were sick people, he could not live under the same roof with such sick, selfish people! (Joyce Carol Oates, *Pilgrim's Progress*)
>
> [Compare the direct form: 'They are sick people, I can not live under the same roof with such sick, selfish people.']

The article goes on to say that in some cases, however, 'the author is not completely silent', where, 'from the semantic point of view, we have a combination of two voices': that of the author, and that of the character. This point is exemplified by:

> It was difficult to refuse! But why give the thing to him to do? That was surely quite unbecoming.... (Galsworthy, *The Man of Property*)
>
> [Compare the direct form: 'It is difficult to refuse! But why give the thing to me to do? That is surely quite unbecoming....']

It is clear that the two examples are essentially the same in terms of the author's or narrator's voice. According to the mono-voice model, both of them do not contain any authorial voice (only the character's voice is shown or represented by the text *qua* text). But according to the dual-voice model, both of them do contain the author's reporting voice as reflected in the switch from the first person reference to the third, and from the present tense to the past. When the two opposing English models, each consistent in itself, are 'translated' into this Chinese version, what we get is a superficially unified model with internal inconsistencies and contradictions. The contradictory viewpoints are in no way clearly marked off from each other, since the article, quite representative of critical writing in Chinese, makes no explicit reference to the works it draws on, except for an attached bibliography.

Interestingly, Banfield's mono-voice examples are sometimes made to illustrate the dual-voice viewpoint in an unwittingly distorted way. And the case is further complicated by the added explanations of the 'translators'. Let's have a look at the following passage taken from the article:

> This does not mean that the author is speaking in place of the character, for the author's voice is only an accompanying one. Although the author's viewpoint coincides with the character's, the language has to be the character's own.
>
> (4) a. Up before breakfast and off to paint, he (mistakenly) believed alone.

(Woolf, *To the Lighthouse*)

If 'mistakenly' is inserted into example (4), the sentence cannot hold water, because in terms of logic, free indirect speech only expresses the character's inner speech.... If 'mistakenly' is added to the sentence, it apparently will become subjective judgment made unilaterally by the author. Thus, the sentence will contain only the author's voice. In fact, the author, who is not the omniscient God, cannot have full access to the character's inner world. Such purely subjective comments made by the author (including 'falsely', 'mendaciously' etc.) cannot therefore be accepted.

b. Which looked best against her black dress: Which did indeed? said Mrs Ramsay *absent-mindedly*. (*ibid.*)

Here, the term 'absent-mindedly' is, however, acceptable, because it expresses both the tone of the character's speech and the author's comment, which is in accordance with the dual voice analyzed above. The same goes for terms like 'ironically' and 'emphatically'.

The above examples are all taken from a section in Banfield's book titled 'Parentheticals as the Type of Speakerless Sentences'. Banfield is concerned only with the parentheticals (such as, 'said Mrs Ramsay absent-mindedly'), and is arguing against the dual-voice position. According to the dual-voice model, such parentheticals are comments made by the reporting narrator, and are therefore to be distinguished from the reported speech or thought of the character. As the narrator is free to pass judgement on the character, the parenthetical 'he (mistakenly) believed alone' is perfectly acceptable. By contrast, in Banfield's mono-voice model, no room is left for the narrator's (or author's) commenting voice, and parentheticals are treated as either purely (speakerless) descriptive statements or part of the character's consciousness. Thus, the parenthetical 'he (mistakenly) believed alone,' which contains a separate commenting voice, is deemed unacceptable, whereas 'said Mrs Ramsay *absent-mindedly*,' whose information is known to the character and may be taken as part of the character's consciousness, is acceptable.

In the Chinese version, the parentheticals are, so to speak, 'absorbed' into the character's 'inner speech,' since they are not even mentioned or discussed separately. This is one step further than Banfield in the mono-voice direction, and clearly goes against the dual-voice model. Nevertheless, the model that the article unequivocally subscribes to is no other than the dual-voice one. Failing to get at the rationale underlying Banfield's argument, the article imposes a dual-voice interpretation on her parentheticals. While Banfield holds that a parenthetical clause is acceptable only when it does not contain the voice of the narrator, the Chinese version asserts that it is acceptable only when it contains both the character's voice and the author's voice. Moreover, in discussing the case 'Up before breakfast and off to paint, he (mistakenly) believed alone,' the Chinese version attributes, due to the failure to catch the true intent of Banfield's argument, the unacceptability of the adverb 'mistakenly' to the author's lack of omniscience. This added explanation is something with which both Banfield and the dual-voice critics would disagree, for the author is obviously omniscient, otherwise she would not have access to the character's inner thought, 'Up before breakfast and off to paint'.

When it comes to the coexistence of the shifted past tense and deictics indicating the character's *here/now*, a phenomenon characteristic of free indirect speech, the article's explanation is no less confusing, as is clear from the following example:

> She [Ruth] imagined how he would kiss her when he came back from work. And this evening, while she sewed, he would read aloud....
>
> [Compare: Ruth thought: 'And this evening, while I sew....']

The comment on this example in the article is this: 'Here Ruth uses "this evening" instead of "that evening" to refer to what is going to happen in the evening. Thus, psychological time indicating future ("this evening") overlaps the time of the narrated action....' Again, this statement is something with which both the mono-voice and the dual-voice model would disagree. According to the mono-voice model, it is the text which shows or represents 'this evening' in Ruth's thoughts. According to the dual-voice model, it is the narrator who preserves Ruth's 'this evening' instead of changing it into 'that evening' in reporting her thoughts. Here, the article contradicts its own dual-voice framework by totally neglecting the narrator's voice. No less regrettable is the fact that, while only acknowledging the voice of Ruth, it deviates from Banfield's mono-voice model by saying 'Ruth uses "this evening" instead of "that evening",' which implicitly and quite absurdly imposes the role of the narrator on the character.

From this article we can see that, as distinct from 'translation proper' which deals with only one original text, interlingual exposition as a kind of translation runs the risk of mixing up different original texts or analytical models. And the confusion may be aggravated by the translator's own interpretations or explanations. But in this kind of translation, sometimes only one original text is involved. In such cases, misreading may occur as a result of the translator's neglect of the original historical context.

NEGLECTING THE ORIGINAL HISTORICAL CONTEXT

A literary theory or idea, as Edward Said points out, is always 'a response to a specific social and historical situation' (1983:237) and is therefore often bound to that particular context. Failure to realize the 'context-bound' nature of theory may lead to misreading and distortion of the original theory in the translating process.

More than two thousand years ago, Aristotle defined plot as 'the arrangement of incidents'. In the twentieth century some Russian Formalists and later certain Structuralists, too, regarded plot as the arrangement of events. The superficial similarity has led some critics to equate the two concepts. In *Story and Discourse*, for instance, Seymour Chatman offers the following structuralist explication of Aristotle's concept of plot:

> Aristotle defined plot (mythos) as 'the arrangement of incidents'. Structuralist narrative theory argues that the arrangement is precisely the operation performed by discourse.... Its order of presentation need not be the same as that of the natural logic of the story. Its function is to emphasize or de-emphasize certain story-events, to interpret some and to leave others to inference, to show or to tell, to comment or to remain silent, to focus on this or that aspect of an event or character. (1978:43)

Such an explication functions to turn Aristotle into a modern structuralist who, in the investigation of 'plot', can take for granted what is represented and concentrate on the manner of representation: whether to show or to tell, to comment or to remain silent, to begin *in media res* or to go against the chronological sequence of the story-events in one way or another for various purposes.

In fact, in ancient Greek when the canons of tragedy were not yet established, Aristotle in discussing 'plot' had to deal with a more 'elementary' kind of arrangement, that is, the proper construction of the fictional reality. He had to assert that 'the plot being a representation of a piece of action must represent a single piece of action and the whole of it [with a beginning, middle, and end]; and the component incidents must be so arranged that if one of them be transposed or removed, the unity of the whole is dislocated and destroyed' (35). The incidents, that is to say, must be causally connected. Aristotle even had to put forward the idea that:

> The successful plot must then have a single and not, as some say, a double issue; and the change must be not to good fortune from bad but, on the contrary, from good to bad fortune, and it must not be due to villainy but to some great flaw in such a man as we have described, or of one who is better rather than worse.... The plot should be so constructed that even without seeing the play anyone hearing of the incidents happening thrills with fear and pity as a result of what occurs. (47–9)

It is clear that Aristotle was writing for an audience not yet sure about what a tragedy ought to represent, and that his 'arrangement' essentially concerns the issue of what is to be represented rather than the manner of representation, the latter being the concern of the modern structuralist's 'arrangement'. Chatman's exposition of Aristotle's 'arrangement' in modern structuralist terms has greatly changed the ancient concept, a concept that is now made to lend support to the modern structuralist distinction between story and discourse.

To see some essential similarity between misreading in interlingual exposition as a kind of translation and that in 'translation proper', we now turn to a case occurring in the latter. In section six of *The Poetics*, Aristotle makes a careful distinction between 'pratton' (agent) and 'ethos' (the character or moral nature of an agent). When translated into English, however, 'ethos' is invariably put into the potentially ambiguous term 'character.' Thus the distinction is blurred as the English term 'character' has come to refer not only to the moral nature of a person but also to a person portrayed in a drama, novel, or other artistic piece. In *Aspects of the Novel*, E. M. Forster cites Aristotle's words, 'Character gives us qualities...' (1966:91), which means that the moral nature of people determines their qualities. This observation is wrongly rendered by the Chinese translator Shu Bingwen into 'From the persons portrayed we can see the special qualities of the work' ('Women cong renwu keyi kanchu zuopinde tese' [1984:73]).

The primary factor underlying this case of misreading and mistranslating is surely the ambiguity inherent in the English term 'character'. Nevertheless, the misrendering is not only ascribable to the given linguistic difference between Greek and English but also attributable to the dissimilarities between the relevant critical contexts. In modern times, one cannot refer to an actor or a protagonist without involving his/her qualities since a person portrayed in a work of art is more closely associated with his/her moral nature. Given the statement 'A novel has three essential components: plot, character and setting', 'character' would naturally be taken as the persons described with their moral nature or dispositions implied. This forms a sharp contrast to the Aristotelian context where 'character' among the six constituents of a tragedy refers exclusively to 'that which determines the quality of the agents' (25). In modern times, in effect, it sounds odd or superfluous to state that one's character or moral nature determines one's qualities. These factors are very likely to be responsible for the translator's taking 'character' not as moral nature but as the persons depicted instead.

The intercultural transference of a theory or an idea, no matter whether in the form of exposition or 'translation proper', always involves at least two socio-historical contexts, which often differ in multiple aspects. As illustrated here, the translators, in introducing a theory from one context into another, tend to operate on the false assumption that the two contexts are similar, thus making for unconscious distortion of the original theory. Although we ourselves cannot escape our own interpretive assumptions, it behoves us to scrutinize such cases of misreading or mistranslating, a kind of scrutiny that may in one way or another help reveal the underlying cultural conventions or practices involved, which tend to remain opaque within the boundary of a single culture.

CONCLUSION

In recent years, misreading in intercultural transference has attracted much critical attention. Edward Said tends to attribute such misreadings entirely to the limits, demands and pressures of the socio-historical contexts involved (1983:236–7). In his view, misreading or transformation of the original theory is quite necessary, since 'there is no theory capable of covering, closing off, predicting all the situations in which it might be useful' (241). By contrast, Robert Holub takes a much more negative stance towards misreadings in interlingual exposition, which are ascribed by him either to the 'biases' of native social, political and intellectual traditions or to some undesirable personal reasons, such as hasty reading habits (1992:56). He attempts to establish a framework 'designed to ensure that future border crossings will not be susceptible to the types of distortions and misunderstandings' as discussed in his book (xi).

It seems to me that the choice between the two stances depends on what kind of misreading is involved. In this paper, we have only examined two kinds of misreading in intercultural transference. Although the latter kind is closely associated with the change in socio-historical context, the responsibility for the misreading seems to rest more with the translator than with the given context. As to the former kind, it is very much a matter of personal misunderstanding. Such misreadings, I would argue, should be guarded against and carefully avoided in translation.

Peking University

Works Cited

Adamson, Sylvia 1994 'Subjectivity in Narration: Empathy and Echo' in M. Yaguello (ed.) *Subjecthood and Subjectivity.* Ophrys, Paris: pp. 193–208.

Aristotle 1982 *The Poetics,* vol. 23. The Loeb Classical Library. Harvard University Press: pp. 22–9.

Banfield, Ann 1973 'Narrative Style and the Grammar of Direct and Indirect Speech' in *Foundations of Language* 10: pp. 1–39.

—— 1982 *Unspeakable Sentences: Narration and Representation in the Language of Fiction.* Routledge, Boston.

Chatman, Seymour 1978 *Story and Discourse: Narrative Structure in Fiction and Film.* Cornell University Press

Cohn, Dorrit 1978 *Transparent Minds: Narrative Modes for Presenting Consciousness in Fiction.* Princeton University Press.

Forster, E. M. 1966 *Aspects of the Novel.* Penguin, Harmondsworth. (Tr. Chinese by Shu Bingwen 1984, Huacheng, Guangzhou.)

Gorlée, Dinda L. 1994 *Semiotics and the Problem of Translation, with Special Reference to the Semiotics of Charles S. Peirce.* Rodopi, Amsterdam.

Hamburger, K. 1973 *The Logic of Literature,* tr. M. J. Rose. Indiana University Press.

Holub, Robert C. 1992 *Crossing Borders: Reception Theory, Poststructuralism, Deconstruction.* University of Wisconsin Press.

Jakobson, Roman 1959 'On Linguistic Aspects of Translation' in *On Translation,* ed. Reuben A. Brower. Harvard University Press: pp. 232–9.

—— 1977 'A Few Remarks on Peirce, Pathfinder in the Science of Language' in *Modern Language Notes* 92. pp. 1026–32.

McHale, B. 1978 'Free Indirect Discourse: a Survey of Recent Accounts' in *Poetics and the Theory of Literature* 3: pp. 249–87.

Ron, M. 1981 'Free Indirect Discourse, Mimetic Language Games and the subject of Fiction' in *Poetics Today* 2, 2: pp. 17–39.

Said, Edward 1983 *The World, the Text, and the Critic*. Harvard University Press.
Wang Liyun and Zhang Wenhao 1989 'Free Indirect Speech in Fiction' in *Foreign Language Teaching and Research* 3: pp. 59–63.

ZHANG YINDE

Transposition de l'Onomastique Littéraire

Nous avons choisi de traiter ce problème en partant de deux constatations corrélatives, liées en partie à des expériences pédagogiques que nous avons vécues avec des étudiants de lettres non sinisants. D'abord, l'impact qu'exerce l'onomastique sur la lecture romanesque dans la tradition occidentale. L'onomastique, notamment les noms propres des personnages, servent en effet de marques récurrentes qui organisent le personnage comme foyer d'information et la mémoire que le lecteur a de son texte. La lecture d'un roman est souvent fonction de la prise en considération par le lecteur du jeu textuel qui se tisse entre le signifiant discontinu qu'est le nom du personnage et son signifié.[1] La seconde constatation dérivée de la première est que ces incidences ainsi attestées concernant la lecture d'un roman indigène s'intensifient ou se problématisent lorsqu'un lecteur se trouve devant un roman traduit, et surtout du chinois, où le nom relève d'un système linguistique et anthropologique particulier, pour ne pas dire unique.

Viviane Alleton a évoqué les difficultés de transposer les noms chinois en langues européennes. Elle commence et termine son ouvrage en constatant un même dilemme: traduit ou transcrit, 'un prénom chinois transposé dans une langue européenne souffre d'un excès ou d'une insuffisance de sens'(1994:7). L'amputation ou l'hypertrophisation sémantique ainsi introduite ne pourra pas être sans incidence sur la lecture; elle impose nécessairement une certaine orientation à l'activité herméneutique du lecteur. L'objectif de cet exposé n'est donc pas d'élaborer des recettes ni de porter des jugements de valeur sur les travaux de traduction réalisés, même si la question les concerne au plus haut point, mais de s'attacher à examiner des velléités d'interprétation qui s'esquissent à partir des noms transposés chez ceux pour qui l'accès à la littérature chinoise passe exclusivement par la traduction, et à qui cette dernière s'adresse en premier chef.

Pour ce faire nous devrons d'abord dresser un recensement rapide des pratiques existantes avant de focaliser notre analyse sur les effets de lecture qu'elle provoquent.

On passera d'abord en revue les différentes pratiques existantes dans ce domaine. Nos investigations se limitent à des textes de la littérature chinoise moderne et contemporaine, traduits en français et parus pendant les dernières décennies. Corpus modeste, qui offre néanmoins un éventail assez large, devant permettre de rendre compte de la diversité des choix en la matière. Sans être comparable aux romans chinois traditionnels où l'onomastique joue un rôle déterminant dans la composition narrative par la myriade des personnages et par les motivations auxquelles les romanciers les soumettent systématiquement, le roman chinois moderne n'en demeure pas moins conditionné par un système désignatif complexe, largement inspiré de la potentialité référentielle. Il suffit pour s'en convaincre de se reporter à tout un travail de reconstitution archéologique effectué par Lu Xun, l'auteur d'*Histoire d'A Q*, au début de sa nouvelle à propos de l'identité de son personnage, ou à *Un fils tombé du ciel* de Lao She, où le choix du nom de l'enfant retrouvé dans la rue offre un épisode initial pittoresque et savoureux. L'importance perpétuée des noms ne laisse pas indifférents les traducteurs, qui sont nombreux et qui, dans leurs propositions diverses, transcendent la simple distinction de traduction ou de transcription.

La diversité des solutions s'affirme quand nos enquêtes s'étendent sur l'ensemble des désignateurs dénominatifs, comprenant à la fois noms propres (il s'agit le plus souvent, bien sûr, de prénoms), surnoms et toutes sortes d'appellations. La complexité des pratiques augmente encore si l'on prend en compte le recours à certains dispositifs explicatifs comme liste de personnages, notes infra-paginales ou paraphrases multiples. Du point de vue de la lecture, ces pratiques de transposition mélangées, entrecroisées, provoquent des effets de réceptions complexes.

Examinons en premier lieu les noms propres ou plus précisément les prénoms. La transposition des noms propres nous révèle d'abord le choix croissant et majoritaire du phonétisme au détriment des considérations sémantiques. La traduction systématique semble en tout cas péricliter. La tentation traductrice subsiste encore, elle se fait toutefois sélective et localisée et ne se manifeste et s'actualise que dans la mesure où la motivation textuelle est explicite et incitative ou que les frontières se brouillent entre le prénom et le surnom.

Famille de Pa Kin constitue ainsi, dans le corpus que nous avons délimité, l'unique cas qui bénéficie d'une traduction systématique des noms de l'ensemble de ses personnages. Ce choix provient du souci que les traducteurs de ce roman ont eu d'éviter la confusion que pourrait engendrer dans l'esprit des lecteurs le nombre important des personnages, dont les noms sont phonétiquement proches les uns des autres (1989:19). La traductrice de *Printemps* et

Automne qui, avec *Famille*, font partie de la trilogie de *Torrent* semble moins préoccupée de ce risque de confusion et rompt avec l'entreprise. Après avoir été traduits dans le premier volet en Eveil du Nouveau, Eveil du Peuple, Eveil de l'Intelligence, Double Jade, Cithare, Chant de Phénix, etc., les personnages de Juexin, Juemin, Juehui, Ruijue, Qin, Mingfeng, dans les second et troisième volets, reviennent à la forme phonétique. La discontinuité est remarquable malgré la liste des personnages, le tableau généalogique, l'avertissement de la traductrice et même des notes infra-paginales, qui contribuent à faire comprendre le système familial chinois et le lignage. Ce retour au phonétisme s'expliquerait non seulement par une autre sorte de souci de clarté, mais par des difficultés d'harmonisation générale que l'on rencontre dans la traduction systématique. Ainsi la forme grammaticale de la combinaison de déterminant-déterminé, la plus couramment adoptée, appliquée ici dans la série des noms qui marquent la génération des oncles, aboutit-elle parfois à des traductions un peu forcées: Maîtrise des Lettres (Kewen), Maîtrise de Lumière (Keming), Maîtrise de Quiétude (Ke'an), Maîtrise de Détermination (Keding). On reviendra plus loin sur les inconvénients occasionnés par l'harmonisation grammaticale de la série. On éprouve au demeurant la même difficulté quant à la fixation du rapport même de déterminant-déterminé dans le nom de Mingfeng, traduit par Chant de Phénix, et non par Phénix qui Chante ou Phénix chantant, plus proche pourtant de l'idée chinoise. C'est sans doute pour éviter ce genre de complication que l'on choisit, dans *Ordination*, d'indiquer en bas de page le sens du premier caractère qui se retrouve dans les noms des trois condisciples — Ren (Bienveillance) : Ren Shan, Ren Hai, Ren Du — sans tenter de donner à chacun d'eux un sens global ou un sens composé.

Le plus grand nombre des traductions ont ainsi opté pour le phonétisme des noms qu'elles appliquent d'un bout à l'autre. On peut citer *Forteresse assiégée* de Qian Zhongshu où les traducteurs ont adopté la translittération systématique, avec les personnages haut en couleur comme Hongjian, Xinmei, Roujia. Dans un autre roman plus récent, *Epouse et concubine*, de Su Tong, les noms de Songlian, Zhuoyun et Meishan revêtent aussi la simple forme transcrite.

Si ces romans ont incité leurs traducteurs à une option bien tranchée, d'autres semblent orientés vers des choix plutôt panachés, en faisant cohabiter la traduction et la transcription. *Le Passeur de Chadong* de Shen Congwen nous donne à lire le nom de Cuicui en Emeraude, alors que les deux frères, Tianbao et Nuosong, se contentent de leur phonétisme. Un cas similaire s'observe avec *Le Pousse-pousse* de Lao She où le personnage féminin, Huniu, est bel et bien mis en vedette avec le nom traduit de Tigresse, tandis que l'autre protagoniste, Xiangzi, voit son nom rester dans l'obscurité sémantique.

Les deux traductions sélectives semblent obéir aussi bien à l'exhortation des textes originaux qu'aux exigences de la langue d'arrivée. Le nom de Cuicui est traduit car le texte explique bien les circonstances dans lesquelles il est donné: 'Les montagnes avoisinantes étaient couvertes de bosquets de bambous d'un vert éclatant, aussi le vieux batelier donna-t-il à la pauvre orpheline le nom d''Emeraude' (1990:11). Le nom traduit emmagasine et incarne ainsi les informations concernant l'harmonie dans laquelle la jeune fille vit avec la nature. La traduction du seul nom de la protagoniste entraîne deux constatations supplémentaires. D'abord, le texte livre aussi le sens des noms des deux frères, Tian Bao et Nuo Song, qui ne sont pourtant pas traduits. On pourra s'interroger sur ce traitement inégal. S'agit-il là d'une façon de privilégier le personnage féminin ('Protégé du Ciel' pour Tian Bao, 'Envoyé du dieu qui détourne les maladies' pour Nuo Song (28)) ou des difficultés imsurmontables de rendre en français les deux noms dont le sens est trop compliqué? En ce qui concerne le nom d'Emeraude lui-même, du point de vue lexical et stylistique, on peut remarquer que le prénom chinois en question résulte de la réduplication du caractère Cui, constituant une sorte de diminutif hypocoristique. Sa traduction française en un seul mot efface ce redoublement et entraîne certaines conséquences sémantiques: le caractère intime et affectif du nom se fait donc moins sentir en français, à la différence de la motivation du texte original: 'Aussi le vieux batelier donna-t-il à cette pauvre orpheline *un nom qui la garde proche de lui*: Cuicui' (la partie en italique n'est pas traduite). Il s'agit donc d'une double allusion à la nature et à l'affectivité, une motivation morphosémantique qu'il paraît difficile à restituer entièrement.[2]

Quant à la traduction du *Pousse-pousse*, la sélection favorisant le nom de Huniu semble s'expliquer par un prénom qui se confond avec le surnom, et semble suggérée par la classification des physionomistes: 'Pour toute progéniture, il [Quatrième Seigneur] n'avait qu'une fille qui appartenait, elle aussi, à la catégorie des tigres. Avec une tête qui lui avait d'ailleurs valu le surnom de "Tigresse", justement, elle faisait peur même aux hommes' (1991:42). Par rapport à Huniu, le nom de Xiangzi prête moins à confusion, il ressemble plus à un prénom qu'à un surnom. On a de bonnes raisons d'hésiter à le rendre par Veinard. La version française proposée par les éditions de Pékin a pourtant cédé à la tentation, en le traduisant ainsi. Elle dote même les deux noms d'une égale couleur de surnoms en les précédant d'un article défini: La Tigresse et Le Veinard.

Passons maintenant aux désignations appellatives et aux surnoms, qui n'en demeurent pas moins l'objet de transpositions hétérogènes, même si, a priori, ils invitent plutôt à la traduction. Les traducteurs se révèlent prudents devant les déterminants comme Lao et Xiao qui préfixent les noms de famille, sans les traduire par Vieux ou Petit. Le domestique dans *Famille* s'appelle encore Vieux Zhao. Si dans *Le Roi des arbres*, Lao Xiao n'est pas traduit par Vieux Xiao, le traducteur met toutefois en bas de page une note qui explique le sens de ce terme en le situant dans le contexte chinois (1988:96). De son côté, *La Cage entrebâillée* nous donne à lire les noms de Lao Li et de Xiao Zhao, indifférenciés d'un nom propre transcrit.

En ce qui concerne d'abord les termes de parenté, ils sont généralement traduits tels quels. Le personnage principal de *Rides sur les eaux dormantes* de Li Jieren s'appelle Belle-Soeur Cai, tout comme Belle-soeur Xianglin dans *Sacrifice du Nouvel An* de Lu Xun. Ce n'est pourtant pas le cas de *La Cage entrebâillée*, où l'entremetteur, qui s'appelle dans le texte original Grand frère Zhang (Zhang Dage) se fait appeler Zhang Dage[3] et, sa femme, Belle-Soeur Zhang (Zhang Dasao) prend l'appellation de Madame Zhang.

Le phonétisme entraîne une sorte de neutralisation du rapport social particulier contenu dans le système appellatif chinois. Ce déficit en signification sociale est toutefois contrebalancé par l'appellation du seul nom de famille, Zhang, qui fait ressortir une certaine familiarité dans le registre français. On peut seulement ajouter, au passage, qu'une telle pratique peut provoquer des effets de confusion très inattendus pour un sinisant. Premièrement il n'est pas précisé que Lao est un préfixe; en plus, les noms de Madame Zhang et de Madame Li nous indiquent en toutes lettres que Zhang et Li sont les noms de famille. Dans ces conditions on a toutes les raisons de soupçonner que Lao, dans Lao Li, est sans doute son prénom. Deuxièmement Zhang Dage prend son nom dans l'ordre invariable de nom de famille + 'le prénom' (on oublie au fur et à mesure que Zhang Dage veut dire grand frère), ou sous la forme abrégée de Zhang. Le nom de Lao Li, du même coup, paraît s'écrire dans un ordre inversé et toujours en entier. Aussi ne peut-on s'empêcher de s'interroger sur la signification éventuelle de ce dernier: Lao Li, avec la permanence de son prénom, serait un personnage mal intégré au groupe social et tourmenté par le problème de l'individualité. En tout cas on comprend que le choix du désignateur rigide ou des appellations occidentales consiste à privilégier les exigences de la langue d'arrivée au détriment du particularisme de la langue de départ. De ce point de vue l'exemple le plus frappant en revient sans doute à *Printemps et Automne*, où le nom de Zhang Shi désigne en réalité Troisième Dame Gao, née Zhang, et où, par ailleurs, il semble plus clair à la traductrice de donner l'appellation de 'cousin(e)' suivi du prénom, plutôt que de traduire Quatrième Frère ou Deuxième Soeur, comme cela est inscrit dans le texte original.

Quant au surnom ou sobriquet, généralement rendu tel quel, il donne lieu pourtant à des arrangements ou à des renonciations à cause sans doute des subtilités ou des allusions qui défient la traduction. Luo Waizui et Cai Shazi, dans *Rides sur les eaux dormantes*, sont respectivement traduits par Luo Bouche Torte, Cai l'Idiot et Xiao Geda, dans *Le Roi des arbres*, par Xiao Le Noueux. Avec une légère modification Jiaoluan (jambes-couilles), ami du fou des échecs dans *Le Roi des échecs*, s'appelle plus pudiquement Longues Pattes. La traduction ne paraît pas rendre le caractère 'très grossier' du sobriquet dont le personnage porteur parle.[4] Pour des raisons diverses, on voit aussi des surnoms transcrits comme un nom propre. Minghai, le nom bouddhique de ce jeune garçon dans *Ordination* de Wang Zengqi, reste sous sa forme phonétique, et son sens de Océan de Clarté est seulement noté en bas de page. Wang Shouwu, amateur de poèmes, dans *Les Trois amis de l'hiver* du même auteur, est aussi exempt de traduction; seules deux notes séparées expliquent le sens de Shou (maigre) et de Wu (je ou moi teinté d'une connotation littéraire), sans que le sens d'ensemble tiré de la référence à un poème de Song soit traduit ou indiqué. Dans *Un Enfant tombé du ciel* (Niu Tianci), le sens figure dans le titre, adopté d'après le nom du personnage, alors qu'à l'intérieur du texte, il est donné simplement en pinyin.

EFFETS DE LECTURE

Les options observées plus haut conditionnent le déchiffrement et créent des effets de lecture divers. Réexaminons d'abord les noms traduits. La traduction invite un lecteur, qui ignore le mécanisme anthropologique et culturel du nom chinois, à identifier les noms traduits à un acte de motivation spécifique de l'auteur, et partant, à faire intervenir assez tôt le travail interprétatif. Ces noms, dont le sens est explicite et reconnu d'emblée par les lecteurs, leur servent de référence prospective, d'horizon d'attente pour 'prévoir' le personnage, à qui ils attribuent tel ou tel contenu moral, caractériel, idéologique ou esthétique. Ces interprétations anticipées se voient, au fur et à mesure de la lecture, confirmées ou démenties. Les aléas sont fonction, certes, des compétences encyclopédiques, génériques ou idéologiques du lecteur. Néanmoins les traductions données ne manquent pas d'infléchir l'interprétation dans une certaine direction.

Que des lecteurs trouvent dans le nom d'Emeraude une note poétique, cela ne s'éloigne pas excessivement du climat idyllique qui règne dans *Passeur de Chadong*. Il est en revanche plus problématique de croire déceler des effets lyriques à travers des noms féminins de *Famille*: Chant de Phénix, Double Jade, Prunier de frimas, Cithare. C'est ignorer que ces derniers s'inscrivent dans l'un des registres les plus conventionnels que l'on puisse observer à l'époque dans le milieu décrit et que Pa Kin reprend pour appuyer l'ancrage référentiel de son roman.

Les trois protagonistes du même roman n'en mobilisent pas moins des tentatives d'interprétation orientées vers la monosémie de la désobéissance. On pense voir dans le morphème Eveil (Jue), qui relie les prénoms des trois frères: Eveil du Nouveau, Eveil du Peuple et Eveil de l'Intelligence, le signal d'une prise de conscience qui renvoie à la révolte des jeunes protagonistes contre l'autorité patriarcale et contre le carcan du système familial traditionnel. C'est aussi ignorer le sens bouddhique de ce terme. Dans le cas de Juehui, le plus révolté de tous, les deux caractères, l'un comme l'autre, appartiennent au champ lexical du bouddhisme, Jue désignant l'éveil, et Hui la sagesse. Son nom de Juehui renvoie même à sa forme anagrammatique de Huijue: éveil, ou fruit de la sagesse. Si l'aîné s'appelle Eveil du Nouveau, ce prénom fait d'abord allusion, on le sait, à la naissance de la nouvelle génération et à l'extension de la famille puisqu'il est le premier né de la première branche. Sympathisant avec ses deux frères dans leur révolte, il est pourtant tiraillé entre le devoir et les idées modernes, et victime de bien des drames. Son parcours dément une quelconque interprétation de son caractère comme novateur.

On ne peut pas, bien entendu, exclure l'hypothèse que Pa Kin investisse les noms de ces personnages d'un sens de prise de conscience ou de révolte. Il s'agira là non d'un sens monolithique, mais d'une polysémie, corrélée à un acte de dénomination qui se situe à deux niveaux. Dans l'univers diégétique on peut penser que le dénominateur légitime est vraisemblablement le père ou le grand-père même si ce rôle ne leur est pas formellement assigné. Lettrés confucéens et défenseurs de la morale ancienne, ils ne peuvent donner que des noms qui correspondent à leurs propres visions et souhaits. L'auteur intervient en tant que, pour ainsi dire, le second dénominateur de ses personnages. Il doit respecter la vraisemblabilité des noms donnés dans de tels contextes familiaux, avant de pouvoir jouer avec la polyvalence de ces termes. C'est au fond une question de remotivation ignorée par les lecteurs: il est un fait culturel et extratextuel que les prénoms chinois ont un sens, qui ne résulte pas d'un travail spécifique de l'auteur. Dans un roman la remotivation est possible, mais pas systématique et elle s'effectue par superposition et par recréation.

Les limites de la compétence linguistique et encyclopédique des lecteurs ne sont pas les seuls éléments générateurs de l'interprétation monolithique ou faussée. Cette dernière peut être favorisée aussi par des traductions infléchies sous les contraintes de la langue d'arrivée. On a vu que dans *Famille*, les garçons de la troisième génération portent dans leur prénom le caractère de Jue (Eveil). Pour marquer cette continuité et l'harmonie de la série, le traducteur le conserve en l'insérant dans une structure grammaticale systématique de combinaison: nom + complément. Mais comme l'indique Viviane Alleton, en chinois 'la suite de deux syllabes dans un prénom peut être une simple juxtaposition, un syntagme ou la condensation d'un énoncé' (1994:71). Les deux caractères qui se suivent ne forment pas nécessairement un mot morphologiquement marqué par la combinaison du type déterminant + déterminé. De ce point de vue, les noms d'Eveil de l'Héroïsme, Jueying (fils aîné de Maîtrise de Lumière) et d'Eveil de l'Avant-garde, Juexian (troisième fils de Maîtrise de Quiétude) sont problématiques sur le plan grammatical comme sur le plan sémantique. Il s'agit en chinois, pour le premier, de la juxtaposition de deux notions: éveil et talent éminent, et pour le second, de la condensation d'un énoncé qui, par la structure d'un verbe substantivable + un adverbe, exprime un souhait — quelqu'un qui atteint l'éveil précocement ou avant les autres. La traduction française, qui se plie à la nécessité de la langue d'arrivée, entraîne une certaine distorsion sémantique qui fausse les données textuelles et fourvoie l'interprétation.

Essayons de voir les conséquences qu'entraînent les noms transcrits au niveau de la lecture. Par rapport aux noms traduits, des noms réduits au phonétisme ne sont pas de nature à susciter des interprétations précoces, partielles ou indigentes. Assignés au statut de noms propres, ils sont au départ un mot blanc, un asémantème (cf. Hamon 1973:145), qui met la lecture en face d'un fonctionnement cumulatif de signification. Le lecteur les charge de sens au fur et à mesure des transformations dont ces morphèmes 'vides' à l'origine auront été le support et l'agent. Ainsi un lecteur doit-il s'engager assez en avant dans sa lecture, ayant connu des échecs subis par Fang Hongjian et son absence systématique de réactions, pour être à même d'en tirer une certaine richesse sémantique relative à ce personnage. De ce point de vue, il n'aura pas perdu beaucoup d'informations par rapport à un nom traduit. La différence réside peut-être dans le fait que la lecture ici prend une forme plus rétroactive, qui charge petit à petit le nom transcrit de significations en fonction du signifié du personnage. Pourtant le défaut de traduction cause fatalement des pertes d'informations et des déficiences sémantiques que l'on peut observer sur plusieurs plans.

Un nom qui n'est pas traduit laisse dans son opacité une partie de la richesse de l'oeuvre et du personnage dans ses propres transformations comme dans les relations qu'il entretient avec d'autres personnages. Un étudiant attentif décèle dans *Famille*, à juste titre, la codification et la hiérarchisation d'un système familial traditionnel grâce à la traduction des noms compartimentés selon la génération, le sexe, et révélateurs d'une attribution inégale: les hommes ont souvent un prénom plus abstrait et plus recherché, chargée d'une qualification positive ou d'une volonté d'agir sur le destin, nomen-numen, alors que les femmes portent un prénom qui renvoie simplement à la beauté comparée aux fleurs ou aux pierres précieuses — Anneau de Turquoise (Cuihuan), Fleur Cachée (Yunhua), Pur Hibiscus (Shurong) — mis à part les prénoms à vertus typiquement féminines, tel Pure Chasteté (Shuzhen). Lorsqu'on est en présence de la simple transcription la situation devient différente. Reprenons l'exemple tiré de *La Cage entrebâillée*. Si Lao She a choisi de nommer, dans ce roman, la plupart de ses personnages non pas d'après leurs prénoms mais d'après leur appellation qui repose soit sur le modèle du nom de famille précédé de Lao ou Xiao, soit sur d'apparents liens de parenté, c'est parce que ce système appellatif est particulièrement révélateur des rapports sociaux que décrit l'auteur dans ce roman. La simple transcription phonétique et l'absence de notification empêchent donc les lecteurs d'accéder à cette référence sociologique et anthropologique, qui est pourtant nécessaire à la compréhension des faits normatifs et de la déviance introduits dans le texte. Grâce à une note jetée en bas de page (1986:286), on comprend mieux pourquoi Xiao Zhao abrège le nom de Ding Erye en Ding Er.[5] En revanche un lecteur non initié a des difficultés à saisir pourquoi Lao Li, d'un caractère foncièrement intègre et probe a toujours refusé d'appeler Xiao Zhao, un de ses collègues débauché et crapuleux.

Examinons maintenant la question du point de vue proprement narratif. Le nom de Xiangzi du *Pousse-pousse*, qui présage le bonheur et le caractère honnête d'un homme, doit permettre à l'auteur d'adopter une double stratégie positive et déceptive dans la construction du personnage. Ce prénom est en concordance avec un caractère foncièrement honnête et intègre, mais en parfaite contradiction avec un parcours narratif descendant et le destin tragique qui lui est réservé, aux antipodes du souhait que son créateur a formulé à travers sa dénomination. A cela s'ajoute encore le rapport entre le discours textuel et le discours intitulant, qui aurait des conséquences non moins importantes sur l'orientation de la lecture. A la différence du titre chinois où figure le nom même du protagoniste, nous avons donc un titre réifié et désanthropomorphisé. En laissant peut-être un peu de côté l'intention première de l'auteur, qui, en adepte de Dickens, aurait voulu placer son héros au centre de son histoire, la traduction suggère par là même une lecture qui ne s'éloigne pas outre mesure du discours textuel global en mettant en relief l'idée de l'objectivation et de l'aliénation du personnage. Encore a-t-il fallu aux traducteurs, pour cette modification, réaménager discrètement et habilement l'incipit de façon à effacer le hiatus qui aurait séparé le titre du texte, puisque la version originale commence par l'explication du nom de Xiangzi et de son surnom, Le Chameau, faisant écho au titre, Xiangzi le Chameau, alors que par le titre du *Pousse-pousse* on a dû introduire dans le passage initial, juste derrière le nom de Xiangzi, une apposition, 'le tireur de pousse-pousse', de façon à assurer un enchaînement entre le titre et le personnage ici présenté (1991:9).

A l'occultation ou à la modification des fonctions narratives et psychologiques des noms de personnages se joignent encore celles de leurs fonctions rhétoriques. Xiangzi le Chameau, qui n'est pas traduit dans le titre, aurait mis en évidence le réseau métaphorique de la bestialité, constituant le contrepoint significatif de Tigresse dans la mise en place du couple oppositionnel de domination/soumission. Dans *La Forteresse assiégée*, c'est l'ironie qui est en jeu. Le nom de Fang Hongjian constitue ainsi une antiphrase de son destin. Hong signifie l'oie sauvage, souvent associée à l'idée de projet ambitieux, de plan grandiose (Hongtu), ou de nobles aspirations (Hongye), tandis que Jian, désignant le 53e hexagramme du *Livre des Mutations*, renvoie à l'idée du développement régulier, le moment où une nouvelle étape est franchie dans la marche vers un accomplissement final. Cette ambition que les parents, probablement, appellent de leur voeu, se voit constamment démentie par des échecs réitérés et une vie d'une platitude désespérante. Son nom contradictoire rejoint celui de sa femme, Sun Roujia, qui, d'après son prénom, doit offrir l'image d'une femme douce, tendre et heureuse. Mais c'est une véritable mégère indomptable qui enfonce chaque jour davantage Hongjian dans ses désillusions et sa déchéance. Le même procédé s'étend jusqu'au nom de Gao Songnian, le recteur de l'université de Sanlü, qui sur un poste qu'il monopolise depuis trop longtemps tyrannise ses collègues avec ses connaissances scientifiques vieillissantes. L'auteur y fait allusion par le choix de son prénom, Songnian (Song — pin, Nian — âge). Le pin étant l'emblème de la longévité, l'homme atteint en effet un âge plus qu'honorable. Le nom de famille même renforce l'idée: Gao, associé à des expressions comme Gaoling, âge avancé ou

Degaowangzhong, vertu éminente et grand prestige. Un charisme donc lié à la doyenneté. De telles notes ironiques se dégagent des noms de ces personnages à la moindre sollicitation d'un lecteur chinois, mais demeurent opaques en français en raison de la transcription.

A l'inaccessibilité du sens s'ajoute encore un dernier point: la restriction du sens, due à l'impossibilité, dont sont souvent prisonniers des lecteurs timides ou inexpérimentés, de reprendre des transcriptions phonétiques, notamment du pinyin, à cause de leur caractère imprononçable. Il en résulte que les noms propres, chargés de la permanence et de la conservation de toutes les informations, sont souvent remplacés par des désignations descriptives comme les titres, les fonctions ou les rôles, avec une densité sémantique plus localisée. Ainsi Roujia est la femme insupportable de celui qui revient de France avec un diplôme bidon, Xiao Zhao, la crapule, Zhang Dage, l'entremetteur, et enfin, Xiangzi (Siang-tse), souvent le protagoniste ou le tireur de pousse-pousse.

Devant ces handicaps aussi bien sémantiques que phonétiques qui affectent la lecture, pourra-t-on imaginer un jour, est-ce une utopie, des solutions qui réinventent des noms à la fois prononçables et contenant un sens maintenu dans sa suggestion discrète?[6]

Université de la Sorbonne Nouvelle (Paris III)

Notes

[1] Les personnages: constitués par des signes linguistiques, des procédés de dimensions variables. Hamon propose de nommer étiquette cet ensemble disséminé de marques: 'Le personnage, "l'effet-personnage" dans le texte n'est, d'abord, que la prise en considération, par le lecteur, du jeu textuel de ces marques, de leur importance qualitative et quantitative, de leur mode de distribution, de la concordance et discordance relative qui existe, dans un même texte, entre marques stables (le nom, le prénom) et marques instables à transformations possibles (qualifications, actions). L'ensemble de ces marques, que nous appellerons "l'étiquette du personnage", constitue et construit le personnage. Le retour des marques stables organise le personnage comme foyer permanent d'information, organise la mémoire que le lecteur a de son texte; leur distribution aléatoire et leurs transformations organisent l'intérêt romanesque.' Philippe Hamon 1983 *Le Personnel du roman*, Droz, Paris: p. 107.

[2] Un élément pratique, indiqué par la traductrice, doit entrer en considération: la transcription phonétique de Cuicui prêterait à confusion car on le lirait comme le mot onomatopéique, en français, de cui-cui, qui imite le pépiement d'oiseau.

[3] Cette appellation est traduite dans la première ligne du roman, mais qualifié de 'surnom' et abandonné pour toujours dans le reste du texte, sauf dans quelques dialogues: 'Zhang n'avait pas volé son surnom de "grand frère"', Lao She, *La Cage entrebâillée*, p. 13.

[4] 'Je m'appelle Ni Bing. Comme j'ai de longues jambes, tout le monde m'appelle Longues Pattes. C'est un surnom très grossier, n'y prête pas attention...' *Les Trois rois*, p. 45. Dans le texte chinois, le commentaire sur le grossièreté porte sur le seul caractère de couilles (luan).

[5] La note nous indique: 'Littéralement, Erye signifie "Deuxième seigneur". En l'appelant Ding Er, Xiao Zhao traite le vieillard comme un simple domestique.' *La cage entrebâillée*, p. 286.

[6] Qu'on se rappelle, avec Viviane Alleton (*Les Chinois et la passion des noms*, p. 64), le procédé utilisé par Rabelais dans le baptême de ses personnages, Panurge, Epistemon ou Eusténès. Panurge, par exemple, à la fois est lisible dans la langue vulgaire, notamment dans la bouche du

personnage lui-même: 'c'est le pain dont j'ai un besoin urgent', et rappelle son étymologie grecque, panourgos, 'apte à tout faire' (d'où 'habile, fourbe'). Pourquoi ne pas réinventer des procédés de transposition des noms chinois qui, associant le son et le sens, suggère à la fois l'exotisme et la conformité au système européen?

Oeuvres Citées

A Cheng 1988 *Les trois rois*, tr. Noël Dutrait. Alinéa, Paris.

Alleton, Viviane 1994 *Les Chinois et la passion des noms*. Aubier, Paris.

Ba Jin (Pa Kin) 1989 *Famille*, tr. Li Tche-houa et J. Alezaïs. Livre de poche, Paris.

—— 1982 *Printemps*, tr. E. Simar-Dauverd. Flammarion, Paris.

—— 1989 *Automne,* tr. E. Simar-Dauverd. Flammarion, Paris.

Hamon, Philippe 1973 *Poétique du récit*. Seuil, Paris.

—— 1983 *Le Personnel du roman*. Droz, Paris.

Lao She 1991 *Le Pousse-pousse*, Philippe Picquier, Arles.

—— 1986 *La Cage entrebâillée,* tr. P. Bady et Li Tche-houa. Gallimard, Paris.

—— 1992 *Un Fils tombé du ciel*, tr. Lu Fujun et Christine Mel. Livre de poche, Paris.

Li Jieren (Li Tie-j'en) 1982 *Rides sur les eaux dormantes*, tr. Wan Chunyee. Gallimard, Paris.

Lu Xun 1990 *Nouvelles choisies*. Ed. en langues étrangères, Pékin.

—— 1989 *Histoire d'A Q, véridique biographie,* tr. M. Loi. Livre de poche, Paris.

Qian Zhongshu 1987 *La Forteresse assiégée*, tr. S. Servan-Schreiber et Lou Wang. Christian Bourgois, Paris.

Shen Congwen 1990 *Le Passeur de Chadong*, tr. Isabelle Rabut. Albin Michel, Paris.

Su Tong 1992 *Epouses et concubines*, tr. Annie Au Yeung et Françoise Lemoine. Flammarion, Paris.

Wang Zengqi 1989 *Les Trois amis de l'hivers*, tr. Annie Curien. Philippe Picquier, Arles.

Muriel Detrie

L'Ecriture Chinoise en Occident: Un Mythe Productif

La situation linguistique de la Chine ancienne présente un cas de figure tout à fait original avec la co-existence de deux langues, une langue parlée (*kouyu*) qui a considérablement évolué au cours des siècles et dont les variétés dialectales sont nombreuses aujourd'hui encore, et une langue écrite (*wenyan*) qui n'a jamais servi et ne saurait servir à la communication orale et qui est demeurée quasiment inchangée au cours d'une longue histoire de près de trois millénaires. Les signes de l'écriture chinoise qui constituent cette langue écrite ont aussi été utilisés — et le sont encore — pour noter la langue parlée, ce qui explique la confusion qui a longtemps été faite par les commentateurs occidentaux entre les deux langues. Depuis la découverte et l'étude consécutive des *jiaguwen* ou inscriptions oraculaires sur os et écailles de tortue, dans la première moitié du siècle, on pense que cette écriture a servi à l'origine, non pas de moyen de communication entre les hommes, mais de moyen d'enregistrement de tout ce qui concerne les rapports des hommes avec les esprits. Les traits incisés sur les supports divinatoires et les craquelures obtenues par l'action du feu sur ces derniers ont été combinés et développés par les devins pour former des signes d'une plus grande complexité qui ne servaient pas à noter les mots de la langue parlée mais qui constituaient des mots en eux-mêmes.

L'écriture proprement dite est née lorsque l'on a commencé à associer signes graphiques et mots de la langue parlée, et donc syllabes puisque le chinois était monosyllabique. Les premiers signes étaient des pictogrammes et des idéogrammes, c'est-à-dire des dessins très stylisés des choses ou des symboles des idées. Mais l'association qui s'est faite entre signes et syllabes a entraîné la création de nouveaux signes — appelés idéophonogrammes ou *xingshengzi* —

par combinaison de caractères pris pour leur valeur sémantique et de caractères pris pour leur valeur phonétique. Les signes de l'écriture chinoise ainsi constitués représentent environ 90% de l'ensemble des caractères (le pourcentage varie un peu selon le lexique de référence choisi), proportion considérable qui bat sérieusement en brèche le mythe d'une écriture purement idéographique. Et pourtant, durant plusieurs siècles, les Occidentaux, qu'ils soient philosophes ou poètes, n'ont cessé de bâtir des systèmes, de rêver et de créer à partir de cette écriture parce qu'à tous elle leur est apparue comme une écriture parlant directement à l'esprit ou à l'imagination, sans l'intermédiaire des sons, une écriture, par conséquent, capable de remédier au désastre de Babel.

La Découverte de L'Ecriture Chinoise par les Européens

Marco Polo ne dit rien de l'écriture chinoise et il faut attendre le milieu du seizième siècle pour voir apparaître sous la plume d'un Européen, François-Xavier, les premières remarques relatives à l'écriture chinoise. Et significativement, ce n'est pas en Chine, mais au Japon, sous la forme des *kanji*, que sont découverts les caractères chinois, qui sont ainsi d'emblée perçus comme des signes d'écriture indépendants de la parole. 'L'apôtre des Indes' note en effet que l'écriture chinoise, qui est enseignée au Japon, permet à Chinois et Japonais de se comprendre parce que:

> ...chaque lettre de la Chine signifie une chose; ainsi, quand les Japonais l'apprennent, lorsqu'ils tracent une lettre de la Chine, ils peignent au-dessus de cette lettre ce qu'elle veut dire ... lorsque celui qui est japonais lit ces lettres, il les lit dans sa langue du Japon et celui qui est chinois dans sa langue de la Chine. Ainsi quand ils parlent, ils ne se comprennent pas; mais quand ils écrivent, c'est par l'écriture seulement qu'ils se comprennent, car ils connaissent la signification des lettres, les langues restant toujours différentes. (1987:386)

Et François-Xavier tire aussitôt profit des avantages de ce système d'écriture puisqu'il compose 'dans la langue du Japon un livre qui traite de la création du monde et de tous les mystères de la vie du Christ', qu'il écrit ensuite (ou plus probablement fait écrire) 'en écriture de Chine' afin, dit-il, 'de pouvoir me faire comprendre lorsque j'irai en Chine, jusqu'au moment où je saurai parler le chinois.'

Se fondant sur les témoignages des premiers missionnaires en Asie, le P. José de Acosta, dans son *Historia natural y moral de las Indias* parue à Séville en 1590,[1] va contribuer lui aussi à répandre cette idée d'écriture non phonétique en soulignant que le chinois, qui associe à chaque notion un caractère, est impropre à noter les sons des mots étrangers. L'ouvrage de Mendoza *Historia de las cosas màs notables, ritos y costumbres del gran Reyno de la China* (1585, traduit en français et en anglais dès 1588), qui a connu un énorme succès en son temps, donnait quant à lui des informations succinctes sur l'écriture chinoise, mais ce fut le premier livre imprimé en Europe à reproduire des caractères chinois et à ce titre il mérite d'être signalé car la contemplation des caractères sera pour les non-initiés une source d'inspiration non moins grande que les discours tenus sur ceux-ci. Mieux documentée, mais non illustrée, est l'*Histoire de l'expédition chrétienne au royaume de la Chine,* rédigée initialement en latin (1615, traduit en français l'année suivante) par le jésuite Nicolas Trigault à partir des notes du P. Matthieu Ricci qui fut le premier missionnaire à pénétrer au coeur de la Chine. En tant que promoteur de la politique d'évangélisation des jésuites dont le mot d'ordre était l'accommodation à la culture du pays-cible, le P. Ricci eut une connaissance approfondie du chinois, aussi bien la langue parlée officielle (*guanhua*) dont usaient les mandarins d'un bout à l'autre de la Chine que la langue écrite (*wenyan*) dans laquelle il rédigea plusieurs ouvrages d'apologétique. Aussi sa première remarque est-elle pour noter la différence entre la 'façon d'écrire et composer' des Chinois et la 'façon de parler', quand bien même 'tous les mots de l'un et l'autre langage sont communs ès devis familiers et plus graves écritures' (1978:91). Toutefois, la nature des signes d'écriture n'apparaît pas clairement: en effet, il note que 'tous les mots ... sont d'une syllabe' et qu'il 'n'y a pas moins de lettres que de mots' — ce qui pourrait laisser croire à une écriture phonétique où chaque signe correspondrait à une syllabe — mais ces 'lettres' (entendez: ces signes d'écriture) sont comparées aux 'figures hiéroglyphiques des Egyptiens' (91), c'est-à-dire considérées comme des symboles, ce qui alimentera la thèse du chinois comme langue purement idéographique. Un peu plus loin il ajoute: 'la plupart de ces lettres sont d'un même son, non même figure, voire aussi non d'une signification: d'où provient qu'on ne trouve aucun autre langage tant équivoque' (92), remarque propre à entretenir la confusion entre langue et écriture. Mais malgré tout, Ricci, comme déjà ses devanciers, est sensible au fait que les Chinois, d'une province à l'autre, mais aussi 'les Japons, Corains, Cocincinois, Leuthiens ont des livres communs' et 'entendent tout le même sens des livres, encore qu'ils n'aient connaissance d'aucune autre langue que de la leur propre' (93). Les promoteurs d'une écriture universelle trouveront là une bonne raison de s'intéresser de près à l'écriture chinoise.

Après l'ouvrage de Ricci-Trigault, les *Lettres édifiantes et curieuses* ainsi que les autres écrits des jésuites continuent tout au long des dix-septième et dix-huitième siècles à renseigner l'Europe sur la langue et sur l'écriture chinoises, mais on y trouve non tant des éléments objectifs nouveaux que des interprétations personnelles nouvelles, si bien qu'ils nous intéresseront plus comme expressions du mythe de l'écriture chinoise que comme sources d'information.

Langue Primitive ou Langue Universelle?

La connaissance de l'écriture chinoise s'est produite à une époque où, à la suite de la découverte de grandes civilisations qui se sont développées en dehors de la sphère judéo-chrétienne, s'est posée avec acuité la question de la communication entre les peuples. Le mythe de Babel, en faisant de la *confusio linguarum* une réponse de Dieu à l'orgueil des hommes, ouvrait la voie à la recherche, soit des vestiges de la langue adamique d'avant Babel, soit des fondements d'une langue universelle capable de reconstituer l'unité perdue. Les tentatives dans ce domaine ont été nombreuses, surtout au dix-septième siècle, ainsi que l'a montré récemment l'importante synthèse d'Umberto Eco, la *Recherche de la langue parfaite* (1994). Dans ce foisonnement d'idées, de théories, de systèmes tous plus fous les uns que les autres, l'écriture chinoise a joué un rôle non négligeable de modèle.

Le jésuite Athanase Kircher fut l'un des premiers à s'interroger sur les écritures non alphabétiques — amérindienne, égyptienne et chinoise — pour essayer de remonter vers la langue primitive. Sensible comme beaucoup de ses contemporains aux ressemblances entre hiéroglyphes égyptiens et caractères chinois, il établit une filiation des uns aux autres en faisant de Fohi (Foxi), considéré comme l'inventeur de l'écriture chinoise, un descendant de Cham, fils de Noé, dont les colonies auraient essaimé d'Egypte en Chine, via la Perse et l'Inde, y introduisant l'écriture hiéroglyphique. Mais si, sous leur forme primitive, les caractères chinois de même que les hiéroglyphes étaient des 'figures tirées de diverses choses naturelles', leur graphie a évolué si bien qu'ils ne gardent plus en eux que quelques vestiges de la révélation: ainsi la croix, qui signifie pour les Chinois 'la mesme chose que parmy les Egyptiens, sçavoir le nombre de dix qui est le symbole de la perfection', se retrouve dans un certain nombre de caractères, tels ceux qui, par ajout à chaque fois d'un trait, signifient respectivement 'terre' 土, 'Roy' 王 et 'pierre précieuse' 玉, et qui tous comportent l'idée de perfection (Kircher 1980:311). Cependant, malgré ces vestiges d'un savoir oublié, les caractères chinois tels que nous les connaissons présentent pour Kircher le grave défaut de ne comprendre 'rien autre chose que la signification des mots et des paroles sans enfermer aucun mistère, ny aucune chose digne d'estre sçeue' alors que 'les lettres hiéroglyphiques n'estoient pas des simples mots puisqu'ils (sic) exprimoient des idées générales et des concepts entiers' (311).

Nourri de lectures cabalistiques et occultistes, et hanté par l'idée d'une sagesse primordiale cachée, Kircher ne pouvait assurément trouver dans l'écriture chinoise, dont il n'ignorait pas qu'elle était toujours d'usage courant malgré sa lointaine antiquité, la profondeur et le mystère que l'écriture égyptienne semblait recéler à ses yeux. Plus poète que savant, Kircher a cependant été séduit par les 'agréables inventions' que révèle la décomposition des caractères complexes en éléments simples. Par exemple, remarque-t-il, le caractère *men* 悶, qui signifie 'estre affligé', se compose de deux autres dont l'un signifie le 'coeur' et l'autre la 'porte', 'comme si on disoit que la porte du coeur est fermée', ce qui lui paraît une jolie trouvaille car il est vrai que 'quand l'homme est dans l'affliction tous les esprits se renferment et resserrent, et se concentrent dans le coeur'. Sous la plume de Kircher, le caractère devient ainsi métaphore révélatrice des 'secrètes significations des choses' (312–13), ce qui se retrouvera chez certains poètes quelque deux siècles plus tard.

S'ils ne font pas des Chinois des descendants des patriarches, un groupe de missionnaires qu'on appelle les 'figuristes' vont cependant chercher et trouver dans l'écriture chinoise des traces de la révélation primitive qui aurait été faite autrefois à la Chine avant que d'être oubliée par les habitants. De même que Kircher, ils considèrent les caractères comme des 'figures hiéroglyphiques', c'est-à-dire des symboles indépendants de la langue parlée. Mais pour eux, à la différence de l'auteur de *China...illustrata*, ceux-ci ne seraient pas inférieurs aux hiéroglyphes égyptiens en signification symbolique. Certes les Chinois n'entendent plus leurs caractères que dans leur sens vulgaire, mais pour les initiés, c'est-à-dire les chrétiens, ils auraient un sens caché qu'il serait possible de retrouver par l'analyse des figures simples qui les composent. C'est ainsi que le caractère qui désigne le navire, *chuan* 船, peut être décomposé en trois éléments: *zhou* 舟, qui signifie lui aussi 'bateau', *ba* 八 qui signifie 'huit' et *kou* 口 qui désigne la 'bouche'; ce serait là un symbole de l'arche de Noé qui transporta en tout huit personnes (Noé et sa femme, leurs trois fils et les épouses de ceux-ci).[2] Toutes les vérités essentielles du christianisme (celles de l'Ancien Testament, qui préfigurent elles-mêmes celles du Nouveau Testament) seraient ainsi cachées dans les caractères dont il suffirait de révéler les significations allégoriques aux Chinois pour que ceux-ci retrouvent le chemin de la vraie religion.

Il y eut dès la fin du dix-septième siècle, et davantage encore au siècle suivant, bien des esprits pour mettre en doute les thèses figuristes, y compris parmi les jésuites, mais surtout parmi les savants et les philosophes. Ceux-ci eurent cependant aussi leur préjugé à l'égard de l'écriture chinoise tant la fascination que celle-ci exerçait sur tous était grande. Ce préjugé, qui faisait de l'écriture chinoise un modèle de langue universelle capable de remédier à la diversité et à l'imperfection des langues connues, prenait son origine dans l'analyse de l'écriture chinoise comme notation d'idées, indépendante du parler. De même que les partisans du chinois comme langue primitive, les promoteurs du chinois comme langue universelle méconnurent donc la dimension phonétique des caractères, mais alors que les premiers virent en ceux-ci des figures des choses et des emblèmes religieux, les seconds, au premier rang desquels Leibniz, voulurent y voir au contraire des symboles de type mathématique, c'est-à-dire non figuratifs et arbitraires.

Après s'être demandé un temps, comme ses contemporains, si le chinois ne serait pas la langue originelle, Leibniz pensa qu'il fallait plutôt y voir un modèle d'écriture universelle, d'une part parce qu'elle était comprise de plusieurs peuples ne parlant pas la même langue, d'autre part parce que, à la différence des hiéroglyphes égyptiens 'plus populaires' et 'trop à la ressemblance des choses sensibles', les caractères chinois lui semblaient 'plus philosophiques' et 'bâtis sur des considérations plus intellectuelles, telles que donnant le nombre, l'ordre et les relations' (in David 1965:65). Une langue 'philosophique' doit en effet, selon lui, non seulement exprimer directement les idées par des signes purement visuels, mais encore servir le raisonnement en classant les notions. Mais le système d'écriture chinois est-il vraiment fondé sur un classement raisonné des choses? Le philosophe finit par en douter, la multiplicité des caractères, aussi variés que les choses elles-mêmes, lui apparaissant finalement comme un inconvénient majeur à l'adoption du chinois comme langue philosophique.

L'UTILISATION DE L'ECRITURE CHINOISE PAR LES POÈTES
Au début du dix-neuvième siècle la sinologie commence à se développer en Europe et ses représentants, même s'ils ne sont jamais allés dans l'Empire du Milieu qui est désormais fermé, publient ces études et ouvrages de référence que Nicolas Fréret un siècle plus tôt appelait de ses voeux:[3] citons par exemple, d'Abel Rémusat, l'*Essai sur la langue et la littérature chinoises* (1811) et les *Eléments de la grammaire chinoise* rédigés en 1822 et publiés pour la première fois en 1857. Les savants et les philosophes, étant désormais mieux informés, cessèrent donc de fantasmer sur le chinois, mais il n'en alla pas de même dans le public en général ni parmi les écrivains en particulier.

Pour ce qui est du grand public, ses préjugés anciens ne furent pas tant dissipés par les travaux scientifiques, qu'il ignorait, que remplacés par un nouveau préjugé: l'idée que l'écriture chinoise, comme toute la civilisation chinoise d'ailleurs, est 'primitive', au sens péjoratif du terme cette fois, c'est-à-dire non développée, encore dans l'enfance puisque n'ayant pas connu le développement considéré comme naturel de la pictographie et de l'idéographie à la notation phonétique. Mais les poètes, à la recherche d'une langue qui fût au plus près des choses, envièrent à leurs homologues chinois leur écriture visuelle et poétique et tentèrent d'inventer sur le modèle de celle-ci un langage poétique délivré de la parole et de l'arbitraire du signe.

L'utilisation par les poètes de l'écriture chinoise mériterait une étude à part qui ne peut être ici qu'esquissée.[4] Remarquons tout d'abord que, à l'exception de Victor Segalen qui a véritablement appris le chinois, aussi bien écrit que parlé, pendant plusieurs années et en Chine même, les poètes dont il va être question ont tous été amenés pour des raisons diverses à s'intéresser de près ou de loin au chinois, à lire à son sujet des ouvrages sinologiques et à consulter des dictionnaires, sans toutefois jamais en acquérir la maîtrise. Mais sa connaissance approfondie du chinois n'a pas empêché Segalen, à l'instar des autres poètes de son temps et des écrivains des siècles précédents, à s'intéresser surtout à l'écriture chinoise en tant qu'écriture idéographique. Il dit des caractères en effet, dans la préface à son recueil *Stèles*, composée en 1910, qu''ils dédaignent d'être lus. Ils ne réclament point la voix ou la musique. Ils méprisent les tons changeants et les syllabes qui les affublent au hasard des provinces. Ils n'expriment pas; ils signifient; ils sont.' Et il résume leur aspect mimétique et symbolique tout à la fois dans la belle formule: 'symboles nus courbés à la courbe des choses' (1982:38). Une quinzaine d'années plus tôt, Claudel, dans 'Religion du signe' (1896), avait pareillement remarqué qu''à la Chine': '...l'écriture a ceci de mystérieux qu'elle parle. Nul moment n'en marque la durée, ici nulle position, le commencement du signe sans âge: il n'est bouche qui le profère. Il existe, et l'assistant face à face considère le nom lisible' (1974:54). Et une trentaine d'années plus tard il écrivait encore: 'L'idéogramme chinois est synthétique. Vous voyez d'un seul coup devant vous le portrait de la chose représentée' (1965:89). Michaux lui aussi est sensible à l'aspect concret et mimétique des idéogrammes, même s'il déplore qu'ils soient devenus des 'idéogrammes sans évocation', leur évolution les ayant conduits vers une abstraction de plus en plus grande: 'Il y eut pourtant une époque, où les signes étaient encore parlants, ou presque, allusifs déjà, montrant plutôt que choses, corps ou matières, montrant des groupes, des ensembles, exposant des situations' (1975:n.p.). Ezra Pound quant à lui, dans son petit essai *The Chinese Character as a medium for poetry* rédigé en 1918 à partir des notes laissées par le japonologue Ernest Fenollosa, parle des caractères comme de 'vivants dessins abrégés d'actions ou de procès naturels' (1972:30–1). Le poète américain aborde aussi la question de la langue, mais il affirme péremptoirement qu'elle 'ignore naturellement la grammaire' et il y voit à l'oeuvre le même procédé qui préside à la formation des idéogrammes à partir des pictogrammes originaux, à savoir la juxtaposition d'éléments simples ou concrets pour suggérer des rapports complexes ou abstraits. Enfin Gérard Macé, se souvenant manifestement de la préface de *Stèles*, fait lui aussi de l'écriture chinoise une mimographie visuelle: 'Méprisant les désinences et les parlers divers, mais liés à l'espace de l'empire, les caractères chinois, dans le carré qu'ils occupent, retracent les fleuves et les défilés du Milieu, le feu du ciel et les labours de la terre', faisant ainsi 'danser devant nos yeux l'illusion d'une langue naturelle' (1981:25).

Telle qu'elle est analysée par nos poètes, l'écriture chinoise présente donc l'avantage, par rapport à l'écriture alphabétique, de donner à voir le monde directement, sans passer par l'intermédiaire des sons et sans user de symboles arbitraires: ses signes sont au plus près des choses, non pas tant parce qu'ils en seraient des dessins exacts, que parce qu'ils en manifestent la signification profonde. Aussi tentèrent-ils d'échapper à la linéarité obligée du langage et de donner à leurs oeuvres la spatialité de l'écriture chinoise en recourant à divers procédés tels que l'insertion de caractères chinois, sous la forme de 'titres' accompagnant chaque poème (*Cent Phrases pour éventails* de Claudel), de sceaux et d'épigraphes (*Stèles* et *Peintures* de Segalen), ou dans les marges voire au sein même du poème (*Cantos* d'Ezra Pound), ou encore sur les pages de gauche, les pages de droite étant réservées au texte français (*Idéogrammes en Chine* de Michaux). Bien que dans toutes ces oeuvres le texte français ou anglais reste premier, la présence d'idéogrammes, parce qu'elle s'impose au regard, permet de retarder ou de suspendre la lecture linéaire. Par ailleurs, ils ont transféré sur le plan de la composition de l'oeuvre les qualités visuelles de l'idéogramme, donnant à celle-ci une forme ('stèle' ou 'éventail' par exemple) et une structure signifiantes qui soient perceptibles à l'oeil, globalement, dans la matérialité même du livre. Claudel est allé plus loin encore dans sa tentative d'imitation de l'écriture chinoise puisqu'il a, dans *Cent Phrases pour éventails* ainsi que dans *Idéogrammes occidentaux*, adopté une écriture manuscrite qui, par la forme et la disposition des lettres, offre 'une certaine représentation des objets qu'elle signifie' (1965:82).

Mais l'écriture chinoise n'a pas seulement influencé les poètes dans leur recherche de moyens d'expression visuels, elle les a aussi amenés à concevoir un langage métaphorique qui fonctionne sur le mode de l'idéographie, c'est-à-dire qui exprime des idées, des sentiments, non par désignation directe et univoque, mais par association de plusieurs figures simples. Claudel semble avoir été le premier à utiliser le procédé, en particulier dans *Le Repos du septième jour* où les images sont souvent accompagnées d'une référence explicite aux caractères chinois qui les ont inspirées. Ainsi en va-t-il dans ce passage: 'Comme l'indique votre caractère "l'Orient", le Soleil / A tiré l'arbre de la terre par la vertu de sa face: / Comme l'arbre élève ses branches vers le ciel, il enfonce des racines dans la terre' (1965:74), où l'on reconnaît l'idéogramme *dong* 東 désignant l'est, qui se compose du pictogramme du soleil 日 et de celui de l'arbre 木 qui lui-même dessine dans sa graphie ancienne ᙂ un tronc avec branches et racines.

Claudel, du moins dans cette oeuvre, montre qu'il a lu les jésuites figuristes car, comme ceux-ci, il découvre dans les figures dont se composent les caractères les symboles du christianisme (ainsi 'le caractère Dix' est-il présenté comme 'la figure de la Croix humaine' (111)) et la préfiguration des événements bibliques (ainsi l'arche de Noé se trouve-t-elle annoncée par 'le caractère *barque* qui signifie *huit bouches*', Noé — 'celui que vous appelez Fou-Hi' dit Hoang-Ti à l'Empereur — 'ayant avec lui sa femme / Et trois fils avec ses trois brus' (39–40)[5]).

Segalen se moquera de ce judéo-centrisme de Claudel en adoptant pour sa part un regard sino-centriste: dans *Peintures*, la croix portée par les envoyés d'une nation chrétienne qui défilent dans les 'Cortèges et trophée des tributs des royaumes', est en effet présentée comme 'un signe déjà connu: ce caractère: 十 CHE, 'dix', dont les traits en croix ont peut-être une signification nouvelle'(1983:122). Segalen n'essaie donc pas de retrouver dans les idéogrammes des vérités connues, mais il interroge lui aussi leur graphie pour en tirer des images qui révèlent la nature profonde des êtres ou des choses. Par exemple, il dit de l'empereur qu''Il est l'Unique sous le Ciel qu'il joint de la tête aux pieds à la Terre' (128), ce qui renvoie au caractère *wang* 王, 'souverain', qui se compose de trois traits horizontaux superposés — le supérieur représentant le ciel, l'inférieur la terre, le médian le monde des hommes — reliés entre eux par un trait vertical symbolisant la fonction unificatrice de l'empereur.

Chez Ezra Pound nous trouvons peu de métaphores ou de comparaisons s'inspirant manifestement de la graphie des idéogrammes; citons seulement ces vers: 'Their aims as one / directio voluntatis, as lord over the heart / the two sages united' (1986:467), qui sont accompagnés en marge du caractère *zhi* 志, traduit par Pound en 'direction of one's will'. Ce caractère se compose du pictogramme représentant le coeur, *xin* 心, et de l'idéogramme *shi* 士 désignant le lettré, d'où la comparaison 'as lord over the heart'. Mais Pound n'a pas seulement tiré de la contemplation des caractères quelques images inattendues. Il en a déduit aussi une méthode de composition poétique, la 'méthode idéogrammatique'. Celle-ci consiste à juxtaposer des images simples, concrètes, pour suggérer 'une relation fondamentale entre elles'(16). De même que le Chinois, selon Ezra Pound, lorsqu'il a voulu 'définir le *rouge*', a réuni 'les dessins abrégés des choses suivantes:

        une rose   une cerise
        de la rouille   un flamant rose (1967:16)[6]

de même le poète a accumulé dans les *Cantos* les exempla, lieux, personnages, actions, époques, objets, éléments bruts, pour exprimer des notions abstraites et fondamentales à ses yeux comme l''usure', la 'vérité'.

Enfin, les caractères peuvent être aussi la source d'inspiration du poème, non pas en tant que leur étymologie, réelle ou supposée, suggère des rapports nouveaux entre les choses, mais en tant qu'ils sont des énigmes, des noeuds de significations latentes qu'il appartient à chacun de dénouer. Par leur graphie évocatrice, les signes de l'écriture chinoise, pour qui n'en connaît point le sens, constituent un réservoir de formes où il peut lire, comme dans un miroir, les secrets de son être profond. 'Les signes chinois provoquent l'imagination', remarque Ezra Pound (15). Ainsi le narrateur de *René Leys*, devant l'énigmatique reçu 'de la première nuit d'amour au palais', couvert de caractères, que lui a remis son ami, laisse-t-il son imagination combler le déficit du sens:

> J'ai déjà tenté de le déchiffrer. Mais suis-je mauvais élève, ou le devoir trop dur? Ces caractères représentent des objets redoutables: des couteaux, une lance à croc; des yeux en long ou dressés en hauteur, des fleurs, des dents de rat, des femmes se cachant le ventre, des puits, des creux, des tombes, des trous lutés d'un couvercle... un fourneau magique... une bouche vide... un bateau... (Segalen 1978:235)

Dans cette énumération d'images hétéroclites et sans lien apparent se devinent les fantasmes de dévoration, d'enfermement et d'engloutissement que le narrateur partage, sans le savoir vraiment, avec son ami René Leys qui est aussi son double. Henri Michaux remarque de même que 'toute page écrite, toute surface couverte de caractères, devient grouillante et regorgeante... pleine de choses, de vies, de tout ce qu'il y a au monde... au monde de la Chine': suivent deux pages où sont évoquées les multiples 'scènes' chinoises qui, aux yeux du poète, émanent des caractères, 'groupes pour résulter en idées / ou pour se résoudre en poésie' (1975:n.p.). Tel un test de Rorschach, les idéogrammes, en suscitant un flot d'images, révèlent les désirs, les peurs, les fantasmes. 'La plupart des idéogrammes ... amorcent un récit en nous invitant à lire leur histoire', remarque Gérard Macé: 'notre histoire' serait plus juste car dit-il, 'apprendre le chinois, c'est rééduquer une main morte, en paralysie depuis toujours à l'orient de soi-même' (1981:26). 'Mais pour réveiller quoi, dans un coin perdu de quel hémisphère?' (13) se demande aussi le poète au seuil de son initiation. Son voyage dans la forêt des caractères, vers ce qui lui est le plus étranger, se révèle finalement une anabase qui le ramène au plus près de lui-même, vers le pays et la langue de son enfance, 'celle des contes de nourrices et des messes basses' (50); car 'du français au chinois, tout est presque toujours inversé. / Ecriture en miroir, et parole prise à revers: la bibliothèque tourne sur ses gonds, et je retrouve dans mon dos le jumeau qui me dévisageait' (42).

Ainsi l'écriture chinoise apparaît-elle en définitive comme une matrice à partir de laquelle chacun peut parler dans sa langue, précisément parce qu'elle n'est censée noter aucune langue particulière, ou encore, pour reprendre les mots de Roland Barthes, parce que 'c'est un vide de parole qui la constitue' (1970:12).

❖

Par delà la diversité des systèmes, des théories, des rêveries qu'a suscités l'écriture chinoise, il est possible de dégager quelques constantes. Tout d'abord on constate que les caractères, qu'ils soient considérés comme des signes motivés ou des signes conventionnels, sont toujours perçus comme des idéogrammes au sens propre du terme, c'est-à-dire des symboles des choses et des notions, qui s'adressent à l'esprit sans passer par l'intermédiaire des sons d'une langue. C'est méconnaître la dimension phonétique de la majorité d'entre eux et oublier le lien qu'ils entretiennent avec la langue chinoise. L'exemple des Japonais, pour ne pas parler des Coréens ni des Vietnamiens, qui n'ont pu utiliser cette écriture pour noter leur langue qu'au prix d'aménagements particuliers, montre bien *a contrario* l'adéquation de la langue et de l'écriture chinoises: les caractères sont parfaitement adaptés à une langue isolante et monosyllabique comme le chinois, non à une langue agglutinante et polysyllabique comme le japonais.

La seconde remarque qui s'impose concernant l'attitude des Occidentaux à l'égard de l'écriture chinoise est qu'ils ne considèrent jamais les caractères comme constitutifs d'un texte mais toujours isolément.[7] Il semble que le caractère parfait, originel, universel, naturel ou encore matriciel des signes chinois ne puisse être préservé qu'au prix d'un oubli de leur capacité à s'assembler pour signifier des énoncés, c'est-à-dire, une fois encore, à noter une langue effective. Or, pris isolément et non en tant qu'éléments d'un code, les caractères cessent d'être des signes linguistiques pour devenir des signes iconiques : alors que les premiers se doivent d'être transparents en quelque sorte, c'est-à-dire de s'effacer devant leur signifié, les seconds sont opaques, ils n'obéissent à aucun code, ou alors ils lui échappent toujours plus ou moins. A l'intérieur d'une langue, la valeur de chaque signe est déterminée par un ensemble de règles (morphologiques, syntaxiques) qui visent à la clarté du message. En revanche, l'image a une opacité qui la rend inépuisable et permet à chacun de lui trouver un (ou plusieurs) sens sans passer par un code qui imposerait un sens unique.

Considéré comme une image, le caractère chinois acquiert ainsi une profondeur, une ambiguïté, une plurivocité qu'il ne saurait avoir pour celui qui, connaissant la langue chinoise, ne voit en lui qu'un mot à l'intérieur d'une séquence signifiante.[8] La fascination exercée par l'écriture chinoise et les rêveries dont elle s'est trouvée investie ne s'expliqueraient-elles pas en définitive par le fait que ses signes ont été considérés comme une écriture douée des pouvoirs et prestiges de l'image, et paradoxalement dégagée des limites inhérentes à toute écriture? Mais il faut admettre qu'il s'agit là d'un mythe — certes particulièrement productif — car si l'écriture chinoise a effectivement le pouvoir de signifier visuellement, elle signifie aussi, d'abord et avant tout, verbalement, et pour celui-là seul qui a fait l'apprentissage de la langue chinoise.

Université de Tours

Notes

1 L'ouvrage est paru en français, dans une traduction due à Robert Regnault, en 1598, sous le titre *Histoire naturelle et morale des Indes, tant orientales qu'occidentales*; une traduction anglaise est parue en 1604.

2 L'exemple est cité, parmi d'autres, dans l'Europe chinoise d'Etiemble (vol. 2, 1989, Gallimard, Paris: p. 230). Il est emprunté à la *Lettre de Pékin sur le génie de la langue chinoise* (1773).

3 Dans une lettre au P. Gaubil datée de 1735, ce savant qui fut le premier sinologue européen non missionnaire écrivait: 'ce n'est qu'à la Chine que l'on peut apprendre le chinois et se mettre en estat de l'enseigner aux autres par des Grammaires et des Dictionnaires bien faits. Lorsque les Missionnaires nous auront donné de semblables ouvrages, peut-estre pourra-t-on s'appliquer avec fruit à l'estude du chinois mais je suis convaincu que sans cela on ne fera que perdre son temps' (in Virgile Pinot 1932 *Documents inédits relatifs à la connaissance de la Chine en France de 1685 à 1740*, Geuthner, Paris: pp. 82–3).

4 Qu'on me permette de renvoyer à quelques articles où j'ai déjà abordé certains aspects de la question: 'Le *Livre de jade* de Judith Gautier, un livre pionnier' dans *Revue de Littérature Comparée*, no. 3, 1989: pp. 301–24; 'Translation and reception of Chinese poetry in the West' in *Tamkang review*, vol. XXII, no. 1–4, Autumn 1991–Summer 1992: pp. 43–57; '*Un Coup de dés* a-t-il été imité?' dans *Mallarmé a-t-il eu des disciples... après sa mort?*, Littérature et Nation, Publication de l'Université de Tours, 15/1995: pp. 13–34; 'L'inscription de la langue et de l'écriture chinoises dans l'Oeuvre de Victor Segalen' in *Actes du XIV Congrès de l'A.I.L.C.*, Edmonton, 1994, à apparaître.

5 Significativement, Claudel oublie le troisième élément du caractère.

6 Est-il besoin de le préciser, il n'existe aucun caractère désignant la couleur rouge qui serait ainsi composé, mais l'exemple est parlant même s'il est tout à fait fantaisiste.

7 Significatif à cet égard est le fait que tous les auteurs dont il a été question ici, à l'exception une fois encore de Segalen, ont eu accès aux caractères chinois non à travers des textes mais à travers des listes, des lexiques ou, pour l'époque moderne, des dictionnaires.

8 La différence de nature entre la lecture d'un texte et la 'lecture' d'une image est corroborée par les travaux des psycholinguistes qui ont montré qu'ici et là les mecanismes engagés et même le lobe du cerveau concerné étaient différents. Pour ce qui est de l'écriture chinoise, en tant que texte elle est traitée par le côté gauche du cerveau, comme n'importe quelle écriture alphabétique, et ce n'est que comme image qu'elle l'est par le côté droit (voir Viviane Alleton 1994 'L'oubli de la langue et 'l'invention' de l'écriture chinoise en Europe' in *Etudes chinoises*, vol. XIII, no. 1–2, printemps-automne: pp. 279–80). Le traitement accordé par les Occidentaux au caractère est cependant justifié lorsque celui-ci, étant calligraphié et non simplement écrit ou imprimé, devient un objet esthétique.

Oeuvres Citées

Barthes, Roland 1970 *L'Empire des signes*. Skira, Genève.

Claudel, Paul 1965 *Le Repos du septième jour*. Mercure de France, Paris.

—— 1965 *Oeuvres en prose*. Bibliothèque de la Pléiade, Paris.

—— 1974 *Connaissance de l'Est*. Gallimard, Paris.

Eco, Umberto 1994 *La Recherche de la langue parfaite dans la culture européenne*, tr. Jean-Paul Manganaro. Seuil, Paris.

Fenellosa, Ernest 1972 *Le Caractère écrit chinois, matériau poétique*. Ed. de l'Herne, Paris.

François-Xavier 1987 *Correspondance, 1535-1552*. Desclée de Brouwer, Paris.

Kircher, Athanase 1980 (1670) *La Chine illustrée*. L'Unicorne, Genève.

Leibniz cité dans Madeleine V. David 1965 *Le Débat sur les écritures et l'hiéroglyphe*. SEVPEN, Paris.

Macé, Gerard 1981 *Leçon de chinois*. Fata Morgana, Fontfroide.

Michaux, Henri 1975 *Idéogrammes en Chine*. Fontfroide, Fata Morgana.

Pound, Ezra 1967 *ABC de la lecture*. Gallimard, Paris.

—— 1986 *The Cantos*. Faber & Faber, London.

Ricci, Matthieu et Nicolas Trigault 1978 *Histoire de l'expédition chrétienne au royaume de la Chine, 1582–1610*. Desclée de Brouwer, Paris.

Segalen, Victor 1978 *René Leys*. Gallimard, Paris.

—— 1982 *Stèles*. Mercure de France, Paris.

—— 1983 *Peintures*. Gallimard, Paris.

Jean-Marc Moura

Dialogue ou Malentendu Culturel? La Chine dans la Littérature Française des Années Cinquante à Soixante-dix: Quelques Aspects

Dans le domaine de la représentation de l'étranger, il est facile (et donc courant) de montrer que l'image littéraire est essentiellement un mirage. Le plus souvent, elle est en effet un miroir, l'utopie d'une conscience rêvant l'ailleurs selon ses propres schèmes. Il n'est plus question alors de relativisme culturel mais bien plutôt d'utopisme culturel. Les images de la Chine dans les écrits français, théoriques aussi bien que fictionnels, des années 1950 à 1970 sont un excellent exemple de cette tendance à la transformation de l'altérité, métamorphose qui n'est pas forcément inintéressante du point de vue esthétique. La Chine extraordinairement idéalisée du mouvement maoïste correspond ainsi à une utopie, non seulement au sens usuel du terme mais aussi au sens plus précis, où l'entendent Karl Mannheim et Paul Ricoeur. Parallèlement, le genre du 'retour de Chine' est propice à l'autobiographie, soit sous la forme d'un roman aux résonances autobiographiques (Pierre-Jean Rémy), soit sous celle d'une autobiographie explicite. Deux oeuvres, radicalement différentes, présentent ainsi une Chine toute personnelle: les *Antimémoires* d'André Malraux et le *Journal de Chine* de Michel Leiris, écritures très éloignées de l'idéal commun du dialogue culturel.

L'Utopie

Des années 1960 au milieu des années 1970, le tiers-mondisme est un courant important de la vie intellectuelle française.[1] Dans ce contexte, l'instauration par le 'prolétaire du tiers monde' d'une nouvelle société, meilleure et dépouillée des influences occidentales, va paraître se réaliser en Chine. La conversion de l'histoire, à laquelle invitaient de fortes voix comme Sartre et Fanon, est annoncée dans l'un des grands pays du tiers monde.

Relevant à la fois d'une sinophilie propre aux intellectuels français et d'une fascination tiers-mondiste plus internationale, le maoïsme se présente en France comme une interprétation idéalisante des transformations sociales chinoises de l'époque. Du point de vue politique, il se définit comme l''Ensemble des organisations marxistes-léninistes se réclamant tant sur le plan international que sur le plan intérieur de la lutte contre le révisionisme moderne, lutte engagée par l'Albanie et la Chine' (Kessel 1972:15). Il se veut une voie marxiste contre la 'bureaucratie', en accord avec les thèses du Parti communiste chinois sur la question du passage au socialisme, et hostile au Parti communiste français. Mais c'est sur le plan idéologique qu'il va surtout se développer. Les tenants du maoïsme imaginent en effet une société socialiste idéale à partir de la dénomination trompeuse de 'révolution culturelle'[2] et du peu d'informations dont ils disposent sur la Chine. Une mythologie chinoise va ainsi voir le jour, dont une citation de Maria-Antonietta Macciocchi résume la tonalité, souvent dithyrambique :

> Des millions d'ardents militants se lèveront dans toute la Chine: une marée invincible. Ils ont grandi durant la révolution culturelle et se sont furieusement éduqués au courage, à l'héroïsme, au dévouement, à la loyauté, au sacrifice, à la pureté, à la modestie, au mépris de la mort. Voilà le lait dont ils se sont nourris. Une somme de vertus à donner le vertige...
> Ainsi, la révolution culturelle 'a ressoudé travail manuel et travail intellectuel, ... a restructuré l'enseignement, du primaire à l'université, en un système d'éducation qui opère la synthèse entre théorie et pratique, ce qui fait que l'homo sapiens et l'homo faber forment un être complet, un homme total.' (1974:377)

Outre nombre d'essais, une revue va plus particulièrement contribuer à l'exaltation de cette 'sinisation du marxisme', *Tel quel*.[3] Les travaux manquent encore sur cette idéologie, mais il semble bien qu'elle réponde à une structure archétypale triplement fondée:

— une théorie de la séparation, développant le thème des divisions de la société industrialisée, où s'opposent bourgeoisie et prolétariat, peuple et pouvoir, ainsi que d'autres clivages présentés comme néfastes: désir/interdit, manuel/intellectuel.

— une théorie de la subversion, portant la volonté d'abolir toutes les séparations. Cette hantise de l'unité a pour élément fondateur le prolétariat, où se conjuguent abolition de l'ordre existant et réalisation d'une société nouvelle autant qu'unanime;

— les principes de l'action subversive, faisant l'objet de débats incessants entre partisans d'une organisation centralisée et spontanéistes.[4]

On peut ainsi définir le maoïsme comme la tentative d'institution imaginaire dans un pays du tiers monde du contre-modèle d'une société industrialisée dont la dénonciation connaît un paroxysme en mai 1968. Cette construction intellectuelle, fort peu illustrée par la fiction, ne durera pas. Les sinologues, tels Mandares et Wang,[5] Simon Leys,[6] Etiemble,[7] vont rétablir certaines vérités, assez généralement acceptées à la fin des années soixante-dix.[8]

Cette Chine des maoïstes français est certes une utopie, mais en un double sens. Elle l'est d'abord au sens traditionnel; il s'agit d'un modèle social idéalisé répondant à une triple détermination: utopie d'une société sans classes; utopie d'un monde où le prolétariat a subverti les cadres autoritaires désuets afin de libérer des forces créatrices nouvelles; utopie d'une société où la subversion de la coercition bureaucratique est instituée en règle et devient, dans son perpétuel dépassement, source d'une histoire régénérée. Le fantasme chinois est celui d'un idéal en réalisation qui doit, par son irrésistible exemplarité, entraîner le (tiers) monde vers un renouveau. Mais elle est aussi utopie au sens où l'entendent Mannheim et Ricoeur.

On sait que le sociologue et le philosophe ne définissent pas ce phénomène imaginaire par son contenu mais par sa fonction sociale. Mannheim tient l'utopie pour 'un écart entre l'imaginaire et le réel qui constitue une menace pour la stabilité et la permanence de ce réel'. Malgré les errances utopistes, elle a pour vertu de 'maintenir ouvert le champ du possible', de permettre donc 'l'écart entre l'espérance et la tradition' (Mannheim cité de Ricoeur 1986:389). Allant plus loin, Ricoeur distingue trois niveaux de sens du phénomène utopique. A un niveau fondamental, 'l'utopie met essentiellement la réalité en question, là où l'idéologie la préserve et la conserve. Elle est la 'fonction de la subversion sociale' (231). A un second niveau, elle constitue une remise en question permanente de l'autorité. Enfin, s'observe la pathologie spécifique de l'utopie: 'faire évanouir le réel lui-même au profit de schémas perfectionnistes' (390).

L'utopie maoïste est parfaitement définie par ces trois niveaux. Elle a effectivement servi les groupes gauchistes dans leur entreprise de contestation d'un pouvoir français qu'ils rejetaient. En ce sens, elle a été une remise en question des canaux de l'autorité dans la société industrialisée. Mais il est avéré qu'elle a fortement souffert de la 'pathologie' utopiste qui l'a conduite à une contestation où le réel chinois s'évanouissait dans la quête d'une perfection sociale fantasmatique, n'existant nulle part.

Cette utopie a davantage, voire exclusivement, mobilisé les essais, pamphlets et ouvrages politiques que la fiction. Elle est demeurée pour l'essentiel une utopie théorique, car à la même époque, récits et romans ont plutôt cultivé la tendance autobiographique.

AUTOBIOGRAPHIES CHINOISES

Le Sac du Palais d'Eté de Pierre-Jean Rémy (1971) est l'un des meilleurs exemples de roman 'chinois' aux résonances autobiographiques. L'auteur, diplomate français en poste à Pékin, évoque la Chine de la fin des années soixante. Dans son oeuvre, il nous présente des Occidentaux devenus les témoins perplexes d'une révolution culturelle à laquelle ils ne comprennent presque rien. L'un des personnages centraux, Guillaume, attaché de presse à l'ambassade de France, et en qui l'on pourrait reconnaître un portrait distancié de l'auteur,[9] s'intéresse davantage à ses amours cosmopolites et à la poésie de Victor Ségalen qu'à une actualité politique chinoise dont il ne perçoit que la surface. Signe du présent idéologique, un autre personnage, Wilhelm, un étudiant allemand, maoïste, est, lui, fasciné par ce qu'il croit comprendre des transformations chinoises. Wilhelm finira par repartir en Europe pour militer dans les milieux gauchistes et propager l'utopie dont je viens de parler. Le livre présente ainsi diverses silhouettes par lesquelles Rémy recrée le Pékin qu'il a connu. Mais sa forme fragmentée interdit de le réduire à la simple autobiographie déguisée. Le récit se déroule en effet sur plusieurs époques: celle de l'événement qui lui donne son titre, celle de la Chine où a vécu Segalen, et celle de la Chine contemporaine.

La Chine, à travers le temps, apparaît ainsi comme le pays de l'exil total, celui d'une altérité que les Occidentaux n'ont de cesse de tenter, vainement, de comprendre et d'aimer. Mais leur trace dans la terre chinoise ne sera pas plus brillante ou solide que le Palais d'Eté, construit par les jésuites au dix-huitième siècle et que des soldats européens ont rasé pour témoigner de leur dérisoire puissance. Les résonances autobiographiques tiennent donc plutôt à une fascination qui se détache de la Chine contemporaine (dont la réalité demeure une pure énigme pour l'auteur) et qui détermine un mythe personnel chinois, où sont cultivés le goût de la tradition chinoise, l'intérêt pour la poésie de Segalen et un rapport simultanément euphorique et fantasmatique à l'altérité assez typique de l'oeuvre ségalénienne.

❖

Avec les oeuvres de Malraux et de Leiris, on quitte le domaine romanesque pour celui de l'autobiographie avouée, ce qui ne signifie du reste pas que nous nous séparons tout à fait de la fiction. Les deux oeuvres appartiennent à deux périodes différentes: les *Antimémoires* sont publiés en 1967 (révisés par la suite), le *Journal de Chine* date d'un voyage fait en 1955, mais il ne paraîtra qu'en 1994, après la mort de l'auteur. A vrai dire, les divergences chronologiques sont peu significatives tant la Chine qu'on nous présente est influencée et même recréée par la personnalité de l'écrivain plus que par les contingences événementielles ou les velléités du témoignage. Ajoutons —et cela soulignerait, si besoin en était, le vague de la catégorie d'autobiographie — que la Chine est probablement l'un des seuls points communs entre ces deux oeuvres.

Si l'on voulait trouver une illustration de la grande différence séparant l'oeuvre de Malraux de celle de Leiris, on pourrait se reporter à Simone de Beauvoir, qui condamnait les *Antimémoires* au nom du modèle des vertus autobiographiques qu'elle trouvait chez le Leiris de *La Règle du jeu* (Beauvoir 1972:173–5). Il est exact que les *Antimémoires* montrent le goût de Malraux pour la transposition des éléments de son existence voire pour ce que d'aucuns appelleraient la fabulation. Comme les *Mémoires d'outre-tombe*, qui leur servent de référence, les *Antimémoires* associent autobiographie et mémoires historiques. Malraux, comme Chateaubriand, se croit fondé à se situer au premier rang dans l'histoire de son temps, à la faveur d'une épopée dont il est à la fois aède et acteur. Pas question pour lui de se livrer à des aveux, confessions ou remords. Le fait que Malraux soit le ministre du général de Gaulle et son émissaire planétaire ne facilite d'ailleurs pas le jeu confessionnel. Mais l'ellipse qui préside à la reconstruction de son existence va l'amener à nombre d'omissions que lui reprocheront les biographes. Il s'agit pourtant là d'un fait typique des écrivains de la génération de Malraux.[10]

Le 'mentir-vrai' d'Aragon ou Cocteau, prétendant être 'un mensonge qui dit la vérité', aident à comprendre l'esprit général dans lequel ont été composés les *Antimémoires*. Mais alors ne manque pas de se poser la question: sont-ce encore des mémoires?

Le genre des mémoires se définit généralement par l'usage d'une même identité nominale regroupant l'auteur, le narrateur, le protagoniste. Les *Antimémoires* se conforment à ce dispositif. Par ailleurs, le genre répond à un pacte autobiographique, externe ou interne au livre. Chez Malraux, ce pacte se veut original comme l'indique d'emblée le préfixe 'anti'. L'auteur justifie ce titre de deux manières :

— il répondrait avant tout à une question fondamentale: 'Qu'est-ce qui survit en l'homme à sa mort approchée, à la mort des autres, à l'humiliation?' Le trait est somme toute assez commun chez les mémorialistes. Chateaubriand, par exemple, ne cesse de dialoguer avec la mort;
— par ailleurs, 'anti-' serait justifié par la présence du farfelu. Mais la thématique farfelue est somme toute plutôt réduite,[11] d'autant qu'elle est encore amputée en 1972, lors des révisions du récit. En outre, le grotesque ou la fantaisie ne sont pas uniquement l'apanage de Malraux (grotesque chez Montaigne, jeu de mots et onirisme chez Leiris).

L'écart de Malraux par rapport au pacte autobiographique n'est donc pas dans ces deux libertés qu'il s'arroge, mais dans le droit qu'il prend d'inclure des séquences de romans dans ses mémoires, ce qu'il nomme des 'scènes autrefois transformées en fiction' (18). Ainsi: 'La richesse de l'autobiographie malrucienne est de ne jamais sacrifier la part de l'imaginaire, et d'intégrer des "noyaux" romanesques dans une forme ouverte, et même éclatée, de l'autobiographie'(Lecarme 1995:46).

La Chine des *Antimémoires* relève de cet imaginaire. Elle appartient à ce continent ambivalent qu'est l'Asie pour l'auteur: symbole de la jeunesse de Malraux et refuge de vieilles sagesses, territoire du souvenir individuel et des mythes immémoriaux, où s'échangent tous les moments de son existence. Contre l'Occident, 'la première civilisation capable de conquérir toute la terre, mais non d'inventer ses propres temples, ni ses tombeaux' (11), l'Asie contribue à entretenir ce que le Walter des *Noyers de l'Altenburg* appelle la 'part divine' de l'être humain (50).

Les trois pays asiatiques privilégiés par Malraux sont l'Inde, la Chine (et Singapour, où 'l'agonie de ce qui fut la Chine s''... est réfugiée' (384)) et le Japon. Dans ces contrées, grâce aux dialogues menés avec des hommes qui en perpétuent ou en incarnent les traditions, la méditation malrucienne peut se développer. En Chine, Malraux rencontre et dialogue successivement avec Chen Yi, maréchal-ministre, Chou En-lai et Mao Tsé-toung, le dialogue avec Mao étant le plus important.

Dans les *Antimémoires*, deux grandes figures historiques asiatiques apparaissent en effet: l'Indien Nehru et Mao. Ils sont envisagés selon le même point de vue général, peu soucieux des contingences présentes. Chefs d'Etat, ils sont éloignés du simple homme politique. La dimension spirituelle que leur reconnaît le narrateur s'accorde à la civilisation qui forme leurs racines. L'Indien est le 'chef de l'idéalisme politique le plus efficace que le monde ait connu', Mao, lui, tout bonnement, 'est la Chine' (341, 562). Il y a certes dialogue, c'est-à-dire échange actuel, entre Malraux et ces hommes, mais seul leur passé compte en fait: le combat gandhien pour l'indépendance, la Longue Marche de Mao, événements fondateurs de l'Asie contemporaine. Malraux s'intéresse en eux à une permanence dans l'histoire, où se mêlent 'ces hommes, les temples et les tombeaux ... parce qu'ils expriment de la même façon "ce qui se passe"'(17). Nehru et Mao deviennent ainsi de véritables figures légendaires dont les actions sont inscrites dans la perspective du devenir millénaire de leurs civilisations. Le récit finit par ne plus les présenter comme des êtres de chair mais comme des entités culturelles qui ont 'puissamment secoué l'histoire' (560).

D'autant plus saisissante est la confrontation de ces statues animées avec la mort. Selon Malraux, Mao est 'hanté par une pensée géante': celle du soulèvement des pays du tiers monde contre le riche Occident (561). Mais le Chinois sait qu'il ne vivra pas assez longtemps pour voir cette 'révolution planétaire'. Et l'auteur de conclure devant la fragilité du grand vieillard: 'Il m'a fait penser aux empereurs, et il me fait penser maintenant, debout, aux carapaces couvertes de rouille des chefs d'armée qui appartinrent aux allées funéraires, et que l'on voit abandonnées dans les champs de sorgho' (561).

Mao rejoint l'indifférence végétale, s'effaçant dans l'inexorable dérive de l'histoire. Ne resteront que les éléments légendaires du grand homme, les récits de ses gestes historiques, dont Malraux livre ici comme les esquisses.

La Chine des *Antimémoires* est ainsi celle de quelques hautes figures, dont les actes et les paroles expriment la fascination malrucienne pour les artisans de l'histoire, et le sentiment, dominant dans ce récit de fin de vie que sont les *Antimémoires*, du néant et de la mort. Elle est une partie de la vaste fresque aux perspectives universelles par laquelle Malraux tente de dessiner et de comprendre son existence. On pourrait dire qu'elle est constituée de sculptures monumentales dont les modèles sont interprétés en fonction des préoccupations esthétiques et métaphysiques de l'auteur. Aux antipodes, si l'on peut dire, le journal de Michel Leiris se concentre sur la Chine du quotidien et des gens du peuple.

❖

A l'automne 1955, Michel Leiris fait partie d'une délégation de l'Association des amitiés franco-chinoises invitée par l'Institut populaire des Affaires étrangères de Pékin à visiter la 'Chine nouvelle'. Le séjour durera cinq semaines. L'écrivain tient un journal qu'il rédige chaque soir, du 17 septembre 1955 au 3 novembre 1955. Ce voyage est pour lui celui qui lui a donné 'le plus de contentement' (1994:10), la Chine lui apparaissant 'comme le pays où plus que partout ailleurs, nature (dont les poissons), choses fabriquées (dont les idéogrammes) et les gens sont en parfaite harmonie' (44).

Dans *Fibrilles*, ce voyage idyllique est examiné de manière psychanalytique. Leiris tente d'expliquer la plénitude rencontrée et le désarroi ultérieur:

> Sans m'attarder par trop à faire précéder la Chine de toute ma 'pré-Chine' et ne cédant qu'à moitié à cette manie qui m'est restée d'aborder par un biais — le plus souvent après maints détours — une question à quoi j'attache de l'importance, je livrerai ici des chinoiseries tirées de mon passé proche ou lointain et notées presque toutes (comme si l'énonciation de ce que j'ai à dire exigeait ce prodrome) alors que le voyage en Chine était déjà derrière moi, et devant moi une étape nouvelle du voyage non localisé que j'effectue avec pour tapis volant ma table de travail. (1948:8)

Cette Chine n'est pas seulement le pays d'un voyage, elle devient rétrospectivement ce qui organise tout un pan de la vie psychique de l'auteur, de telle sorte que la multiplicité des 'chinoiseries' acquière sens et nécessité. Mais comme cette partie de l'oeuvre de Leiris est bien connue et fort commentée, je voudrais plutôt aborder la question du journal, qui a été publié récemment.

Par rapport aux écrits autobiographiques habituels chez Leiris, il est fort singulier et même décevant. Les rêves, humeurs, états d'âme, retours sur soi en sont absents au profit de l'immédiateté des gens et des choses, de la brutalité du fait. A la différence des autres écrits de l'auteur, on n'y trouve ni lyrisme ni leirisme. Il s'en explique en comparant la Chine de son voyage à l'Afrique:

> Sur l'Afrique Noire j'avais bâti un mythe avant même d'y aller et j'étais demeuré attaché à cette construction sentimentale ... durant tout mon séjour [en Chine], j'avais su tenir en laisse mon imagination alors même que je m'enthousiasmais et j'avais regardé non pour retrouver ce que j'avais mis d'avance dans l'objet considéré mais simplement pour essayer de juger. (272)

Ces limites imparties à l'imagination n'impliquent nullement que Leiris considère la Chine avec les yeux du professionnel de l'ethnologie qu'il est. Comme le remarque Jean Jamin, dans la présentation qu'il fait de ce journal, la Chine semble représenter un défi pour l'ethnologue par ses excès de toutes sortes (excès d'histoire, de populations, d'Etat, d'écriture, de paysages...), excès d'autant plus intéressants qu'ils sont radicalement distincts des cultures dont s'occupe l'ethnologie africaine, le plus souvent placées sous le signe du manque. La Chine constitue ainsi un défi méthodologique que Leiris ne put ou ne sut relever, comme il le reconnaîtra :

> Le fait est que j'ai mal organisé mon travail en Chine: j'ai visité le plus de choses possibles et me suis en même temps renseigné, succinctement sur les questions les plus diverses. J'aurais dû soit faire carrément le flâneur et le touriste ... soit m'attacher à une seule question.... Je me suis assis, somme toute, entre les deux chaises du devoir et du plaisir. (1992:490)

La surcharge de sens et d'événements rencontrée en Chine a donc troublé le voyageur et l'ethnologue au point de brouiller les catégories usuelles du travail et du loisir itinérants.

Le familier des oeuvres de Leiris pourrait s'attendre, puisque l'ethnologie est laissée de côté, à ce que l'écrivain s'engage dans une introspection, un leirisme, qui lui est assez coutumier. Pas du tout. La volonté de se dégager du rêve est manifeste et même explicite: 'Il faudra maintenant s'employer à ce que tout cela n'ait pas été purement et simplement rêvé.' (208). Nombre de traits stylistiques — phrases courtes, parfois style 'télégraphique', appel aux sens (vue, ouïe, goût) pour traduire la difficulté à parler de la Chine, minutie des descriptions avec les inévitables évocations touristiques (tombeau des Ming, Grande Muraille), constats chiffrés du développement social chinois (cf 155–6) — visent ainsi à préserver la fraîcheur de la notation, pour éviter qu'elle ne se réduise à une archive. On pourrait parler d'une écriture de la spontanéité, soutenue par le refus de la transposition dans l'espace autobiographique où les faits auraient perdu de leur fraîcheur et seraient devenus objets de contemplation. Leiris s'interdit 'le tressage de ses niveaux de conscience auquel le rêve peut donner lieu. La Chine n'est pas soi, ni même un miroir de soi'(1994:20).

On n'en parlera pas pour autant d'objectivité. La Chine que nous présente Leiris est presque aussi idéalisée que celle de Malraux. Son séjour chinois apparaît 'comme un rêve, fait de fragments et d'éclats de réalité, d'autre part, comme une sorte d'utopie sociale que la campagne des Cent Fleurs lancée en mai 1956 à l'initiative de Mao Zedong et invitant le peuple chinois à exprimer librement ce qu'il pense du régime — mais qui se soldera par une violente épuration — viendra mettre au jour' (17). Leiris n'a-t-il donc rien vu rien perçu du contexte politique?

La situation lui interdisait d'abord d'être trop critique. Appartenant à une délégation de l'Association des amitiés franco-chinoises, pour la plupart sympathisants de la révolution chinoise, invité donc du gouvernement chinois, il n'est pas dupe des discours officiels,[12] mais la simple courtoisie l'incitait à ne pas se montrer trop soupçonneux. Ainsi, pas plus que Sartre et Beauvoir, en voyage en Chine à la même époque que lui,[13] il ne dit mot de la violente épuration de la campagne des Cent fleurs.[14] Leiris précise d'ailleurs la difficulté de son rôle :

> Il est facile de s'engager dans l'anti-colonialisme, par exemple, ou dans la réprobation de la répression, car on est sûr d'avoir le beau rôle; il est plus difficile de prendre parti publiquement pour une révolution triomphante, car on peut alors vous reprocher de fermer les yeux sur un certain nombre d'injustices imputables à cette révolution. (1992:18)

Leiris insiste ainsi sur les progrès de la Chine, et sur la gentillesse, la courtoisie, l'amabilité des Chinois à l'égard des Européens. Son journal est le procès-verbal d'une rencontre harmonieuse, pièce à conviction et pièce de conviction sur 'une société certes exotique mais qui se présente comme un monde possible à vivre' (1994:18).

L'étrangeté de ce journal vient de là: sa spontanéité saisissante par rapport au style habituel de l'auteur — et qui est d'abord mise en pratique de la technique de l'ethnographie inspirée par la consigne de Marcel Mauss, déjà utilisée pour *L'Afrique fantôme*: 'La première méthode de travail consistera à ouvrir un journal de route, où l'on notera chaque soir le travail accompli dans la journée'(1947:4) —, son refus des analyses trop fouillées, curieux pour un ethnologue rompu à l'étude de l'altérité. Leiris parlait de 'tenir son imagination en laisse', mais ce n'est pas uniquement l'imagination qui est ici bridée. L'écrivain-voyageur s'efface devant l'harmonie du pays qu'il a parcouru. Il enregistre ses impressions sans les creuser ni psychologiquement ni sociologiquement, soucieux de ne pas troubler la douceur de son itinéraire:

> Plus que partout ailleurs, impression de se retrouver en face — ou, plus exactement, au sein — d'une civilisation incomparablement raffinée.... Une fois de plus, on constate un prodigieux accord entre passé et présent, monuments et vivants. Jamais, sans doute, on a poussé aussi loin l'art de vivre: dans tout autre pays — sauf peut-être en Italie, où les enfants savent si bien se mêler aux barbes des dieux marins sculptés — la foule déparerait les monuments par sa vulgarité. Ici, il est certain au contraire qu'elle en accentue la beauté...' (1992:141)

Une double révélation préside à ce voyage: 'la découverte concrète de l'Extrême-Orient et celle du socialisme en train de s'édifier sur le vieux fond de la civilisation chinoise'(225). La précision documentaire voire la sécheresse du journal visent ainsi à préserver l'harmonie d'un séjour que des explications ou des analyses seraient seulement venues ternir *a posteriori*. La relative déception du lecteur devant ce journal provient sans doute de là: Leiris n'a pas 'problématisé' son voyage en Chine. Il n'est pas revenu d'une manière soupçonneuse sur l'harmonie qu'il y découvre non plus qu'il n'a tenté une analyse ethnologique ou sociologique. D'où la sécheresse d'un récit où les faits mentaux et concrets sont avancés sans la rigueur de l'examen (de soi, des autres) qui fait la spécificité, le style d'autres oeuvres de l'auteur.

❖

A partir des quelques exemples que l'on vient d'examiner, peut-on parler de dialogue interculturel? A l'évidence mieux vaut évoquer la captation de la Chine contemporaine — et millénaire, car il y a un mythe français de la Chine immuable, inchangée, de l'empire jusqu'à Mao — à des fins idéologiques (maoïsme) ou autobiographiques. Pour le domaine littéraire, les oeuvres autobiographiques sont les plus intéressantes, de la redécouverte de la Chine par Malraux à sa découverte par Leiris. Sans doute peut-on parler de ces récits comme de malentendus esthétiques, c'est-à-dire au fond de beaux sous-entendus par lesquels la Chine permet à l'auteur d'exprimer des vérités qui lui sont essentielles à lui. La Chine de Mao est le symbole de la légende et de l'histoire en marche pour Malraux, elle est le pays d'un grand bonheur possible (mais seulement aperçu et pas vraiment analysé) pour Leiris. Les deux oeuvres sollicitent principalement (voire exclusivement) un certain aspect de la réalité chinoise, le plan politique et historique pour les *Antimémoires*, le pays concret, quotidien, pour le *Journal de Chine*, l'une développe ses virtualités mythiques, l'autre se veut fidèle à la sensation de bonheur qu'elle lui a donnée. Par des chemins différents, toutes deux donnent de la Chine un mythe personnel engagé par une subtile et parfois belle méconnaissance. Comme quoi le malentendu culturel peut devenir une clef de la réussite artistique.

Université de Paris III

Notes

1 Cf. J. M. Moura 1992 *L'Image du tiers monde dans le roman français contemporain*. P.U.F., Paris.

2 On sait qu'il s'agit d'un américanisme. 'Cultural' a un sens plus extensif, et moins prestigieux, que le français 'culturel'.

3 Cf. le numéro 50 (juillet 1972) et le numéro spécial 'En Chine' de décembre 1974.

4 Sur cette structure archétypale, cf. Y. Lescot et P. Pharo 1977 *Mentalité et philosophie du gauchisme de mai 68*, thèse de doctorat, Paris VII, dactylographiée.

5 1974 *Revo Cul dans la Chine pop* (parution anonyme), U.G.E., Paris.

6 Notamment 1974 *Ombres chinoises*, U.G.E., Paris.

7 Cf. 1976 *Quarante ans de mon maoïsme*, Gallimard, Paris.

8 Sur les ouvrages qui contribuent à cet épuisement, cf. J. M. Moura 1987 *L'Image du tiers monde dans le roman français de 1968 à 1980*, Atelier national de reproduction des thèses, Lille. pp. 73 sqq.

9 Il est par exemple né la même année que l'auteur et lui aussi est fasciné par la poésie de Segalen.

10 'Aragon, Montherlant, Cocteau, Cendrars, Céline. Cette génération semble n'avoir éprouvé que répulsion pour la platitude de l'énoncé autobiographique, que fascination pour les jeux du men-

songe et de la mystification.' J. Lecarme 1995 'Malraux et l'autobiographie' in *Revues des Lettres Modernes* 9: p. 38.

11 Elle est concentrée autour du personnage de Clappique.

12 En témoigne sa rencontre avec Sartre et Beauvoir: 'Eux aussi sont d'accord avec ce qui se fait mais point satisfaits de ce qui se dit: quasi impossibilité d'obtenir autre chose que des exposés officiel.' (1992:129).

13 Cf. S. de Beauvoir: 1957 *La Longue marche*. Gallimard, Paris; 1963 *La Force des choses II*. Gallimard, Paris. J. P. Sartre 1955 'La Chine que j'ai vue' in *France-Observateur*, 1 décembre et 8 décembre.

14 Dont Robert Guillain quant à lui, a rendu compte dans *Le Monde*.

Oeuvres Citées

Kessel, Patrick 1972 *Le Mouvement maoïste en France*, t. I. U.G.E., Paris.

Macciocchi, M. A. 1974 (1971) *De la Chine*. Seuil, Paris.

Ricoeur, P. 1986 *Du Texte à l'action*. Seuil, Paris.

Beauvoir, Simone de 1972 *Tout compte fait*. Gallimard, Paris.

Lecarme, J. 1995 'Malraux et l'autobiographie' in *Revue des Lettres Modernes*, 9.

Leiris, Michel 1948 *Fibrilles*. Gallimard, Paris.

—— 1992 *Journal*. Gallimard, Paris.

—— 1994 *Journal de la Chine*, établie par J. Jamin. Gallimard, Paris.

Mauss, Marcel 1947 *Manuel d'ethnographie*. Payot, Paris.

JOHN NEUBAUER

Literary 'Misreadings': Brink and Coetzee

What presuppositions does the notion of cultural 'misreadings' silently carry with it? In the first place, 'misreadings' presuppose a 'correct' reading, not only theoretically but also as a yardstick against which we set off incorrect ones. And this implies that cultures, like texts, can be defined with clarity, with coherent and unique meanings. This is a large assumption if we value dialogue and misunderstanding within a culture as much as between cultures; if we hold multiculturalism within a society in as high an esteem as coexistence and understanding in the symphony of cultures. Indeed, one of the most common intercultural misreadings is to reduce the variety within another culture to a monolithic homogeneity, to take one feature of that culture for its totality. This way, the Germans become Prussians, the Americans materialistic, the Dutch and the Scots penny-pinching, the Japanese hard-working and disciplined, and the Iranians muslim fundamentalists.

Yet, not all intercultural readings that deviate from the conventional self-image of a culture are 'misreadings'. If cultures are, indeed, heteroglossic mosaics of subcultures and contradictory features, then a reading from outside may set the accents among the constituent elements differently from the way the culture sees itself, and apparent misreadings may in fact be innovative and refreshing new perspectives, focalizations from another vantage point rather than errors. Within such a more 'positional' approach to cultural readings, one of the most difficult questions then becomes how to draw the line between acceptable readings and truly erroneous misreadings.

❖

Literary texts tend to be particularly heteroglossic; polyvalence and resistance to reductive reading may even be their defining feature. We will have to draw a line between acceptable and unacceptable readings even here, but the notion of misreading will become highly problematic: an intercultural or historically later reading of a text may uncover hitherto unperceived, 'dormant' features of the text, yet become labelled a 'misreading' simply because it deviates from conventionally canonized readings. Seen in this light, literary texts may warn us not to reject in an off-hand manner cultural readings that appear at first sight misreadings: a culture may miss the opportunity to readjust critically its self-image if it hastily brushes off an intercultural reading of itself as misreading.

What further roles may literature have in cultural communications and misunderstandings? For ethical and political purposes it would, of course, be convenient to claim that literature's primary function is to mediate between different ethnic groups, religions, nations and cultures. No doubt some great works of literature have been written with that purpose: *Max Havelaar*, for instance, a major nineteenth-century Dutch novel by Multatuli, which was a passionate defence of poor Indonesians against the tyranny of the Dutch colonizers and their local native supporters, E. M. Forster's *Passage to India*, and Romain Rolland's *Jean-Christophe* which was written to mediate between France and Germany. But such artistic projects, however successful they may be in exacting from us ethical and political support, are ever in danger of striking us as sermons or political pamphlets rather than works of art. Let us remember also that next to works that mediate and reconcile there are also others, often of considerable literary quality, that foster cultural misunderstanding by misrepresenting other nations and cultures, or their own culture in terms of clichés and stereotypes. Suffice to remember Shylock in Shakespeare's *Merchant of Venice* and the French in his *Henry V*, or some of Dostoyevsky's women and holy men who contributed in no small measure to notions of the 'Russian soul' around the world.

The literature I want to discuss here lies somewhere between the cited positive and negative examples; better said, it is their amalgamation. I am interested in cases where literature deliberately misreads culture in order to force its reconsideration. Such works are special examples of the misreading one finds in subversive satires, ironic 'misstatements' and exaggerations of everyday experience. Much of great literature, from Rabelais through Swift and Stern to Kafka and Borges, is precisely such a deliberate misreading, in which fiction displays a referential irresponsibility in order to change our perceptions of the world or to force upon us reflections on the function of language and literature.

Much of literature is not a true picture of the world, and moralists and ideologists, Plato among them, have accused artists of being prone to lie. Yet, as Lu Xun's *A Madman's Diary* so well illustrates, writers deviate from the norms that happen to dominate their society by using alienating perspectives, figurative language, satire, exaggeration, and imaginary worlds in order to reshape our perception of the past and of the cultural *other*. In providing such referentially irresponsible images, literature comes into conflict not only with historical writing, sociology and cultural anthropology, but also with the official images that those in power deem fit to propagate.

It is this politically and ethically subversive referential irresponsibility of literature that I want to illustrate with works of two South African novelists, André Brink and J. M. Coetzee, which were written during the years of apartheid and opposed the officially promoted historical and cultural images of apartheid with misreadings that deliberately veer away from verisimilitude.

❖

All of Brink's recent contemporary and historical novels are set in South Africa and include some information that is consistent with the author's own life. In *States of Emergency*, for example, the narrator works on *The Lives of Adamastor*, a title that anticipates Brink's own later book. At the same time, these novels frequently incorporate fictional foreign texts. *Looking on Darkness* is a fictional diary of a black actor who awaits his execution; the narrator of *A Dry White Season* reconstructs notes entrusted to him by an acquaintance who was murdered by the Secret Police; *States of Emergency* ingeniously interweaves the narrator's own fictional love story with two other love stories: a fictional one, whose manuscript was entrusted to him by a woman before she committed suicide, and the 'real' love story of that woman. The novels almost playfully intermingle documents with fictional authors and fictional fiction.

We are, of course, familiar with such intertextual 'retellings' and 'interweavings' as hallmarks of postmodern fiction; in Brink's engaged writing these apparently formalistic devices acquire a social purpose. His 'ordinary' protagonists are confronted with extraordinary experiences and compelled to report about them, even though they have to struggle with writing. What they leave behind — a polished story, a dull enumeration of facts, or a jumble of barely decipherable notes — is always a desperate appeal to some reader to make sense of what they could only dimly grasp. They throw, as it were, embottled legacies into the sea, hoping that some sympathetic reader might take the message to heart and continue the writing, eventually making the text available to the public. Indeed, the narrators of *States of Emergency* and *A Dry White Season* are just such readers who finally incorporate the inherited text into their own. Here, the intertextual embedding of received texts functions to keep counter-official accounts alive.

In Brink's historical novels, the 'foreign' texts are historical documents and other novels. Thus *On the Contrary* contains the fictitious memoirs of the historically documented adventurer, Estienne Barbier, whom Brink recreated from carefully researched historical documents but blended with the figures of Jeanne d'Arc and Don Quixote (perhaps also Michael Koolhaas and Max

Havelaar). After dutifully acknowledging all his borrowings, Brink adds: 'Most of the rest, I think, is invention. But one never knows' (376). *The First Life of Adamastor* rewrites the legend of the towering rock at the tip of Africa near Cape Town that Camoes eternalized in the Fifth Canto of *Os Lusiadas* (1572). *An Instant in the Wind* uses eighteenth-century diaries and official reports, but then gives free rein to the imagination. *A Chain of Voices* is based on court proceedings on a nineteenth-century uprising of slaves.

In all these cases, the foreign sources serve as a point of departure for writing conjectural history that may in fact be a misreading. Thus *An Instant in the Wind* picks the obscure phrase, 'This no one can take away from us' from the rather dull diary of the middle-class Elisabeth Larsson in order to read, perhaps deliberately misread, it to mean that she had a love affair with a fugitive slave. Elisabeth may have meant something very different and the love affair may not have taken place at all. But even if Brink deliberately misunderstood his source, he spun a story that subverts official apartheid histories of South Africa which are no less fictitious and often downright mendacious. The appropriation of older texts, legends, and documents leads to the writing of second-hand stories that reinvent history.

Blurring the boundary between history and novel, fact and fiction, Brink imaginatively invents alternatives to official stories. Rewriting the legend about Adamastor as a love affair between a native and a white woman; teasing an inter-racial love affair out of Elisabeth Larsson's diaries; imagining that the adventurer Estienne Barbier had made peace with the natives before he was executed by the colonialists; portraying in contemporary novels the struggle to find the truth behind the lies of the Secret Police — in all these cases he is questioning presumed facts, he is writing history 'on the contrary'. The deliberate misreadings of the officially presented evidence replace the fictions of the Secret Police and the histories written to justify apartheid with genuine fiction. The misreadings suggest an alternative history of South Africa — a functionalized fictional history that may further future friendly race-relations that may or may not have existed in the past.

Brink's historical as well as the contemporary novels represent alternatives to or misreadings of official stories. But whereas the contemporary fiction attempts to reveal the true story that the officials try to conceal, the historical ones invent counter-factual histories, in order to help construct a new self-image for South Africa.

❖

In contrast to Brink, J. M. Coetzee does not confront the official stories and histories of South Africa in a contestatory manner. Of his seven major novels to date, four — *Dusklands, In the Heart of the Country, Life and Times of Michael K,* and *Age of Iron* — are situated within South Africa, and these disregard documentary or historical material. Indeed they often deliberately blur time and place. Although he has been criticized for not addressing more directly the conditions in South Africa, Coetzee refuses to make fiction a rival of historical and sociological writing.

Coetzee's seeming 'referential irresponsibility' was then to have avoided thematizing directly the suffering and the outrage in his society. But was this deliberate shunning of verisimilitude an ethical irresponsibility, as some of his critics have charged, or rather an attempt to address the issues that Coetzee considered appropriate for literature, namely by way of indirection? I tend to agree with Attwell, who writes: 'Coetzee's polemics engage the politics of historical discourses; in order to preserve their rhetorical force, they are silent about the referents of these discourses' (1990:588). Let me illustrate the point by showing how two of Coetzee's non-South African novels deal with the problem.

Waiting for the Barbarians is told in the present tense by an unnamed aging magistrate of a small imperial outpost in a geographically and historically indefinite colonial empire. Since the empire is built on racial suppression, some of its problems evidently mirror those of South Africa, yet since the general structure is colonial the problem is projected back into a nineteenth-century situation of Conrad's *Heart of Darkness*, which may, indeed, have been Coetzee's chosen subtext.

The magistrate realizes that a military emissary of the headquarters is torturing nomad people to extort information about an alleged 'barbarian' invasion. He picks up a girl who survived the torture half-blinded and with broken legs; he nightly bathes her limbs, but the atonement brings no reconciliation, for they fail to communicate and he falls asleep desireless upon her naked body. Finally he undertakes an arduous expedition to return the girl to her native territory and is accused of treason upon return by his own military, which tortures and humiliates him. The military expedition against the alleged barbarian threat is decimated by the hostile climate and terrain, the imperial forces retreat, leaving the magistrate behind in the squalor of the plundered outpost.

Like Brink in *A Dry White Season*, Coetzee portrays how a white male gradually discovers the barbarism of his own state behind the official lies. Just as Brink's white characters find themselves in a cultural limbo once they start to question the official stories, so too the magistrate becomes alienated from his own culture. The fact that Brink depicts a concrete historical moment and condition of South African apartheid and Coetzee portrays, as Marianne Moore would say, 'real toads in imaginary gardens', does not in any sense mitigate the horror of his fictional world.

Indeed, one could argue that the mental anguish is more intense in Coetzee's novel. In *A Dry White Season* the alienation of a white person from his society is minimally compensated by a certain solidarity between whites and blacks, which, to be sure, does not lead to any comradery, for whites and blacks may work for a common cause but remain socially and psychologically apart. But in Brink's historico-fictional *An Instant in the Wind* and *The First Life of Adamastor*, physically and spiritually meaningful miscegenation becomes possible, if only for moments, in spite of the social injunctions against it. In contrast, the non-communication and misunderstanding between the magistrate and the nomad woman in *Waiting for the Barbarians* is due to internalized cultural differences rather than external pressure.

Similar gaps in intercultural communication are thematized in *Waiting for the Barbarians* in descriptions of the magistrate's unsuccessful attempts to decipher the signs he finds on the wooden slips of another civilization. What was originally just a hobby becomes a matter of self-reflection once he starts to write his own story and realizes that his desire to leave behind a record of his story and civilization is similar to the one that resulted in the coded wooden slips. Although the sense of this commonality further alienates him from his own culture, which considers itself superior to all the native cultures of the soil, it does not bring him any closer to the past cultures that he cannot decipher. Like the girl he nursed, the historical native culture remains closed to him. Whatever he will write about the cultural *other* of the past and present will necessarily be based on misunderstanding since he has no access to them.

❖

Foe, like Brink's *The First Life of Adamastor*, is an interrogation of a European classic, a rewriting that presents itself as a pre-text of the canonized version. But the two archaeologies are differently motivated. Brink reconstructs a Rabelaisian as well as idyllic and melancholic ur-text that is morally and socially superior to Camoes' nationalist version; Coetzee has nothing better to offer and focuses on the losses and misunderstandings that may have occurred between some hypothetical real events and their textualization as Defoe's *Robinson Crusoe*.

The truncated name in Coetzee's title emblematizes how this archetypal colonialist novel inevitably misunderstands and misstates its subtexts.

The new version is told by a woman, Susan Barton, who had searched for her wayward daughter in Brazil and subsequently been cast on the island of Cruso(e), and Friday, who is, in this version, a tongueless slave from Cruso's former ship. The three are finally saved but Cruso dies on the journey home. This revision of *Robinson Crusoe*, the first part of Coetzee's novel, is presented as the manuscript that Susan entrusts to the famous writer, Mr Foe, in order to turn it into a successful novel. The second part is a series of letters that the increasingly anxious Susan writes to Foe. The third one is a series of dialogues between Susan and Foe, while the concluding short part is a rather mysterious epilogue by a new narrator that leaves everything unresolved.

Thus Coetzee thematizes the misunderstandings and losses that occur in communication and the writing of fiction: 'Our craft is all in reading *the other*: gaps, inverses, undersides; the veiled, the dark, the buried, the feminine; alterities' (1988:81).

The novel's two types of communicational gaps, those of gender and race, are qualitatively different. Friday, like the nomad girl in *Waiting for the Barbarians*, is a 'black hole', a silent and impenetrable world, whose story even Susan cannot retrieve: 'To tell my story and be silent on Friday's tongue is no better than offering a book for sale with pages in it quietly left empty. Yet the only tongue that can tell Friday's secret is the tongue he has lost!' (67 cf. 118).

What to do then? Susan recognizes that Friday 'utters himself only in music and dancing' (142), yet, upon Foe's advice, she tries to teach him to speak English, and when this fails she tries to teach him the alphabet. Writing, explains Foe, who knows his Derrida, 'is not doomed to be the shadow of speech' (142). By the end of the story Friday can write the letter 'o', and Foe instructs Susan to teach him 'a' the next day (152). The project of teaching Friday the language of the *other* seems mired between omega and alpha.

The possibility of letting Friday communicate in his own tongue is *a priori* excluded, and Susan realizes that she, and the world, are taking imperial possession of him:

> Friday has no command of words and therefore no defence against being re-shaped day by day in conformity with the desires of others. I say he is a cannibal and he becomes a cannibal.... Friday is Friday. But that is not so. No matter what he is to himself (is he anything to himself? — how can he tell us?), what he is to the world is what I make of him. Therefore the silence of Friday is a helpless silence. (121–2)

Although Susan has power over Friday, she faces similar problems when trying to communicate her story. Not only does she discover that narration has its own conditions, that the storyteller 'must divine which episodes of his history hold promise of fullness and tease from them their hidden meanings' (88–9), she must accept that her words will merely serve as a subtext to those of Foe. First she confidently allows him to set the story 'right' (47) in order to make it not only true but also pleasant to its readers (63), but she gradually realizes that Foe's referential irresponsibility, his liberties with truth in the name of a 'good story', encroach on the integrity of her story as well as personality.

Foe first wants to fill the gaps in her story and add exciting elements: did Cruso perhaps save a musket from the wreck (53)? Perhaps even a carpenter's chest to build his ship (55)? Was Cruso not younger and more amorous (83) and Friday not more evidently a cannibal? To Susan's melancholy insight that her true story is dull, Foe replies that it is not dull 'so long as we remind ourselves it is true. But as an adventure it is very dull indeed' (127). Hence Foe decides that the events on the island must be set within a larger five-part epic:

> ...the loss of the daughter; the quest for the daughter in Brazil; abandonment of the

quest, and the adventure of the island; assumption of the quest by the daughter; and reunion of the daughter with her mother. It is thus that we make up a book: loss, then quest, then recovery; beginning, then middle, then end. (117)

Susan now adopts a new strategy: if earlier she protected her story on the grounds of verisimilitude, she now argues both that her story is well-made and that she must reject the reduction of 'the island to an episode in the history of a woman in search of a lost daughter' (121) as an intrusion on her authorial rights.

Insisting on her power to shape her story, Susan wants to define herself against the powerlessness of Friday. She can decide whether to be silent about parts of her life: 'There was a life before the water which stretched back to my desolate searchings in Brazil, thence to the years when my daughter was still with me, and so on back to the day I was born. All of which makes up a story I do not choose to tell' (131). She struggles to remain 'the father' (!) of her story by retaining the right to guide, amend and withhold it (123). At stake by now is obviously no longer merely her story but her power to master it and hence her identity — a struggle that bears resemblance to Dora's struggle with Freud in putting together the history of her childhood. Accepting Foe's expanded story she would be reduced to the status of Friday, who now becomes a sort of negative mirror for her.

Friday's life seems wholly written by others, including Susan who undertakes an arduous and finally futile journey with him to Bristol in order to ship him back to Africa (an inversion of returning the girl to native territory in *Waiting for the Barbarians*). Susan believes she is more of a master of her own life until her faith is shaken by sinister events, probably designed by Foe: a girl, whom Susan does not recognize, appears and claims to be her lost daughter, recounting a childhood that bears no resemblance to Susan's recolletions (90-1). The distinction between fact and fiction, real and fictional characters, memory and invention, identity and conjecture gets blurred, but Susan refuses to accept it. When the girl returns with a woman she claims was her nurse, Susan responds with words that oppose *avant la lettre* the postmodern fictionalization of reality and personality:

> It would be a waste of breath, Mr Foe, for me to say that these women are strangers to me, for you will only reply that I have forgotten, and then you will prompt them and they will embark on long stories of a past in which they will claim I was an actor too. What can I do but protest it is not true? I am as familiar as you with the many, many ways in which we can deceive ourselves. But how can we live if we do not believe we know who we are, and who we have been? (130)

Susan continues to insist that a story, which may be shaped this way or that way, is different from 'a substantial being with a substantial history in the world' (131): she is not a bottle bobbing on the waves with a scrap of writing inside, not 'a mere receptacle ready to accommodate whatever story is stuffed in me ... I am a free woman who asserts her freedom by telling her story according to her own desire' (130–1).

❖

We should not conclude from Susan's last quoted words that *Foe* is an idealistic defence of the autonomous person; neither is it a political pamphlet against racism and sexual discrimination, even if it thematizes the social suppression of blacks and women, and literature's complicity with it. By the time Susan and Foe reach the end of their dialogues, Susan no longer proclaims her autonomy and admits that her life 'grows to be story' and nothing of her own is left to her:

> I thought I was myself and this girl [her alleged daughter] a creature from another order speaking words you made up for her. But now I am full of doubt. Nothing is left to me but doubt. I am doubt itself. Who is speaking me? Am I a phantom too? To what order do I belong? (133)

Foe has no answer to the question 'who among us is a ghost and who not' (134). Far from singing the praise of fiction he melancholically admits that as a writer he is a whore 'who should ply her trade only in the dark'; Susan must ironically console him that it is 'not whoring to entertain other people's stories and return them to the world better dressed' (151–2).

Literature as a pretty dress that hides the naked and perhaps ugly truth underneath? Would fiction, in this view, not be a source of misunderstanding, a means of avoiding uncomfortable truths? Perhaps, but Susan's consoling statement is only one of several perspectives on fiction that Coetzee's fiction entertains. This novel seems to say that *Robinson Crusoe* is, perhaps unavoidably, a misrepresentation of its pre-texts. Some of the reasons for this, like Friday's muteness, are social, and hence amenable to improvement, others are radicated in historical notions of the novel that may also be amended: while Foe insists that stories must have an end, Coetzee's is actually lacking one. But having come to the end of Coetzee's novel we cannot but help sensing also a certain aporia of communication and fiction writing.

Facing that ineradicable residual misrepresentation and misunderstanding, Coetzee's *Foe*, like all fiction, can merely muster the courage to become self-reflexive, to obsessively encircle its own shortcomings.

University of Amsterdam

Works Cited

Attwell, David 1990 'The Problem of History in the Fiction of J. M. Coetzee' in *Poetics Today* 11, pp. 579–615.

Brink, André 1976 *An Instant in the Wind*. W. H. Allen, London.

——— 1979 *A Dry White Season*. W. H. Allen, London.

—— 1982 *A Chain of Voices*. Faber and Faber, London.
—— 1988 *States of Emergency*. Faber and Faber, London.
—— 1993 *The First Life of Adamastor*. Secker and Warburg, London.
—— 1993 *On the Contrary*. Secker & Warburg, London.
Coetzee, J. M. 1983 (1974) *Dusklands*. Penguin, New York.
—— 1982 (1977) *In the Heart of the Country*. Penguin, New York.
—— 1982 (1980) *Waiting for the Barbarians*. Penguin, New York.
—— 1987 (1983) *Life and Times of Michael K*. Penguin, New York.
—— 1987 (1986) *Foe*. Penguin, New York.
——1988 *White Writing. On the Culture of Letters in South Africa*. Yale University Press.

WANG YIMAN

Misreading at the Meeting of Two Hermeneutics: Ezra Pound's Invention of Chinese Poetry

Misreading as 'part of a historical transfer of ideas and theories from one setting to another' (Kenner 1971:236) has been accepted as an inevitable phenomenon in cultural communication. The gap between the new version and the original can be both intentional and unexpected. The former indicates a specific reading technique, while the latter stems from the reader's mental habits, including cultural background and personal preoccupation. Instead of being 'a farcical repetition' of the original tragedy as Marx describes in *The Eighteenth Brumaire of Louis Bonaparte* (cited in Said 1983), misreading has been viewed as a creative strategy both in dealing with the paternal cultural heritage (Harold Bloom) and an alien culture. During its reproduction, the cultural *meme* (to borrow a word coined by Richard Dawkings, indicating the abiding cultural phenomenon or mental position) undergoes variation, omission, rearrangement, as well as repetition, according to the particular time and place.

The result is 'cultural mutations'. The mutation refers to both change and enrichment, even the generation of a new culture. Viewed in this light, we may regard Ezra Pound, the modern American poet, as the paragon misreader, or 'the inventor of Chinese poetry of our time', according to T. S. Eliot. Pound attempted to exhume the original poetry, which he was convinced had been crystallized in Chinese ideograms. By simply staring at the structuring of the radicals and dramatizing the interrelations between the strokes, he literally invented a Chinese poetry, or to be more exact, a poetry of Chinese characters, if 'invent' is used in the Vician sense of 'finding and exposing things that otherwise lie hidden beneath piety, heedlessness or routine' (Said 1983:53).

It has been noted that Pound's interest was not Chinese culture as it is. On the contrary, he misreads it, so as to adapt it to his own social and literary conceptions. Analogous to his conception of the 'vortex' as the patterned energy made visible by water, rather than water itself (Kenner 1971), Pound's writing or rewriting of foreign poems is not a mere correspondence of the original, but his own mental framework made visible by the *other*'s writing. Pound's creative misreading is a renowned fact, which I do not want to contradict. My focus is not the result of his misreading, but how he misread Chinese culture, especially Chinese ideograms. By analyzing his approach I hope to show that, despite his modernist preoccupation, his interpretive strategy (which eventually led to his misreading) does display some affinity with traditional Chinese hermeneutics.

❖

Interpretation is not eliciting meanings from the texts, but 'the means of synthesizing and carrying on a whole structure' (Kenner 1971:236). Its necessity is determined by the human need for 'traditional ideas, which are continuous with time-tested experience and not unprecedented insights with uncertain consequences' (236). This applies to both Western and Eastern hermeneutics. Yet the hermeneutic method varies according to the specific cultural tradition and contemporary concern. The dividing-line between the Western and the Chinese strategies is by no means clear-cut. Nevertheless, we can discern two different trends, which will help us locate Pound's misreading. Therefore, before discussing Pound, I will first chart the two trends by comparing two representative interpreters, Steven Owen and Wang Bi (AD 226–249).

The postmodern attempt to de-ontologize language testifies to the linguistic orientation in Western thought. As a result of the effacement of the author and the original meaning, the text is treated not as a material embodiment of the author's ideas but as a linguistic instigator of the critic's own concern. In other words, the interpreter replaces the author as a creator, or a poet in its original meaning of 'maker'. By assimilating the text into his own theoretical framework, he substitutes his own creation for the original. To generalize it in terms of figure of speech, the Western interpretation is metaphorical.

This reactionary mentality is implied in Steven Owen's reading of classical Chinese poetry. When analyzing a Tang poem, 'The Mountain Temple at the Yong Lake' by Zhang Yue (AD 667–730), Owen proposes a defiant reading as an alternative to the traditional author-guided interpretation. The last line is traditionally understood as, 'If the two recluses Cao and You can share my feeling, they will surely not exchange seclusion for officialdom'. This rendering is based on the reader's intuitive grasp of the poet's intention. After noting the importance of following the authorial guiding, Owen shifts to the opposite side and interprets it as 'If the recluses can share my feeling, how can they resist exchanging seclusion for officialdom?' Since I need not become a recluse to appreciate seclusion, the recluse can also taste the joy of secluded life without giving up officialdom (Owen, tr. Jia 1987). This rendering gives a twist to the poet's intention, thus contradicting the Chinese convention of recluse poetry (which involves the poetic gesture of fleeing officialdom for unrestrained freedom; the most typical example is 'Back to Rural Life' by Tao Qian [AD 365/372/376–427]). The twist, however, is not totally unjustified, since the verbal line itself does not exclude it. That is to say, the new meaning endowed to the line by the interpreter disregards, even threatens, the original meaning.

The new spirit that inhabits the classical Chinese poem is the Western anti-authorial tendency. Despite his awareness of the two different modes of interpretation and his emphasis on Chinese poetic convention, Owen's own reading is conditioned by the text-oriented new critical and structuralist approach. Owen is certainly no self-styled misreader of Chinese poetry. Neither is he an absolute champion of the hermeneutics of recovery. By amply adducing the poets' biographies, the contemporary milieu and the literary convention, Owen hopes to trigger the historical imagination so as to give the poem a more accurate and more meaningful interpretation. Nevertheless, his textual documentation is balanced, sometimes overbalanced, by his meticulous textual analysis. Classical poetry, whose ineffable message is supposed to be retrieved only intuitively, takes on a new look under Owen's creative scrutiny.

Generally speaking, Owen's analysis hinges on two major structuralist concepts: the universal basic framework and binary opposition. In Appendix I of his *Early T'ang Poetry*, he describes his task as representing the early Tang palace poetry convention as a matrix 'language' of high Tang poetry. His purpose is to reconstruct the *langua*, or the depth grammar, from the *parole*, or the individual poems, so that the poetry written in this 'language' will be read in a proper framework. The structuralist approach enables Owen to crystallize various palace poems into a basic tripartite structural scheme: introduction of the topic, descriptive elaboration and emotional response. The relative positioning of the component in the whole structure determines its meaning and the reader's expectation. Therefore, the topic introduced at the beginning is re-evaluated at the end in the light of the whole poem. In addition to the tripartite structure, the antithetical couplet also contributes to the adhesive inner tension, hence the poetic unity.

Although not openly contradictory to the Chinese conception of the antithetical couplet, Owen obviously plays down the postulated underlying *yin-yang* interaction, which is the keystone of the couplet device. He plays the structuralist binary opposition against the Chinese bipolar complementarity. According to him, the antithetical opposition is a structural device for orchestrating different elements into a verbal net in which every element is explained in relation to its counterpart. Yet instead of tracing this particular structure to an extra-textual metaphysical power which, according to the Chinese mind, shapes everything in couples, Owen adopts a purely linguistic view and stops at the verbal structure itself. His analysis is based on the very identification of the Chinese poetic device with the structuralist binary opposition. Owen's writing provides a list of opposing concepts: the personal poem and the palace poem, the descriptive and the imaginary, poetry as self-expression and as artefact, inspired writing and imitative writing, the poet as a private writer and as a public figure. All these concepts reflect Northrop Frye's two-fold division: the division of nature into context (which provides the raw material) and text (which re-presents the selected material), and the division of the poet into an actual person in real life and a dramatic persona.[1] This shows that Owen's framework is rooted in the Western fictional conception of literature with its two cardinal ideas of making and structuring. Owen's analysis actually converts Chinese poetry into a quarry for structuralist hunting.

This is not to say that he deliberately uproots Chinese poetry and transplants it into an alien theoretical grid. But it points up the role of cultural heritage in shaping his approach. His highlighting of a peculiar aspect of the Chinese poetry, such as the antithetical couplet, is achieved only through comparing it with a Western counterpart, or lack of a counterpart. This again testifies his Occidental orientation. Owen's reading converts a flowery, insignificant type of poetry into a well-structured verbal unity, which forms the matrix for the later flourishing Tang poetry. In this sense, Owen plays the poet who creates a verbal icon out of classical Chinese poetry.

Contrary to revisionary Western hermeneutics, traditional Chinese literary criticism can be called a hermeneutics of recovery or restoration. The goal of the critic is to retrieve the original meaning by examining the poem in the light of the poet's life experiences and social environment. Consequently, the focus of critical attention is not the text, but the poet's temperament and intention, which are often apprehended through non-textual means, such as intuition and non-literary documents. The emphasis on the poet's actuality is captured in a remark by Mencius (ca. 372–289 BC): 'Those who are good at commenting on poetry peel off the embellishment so as to get the words, then penetrate the word to grasp the poet's intention. To understand is to meet the author's intention with one's own intuition' (*Mencius, Wanzhang* 1). This approach presupposes a time-transcending psychological affinity between the poet and the reader. The confidence in direct communication leads to the dominance of authorial intention at the expense of the material text. In a later introductory comment on Lao Zi (ca. 585–500 BC), Wang Bi also stresses authorial intention as the fountainhead and aim, and describes reading as an act of 'exploring its [the text] cause, tracing to its origin, so that the words do not get dissociated from the executive mind, and the accounting does not get out of the poet's control'. Words are derived from and subordinate to the original intention. This view is diametrically opposite to the Western textual concern. The hermeneutics of recovery seeks to transcend the text, so as to forge a bond with the poet. This reading is not metaphorical, but metonymical. It continues and restores (at least it professes to do so) the poet's line of thought. The Chinese critic re-enacts the poet's performance, while the Western critic directs his own drama, so to speak.

We can follow Roland Green's distinction (cited in Allen) and call the Chinese approach the 'ritual' mode of apprehension, in contrast to the Western fictional mode. The word 'ritual' suggests the self-expressive nature of Chinese poetry, as indicated in the well-quoted remark, 'Poetry articulates the intention'. The emphasis on expression determines the poet's personal presence and the dominant position of subjectivity, which in turn occludes the critic's independent recreation. As a result, the material text is regarded as a vestige or trace of the poet's intention. It can hardly capture the original commotion, and functions at best as a makeshift pointer to the object. Rather than constituting a fundamental structure (whose discerning is the goal of structuralism), the words and images in Chinese criticism serve as an index of the extra-textual message. Having bridged the poet and the reader, they must be dispensed with once the message is retrieved.

This functional view of the text is expressed by Wang Bi in 'The Explanation of the Image' in *Brief Exemplification of the Zhou Yi*. According to him, the word expresses the intention; the image embodies the word. They are the best means available for grasping the original meaning. Yet they function as the trap for rabbit-hunting and the net for fishing. Whoever sticks to the tool will lose sight of the goal. Wang Bi actually postulates the discarding of the image and the word after having grasped the poet's intention. Consequently, the linguistic text is not only dispensable but also replaceable: 'Whatever signifies the same type can be its image. Whatever matches the message can be its index.' Apparently, the replaceability of the text resembles the interchangeability of the surface manifestations of the basic structural pattern, as proposed in structuralism. Yet the difference is significant. In structuralism, the multiple manifestations share a common pattern embedded in the text, while in Chinese hermeneutics the verbal signs are ultimately determined by the extra-textual executive power.

Just as Owen's reading of Chinese poetry betrays his structuralist orientation, Wang Bi's interpretation of *The Book of Changes* bespeaks his typical Chinese approach, which stresses the original intention and the resultant functional view of the verbal text. Wang's restoring hermeneutic, together with Mencius's biographical approach, helps to shape Chinese authorial essentialism. While reflecting on the Buddhist scripture, Zhu Daosheng (AD 375–434), a Buddhist disciple, realizes that:

> ...the image embodies the message, and is to be dropped once the message is comprehended. The word shows the principle, and is to be silenced once the principle is

revealed. The newly introduced scriptures have been garbled and obfuscated by the translators. Only when one gets rid of the boggling words, can one see the uncluttered original meaning. The Dao is revealed only when the fishing net is dropped. (Hui 1991:46)

A corollary of the restoring hermeneutics (which reaches for the original intention at the expense of the text) is that the ideal translation does not stick to the original text, but reverbalizes the original message, a rewriting based on transverbal comprehension.

Having delineated the two distinct (Western and Chinese) interpreting trends, which are analogous to metaphor and metonymy, we can now locate Pound's reading of Chinese poetry. Pound's interest is in the image, both those constructed in the poem and those crystallized in the ideograms. He invents a poetry out of the intrinsically imagistic, hence poetic, Chinese language (an inspiration he gets from Fenellosa's study of Chinese characters). This linguistic starting point shows his affinity with Western verbal preoccupation. His viewing ideograms as the matrix of poetry suggests his sympathy with the Romantic idea of a universal language. This also parallels the structuralist quest for a basic pattern. Besides, he treats the characters in much the same way as the structuralists do texts — lifting a single word out of its history so as to reinvest it with a pure aesthetic message. In these aspects, Pound's reading of Chinese poetry has a Western verbal orientation, which goes against the expressive and volitional nature of Chinese poetry, therefore producing a counter-version of it.

Nevertheless, Pound's conception of the vortex points to the other side of the coin, that is, his extra-textual concern. Visualized as a patterned energy, the vortex not only exists beyond the text, but also governs its composition. The extra-textual energy connects him to Chinese restorative hermeneutics. The common concern leads to similar interpretive strategies. A comparison of his dramatization of the Chinese characters and Wang Bi's interpretation of the trigrams and the hexagrams in *The Book of Changes* will clarify this point. When dissatisfied with the crib or puzzled with it, as Zhu Daosheng is by the poor translation, Pound has nothing but the 'look of the characters and the radicals to go on from' (Kenner 1971:448). The pure look of the characters prompts his wishful etymologizing, or the so-called 'method of intelligent reading' (159) — to read the various possible meanings in light of the dominant overtone. This dominant overtone is determined by the common radicals in a phrase. By breaking down the characters into the constituting radicals, then rearranging them into a proto-plot, Pound is able to improvise a narrative on the basis of the physical look of the characters.

This impromptu dramatizing is also adopted in Wang Bi's decoding of the trigrams and the hexagrams. Similar to Pound, Wang bases his exegeses on the enigmatic 'picture' of the trigrams and hexagrams. Through his elaboration, a static linguistic sign becomes a picture, even a dynamic process. The dramatizing approach presupposes the automatic connection between the visual forms and the root ideas of the language, or the transparency of the linguistic sign. (This does not necessarily mean the adequacy of language however. The signifying nature of the language system is not the same thing as its congruence with the objective world.) The pictorial view of language designates the mutual dependence of the non-textual intention and the textual existence, therefore legitimizing the human factor in literature. The bedrock of human agency results in a functional view of language, and makes possible the trans-temporal and trans-spatial communication. In Pound's words, all honest men (he picks up the Confucian gentlemanly virtue of sincerity (*cheng*), and adapts it to his framework) far apart in space and time can achieve a consensus in their reading. That is why he observes in *Spirit of Romance* that 'All ages are contemporaneous.... What we need is a literary scholarship, which will weigh Theocritus and Yeats with one balance' (cited in Yip 1993:21). This one balance is tuned exactly to human agency.

Pound and Wang Bi call the human element vortex and *yi* (message and intention or will) respectively. Vortex, meaning patterned energy, seems to lack the personal aspect, which is essential to *yi*, meaning the poet's intention. And yet *yi*, in its most profound form, also indicates an impersonal cosmic will, called Dao. Conversely, Pound's patterned energy depends on the underflow of personal commotion, just as T. S. Eliot's personalization stems from unfeigned personal emotion. Thus both vortex and *yi* have the dual aspects of the personal and the impersonal, and both of them suggest concern with human agency, rather than the material text. The subordination of language to message eventually leads Pound to describe his translation as 're-writing as if you didn't know the words of the original and were telling what happened' (Kenner 1971:150). This kind of translation is meant to convey the energetic pattern with little regard for the original language. It is based on what Zhu Daosheng conceives as a non-verbal comprehension of Buddhist scripture. The tendency to bypass the text removes the linguistic constraint and allows the reader to approximate the original meaning from a more sympathetic perspective. Therefore, Pound can deliberately distort the original word in order to keep consistent with his opening or the overtone of the whole writing. This distorting naturally leads to misreading, yet it is the result more of Chinese restorative hermeneutics than of structuralist revisionist hermeneutics.

In his exegesis of *The Confucian Analects*, Wang Bi also deviates from the recorded words so as to adjust them to the extra-textual intention (which is often based on the reader's sympathy with the author) dictating the overtone of the text (Cheng 1990:958). In their reading of ancient or foreign texts both Pound and mainstream Chinese scholars sacrifice the text for the message (either the patterned energy or the poet's intention). The result is not a totally different work, but a 'displaced' text (as Northrop Frye uses the term, meaning to modify the text according to the specific context). The archetype and the message are re-presented, yet unchanged essentially. This reverbalization is possible because of the replaceability of the words and the images. As mentioned above, both the word and the image are expedient and replaceable by the cognate signs which may be more appropriate in a different situation. For example, the pair of fundamental trigrams in *The Book of Changes* are *yin* and *yang*, meaning obedience and *puissance*. Yet the idea of *puissance* is symbolized in a variety of images other than the stallion; neither does obedience have to be symbolized by the mare. What is important is the symbolized meaning, not the symbol itself. To stick to a particular verbal sign is to lose sight of the real meaning. Significantly, Pound holds the same provisional view about the image. He defines the vortex as patterned energy made visible by water, but not water itself. That is to say, water is only one of the images that can manifest the underlying energy, but not essential or indispensable to the latter. The extra-textual energy determines the sign to be chosen, not vice versa.

❖

The similar hermeneutic strategies employed by Pound and Wang Bi (the latter, to a great extent, helped shape Chinese classical hermeneutics) testify to their common concern with something bigger and beyond the text. Pound undoubtedly invents a Chinese poetry in order to illustrate his poetic theory, just as the image of water is used to manifest the vortex. Nevertheless, his misreading does not prove his Orientalism. The difference between his assimilation of the *other* and the crude subordination of the East to the West is revealed in his specific approach to Chinese culture, and poetry in particular. On the one hand, he inherits the Western verbal preoccupation and the Romantic quest for a universal language. On the other, he treats verbal signs as an expedient and replaceable manifestation of a non-textual messsage, and subordinates the former to the latter. This shows his affinity with the Chinese hermeneutics of restoration, as opposed to the Western hermeneutics of revision. People may argue that, since Pound's theory demonstrates a directional will of his own, rather than that of the original author, his is still a hermeneutics of revision. This is true to an extent. Yet his attention to human agency (either his own or the original author's) as opposed to verbal structure separates him from the mainstream of Western logo-centrism. Actually, even in Chinese hermeneutics, the restoration of original intention often coexists, even collaborates with, the triggering of the interpreter's intention. What is important is not the exclusion of the interpreter's creativity (an idea now recognized by many critics), but the emphasis on the non-textual message.

When identifying the Western poet and the Chinese character *ling* (lit. soul or witch), Pound affirms the two-fold nature of poetry-writing: the active bringing things into existence and the ritualistic dancing and miming of some greater process. These two aspects correspond exactly with the two modes of comprehension, the Western fictional and the Chinese ritual. Pound's contribution to East-West communication is represented by the combined strategy in his invention of classical Chinese poetry.

Peking University

Note

1 Frye's ideas cited here underpin Owen's arguments, and are scattered throughout his various writings.

Works Cited

Allen, Joseph R. 1993 'Macropoetic Structures: The Chinese Solution' in *Comparative Literature* 5.4. Pennsylvania State University Press.

Cheng Shude 1990 *The Confucian Analects*, vol. 3. Zhonghua shuju, Beijing.

Hui Jiao (comp.) 1991 (repr.) *Biographies of Master Monks*. Shanghai guji chubanshe.

Kenner, Hugh 1971 *The Pound Era*. University of California Press.

Owen, Steven 1987 *Early T'ang Poetry*, tr. Jia Jinhua. Guangxi renmin chubanshe.

Said, Edward W. 1983 *The World, the Text and the Critic*. Harvard University Press.

Wang Bi (ed.) 1989 *Guide to Lao Zi*. Shanghai guji chubanshe.

—— (ed.) n.d. *Brief Exemplification of the Zhou Yi*. Shanghai guji chubanshe.

Yang Junbo (ed.) 1963 *Mengzi*. Zhonghua shuju, Beijing.

Yip Wai-lim 1993 *Diffusion of Distances: Dialogues Between Chinese and Western Poetics*. University of California Press.

TANAKA TAKAAKI

From Short to Long Forms of Narration: *Genji Monogatari* and Tang *Chuanqi* Tales

INVENTED HISTORICAL NARRATIVE IN *GENJI MONOGATARI*
The 'Kiritsubo' section of *Genji Monogatari* (*The Tale of the Genji*) is known to contain numerous quotations from 'Changhen ge' (Song of Everlasting Sorrow) by Bai Juyi,[1] but I believe that it may be more closely related to Chen Hong's tale 'Changhen ge zhuan' based on this poem, and which would have been read with it.

Just after the opening of 'Kiritsubo' it is described how people at court begin to voice their criticisms when the emperor's special affection for one low-ranking concubine upsets the order of the court:

> His court looked with very great misgiving upon what seemed a reckless infatuation. In China just such an unreasoning passion had been the undoing of an emperor and had spread turmoil through the land. As the resentment grew, the example of Yang Guifei was the one most frequently cited against the lady. She survived despite her troubles, with the help of an unprecedented bounty of love. (1978:I, 3)[2]

At the same time as it introduces the characters, this early passage contrasts Japan with China. In the narration of a story about Japan — purportedly historical — it is extraordinary to make such reference to China. The reference to the 'example of Yang Guifei' makes it clear that the tale of Emperor Xuanzong and Yang Guifei underlies this tale of the Emperor of Japan and the concubine. This is shown both by the source of expressions and the narrative style of the tale itself. Because it may seem as if there are few direct quotations from Chen Hong's tale, there are those who deny its influence on the *Genji*, but in the original of the passage just quoted, the first sentence is based on a quotation from

'Changhen ge zhuan'. Manuscripts from the Kanazawa and Masamune archive collections indicate how the tale was read in the Heian period.³ Cleverly changing the reading for 'the capital and high officials' to 'the senior nobles and courtiers', the author of the *Genji* continues by quoting this *kundoku* reading.

THE AUTUMN STORM SECTION OF 'KIRITSUBO' AND 'CHANGHEN GE ZHUAN'
The most memorable scene in 'Kiritsubo' is the section beginning 'The autumn tempests blew...' which describes how after the lady's death the emperor sends Yugei-no-myobu to visit her mother (7). Although this is often said to be based on the episode in 'Changhen ge' where the Taoist priest sent by Emperor Xuanzong in search of Yang Guifei's spirit discovers her on Mount Penglai and returns with her shell box and gold hairpin, it looks rather more like a skilful reworking of the same episode in 'Changhen ge zhuan'. Again, the wording in 'Kiritsubo' is very similar to that of the text of the 'Changhen ge zhuan' in the Kanazawa and Masamune collections, as I have shown elsewhere (Tanaka 1993:19).

I believe that it is possible to say that the structure and plot of 'Kiritsubo' corresponds more closely to the structure and plot of the tale 'Changhen ge zhuan' than the poem 'Changhen ge'.

Furthermore, without going into specific examples, what is important to note is that 'Kiritsubo' adopts narrative techniques from the tale. 'Changhen ge' ends in a mood of poetical lyricism far removed from historical actuality, while 'Changhen ge zhuan' is narrated from beginning to end as historical record. Despite its many fictional elements and suppression of important historical facts, the tale as a whole is in the form of a historical narrative.

What is also interesting is the way Chen Hong ends 'Changhen ge zhuan' by explaining the circumstances which led him to write the work, that he merely made the poem 'Changhen ge' into a 'zhuan'. There are two interpretations of the meaning of 'zhuan' here, as 'commentary' or 'tale'. I believe that the latter is preferable: he narrates the 'Changhen ge' as a tale. However this should be understood as narration of a historical tale based on actual fact, and not as the invention of a fictional tale. In terms of its relations with *Genji monogatari*, we can affirm not only that *Genji monogatari* quotes from the 'Changhen ge zhuan', but also that the Japanese author learned from the techniques of the Chinese storyteller. To put it simply, 'Kiritsubo' transforms 'Changhen ge' into a story of the Japanese court by techniques very similar to those used by Chen Hong to make a 'zhuan' or tale from the same poem. Although it is obviously true that 'Kiritsubo' has a greater proportion of fiction in comparison with 'Changhen ge zhuan', it is narrated as history, with historical fact woven into the tale in the same way.

The story told in *Genji monogatari* is Japanese through and through, yet in the passage quoted above, the narrator makes her debt to 'Changhen ge' explicit through expressions that introduce Chinese precedents and the example of

Yang Guifei. The narrator shows her strong awareness of China, but at the same time she emphasizes differences by the contrast with China. When later she has the emperor look at actual pictures by Uda and poems by Ise on the theme of the 'Song of Everlasting Sorrow', this allows her to describe how much the lady the emperor loved was unlike the Yang Guifei known through the paintings. The story is based on that of Xuanzong and Yang Guifei, but makes especially clear the differences in the characters of the lady and Yang Guifei. Poetic phrases from 'Changhen ge' are repeatedly quoted in order to express the intense grief of the emperor on the loss of the lady, with the first half of 'Kiritsubo' ending thus:

> ...and now to neglect his duties so — it was altogether too much. Some even cited the example of the Chinese emperor who had brought ruin upon himself and his country. (13)

THE HISTORICITY OF TANG TALES AND *GENJI MONOGATARI*

'The days and months passed and the young prince came to the palace' (13). So begins the latter half of 'Kiritsubo', with the appearance of the young prince Genji, the Shining One. Whereas both 'Changhen ge' and 'Changhen ge zhuan' end tragically with the love of Xuanzong for Yang Guifei, one could say that it is from this point that *Genji monogatari* really begins.

The living Fujitsubo takes the place of the spirit of Yang Guifei for which Xuanzong searched, as Yan Shaotang has said (1987:276), while Genji is the keepsake which the lady leaves behind for the emperor, as Japanese scholars have pointed out. Once the spirit of Yang Guifei can be found, the story must end, but the two substitutes that remain behind in the world bring about a new story in courtly society. This goes beyond the short story form of the Tang tale and opens the way to a long tale.

One striking way 'Changhen ge zhuan' and other Tang tales influenced *Genji monogatari* was in their historicity. Characters and events in the *Genji* are basically fictitious, but historical facts are interwoven so that the work takes on the style of historical narrative: 'In a certain reign there was a lady not of the first rank whom the emperor loved more than any of the others' (3).

'In a certain reign' or, more literally, 'In whose reign was it?', resembles the opening of 'Changhen ge zhuan'. It may seem a vague expression, but the fact that it refers to the reign of a particular emperor later becomes clear:

> He had become addicted to illustrations by the emperor Uda for 'The Song of Everlasting Sorrow' and to poems by Ise and Tsurayuki on that subject, and to Chinese poems as well. (10–11)

Emperor Uda is referred to in the original by his name after abdication, Teiji-no-in. All facts are historically correct, except for the statement that Tsurayuki had written poems for the illustrations.

Because there are no direct quotations from 'Changhen ge' or 'Changhen ge zhuan' in the second half of 'Kiritsubo', we will not cite the original Japanese. We should note, however, that the hero's childhood is narrated in the style of records of public functions.

I believe that this method of narration in 'Kiritsubo' was learnt directly from 'Changhen ge zhuan', and that the narrative style of *Genji monogatari* was created by the incorporation of methods from this and other Tang tales.

THE NARRATIVE COMMENTARY IN *GENJI MONOGATARI* AND THE TANG TALES

'Kiritsubo' ends as follows: 'The sobriquet "the shining Genji", one hears, was bestowed upon him by the Korean' (19). A little earlier it had been said that 'People called [him] "the shining lord"' (16). Now the narrator says that there is a tradition that it was in fact the physiognomist from Korea ('Koma' or Pechili) who gave Genji this name. A term from a medieval commentary is used to refer to such passages: *soshiji*. The narrator in these passages of special explanation is not the same as the narrator elsewhere. There are relatively long *soshiji* at the beginning of 'Hahakigi' and the end of 'Yugao', the second and fourth chapters (*maki*) respectively:

> 'The shining Genji': it was almost too grand a name. Yet he did not escape criticism for numerous little adventures. It seemed indeed that his indiscretions might give him a name for frivolity, and he did what he could to hide them. But his most secret affairs (such is the malicious work of the gossips) became common talk. (20)

> I had hoped, out of deference to him, to conceal these difficult matters; but I have been accused of romancing, of pretending that because he was the son of an emperor he had no faults. Now, perhaps, I shall be accused of having revealed too much. (83)

In both cases these passages explain the circumstances behind the telling of Genji's tale from the personal viewpoint of the final narrator. In this regard, I have argued elsewhere that passages of editorial commentary in Sima Qian's *Shiji* may have given rise to *soshiji* like these. The so-called *lunzan* passages containing direct comment in the person of Sima Qian himself and beginning with the phrase 'Taishigong yue' (The Grand Historian says) occur both in the course of and at the end of episodes in the Basic Annals, Hereditary Households, Memoirs and other sections. I still believe in the possibility that *Shiji* and its editorial commentary were the ultimate source of the *soshiji* in *Genji monogatari*, but now think that the direct influence was the passages in Tang period tales where the authors explain how they came to write the stories, passages which themselves evolved from the *lunzan* passages in *Shiji*.

In the case of 'Changhen ge zhuan', the passage in question begins 'In the first year of the Yuanhe era...' in the version preserved in the compendium 'Wenyuan yinghua' (Finest Flowers of the Preserve of Letters). This gives an account of how the 'Changhen ge zhuan' was written, but is very probably untrue. The *soshiji* in *Genji monogatari* are naturally also a plausible invention told by a fictitious narrator.

The 'Yugao' story is nearly certainly based on 'Renshi zhuan' (see Shinma Kazumi 1982:45). This Tang tale (*chuanqi*) is the story of the love between a man and a fox which has taken on a woman's form. At the end the author, Shen Jiji, has the protagonist directly express his feelings on hearing the story, and it is explained that this character, Wei Yin, is based on an actual person. What this has in common with the *soshiji* at the end of 'Yugao' is the way an implausible lie is said with a straight face. This is not an isolated case, however, similar passages from many other Tang tales were adopted in *Genji monogatari*.

From Short to Long Forms of Narration

The Tang *chuanqi* are all short narratives. *Genji monogatari* is divided into fifty-four *maki*, but some of these are partially independent, short narratives in their own right. This is particularly the case in 'Hahakigi', 'Utsusemi', 'Yugao' and 'Suetsumuhana', the *maki* that follow 'Kiritsubo', and is probably due to the influence of the Tang tales. At the same time, however, the Genji begins to take the form of a long narrative from the latter half of 'Kiritsubo'. The emperor's concubine reborn in the young Genji and Fujitsubo corresponds to Yang Guifei's spirit, as we saw earlier. This is the element in the story that creates a longer narrative, and comes as part of the influence from 'Changhen ge' and 'Changhen ge zhuan'. The fact that the Tang tales were narrated as history was still more important. The historicity of *chuanqi* can already be seen in the the earlier genre of *zhiguai* (record of marvels). Discussing one of the best of these prose works, *Hanwu gushi* (Stories of Emperor Wu of the Han), Li Jianguo (1984:178) concluded that it was characterized by the close cohesion of its historical and fantastic elements. This trait was inherited by the Tang *chuanqi*, and adopted in turn by *Genji monogatari*.

Concerning the extended structure of *Hanwu gushi*, Kominami Ichiro comments that it revealed the possibility of development into long works of narrative fiction (1984:136). In China it was not until long afterwards that this actually happened, but meanwhile *Genji monogatari* had succeeded in creating a long narrative, having inherited from China the potential for long fiction, probably through the medium of the Tang tales. Though a fictional tale, *Genji monogatari* adopts the style of historical accounts, making use of the format of *lienü zhuan* biographies of women in Chinese histories and quoting from *Shiji* and *Hanshu*. The different ways in which historical works have been incorporated in the structure of the *Genji monagatari* are what made possible its success as long narrative fiction.

Waseda University

Notes

1 The name of the poet also appears in Western sources as Bo Juyi or Po Chü-i.
2 The translation used here is that by Edward G. Seidensticker 1978.
3 The edition of the tale in the Kanazawa Bunko collection of Bai Juyi (Hakushi Monju) is, like the poem, entitled 'Chogonka' (the Japanese reading of 'Changhen ge') while that in the Masamune Atsuo Bunko collection is called 'Chogonkaden' (Changhen ge zhuan).

Works Cited

Abe Akio, Akiyama Ken and Imai Gen'ei (eds) 1970 *Genji monogatari*. Shogakukan, Tokyo.

Kominami Ichiro 1984 *Chugoku no shinwa to monogatari* (Chinese Myths and Tales). Iwanami shoten, Tokyo.

Imai Gen'e 1994 'Kanseki, shisho, butten in'yo ichiran' (Index of quotations from Chinese, historical and Buddhist texts), in *Genji monogatari*, vol. 1, Shinpen Nihon koten bungaku zenshu, Shogakukan, Tokyo.

Li Jianguo 1984 *Tangqian zhiguai xiaoshuoshi* (History of Pre-Tang zhiguai tales). Nankai University Press, Tianjin.

Seidensticker, Edward G. (tr.) 1978 *The Tale of Genji*. Charles E. Tuttle, Tokyo.

Shinma Kazumi 1982 'Mo hitori no Yugao: Hahakigi sancho to *Jinshi no monogatari*' (Another Yugao: the three 'Hahakigi' chapters and 'Renshi zhuan') in *Genji monogatari no jinbutsu to kozo* (Characters and structure of *The Tale of Genji*). Kazama shoin, Tokyo.

Tanaka Takaaki 1993 Genji monogatari *rekishi to kyoko* (*The Tale of Genji* and historical fiction). Benseisha, Tokyo.

Yan Shaotang 1987 *Zhongri gudai wenxue guanxi shigao* (History of Japanese-Chinese classical literary relations). Hunan Wenyi Press, Wuhan.

Manfred Schmeling

Kafka en France: La Productivité Littéraire du Malentendu

La question du 'misreading' prend, dans un contexte comparatiste — c'est à dire interculturel et international — une valeur tout à fait particulière. La formule simple selon laquelle un texte, dans un contexte historiquement postérieur, transmet un message différent de celui qui se dégage à l'époque de sa production, cette formule est insuffisante pour décrire le processus de la réception dans ce cas. A la relation entre 'autrefois' et 'plus tard' s'ajoute une synchronie qui dépasse largement l'horizon d'une littérature nationale. La situation d'interprétation est marquée par le fait que du côté du récepteur ne règnent pas les mêmes données culturelles que du côté de l'émetteur. Le malentendu ou la trahison créative sont le résultat d'une distance qui est d'abord linguistique. Le matériau étranger (au point de vue du récepteur) qu'est la langue de l'original complique encore davantage l'accès à ce qui est déjà en soi-même assez difficile à reconstruire, l''intention de l'auteur'.

Il est intéressant de constater que l'idée de reconstituer l''intention de l'auteur' ou en l'occurrence, l'intention du texte, est reprise aujourd'hui en relation avec Kafka par Milan Kundera. Selon lui les traducteurs français auraient trahi l''intention esthétique' de l'auteur praguois (Kundera 1993). La sociologie de la littérature véhicule cette idée depuis les années soixante-dix et le terme même de la 'trahison créatrice' est attribué à Robert Escarpit:

> Une lecture donnée constitue une trahison créative lorsque nous avons à faire à une signification de l'oeuvre qui n'a pas été voulue par l'auteur — voilà la trahison — et lorsque cette signification qui n'a pas été voulue ne prive pas l'oeuvre de sens, mais lui en donne un nouveau. (1970:28)

Une particularité de la réception de Kafka, et pas seulement en France, est le fait qu'on ne savait d'abord quasiment rien du 'contexte originel' — la langue de Kafka, sa situation historique et biographique, l'arrière-plan littéraire. Les préfaces des premiers traducteurs ou les premiers comptes rendus de son oeuvre témoignent moins d'un malentendu que d'une ignorance. L'édition française du *Procès* en 1957 contient une 'introduction' du traducteur Alexandre Vialatte, qui confirme cet état de choses sans pour autant le dépasser en pensée: là non plus, pas le moindre mot de l'environnement socio-culturel de l'auteur. 'Il débarquait dans la littérature comme un Martien sur le globe terrestre', écrit Vialatte; et il ajoute, faisant allusion à l'absence totale de réception pendant la domination nazie:

> Après sa mort il s'amenuise encore. Pendant toute la période nazie, il disparaît triplement de la terre qu'il n'avait au surplus jamais bien habitée. Il n'est plus que l'ombre d'une ombre et cette ombre d'ombre est traquée. Ses éditeurs allemands ont été supprimés, ses livres ont été brûlés, ses traductions ont été interdites, ses manuscrits s'égarent, les démons de l'échec qu'il avait déchaînés s'acharnent sur tout ce qui le touche. (32)

On est tenté de prendre au mot la thèse postmoderne de la 'disparition de l'auteur' et de l'antidater de quelques décennies. C'est le destin de Kafka de n'avoir correspondu en rien, selon le point de vue de l'époque, à l'idée de ce que devait être un écrivain, qu'il s'agisse d'origine nationale, de statut social ou de respect du canon. Marthe Robert dont personne, même hors de France, ne devrait mettre en doute la compétence en ce qui concerne Kafka, fait apparaître non sans ironie le vide herméneutique grâce auquel un espace de liberté s'offre aux exégètes et aux littérateurs:

> Kafka est apparu comme un citoyen de nulle part, un solitaire que rien ne précédait et dont on ne savait même pas très bien dans quelle langue il avait écrit son oeuvre. Comme il semblait libre de toute contrainte historique ou géographique, il a été adopté sans arrière-pensée, on pourrait même dire presque 'naturalisé' car il s'agissait bien d'une sorte de naturalisation qui a fait naître un nouveau Kafka, un Kafka français, évidemment bien éloigné du vrai. (1966:310)

La critique que Marthe Robert adresse à ceux qui se sont approprié Kafka, les surréalistes, les existentialistes ou les philosophes chrétiens comme Groethuysen ainsi qu'aux traducteurs tendencieux comme Vialatte, repose, c'est bien évident, sur l'hypothèse que même Kafka — elle parle du 'vrai' Kafka — a droit à l'objectivité et ainsi à une réception adéquate. Or, il n'est pas d'auteur qui ait été plus que Kafka soumis à la subjectivité des récepteurs ou, d'une façon plus générale, à la manipulation de la culture-cible. En ce qui concerne la France, on trouve les noms de Breton, Klossowski, Vialatte, Camus, Sartre, Robbe-Grillet, Sarraute, Pérec et bien d'autres. Déjà les premières traductions, celles des recits de Kafka, qui d'ailleurs avaient été faites non par des traducteurs professionnels mais par des écrivains d'obédience surréaliste, ces traductions révèlent bien la prédominance de la culture-cible sur l'oeuvre importée. On pourrait appliquer au moins à cette phase initiale de la réception de Kafka en France ce qu'écrit un sémioticien et théoricien de la traduction, l'Israélien Itamar Even-Zohar, à propos du statut 'périphérique' de la littérature traduite: cette dernière 'is modelled according to norms already conventionally established by an already dominant type in the target-literature' (1990:48). On peut même se demander si la traduction, dans ce cas, ne va pas à l'encontre de ce qui est son objectif: être productive et apporter un renouvellement à la culture-cible.

Mais il est possible que cette évolution repose sur une prédominance seulement passagère de la culture-cible. Les traductions mystificatrices de Klossowski, de Carrives ou de Vialatte qui, nous l'avons dit, s'adaptaient à la tradition stylistique et aux tendances intellectuelles alors en vigueur ont influencé la réception surtout dans les premières années de l'après-guerre. Les traducteurs ont pratiqué ce qu'on pourrait nommer un 'rétrécissement de l'ouverture sémantique' (Schmeling 1979:34). C'est ainsi par exemple que dans la traduction du *Château* par Vialatte, le petit mot de 'Schuld' ('faute') est rendu par différents synonymes, entre autres, 'péché'; le mot 'Offenbarungswort' ('révélation') par 'le texte d'un évangile'. Les 'Bittgänge' ou les 'Gänge' ('démarches') vers le maître du Château se transforment en 'pèlerinages'. Ce n'est que beaucoup plus tard qu'il a été possible de corriger de telles transpositions auxquelles des connotations bibliques avaient donné une valeur réductrice: par exemple dans la nouvelle traduction de Bernard Lortholary parue en 1983 l'expression 'nicht viel schuldiger' que Vialatte avait traduite par 'sans plus de péché' se sécularise pour devenir 'presque aussi innocemment' (1984:230).

L'exemple que nous venons d'évoquer (Lortholary) suggère l'idée que les manipulations dues à la hâte ou au malentendu ne sont pas indéfinies, qu'elles peuvent être revues et corrigées, même si, peut-être, d'autres malentendus peuvent se produire à d'autres endroits. Cette expérience devrait suggérer une question de principe: la relation entre l'original et la traduction ne s'est-elle pas déplacée, au cours de l'histoire de la réception de Kafka, en faveur d'une position 'centrale' de Kafka à l'intérieur de la culture étrangère? Incontestablement on a tendance aujourd'hui à rendre justice au style particulier, à l'expression de la situation socio-linguistique de l'écrivain praguois. Des formes d'expression 'inorthodoxes' à l'allure 'étrangère' se sont tout à fait intégrées à la culture-cible — tout aussi bien que certains thèmes kafkaïens se sont intégrés à la littérature en général. Le mot d'emprunt 'kafkaesque', ou 'kafkaïen', dont la critique française fait usage pour caractériser les productions culturelles nationales, n'est-il pas la preuve de l'impact international des stratégies esthétiques de l'écrivain praguois? Et à ce point de vue, ne doit-on pas reconnaître à la littérature traduite une position de 'force' susceptible en même temps de libérer les pouvoirs d'innovation littéraire à l'intérieur de la culture-cible? En effet, plus une culture-cible subit l'influence des caractères particuliers du texte étranger — c'est à dire plus une traduction peut être considérée comme 'a reproduction of the dominant textual relations of the original' (Evan-Zohar 1990:50) — plus grande semblera la distance avec sa propre tradition.

❖

Bien que la traduction de Kafka en tant que type de texte constitue également une forme de réception littéraire, elle n'obéit pas tout à fait aux mêmes règles que l'influence littéraire de Kafka dans son ensemble. Le roman français moderne, dont il va s'agir ici encore une fois à titre d'exemple, n'est censé s'en tenir ni à la règle d''adéquation' ni à celle de 'fidélité'. Le 'malentendu' et la 'trahison' sont justement les conditions du renouvellement culturel.

Avec son roman *Le Fidèle berger* (1942) Alexandre Vialatte est un représentant typique de la première phase de la réception de Kafka en France, qui se distingue nettement d'une seconde que je ferais commencer à la naissance du nouveau roman. L'oeuvre de Vialatte, quelles que soient nos réserves, apparaît comme un maillon important dans une chaîne de réactions parce que l'auteur, en tant que traducteur de Kafka (*La Métamorphose* 1928; *Le Procès* 1933), a naturellement subi l'influence textuelle de ce dernier sur ses propres oeuvres plus fortement que d'autres romanciers. Effectivement les mystifications religieuses et les accents surréalistes des traductions ont laissé leurs traces dans *Le Fidèle berger*, d'abord à un niveau thématique: le héros, victime de la guerre entre la France et l'Allemagne, subit en tant que prisonnier le destin de l'accusé qui ne sait pas de quoi on l'accuse et qui, à la limite de la folie, finit par se suicider.

Le fait que la conception du roman ait été marquée par la deuxième guerre mondiale et qu'il véhicule, dit-on, le point de vue spécifique des Français, ne l'empêche pas d'être classé parmie les épigones. Voici un monologue du héros dans lequel nous trouvons le thème de l''emprisonnement' devenu un labyrinthe existentiel:

> — Je suis fou! se dit-il. Mais si c'était ça, on m'expliquerait! On ne me laisserait pas dans l'énigme.... Que me veut-on?... C'est qu'il y a contre moi une mauvaise volonté dont j'ignore l'origine! Nécessairement, sans quoi on m'eût interrogé! On ne condamne pas ainsi quelqu'un sans jugement! Où suis-je? Dans une prison ou dans un hôpital? (112)

On ne manquera pas non plus de trouver des réminiscences bibliques: 'L'oeil de Caïn dans la tombe. L'oeil du remords. L'interprétation était plausible! Il fallait donc qu'il y eût remords! S'il y avait eu remords, c'est qu'il y avait eu faute!'(118).

Dans cette jungle de mystères et d'hypothèses abstraites, nous rencontrons beaucoup de kafkaesque, mais très peu de Kafka. La logique labyrinthique de Kafka sur le thème de la faute a fait des émules; ce qui, dans le monde procédurier du *Procès*, est resté ouvert est explicité sous la forme du combat contre un *deus absconditus*. Certaines formulations du roman rappellent textuellement la préface de Groethuysen à la traduction de Vialatte. La métaphysique de l'absurde constitue à cette époque autour du thème de l'existence ('exister, c'est être jugé', écrit le philosophe dans la préface de 1933) une aura omniprésente dans laquelle baignent non seulement Vialatte, mais aussi Camus, Sartre ou bien Gide.

Si contestable scientifiquement que risque de paraître l'idée qu'un écrivain, un romancier puisse avoir des dons 'prophétiques', dans le cas de Kafka cette opinion si souvent exprimée fait preuve d'une certaine logique. En effet la dictature hitlérienne et ses conséquences, l'extermination des Juifs et la seconde guerre mondiale, contribuent aussi, et particulièrement en France, à une lecture qui fait de l'oeuvre de Kafka *a posteriori* une anticipation de l'histoire.

Mais alors que Vialatte représente la terreur sous la forme d'interrogatoires menés par les occupants allemands, Albert Camus, lui, trouve une autre voie en écrivant *L'Etranger* (1942) et *La Peste* (1947). Si la lecture de Kafka, alors, joue un rôle, c'est d'une manière très abstraite, philosophique. L'idée de la 'révolte' qui le fascinait chez Kafka et qui l'a poussé, concrètement, à entrer dans la résistance, ne prend dans les romans une dimension historico-politique que de façon très indirecte, allégorique.

Camus avait lu *Le Procès* dès 1938, si bien que l'éventualité d'une influence directe sur un roman écrit en 1941 et publié en 1942 semble acceptable, au moins chronologiquement. Etant donné que dans le roman lui-même — mises à part des affinités thématiques frappantes, on ne trouve aucune réminiscence explicite de Kafka — *Le Mythe de Sisyphe* qui date de 1942 et le modèle de l'"homo absurdus" qui s'y exprime prennent une valeur particulièrement éclairante. Le recours à ce modèle pour expliquer le héros kafkaïen apparaît dans un chapitre publié séparément en 1943 sous le titre *L'Espoir et l'absurde dans Kafka*. K. ou l'Arpenteur représentent ici globalement ce que Camus entend par existence absurde: l'indifférence, l'impression d'être un étranger, une vie sans progression (et qui en tant que telle est libérée du souci de l'existence), la révolte de la chair, l'expérience d'une existence purement matérielle. Tandis que, dans ce texte philosophique sur l'absurde, le processus de la compréhension concernant Kafka devient explicite, Camus romancier est beaucoup plus discret. Certes les parallèles extérieurs entre *Le Procès* et *L'Etranger* ont été souvent constatés: Joseph K. et Meursault montrent peu de réaction devant tout ce qui se passe, ils ne participent guère aux évènements; leur relation avec les femmes est essentiellement physique, les entretiens avec les juges instructeurs et les aumôniers de la prison se déroulent sans résultats ni pour l'un ni pour l'autre. Mais surtout on a les thèmes communs: l'arrestation, l'accusation, la faute, la peine de mort, en somme tout le procès. A la fin du roman, les deux héros réagissent par l'indifférence: K. s'abandonne aux bourreaux ('Il ne songea qu'à l'inutilité de sa résistance' (1957:293)) et Meursault peu avant sa mort, s'offre à la 'tendre indifférence du monde' (1962:1211).

Mais si Camus se présente à nous comme un lecteur de Kafka, toutefois il place fermement ses propres accents (le meurtre de l'Arabe par Meursault n'est pas comparable à la faute abstraite de K.) et, dans *L'Etranger* d'abord, il se rebelle, en particulier contre Dieu et l'église ('que m'importait son Dieu?' (1210)). Il fera une autre tentative avec *La Peste* où, face au dogme du péché originel ('l'origine divine de la peste et le caractère punitif de ce fléau' (1299)) il pose la force de l'action individuelle (Rieux) aussi bien que collective. Avec ce modèle dialectique, le romancier français dépasse Kafka, dépasse aussi sa propre théorie de l'absurde. Le fait que l'histoire de la victoire sur la peste ait pu être et soit encore lue comme une parabole de la lutte européenne contre la domination nazie relie historiquement Camus à son époque tout en le rapprochant de l'écrivain praguois dont il exploite l'écriture parabolique.

Mais les nouveaux romanciers français vont bientôt renoncer à des significations aussi substantielles. Alain Robbe-Grillet, dans son esquisse de programme romanesque, *Pour un nouveau roman*, déclare la guerre à la tradition humaniste de la 'profondeur des choses', de la pensée analogique ou allégorique. Et il le fait explicitement au nom de Kafka ('La mésaventure de Kafka dans ce domaine est exemplaire.' (1963:178)) en lui prêtant une écriture purement 'objective', c'est à dire anti-symbolique. Après avoir été réquisitionné par les surréalistes et les existentialistes, voilà Kafka cité pour la défense d'une nouvelle conception du roman selon laquelle seule compte 'l'évidence des objets, gestes, paroles etc...' (179) et non leur signification absurde. A une esthétique de la profondeur le Nouveau Roman oppose une esthétique de la surface. Le langage de la mythologie et du symbole ne doivent plus être des moyens d'expression, mais tout au plus un matériau avec lequel le romancier réalise sa création.

Nathalie Sarraute, dans *L'Ere du soupçon* (1964), ramène aussi à l'influence de Kafka d'importants facteurs de la nouvelle évolution: la disparition du héros et de l'intégrité narrative, les contradictions du dialogue, la narration qui n'avance pas, la méfiance vis à vis des significations fermées. Et pourtant il semble évident que de telles conceptions théoriques ne peuvent se réaliser que très partiellement dans la pratique romanesque. Le roman de Robbe-Grillet *Les Gommes* (1953) est aussi peu immunisé contre les interprétations symboliques que *Dans le labyrinthe* (1957): il est évident que les errances labyrinthiques du héros dans le temps et dans l'espace — comme chez Kafka — évoquent pour le lecteur un certain nombre d'expériences fondamentales, existentielles et constituent — nommons-les! — des archétypes.

Le jeu intertextuel et la déconstruction systématique de modèles d'interprétation psychanalytique et mythologique sont censés s'opposer à de telles lectures. Dans *Les Gommes*, ce n'est pas par hasard que des réminiscences de Kafka (par exemple la 'rue des Arpenteurs') et des situations oedipiennes s'imbriquent les unes dans les autres. Le protagoniste, à l'instar de K. dans *Le Château*, descend d'abord dans une auberge: 'cet obscur bistro de la rue des Arpenteurs' (1953:15). La situation labyrinthique du détective fait penser à

Sophocle, à Kafka et à Edgar Wallace: parti à la recherche du meurtrier et de son propre moi, il rencontre sa propre amnésie et une sorte de culpabilité obscure.

Le roman de Nathalie Sarraute, *Martereau*, est lui aussi le résultat d'une lecture productive de Kafka. D'abord, presque tout, dans ce roman, se présente comme l'extériorisation de la vie intérieure du je-narrateur; de plus la scène finale semble également sortir du *Procès*. Ici, Joseph K. entre deux messieurs pâles, 'surmontés de hauts-de-forme qui semblaient vissés sur leur crâne' en route vers l'exécution, et, là, dans *Martereau*, comme un reflet de la réalité intérieure du sujet: 'On dirait la scène finale du *Procès* de Kafka! [...] Et moi comme le héros du procès, je me laissais faire, consentant, presque complice, un peu écoeuré.... Ridicule, évidemment' (1964:202). Le leitmotiv de la disponibilité, de la flexibilité du héros, 'cette malléabilité' que Nathalie Sarraute, déjà dans *L'ère du soupçon*, observe chez Kafka (1964:63), est interprété ici essentiellement de manière structurelle — comme les hésitations et la méfiance du sujet de la narration vis à vis de son objet. Contrairement à Camus qui récupère la scène finale du *Procès* pour exprimer sa conception d'une existence absurde, il ne s'agit pas pour Sarraute de positions philosophiques mais, de façon primordiale, de la maîtrise de la représentation artistique dans le cadre d'une écriture fondamentalement nouvelle.

Cette nouvelle écriture trouve aussi en Georges Pérec un adepte qui, dans *La Vie mode d'emploi* (1978), fait d'un 'puzzle' inachevé à la fois le leitmotiv et le modèle structurel de son roman. Ce dernier, un puzzle intertextuel, confronte le lecteur, entre autres textes, avec une variante d'une nouvelle de Kafka dont le héros est un artiste, *Erstes Leid*, et marque la relation avec Kafka par un réseau de citations, de réminiscences et de parodie. Alors que l'artiste trapéziste de Kafka en principe ne quitte pas son trapèze, nous lisons chez Pérec: 'Le trapéziste ouvrit les mains et avec un long hurlement alla s'écraser sur le sol au terme d'une impeccable parabole' (72). D'une part, l'expérience que fait Kafka d'un art qui menace la vie sert à donner une signification à la nouvelle; d'autre part cette interprétation justement est mise en question par le coup de théâtre final (s'écraser) et par le double usage de la parabole, courbe mathématique et technique narrative. (Songeons à ce propos au nom de l'impresario chez Pérec: Rorschash. On a longtemps considéré que les paraboles de Kafka ressemblaient aux tests de Rorschach.)

On peut considérer que de telles instrumentalisations de la lecture de Kafka ouvrent une ère nouvelle dans la réception. Il ne s'agit plus du questionnement de l'oeuvre de Kafka, mais d'un réseau intertextuel dans un monde pluraliste et diffus. Même des productions récentes, comme le roman de François Rivière, écrit en 1992 d'après un scénario destiné au cinéma et totalement centré sur l'écrivain praguois et son oeuvre, restent le résultat de l'émiettement postmoderne. De tels montages — passages biographiques, jeu sur les formes de la réception (scène du film avec Kafka comme protagoniste) et réminiscences intertextuelles — nous rappellent les observations du premier traducteur français de Kafka, Claude Vialatte, qui parlait de l''ombre de l'ombre' de Kafka. Encore plus que les traductions dont elles sont le résultat, bon ou mauvais, les réceptions 'littéraires' au sens étroit du terme sont condamnées à mener une existence d'ombre.

Universität des Saarlandes

Oeuvres Citées

Camus, Albert 1962 'Le Mythe de Sisyphe' dans *Essais*. Gallimard, Bibl. de la Pléiade, Paris: pp. 89–211.

—— 1962 *L'Etranger* et *La Peste* dans *Théâtre, Récits, Nouvelles*. Gallimard, Bibl. de la Pléiade, Paris.

Escarpit, Robert 1970 *Le Littéraire et le social*. Flammarion, Paris.

Even-Zohar, Itamar 1990 'The Position of Translated Literature within the Literary Polysystem' in *Poetics Today*, 11, 1. spring: pp. 45–51.

Kafka, Franz 1957 (1933) *Le Procès*, nouvelle édition enrichie des variantes du texte original, tr. Alexandre Vialatte, préface de Bernard Groethuysen. Gallimard, Paris.

—— 1984 *Le Château*, tr. Bernard Lortholary. Flammarion, Paris.

Kundera, Milan 1993 *Les Testaments trahis*. Gallimard, Paris.

Pérec, Georges 1980 *La Vie mode d'emploi*. Hachette, Paris.

Rivière, François 1992 *Kafka*. Calmann-Lévy, Paris.

Robbe-Grillet, Alain 1953 *Les Gommes*. Ed. de Minuit, Paris.

—— 1963 *Pour un nouveau roman*. Gallimard/NRF, Paris.

Robert, Marthe 1966 'Kafka in Frankreich' in *Akzente* vol. 13: p.p. 310–320.

Schmeling, Manfred 1979 'Das "offene Kunstwerk" in der Übersetzung' in *Arcadia* vol. 14. no. 1: pp. 22–39.

Sarraute, Nathalie 1964 *L'Ere du soupçon*. Gallimard, Paris.

—— 1964 *Martereau*. Gallimard, Paris.

Vialatte, Alexandre 1984 *Le Fidèle berger*. Gallimard, Paris.

Maria Alzira Seixo

Malentendu Culturel et Poétique Narrative: Fernão Mendes Pinto et Gaspar da Cruz

Un des domaines privilégiés de la narratologie est celui de la détermination des conditions qui permettent à un ensemble de données de discours constituant un rapport, de devenir (et notamment dans le registre écrit) une histoire que l'on raconte. Barthes le notait déjà, il y a trente ans, dans son 'Introduction à l'analyse structurale des récits':

> Dans tout récit, l'imitation reste contingente; la fonction du récit n'est pas de 'représenter', elle est de constituer un spectacle qui nous reste encore très énigmatique, mais qui ne saurait être d'ordre mimétique; la 'réalité' d'une séquence n'est pas dans la suite 'naturelle' des actions qui la composent, mais dans la logique qui s'y expose, s'y risque et s'y satisfait. (1966:26)

La poétique narrative a toujours insisté sur les possibilités de décalage des niveaux de la représentation que chaque récit peut manifester et qui, sans écarter la fonction mimétique qu'ils développent, permet toutefois l'analyse de leur travail respectif dans une certaine autonomie qui peut souligner les références du texte, qu'elles soient historiques, idéologiques ou culturelles. Cette indépendance relative des niveaux du récit ne va pas sans tester les positions analytiques qui les considèrent, ainsi que leur caractère plus ou moins partiel dans l'élaboration des synthèses historiques qui les soutiennent. Une des tentatives les plus fructueuses développées dans ce sens a été celle de Louis Marin, tout au long de sa carrière (malheureusement trop tôt interrompue), et notamment son travail de repérage des dispositifs d'énonciation qui permettent aux données discursives d'un certain rapport de devenir un récit organisé. Dans son livre *Le Récit est un piège*, il essaie de décrire les tours de la représentation dans une fable de La Fontaine et dans 'Le Chat botté' de Perrault, et aussi dans les mémoires de Retz et dans un fragment du journal de voyage de Racine, tout en montrant que l'organisation d'un récit peut orienter la constitution d'un pouvoir et, surtout, que ce pouvoir peut être déjoué par la mise en évidence, par le récit lui-même en tant qu'il est gouverné par son narrateur, des mécanismes qui l'organisent, en prospection autonymique ou, sur le plan sémantique, par la construction critique du doute, du soupçon et du rire. Louis Marin écrit:

> ...ce narrateur léger et habile racontera des histoires et non plus l'Histoire; il ne tiendra pas de discours critique sur le Récit mais il dira des récits dont toute l'efficace tiendra à ce que — pour un moment — il conte au pouvoir la façon dont le pouvoir se raconte et, du même coup, le piègera à son propre piège par le plaisir que le pouvoir y prend. (1978:10)

Or il est curieux de voir que Marin travaille sur l'analyse de ces procédés dans trois types de textes: descriptifs-prescriptifs (la fable), descriptifs-subjectifs (mémoires), narratifs-mythiques (le conte de fées) et descriptifs-topiques (journal de voyages). Et j'aimerais souligner le fait que le récit de voyage, dans sa conception générale, survole les quatre catégories, tout en insistant sur certains modes en fonction des époques ou des conceptions qui les soutiennent, et qu'il s'agit là d'un genre qui est justement un terrain de privilège pour le récit piégé, tel que le conçoit Louis Marin. Dans un autre travail bien connu, consacré à l'étude de l'utopie, ce même auteur considère le récit de voyage comme la temporalisation d'une description, et, partant, une temporalisation qui, comme il dit, rend historique la carte géographique, et 'qui est à la fois celle du discours en tant que linéarité syntagmatique et celle du récit proprement dit par l'introduction d'un acteur' (1973:65).

Le thème en débat, qui relève des problèmes de la communication entre les cultures, et, partant, d'une temporalisation qui confronte la diversité des espaces (souvent paradigmatisée: antérieur/postérieur; ancien/nouveau; même/autre), trouve dans le récit de voyage l'exercice de la communication (écrite, littéraire) de cette même communication, et des mésaventures que le dialogue (en récit bifurqué, et, donc, 'mal entendu') peut développer. Constituant de façon souvent prioritaire un rapport, et ceci même dans le double sens du mot, on peut penser que l'intérêt de ces textes porte souvent sur les malentendus de l'approche et de l'interprétation, et que leur caractère littéraire pourrait justement se trouver, du moins pour le lecteur contemporain, dans les pièges d'un récit qui n'est pas étranger au contact de l'exercice du pouvoir et de l'état du désir, tout aussi bien que d'un savoir acquis pouvant s'orienter dans les deux modalités mentionnées.

Les textes dont je vais parler appartiennent à un monde idéologique pareil a celui de ceux qui sont étudiés par Louis Marin, et développent des situations narratives d'un type identique. Il est vrai que le contact profond qu'ils supposent avec des mondes nouveaux, et le fait qu'ils sont écrits du point de vue du voyageur qui est là-bas, dépendant d'une *hétérotopie* (Seixo 1995:12) narrative, fait que leur rapport avec le pouvoir monarchique de l'ancien régime devient plus particulier. La *Pérégrination* de Fernão Mendes Pinto est un texte écrit avant 1580, quoique publié seulement en 1614, et rend compte des années quarante et cinquante en Asie; le *Traité de la Chine* de Gaspar da Cruz couvre une observation de la Chine pendant les années quarante. Les deux rendent compte de longs voyages, mais l'enjeu de leurs déplacements est différent: Pinto a en quelque sorte voyagé malgré lui, menant une vie d'aventures pendant une vingtaine d'années, s'exposant aux dangers, aux joies, aux acquisitions et aux pertes de biens dans des situations qu'il n'a pas souhaitées et qui l'effraient, et il ne dépasse pas le niveau le plus commun des hommes d'équipage et des marchands anonymes; Gaspar da Cruz est un frère dominicain qui a passé, tout comme Pinto, vingt ans en Orient, habitant surtout Goa et Malaca, et qui décide d'aller (ou plutôt de venir) en Chine où il a été, paraît-il, le premier frère prêcheur de l'Evangile. Les deux ouvrages se présentent comme des récits d'évènements (aventures mouvementées chez Mendes Pinto, et bizarreries observées chez Gaspar da Cruz), où la description joue un rôle éminent, subordonnée cependant à l'action; dans ce cas le texte s'organise d'après une sorte de catalogue plus ou moins systématisé des réalités observées. Le savoir domine donc le niveau des modalités, dans le *Traité des choses de la Chine*, et les situations croisées de désir et de hasard, en un mot, la volonté devenue contingence, dominent la *Pérégrination*.

Mendes Pinto parcourt tout l'Orient, depuis Ormuz jusqu'au Japon, mais l'essentiel de son livre se passe dans les mers et dans les villes de Chine. Parmi de nombreux épisodes déroulés dans cet espace, susceptible d'être géographiquement vérifié, soulignons l'importance de deux séquences: celle de l'île de Calemplui et celle de la traversée de l'intérieur de la Chine. De façon correspondante, je mettrai en relief les chapitres de Gaspar da Cruz consacrés à l'étude des villes chinoises, des mariages locaux et du goût des voyages.

L'épisode de l'île de Calemplui constitue une des plus belles séquences de *Pérégrination*. Le héros en est un certain Antonio de Faria, corsaire portugais courageux et sans scrupules, qui poursuit les navires des mers de Chine, et devient à un certain moment curieux et rêveur en ce qui concerne une île perdue où sont gardés les trésors des empereurs. Il parvient à aborder l'île, s'empare des richesses qui y sont religieusement gardées, mais il est puni par le 'typhon', qui fait faire naufrage son bateau et noyer la plupart des siens, lui-même et les trésors disparaissant de façon mystérieuse. (Chose curieuse, Gaspar da Cruz conclut son texte par l'action du typhon, qui a ici aussi une fonction punitive, mais cette fois sur les chinois, à cause de leurs péchés, précise le prêtre.) Revenant à la tragédie de Calemplui, les rescapés, y compris le narrateur, gagnent la terre et errent pendant plusieurs semaines au sein du territoire chinois, y sont faits prisonniers, et Mendes Pinto fait des éloges enthousiastes des villes de Nanquin et de Pékin, qu'il décrit longuement et avec minutie. Ils profitent finalement de la guerre avec les Tartares pour obtenir des envahisseurs leur liberté.

Gaspar da Cruz, dans son *Traité des choses de la Chine*, commence justement par la mention des villes, s'occupant de Canton (où apparemment il est resté la plus grande partie de son voyage) mais soulignant qu'il s'agit d'une des moins belles villes de la Chine, et hyperbolisant les autres, comme Nanquin et Pékin. Il parle de l'organisation économique et politique des provinces, mentionne largement les us et coutumes, et notamment les mariages, la religion et la circonscription des chinois dans leur propre pays, duquel il leur est interdit de sortir, dit-il, sous peine de graves punitions. La méthode narrative de Gaspar da Cruz est contrôlée, exhibant de petites histoires comme exemples des observations qu'il énumère dans son inventaire, et suivant un rythme d'écriture lent et régulier, contrairement au rythme entrecoupé des aventures de conquête et de désastre de la *Pérégrination*. Gaspar da Cruz insiste sur le fait que les villes chinoises sont riches de préciosités et bâties selon des plans d'une architecture en avance sur les plans des villes occidentales. Cependant, son projet de voyage en Chine étant celui de l'évangélisation, pour lequel il avoue avoir été trompé en raison des difficultés que la région offre à cet égard, ses sentiments de déception se changent en une immense admiration devant les richesses du pays et le bien fondé de son organisation économique, et il rend pittoresque son plaidoyer par quelques traits négatifs qu'il cherche à mettre en évidence. Dans le chapitre sur le travail, il écrit:

> On soigne bien tous les morceaux de terre en Chine car, comme la population est excessive, et les hommes dépensent sans compter, et ils se soucient de bien manger, et bien boire, et bien s'habiller, et d'avoir de jolies maisons, mais surtout puiqu'ils sont de gros mangeurs, chacun s'occupe d'avoir de quoi faire pour travailler, et ceux qui ne travaillent pas ne mangent pas. (820)

Et il ajoute, dans le chapitre suivant, consacré aux marchands et aux métiers, et de façon idéologiquement marquée:

> Dans les produits d'argent ils mélangent l'alliage, et c'est pourquoi l'argenterie y est bon marché. Les marchands y sont en général malhonnêtes et menteurs, et font ce qu'ils peuvent pour tromper leurs clients, car leur conscience ne les accuse point, s'étant toujours adonnés à la pratique du mal. (827)

Si pour les voyages il observe le caractère compulsif de l'isolement des chinois, il le dit aussi à l'égard des mariages, qui se réalisent à un même niveau social, qu'il décrit en tenant compte surtout des mariages des rois. Ces deux traits se rapportent à une même attitude de circonscription, à la fixité (sociale et spatiale), et il est curieux de remarquer que Mendes Pinto les représente de façon concrète, soit pour l'île de Calemplui, soit pour le pèlerinage des prisonniers à travers les campagnes et les villes de Chine. Calemplui est le réduit du signe de l'Empereur, bien gardé et inaccessible, entouré d'une philosophie morale qui sert au gardien Hiticou à menacer Antonio de Faria: 'le sillon de ton aveuglement, en pilote d'enfer, vous conduit, toi et les autres, vers la profonde concavité du Lac de la Nuit. Car au lieu de rendre grâce à dieu pour cet immense bienfait qu'il t'a dispensé, tu viens le voler' (238).

L'existence de ce gardien moral ressemble à la protection matérielle de la Grande Muraille de Chine, que Mendes Pinto décrit de la façon qui suit:

> J'ai vu plusieurs fois et mesuré cette muraille. Elle compte généralement six brasses de haut et quarante empans de large au gros de la paroi. Mais les quatre brasses du bas sont augmentées d'un remblai à la manière d'un terre-plein dont la face extérieure est enduite d'un bitume pareil à un mortier, remblai qui, près de deux fois plus large que la muraille elle-même, forme une escarpe, par laquelle elle est rendue si robuste que mille *basiliscos* (i.e. canons) ne pourraient la mettre à bas. En place de tours ou de bastions, elle possède des guérites de deux étages, dressées sur des poteaux d'un bois noir qu'ils nomment *caubesi*, ce qui veut dire 'bois de fer', gros comme des barils fort élevés; de sorte que ces guérites sont, semble-t-il, bien plus robustes que si elles étaient de pierre et de chaux.
>
> Cette muraille ou *Chanfacau* comme ils l'appellent, c'est-à-dire 'Forte Résistance', s'étend en tout lieu d'une façon égale, jusqu'aux escarpements des montagnes qui sur son chemin se présentent, lesquels, afin de servir également de muraille, sont chamfreinées à la pioche, formant un ouvrage plus robuste encore que la muraille elle-même. On comprendra donc que sur toute cette étendue, il n'y a d'autre muraille que celle qui couvre les espaces s'étendant de sommet à sommet. Pour le reste, les montagnes elles-mêmes tiennent lieu de mur.
>
> Au long de ces trois cent quinze lieues il n'y a d'entrées que celles que font en ces régions les cinq fleuves de Tartarie, par lesquelles, avec l'impétueux courant qui leur permet de couper l'intérieur du pays sur plus de cinq cent lieues, ils vont se jeter dans la mer de Chine. (291)

La muraille garde la ville de Pékin, ou, comme il dit, 'sa richesse, son organisation et sa grandeur', par quoi on peut l'appeler 'capitale de la monarchie du monde' (326); je ne peux pas rendre compte ici de la façon attentive et détaillée dont Mendes Pinto, dans sa *Pérégrination*, rend compte de cette richesse, de cette organisation et de cette grandeur, tout au long d'une bonne dizaine de chapitres où c'est en fait l'organisation sociale qui, en véritable formation utopique, séduit particulièrement le narrateur. Mais on peut aisément comprendre la fascination utopique qui le saisit, et qui rôde autour des écrits de voyage, signifiant justement un mode de perception des autres civilisations qui rend dialogues et malentendus souvent inextricables. L'organisation poétique de ces récits semble être polarisée par des extrêmes de rejet et d'attirance que la composition du texte rend simultanés, soit au niveau de l'information communiquée (différence de niveaux orient/occident qui n'empêche pas une comparaison implicite et parfois explicite), soit au niveau de l'expérience acquise par le narrateur ou des émotions éprouvées par les personnages, et ceci dans des conditions éthiques et esthétiques contradictoires, signifiant la sémantisation de formes complexes de l'altérité, qui dépassent l'incompréhension des phénomènes que l'on observe, et que l'on interprète à plusieurs reprises de façon erronée, ou que l'on cherche même à évincer. (C'est le cas, pour ces deux textes, de l'omission de l'ambassade de Tomé Pires, qui a été la première incursion officielle des Portugais en Chine, d'effets désastreux, et que le rapport de ces textes à une situation de pouvoir occidental — la situation de découverte — réduit à un rôle insignifiant. Cette omission est surtout frappante chez Mendes Pinto, qui organise tout un très beau chapitre autour de la rencontre inattendue d'une chrétienne par les rescapés du naufrage parcourant le territoire chinois, et qui est justement Inês de Leiria, la fille de l'ambassadeur Tomé Pires, resté là-bas prisonnier, torturé et exilé jusqu'à sa mort.)

Cette perception des autres cultures est donc l'occasion d'une interception dans plusieurs sens. J'aimerais revenir sur la question des mariages pour souligner que, dans la *Pérégrination*, Mendes Pinto raconte deux épisodes qui se ressemblent. Dans le premier, le groupe du narrateur et Antonio de Faria admirent, de leur navire, un cortège de mariage où la fiancée, accompagnée de sa famille, vient à la rencontre de son futur époux, et prend le bateau des Portugais pour une des embarcations du cortège. Les Portugais les attaquent, prennent la jeune fille et tuent ceux qui l'accompagnent, trompant par la suite le jeune homme qui arrive à la rencontre de sa fiancée, et se moquant de lui. Dans l'autre épisode, un portugais, Diogo Soares, enlève aussi une jeune fille au moment de son mariage, tout en tuant son époux et d'autres personnes de sa famille qui essayaient de l'en empêcher. La jeune fille finit par se suicider, et son père, avec une foule de gens révoltés, réussit à poursuivre Soares pour le lapider — et cette fois Mendes Pinto de commenter: 'Et que l'on me pardonne de ne pas conter intégralement les détails de cette vilaine affaire: je le fais pour l'honneur du nom portugais' (649). Le fait est qu'il nous le raconte en détail, mais que, dans le premier épisode, où il est participant, il n'est pas dit ce qui arrive à la jeune fiancée, et il ne nous présente pas ses commentaires négatifs qu'il suggère pour le cas présent.

Ces textes ont la particularité de parler d'une intégration effective de l'homme occidental dans le monde nouvellement connu par l'Occident, tout en développant des malentendus culturels de part et d'autre que l'interception des valeurs étrangères et leur mise en place dans les systèmes familiers rend en quelque sorte objectifs dans la communication des cultures, faisant en même temps qu'ils deviennent déterminants dans la construction poétique du récit. Ils énoncent de façon décisive le pouvoir de l'idéologie qu'ils représentent, mais montrent aussi leur soumission au pouvoir de l'"autre' monde (qui pratique une sorte d'hypostase, dans le regard occidental, de cette altérité, de l'imagination perceptive et du récit de fiction), notamment dans l'expression courante par laquelle le narrateur de *Pérégrination* se désigne lui-même dans le récit (par exemple: 'Dieu sait comment le pauvre de moi était dans ce moment, plus mort que vif'), et prêtent aussi leur voix aux critiques du comportement occidental (comme dans l'exemple d'un enfant chinois qui adresse des critiques violentes directes à Antonio de Faria).

Le mode utopique du désir et de la volonté construit en partie, il est vrai, la modalité prédominante de ces écrits, mais le 'neutre' et le 'fixe' que l'utopie implique y sont dépassés par les marques de l'historicité que le statut du narrateur toujours implique (à travers les spécificités du point de vue, le lieu de la parole et l'entrecroisement des voix que le texte enregistre). Dans *Comparative Poetics*, Earl Miner souligne les superpositions culturelles et textuelles développées par la construction d'un récit, et il écrit notamment:

> Since an unnarrated narrative is a contradiction, narratorship extends from beginning to end, affording one of the principal features of continuities and sometimes of fulfilment as well. The plural, continuities, is required, both because a wide range of effects is involved and because point of view may be shifted.... Since narrators are versions of people, there is renewed testimony to the importance of people over places and times in narrative. The concept, the fact, is not only important but also fraught with a number of uncertainties, matters that we are only beginning to understand. (1990:181)

Le dialogue des cultures manifesté dans les textes de Mendes Pinto et de Gaspar da Cruz, avec tous ses malentendus possibles et effectifs, détruit le simplisme des paradigmes, et donne par là conscience au monde occidental d'être lui aussi un 'autre' monde, que le travail de l'écriture et sa capacité critique soulignent et reconsidèrent sans cesse.

Université de Lisbonne

Oeuvres Citées

Barthes, Roland 1966 'Introduction à l'analyse structurale des récits' dans *Communications*, 8. Seuil, Paris.

Cruz, Gaspar da 1984 *Peregrinaçao de Fernão Mendes Pinto e Itinerario de Antonio Tenreiro, Tratado das Cousas da China, Conquista do reino de Pegu*. Lello, Porto.

Marin, Louis 1973 *Utopiques: Jeux d'espaces*. Minuit, Paris.

—— 1978 *Le Récit est un piège* Minuit, Paris.

Miner, Earl 1990 *Comparative Poetics. An Intercultural Essay on Theories of Literature*. Princeton University Press.

Pinto, Fernão Mendes 1991 *Pérégrination*. La Différence, Paris.

Seixo, Maria Alzira 1995 'Two Portuguese in Japan: From Wanderlust to a Second Homeland (Mendes Pinto, XVI, and Morais, XIX–XX)' dans *The Force of Vision, 1: Dramas of Desire*, ed. Ziva Ben-Porat and Hana Wirth-Nesher. Proceedings of the XIIIth Congress, ICLA 1991, Tokyo.

JEAN BESSIÈRE

Malentendus Romanesques et Données Culturelles: Quelques Exemples Francophones

L'hypothèse d'un malentendu culturel, interculturel est, en elle-même, ambiguë. Elle suppose une part d'inintelligence, d'inintelligibilité entre cultures. Elle suppose aussi le point de l'intelligibilité, de l'intelligence de ce malentendu; elle suppose en conséquence un certain type d'entente qui rende compte de cette inintelligence, de cette inintelligibilité. Cette hypothèse relève d'un constat: il y a des désaccords culturels. Elle relève également d'une manière de correction implicite de ce désaccord: celui-ci peut être interprété parce qu'il a pour condition que puisse être conçu le lieu commun de l'inintelligibilité, de l'inintelligence. Le malentendu dit à la fois le désaccord certain et l'herméneutique possible de ce désaccord. Cette herméneutique peut être construite, reconstruite par la critique. Elle peut être la donnée même des oeuvres littéraires qui entreprennent de dire un tel malentendu. Celui-ci, à sa fonction de figurer des désaccords, ajoute une fonction proprement dialogique et interprétative: les désaccords sont donnés, se lisent sur le fond de l'élaboration d'une intelligibilité qui, à défaut d'être explicitement commune, suppose, expose l'échange entre les cultures qui sont placées sous le signe du malentendu.

Les oeuvres littéraires qui traitent d'un tel malentendu peuvent se définir dans ces termes: ces oeuvres reconnaissent le malentendu, s'investissent dans le malentendu, en font comme leur propriété, et rapportent cette implication précisément un mouvement d'interprétation qui n'exclut pas que soient maintenus la notation de la distance des cultures, le rappel de l'épreuve de la différence. Ces notations commandent une première conclusion. Le malentendu est un constat et une épreuve. Il est aussi connaissance — connaissance de ce malentendu, connaissances sur les cultures liées à ce malentendu, qu'implique cette connaissance qu'est le malentendu. De façon paradoxale, le malentendu traduit une dette réciproque des cultures auxquelles il renvoie, comme il suppose que celui qui écrit dans ce malentendu et de ce malentendu est dans une dette à l'égard de ce malentendu et qu'il ne cesse précisément de le reprendre, de l'exposer, de l'interpréter sans le récuser. Il peut être dit, dans ces conditions, une double vérité du malentendu: la vérité du malentendu même — le désaccord est répété; la vérité de l'exposition, de la narration du malentendu — ce malentendu, pris dans un récit, dans une fiction, trouve une vérité dans le jeu de la répétition du désaccord et de cette mise en fiction.

Ce malentendu et ce jeu littéraire, herméneutique, qui lui est attaché, sont comme redoublés dans le cas où ils sont mis en oeuvre à propos de cultures différentes qui possèdent une langue commune. Ainsi, tels romans, écrits en français, mais issus d'aires culturelles étrangères à la France même — nous retiendrons les romans antillais de Patrick Chamoiseau, *Solibo le Magnifique*, *Chronique des Sept Misères*, *Texaco*, le roman algérien de Rachid Boudjedra, *Topographie idéale pour une agression caractérisée*, le roman marocain de Tahar Ben Jelloun, *La Réclusion solitaire* — disent le champ linguistique commun, la proximité historique des cultures considérées, cultures antillaise, marocaine, algérienne, française, et font de ce champ linguistique, de cette proximité historique le premier moyen du constat du désaccord et du malentendu. Mais ce même champ linguistique, cette même proximité historique sont aussi les moyens de l'interprétation du constat. Dans *Solibo le Magnifique*, *Chronique des Sept Misères*, et *Texaco*, les agents romanesques savent à la fois la France et les Antilles. Dans *Topographie idéale pour une agression caractérisée*, narrateur et agent romanesques savent à la fois l'Algérie et la France. Dans *La Réclusion solitaire*, narrateur et agents romanesques savent à la fois la France et le Maroc. Le malentendu se résume dans des fables explicites. *Solibo le Magnifique*: les 'djobeurs', ces vendeurs qui sont aussi des conteurs, disparaissent de la culture antillaise et figurent ainsi l'impossible reconnaissance et l'impossible pratique d'une parole authentiquement locale, et l'inévitable malentendu puisque s'efface la dualité de l'expression culturelle. *Chronique des Sept Misères*: le conteur antillais meurt, d'une sorte de trop de parole, mais aussi du défaut de reconnaissance du conteur. *Texaco*: la ville noire disparaît — par quoi se figure encore la fin d'une dualité culturelle explicite. *Topographie idéale pour une agression caractérisée*: un Algérien à Paris, dans le métro parisien, ne peut que mourir — où il y a la refiguration de toutes les antinomies de l'histoire de la colonisation. *La Réclusion solitaire*: un immigré marocain meurt, en France, de solitude, de réclusion symbolique — où il y a une manière de dire à nouveau les antinomies de la colonisation et de noter l'impossibilité de l'entente culturelle. Ces fables explicites du malentendu sont écrites par ceux-là mêmes qui appartiennent à la culture qui n'est pas reconnue. Ces fables peuvent être lues comme des thèses. Ces thèses ne sont pas cependant les mots derniers de chacun de ces romans. Elles sont le cadre que se donnent ces romans du malentendu.

Ce cadre ne définit pas, en conséquence, le tout de l'expérience et de l'herméneutique du malentendu. Car, chaque fois, le narrateur et l'agent romanesque sont l'interprète de ce cadre, alors même qu'ils se définissent comme les victimes de ce malentendu. Les romans de Chamoiseau, de Boudjedra, de Ben Jelloun se prêtent ainsi à une manière de formulation extrême. Il convient de dire l'état de maladie qui est la figuration exacte du malentendu culturel — c'est pourquoi la notation de la souffrance est constante dans ces romans. Il convient, de plus, de marquer en quoi l'exposition et la figuration de cette maladie révèlent l'existence d'un processus dont les personnages sont le théâtre et qui symbolise la manifestation d'une pensée possible sur le malentendu, sur la communauté humaine partagée.

Patrick Chamoiseau, Rachid Boudjedra, Tahar Ben Jelloun redoublent le jeu du malentendu et de l'inintelligibilité dans la mesure où ils font du malentendu un des moyens d'interpréter le malentendu: le malentendu est considéré en lui-même et suivant un rapport au savoir et au fantasme —savoir et fantasme du malentendu, savoir et fantasme qui résultent de cette dualité de l'approche du malentendu. La fonction dialogique et herméneutique du malentendu est là: en rester au malentendu pour finalement expliquer par le malentendu même, sans qu'il soit prêté à ce malentendu un caractère de causalité — la maladie des hommes, tels que les décrivent Chamoiseau, Boudjedra, Ben Jelloun, ne se comprend pas par la seule référence au malentendu. Le malentendu est également l'interprétant de cette maladie. Aussi ces romans sont-ils dans leur traitement du malentendu culturel équivoques. Les cultures dans leurs désaccords présentent des signes de réciprocité qui permettent de marquer que le malentendu n'exclut pas les corrélations et qu'il doit être moins considéré en lui-même que selon les figurations lisibles qu'il met en oeuvre. Ces romans de Chamoiseau, de Boudjedra, de Ben Jelloun, sont, en conséquence, contradictoires, à quelque degré, dans leur propos.

La fable explicite du malentendu, qui est au fond une fable idéologique, interprétable dans le contexte postcolonial et dans celui d'une paupérisation du Tiers Monde, est une fable contradictoire parce qu'elle reconnaît à la fois la pertinence de ce malentendu en termes postcoloniaux et l'impossibilité de dire de manière positive et autrement que par la notation d'un rapport d'aliénation le rapport des cultures. Il y a là même une caractérisation, implicite, explicite, de la culture postcoloniale, considérée dans sa différence avec la culture française. Cette culture postcoloniale est d'une identité faible, qui se dit par son propre deuil. La notation du deuil apparaît ambivalente: elle traduit le drame de la différence; elle traduit que l'allégeance au monde postcolonial est peut-être une allégeance vaine dans la mesure où cette allégeance ne peut fonder la pertinence d'un récit du malentendu culturel.

Dès lors, la fable du malentendu culturel construit une double image du deuil. D'une part, l'image du deuil qui résulte du malentendu culturel, noté d'abord par la thématique de l'étrangeté — étrangeté du 'djobeur', de celui qui entreprend de dire la ville noire dans *Texaco*, étrangeté de l'immigré algérien, marocain, en France. D'autre part, l'image du deuil est indissociable de l'épuisement de l'identité postcoloniale. Cette double image du deuil est, dans ces romans, le premier témoin de la réciprocité des cultures évoquées, représentées sous le signe du malentendu. La mort est sans doute le symbole achevé du malentendu; elle est aussi le symbole de ce par quoi communiquent les cultures, placées sous ce signe du malentendu. Cela fait entendre très explicitement: la vérité du malentendu culturel est certaine cause de la différence et de l'inégale importance politique des cultures; elle est aussi certaine parce que ce malentendu doit s'interpréter comme l'impossibilité actuelle de dire et de médier l'altérité dans les cultures qu'évoquent Chamoiseau, Boudjedra, Ben Jelloun.

La fable du malentendu peut donc se lire doublement: suivant sa thèse expresse — le malentendu des cultures participe d'un affrontement et d'une inégalité de pouvoir de ces cultures; suivant sa thèse sous-entendue — le malentendu est peut-être interculturel, il est également et plus essentiellement proprement culturel, au sens où une culture, en elle-même, ne peut médier ses propres altérités, ses sujets mêmes, en tant qu'ils sont considérés comme des singularités. C'est pourquoi le monde antillais que décrit Patrick Chamoiseau reste un monde ambivalent: monde qui se réclame de sa tradition orale et cependant, dans les termes de Chamoiseau, monde inédit parce que toute expression de ce monde, y compris l'expression proprement locale, est une expression inadéquate.

De la même manière, dans *Topographie idéale pour une agression caractérisée*, Rachid Boudjedra marque manifestement la clôture de la culture française, mais également la lucidité de celui, algérien, qui est pris dans une telle clôture: cette épreuve de la différence et de l'étrangeté est sans doute une épreuve française; elle est indissolublement une épreuve algérienne dans la mesure où celui qui affronte la différence le fait parce qu'il y a là un mouvement qui est commandé par la réalité, la culture algérienne même.

L'argument de *La Réclusion solitaire* de Tahar Ben Jelloun est similaire. La nostalgie qu'éprouve ici l'immigré pour le Maroc, traduit sans doute le jeu du malentendu culturel, mais elle marque aussi l'inaptitude de la culture indigène à être autre chose que sa propre apparence et nourrir autre chose que le rêve de la nostalgie.

Une conclusion s'impose, qu'il s'agisse des fables de Chamoiseau, de celle de Boudjedra, ou de celle de Tahar Ben Jelloun: la maladie que figure le malentendu culturel, n'est pas seulement la maladie que suscite l'épreuve de la différence, elle est aussi la maladie de ces cultures, l'antillaise, l'algérienne, la marocaine, où rien du drame du réel, rien de ce monde manichéen, ne peut être refoulé, et où la lucidité du sujet se confond avec la conscience de ce défaut de refoulement.

Le malentendu culturel doit en conséquence se réinterpréter. Il prend dans ces romans, *Solibo le Magnifique*, *Chronique des Sept Misères*, *Texaco*, *Topographie idéale pour une agression caractérisée*, *La Réclusion solitaire*, la forme extrême de l'inintelligence du colonial et du postcolonial. Dans cette forme extrême, il fait apparaître que le traumatisme de la différence a un antécédent dans le traumatisme de la culture natale. Aussi le malentendu se lit-il triplement: suivant l'explicite de sa fable; suivant le traumatisme de la culture natale; suivant la chance qu'offrent le traumatisme de la différence et celui de la culture natale. A cause de ces traumatismes, le monde auquel l'homme, celui qui vient de la différence, est confronté, n'est pas pleinement lisible. C'est ici l'argument que suggère la fable du malentendu culturel: parce que ce monde n'est pas pleinement lisible, il laisse une place à la lecture de l'individu, du sujet singulier. Tous les romans cités sont de la part de leurs narrateurs, de leurs agents, de telles entreprises de lecture qui supposent le malentendu, et qui constituent une manière de savoir. Ce savoir est spécifique: celui du sujet, cet individu pris dans le malentendu cuturel, qui, parce qu'il peut voir, entendre, fût-ce dans une certaine inintelligence des cultures, a la capacité d'assumer l'activité et la force de la subjectivité face à l'histoire.

Cette histoire est, dans ces cinq romans, une histoire postcoloniale. Celle d'une dépossession et d'un malentendu. Celle d'une possiblité de lire et de dire, qui, pour le sujet postcolonial, a partie liée avec la déchirure de l'intelligence que porte d'abord le malentendu des cultures.

Ces romans sont donc les romans de l'inversion des signes du malentendu culturel. Ce malentendu ouvre, en un premier temps, une herméneutique paradoxale: il ne doit pas tant être interprété en lui-même que comme le symptôme de l'égale maladie des cultures qui se mésinterprètent. En un second temps, il désigne l'inintelligence des cultures comme le moyen de fonder l'intelligence libre du sujet, qui commence par le regard et par cette parole qui sait qu'elle ne dispose plus d'une tradition, mais seulement de la nostalgie d'une identité culturelle certaine.

Dès lors, par un autre paradoxe, celui qui témoigne du malentendu culturel — les conteurs de *Chronique des Sept Misères* et de *Solibo le Magnifique*, le narrateur de *Texaco*, l'homme enfermé dans le métro parisien de *Topographie idéale pour une agression caractérisée*, l'immigré reclus de *La Réclusion solitaire* — devient l'interprète des signes de chacune des cultures, en les lisant, en les disant tout simplement. Il est le témoin réciproque qui ne lève pas l'inintelligence, puisque, dans l'énigme de l'inintelligence, il y a la possibilité de l'entente libre. C'est pourquoi la notation de l'étrangeté et du deuil commune à tous ces romans, se lit la fois comme l'indication du malentendu, des conséquences de ce malentendu, et comme l'indication de cette interprétation du malentendu, qui ouvre l'espace d'une possible intelligence.

Le malentendu culturel, au-delà du constat qu'il suscite, est la condition d'une manière de double regard, de la part des narrateurs, des agents romanesques. On perçoit la discontinuité des cultures — cela que ressassent *Solibo le Magnifique, Texaco, Topographie idéale pour une agression caractérisée, La Réclusion solitaire*. On perçoit, avec une égale netteté, les deux cultures à la fois — l'Antillaise et la Française, l'Algérienne et la Française, la Marocaine et la Française. Le malentendu culturel et sa fable extrême n'excluent ni l'objectivité, ni une manière d'objectivisime. La fable du malentendu se formule doublement: donner l'évidence et les causes du malentendu, passer le témoignage du malentendu pour caractériser celui qui connaît l'épreuve du malentendu comme le témoin de réalités opposées.

Grâce à un tel traitement du malentendu, les entreprises romanesques de Chamoiseau, de Boudjedra, et de Ben Jelloun présentent l'intérêt de préserver ce qu'implique la notation du deuil: le défaut de réciprocité des cultures, et cependant de tirer de ce défaut le moyen d'un dialogisme implicite. C'est pourquoi il est constamment dit la distance culturelle. Cette distance est figurée dans *Solibo le Magnifique, Chronique des Sept Misères, Texaco,* par l'éloignement de l'oral et de l'écrit, dans *Topographie idéale pour une agression caractérisée,* par la caractérisation du personnage de l'immigré algérien comme l'errant du métro de Paris, dans *La Réclusion solitaire,* par la comparaison de la chambre où vit l'immigré marocain à une malle. C'est pourquoi il est encore constamment dit la présence de l'Antillais, de l'Algérien, du Marocain, et de l'autre culture — fût-ce sous le signe de la souffrance et de la dépossession.

Cette dualité du traitement du deuil et de la distance place les romans sous une série de contraintes. Ainsi narrer revient raconter deux choses à la fois: la dépossession et l'assimilation, sous le signe de l'objectivité, de l'autre culture. Ce n'est pas un des moindres paradoxes des romans de Chamoiseau que d'affirmer une identité antillaise, de la déclarer simultanément inédite, et de placer l'écrivain dans une manière de discordance avec cette culture — les moyens dont celui-ci dispose sont, par définition, inadéquats au dessin d'un devenir de l'identité culturelle martiniquaise.

Une ambiguïté similaire est lisible dans *Topographie idéale pour une agression caractérisée* et dans *La Réclusion solitaire*. Boudjedra, en faisant de son personnage, un étranger, l'étranger, qui reste cependant caractérisé par des références spécifiquement algériennes, figure un extrême du malentendu, mais il suppose aussi — et par ces mêmes moyens — que la culture algérienne est à quelque degré indicible par elle-même, ou, plus exactement, qu'elle ne se dit que par ce jeu du malentendu, de l'étrangeté. Ben Jelloun reprend cette thématique extrême de l'étranger; il n'exclut pas cependant des références à la culture marocaine, mais il les donne expressément pour des images. Il est dit en conséquence, dans chacun de ces romans, une évidence, fût-ce au moyen de la notation de la souffrance, l'évidence de l'autre culture et l'évidence de la culture natale.

Ces ambivalences de la narration place les romans de Chamoiseau, de

Boudjedra, de Ben Jelloun, sous le signe de l'enquête. Enquête explicite, puisqu'elle est policière, dans *Solibo le Magnifique*. Enquête dans *Texaco*: l'argument du roman consiste à dire pourquoi la ville noire a disparu. Enquête dans *Topographie idéale pour une agression caractérisée*: l'étranger est celui qui démontre la réalité de l'autre culture. Enquête sur soi-même que mène l'étranger dans *La Réclusion solitaire*, et qui est une enquête sur le malentendu culturel, sur cette juxtaposition, dans ce personnage de l'étranger, de deux cultures, celle de sa nostalgie et de ses fantasmes, celle qu'il figure, la culture française, par sa propre souffrance. Ces enquêtes sont sans solution. L'énigme du malentendu subsiste. Ce que Chamoiseau dit en notant que les causes de la mort de Solibo ne sont pas connues, que l'histoire de la ville, dans *Texaco*, ne peut être l'histoire d'une prospective. Ce que Boudjedra marque en notant que, pour cet étranger, ce qu'il perçoit de la métropole reste un ensemble de signes qu'il peut seulement identifier. Ce que Ben Jelloun note en résumant l'itinéraire d'un expatrié — qui va de la misère locale, celle du pays d'origine, aux images, tout à la fois de ce pays et du pays d'accueil. Dès lors que subsiste l'énigme du malentendu, dire les cultures devient exercice de citation. Ainsi que Chamoiseau ne cesse de citer les témoins de l'oralité et les témoins de cette culture de l'écriture — assimilée à la culture française. Ainsi que Boudjedra fait de l'itinéraire dans le métro parisien l'occasion d'une manière de relevé ethnologique des comportements, des signes, des spectacles, des images. Ainsi que Ben Jelloun, dans la fiction d'un discours intérieur, prête au personnage de l'expatrié une série de notations, souvent mémorielles, qui sont autant d'images de l'une et l'autre cultures.

Sous le signe de l'énigme de l'autre culture, qui n'exclut pas que la culture natale devienne aussi une manière d'énigme, dès lors que les conditions de son expression ne sont plus réunies — c'est la thématique explicite et constante de Chamoiseau, c'est la thématique plus indirecte de Boudjedra et de Ben Jelloun qui font de la culture natale à la fois une nostagie et un inexprimé — le malentendu culturel n'exclut pas, cause de cette énigme même, qu'il y ait, dans ces romans, une lecture certaine de l'une et l'autre cultures. La lecture des signes de ces cultures, de ces signes évidents dans l'actualité, dans la mémoire, dans l'histoire. Le malentendu culturel n'est pas dissociable d'une manière d'objectivisme.

Par un nouveau paradoxe, le malentendu culturel n'appelle donc pas, dans ces romans, son propre traitement explicite. La notation du deuil, l'objectivisme, les données narratives, la fable de l'enquête, le jeu citationnel — fantasmes, images, paroles, textes — disposent explicitement l'évidence de l'altérité et les témoins de l'altérité. Le témoin est celui qui voit, fait l'expérience de l'autre culture. Dans cette expérience, l'altérité est reconnue pour elle-même, ainsi que le témoin se reconnaît. Le malentendu devient l'occasion de l'exposé d'une transparence des cultures. Aussi Chamoiseau, Boudjedra, Ben Jelloun ne proposent-ils aucune comparaison des identités culturelles, aucune explication du malentendu. Ce malentendu suppose, de fait, une sorte de savoir. Savoir sur les cultures natales: elles sont des cultures de la fin — telle est, dans *Solibo le Magnifique* et *Chronique des Sept Misères*, l'argument de Chamoiseau — et de l'exclusion — telle est la notation explicite de Boudjedra et de Ben Jelloun. Savoir de la culture autre: la culture française figure l'altérité quasi absolue, et manifeste une méconnaissance d'elle-même, comme le suggère Chamoiseau en marquant, dans *Texaco*, que le rapport de la Martinique avec la France ne dit pas ce que peut être une conscience de l'identité française, comme le suggère aussi Boudjedra dans *Topographie idéale pour une agression caractérisée* en soulignant que l'univers français est d'abord un univers sémiotique qui ne fait pas sens en lui-même. Aussi le savoir du malentendu devient-il, puisqu'il n'est pas le savoir du malentendu en lui-même, le savoir d'une sorte de dramaturgie. Parce que le constat du malentendu n'est pas séparable du deuil, c'est-à-dire du caractère mortifère et de la culture natale et de la culture autre, le savoir, dont il est indissociable, est savoir de l'action et du drame que fait chaque culture et que font les cultures ensemble. Ce drame est explicitement le drame des identités culturelles, vouées tantôt à figurer l'altérité et la méconnaissance d'elles-mêmes, tantôt à exposer leur caractère fantasmatique ou imaginaire. Le fait et l'exposé du malentendu apparaissent comme les moyens de dire des identités culturelles, sans qu'elles soient reportables sur le malentendu.

Le malentendu définit un champ d'intelligibilité: celui du caractère manifeste des cultures, celui du libre regard que permet ce malentendu. Aussi Chamoiseau, Boudjedra et Ben Jelloun rapportent-ils cette intelligibilité à une manière d'herméneutique objective, qui procède du constat que rien ne peut médier l'altérité — c'est cela que fait comprendre la thématique de l'étranger dans *Topographie idéale pour une agression caractérisée*, dans *La Réclusion solitaire* — et que, par là, toute différence, cela qui maintient le malentendu, est lisible, caractérisable, non pas suivant un jeu de comparaison, mais selon ce qu'elle fait voir. Ce mouvement d'intelligence suppose que les diverses cultures et identités culturelles soient laissées elles-mêmes.

Laisser les identités culturelles à elles-mêmes fait comprendre que le malentendu est inaltérable. Les romans de Chamoiseau, de Boudjedra, de Ben Jelloun figure cet inaltérable en marquant une dissymétrie entre la culture natale et la culture autre, la culture française. Cette dissymétrie est une façon de redire le pouvoir historique et encore actuel de l'autre culture. Elle est encore le moyen de souligner ce que peut être le bon usage de l'altérité pour celui qui en fait l'expérience et l'épreuve. Les personnages martiniquais de Chamoiseau, le personnage algérien de Boudjedra, le personnage marocain de Ben Jelloun, à défaut d'être explicitement reconnus par l'autre culture — où il y a une autre caractérisation du malentendu culturel — reconnaissent les témoins de l'autre culture, les identifient comme tels. L'alliance de la dissymétrie et de cette reconnaissance fait entendre, d'une part, que le constat de l'altérité lève toute tentation de prêter aux témoins propres de l'autre culture un geste d'introspection et de les placer sous le signe d'une identité réfléchie. Elle fait entendre, d'autre part, que celui qui fait l'expérience de l'autre culture ne peut se prévaloir ultimement de son identité — où il y a une nouvelle justification de l'absence de comparaison des identités culturelles — mais que, puisqu'il ne lui est jamais donné l'occasion d'être lui-même, il peut regarder, imaginer, parler de lui-même et de l'autre, suivant l'évidence de ce qui vient de l'autre culture. Par un paradoxe supplémentaire, pour celui qui fait l'expérience de l'autre culture, l'évidence de l'autre est celle de celui, de cela qui n'est pas moi-même, et grâce à laquelle je ne puis me concevoir autre que je ne suis. L'intelligibilité ultime du malentendu est là.

Dans ce présent commun, celui de l'autre culture et du témoin étranger de cette culture, narrer le malentendu porte doublement sens. Cette narration fait de ce présent sa propre représentation. C'est pourquoi les romans de Chamoiseau, de Boudjedra, de Ben Jelloun, identifient le malentendu culturel à une précise actualité. Cette narration, parce qu'elle est la narration du malentendu, dit celui qui fait l'expérience de l'altérité. Autant il ne peut y avoir de discours plénier de l'autre culture, autant, cause de cela-même, il peut y avoir un discours de celui qui ne peut se concevoir autre qu'il n'est. Ce discours est, sans doute, celui de la déréliction, de l'aliénation. Il est cependant plus: parce que l'autre culture, dans le jeu du malentendu, est en quelque sorte disponible, elle peut devenir le moyen d'une écriture de soi, de celui qui fait l'expérience de cette autre culture. La disponibilité fait entendre que le malentendu n'exclut pas que la culture autre soit dite suivant ses spectacles, suivant ses données les plus manifestes, et que cette manière de dire fonde la possibilité d'un portrait éthique de celui qui fait l'expérience de cette autre culture.

Puisque le malentendu culturel instruit que rien ne peut médier l'altérité, et que celui qui fait l'expérience de l'autre culture est amené élaborer un discours de lui-même, les personnages martiniquais de Chamoiseau, le personnage algérien de Boudjedra, le personnage marocain de Ben Jelloun deviennent plus que les témoins, les porteurs de leur propre identité; ils deviennent ceux qui disent l'objectivisme de l'autre culture et qui se disent, ceux qui exposent à la fois le jeu de la culture française et le jeu de leur propre culture, figuré par le discours personnel qu'ils tiennent. Il y a là un portrait éthique parce que celui qui fait l'expérience de la culture autre donne un droit de cité égal à la culture autre et à lui-même. Ces personnages entreprennent de placer leur propre singularité face au spectacle de l'autre culture, deviennent les transcripteurs libres de cette autre culture, comme ils sont finalement capables de se dire, et, par là, de renvoyer à leur propre culture. Le malentendu est essentiellement l'occasion de cet exercice qui est exercice d'intelligibilité. Non pas au sens où il serait proposé une interprétation continue du face à face des cultures, mais au sens où le défaut de médiation de l'altérité est à la fois la condition du malentendu et la condition de cette exercice de compréhension qui consiste à reconnaître le fait de l'autre culture et à se dire.

Ces notations appellent une conclusion importante. Dans ces romans, le malentendu culturel impose de laisser les cultures elles-mêmes, mais exclut de concevoir les mondes extérieurs des cultures comme des entités douées d'existences autonomes. Les personnages de Chamoiseau, de Boudjedra, de Ben Jelloun savent que les mondes de ces cultures sont un même monde — celui du malentendu. Le malentendu s'interprète alors comme l'inadéquation des diverses représentations que l'on peut avoir de ces cultures. Par là, le malentendu est indépassable. Comme on l'a dit, ces romans présentent cependant ce malentendu comme une chance. Il marque les limites de ce qui peut être dit, de ce que peuvent dire ces cultures d'elles-mêmes. C'est pourquoi ne pas aller contre le malentendu permet de reconnaître cette limite et d'engager l'intelligibilité de cette limite.

Il y a là le moyen de relire les romans de Chamoiseau, de relire *Topographie idéale pour une agression caractérisée*, *La Réclusion solitaire*. On a noté que les romans de Chamoiseau, et particulièrement *Texaco*, concluent sur un inédit de la culture antillaise. Cette conclusion est paradoxale en ce qu'elle suppose la culture martiniquaise et qu'elle la déclare en quelque manière non dite. Il convient de souligner: cette culture n'est peut-être pas dite en elle-même; elle n'est peut-être pas dite comparativement; elle est sans doute dite sur le mode de la parole perdue; mais elle est aussi dite sur le mode de la réflexion que suscite le constat du malentendu — cette reflexion que figure l'exercice narratif. En ce sens la notation et l'usage du malentendu culturel sont certainement, dans les romans de Chamoiseau, les moyens de représenter la parole martiniquaise sous le signe de sa propre altérité, et, en conséquence, de fonder, particulièrement dans *Texaco*, ce que nous avons appelé ailleurs le jeu de la poétique implicite. Celle-ci s'oppose la poétique explicite qui identifie l'écrivain à une sorte de conteur et le définit, dans les termes de Chamoiseau, comme un 'marqueur de paroles'. Cette même poétique implicite se caractérise de la manière suivante: puisque la seule représentation de la parole est vaine, puisque la seule reconnaissance de la logique du récit romanesque contredit la représentation de la parole, l'alliance de cette représentation et de cette logique vaut pour elle-même contre ce qui serait le seul droit de la représentation de la parole ou le seul droit du récit et de la logique qu'il porte. Le malentendu culturel apparaît comme le moyen de définir un discours de l'identité antillaise, qui échappe aux impossibilités de dire directement une telle identité. Boudjedra et Ben Jelloun proposent un usage similiaire du malentendu culturel. Ni *Topographie idéale pour une agression caractérisée*, ni *La Réclusion solitaire* ne viennent à une caractérisation positive de l'identité de la culture natale — cette identité est également une identité partiellement inédite parce qu'elle porte en elle-même des jeux de malentendus.

Cependant, grâce au malentendu des cultures, cette identité acquiert droit de cité: elle est l'occasion, dans l'intelligence du malentendu, d'une représentation réfléchie. Dans *Topographie pour une agression caractérisée*, cette représentation réfléchie résulte de l'objectivisme qui est indissociable de l'évocation de l'autre culture. Dans *La Réclusion solitaire*, cette représentation réfléchie est liée au jeu d'opposition et de citation des données de la culture française et de la culture marocaine, fût-il placé sous le jeu du fantasme.

Au total, l'exposé du malentendu culturel permet, dans ces romans, d'exposer les conditions d'une dicibilité des identités culturelles postcoloniales, dans le rappel de la condition coloniale et dans l'évidence de la culture française, culture autre, dont l'approche objective et objectiviste transforme le malentendu culturel en une intelligence de la communauté des cultures et de la culture postcoloniale.

Université de Paris III

Oeuvres Citées

Ben Jelloun, Tahar 1976 *La Réclusion solitaire*. Denoël, Paris.

Bessière, Jean 1995 'Patrick Chamoiseau et le récit de l'inédit. Poétique explicite, poétique implicite' dans Pierre Laurette et Hans-Georgre Ruprecht (eds) *Poétiques imaginaires. Francopolyphonie littéraire des Amériques*. L'Harmattan, Paris.

Boudjedra, Rachid 1975 *Topographie idéale pour une agression caractérisée*. Denoël, Paris.

Chamoiseau, Patrick 1988 (1986) *Chronique des Sept Misères*. Gallimard, Paris.

—— 1991 (1988) *Solibo le Magnifique*. Gallimard, Paris.

—— 1992 *Texaco*. Gallimard, Paris.

Margarida L. Losa

Literature and Desire

WHY FICTION IS NOT TO BE READ LITERALLY[1]
A first reason for the figurative character of fiction resides in its incorporation of the author's personality and point of view.[2] Even an advocate of impersonal naturalism such as Zola states that the novelist who depicts a portion of reality (*un coin de la nature*) must do it through his own personality (*à travers un tempérament*) (1971:140). In the process of literary creation the writer's 'raw materials' are shaped by his or her ideological interpretations and emotional preferences. This is one reason why writers are considered the authors of their works and are entitled to copyright. From this evidence it follows that when we wish to describe the textual content of a literary work we ought to keep in mind that, somehow, it includes its author, and that this is so even when there is not a single word testifying to such an inclusion.[3]

In fact authors, because they have personalities, will react to a portion of reality rather than depict it. This provides the literary text with an intrinsic 'duality' of content. Even when, in appearance, it is either strictly objective or, on the contrary, strictly fictional, it incorporates the 'invisible' presence of the author. Because it is unique and irreplaceable this presence provides the work of art with a lasting 'aura' of originality.[4] Readers and their interpretations will vary but while the aura lasts the work remains somehow attached to its source. The author radiates from the text itself and, if in no other way, the style of the work testifies to it. The style is an important part of the content of the literary work.

Secondly, fiction cannot be read literally because it does not exist in a social void. It has a context. Writers presuppose that certain things are known to their readers. They may even be unaware of these presuppositions because as members of a given cultural community they take them for granted. On the other hand, writers do not wish to repeat what others have already done because their trade requires 'originality'. Novelty is part of the consumers' 'horizon of expectations', even of those consumers who are likely to defend the aesthetic traditions they know best.[5] Without having to make it explicit, authors react against what is already in existence in the field, generating thereby a sort of negative 'intertextuality'.[6] The latter, too, will become a kind of 'invisible' subject matter to which an informed 'community of readers' will respond while other communities, unaware of such intertextuality, will not.[7] To put it briefly, under contextualization we may subsume factors such as cultural codes, literary conventions, aesthetic trends, political constraints and market demands. (All these aspects are now studied in conjunction under the general label of systemic studies.) The author will be writing within a given cultural 'system' — even when he/she is reacting against it — but nothing in the text will have to say so explicitly. We may conclude from the above, then, that an important part of the meaning of the literary work is inferred from its extra-textual context.

A third and in my opinion most important reason why literary fiction is not to be read literally is based on the fact that what actually appears written on the page is not necessarily what the work is saying.[8] There is a particular duplicity in the literary text. First, as Michael Riffaterre (1990), for example, succintly explains in his essay on undecidability, the construction of meaning is a gradual and in part retroactive process. Readers 'travel' with the text and the total clues to an understanding are realized only at the end. This is the more so when texts have plots, as is the case of narrative and dramatic fiction.[9] This dynamics of reading explains how one episode can mean something at one stage of reading and something else at a subsequent stage.

However, this idea of duplicity is connected with other aspects of the literary text as well, such as its metaphoric quality, for example. In his *Le Roman Expérimental*, Zola spoke of the writer as an experimentalist. In a different manner from the lab scientist — whom Zola wished to emulate — the writer's experiment consisted in letting the characters speak and act on their own, as it were, leading readers to discover by themselves the laws that governed the characters' behaviour. Or, as Lao She wrote in his 1945 Afterword to *Camel Xiangzi*:

> Once I had my characters, it was comparatively easy to work out the plot. Since Xiangzi is the main character, everything in the story must revolve around rickshaw pulling. As long as all the people were linked in some way with the rickshaw, I had Xiangzi pinned down exactly where I wanted him. (1988:233)

Several writers have stressed this principle that the events must speak for themselves, from which we infer that there are meanings to be extracted from the text which the author does not feel should be spelt out. They have to be discovered and appropriated by the reader. The cooption of the reader to participate in the diagnosis of the text's semantic content enhances not only the dialogic nature of fiction but also the reader's aesthetic enjoyment itself. Naturally, this hide-and-seek strategy entails the risk that different readers will infer different meanings from what is left unsaid. It is a 'calculated risk', one on which the value of fiction as aesthetic object probably depends. This is also why, among other consequences, a good work of art is seldom very reliable propaganda (however much art and propaganda have been close partners throughout history), and good, reliable propaganda is usually an impoverished substitute for art. By contrast the very flexibility of meaning of the literary text is probably what causes it to be more easily transposed to another culture.

To borrow two concepts from Sigmund Freud's theory of the interpretation of dreams, the aesthetic object, like the dream, has one 'manifest content' and a different conceptual content under the surface, the 'latent content'. The latter is the 'true content' or rather 'the content of truth' which hides inside fiction. Fiction is the alibi of the latent content, as it were.[10] In this connection one suspects that fiction lies, invents, disguises or simply 'distances' itself from the real world so as to elude the repressive powers that exist in it and to probe the meanders of human and social truths.[11]

Literary fiction is related to the world of dreams, daydreams, creeds and, in short, desires. When someone imagines the fulfilment of a desire and then presents that fulfilment to others as if it had actually occurred he or she is either lying or 'fictionalizing'. In this sense fiction has a power of its own. It is intertwined with human culture at large in a complex way. Fictions of all sorts, posing as reality, circulate among us. From a sociological and political point of view, because they are a powerful means of intersubjective communication, fictional texts are often deemed pernicious, addictive or, to say the least, irresponsible. They are seen as obfuscating common sense and interfering with productive behaviour.

In the sense I am proposing now, all fiction, even the most fantastic, is realistic because it bases itself on the power of figuration of the mind, on our capacity to articulate in speech what has been imagined. Whether an author chooses to represent the real world of suffering migrant workers as did John Steinbeck in *The Grapes of Wrath* (1939), or the fantastic life of a lab-generated monster as did Mary Shelley in *Frankenstein* (1818), what is being conveyed to the reader is a figuration of human suffering. Steinbeck's metaphor, by taking its raw materials from historical reality, operates with an *effet de réel*, to use Barthes' expression (1982). Shelley's metaphor operates with an effect of the uncanny and the fantastic, and part of her raw materials, as she herself claimed, were taken from a dream she had. In more senses than one both novels are parables because they tell a tale on the surface and convey 'a different story' underneath. Not all readers will verbalize or 'interpret' the latter. But, even when they do not they will have responded to it emotionally, 'understanding' and sympathizing with both the monster's point of view and that of Tom Joad and his migrant family.[12]

❖

Let us now focus on what can be called the dialectical nature of reception. As the text goes out of the author's hands it undergoes a process of confrontation with the reader so that the meaning emerges as a kind of synthesis of the positions of both entities. In Albert Camus's formulation of this dialectical process, in art, to name a need is already an imaginary surpassing of that need and that is why 'even if the novel speaks only of nostalgia, despair, the unachieved, it still creates the form and the salvation. To name despair is already to go beyond it' (1983:51). One way of explaining this phenomenon is the following: authors presuppose the existence in their readers of unfulfilled desires for happiness. So, while they ostensibly write about sorrows they implicitly commune with their readers about the desire that such sorrows ought not exist. Exposing what one fears or dislikes can have the effect of an exorcism. Conversely, writing about rose-colored worlds of wish-fulfilment, because it establishes a depressing contrast with a not so appetizing reality, may either be received as parody or else become an addictive enterprise inducing desire in the reader for more escapist, vicarious wish-fulfilment. This dialectical nature of reception is what explains, for example, that naturalist novels dealing with human degradation can be read, and as a rule were meant to be read, as literature of protest in the name of a better future.[13]

Fictional literature is therefore intrinsically and extrinsically ironic; it is likely to mean something other than what it says and the reader is likely to have to understand something other than what is written. The two ironies may not coincide because the text is to be confronted with the reader's real world and that may no longer be the same as the world with which the author expected the text to be confronted. In any case much is to be inferred from the confrontation. More likely than not the irony implicit in literary fiction is of a romantic nature since it feeds on need, frustration and desire.

So, this fourth reason why fictional literature is not to be read literally resides in the fact that it is a form of communication and of confrontation. The text is addressing someone and that someone is going to set the text against the real world he or she lives in. This happens even when the implicit dialogue takes place across a gulf of unknown barriers. The actualized meaning of the message fluctuates according to who, when and where the receiver is. One thing is certain, however, and the writer knows it: the receiver is always someone different from himself or herself. In fact, not only will the reader bring into the reading a different personality or 'temperament' and, often, a different explicatory context, he or she will also project his or her own 'authorship', as it were, into the text. Readers select what is important for them: they retain certain scenes and characters and neglect to take notice of others. Some readers identify with a certain protagonist, others identify with another, and so on. Reading is a process riddled with unconscious projections. Readers understand only what they can understand. No reader is 'innocent'. In this sense every reading is a personalized 'misreading' and even authors themselves will misread their own work.

It should be noted, however, that authors are the first to know the game they are playing. They know they are speaking on behalf of, as well as to, a plurality of readers. In modern times, they know about the existence of different worldviews and it is likely that they will construct the text so that dialogue is possible with a wide spectrum of readers.

WHY FICTIONAL LITERATURE PROMOTES INTERCULTURAL DIALOGUE

Having reviewed some of the reasons in favour of the argument that fictional literature is not to be read literally, I will consider the apparent paradox of how the very same fictional literature whose literal meaning is irrelevant or even non-existent — in spite of the well-ordered words on the page — nonetheless, historically speaking, has been a privileged ambassador between different cultures.

Lao She tells us in his 1945 Afterword to *Camel Xiangzi* how in the process of planning the story he:

> ...began to consider that a rickshaw puller like everyone else would have problems other than simply his daily bread. He would have ideals and desires, a family and children. How would he solve these problems? How could he? In this way, the simple story I had heard developed into a story of dimensions huge enough to encompass a whole society. (1988:233)

And in fact this widely translated book became a sort of intercultural introduction to pre-revolutionary China and, indirectly, to the circumstances that brought about the victory of the Chinese communists over the Nationalist government. British writer Doris Lessing was born in 1919, twenty years after Lao She, and she wrote that she had come to know nineteenth-century Russia through reading Tolstoy's *Anna Karenina*, and nineteenth-century France through reading Stendhal's novels. She declared that her intention in writing her own novel, *The Golden Notebook*, was to achieve a similar goal concerning mid-twentieth-century European civilization. And I believe that she succeeded even if, at the more obvious level, the story revolves around the psychological breakdown of one single protagonist, Anna Wulf, after she quits her political party and, on the same day, the man she loves abandons her. One way of reading Anna's story is to see that it is about the failure of revolutionary ideals in Europe. Naturally there are many ways of understanding the novel. As Lessing herself recognizes with misgivings in the Preface to the 1972 edition, the novel became a bestseller largely because it was appropriated by the women's movement. The differentiated feminine point of view is, in fact, an important ingredient of the book.

How can a single novel be so pertinent to so many people and be so relevant to our understanding of the non-fictional reality of a given historical period? I will divide my own attempt to answer this into four points.

The universal underground theme. Human beings aspire to happiness. To be happy they require food, shelter, health, freedom of movement, love, affection, social integration and the sense of individual worth and dignity. No civilization known to us to this day has found a way of providing this kind of happiness for all its citizens. It is normally believed that, on earth, this is impossible, utopian. Because fiction draws its basic sustenance from human imagination it is understandable that in every culture the unfulfilled desire for happiness should seek imaginary compensation. It does so in religion, in art and in play.[14] There are no historical or geographical barriers to be considered in this respect. It is a universal source of fictionalizing. If there is a multitude of ways in which human beings can seek imaginary compensation for the insufficiencies of reality, there is nonetheless this thematic original source which literary works of fiction everywhere, at all times, share.[15] This shared germinating ground (or let us preferably call it underground) facilitates the understanding of the surface variations that each individual literary work makes manifest. Our desires may appear complex as visible epiphenomena but they are in all likelihood much simpler at the basic biological, deep-psychological level. It is probably because they share this subjective, emotionally-charged 'underground' that works of fiction are more easily accepted than non-fictional expository texts when they are made to travel across geographical and temporal boundaries. In this manner, as a kind of side-effect, they often contribute in introducing foreign cultures to one another.

It has been written that fiction has the capacity to defamilarize the familiar. By the same token fiction also has the capacity to familiarize us with the unfamiliar, to make us accept what we do not know.[16] This is so perhaps because we expect literary fiction to be about other worlds anyway. In a sense, fictional worlds are always new to us. To know about the other, the foreign culture, for example, is also a way of making us see ourselves in a new light. In a certain sense, fiction writers are always introducing the reader to a 'foreign world', and so they are prepared to act as guides. In their trade it is natural to become an ambassador between cultures.[17]

The intrinsic dialogism of fiction. Extrinsically speaking, fiction is a dialogic instrument in the sense that the author (either one individual or a restricted number of individuals), addresses an indefinite number of recipients. This communicative function is part of the strategy of literary production in general. I would like to call your attention now, however, to the intrinsic dialogism of narrative fiction, such as Bakhtin has defined it in his essays (1981, 1986). Since the Renaissance, narrative fiction has been a literary genre characterized by a 'dialogue' between a speaking subject, personified, for example, in the omniscient narrator or in one of the protagonists as a surrogate for the author, and the represented Other, personified in the other protagonists and characters in general. The Subject, the implicit or explicit I, is directly experienced from the inside; and the Object, the Other, is observed from the outside. In addition the latter also functions as a mirror for the I who cannot otherwise perceive itself from the outside. This structuring dialogue between two qualitatively different points of view is part of the expressive/mimetic nature of fiction.

Because it departs from this intrinsic conflict of points of view, and because, extrinsically, it is also addressing itself to a diffuse, often unpredictable Other, literary fiction, at least that of a 'readable' sort,[18] contrary to monological literature or political and religious propaganda, turns out to be, indeed, a good vehicle for promoting intercultural and inter-ideological dialogue. This is so even when one observes the authors' counterbalancing propensity for reinforcing their authorial and authoritative points of view, subordinating other voices to their own voices so that, as will be seen next, the work's identity is retained and with it its distinctive aura.

The author's authority and the umbilical aura of the work. The more the author predicts that his or her tale will travel far and wide, the more he or she will try to saturate the text with all possible pointers to what is deemed to be its essential message. In this manner the text will remain the author's text and retain the aura of its origin. If much is 'undecidable' in terms of the effect the text will generate on the reader, and also because the reader is an unknown variable, much is also decisively interwoven into the text so that a certain amount of self-sufficiency is attached to it once it separates itself from its originator. As Roland Barthes has maintained in relation to his analysis of Honoré de Balzac's tale 'Sarracine' in *S/Z*, the so-called 'readable' text is over-determined as to the message it is supposed to convey. In this manner the reader, the very embodiment of the Other, will be forced to establish a 'dialogue' with the tightly knit text, never his or her own text, even across temporal, geographical and cultural borders, and will not easily miss the core of its message. The changing interpretations which we perceive to be possible of one and the same text have as a corollary the stability of its core content. The 'manifest content' impregnated as it may be with transient historical information, is prone to acquire ever new colourings and meanings. The 'latent content', on the other hand, ought to be more resilient. It is closer to the deep structure of the work. It permits the latter not only to survive a multiplicity of interpretations but also to undergo translation into other languages and other media without ceasing to be itself.

Redundancy and internal coherence. Barthes showed how repetition and redundancy makes it almost impossible for any reader of 'Sarracine' to miss its cumulative central theme: the uncanny articulation of castration with beauty. This happens irrespectively of the manner in which readers interpret this same articulation and independently of its having any particular significance for them. I would venture to propose that the more ineffable the message the more redundant and coherent must be the text. Taking as an example just two pages describing an amorous encounter in D. H. Lawrence's 1921 expressionist novel *Women in Love*, I counted eight instances of the word *dark* or its derivatives; four of the word *mystery*; eight of the adjective *strange*, and five of phrases relating the concept of electricity to that of love.[19] It will be difficult for any reader not to understand the author's concern with the importance of, but also his fear about, the ominously evanescent character of sexual passion between a man and a woman. Whether the reader finds this a meaningful, significant interpretation of love is another matter.

In an altogether different style, semantic overdetermination of the core literary content is also evident in Lao She's social realist novel *Camel Xiangzi* (orginally translated into English as *Rickshaw Boy*). There can be no doubt that the central message of the book is reinforced chapter after chapter, making readers understand that the Xiangzis of this world deserve a better fate. Xiangzi's obsession with owning his own rickshaw is a metaphor for the cruelest of realities: not even such a wretched dream as owning one's own rickshaw is achievable within the boundaries of an exploitative class society, a society in which an affluent minority lives off the dehumanized labour of the majority of the population. Whether or not readers will infer a plea for social revolution from the parabolical structure of the story, they will certainly not misunderstand the overcoded message that the Xiangzis of this world deserve a better fate. Unless they dismiss the novel altogether, readers will identify and sympathize with Xiangzi irrespectively of which class, cultural group or country they belong to. The core message will resist alternative interpretations and, in addition, the novel will continue transporting its cultural and historical contents across national borders and continents and beyond its original social and political context.

❖

These four characteristics of fiction may be subsumed under a single one, that of the so-called 'autonomy' or 'self-sufficiency' of the fictional text. Literary works of fiction are not just documents of a given historical period; they are also monuments to it. Their resilient nature allows them to continue to yield meaning to different historical publics. They are capable of encapsulating a great amount of information about a particular day and age, or about a given cultural tradition, and of making it travel far and wide, because such information, which might otherwise be misunderstood or found unacceptable, is articulated with the more enduring and universal world of desires and their imaginary fulfilment. This alternative world of fiction is not only dense and cohesive in its metaphoric nature, it also deals in human emotion and affect, indispensable ingredients for the preservation and applicability of knowledge.[20]

When Lao She wrote *Camel Xiangzi* he probably had in mind not only the ethical usefulness of lending his voice to the abused, illiterate workers but also the pragmatic possibility of using fiction to inform readers from better off social strata and, possibly, from other nations as well, about the untenable conditions in which the majority of the Chinese people were living. So much has happened since then and yet, in its consistent and stark simplicity, the novel permits today's reader not only to travel back in time and understand what China was like before the communist victory (and perhaps, too, why there was immense support for the communist movement), but also, at the same time, it permits him or her to confront Xiangzi's destiny with the destiny of our world of today. At the same time as it introduces readers to cultural aspects of a given period of Chinese history which they may find unfamiliar and exotic, the novel also establishes an 'underground dialogue' with probably every reader on the universal theme of the search for human happiness. Several details and secondary meanings may escape the reader, especially the reader who, like me, must use a translation, but the tragic irony of Xiangzi's frustrated desire to become an established rickshaw owner is so strongly emphasized that it is impossible to miss the unwritten yet overcoded message that the honest, hardworking Xiangzis of this world deserve a better fate. The story is a metaphor. Besides being his own fictional self — a simple, honest, stubborn young man of few words — Xiangzi, a struggling and guiltless young Sisyphus of the Beijing slums, barely surviving in an inhumane urban environment — is also all and any of us. The immutable, intrafictional world of the rickshaw puller provokes an ongoing, unending, unpredictable dialogue with ever-changing, extra-fictional reality, inviting us to see how many Xiangzis there still are in this world of ours and leading us to ask ourselves how can this be and what is to be done about it. That fictional texts are capable of leading us to formulate such uncomfortable questions is one more reason why, in my opinion, they are such great ambassadors between cultures.

University of Porto

Notes

1 The first part of this paper was presented at 'The International Conference on Cultural Dialogue and Cultural Misreading,' held at Peking University, 9–11 October 1995. The second part was presented at the Conference on 'Cultural Dialogue and Cultural Misunderstanding' organized by Instituto Cultural de Macau, 13–14 October 1995.

2 Cf. Wayne C. Booth (1961, 1975), p. 71: 'Our present problem is the intricate relationship of the so-called real author with his various official versions of himself.' Interesting as this may be, I am not concerned here with the so-called 'implied author', but rather with how authors are part of their texts independently of how much they are aware of it. I am postulating therefore the interdependence and complementarity of the extratextual and the intratextual author, and also that authors are part of their texts and remain so even when they themselves no longer exist.

3 For my understanding of the author's 'excedentary' presence in the literary text I am indebted to Mikhail Bakhtin's *Speech Genres and Other Late Essays* (1986).

4 For the concept of aura I am indebted to Walter Benjamin's 'The Work of Art in the Age of Mechanical Reproduction (1936)' in *Illuminations* (1969).

5 For the theoretical concept of 'horizon of expectations' see Hans-Robert Jauss's 'Literary History as a Challenge to Literary Theory (1970)' in *Towards an Aesthetics of Reception* (1982).

6 On negative intertextuality and 'poetic misprision' see Harold Bloom (1973).

7 For the theoretical discussion on 'communities of readers' see Stanley Fish's essays (1980).

8 Cf. Wolfgang Iser (1978) p. 45: 'Effect and response arise from a dialectical relationship between showing and concealing — in other words from the difference between what is said and what is meant.' Iser's book is a thorough theoretical discussion of this question.

9 Or so we have been telling ourselves in the West at least since we studied Aristotle's definitions. Earl Miner (1990) suggests that there can be narrative without plot, exemplifying this view with the Japanese *monogatari* among other types of literary texts.

10 Relating literature to psychoanalysis, Norman Holland introduces the concepts of 'form as defense' and 'meaning as defense.' Cf. *The Dynamics of Literary Response* (1968, 1989), p. 105: 'Virtually all the familiar entities of literature — plot, character, and form — serve at least partly as defensive modifications of unconscious content.'

11 Similar issues are thoroughly discussed by Thomas Pavel (1986). On distance cf. p. 145: 'Creation of distance could well be assumed to be the most general aim of imaginary activity: the journey epitomizes the basic operation of the imagination, be it realized as dreams, ritual trance, poetic rapture, imaginary worlds, or merely the confrontation of the unusual and the memorable.' Jean Bessière also discusses all these questions of duality, distancing, double meaning and so on (1990). Contrary to Bessière's book which deals with the literary in general, I discuss literary fiction only. Not all literature is fictional and not all fiction is literary or even artistic, even if lying is called 'an art'. I consider it important that my readers keep this distinction in mind.

12 Similarly, a feminine reader, or a reader of feminine sensitivity, may cry towards the end of Tolstoy's *Anna Karenina* without ever having a chance to consider why she, or he, is crying over a fictional character. In fact it is because Anna Karenina stands for real women, including the reader herself. The latter does not have to interpret the text as, say, a critique of patriarchal society in order to go through an emotionally active reception of the text. Cf. also Thomas Pavel's *Fictional Worlds*, pp. 55 and 145, where this example is brought up. According to Pavel the reader's reaction could be subsumed in the phrase: 'Since this can happen to anyone, it also can happen to me.' Naturally this is a simplification of a rather complex process of identification, transference, and so on, as studied by psychologists. Norman Holland (1968, 1989) analyses readers' response from a psychoanalytic point of view.

13 For a theoretical and historical examination of the concept of catharsis cf. Hans-Robert Jauss's chapter on the same (1982:92–111). Contrary to Jauss, who stresses the reconciliatory aspect of catharsis, I believe that in relation to the constraints of reality catharsis can also be of a liberating kind.

14 Basing himself on Kendall Walton's essays, Pavel writes: 'Works of fiction are not mere sequences of sentences but props in a game of make-believe, like children playing with dolls or pretending to be cowboys' (1986:55). For some reason, Pavel does not mention Freud's comments, many years earlier, on this connection. In the essay 'The Relation of the Poet to Daydreaming (1908),' for example, Freud wrote: 'Now the writer does the same as the child at play; he creates a world of phantasy which he takes very seriously; that is, he invests it with a great deal of affect, while separating it sharply from reality.' (Cited in *Character and Culture*, ed. Philip Rieff (New York, 1963) p. 35.

15 Pavel also mentions this universal heritage of fictional themes: 'In almost every place and time we find a more or less complete thematic set, covering the main human concerns, social or existential. Birth, love, death, success and failure, authority and its loss, revolution and war, production and distribution of goods, social status and morality, the sacred and the profane, comic themes of inadequacy and isolation, compensatory fantasies, and so much more, are always present, from early myths and folktales to contemporary literature. Changes of taste or shifts of interest seem to affect the inventory only marginally' (1986:147–8). I would subsume the major uni-

versal themes of fictional literature under the single designation of compensatory fantasies, including therein even realistic literature if understood in the dialectical way I have tried to explain in my paper. My Portuguese colleague Manuel Frias Martins chose the concept 'dark matter' to designate the underground, universal thematic source of all fictional literature in *Matéria Negra: Uma Teoria da Literatura e da Crítica Literária* ('Dark matter: A Theory of Literature and Literary Criticism', 1993). I am indebted to him throughout my paper.

16 Cf. Wolfgang Iser: 'By means of this foreground-background relationship, the principle of selection exploits a basic condition for all forms of comprehension and experience, for the as yet unknown meaning would be incomprehensible were it not for the familiarity of the background it is set against' (1978:93).

17 Not necessarily between different geographic regions only. Also between different cultures within one and the same nation. Reverting to the case of Émile Zola mentioned in Part I of this paper, one can value his novel *Germinal* as a sort of embassy between bourgeois and working-class cultures within France. Most social realist writers wished to serve this purpose. *Camel Xiangzi* is another good example.

18 I am borrowing the term from Roland Barthes's essay *S/Z* (1970). In this essay Barthes analyses Balzac's tale 'Sarracine' line by line after having included it in 'readable literature,' (*littérature lisible*) as opposed to 'writerly literature' (*littérature scriptible*). The latter, more characteristc of modern times, already presupposes the reader's active collaboration in the constitution of the final literary product.

19 The novel is saturated with the word darkness, its derivatives and synonyms as I had occasion to discuss in my unpublished Master's Dissertation (Lisbon, 1970). It is well-known how concerned D. H. Lawrence was with having fiction restrict itself to the basic vital themes, also the most difficult to put into words.

20 See the recent book (USA 1994; Lisbon 1995) by University of Iowa neurologist, Antonio Damâsio (Portuguese by birth). It reports on findings that reveal how the affective component is indispensable for memory and reason to operate.

Works Cited

Bakhtin, Mikhail 1981 *The Dialogic Imagination*. University of Texas Press.

—— 1986 *Speech Genres and Other Essays*. University of Texas Press.

Barthes, Roland 1970 *S/Z*. Seuil, Paris.

—— 1982 [1968] 'L'Effet de réel' in *Littérature et Réalité*, ed. Roland Barthes. Seuil, Paris.

Benjamin, Walter 1969 (1936) 'The Work of Art in the Age of Mechanical Reproduction' in *Illuminations*. Schocken Books, New York.

Bessière, Jean 1990 *Dire le littéraire: Points de vue théoriques*. Mardaga, Bruxelles.

Bloom, Harold 1973 *The Anxiety of Influence: A Theory of Poetry*. Oxford University Press.

Booth, Wayne 1975 (1961) *The Rhetoric of Fiction*. University of Chicago Press.

Camus, Albert 1983 (1952) 'Art and Revolt' in *Writers and Politics: A Partisan Review Reader*, eds Edith Kurzweil and W. Phillips. Routledge and Kegan Paul, London.

Damâsio, António 1994 *Descartes' Error: Emotion, Reason and the Human Brain*. Grosset/Putnam, New York.

Freud, Sigmund 1963 [1908] 'The Relation of the Poet to Daydreaming' in *Character and Culture*. Macmillan/Collier, New York.

Fish, Stanley 1980 *Is There a Text in This Class? The Authority of Interpretive Communities*. Harvard University Press.

Holland, Norman 1989 (1968) *The Dynamics of Literary Response*. Columbia University Press.

Iser, Wolfgang 1978 *The Act of Reading: A Theory of Aesthetic Response*. Routledge and Kegan

Paul, London.
Jauss, Hans-Robert 1982a (1969) 'Literary History as Challenge to Literary Theory' in *Towards an Aesthetic of Reception*. University of Minnesota Press.
—— 1982b *Aesthetic Experience and Literary Hermeneutics*. University of Minnesota Press.
Lao She 1988 (1937, 1945) *Camel Xiangzi*. Foreign Language Press, Beijing.
Lessing, Doris 1973 (1962) *The Golden Notebook*. Panther Books, London.
Martins, Manuel Frias 1993 *Matéria Negra: Uma Teoria da Literature e da Crítica Literária*. Cosmos, Lisboa.
Miner, Earl 1990 *Comparative Poetics: An Intercultural Essay on Theories of Literature*. Princeton University Press.
Pavel, Thomas 1986 *Fictional Worlds*. Cambridge University Press.
Riffaterre, Michael 1990 'Undecidability as Hermeneutic Constraint' in *Literary Theory Today*, eds Peter Collier and Helga Geyer-Ryan. Cambridge University Press.
Zola, Emile 1971 (1875) 'Le Naturalisme au Théatre' in *Le Roman Expérimental*, ed. André Guedj. Garnier-Flammarion, Paris.

TAO JIE

The (Mis)Reading of *Uncle Tom's Cabin*

Uncle Tom's Cabin was translated into classical Chinese under the title *Black Slaves Appeal to Heaven* and published in 1901 when China was still under the rule of the Qing Dynasty. Lin Shu, the translator, and his collaborator, Wei Yi, selected the book mainly for its political nature. At the turn of the century, there was strong anti-China sentiment in the United States and Chinese labourers who helped build the Trans-Pacific Railroad were badly treated and discriminated against. However, the inept Qing government was unable to do anything for them. Lin and Wei saw similarities between the misery of the black slaves depicted by Mrs Stowe in her novel and the persecution and maltreatment suffered by Chinese labourers in the United States. They believed that Mrs Stowe's book could be used to warn Chinese readers of the possibility that they could be reduced to slaves. In his preface, Lin Shu declares:

> Now the United States has been applying to the yellow people what they used to do to the black slaves.... The yellow race is being maltreated, even worse than the blacks.... It is my hope that this translation will sound the alarm to wake them up. (1981:1)

The Chinese version of *Uncle Tom's Cabin* caused a sensation in China and the response of the reading public was immediate and intense. It helped to start a protest movement against the USA government and strengthened general disillusionment with the Qing Dynasty on the part of educated people. A reader writing with the pen name of Xing Shi (Awakened Lion) to the *Xinmin congbao* newspaper in 1903 stated that: 'When we think of the grim future of the yellow race, it is not for the black slaves that we should grieve.' Another reader, Hui Yun, wrote to the *Guomin ribao* daily newspaper: 'Chinese labourers are now shut up in stockades by the Americans. How sad it is that China has become weak, and lost even its national sovereignty. Seeing ourselves in the black slaves, I cannot refrain from weeping for the yellow race' (Tian 1961). Ling Shi summed up the feelings of all readers in his article 'Upon Reading *Black Slaves Appeal to Heaven*': 'I am glad that the situation of my compatriots is not as terrible as that of the black slaves, but I am worried for my compatriots because they are indifferent to their country's plight and are likely to degenerate into being just like those black slaves.... I weep for us yellow people in the same way as I grieve for the black people.' He then called upon every Chinese to read the book and urged actors, entertainers and storytellers to make good use of Mrs Stowe's novel and to try their utmost to provide vivid presentations of the sorrows of the slaves and the cruelty of the slave owners to 'arouse large audiences' (A Ying 1961:282).

This understanding of the book as a political novel corresponds with Mrs Stowe's purpose in writing the book — to expose and attack slavery. She had written the novel at the request of her sister-in-law 'to write something that will make this whole nation feel what an accursed thing slavery is'. She confided to her brother Henry her desire to write a series of sketches 'to illustrate the cruelties of slavery' and wrote to her husband that she was 'projecting a sketch for the *Era* on the capability of liberated blacks to take care of themselves' (Sundquist 1986:7–8). Mrs Stowe's desire to reform was rightly interpreted in her own time. The book was greeted by the anti-slavery press with great enthusiasm. It was accepted in the western hemisphere as 'a plea for the oppressed of all races and nationalities' (Mott 1947:121) shortly after its publication, as it was in China fifty years later. We can even hear echoes of Ling Shi's call in the shout of the *Independent*: 'Spread it round the world!' (120). This political purpose was much emphasized by Lin Shu in the introduction: 'The book tells a fictitious story. But it may be a good lesson to Chinese labourers in the United States.... It is my hope that my readers will not take the story merely as fantasy' (1981:8). To reiterate this point, he also wrote a postscript in which he states:

> Mr Wei and I have collaborated in the translation of this novel. It is not our intention to bring our readers to tears with a story of pathos and grief. We have to cry for the masses because we are in danger of being reduced to slaves.... This book of ours is to be published at a time of political reform when everyone is looking for new ideas and new theories to replace the old. Although it is not an important book and does not deal with any profound subject, it will make its contribution to enhance the awareness of our readers, promote patriotism, and strengthen our determination to protect our people and preserve our heritage. (206)

Lin Shu's patriotism was shared by Wei Yi, who describes in his preface America's chauvinistic discrimination against Chinese labourers and compares the novel to be bells and drums that ring out warnings against lurking dangers.

The political import of *Uncle Tom's Cabin* seems to be the only thing accepted by its Chinese translators or readers. Lin Shu and Wei Yi did not seem to notice that the novel was written by a woman with strong feminist sentiments. Neither did they understand that the work was written as a gothic romance, traditional to women, and was addressed to a female audience. Mrs Stowe was thinking of her women readers when she adopted the title *Uncle Tom's Cabin* — 'Tom' being a common name, 'uncle' a conventional sign of kinship and familiarity in slave life, and 'cabin' a well-known term for the residence of slaves. To make this clearer, she added the subtitle 'or, Life of the Lowly', and wrote in a simple language and adopted 'a vital story' that had the effect of 'striking with extraordinary directness to the heart of fundamental human feelings and relationships'(Mott 1947:121). Although Lin Shu and Wei Yi were, like others, moved by the pathos of the story, they probably had in mind only a male audience. Furthermore, Lin Shu changed the title into *Black Slaves Appeal to Heaven*, believing that the original title was not refined enough. Although Lin Shu shared Mrs Stowe's view of making fiction a unique weapon in the battle against oppression, the changes he made showed that his were the viewpoints of a Chinese male scholar. His concern was to arouse those of his class to patriotic action.

If Lin Shu failed unconsciously to perceive the feminine perfection of the heart or that 'it is the women in the book who most clearly represent the supremacy of right feeling' (Levin 1994:40), he was deliberate in deleting passages about Christianity in the original text. Surrounded by a family of ministers, Mrs Stowe could not but accept the power of Christianity and used it as a solution to the slavery issue, even though she was well aware 'that true Christianity often play(ed) into the hands of exploiters'(45). Stowe created both Tom and George Harris as 'a kind of bifurcated black anti-slavery hero', with the former as an emblem of 'exalted Christian faith' and the latter that of 'African colonization' (Stepto 1986:142). As a result, Tom has to be a martyr who dies for his faith while the only way out for George is to go to Canada, since Mrs Stowe had no intention of starting a revolution. To her Chinese translators, however, the plot is more important and the job of appealing to the reader's emotions should only be done with descriptions about the misery and sufferings of the slaves. Lin Shu states in his introduction, 'There is too much discussion of Christianity in the novel. Mr Wei has done away with passages and descriptions that have nothing to do with the development of the story so as to make it easier for the reader to follow the plot. I hope our readers will not blame us for the deletion' (3).

It was not Lin Shu or Wei Yi alone who did not like the role of Christianity in *Uncle Tom's Cabin*. In 1907 at a time when the anti-Qing movement was at its height, a group of patriotic Chinese students in Japan was attracted by the novel and its political implications. Zeng Xiaogu, a playwright, dramatized Lin Shu's rendition and the Chunliu Drama Club performed the play on 1–3 June 1907 in Tokyo as an expression of protest against the Qing government. It is interesting to notice that this five-act play focuses mainly on George Harris and his struggle for freedom. The ending is quite different from the original novel. In Act V, George meets Eliza and their son in a mountain on a snowy day, fights bravely with their pursuers and kills his master, winning final freedom for himself and his family. What is more, Tom is with them in their flight from the slave owners (Chen 1987:20). Evidently, the playwright and other Chinese students in Japan believed in fighting for freedom rather than placing hope in Christianity. Eighty years later, this deliberate misreading of Mrs Stowe's novel was still much praised in China. The historian Cao Xiaoqiao commends Zeng Xiaogu for 'removing the Christian elements of the original text and emphasizing racial conflicts and class struggle so as to applaud and glorify freedom, self-reliance, and the spirit of rebellion', and maintains that the play is a good example in 'the borrowing of ideological content, the sentiment of national independence and national equality' (1987, I:288).

❖

This interest in *Uncle Tom's Cabin* as a political novel remained strong after the downfall of the Qing dynasty. Its rendition in classical Chinese was still in print in 1920, almost twenty years after its first appearance. As the classical language was difficult for common readers, abridged versions of the novel in vernacular Chinese began to appear in the 1930s and early 1940s. It may have been because of the imminent danger of the Japanese invasion that an edition entitled *Souls of the Black Slaves* was especially popular and was also serialized in a children's magazine.

A later revival of the novel appeared in the early 1960s when there was no danger of the Chinese people being reduced to slaves. This time, the emphasis on the work as a protest novel was even greater. To a certain extent, this was due more to cultural, even personal, needs than political purposes.

The year 1957 saw the fiftieth anniversary of the rise of the new drama movement in China that began with the dramatization of *Black Slaves Appeal to Heaven* in Tokyo. There was a suggestion that the play should be staged again as part of the activities to commemorate the birth of Chinese drama. Ouyang Yuqian, one of the founders of the Chunliu Drama Club and one of the actors in the play, began to think seriously of writing a new scenario for a rehearsal. Unfortunately, he had to give up the project because of the political situation at the time.

As *Uncle Tom's Cabin* had always been closely associated with racial discrimination and the struggle for freedom and independence, Ouyang Yuqian saw a chance for its revival in 1959 when some African states began winning freedom and when protests against racial discrimination began to take place in the United States. He told Sun Weishi, the director of the Experimental Drama Troupe of the Central Drama Institute, repeatedly, '*Black Slaves Appeal to Heaven* still has its practical and immediate significance. We have to work on it and make a good job of it' (Sun 1962:20). Within ten days, the ten-act play under the title of *Hatred of Black Slaves* was completed. It was published in November 1960 and was soon staged in Shanghai, Beijing, and several other places. Although, as Ouyang Yuqian stated in the postscript that 'the play is based on the text written by Mrs Stowe published in Chicago in 1897, with Lin Shu's translation as reference' (1962:93), it was more a product of the 1960s when politics was of first priority in almost every aspect of social life. Ouyang Yuqian openly admitted, 'Because of differences in viewpoints, changes have had to be made in the plot, especially in characterization. It is impossible for my characters to think or act in the way Mrs Stowe prescribed in the original text...' (93).

Ouyang Yuqian also changed the title to *Hatred of Black Slaves* to highlight the theme of oppression and rebellion. Obviously, Mrs Stowe's novel was totally misread and distorted to serve the need of a Chinese writer who was eager to commemorate the drama club he had founded many years ago. After some preparation, dramatization of *Hatred of Black Slaves* began in Beijing in July 1961 to commemorate the 110th anniversary of the publication of the novel. Had she attended the performance, Mrs Stowe would have been shocked to hear Tom speak eloquently about blood to be paid by blood before he was burnt to death. Almost without exception, the reviews stressed the political content of the play. Tian Han, the renowned playwright and literary critic, represented the general view when he wrote in 1961:

> The dramatization of *Hatred of Black Slaves* is not just to commemorate the rise of the new drama movement. It is also a significant support to the liberation movement of the black people in Africa and the United States.... The play is a powerful exposure of the United States ... a powerful exposure of the reactionary nature of United States imperialism.

Criticizing Mrs Stowe for placing too much hope in Christianity, he complimented Ouyang Yuqian for looking at slavery from the perspective of 'socialist ideology' by creating a most touching character in Tom and 'endowing him with class consciousness at the time of his death'.

Obviously, the favouring of politics over aesthetics was the trend of the 1960s, and no-one could avoid its influence. As a result, Mrs Stowe's crusade against slavery was distorted into a piece of propaganda to meet the political and cultural need of China of that period.

❖

Because of the its political significance, *Uncle Tom's Cabin* has always been considered great literature in China, despite its ups and downs in the United States. After the Cultural Revolution ended in 1976 and China started to open up to the outside world, there was a renaissance in the publication of foreign literature. *Uncle Tom's Cabin* was retranslated and republished many times by different publishers in the late 1970s and 1980s. Mrs Stowe was included in dictionaries such as *Famous Foreign Writers* (Social Sciences Press 1979), the *Foreign Literature* volume of *Encyclopedia Sinica* (Encyclopedia Sinica Press 1982) and *Dictionary of Foreign Women's Literature* (Lijiang Press 1989); in anthologies of American literature compiled by university professors; and in two histories of American literature written by Chinese scholars. This coincided with its revival in the United States, the only difference being that Chinese scholars still limited their discussion of the novel to its political import. For instance, in the introduction of the most important Chinese edition published in 1982 whose first print-run was a record high of 59,000, almost half of the space is taken up by detailed descriptions of slavery in the United States and the influence of *Uncle Tom's Cabin* in speeding up the abolition movement and even the Civil War. Huang Jizhong, the translator, does not go beyond the conclusions of critics before him when he criticizes Mrs Stowe for her 'overzealous Evangelist desire' and for creating a Christian martyr in Tom out of 'her religious bias'(1982:13). Among all the reviews and essays written during the period, not one was about the novel as a feminist book. Only one critic, Xiong Yupeng, spoke in a different voice by pointing out Mrs Stowe's satire on the more liberal or kindhearted slave owners like Shelby and St Claire and her exposure and renunciation of Christianity. Xiong states:

> Out of deep sympathy for the slaves and their misery, out of a deep sense of justice, Mrs Stowe, as a serious realist writer, could not but attack and expose religious propaganda that served the need of slavery. However, as a humanist growing up in a religious environment, she had no choice but to turn for help to the God that she was most familiar with. (1983:44)

This revival of *Uncle Tom's Cabin* was more an attempt to meet the cultural needs of the time than to understand Mrs Stowe or her work. What is most interesting is that, while Mrs Stowe's book is now gaining more attention in the United States, it is on the decline in China. Since the late 1980s, it has not received any new reviews. Also, no research papers have been written to explore Mrs Stowe's 'entanglements among the role of woman, the place of blacks in American history and society, and the radical powers of Christianity'(Sundquist 1986:7) which are very much in vogue in the United States. It was not until 1995 that two short articles appeared to introduce Joan Hedrick's book *Harriet Beecher Stowe: A Life*.

There are many reasons for this unintentional neglect of Mrs Stowe and her novel. For one thing, Chinese readers are fed up with politics and political novels and with realist writing. After being isolated from the world for so long, they are thirsty for new themes and new techniques. Their interest has shifted to modernist writings, such as William Faulkner's *The Sound and the Fury*, James Joyce's *Ulysses* or the more experimental fiction like *Catch 22*. Also, women's liberation and equality among ethnic groups in China have always been granted from above and ensured by the government. Writers or critics do not often see the importance of establishing a special women's literature (minority literature has always been encouraged) or to work on the reevaluation of past or foreign literature. The Chinese are seeking new things in the West — its new machinery and technology, its more 'effective' way of business management, even its fast food and rock music — and are working hard to make these things serve the new and more urgent needs of their country. For them, *Uncle Tom's Cabin* is a thing of the past that has played its role in serving Chinese purposes and should now be placed on the shelf.

All this proves that the travel of a foreign novel, like the movement of ideas and theories, also undergoes 'acceptance ... resistance ... toleration' and that its transformation 'by its new uses, its new position in a new time and place' (Said 1983:227) is often closely connected with the political or cultural needs and traditions of the new place.

Peking University

Works Cited

Ammons, Elizabeth 1986 'Stowe's Dream of the Mother-Savior: *Uncle Tom's Cabin* and American Women Writers Before the 1920s' in *New Essays on Uncle Tom's Cabin*, ed. Eric J. Sundquist. Cambridge University Press.

A Ying 1961 *Studies of Fiction and Operas of the Late Qing Dynasty*. Zhonghua Publishing House, Beijing.

Cao Xiaoqiao 1987 'Imported Goods Versus Leftovers: On Sources of Early Chinese Drama' in Editorial Board of the Chinese Drama Press *Studies of Drama*. Chinese Drama Press, Beijing.

Chen Dingsha 1987 'The History of the Chunliu Drama Club' in Institute of Drama of the Academy of Chinese Art *Collections of Historical Records of Chinese Drama*. Art and Literature Publishing House, Beijing.

Huang Jizhong 1982 'Introduction' to *Uncle Tom's Cabin*, tr. Huang Jizhong. Shanghai Translation Press.

Levin, David 1994 'American Fiction as Historical Evidence: Reflections on *Uncle Tom's Cabin*' in *Forms of Uncertainty: Essays in Historical Criticism*. University Press of Virginia.

Lin Shu 1981 'Preface' to *Black Slaves Appeal to Heaven*. Commercial Press, Beijing.

Mott, Frank Luther 1947 *Golden Multitudes: the Story of Best Sellers in the US*. Macmillan, New York.

Ouyang Yuqian 1962 'Postscript' in *Hatred of the Black Slaves*. Chinese Drama Press, Beijing.

Said, Edward 1983 *The World, the Text, and the Critic*. Harvard University Press.

Sun Weishi 1962 'Recollections on the Writing of *Hatred of the Black Slaves* by Comrade Ouyang Yuqian' in *Hatred of the Black Slaves*. Chinese Drama Press, Beijing.

Sundquist, Eric J. 1986 'Introduction,' in *New Essays on Uncle Tom's Cabin*, ed. Eric J. Sundquist. Cambridge University Press.

Tian Han 1961 'On *Hatred of the Black Slaves*' in *People's Daily*, 12 July.

Xiong Yupeng 1983 '*Uncle Tom's Cabin*: Harbinger of American Realism' in *Academic Journal of East China Normal University*, no. 6. Shanghai.

PART THREE

Identity

ANTON KAES

Media and Nations: Global Communication and Cultural Identity

What follows is an exploration of the role of cinema and mass media in the construction, affirmation, and defence of national identity. The often hidden nexus between media and nations surfaced as a widely discussed political issue when in recent GATT negotiations the French government vehemently opposed Hollywood's purported imperialism. The French (in union with many European intellectuals) argued that American media culture threatened to marginalize French national cinema and, by implication, disparage and destroy France's cultural and national identity. Hollywood appeared as the ultimate colonizer — appealing and insidious. Taking our cue from this culture clash, we might begin by asking ourselves whether such fear of cultural subjugation is justified; whether a link exists between global media culture and rekindled nationalism; and whether there's a good explanation for the seemingly universal appeal of Hollywood's mass culture. We might also speculate whether new communication technologies (such as satellite transmission and the internet) will alleviate or exacerbate the perceived problem.

In his influential book, *Imagined Communities*, Benedict Anderson defined nation as an imagined political community — imagined because 'the members of even the smallest nation will never know most of their fellow-members, yet in the minds of each lives the image of their communion ... all communities larger than primordial villages of face-to-face contact (and perhaps even these) are imagined' (1993:6). They are imagined and yet so real that millions of people have been willing to die for such imaginings. In order to understand why the concept of a nation has been such a successful instrument for political mobilization and cultural homogenization, we have to look at the ways in which the political structure of the state has been linked to the cultural conception of the nation. The idea of the nation gives legitimacy to the political structure of the state, while the state provides an institutional framework of cultural and social homogenization, an efficient infrastructure for culture-building. For Anderson, it was the invention of the printing press that laid the basis for national consciousness: print gave fixity to spoken language; it also made it possible to be connected to thousands if not millions of fellow-readers. One became aware that one belonged to a particular language-field and that others outside one's language did not belong: 'These fellow-readers to whom one was connected through print, formed, in their secular, particular, visible invisibility the embryo of the nationally imagined community' (44).

However, Anderson's analysis leaves several questions unanswered. Apart from the fact that his concept of a nation tends to be much more homogeneous and unified than any nation ever was, I think it is odd that he does not take his argument into the twentieth century: for the last hundred years, the visual media — film, television, video, and, more recently, electronic networks — have to a large degree superseded languages fixed in print. Visual communication does not need translation, it transcends national borders. One does not need to know any language to 'read' and intuitively understand a photograph, a silent film, or a video clip. If, for Anderson, print is the basis of the imagined nation, what then are the effects of film or television on national identity formation? Does global communication challenge and undermine national identity? What is the relationship between national and cultural identity? What is a national cinema? Is there such a thing as a national style of filmmaking? How does a domestic cinema maintain its cultural signature in face of Hollywood's world-wide domination? As media go global, what are the chances for the survival of a distinct national culture? Do Hollywood and the television networks control what one nation knows and thinks about another? Does television equalize by making information available to anyone in the world who owns a television?

The inevitable expansion of informational media enables cultures and subcultures of all kinds to gain access to a public sphere that transcends nationhood. (The revolutions in Eastern Europe in the late 1980s would not have been possible without a media network that knows no border police, barbed wire or walls.) Does, then, the proliferation of communication across borders equip the world for the recognition of diversity and difference? Or does it flatten out difference and obliterate distinct cultural identities? Such questions are notoriously hard to answer because they often rest on unquestioned assumptions. One such assumption is a fixed national and cultural identity.

In his essay, 'Cultural Identity and Cinematic Representation', Stuart Hall claimed that 'cultural identity is not a fixed essence at all, lying unchanged outside history and culture. It is not some universal and transcendental spirit inside us on which history has made no fundamental mark' (1989:71). Any reclamation of cultural identity for its own sake may act in the interest of a divisive separatism. Paul Gilroy has also recently pleaded for a rethinking of cultural nationalism:

> Getting beyond the national and nationalistic perspective is essential for two principal reasons. One is to do with the postmodern eclipse of the modern nation-state as a political, economic, and cultural unit. Neither political nor economic structures of domination are still co-extensive with the borders of nation-states. *Electronic communication alone erases all borders....* The second concerns the integrity of cultures and in particular the relationship between nationality and ethnicity. (1992:188; emphasis added.)

Film and electronic media erase borders: the yearning for an international language of images over and beyond the national languages and local dialects can be traced back to the early part of the century when, after a terrifying global war, film-makers and intellectuals championed a universal language that everyone could understand — emotionally and without recourse to translation. In the early 1920s the whole world united in appreciating Charlie Chaplin's slapstick. Laughing at his antics was not confined to a specific nation; it was a communal experience reverberating around the globe. Thanks to television (which nowadays is the main supplier and distributor of Hollywood cinema) film and mass culture have never had more power: they set political and social agendas, they influence attitudes and behaviour, and, above all, they shape the image we have not only of our own nation but also of other nations of whose existence we often only know through film and television in the first place. Using fictional and semi-fictional devices, the media unscrupulously create narratives (illustrated with stereotypical images) about 'America' and 'the' American people or about 'the' Germans or 'the' Chinese. By pretending to represent a national identity, they create it. If national identity is indeed a cultural construct, we need to know where, how, and to what end it is constructed. It is my basic argument that cinema and mass media play a major part in this construction.

The complex relationship between nations and media can be traced along three axes.

Along the historical axis one will have to focus on the role that cinema played (and still plays) in the service of a nation's self-representation and self-fashioning, ranging from D. W. Griffith's *Birth of a Nation* (1914) or Fritz Lang's *Nibelungen* (1924) or Abel Gance's *Napoleon* (1928), to the European art film of the 1960s and further to the postcolonial cinema of the 1970s and 1980s, both of which have programmatically looked for alternatives to the classical Hollywood film. When did Hollywood start to dominate world cinema? Is avant-garde counter-cinema the only antidote to American mass culture? What relations exist between the popular and the national at different times?

Along the theoretical axis, one needs to question the use of such terms as national cinema, national character, and cultural identity. Here, recent discussions of postcolonial discourse theory, hybridity, assimilation, cooptation, cultural mimicry, and the vicissitudes of visual representation will have to be examined.

Along the political axis, the consequences and effects of Hollywood's domination on both the First and Third World will need to be interrogated. What are the ideological implications of countries being colonialized by mass media? Today electronic communication by fax and on the internet transcends national boundaries even more radically than the 'international language' of the movies.

The accelerating processes of globalization of media culture confronts us with an extensive cultural and historical diversity that correlates with an increased heterogeneity in the world. The dislocation of millions of Third-World inhabitants into the urban centres of the First World requires a rethinking about unquestioned terms such as origin, identity, blood and soil (*blut und boden*), nation, and homeland (*heimat*) — terms that seem permanently fixed but are in fact extremely elusive. As national and cultural borders are crossed more easily today than ever, both *realiter* and in virtual reality, it is no coincidence that questions of movement and migration, immigration and displacement, exile and diaspora have assumed an unprecedented urgency.

Migrancy and exile, as Edward Said points out, involve a 'discontinuous state of being', a form of picking a quarrel with where you come from. It has thereby been transformed 'into a potent, even enriching, motif of modern culture':

> The exile knows that in a secular and contingent world, homes are always provisional. Borders and barriers, which enclose us within the safety of familiar territory, can also become prisons, and are often defended beyond reason or necessity. Exiles cross borders, break barriers of thought and experience. (1992:365)

The radical reconfiguration of the displaced person as the norm challenges the craving for the phantasm of a lost community, the memory of primary loss, and the energies spent on recuperating a sense of plenitude, centre, and origin. Instead we must recognize the need for a mode of thinking that is neither fixed nor stable, but is one that is open to an 'other' text, an 'other' voice, an 'other' world. It is global communication that has the potential to accelerate modernization and inject a degree of diversity into national cultures. Confrontation with diversity produces a measure of relativity of one's own culture which then becomes mixed, impure, and in constant dialogue with other cultures. But this utopia has a price.

It is to be expected that the dynamic push for economic and cultural internationalism may produce a reaction, even a backlash, that articulates itself as a return to political nativism and a renewed insistence on cultural difference. Given the rapid globalization of communication and the inexorable expansion of Hollywood mass culture, one question will be of the essence: how to negotiate between the universalism of mass culture and the partly timid, partly defiant, particularism of local cultures. I suspect that debates about mass media and their impact on national narratives of identity will become more heated as national borders appear increasingly pointless in a global culture. These debates constitute a rich, dynamic, and heavily contested field where politics and aesthetics, visual culture and social history intersect.

University of California

Works Cited

Anderson, Benedict 1991 *Imagined Communities*. Verso, London and New York.

Gilroy, Paul 1992 'Cultural Studies and Ethnic Absolutism' in L. Grossberg et al. (eds) *Cultural Studies*. Routledge, New York and London, pp. 187–98.

Hall, Stuart 1992 'Cultural Identity and Cinematic Representation' in *Framework* 36: pp. 71*ff*.

Said, Edward 1992 'Reflections on Exile' in Russell Ferguson et al. (eds) *Out There: Marginalisation and Contemporary Cultures*. MIT Press.

SVEND ERIK LARSEN

Interplay of Images

WHOSE IMAGE?
The American Image — whose image is it? A European image of the Americans, perhaps thereby mirroring ourselves? Or an image of us, created by Americans whereby they, in turn, try to find themselves? Can you have one without the other? When we approach images, we cross the threshold to the constantly self-referential Babylonian library of Borges. We are therefore left with an open question concerning the centre of the image: where is it? In the subjects producing it or using it? In the objects it refers to? In the structure of the image itself? To go a step further and ask for the origin of the image will not be of much help: does the image emerge from the object, the subject or the context of other images?

Even if we rely on common sense and simply try to see what an image looks like, we will never be able to escape the basic complexity of images. If we presume that an image looks like something we can recognize, this likeness is only perceived because of a more basic difference between the image, its object, and its user. In an image we look at something which, being imagined, is different from ourselves and our immediate experience of the world around us. It offers a way to explore ourselves and our world through the medium of what is different from ourselves. Images always work at a distance. The identity of the image is the result of a continuing process that disguises the presupposed differences without which there would be no images at all, and transforms them, if only temporarily, to an image with an identity.

That is why the American image — or, rather, images — automatically opens a comparative perspective. An image will never simply have an immediately readable content. To see what is in an image always implies the oscillation between the point of view of the image and the point of view of those using it or producing it. And the centre of the image is located in neither of these positions, but in what emerges between them.

In the following I shall try to exemplify the interplay of four instances of mutual Euro-American images: the spatial, the conceptual, the institutional and the existential images. Each of them is stereotypical, but brought together they create a new horizon for cultural dialogue.

SPATIAL IMAGES

I am approaching Le Mans, the capital of the *département* of Sarthe in Western France, a city of about 200,000 inhabitants. On the national highway 157 from Laval I find, at a certain distance from Le Mans, advertisement boards for hotels, restaurants and shops. When I come closer I have to decide whether to enter the city or to take the bypass around it. The road sign indicates a forked road — *centre ville* or *autres directions*. I take *autres directions*, and a little further down the highway, a new dichotomy guides me: take the exit towards Tours and Blois or continue in *autres directions*. Whenever you come to a forked road, choose.

Had I approached my home town, Odense, the capital of the county of Fyn, also with about 200,000 inhabitants, the road signs would have looked very similar, although less simple. As you may know, the images of the Danes have always shown us as more sophisticated than the French. In contrast to the simple dichotomy we have a more complex one: *centrum* is opposed to several destinations in different directions that are not subsumed by *autres directions* (Kerteminde, Otterup, Svendborg). But the centre of the city still constitutes one of the options.

When I approach Trenton, the capital of New Jersey, a city of about 100,000 inhabitants, it is different. I take Exit 7A from the New Jersey Turnpike in order to arrive at Trenton via Interstate 195. I have to know that the three-digit number beginning with an odd number indicates a road leading to the city (while 295 is a bypass). However, following the Interstate 195 I am still somewhat confused. There are no road signs for the centre of the city or for downtown. But at every exit there are names of major streets (such as Kennedy Boulevard, Market Street) and, honestly, I do not know how to get into the city. Asking people for the centre was not of any help: 'Do you mean the Capitol or the public parking lot near the police headquarters?'— how should I know? I crossed the Delaware River a couple of times before I finally, by chance as it were, reached a kind of centre.

We see two distinctly different city images at work here: that of the centred place, and that of the expanding and decentred grid. The classical European image of space as closed, a focus, a point of departure or a final destination, is opposed to the American notion of space as endless openness, in which locations are islands, more network intersections than centres.

The history of European cities is the history of centres reaching out to immediate and more distant surroundings, often in competition with one another, the cities themselves being centred structures. The history of American cities is, until the mid-nineteenth century, the history of isolated and peripheral places, each of them more related to London as satellites than to each other. The conception of the city itself as a congested space was invested, heavily and negatively, with a symbolic Europeanness.

The anti-Americanness in European urban thought and the anti-Europeanness in American urban thought are both American images: images made of America or by America. Nevertheless, the European city spills over its borders, and the American cities revitalize their non-existing centres, both processes strongly influenced by the same functionalistic planning of urban expansions common to both continents during the twentieth century.

Global urban development produces images in which European and American images of cities are merging into an image of a mixed Euro-American character, and the new phenomenon of edge cities, urbanized fabrics related to administrative headquarters, communication networks and shopping centres, is an urban trend beyond the Euro-American images. They are centres of urban networks, like the classical European city, and also open-ended decentred structures, like the prototypical American city (see Garreau 1991).

Conceptual Images

In 1977 the debate between Jacques Derrida and John Searle in *Glyph 1* and *2* inaugurated the deconstructionist debate in the USA (Derrida 1977a and 1977b, Searle 1977). The decentred self, the decentred structure, the decentred text, the decentred everything constituted the agenda of the day, especially if at the same time it was post-something. Although an overwhelming river of words concerned with de- and post-phenomena, large as the Mississippi, has flooded the academic and cultural landscape since then, it seems to me that nothing substantially new has been added to the debate. So I will refer only to the Derrida-Searle argument.

Without challenging the seriousness and depth of the two philosophers, I can not avoid the feeling that they are not addressing philosophical questions only. Searle's viewpoints are filtered through a negative American image of a European, especially French, type of haughty, non-common-sensical thinking. Derrida, on the other hand, argues with a negative European image of an all-too-common-sensical type of Anglo-American, especially American, type of pragmatic down-to-earth thinking. Searle pretends that he does not understand very much (unless he is allowed to interpret Derrida as he, Searle, is used to deal with philosophical problems), and Derrida shows at length and with condescending irony, that he understands more than everything. This is the Jeffersonian yeoman against the French nobility, Horatio Alger against Gustave Flaubert.

In the beginning of his reply Searle approaches allegations of intellectual exotism by stating, 'I should say at the outset that I did not find his [Derrida's] arguments very clear and it is possible that I may have misinterpreted him as profoundly as I believe he has misinterpreted Austin' (Searle 1977:198). In the opening of his rejoinder, Derrida lets us know that, 'I had, first of all, to resist the temptation of contenting myself with a commentary (in the American sense) on the thing' (1977b:163), the 'thing' being Searle plus his reply as a whole, later baptized Sarl with the French abbreviation for a joint-stock company. French refinement against American cool cash.

The pivotal point of the debate is the role of intentionality for the understanding of meaning, text and subject. Searle's claim is that without a conscious intentionality as the conceptual basis, we would never be able to communicate any meaning through texts from one subject to another. Intentionality is the core of meaning production; that is the criteria for the distinction between acceptable and aberrant meanings, between serious talk and jokes, and between ethical commitment to what is uttered and unethical manipulation. No argument for or against anything will be possible without reference to intentionality.

Derrida does not entirely disagree. His point is that, basically, the goal of communication is not to obtain mutual understanding or unanimity, but to get round misunderstandings. Thus, the possibility of misunderstanding is the driving force of communication. Whenever we produce a text, we produce a possible misunderstanding. And whenever we produce a text to escape this misunderstanding, we do so through a new text which itself, clarifying as it may be, opens up the possibility of a new misunderstanding. There is no mastery based on intention, as claimed by Searle, but a limited responsibility as in a joint-stock company, as suggested by Derrida. Like any material product, the text, too, is a thing out in the world, adrift among people and their arbitrary uses. Even if it is carefully produced with the best and most explicit of intentions, the unpredictable intentions of the users may take over the control of its meaning. It has lost its self-imposed centre. So intention is only a reaction to a more foundational decentred context of subject, meaning and texts.

This image of the decentred European subject has had a considerable impact on American intellectual and academic life. At the same time, the image of the centred, voluntaristic American subject is presupposed by a European intellectual. The outcome is that the reverse image of the spatial one occurs: the centred voluntaristic American is living in decentred cities, whereas the decentred European is dwelling in centred spaces. It is no longer possible to talk about an image, in the singular grammatical form, neither on the American, nor on the European side. New images are produced in a dialectical interplay of images, thus making a new dialogue possible and necessary.

INSTITUTIONAL IMAGES
In the summer of 1993, the Mississippi River flooded its banks and neighbouring territories on an unprecedented scale, a catastrophe only comparable to the big flooding of 1927 out of which grew a federal strategy, and responsibility, for the construction and maintenance of levees with the Army

Corps of Engineers as the federal task force.[1]

Watching television, reading the press and passing through the flooded area myself in July 1993, as a European I could not help wondering why houses were swimming down the river. Why on earth do Americans not build solid brick houses instead of these ephemeral shelters of wood and plastic called frame houses? A mobile home without wheels. It corresponds to my stereotypical image of America as the prototype consumer society: do not acquire anything unless you are sure you can get rid of it again. No solid traditions for lasting cities or buildings, but a repeated challenge to the voluntaristic individual to build his own home anew.

More important, this challenge corresponds to the immediate experience of life close to the big river, as reported to the general public by many local people. It is a risky business being a farmer or a barge driver, both in terms of economy and physical survival. Federal aid in case of a devastating natural catastrophe like this cannot be trusted. And insurance is too expensive for most people. You are on your own here, like on the old western frontier. The appeal across the country to a whole army of volunteers sharing this attitude to life, and perhaps also the life experience, is strong. They came spontaneously to give a hand, an immediate responsibility for local living conditions through individual initiative. The decentred, non-institutionalized, individual voluntarism came out as an effective, and definitely not European, social force. But there is another side to the coin.

The general conditions for the course of the catastrophe and the lesson to be learned from it were vividly discussed in public debate. Of course, weather was to blame, but also two other important factors. First, the overexploitation for agricultural purposes of wetland too close to the river. The wetlands are necessary to absorb the water which from time to time cannot be contained in the river bed. No levee system on earth can prevent flooding. The present degree of exploitation, which has developed over the last hundred years, has reached a level where the risks and the costs of the exploitation no longer match the gains. So, there will have to be a federal policy of not reconstructing some of the damaged areas but convincing or forcing people to move out — a federal policy against the tradition of decentred settlements. The general American reluctance to accept federal authority will not make this task easy.

Second, the federal system of levees and dams proved more solid than those built and surveyed by counties and smaller communities. Only on the federal level did the long-term responsibility for maintenance have an effect. On the local level, priorities other than water protection were highlighted after a couple of years with a peaceful Mississippi. And these were the constructions that first yielded to the water pressure and thereby reduced the value of the well-kept walls of protection. Why, asks a European, don't they impose a federal, centralized system on the water defence system? The decentralized local communities cannot handle it? One of the answers is almost eerie: the efficiency of the levees surveyed by the federal engineers added to the catastrophe, because so much water was deprived of a natural outlet that the river, when it finally and inevitably broke through the dikes, was like a ravaging Niagara. As for the expanding European cities of the nineteenth century the lesson now to be learned from the flood is the same: 'Concrete walls aren't best for floods' (headline in *New York Times*, 4 August 1993). A balanced solution, taking into account ecological demands and social needs by restoring some of the wetlands, will have to be found. So what is needed is a federal policy against a federal strategy. That, too, is difficult.

We are here confronted with an ambiguous attitude to federal authority and responsibility as well as to individual initiative and rights. The present-day health care debate in the USA has its centre exactly in this ambiguity. Many Europeans love to think that the Americans are (finally) adopting a European image of public health care. And many Americans love to believe that they are producing a new American image of what the relation between the federal authority and the individual citizen should be. The European and the American image of this relationship is but two sides of the same coin. The actual debate in Europe to reduce the central power structures and enlarge the realm of individual freedom is not accompanied by a denigration of central authority as such, but more by an uncanny feeling about the all too individualized or regionalized fragmentation of society. On the other hand, the American attempts to reinforce the federal power in certain areas has to fight against an image of centralized powers as parasites, held up against the endless possibility of the individual. In Europe the problem is how to allow for more individual freedom without reducing central power too much. In the USA the same problem is looked upon from another angle: how to enlarge federal authority without impeding individual rights.

EXISTENTIAL IMAGES

In his *Journey between the Wars* (1938) John Dos Passos, with a melancholy empathy, briefly describes his meeting with a Mr Hansen in 1928 on the boat to Europe. Mr Hansen is a Dane who has been living and working for twenty-five years in California. He only wanted to earn money enough to be able to return to the old land to spend his third age. The centre of his life was still there. Why should he care about California? He did not get aquainted with anyone in the States, he was just a passer-by.

Dos Passos, too, has had problems with homes and centres: an illegitimate child, born in a hotel, staying during his entire childhood in different places in Europe and the USA, attending different schools, participating as a young man in the devastating experience of the First World War as an ambulance driver — always on the road. Now he is on his way to the Soviet Union, perhaps the new centre of the world. After an intercontinental life of travelling he is profoundly dissatisfied with his homeland in its present state. But, as we know from his later writings, he did not join the communist party (or any other party), but stayed the restless individual.

Paradoxically, then, both Dos Passos and Mr Hansen are always on the road, while firmly believing in the homeland as the centre. They have left home because they could not live without it. They went out, keeping the American and the Danish image alive, shining bright, inside somewhere, real or not. The image became clearer, more simple but also more attractive the more they saw other images: other people's images of them and of America and Denmark. The distance, the otherness of the image, reinforced the power of the centre.

By coincidence Dos Passos meets Mr Hansen again a few days later in Copenhagen in front of Tivoli. Denmark did not quite correspond to his image of twenty-five years ago, and as he did not have images of any other place or any other images of Denmark, he did not know what to do with himself. Maybe he would go back to the USA. Dos Passos leaves him there. When Dos Passos himself left the Soviet Union, he also had troubles with his image of this place. Having no other attractive images, either of the USA or any other place, he, too, was left in a void.

When he is about to leave Moscow he is asked by one of the comrades:

> 'Tell us,' she asked me as I stood beside my sleeper in the steaming trainshed waiting with desperate impatience for the train to leave, 'are you for us or against us? They want you to show your face.' How could I answer? The train was already moving. (1966:196)

This attitude made him turn to the classically conservative American values of Jeffersonian origin, offering a rigid ideological and political centre but no centre in the social and material world. Almost like Mr Hansen.

INTERPLAY OF IMAGES

Mr Hansen and Dos Passos had only one image which referred to the existential centre of their lives. But one image, that is at least one image too little. Images function when they force us to produce contrasting images, through which we produce new centres on the edge of the existing images. Images, like cultures, depend on each other. Even cultures that are supposed to be superior cannot stand alone (cf. Larsen 1991). The following is a description of a personal experience and does not correspond to any single American or European image (Larsen 1990:59*f*). Here spatial, conceptual, institutional and existential images are involved simultaneously and their interplay directs our attention toward a new horizon for cultural dialogue:

> On the paper-white computer screen, we saw the disembodied heads of Osiris, Horus and other Egyptian gods appearing in a row. Just below them, a row of bodies, walking, standing or sitting, some with sceptres or fly whisks in their hands.
> 'By clicking on the mouse, the students can position the heads on the bodies. In the same way, they can identify the names of the gods in hieroglyphic script. They can also learn to write their own names in hieroglyphics,' says the teacher.

'But this is really for the more advanced students. With most of the class we spend nearly all our time on the Greek and Roman civilizations. These are the most important points of reference for Spanish-speaking students, such as those from Latin America.'

'And is Spanish the first language of most of your students, Mr. Ostrovski?' I asked.

'Yes.'

'And what is the biggest ethnic group here at Newcomer High School?'

'Chinese.'

'How can that be?'

'Most of the Chinese students from Peru are Spanish speakers.'

What is European, American or 'other-placean' in this classroom conversation cannot easily be sorted out. Does it imply that the very notion of the American Image, of the European or of any regionalized image for that matter, is obsolete? Or rather: that we constantly have to produce new images with which to define centres in a decentred global reality? When we ask to whose image the screen and the mouse belong, we see that perhaps cultural images based primarily on spatial images, whatever their content, are losing their importance. The very spatiality of the basic images makes them stereotypical. Will cultural oppositions in the future relate more to a technological and informational divide than to national and continental or any other localistic contrasts? Will the image of the mouse open a new dialogue, making the basic localism and territorialism a mousetrap? The answer requires a global and cosmopolitan cultural dialogue.

Odense University

Note

1 My references here are the *New York Times* 1993: July 7 (sect A, p. 7), July 18 (sect. 4, p. 1), July 20 (sect. C, p. 1), July 29 (sect. D, p. 2), August 4 (sect. A, p. 18), August 10 (sect. A, p. 1), August 28 (sect.1, p. 6), Sept. 2 (sect. D, p. 2).

Works Cited

Burnham, Daniel H. and Edward H. Bennett 1970 (1909) *Plan of Chicago*. Da Capo Press, New York.

Derrida, Jacques 1977a 'Signature, Event, Context' in *Glyph 1*. Johns Hopkins University: pp. 172–97.

—— 1977b 'Limited Inc a b c...' in *Glyph 2*. Johns Hopkins University: pp. 162–254.

Dos Passos, John 1938 *Journeys Between the Wars*. Harcourt, Brace and Co., New York.

—— 1966 *The Best Times. An Informal Memoir*. The New American Library, New York.

Garreau, Joel 1991 *Edge City. Life on the New Frontier*. Anchor Books, New York.

Glaab, Charles and Theodore Brown 1983 (1967) *A History of Urban America* 3rd ed. Macmillan, New York.

Larsen, Svend Erik (ed.) 1990 *A Helluva Country. American Studies as a Cross-Cultural Experience.* Odense University Press.

—— 1991 'The Logic of Cultural Exchange' in Rob Kroes (ed.) *US Orbit: Small National Cultures vis-à-vis the United States.* VU University Press, Amsterdam: pp. 91–100.

Lavedan, Pierre 1967 *Histoire de Paris.* Presses Universitaires de France, Paris.

Searle, John 1977 'Reiterating the Differences: A Reply to Derrida' in *Glyph 1.* Johns Hopkins, Baltimore: pp. 198–208.

Taylor, Talbot J. 1992 *Mutual Misunderstanding. Scepticism and the Theorizing of Language and Interpretation.* Routledge, London.

Wolfe, Tom 1981 *From Bauhaus to Our House.* Washington Square Books, New York.

Rien T. Segers

Cultural Identity: New Perspectives for Literary Studies

WHERE DO THE ENGLISH LIVE?
There is an old nursery rhyme which gives an answer to this question:
The Germans live in Germany, the Romans live in Rome,
The Turks live in Turkey; but the English live at home.
This paper concerns the semantics of these two lines of this nursery rhyme, which is — it goes without saying — an *English* nursery rhyme. The main purpose is to explore two questions. How should cultural identity be described? How can cultural identity be related to literary studies? Due to the strongly interdisciplinary character of my subject and its complicated nature, I can only scratch the surface and present a general view.

If we examine the interrelations between cultures now, at the end of the century, we can perceive two contradictory but strong tendencies:

> ...on the one hand, there is the search for cultural authenticity, the return to origins, the need to preserve minor languages, pride in particularisms, admiration for cultural self-sufficiency and maintenance of national traditions; on the other hand, we find the spread of a uniform world culture, the emergence of supranational myths and the adoption of similar lifestyles in widely different settings. Modern technological societies have generated a transnational, composite, mass culture with its own language whose linguistic imprint is already universally evident. (OECD 1989:16)

This paradox between nationalization and globalization can be found in many parts of the world and in many different ways. Concerning European unification, for example, Philip Schlesinger (1994:325) has aptly described this paradox as follows:

> On the one hand, the difficult search for a transcendent unity by the EC — one which must recognise component differences — throws the nation-state into question from above, arguably contributing to crises of national identity. The political and economic developments in the integration process, however, are out of phase with the cultural: what European identity *might* be still remains an open question. On the other hand, the ethno-nationalist awakenings in the former communist bloc and current developments within western Europe — whether neo-nationalist separatisms or racist nationalisms — tend to reaffirm the principle of the nation-state as a locus of identity and of political control.

Schlesinger correctly points at the ultimate paradox of the last decade of the twentieth century: the clash between the indigenous, inner culture of a particular community on the one hand and the global outer culture of a certain constructed *ensemble* of a number of communities. On a programmatic level this paradox goes under different catch words and slogans, such as nationalization versus globalization, 'small is beautiful' versus 'big is necessary and inevitable', individual responsibility versus centralist efficiency. These slogans relate to conflicts at several distinct pragmatic levels: between an individual and his or her direct working environment (say a university department), between a department and a new faculty structure, between the faculty and the development of a new governmental system, between a national government and the regulations of the European Union, and so on.

Arjun Appadurai has suggested that globalization consists of five dimensions, five cultural flows which cross each other at various levels in many parts of the world:

> Firstly, there are *ethnoscapes* produced by flows of people: tourists, immigrants, refugees, exiles and guestworkers. Secondly, there are *technoscapes*, the machinery and plant flows produced by multinational and national corporations and government agencies. Thirdly, there are *finanscapes*, produced by the rapid flows of money in the currency stock exchanges. Fourthly, there are *mediascapes*, the repertoires of images and information, the flows which are produced and distributed by newspapers, magazines, television and film. Fifthly, there are *ideoscapes*, linked to flows of images which are associated with state or counterstate movement ideologies which are comprised of elements of the Western Enlightenment world-view — images of democracy, freedom, welfare, rights, etc. (1990:67)

It is tempting to speculate about which will be the strongest force in the near future: nationalization or globalization. While both tendencies with their completely opposite aims exist at the same place and at the same time, it will be difficult to come up with convincing arguments, as has been tried in a number of publications, implying that the globalization tendency will be a much stronger force than the nationalization tendency. (See, for instance, some papers in Featherstone 1990.)

Let me briefly mention one example. Americanization is an important aspect of contemporary globalization. It is represented in all of the five cultural flows above. Americanization has affected most cultures but, generally speaking, the reception of American culture (or what is regarded as such) might be different according to the specificity of the receiving culture. Important conventions that make up that specificity structure the direction and the depth of Americanization. I would venture the hypothesis that Americanization has been carried out differently in Japan than in The Netherlands. This constitutes an intriguing research object for literary studies.

On the one hand we can observe that 'nationalism is back today with a vengeance all over the world' (Radhakrishnan 1992:83) from Canada to India, from the former USSR to Iraq, from Japan to Turkey. For the time being I belong to those who believe that nationalization will dominate globalization at least in the foreseeable future, and not only outside western Europe as some critics want us to believe, but also to a considerable extent in the countries that belong to the key group members of the European Union. In this context Helmut Dubiel (1994:896) points at new forms of German nationalism, but similar tendencies are alive and well in many other countries of the European Union.

I fully agree with Rolf Dahrendorf's (1994:760) conclusion after his fine analysis of the future of the nation state:

> Auf absehbare Zeit wird der Nationalstaat der Rahmen individueller Rechte und die Aktionseinheit der internationalen Beziehungen bleiben. Das gilt auch in und für Europa. Der Nationalstaat wird hier und da angenagt und angekratzt, bleibt aber in seinem Kern durch neuere Entwicklungen unberührt. Er ist auch der Raum, in dem Menschen Zugehörigkeitsgefühle empfinden können. Einstweilen haben wir noch nichts besseres erfunden als den heterogenen Nationalstaat.

To phrase this in other well-known German words: 'Europa ist ein Kopfgeburt und die Regionen sprechen das Herz an.'

On the other hand we see the severe impact of the five cultural flows of globalization. Globalizaton will persist as an extremely strong tendency, and its strength may even increase. But in the decades to come the nationalization tendency will be able to adopt and adapt many global trends. Globalization will be nationalized to a great extent. That means — to answer the title of this section with a metaphor — that the primary home of the English is England but that their summerhouse stands in a place called the world. Obviously, the same is true for the Germans, the Romans and the Turkish. But let us be realistic, whenever one takes an intellectual ride on a metaphor, it is essential that one knows where to get off (Hannerz 1992:264). It is better to get off this metaphor right here, because reality is much more complex than it can indicate.

Let me add that the threat to the nation or to nationalization does not primarily consist of globalization tendencies, but the threat comes also from within the nation itself. We could think here of Canada, Belgium, Spain, the former Czechoslovakia and Yugoslavia, and we could add, paradoxically, Germany, where the following joke could be heard shortly after the unification: an East

German says to a West German, 'We are one people now!' and the West German replies, 'We too!'

The paradox contained within nationalization versus globalization, however, can only be understood through the concept of cultural identity because this very concept represents the ultimate reason for those serious conflicts between the smaller community and the larger constructed *ensemble* or between two or more smaller communities.

Fields such as philosophy, history, sociology, anthropology, international relations and political science have dealt with the concept of cultural identity on a relatively large scale, but mainly in combination with topics such as European unification, nationalism and lifestyle research. The cultural aspect, to use a narrower sense of the word, has not received too much attention. And here the opening can be found for disciplines with an aesthetic dimension: literary, theatre and media studies, for example.

Comparative literature boasts long-standing expertise in comparing authors and texts, literary movements, literary histories from two or more cultures. But the question of the specificity of a certain culture or of a certain literature, has been raised sometimes, but not answered adequately. What is the Englishness of English literature, the Chineseness of Chinese literature, and so on? The investigation of cultural and literary identity may result in new challenges and promising possibilities.

The Concept of 'Cultural Identity'

Much scholarly research and journalistic writing take as their point of departure well-established stereotypes, based as they are on an ontological belief in the specificity of a certain community. What alternative can we offer which would make it possible to overcome the old ontological, essentialist approach to identity and to by-pass the new extreme relativism which says that identity escapes every attempt at definition?

In his latest collection of essays Ernest Gellner asks for serious attention to be paid to cultural identity:

> [It] is not a delusion, excogitated by muddled romantics, disseminated by irresponsible extremists, and used by egotistical privileged classes to befuddle the masses, and to hide their true interests from them. Its appeal is rooted in the real conditions of modern life, and cannot be conjured away, either by sheer good will and the preaching of a spirit of universal brotherhood, or by the incarceration of the extremists. We have to understand those roots, and live with their fruits, whether we like them or not. (1994:45)

In order to understand the roots of cultural identity we need to understand the semantics of this concept. Here we do not have to go through the work of Sigmund Freud, George Herbert Mead, Erik Eriksson, Talcott Parsons, Jürgen Habermas and others to come up with a well-grounded description of identity. William Bloom (1990:53) offers an elegant summary of current thinking:

>...identification is an inherent and unconscious behavioural imperative in all individuals. Individuals actively seek to identify in order to achieve psychological security, and they actively seek to maintain, protect and bolster identity in order to maintain and enhance this psychological security which is a *sine qua non* of personality stability and emotional well-being. This imperative works from infancy through adulthood and old age. Moreover, identifications can be shared, with the result that individuals who share the same identification will tend to act in concert in order to protect or enhance their shared identity.

These are beautiful words with which we probably all agree. But the problem arises when we try to describe somebody's personal identity or the cultural identity of a particular people. As we all know, talking about personal and cultural identity can be tricky, especially if wishful thinking, stereotypes and a strong belief in the overstressed uniqueness of a particular person or country are the only guidelines.

One of the best recent definitions of 'culture' has been given by Geert Hofstede. His definition unites three important elements. Hofstede's definition shows the decisive value of culture, the importance of cultural relativism and the constructed character of culture. Hofstede (1994:5) distinguishes two meanings of the word culture. There is culture one, which refers to civilization, refinement of the mind which can be found in education, art and literature. This is not the description of culture I would like to refer to. I shall select here Hofstede's culture two, which

>...deals with much more fundamental human processes than culture one; it deals with the things that hurt. Culture (two) is always a collective phenomenon, because it is at least partly shared with people who live or lived within the same social environment, which is where it was learned. It is *the collective programming of the mind which distinguishes the members of one group or category of people from another.*

According to Hofstede culture is learned, not inherited. It derives from one's social environment, not from one's genes. He distinguishes culture from human nature based on the following reasoning: as a human being one can feel fear, anger, love, joy, sadness, and so on. All those feelings belong to human nature. But the way these feelings are expressed is modified by culture. Culture is the software of the mind. It is also distinguished from the personality of an individual. The latter is described as her/his unique personal set of mental programs (s)he does not share with any other human being. Hofstede's description of 'personality' is somewhat naive, but his concept of culture is extremely useful.

Hofstede has a systemic (*in sensu* Niklas Luhmann) conception of culture. He does not see 'culture' as a vast unspecified domain, but as an entity consisting of different levels, which are interrelated. At the same time a person always belongs to a number of the following levels, or indicators of identity, for instance: a national level according to one's country; a regional/ethnic/religious/linguistic affiliation; a gender level; a generation level; a social class level; an organizational or corporate level for those who are employed. The implication is that it is impossible to speak about 'the' identity of a person or of a group; it may vary according to circumstances.

For the concept of 'cultural identity' this implies that the cultural identity of a particular group or people is only partly determined by their national identity. Cultural identity is a broader concept than national identity. In this respect I agree with E. J. Hobsbawm (1990:182) who emphasizes that belonging to a particular state 'is only one way in which people describe their identity among many others which they use for this purpose, as occasion demands'. Whether it is justified to conclude on the basis of that argument that the power of nationalism is receding around the globe, as Hobsbawm does, is another matter and seems to be wishful thinking. The struggle between nationalization and globalization is not yet decided. But based on recent political developments in some parts of the world, on the wars and fighting which are going on, my forecast would differ from that of Hobsbawm. The nationalization trend might hold the winning cards for the immediate future.

Hofstede undertook a large scale intercultural research project, which revealed the following five dimensions, on the basis of which cultures can be classified (1994:13):

1. Social inequality, including the relationship with authority;
2. The relationship between the individual and the group;
3. Concepts of masculinity and femininity; the social implications of having been born as a boy or a girl;
4. Ways of dealing with uncertainty, relating to the control of aggression and the expression of emotions;
5. A long-term orientation in life versus a short-term orientation.

Hofstede's conception of culture has a number of advantages: culture is an ever-changing entity, not a static one; culture is learned not inherited; there are no criteria on the basis of which culture A is 'intrinsically' better than culture B (with the usual theoretical exceptions such as the culture that deliberately and seriously violates human rights); culture is a mental construction rather than an innate property of a certain community. This implies that Hofstede's view of culture is more useful with respect to its application in actual research than many other definitions of culture, which base themselves on ontological or essentialist conceptions.

A weak side of Hofstede's book, however, is that the very concept of cultural identity is not used. This concept is needed to discuss questions whenever two cultures come into contact with each other or — at an academic level — are compared with each other. A key question such as 'How can the distinctiveness or the specificity of this culture be determined?' is in fact a question concerning the *cultural identity* of a particular community. The extent to which a certain culture can be said to have distinctive *and* common traits can only be determined on a comparative basis. As the American sociologists Jepperson and Swidler (1994:368) recently stated: 'The essential strategy for making the invisible visible is *of course* comparative research. And that is exactly why disciplines which have a comparative basis should take the lead in research in this domain' (my emphasis).

Books discussing the cultural identity of a particular nation often refer to certain 'special features', 'characteristics' and 'traits' of a country or its people. Often these observations are principally based on impressions, introspections, myths and — not to forget — jokes rather than on factual evidence or empirical research. Obviously I do not want to deny, for instance, that the thousands of existing jokes concerning national and cultural stereotypes can indicate particular aspects of the cultural identity of a particular community or nation. But they are only indicators and not more than that.

Consider for instance the following two jokes. The first originated in New York, the second in Tokyo.

In a New York hotel an American and Japanese engineer meet for the first time and they introduce themselves, the American first: 'Hello, my name is John Smith. Nice to meet you. I am an electrical engineer and at this moment I am working for Kodak.' After a couple of moments of silence the Japanese says: 'Hello, I am Toyota and my name is nobody.' This joke may serve as an indicator of the American self-image as individualistic, self-confident and successful. The joke also implicitly constructs an image in which Japanese professionals are not individuals, and neither self-confident nor successful.

The Japanese from their side have a pagoda full of American jokes, such as this one. An American and a Japanese meet each other on a safari trip in Africa. They take a walk together, somewhat outside the safe touristic path. Suddenly, they are confronted with a hungry-looking lion. The American immediately starts running. But the Japanese does not move and thoughtfully opens his black leather briefcase in order to take out a pair of gym shoes. Looking back at the Japanese the American shouts: 'Come on, run for your life, leave those gym shoes behind — you don't have a chance anyhow to run faster than the lion does.' The Japanese thinks, waits a bit and says politely, 'The one I have to outrun is not the lion, but you.' This joke may serve to us as an indicator of the Japanese self-image as smart, civilized and competitive, whereas the American is seen as impulsive, thoughtless and pushy.

These jokes not only demonstrate the well-known fact handed over to us from social psychology that the image of a neighboring people is constructed as a negative counterpart of one's own image, on the basis of which the in-group people can identify themselves more easily with their own self-image (Fink 1991:453). But the jokes should also show that the construction of cultural identity involves at least two parts: the in-group and the out-group, the perception of oneself and the perception of the other (*Selbstwahrnehmung* and *Fremdwahrnehmung*). The Japanese looks at the American from a Japanese perspective, and vice versa.

In our time it is of great importance to have an adequate, well-balanced insight into the cultural identity of a particular nation. A distorted view can significantly hamper good understanding and adequate communication with citizens of that nation. Very often political conflicts and wars find their deep origin in distorted visions of one's own and the foreign identity. What has been said so far concerning cultural identity applies also to literary identity, with the apparent exception that a misconception of the literary identity of a particular nation might not have such severe consequences as the distortion of the cultural identity.

Often cultural identity has been seen as a range of characteristics which are unique for a particular culture and 'innate' to a specific people. The Japanese scholarly tradition of *Nihonjinron* (Studies about Japaneseness) is a typical example of this approach. But also in other cultures many examples of this type of thinking can be found, and in many cases not only practised long ago, but even nowadays and also not primarily on the periphery of scholarship.

Another view suggests that cultural identity has a structuralist character, where a particular culture is seen as a set of characteristics which are all related to each other, more or less independent from the people that make that culture.

The alternative for the conception of 'identity' as a set of unique or structural characteristics is the idea of identity as a *construction*. Within such a constructive framework the cultural identity of a particular nation or of a certain ethnic group within that nation can be attached to three factors: (1) the formal characteristics concerning that nation or group at a given time in history; (2) the programming of the mind (to use Hofstede's words) within a particular community on the basis of which the cultural identity by the in-group is being constructed; and (3) the way in which people from outside conduct a process of selection, interpretation and evaluation concerning the specificity of the in-group, which means in other words the outside image of the cultural identity of a foreign nation or group. The relationship between these three elements is a dynamic one. Ideally, the (scholarly) construction of identity should be based on *all three* factors. (For a more extensive explanation see Segers 1992.)

What are formal characteristics with respect to cultural identity? Formal characteristics are 'facts', figures that can be found in statistical handbooks concerning a particular country or an ethnic group and that determine to a great extent the programming of the mind of a given society, and the other way around: for instance, the total number of citizens of a country, the size of the country, the gross national product, average income, percentage of unemployment, the number of museums, the number of books produced, the genres, the relation between 'native' and translated books.

Since we do not have direct access to the way in which people's minds are programmed, we are driven back on visible indicators thereof. We have to look at the style of conduct and communication in a particular community, to use Gellner's (1983:92) more pragmatically oriented definition of culture. This style of conduct and communication of the citizens of a state or the members of a particular ethnic group is their visible cultural identity. This visible cultural identity can be suppressed or thematized by opinion leaders (individuals and institutions) within that particular community. It is impossible to talk about cultural identity without taking into consideration who is defining it and along which lines.

The third element of the identity triangle consists of the constructions made by persons, most of the time opinion leaders or important institutions from outside, concerning the conduct and communication of the people inside.

It would be somewhat misleading to think that the idea of considering national or cultural identity as a construction originated in systems theory (from Ludwig von Bertalanffy to Niklas Luhmann). Scholars working outside this domain arrived more or less at the same conclusion. An interesting example is Benedict Anderson (1983:15), who coined the term 'imagined community'. In an attempt to define the concept of 'nation' he states:

> ...it is an imagined political community — and imagined as both inherently limited and sovereign. It is *imagined* because the members of even the smallest nation will never know most of their fellow-members, meet them, or even hear of them, yet in the minds of each lives the image of their communion.

I am not saying that Anderson's 'imagination' is an equivalent to Luhmann's 'construction'. The similarity is to be sought in the emphasis on the mental processing of a particular object.

To consider cultural identity as a construction means that it is a mental conception which may vary according to the constructor, the time and place of construction. This implies that it is impossible to speak about 'the' cultural identity of a community. In theory there are as many cultural identities of a given community as there are times, places and people that construct that identity. That should not prevent scholars, however, from the necessary task of describing and systematizing the common characteristics based on those several existing identities. Moreover, in reality we are normally confronted with only one *dominant* construction of the cultural identity of a particular country.

The most recent development concerning the concept of cultural identity has been the addition of the prefix 'post', as an attempt to resolve the paradox between globalization and nationalization. The term 'postnational identity' is coined in a recent book by Dewandre and Lenoble (1994). It implies the paradox between the necessity of the construction of one political European identity based on the development of the European Union as against the promotion of the cultural distinctiveness of the several European nations and regions: one political identity versus many distinctive cultural identities, all living under the same roof of a house called postnational identity. This concept of postnational identity looks rather academic, sponsored by wishful thinking 'from Brussels with love'. (For more extensive criticism see Picht 1994.)

There is, however, still another caveat to be considered, which especially applies to cross-cultural or comparative studies concerning cultural identity. Richard Handler has formulated the following reasonable objection in this respect:

> Identity has become a salient scholarly and cultural construct in mid-twentieth-century, particularly in social-scientific, scholarship in the United States. Its prominence in that context, however, does not mean that the concept can be applied unthinkingly to other places and times. (1994:27)

Western notions of collective identity are grounded in individualist metaphors. Attributes of boundedness, continuity, uniqueness, and homogeneity that are ascribed to human persons are ascribed to social groups as well. This leads Handler to his conclusion:

> Thus it seems to me that if other cultures imagine personhood and human activity in terms other than those we use, we should not expect them to rely on Western individualistic assumptions in describing social collectivities. (1994:33)

Clifford Geertz (1980:24–5) tells an anecdote which shows a completely different approach to boundaries and the essence of a community. It concerns the Balinese state where the rulers did not compete for boundaries (territory) but for the allegiance of men:

> The Dutch, who wanted ... to get the boundary between two petty princedoms straight once and for all, called in the princes concerned and asked them where indeed the borders lay. Both agreed that the border of princedom A lay at the farthest point from which a man could still see the swamps, and the border of princedom B lay at the point from which a man could still see the sea. Had they, then, never fought over the land between, from which one could see neither swamp nor sea? 'Mijnheer', one of the old princes replied, 'we had much better reason to fight with one another than these shabby hills'.

LITERARY STUDIES AND CULTURAL IDENTITY

It is impossible to investigate the 'complete' cultural identity of a particular community. The best one can do is to select and investigate some elements that are supposed to form a central part of it. Literature and its reception offer an excellent opportunity to construct basic elements of the cultural identity of a certain nation or group, based on literature's ability to represent important aspects of a particular community.

How should the three cultural factors be described when we talk about the impact of literature on cultural identity? The formal characteristics imply, for instance, the number of literary texts printed in a particular country, sales figures of fiction, statistics concerning library loans, number of translations of foreign literary texts, many other figures that are related to the 'material' side of the literary system and finally social circumstances that directly or indirectly influence literary communication in that country (such as language training, literary education, literary media coverage and censorship).

The second and third factors which are important for the construction of literary identity are based on the specific conventions of writing, processing and reading literature. The second factor concerns the production and reception of a national literature (or the literature of their ethnic group) by writers and readers from inside, *plus* the reception of the foreign literature that plays an important role in that specific country or community. The third factor implies the reception of the literary texts by the outside group belonging to another nation or community. 'Reception' is used here in the broadest sense of the word: including interpretation, translation, canon formation, teaching, writing of travel literature concerning another country.

To give a short but striking example of the power of the outside group, until the end of the 1980s the contemporary Dutch author Cees Nooteboom was considered to be a second-rate author (not very well-known, small sales figures). After he moved to Berlin his work was gradually translated into German. In the early 1990s the highly influential German critic, Marcel Reich-Ranicki, announced in his usual slapstick style in a TV talkshow that Nooteboom would win a Nobel Prize. Soon after, the writer became a celebrity in Germany, and consequently he was also rediscovered by the leading Dutch critics and academics as an outstanding author, belonging to the best that The Netherlands has to offer.

This example represents an interesting case in German-Dutch relations which runs against all stereotypes: the Germans who discover and 'make' Dutch culture. The example not only shows the power of exterior forces, but it also shows the power of media criticism. (For a rich book on literary criticism in the media see Barner 1989, especially the articles by Lämmert and Viehoff.)

What is the relationship between literary studies on the one hand and the study of literary and cultural identity on the other? How can an adequate tie be established? How might research in this domain be structured?

There exists an approach recently introduced to literary studies, which permits research into the specificity of the literary conduct and literary communication of a given group or people. This is the so-called systemic approach. (For an extensive bibliography see Tötösy de Zepetnek 1992.) In short, systemic theory considers literature as a system, which is based on all activities as performed by participants in the literary communication process. Systemic theory is interested in the 'actions' of all agents of the communication process, as opposed to most other approaches which are interested in just one agent. For instance, reception aesthetics mainly focused on the reader or biographical criticism focusing on the author, or structuralism on the text.

Systemic theory deals with five broad categories: actions performed by *authors*, *institutions*, *general readers*; these actions, in turn, take place against the background of a *social context* and are directed at *texts*.

The institutional category is a very broad one and consists of a great number of distinctive agents and corresponding actions: readers for publishing houses and the publishers themselves; critics and reviewers; bookkeepers; teachers and pupils, professors and students; academic researchers; librarians; translators; representatives of several distinctive organizations, such as book clubs, associations of authors and publishers; administrators and bureaucrats dealing with 'culture' on a city, state or national level (see Rusch 1991:24).

If the above five categories and the nine institutional subcategories are the main areas in which literary conduct and communication take place within a particular community, then they also form an adequate basis for a well-grounded study of the cultural and literary identity of a specific people.

Research into literary and cultural identity has a strong comparative nature. For instance, the construction the in-group makes of itself is just one third of the story. This construction should be complemented by a comparison with the formal characteristics and by the construction the out-group makes of the in-group. Within a constructive framework identity is a relational concept, which can only function within a comparative context. To investigate the Englishness of a novel by Virginia Woolf implies the application of criteria that cannot be derived from English modernism alone, but should be based on an understanding of the general principles of modernism (both on an international as well as on an inter-artistic level). To mention another example: the question to what extent there exist specific American reading strategies, which lead to a distinct interpretation and evaluation of certain texts, cannot be answered by a research project geared towards the way only Americans read fiction.

The study of literary and cultural identity is a project pre-eminently fit for a comparative perspective. It is not surprising, therefore, that a discipline such as comparative literature has a respectable tradition in image studies, albeit that most of the research and proposals by Louis-Paul Betz, Fernand Baldensperger, Paul Hazard and Paul van Tieghem have become obsolete, based as they were on old-fashioned psychological and philosophical concepts. In this respect Manfred S. Fischer gives a good account of the developments until 1951. Later work done by Hugo Dyserinck (1981, for a survey on 'komparatistische Imagologie') is more sophisticated.

But the danger of much current and future work within comparative literature on questions relating to literary identity is its lack of synthesis, an old point of criticism against comparative research in general. Yesterday we wrote about *L'Image de la Belgique dans les lettres francaise de 1830 à 1870* (Pichois 1957). Today we write about Flanders in the novels of Georges Rodenbach (Dhuygelaere 1991), and tomorrow maybe on the image of France in the literature of *la Wallonie*. Due to their completely different methodological positions it is hard to relate those studies to each other.

What is currently missing in literary studies is a framework on the basis of which future studies concerning cultural identity can be related to each other. This framework should take into consideration all aspects relevant to research into cultural identity and it should stimulate hermeneutic *and* empirical research. Maybe the constructivist-systemic framework could perform this function.

NEW PERSPECTIVES
In most parts of today's world cultural borders no longer coincide with national borders; cultural diversity within one nation-state is more the rule than the exception. To give just one example, until the late 1960s The Netherlands was a country with hardly any ethnic diversity, a rather homogeneous state, like so many others in Western Europe at that time. On 1 January 1991 the four largest cities of the country (Amsterdam, Rotterdam, The Hague and Utrecht) had a total population of almost two million. Of those two million people more than 400,000 (twenty-one per cent) were aliens (mainly Turks, Moroccans and persons of Surinamese and Netherlands Antilles ethnic origin, according to OECD 1992:71).

All over the world a growing number of severe political and ethnic conflicts have arisen, which find their origin in an imbalance of the relationships between the three cultural factors. The nature of this imbalance may vary from place to place: it may be a wrong, one-sided selection of the material statistics, an inadequate and too strong self-image or a distorted look at the foreign partner. The nature of the imbalance may be different, but the result is always the same everywhere: cultural relativism gives way to cultural absolutism.

It goes without saying that the current political situation in many parts of the world implies that the study of cultural identity has become an important item for scholarship. Literary scholarship also has a task to fulfil here and should not leave this work to other disciplines. Literary and cultural identity represent an *important* and *complex* study object.

This object is important since it leads literary studies back to the relationship between text and social context. By focusing on this relationship literary studies will gain access to the major contemporary and historical social issues. This access had been denied due to the impact of a number of influential twentieth-century critical schools such as Russian Formalism, New Criticism, the German *werkimmanente Interpretation*, and Structuralism. They all more or less locked themselves up in texts, which were cut off from society.

The complexity of the study of literary and cultural identity is caused by the multi-faceted character of its object and by the multi-disciplinary approach it requires. If one sticks to the idea that the study of the literary communication process is the primary target of literary studies, then research into literary identity has not just one face (the text), but as many faces as there are actors in that communication process (authors, publishers, critics, teachers, pupils, general readers). In addition to this multi-faceted character, the complexity of the object is also caused by the interdisciplinary approach which is required here. Cultural and literary identity is an area where philosophy, history, anthropology, sociology, psychology, political science and literary studies meet.

The interest in cultural and literary identity is rising rapidly within literary studies in general and within comparative literature in particular. A large section of the XIVth Congress of the International Comparative Literature Association (Edmonton 1994) was devoted to 'Literature and Identity'. At the Second International Congress of the Portuguese Comparative Literature Association (Porto 1995) and at the International Conference on Cultural Dialogue and Cultural Misreading (Peking University 1995) a large number of papers dealt with problems of identity in a rather explicit way. Also the 1997 Leiden Congress of the International Comparative Literature Association has two large sections ('Nation Building' and 'Colonizer and Colonized') where questions of cultural identity occupy a central place.

There are five categories into which the construction of literary identity can be divided: authors, institutions, readers, social contexts and obviously the texts themselves. In current mainstream scholarship most attention is directed at identity (national, regional, multicultural, feminine) as it can be found in literary texts. A second place is reserved for papers concentrating on the relationship between textual identity and the socio-cultural context.

So far one category is not very well represented. It concerns the activities performed by the several literary institutions. Traditionally they have played a significant role in the construction of a given cultural identity. Activities performed by publishers, reviewers, booksellers, teachers, researchers, librarians, translators, administrators and bureaucrats might be as important to the formation of the cultural identity of a given community as the activities performed in the other four categories mentioned above. All the institutional agents are relatively powerful with respect to the construction or deconstruction of a certain identity. Their role and their power is an interesting and important research object.

In the search for a description of the cultural and literary identity of a given community literary scholarship may direct its attention equally to all five categories of the literary communication process (authors, institutions, readers, social context and the texts themselves). In meeting this challenge a new domain of research and teaching will present itself. This new domain will not only broaden scholarly scope by the necessity to focus on all five categories, it may also lead to another way of reading literature. This will allow literary studies to deal with issues that have a strong social impact.

In principle two methodological positions are possible in respect of research on cultural identity: the hermeneutic and the empirical position. So far most of the research on cultural and literary identity has had a hermeneutic character, where the researcher tries to come up with his or her own interpretation concerning a particular textual aspect of cultural identity. The empirical approach tries to assemble the opinion of authors and all kinds of readers about topics of cultural identity. The focus is here on the description of what others think about a particular literary-cultural item. It can be shown (for instance based on Hofstede's book) that a combination of hermeneutic and empirical research is extremely fruitful (for some elementary results see Segers 1994). If one wants to describe part of the 'mental software' of a particular nation I do not think it is possible to do this only on a hermeneutic basis or only on an empirical basis. Both approaches are needed to tackle this extremely complicated topic.

CONCLUSION

Issues related to cultural identity seem to be and will stay the issues of the last years of this century and the beginning of the next. In one of its many reports the OECD writes:

> Awareness of an ethnic or regional identity, or of a minority status, can be hidden for many decades by the myth of national unity and identity, of ethnic homogeneity, of mass culture or planetary culture. It can also be hidden by an analysis in terms of social groups or the evocation of proletarian internationalism. Today, ethnic or racial claims, nationalist or regionalist movements, and movements for independence or autonomy, have broken up communities which were merely a facade. (1987:43)

This process of breaking up seemingly homogeneous communities and the consequent struggle for identity will undoubtedly continue for a number of years in many parts of the world. To study this process from a literary and cultural point of view offers as many challenges as possibilities for literary studies in the years to come.

This article has tried to show that the English people who, in the nursery rhyme, 'live at home' can be substituted by most other nations or ethnic groups living in a particular nation. As Hofstede has observed:

> Everybody looks at the world from behind the windows of a cultural home and everybody prefers to act as if people from other countries have something special about them (a national character) but home is normal. Unfortunately, there is no normal position in cultural matters. This is an uncomfortable message, as uncomfortable as Galileo Galilei's claim in the seventeenth century that the Earth is not the center of the Universe. (1994:235)

Literary studies in general and comparative literature in particular could show the dangers of this naive nursery rhyme and of thousands of other texts which in fact have the same semantics. This could be done by focussing on the problem of cultural identity as outlined here. It might give literary and comparative studies a new perspective and a new prestige.

Rijkuniversiteit Groningen

Works Cited

Anderson, Benedict 1983 *Imagined Communities: Reflections on the Origin and Spread of Nationalism*. Verso, London.

Appadurai, Arjun 1990 'Disjuncture and Difference in the Global Cultural Economy' in Mike Featherstone (ed.): pp. 295–310.

Bloom, William 1990 *Personal Identity, National Identity and International Relations*. Cambridge University Press.

Dahrendorf, Ralf 1994 'Die Zukunft des Nationalstaates' in *Merkur. Deutsche Zeitschrift für Europäisches Denken* 48, no. 9/10: pp. 751–61.

Dewandre, Nicole and Jacques Lenoble (eds) 1994 *Projekt Europa: Postnationale Identität: Grundlage für eine europäische Demokratie?* Schelzky & Jeep, Berlin.

Dhuygelaere, Doris 1991 '"La petite patrie": La Flandre dans les romans de Georges Rodenbach' in *Yearbook of European Studies/Annuaire d'Etudes Européennes* 4: pp. 137–64.

Dubiel, Helmut 1994 'Über moralische Souveränität, Erinnerung und Nation' in *Merkur. Deutsche Zeitschrift für Europäisches Denken* 48, no. 9/10: pp. 884–97.

Dyserinck, Hugo 1981 *Komparatistik. Eine Einführung,* 2nd ed. revised. Bouvier Verlag Herbert Grundmann, Bonn.

Featherstone, Mike (ed.) 1990 *Global Culture: Nationalism, Globalization and Modernity*. Sage, London.

Fink, Gonthier-Louis 1991 'Das Bild des Nachbarvolkes im Spiegel der deutschen und der französischen Hochaufklärung (1750–1789)' in Bernhard Giesen (ed.): pp. 453–92.

Fischer, Manfred S. 1981 *Nationale Images als Gegenstand Vergleichender Literaturgeschichte: Untersuchungen zur Entstehung der komparatistischen Imagologie*. Bouvier Verlag Herbert Grundmann, Bonn.

Geertz, Clifford 1980 *Negara: The Theatre State in Nineteenth-Century Bali*. Princeton University Press.

Gellner, Ernest 1983 *Nations and Nationalism*. Blackwell, Oxford.

―――― 1994 *Encounters with Nationalism*. Blackwell, Oxford.

Giesen, Bernhard 1991 *Nationale und kulturelle Identität: Studien zur Entwicklung des kollektiven Bewusstseins in de Neuzeit*. Suhrkamp, Frankfurt/M.

Handler, Richard 1994 'Is "Identity" a Useful Cross-Cultural Concept?' in John R. Gillis (ed.) *Commemorations. The Politics of National Identity*. Princeton University Press: pp. 27–40.

Hannerz, Ulf 1992 *Cultural Complexity. Studies in the Social Organization of Meaning*. Columbia University Press.

Hartung, Klaus 1994 'Die Nation gehört nicht der Rechten' in Robert Leicht (ed.): pp. 10–2.

Hobsbawm, E. J. 1990 *Nations and Nationalism Since 1780: Programme, Myth, Reality*. Cambridge University Press.

Hofstede, Geert 1994 (1991) *Cultures and Organizations*. HarperCollins, Hammersmith, London.

Hutchinson, John and Anthony D. Smith (eds) 1994 *Nationalism*. Oxford University Press.

Jepperson, Ronald L. and Ann Swidler 1994 'What Properties of Culture Should We Measure?' in *Poetics* 22: pp. 359–71

Lämmert, Eberhard 1989 'Literaturkritik. Praxis der Literaturwissenschaft?' in Wilfried Barner (ed.) *Literaturkritik: Anspruch und Wirklichkeit*. DFG Symposium, J. B. Metzlersche Verlagsbuchhandlung, Stuttgart: pp. 129–39.

Leicht, Robert (ed.) 1994 *Umdenken. Deutschland, seine Rolle, seine inneren Umbrüche*. Zeit-Punkte nr. 3, Die Zeit, Hamburg.

Luhmann, Niklas 1984 *Soziale Systeme: Grundriss einer allgemeinen Theorie.* Suhrkamp, Frankfurt.

OECD 1987 *Multicultural Education.* Organisation for Economic Co-operation and Development; Centre for Educational Research and Innovation, Paris.

—— 1989 *One School, Many Cultures.* Organisation for Economic Co-operation and Development; Centre for Educational Research and Innovation, Paris.

—— 1992 *Trends in International Migration.* Organisation for Economic Co-operation and Development; Centre for Educational Research and Innovation, Paris

Parker, Andrew, Mary Ruso, Doris Sommer and Patricia Yaeger (eds) 1992 *Nationalisms and Sexualities.* Routledge, New York and London.

Pichois, Claude 1957 *L'Image de la Belgique dans les lettres francaises de 1830 à 1870.* Editions Traces, Paris.

Picht, Robert 1994 'Europa — aber was versteht man darunter? Aufforderung zur Überprüfung der Denkmuster' in *Merkur. Deutsche Zeitschrift für europäisches Denken* 48, no. 9/10, pp. 850–66.

Radakrishnan, R. 1992 'Nationalism, Gender, and the Narrative of Identity' in Andrew Parker et al.: pp. 77–95.

Rusch, Gebhard 1991 'Zur Systemtheorie und Phänomenologie von Literatur: Eine holistische Perspektive' in *SPIEL. Siegener Periodikum zur Internationalen Empirischen Literaturwissenschaft* 10: pp. 305–39.

Schlesinger, Philip 1994 (1992) 'Europeanness: A New Cultural Battlefield?' in John Hutchinson and Anthony D. Smith (eds): pp. 316–25.

Segers, Rien T. 1992 'Research into Cultural Identity: A New Empirical Object. The Case of Japanese "Uniqueness" Between East and West' in *SPIEL. Siegener Periodikum zur Internationalen Empirischen Literaturwissenschaft* 11: pp. 149–62.

—— 1994 'Japanese Cultural Identity and Reading Behavior' in *The Japan Foundation Newsletter* 22, no. 1: pp. 15–20.

Tötösy de Zepetnek, Steven 1992 'Systemic Approaches to Literature: An Introduction with Selected Bibliographies' in *Canadian Review of Comparative Literature/Revue Canadienne de Littérature Comparée* 19: pp. 21–93.

Viehoff, Reinhold 1989 'Literaturkritik 1973 und 1988. Aspekte des literaturkritischen Wertewandels' in Wilfried Barner (ed.) *Literaturkritik Anspruch und Wirklichkeit: DFG Symposium 1989,* J. B. Metzlersche Verlagsbuchhandlung, Stuttgart: pp. 440–59.

THEO D'HAEN

Transcending Borders: Faulkner and Alternative Identities

My starting point is a specific case of 'cultural misunderstanding'. Both Paul Gilroy, in his *The Black Atlantic*, and Chris Bongie, in an essay on '(un)Ending Colonialism: Postcolonial Identities and Postmodern Ambivalence in Edouard Glissant's *Mahagony*', voice their dissatisfaction with J. Michael Dash's English-language translation of French Caribbean writer and critic Edouard Glissant's major essay collection, *Le Discours antillais*. Gilroy, in a discussion of the problematic issue of 'nationalism' in the context of black political discourse in the geographical space of what he calls 'the black Atlantic', asks us to consider:

> ...the case of Edouard Glissant, who has contributed so much to the emergence of a creole counter-discourse that can answer the alchemy of nationalisms. Discussion of these problems suffers when his translator excises Glissant's references to the work of Deleuze and Guattari from the English edition of his 1981 book *Le discours antillais*, presumably because to acknowledge this exchange would somehow violate the aura of Caribbean authenticity that is a desirable frame around the work. (1993:31)

Bongie, in a textual parenthesis, argues that the 'edited translation' of *Le Discours antillais* 'severely downplays Glissant's localized political commitments in the name of his cross-cultual poetics' (8). In a footnote he adds that:

> Dash's edited translation ... plays to North American audiences in its selection of texts: the arguments of most 'universal' application are included, whilst many of the detailed analyses of Martinique are excluded, thus distorting an essential element of the text's dynamic, which tactically alternates between a globalizing and an insular vision. (34)

He ends his note by referring to Gilroy's remark just quoted as pointing out 'a different but intimately related translation strategy'. This is perhaps the place to insist that, strictly speaking, Gilroy and Bongie are taking the wrong man to task. As A. James Arnold told me, in his guise of editor of the series in which *Caribbean Discourse* appeared it was largely he, not Dash, who was responsible for the selection of material to be included. For simplicity's sake, however, and following Gilroy's and Bongie's use, I will continue to refer to 'Dash's edition' while actually meaning 'Arnold's edition/Dash's translation'.

At first sight, Gilroy's and Bongie's remarks seem to point in different directions: for Gilroy, Dash's edited translation aims at making Glissant's text more specific, more 'authentically Caribbean'; for Bongie, Dash's selection 'universalizes' Glissant's concerns, and makes them therefore less 'Caribbean'. Yet, taken together, these two forms of editorial intervention can serve as instances of what happens when, in Edward Said's famous formula, 'theory travels' (1983). Specifically, and in combination, they both rewrite Glissant's original to fit an 'American' paradigm. By thus domesticating or naturalizing Glissant, they also short-circuit the original foreign text's potential for renewal of the domestic paradigm. Putting the 'foreignness' back into Glissant's text might fruitfully address the impasse which the 'American' domestic paradigm has reached in the eyes of many.

On the North-American continent 'literature' in the vernacular, ever since its institutionalization as an academic discipline in the late 1920s, has been perceived primarily as an identity-machine. The assumption that there is such a thing as a recognizable 'American' identity is fundamental to all classics of American literary scholarship, and it is the recognized canon of American literature that projects this identity as both uniquely American and yet universal in appeal (Pease 1994a and 1994b). If what Donald Pease (1994b) has called the 'Old Americanists' until quite recently portrayed 'America' via its canonical literature as the 'Great White Hope', then it has of course by now become a critical commonplace that over the last decade or so this unitary American sensibility has been largely washed away by the rising tide of multiculturalism. Yet, I suggest that the assertion of *difference* multiculturalism proposes reinstates, at a meta-level, the very same unitary consciousness it claims to undo. Indeed, it seems to me that each and every one of the various literatures that under the aegis of multiculturalism constitute themselves as separate and equal within the American cultural context appeal to the very same essentialism they reject with regard to 'American' literature as a whole. Multiculturalism, then, is simply the guise 'Americanness' assumes under postmodernity, extending its citizenship to 'all' Americans, not by ideally and ideologically raising each member of the disenfranchised minorities to a hypothetical 'white' Americanness, thereby — as under the old dispensation — theoretically abolishing minority as an issue in the American context, but rather by downshifting the burden of the Constitution's promise of life, liberty, and the pursuit of happiness to the level of the minorities as themselves constitutive of

'America'. Each American is thereby re-constituted as such only as a member of a minority. In terms of literary definitions, then, it becomes — literally — essential that each of the literatures of American multiculturalism obey the paradox of being at the same time as 'original' and 'authentic' as possible, and as 'universal' as possible, thereby effectively duplicating the requirements traditionally obtaining for 'American' literature.

The apparently paradoxical combination of editorial interventions applied by Dash in the course of his translating Glissant's *Discours antillais* can be read as a double instance of Said's 'traveling theory': an originally 'foreign' theory is literally 'transformed' to fit the prescriptions of its new 'domestic' context, so that its authority can then be invoked to further the claims of domestic 'theory'. Interesting in the specific case under discussion is that it suddenly shows the conjunction obtaining between three of the most potent contemporary paradigms for the study of literature: postmodernism, multiculturalism, and the postcolonialism of which Glissant's own work is usually seen as an instance. Specifically, Dash's edition recasts postcolonialism under the postmodern dispensation as multiculturalism American style. As such it explicitly feeds the fears of those theorists of postcolonialism, such as Helen Tiffin (1991), Stephen Slemon (1991), and Kumkum Sangari (1990), who see the transformation of postmodernism from a term and concept exclusively referring to the 'First World' into a concept also taking in what used to be referred to as the 'Third World' as a sly manoeuver on the part of the West to re-assert its theoretical (as well as political, economic, and cultural) dominance. This basically once more involves a duplication of what I earlier described as the process of recuperation of multiculturalism by 'American' literature. While each postcolonial literature separately is granted its own history and importance, its own 'canon', jointly they are recuperated *as a phenomenon* under the umbrella of postmodernism, a meta-label issuing from the Eurocentric centres of theoretical power.

Glissant's original *Le Discours antillais* resists recuperation by Eurocentrism, and it does so precisely via those elements that Dash has filtered out. As the quotation from Bongie referring to the original French version of *Le Discours antillais* makes clear, Glissant 'tactically alternates between a globalizing and an insular vision' and, as the quotation from Gilroy suggested, it does so precisely via the work of Deleuze and Guattari. Specifically, it invokes the concept of 'minor literature' as coined by Gilles Deleuze and Félix Guattari in their *Kafka: Pour une littérature mineure* (1975). Deleuze and Guattari most succinctly see a 'minor literature' as characterized by 'the deterritorialization of language, the connection of the individual to a political immediacy, and the collective assemblage of enunciation' (1986:18). In another instance of 'traveling theory', this concept in the American context has been almost exclusively[1] taken to apply to 'minority literatures', as for instance in Abdul R. JanMohamed and David Lloyd's *The Nature and Context of Minority*

Discourse (1990), a collective volume gathering essays on a variety of literatures, both multiculturally American and postcolonial. As such, the concept goes to strengthen the 'American' paradigm I earlier outlined. Yet, Deleuze and Guattari themselves explicate their argument with reference to Kafka, a 'major' author in a 'major' literature (German) as well as a 'minor' author in Jewish-Czech-German literature. The point is that Kafka's importance and strength as a 'minor' author are dependent upon his status as a 'major' author *and vice versa*. Elsewhere Deleuze and Guattari invoke James Joyce and Samuel Beckett as other such 'minor' writers. As Deleuze and Guattari put it, 'minor no longer designates specific literatures but the revolutionary conditions for every literature within the heart of what is called great (or established) literature' (1986:18) and 'there is nothing that is major or revolutionary exept (sic) the minor' (26). This revolutionary potential comes out in an author's 'becoming-minor' (27), not in his being a member of a minority. In other words, 'becoming-minor' is a matter of bringing into play the dialectical relationship between major and minor, and of keeping this dialectic alive all the time. It is not a matter of constituting a separate minor/minority literature. This, essentially, is the lesson Glissant also draws from Deleuze and Guattari, and which he applies to his own, and his Martiniquean and by extension Caribbean postcolonial condition in *Le Discours antillais*. This is the lesson that is lost to the American audience of *Caribbean Discourse* (1989) with its rewriting of postcolonialism as multiculturalism.

❖

Putting back into Glissant's *Caribbean Discourse* the Deleuze and Guattari part that Dash took out not only restores this specific text to its specific context, there to do its 'cultural work'; it might also turn it into a useful example with which to approach some of the issues dogging 'American' literature, whether 'Old' style or 'New' style. Specifically, it would free individual works or authors from the necessity of being read as either 'major' or 'minor', expressive of either the traditional and 'classical' unitary 'American' sensibility or the fractal community sensibility of multicultural America. In other words, it would open up the possibility of reading specific major authors as both/and, or, precisely, as 'becoming-minor'. An example in case might be William Faulkner. Of course, Glissant himself discusses Faulkner at some length in *Le Discours antillais*, and the immediately relevant passages are duly included in *Caribbean Discourse*. The excision of the specific Deleuzian/Guattarian theoretical framework in the English-language edition, however, robs the discussion of its cutting edge as *exemplum* from which to tackle the wider context of 'American' literature.

Faulkner has been seen as a spokesman for a national American identity because of his use of certain modes, such as romance (Chase 1957) or historical romance (Dekker 1987), or certain themes, such as male bonding (Fiedler 1960). He has been read as representative of a regional and sectarian Southern identity (Taylor 1983), again because of certain modes, particularly his use of the Gothic, and themes, particularly those touching upon the history of the South, the tense relationship between the South and the North of the United States, and race relations. Faulkner's fiction has also been looked at from an African-American (Davis 1983) and Native-American (Dabney 1974) angle. Combining existing interpretations rather than casting them as mutually exclusive already enables us to 'create' Faulkner as 'becoming-minor' in the sense of not locating him or his work as 'scripting' one or other collective/individual 'identity' (Appiah 1992) exclusively, but as keeping the tensions prevalent in 'America' as social, political, economic and cultural arena alive all the time. Suffice it to think of Dilsey's part in *The Sound and the Fury* as an instance of what Deleuze and Guattari (1986:26–7) call 'mak[ing] use of the polylingualism of one's own language, ... mak[ing] a minor or intensive use of it, ... oppos[ing] the oppressed quality of this language to its oppressive quality, ... find[ing] points of nonculture or underdevelopment, linguistic Third World zones by which a language can escape', to see Faulkner in the act of 'becoming-minor'.

I would want to argue, though, that to read Faulkner in a specifically postcolonial framework such as Glissant's brings out the further 'revolutionary' (in the terms of Deleuze and Guattari) potential of Faulkner's work. In part, what I propose is already being done in some recent re-interpretations of *Absalom, Absalom!* from a transnational, and specifically a pan-American point of view. Such is the case with Ramón Saldívar's 'Faulkner, Paredes, and the Colonial and Postcolonial Subject' (1995), and Hortense Spillers' 'Who Cuts the Border: Some Readings on "America"' in her collection *Comparative American Identities: Race, Sex, and Nationality in the Modern Text* (1993). In Carolyn Porter's words from a recent article in *American Literary History* in which she discusses a number of innovative approaches to 'American' literature, in Spillers' reading *Absalom, Absalom!* 'is not limited to the history of 'the South' or even to that of the USA but instead must now be grasped in the larger context of the Atlantic system from which these histories were themselves generated' (1994:513). In other words, *Absalom, Absalom!* can now be read within the same parameters as Glissant's own work as theorized in *Le discours antillais*.

Instead of seeing *Absalom, Absalom!* as solely tributary to a 'native' American literary tradition, and an American national history, one can now see it as also relating to the wider tradition of European colonial literature, with its specific genres (such as the novel of adventure and the 'plantation novel'), modes (such as the exotic), and themes (such as the fear/temptation of 'going native'). And one can see Faulkner 'becoming-minor' in inverting, true to postcolonial usage, colonial literature's categories. Instead of reading Sutpen's

Caribbean exploits prior to his removal to Northern Mississippi as a colourful interlude, and the time he spends in New Orleans as a topical reminder of Faulkner's own sojourn in that city, we now can read these episodes as references to formative periods in the history of the Americas. Specifically, we can read them as windows on alternative forms of civic organization, not marked by the essentialism of 'American' identity formations. This alternative is literally embodied in Charles Bon, who is usually seen as a minor character in *Absalom, Absalom!*, but who now comes to occupy a pivotal role in the novel. Perhaps we may even speculate that Faulkner himself was articulating a certain preference by baptizing this character, and his lineage, 'Good'. The sad fate of Bon's ultimate descendant, then, as well as the fact that the latter's name modulates into 'Bond', with everything this implies in terms of racial and social relationships, indicates what opportunities have been lost in building 'America'.

Absalom, Absalom! thus involves not, or not solely, a rewriting of the South as an American drama of dissent and reconciliation, but rather the tragedy of how older American formations, involving primarily Romance languages and Latinate cultures of creolization, are being displaced by an Anglo-Saxon culture of racial essentialism. Mississippi becomes a border region not just of the United States but also of what Jonathan Daniels once called 'the Caribbean Republic of Louisiana' (1938:231), and this not only in a geographical but also in a cultural sense. This is where the battle between two mutually incompatible models of social organization is being fought out: one thriving on creolization and hybridity, the other fixated on racial purity and racial discrimination. Sutpen himself is mauled by the clash between these two systems, and *not* so much by the clash between North and South as such. In fact, *both* North and South of the States, whether United or Confederate, are now seen as partaking of the same essentialist culture of racial purity. Faulkner's celebrated use of language, especially in *The Sound and the Fury* and *Absalom, Absalom!*, is not uniquely 'Southern' Gothic, springing from a native English-language tradition, but rather becomes or also becomes an instance of the baroque, which Cuban author Alejo Carpentier saw as typically Caribbean and Latin American. Joe Christmas, in *Light in August*, rather than an example of the dangers of miscegenation, is an illustration of the victimization inherent in American racial and religious (primarily Protestant) essentialism.

In all these matters, Faulkner could be usefully contrasted with Hemingway, who can be read as 'essentialist' in language, race, and identity, and who can thus be rightly construed as typical 'American' in Pease's 'Old Americanist' vein. The topicality of this attitude in the interbellum period undoubtedly goes a long way toward explaining the difference in popularity Faulkner and Hemingway then enjoyed. At the same time, the creole and baroque aspects of his work may have smoothed the way for Faulkner's becoming the example he undoubtedly has been to many major Latin American and Caribbean postwar writers such as Carlos Fuentes, Gabriel García Márquez, and Mario Vargas

Llosa. In other words, whereas Hemingway's work feeds into a dominant ideology of American exceptionalism, Faulkner suggests the possibility of alternative identities akin to those of the continent's other inhabitants, and in fact transcending the geographical borders of the nation state. As such, Faulkner could be seen as functioning not just in an American (that is a United States) continuum, but in a continuum comprising other modernist or postmodern Caribbean authors such as the Cuban Alejo Carpentier, most specifically with *El siglo de las luces* (1962, *Explosion in a Cathedral* [1963]), the Puerto Rican Luis Rafael Sánchez, with *La Guaracha del Macho Camacho* (1976, *Macho Camacho's Beat* [1980]), and the Dutch-Antillean Frank Martinus Arion, with *Afscheid van de koningin* (1975, Farewell to the Queen). By then, we have moved from 'cultural misunderstanding' to 'cultural dialogue'.

Leiden University

Notes

This essay is a shorter version of an essay originally titled 'American Identities and Postcolonial Theories' in Rüdiger Ahrens and Laurenz Volkmann (eds) 1996 *Why Literature Matters. Theories and Functions of Literature*. Winter, Heidelberg: pp. 181–93

1 An exception immediately would have to be made for Louis A. Renza's *'A White Heron' and the Question of Minor Literature* (1984).

Works Cited

Adam, Iand and Helen Tiffin (eds) 1991 *Past the Last Post: Theorizing Post-Colonialism and Post-Modernism*. Harvester/Wheatsheaf, London.

Bongie, Chris (forthcoming) '(un)Ending Colonialism: Postcolonial Identities and Postmodern Ambivalence in Edouard Glissant's *Mahagony*' in Theo D'haen (ed.) *(Un)Writing Empire*.

Dabney, Lewis M. 1974 *The Indians of Yoknapatawpha: A Study in Literature and History*. Louisiana State University Press.

Daniels, Jonathan 1938 *A Southerner Discovers the South*. Macmillan, New York.

Davis, Thadious M. 1983 *Faulkner's Negro: Art and the Southern Context*. Louisiana State University Press.

Deleuze, Gilles and Félix Guattari, 1975 *Kafka: Pour une littérature mineure*. Minuit, Paris. (Tr. Dana Polan 1986 *Kafka: Toward a Minor Literature*. University of Minnesota Press.)

Fiedler, Leslie A. 1967 [1960] *Love and Death in the American Novel*. Jonathan Cape, London.

Gilroy, Paul 1993 *The Black Atlantic: Modernity and Double Consciousness*. Harvard University Press.

Glissant, Edouard 1981 *Le Discours antillais*. Seuil, Paris. (Tr. J. Michael Dash 1989 *Caribbean Discourse*. CARAF Books, University Press of Virginia.)

JanMohamed, Abdul R. and David Lloyd (eds) 1990 *The Nature and Context of Minority Discourse*. Oxford University Press.

Pease, Donald 1994a *Revisionary Interventions into the Americanist Canon*. Duke University Press.

—— 1994b *National Identities and Post-Americanist Narratives*. Duke University Press.

Porter, Carolyn. 1994 'What We Know That We Don't Know: Remapping American Literary Studies' in *American Literary History* 6:3: pp. 467–526.

Renza, Louis A. 1984 *'A White Heron' and the Question of Minor Literature.* The University of Wisconsin Press.

Said, Edward W. 1983 'Traveling Theory' in *The World, the Text, and the Critic.* Harvard University Press.

—— 1993 *Culture and Imperialism.* Chatto and Windus, London.

Saldívar, Ramón 1995 'Looking for a Master Plan: Faulkner, Paredes, and the Colonial and Postcolonial Subject' in Philip Weinstein (ed.) *The Cambridge Companion to William Faulkner.* Cambridge University Press: pp. 96–120.

Sangari, Kumkum 1990 'The Politics of the Possible' in Abdul R. JanMohamed and David Lloyd (eds): pp. 216–45.

Slemon, Stephen 1991 'Modernism's Last Post' in Iand Adam and Helen Tiffin (eds): pp.1–11.

Spillers, Hortense 1993 'Who Cuts the Border: Some Readings on "America"' in Hortense Spillers (ed.) *Comparative American Identities: Race, Sex, and Nationality in the Modern Text.* Routledge, New York. pp. 1–25.

Taylor, Walter 1983 *Faulkner's Search for a South.* University of Illinois Press.

Tiffin, Helen 1991 'Introduction' in Iand Adam and Helen Tiffin (eds): pp. vii–xvi.

MENG HUA

Quelques Réflexions sur la Temporalité du Stéréotype

Vers cette fin du vingtième siècle, lorsqu'on réfléchit sur le problème de la communication entre les différentes cultures — 'dialogue' ou 'malentendu' — on ne peut pas ne pas prêter attention à une forme particulière de l'image de l'Autre: le stéréotype. 'C'est le prêt-à-porter de l'esprit' (Amossy 1991:9) qui est en quelque sorte synonyme d'un 'préjugé', d'un 'cliché', d'une 'idée reçue'. C'est 'une sorte de résumé, l'abrégé emblématique d'une culture' (Pageaux 1994:63), le stéréotype s'inscrit par nature dans notre champ d'études comparatiste.

Dans son récent ouvrage, *La Littérature générale et comparée*, Daniel-Henri Pageaux a consacré plusieurs pages à la mise en lumière des traits spécifiques du stéréotype. Ce travail inspirateur a d'ailleurs éveillé ma curiosité par les lignes suivantes:

> ...porteur d'une définition de l'Autre, le stéréotype est l'énoncé d'un savoir minimum collectif qui se veut valable, à quelque moment historique que ce soit. Le stéréotype n'est pas polysémique: en revanche il est hautement polycontextuel, réemployable à chaque instant. (1994:63)

Avec ces mots-là est soulevé le problème du temps du stéréotype. Certes, cette spécificité de longue durée est valable pour tous les stéréotypes concernant les Européens, tels que 'Anglais buveur de thé', 'Espagnol orgueilleux', ou 'nez crochu' de Juif. Pourtant, j'ai souvent remarqué dans mes propres recherches que les stéréotypes chinois dans la littérature française ne sont pas aussi durables, aussi réemployables. Ils sont souvent au contraire liés étroitement à une certaine période, à un contexte historique donné.

Prenons le cas de 'l'empereur chinois éclairé' comme exemple. Si l'on remonte au début des échanges culturels entre la Chine et la France, on doit évoquer ces pères jésuites installés en Chine. Informateurs principaux de l'Empire de Chine, ils n'arrêtent pas d'exalter avec enthousiasme les Empereurs chinois: vertueux, tolérants, disciples de Confucius, amateurs d'art et de lettres, défenseurs des lois. De cette image, on a tiré une expression simplifiée: 'Empereur chinois éclairé'. Coulée par l'idée du 'roi éclairé', elle devient bientôt un schème qui revient fréquemment sous la plume des écrivains des Lumières. On le retrouve par exemple souvent chez Voltaire, dans l'*Essai sur les moeurs, le Dictionnaire philosophique, Le Siècle de Louis XIV, Lettres chinoises, indiennes et tartares* et *La Princesse de Babylonne*.[1] Il est réemployable également chez les physiocrates, en particulier dans les ouvrages de Quesnay et de Turgot.[2]

Il faudrait avouer qu'au dix-huitième siècle, non seulement la France, mais aussi toute l'Europe utilisent ce stéréotype qui, comme l'a dit M. Pageaux, 'délivre une forme minimale d'information pour une communication maximale ... tendant ... à la généralisation' (1994:63) de l'Empire du Ciel idéal, mis en service de la diffusion de l'esprit des Lumières. Cependant, 'l'empereur chinois éclairé' disparaîtra désormais de la littérature française. On en reparlera de moins en moins au dix-neuvième siècle, et presque nulle part au vingtième.

Il en est de même pour d'autres stéréotypes chinois dont 'le rire jaune'. Celui-ci n'existe pas du tout au dix-huitième siècle, devient au dix-neuvième une expression générale mélangée de mépris et de crainte chez le Français colonialiste. Mais lui aussi, passager, temporel, on ne le retrouve guère dans les écrits contemporains.[3]

La vie passagère des stéréotypes ci-dessus analysés révèle incontestablement une évolution de la connaissance de l'Autre (la Chine) chez le producteur du stéréotype (la France). Et si l'on les compare avec ceux que les Européens utilisent les uns envers les autres, durables et réemployables, le contraste est trop frappant pour qu'on le souligne. Ce phénomène me donne matière à une première réflexion: plus les nations sont proches, plus le va-et-vient est fréquent entre elles, et ce d'autant plus que leurs cultures remontent souvent à la même origine. Cela affaiblit la diversité dans l'altérité d'une part et permet d'autre part au producteur du stéréotype une accumulation de connaissances sur l'Autre à long terme. Ce va-et-vient de longue durée rectifie sans doute dans la psychologie du peuple l'image de l'Autre avant que le schème ne soit figé. Par contre, les pays éloignés, n'ayant pas un accès facile l'un à l'autre, produisent des stéréotypes plutôt selon une impression superficielle et souvent à la hâte afin de répondre au changement de contexte historique.

De tout cela, on pourrait peut-être en tirer une conclusion: à savoir que la durée d'un stéréotype est proportionnelle à celle de son processus de production. Toutefois, le malentendu dû à la distance géographique et culturelle participe activement au processus de production du stéréotype, en particulier autrefois où on manquait de moyens efficaces pour acquérir les informations de première main entre les deux pays à distance.

Cette thèse sera soutenue et complétée par la recherche en sens inverse. Dans la littérature chinoise, il semble que la disparition de stéréotypes occidentaux soit en premier lieu imputable à cette cause, mais celle-ci n'est certes pas la seule.

On sait que la Chine, longtemps isolée du monde extérieur, n'a eu connaissance de l'Occident qu'au début du seizième siècle avec la venue des premiers commerçants portugais. Avides au grain, désireux de femmes, ces derniers ont irrité les Chinois qui les ont fait passer pour 'kou' (bandit), dès lors il n'est pas étonnant que leur image reste essentiellement négative, sinon péjorative. Citons entre autres 'Hongmao fan' (Etranger aux poils rouges)[4] et 'Yang guizi' (diable étranger).

Faute de temps, je n'ai pas pu faire une étude détaillée pour chercher leur véritable origine. Mais les documents tombés entre mes mains m'inclinent à croire que ce genre de stéréotypes a pris la naissance peu de temps après l'arrivée en Chine des premiers Portugais.[5] Or le 'Yang guizi' exprimant une forte haine à l'égard des Occidentaux est devenu une image stéréotypée surtout à mi-dix-neuvième siècle,[6] car c'est à partir de la Guerre de l'Opium (1840–42) que ce terme est 'tenu avec assurance considérable par un grand nombre de personnes' (Amossy 1991:28). A noter pourtant qu'il ne se trouve alors que dans les chansons populaires, les proses et les reportages.

Voici quelques exemples. Dans une chanson populaire intitulée *Waiguo Yangren tan shisheng* (Dix soupirs poussés par les Etrangers), on répète dix fois le terme 'Yang guizi', par example:

> Les diables étrangers venus en Chine poussent le premier soupir: que les Chinois soient fins et habillés de façon correcte.... Les diables étrangers venus en Chine poussent le cinquième soupir: que les opiumanes de Canton soient trompés par l'Occident.... Les diables étrangers venus en Chine poussent le sixième soupir: que les autres Chinois éduqués de confucianisme percent à jour notre complot...[7]

Quant à la prose, la première trace que j'ai découverte se trouve dans *Zhongxi jishi, yuemin yishi ji* (Notes sur les relations sino-occidentales, Insurrection du peuple de Canton) de Xia Xie (1800–1875). Il rapporte dans ses notes ce qui s'est passé lors des premières résistances des Cantonnais contre les envahisseurs anglais en 1840. On y lit (sachant qu'un petit commerçant a été fouetté par le valet du mandarin local qui vient de négocier avec les Anglais): 'les Cantonais sont en rumeur, ils disent: "le gouvernement a balayé la route pour accueillir les diables étrangers, mais tondu la laine sur notre dos."'[8]

Dans le même recueil, le terme 'Yang guizi' apparaît au moins sept fois dans les 78 pages qu'occupent les proses.

Et puisque ce stéréotype est le produit d'une époque troublée, il s'est dissolu tout naturellement à l'heure actuelle avec le changement de contexte social et culturel, suivi d'un changement de mentalité du peuple. Ainsi, avons-nous vu la mentalité, la psychologie du peuple être un facteur non négligeable dans la production de stéréotype.

Si ces exemples nous montrent déjà la vie passagère des stéréotypes dans les échanges littéraires entre les pays qui s'écartent considérablement sur le plan géographique et culturel, j'aimerais maintenant attirer l'attention sur un autre fait intéressant: en Chine, tout comme ailleurs, les stéréotypes décrivant les traits physionomique, donc éthniques, sont vraiment stables, 'réemployables à chaque instant'.

A ce propos, il suffit de voir combien le stéréotype 'da bizi' (le grand nez) reste durable: les Chinois l'utilisent depuis toujours jusqu'à aujourd'hui pour désigner l'Occidental. Cependant on ne peut pas non plus dans ce cas-là parler d'une haute polycontextualité, car sa connotation n'est jamais homogène, elle a changé constamment avec le temps.

Dans un ouvrage de la dynastie des Ming, *Chou haitu bian* (Notes sur les résistances aux envahisseurs étrangers), on décrit les Occidentaux 'tous avec un grand nez et les yeux creux.... Ignorants des rites et de la courtoisie, on les leur a fait apprendre et pratiquer trois jours dans le temple Guanglin avant qu'ils aillent à l'audience (du gouverneur de la province du Canton).'[9] A la lecture de ces lignes, un mépris et une curiosité sautent aux yeux à travers le terme 'le grand nez'.

Mais depuis la Guerre de l'Opium, ce stéréotype connaît, cela va sans dire, le même sort que les autres concernant l'Occidental, auxquels les Chinois outragés, indignés, accordait sans aucune exception un nouveau signifié: la haine, manifestant ainsi violemment leur colère. Et ce 'grand nez' tellement abominable aux yeux des Chinois d'alors aura une connotation différente dans les années quatre-vingts du vingtième siècle avec l'ouverture du pays. Lorsqu'il est réemployé aujourd'hui, on l'entend par là un respect et même un désir.[10] Les nombreuses transformations qu'a connues 'le grand nez', en ce qui concerne sa connotation, confirment le point de vue d'un chercheur israélien, Mme Ruth Amossy qui déclare:

> ...le stéréotype n'existe pas en soi. Il n'apparaît qu'à l'observateur critique ou à l'usager qui reconnaît spontanément les modèles de sa collectivité.... Le stéréotype ... est toujours relatif. Il est tributaire de nos modèles culturels, eux-mêmes variables et changeants. (1991:21–4)[11]

De là découle notre seconde réflexion: le stéréotype ainsi fabriqué pourrait-il se dissoudre avec le dialogue des cultures? La réponse n'est peut-être pas évidente.

Le dialogue en faveur d'une compréhension réciproque, aide certes à franchir la distance culturelle; pourtant le stéréotype est une sorte de langage marqué fortement par la subjectivité du pays-producteur. Voyons dans l'histoire, la production et la disparition de ce genre de stéréotypes dépendaient, dans la plupart des cas, du changement de situation économique, militaire, politique ou de mentalité du peuple; il est donc plutôt un langage idéologique. Si bien que le dialogue exige l'égalité totale

entre les partenaires pour qu'il soit efficace.
Par là, on partage entièrement l'avis de M. Pageaux qui pense que les réflexions concernant le stéréotype:

> ...participent d'une certaine façon à une problématique qui est autant de littérature générale ... que de littérature comparée. Mais les études d'imagerie littéraire, ou mieux culturelle, ont le mérite de réorienter la réflexion du littéraire vers des problèmes d'ordre social et culturel qui ont leur place dans des études justement nommées de littérature générale. (1994:64)

Université de Pékin

Notes

1 A ce propos, cf. la thèse *Voltaire et la Chine* que j'ai soutenue en 1988 à l'Université de Paris-Sorbonne (Paris IV), p. 193–215.

2 On peut citer entre autres: Quenay, *Despotisme de la Chine*; Turgot, *Réflexions sur la formation et la distribution des richesses*.

3 Mme Muriel Détrie (Université de Tours) a traité ce thème dans les interventions qu'elle a données en 1991 à l'Université de Pékin dans le programme de séminaire sur 'L'Image de la Chine dans la littérature française'.

4 Très répandu à Taiwan et à Penghu, ce stéréotype désigne surtout l'Hollandais.

5 En ce qui concerne 'Yang guizi', il se peut que les Chinois en fassent usage au seizième siècle, puisque déjà, dans *Ming shi lu* (Chronique de la dynastie des Ming) et *Ming shi* (Histoire officielle de la dynastie des Ming, 1368–1644), les historiographes ont noté à maintes reprises que les commerçants portugais sont 'méchants, trompeurs', ayant 'dépouillé des hommes, violé des femmes et enlevé des enfants', ils sont considérés comme 'la source du malheur' (voir *Ershiwu shi: 25 Histoires dynastiques*, T.10, Shanghai, Shanghai guji chubanshe, 1986). Cette image de bandit se transformera bientôt en diable: dans un ouvrage intitulé *Shuyu zhouzi lu* (Notes rédigées à partir des sources sur les pays étrangers particuliers, 1574) de Yan Congjian, on peut lire: 'Le pays étranger, le Portugal, n'a eu auparavant aucune relation avec la Chine, ... ils aiment manger les bébés...'; après cela, l'auteur a encore décrit avec précision la façon avec laquelle ces étrangers ont cruellement cuit les enfants: faire bouillir de l'eau dans une grosse casserole, cuire les enfants à la vapeur, enlever leur peau, etc. Ces lignes effrayantes renvoient immédiatement le lecteur à la figure de 'guizi' (diable).

6 Cette idée-là, je la dois beaucoup à Mme Xia Xiaohong. Professeur à l'Université de Pékin et grande spécialiste de la littérature chinoise de l'époque 'wanqing-minchu' (fin de la dynastie des Qing et début de la République), Mme Xia m'a prêté des livres précieux sur la question et signalé l'importance de la Guerre de l'Opium dans cette recherche. Je la remercie donc ici vivement tout en soulignant qu'elle a récemment publié un livre sur *Wanqing wenren funu guan* (Concept sur les femmes dans le milieu des lettrés vers la fin de la dynastie des Qing), Beijing, Zuojia chubanshe, 1995, où elle traite du thème 'xiaojiao' (pieds bandés) qu'on peut considérer également comme un stéréotype de l'ancienne Chine dans la littérature occidentale.

7 Le texte de cette chanson conservé en fait dans la Bibliothèque Nationale de Paris (en version occidentale) a été copiée par un Chinois, Wang Chongmin, et publiée pour la première fois dans le *T'ong Poo*, 1899, pp. 220–1. Ici, je l'ai retraduite du chinois selon le texte publié dans *Yapian zhanzheng wenxue ji* (Anthologie des oeuvres littéraires sur la Guerre de l'opium), Editions de A Ying, Beijing, Guji Chubanshe, 1957, t. 1, p. 253–4.

8 In *Yapian zhanzheng wenxue ji*, op. cit., t. 2, p. 729.

9 In Zhou Jinlian, *Zhongpu waijiao shi* (Histoire des relations diplomatiques entre la Chine et le

Portugal), (rééd.) Beijing, Shangwu yinshuguan, 1991, p. 11–13. Ce livre attribué à Hu Zongxian a en fait été rédigé par un de ses conseillers, un certain Zheng Ruozhen.

10 Le stéréotype 'le grand nez' est parmi les synonymes de l'Occidental les plus utilisés en Chine contemporaine tant dans le langage courant que dans la littérature. Il mérite donc une étude sérieuse que je n'ai pas pu entreprendre jusqu'ici.

11 C'est grâce au Professeur Ziva Ben-Porat que j'ai eu connaissance de l'existence de cet ouvrage.

Oeuvres Citées

Amossy, Ruth 1991 *Les Idées reçues, Sémiologie du stéréotype*. Nathan, Paris.

Pageaux Daniel-Henri 1994 *La Littérature générale et comparée*. Armand Colin, Paris.

HOLGER KLEIN

Laughing at Difference: Maurois, Macdonnell, and Mikes on the English

National and ethnic stereotypes have a terrible destructive potential. Of that we have, sad to say, ample evidence. Depending on historical circumstances, however, they also often have an innocuous and funny side — and usually there is a grain of truth behind the unjustifiably vast generalizations. As George Mikes puts it:

> Stereotyped images die hard and there is always a good reason for their existence.... These pictures may be caricatures, but the trouble with caricatures is that they resemble the original much more than we (if we are the original) care to admit. (1973:7–8)

Mikes should know; he has gently and wittily lampooned many nations since his successful start with the famous *How To Be an Alien* in 1946. Moreover, although he is not usually taken into consideration by academic imagologists, Mikes has developed from a merely funny writer into a serious student of stereotypes, as becomes clear, for instance, from the long and substantial introduction to *The Land of the Rising Yen* (1970). As far as I know, Mikes has not written about China, but this second book on Japan[1] is quite a good introduction to what we have come, since Edward Said's influential study, to call (European) Orientalism.

Probably the most common cluster of stereotypic notions in the West about people in the Far East is their 'exoticness', their 'inscrutability' and the impossibility of ever understanding them. Thus, Karel Capek, the well-known Czech poet and writer, uses the example of China as the archetype in his exotic witty travel impressions of Britain, *Seltsames England: Erlebnisse einer Reise* (1926, tr. 1947). J. B. Priestley's hilarious essay on Americans (1926) uses it too. This essay is worth quoting for a more general reason: it shows an unusual consciousness of the relativity of perspectives. Just when one's indignation is about to burst out, he deftly performs a volte-face:

> The fact is that Americans never seem to me to be real people at all. They are as unreal as Chinamen, but as they look and talk like real people ... I therefore think of them as a kind of magnificent automata.... It is more than likely ... that all the Americans I have met these last few weeks, those hurrying, smiling, loquacious persons, have already arrived at the conclusion that I and my likes are equally unreal. (Tr. 1956:104*f*)

It is exactly such a volte-face which Mikes performs in his book nearly fifty years later. He talks of the Japanese habit of attaching extreme importance to matters of ceremonial etiquette, citing the eighteenth-century novel of *The Forty-Seven Ronin*, in which a courtier tricked another courtier into wearing the wrong sort of trousers for a great occasion:

> The warrior's humiliation is intolerable; and it demands a horrible vengeance. The story itself is the history of this vengeance, the story of forty-seven brave, avenging samurai. All forty-seven are killed before the terrible tale is concluded; villages are pillaged and burnt; countless people ambushed, tortured, massacred.... All because of the wrong pair of trousers. 'Quaint, quaint Orientals...' I thought.
> And at that moment a horrible thought occurred to me. They are not quaint. We are quaint. Quaint, quaint occidentals.
> I thought of a Japanese humorist (in itself a quaint occidental idea) flying westwards — or perhaps eastwards — to his own Far East, New York, and musing thus:
> 'I quite like occidentals and their quaintness certainly adds to their charm. I specially like those lovely old Roman letters they insist on using, flashing with racy agility on the neons signs of Times Square and Picadilly. It's rather exotic and gives one the strongly pleasant feeling of being abroad. And their manners... their strange ceremonies.... Of course, some of these formalities were not so innocent and meaningless. At least 47,000 people died in absolutely pointless duels. They have a celebrated literary work — *Cyrano de Bergerac* it's called — in which a knight is killed because he made a remark about this chap Cyrano's nose. I shouldn't be surprised to hear that a few of them died because — say — someone gave them the advice to wear the wrong pair of trousers on some ceremonial occasion. How stupid can one get?... And those quaint occidental habits! ...they actually wash themselves in the bath — instead of before getting into it — and then sit in their own dirt, feeling proud of their cleanliness; also they have their soup at the beginning of a meal. They must be mad. (1970:19)

I suspect that, where cultures that are very remote the one from the other, either in place or in time are involved, there must be points concerning which such mental agility, such elegant inversion of perspective as demonstrated by Priestley and Mikes will no longer do. Several ancient cultures, for example those of the Etruscans, the Incas, and the Druids, are said to have sacrificed human beings in the context of their religious rites. And, closer to us in time, there were numerous witch-hunts and *auto-da-fés* in the late Middle Ages, the Renaissance and Baroque periods in Europe. Millions of people were gassed and burned in the extermination camps run by Nazi Germany during the Second World War. The difference is not, however, merely one of numbers, but one of basic attitude. To right-minded twentieth-century thinking, the Holocaust was criminal, and to condone it is in itself a crime. There is no room for compromise on these and related questions. And, fortunately, the vast majority in all countries are of this opinion. In the former periods I mentioned it was the mass of right-minded people who thought human sacrifices or the burning of witches and heretics quite an ordinary, indeed a salutary and necessary, measure. One runs up against an impasse here, relativity has its limits. All one can do is to leave well alone. The gap is too wide to be bridged. And, fortunately, there is no need for compromise — such things are historic facts but do not impinge on our lives, whereas what happened in the recent past and what happens very near vitally concern us.

The aspects on which Mikes concentrates in the case of Japan, and the differences provoking comment, unease, criticism and friction among closely related cultures rarely or never concern such basic notions of humanity. However grave the political context in which hostile national stereotypes are aired, and however intense the economic and other power- and greed-related motivations using them to accentuate difference, the various supposed national peculiarities are, in the case of Britain and her Continental neighbours, not in themselves of such a grave nature. Around 1900 we are looking at a broad and important re-alignment. The traditional enmity between France and Britain is receding, not so much in the wake of such dispassionate analyses given in the famous travel book by Hippolyte Taine (1871) than as a result of practical political considerations, which lead to the entente cordiale, heightened during the War of 1914–18 by the sense of common effort and sacrifice — and sanctified, for instance, in Ford Maddox Ford's *Between St. Denis and St. George* (1915). Even earlier on there were flanking movements of individuals making conscious attempts at dismantling misunderstandings and building up mutual appreciation, for which the lady writing under the name of Pierre de Coulevain (1906) may serve as an exponent.[2] Marius-François Guyard (1954) has shown, however, that reserve towards, and even aversion against, the neighbours across the Channel persisted with some novelists; in literature at any rate, no unified shift of reactions to the English can be observed.

Looking in another direction, one may say that the traditional feeling of racial relatedness and of past alliances between German states and Britain began to crumble from around 1900 onwards, indeed to be largely effaced (certainly on the English side) under the impact of industrial, trade and power rivalry which notably the historian Paul Kennedy has analysed in a masterful study. Others — for example Heinz-Joachim Müllenbrock (1967) and Peter Firchow (1986) — have looked at the cultural and specifically the literary manifestations of the process. In Germany, what Goethe had termed Anglomania[3] admittedly was by and large a thing of the past already by the mid-nineteenth century, as, for instance, readings in Theodor Fontane (1944) make clear. Yet there is a great distance separating reports like that in J. J. Weber's *Guide* (1851) for people intending to travel to London[4] or the valiantly impartial account by Carl Peters (1904) and even Karl Bleibtreu's harshly juxtaposing survey (1909)[5] from the kind of acrimonious and patently propagandistic contributions on the image of England — a term widely used to represent the whole of Britain at the time — that appeared during the Great War, and again during the Second World War.[6] An attempt to put the record straight, and an audacious attempt to eschew stereotypes (*'England wie es wirklich ist'* — England as she really is), was presented, many years after 1945, by Karl H. Albers.[7]

Much to my regret, I have not found a deliberately funny book written by a German about England. Yet the general context I have attempted to sketch before turning to my three main subjects is still useful, I submit, because the surprising thing that emerges, when one looks at images of England from the mid-nineteenth to the mid-twentieth century, is their sameness. There may be differences of emphases — and there certainly are differences in tone and connotations as well as implications. Nevertheless, most traits of England and the English, as seen from various continental perspectives and under very diverse circumstances, have remained remarkably constant and alike during this period, never mind the changes which have undoubtedly taken place in reality, even during the space of my own acquaintance with England during the last forty years.

❖

My examples of books chosen for a closer look begin with the first volume of André Maurois' Bramble trilogy, *Le Silence du Colonel Bramble*, which was indeed his very first novel and was a huge success both in French and when it appeared in English translation (1919).[8] It was soon followed by *Le Général Bramble* and, in 1922, by *Les Discours du Docteur O'Grady*. Such sequels have obvious advantages, also found in series of, for example, detective novels like the ones centred on Miss Marple, Hercule Poirot, Lord Peter Whimsey, Nero Wolfe and many others. The cast is familiar, one delights in meeting them again, the circumstances differ — an ideal balance between the already known and the new. However, actual sequels — as opposed to series novels — tend to be weaker than the first book. And from our present point of view, *The Silence of Colonel Bramble* is certainly the most interesting. *The Silence* shows the British (that is, a selection of representatives from all parts of the United Kingdom at the time) overseas, in France during the First World War — nearly three years of it. Although events in the book include the Battle of the

Somme and climax in the death of the padre, the War itself is not at the centre of it. Its main concern is a gallery of typical British officers serving in a regiment of the Highland Brigade: the quiet, fair-minded Colonel Bramble himself, who is Scottish, as is the hot-headed (and pig-headed) though generous Padre MacIvor, while Major Parker, second son of a peer, is English, and the regiment's Medical Officer is Irish — Doctor O'Grady, an extremely well-read atheist and cynic. Captain Warburton, one of the (more peripheral) young subalterns, a real firebrand, is Welsh. And, in a wider circle still more on the periphery, there are numerous further representatives. All these people reveal their characteristics through action and above all through exceedingly funny dialogue, with relatively little comment from the third-person, clearly omniscient narrator, who principally focuses on the thoughts and reactions of a Frenchman, Aurelle (alter ego of Maurois), who is attached to the unit as interpreter and liaison officer.

The most interesting thing here is that the spirit of admiration that Aurelle feels for his British fellow-officers softens the quite substantial criticism that emerges. Here, as in our own private lives, the person of the speaker and our general relations to her or him matter most, and what is actually said is of less importance; we bear even with strongly adverse observations if we like the person who makes them. In a number of the German books on England, for instance, the love of sport, while being mostly praised, is coupled with the assertion of correspondingly less time for mental activities and, hence, their underdevelopment. This is proudly confirmed by Major Parker, the upper-class Englishman, when he argues:

> 'The greatest service which sport has rendered us is that it has saved us from intellectual culture. Luckily one hasn't time for everything, and golf and tennis cut out reading. We are stupid...'
> 'Nonsense, major!' said Aurelle.
> 'We are stupid', emphatically repeated Major Parker, who hated being contradicted, 'and it is a great asset. When we are in danger we don't notice it, because we don't reflect; so we keep cool and come out of it nearly always with honour.'
> 'Always', amended Colonel Bramble with his Scotch curtness. (1918:7–8)

Earlier on Parker had asked Aurelle whether he does not think that in France, 'intelligence is over-estimated' and added, 'It is certainly more useful to know how to box than how to write. [...] We don't go to school to learn, but to be soaked in the prejudices of our class, without which we should be useless and unhappy' (5).

Parker, of course, furnishes an example of ostensible self-deprecation, a frequent trait we shall also meet with in George Mikes. A little later Aurelle reflects on the question and says:

> ...it is a very foolish error to imagine that they are less intelligent than ourselves, in spite of the delight my friend Major Parker pretends to take in affirming the

contrary. The truth is that their intelligence follows a different method from ours. Far removed from our standard of rationalism and the pedantic sentiment of the Germans, they delight in a vigorous common sense and all absence of system. (33-4)

And this is confirmed when he calls the 'aversion to logic a deeply rooted part of the national character' (59).

The reproach against unshakeable pride, the implicit or explicit belief that England and the English, or indeed Britain and the British, and their ways are tops, recurs regularly.

In *The Silence*, this aspect does not come to the fore very much — certainly less than in Mikes, as we shall see. It is very palpable, however, in the way the British officers try to change Aurelle's way of life. He is left alone by his neighbour, a major in the Engineers, at a dinner when he admits that he is not interested in sports. His reaction after much talk about hunting is wonderfully oblique: 'at last he realized that this world is a great park laid out by a gardener god for the gentlemen of the United Kingdoms' (54). Later he is peremptorily informed, 'you must hunt after the War, messiou' (114). Once Aurelle is told, with approval, that he is becoming quite anglicized; and, Major Parker muses, 'if you could only manage to eat tomatoes and underdone cutlets for breakfast you would be perfect' (44). Aurelle, however, modestly prefers to 'remain French'.

O'Grady, next to Parker the most talkative of the group (whereas Bramble really excels in remaining silent, a quality many have noted in the English), tells Aurelle about the Englishmen's (broadly including Scotsmen like Bramble and the padre here) stoicism and contempt of sentimentality. However, nothing emerges more forcefully than the diversity of characters in this group of British soldiers. And most of the comic effects result from their misunderstandings and the juxtaposition of opposed temperaments. Bramble is silent, Parker and O'Grady talkative, the padre egotistical, Bramble always acutely aware of the feelings of others, Gibbon cautious, Warburton raring for battle — in a word, the book demonstrates the futility of any attempt to characterize a vast collective such as a nation. These people are pronounced individuals, bordering on the eccentric, and keen to tease each other as well as Aurelle. This illustrates one statement frequently found in works about the English (*viz*. the British): the contradictoriness of the national characters as these works conceive it. One might equally well say that a national character as such does not exist and never has existed but is, as Manfred Fischer, basing himself on a long line of previous critics, eloquently argues (1981:18-19), nothing more and nothing less than an ideological as well as a literary construct.

The shared qualities of these British soldiers are hardly talked about: a fighting spirit, sense of duty, fortitude, independence, love of liberty — precisely those traits that have often been praised by foreigners in the past. They emerge without comment from action — never more so than Bramble under shellfire in Ypres talking about Dr Johnson. And just to right the picture, there is Tarkington, who does not show these traits in any appreciable measure. In general, despite the constant needling in all directions, an understanding, a vast sympathy and admiration for the neighbours across the Channel emerge from these pages — the very things de Coulevain wanted to promote in 1906 and which also illuminate the two other novels of the trilogy as well as, for instance, *Le Côté de Chelsea,* Maurois' own book of travel to Britain written much later (1932). Other nationalities fare badly in comparison to the English (which here include Scots and Welsh): the Germans, not surprisingly, in some few remarks on the side, and the Irish with their clamours for autonomy; and it is Doctor O'Grady, a Catholic but clearly very Anglo-Irish and Unionist, who is most sarcastic at their expense.

Among the many features of this book that could furnish further elements of imagologic value there is one which even a necessarily cursory account may not pass over: Maurois skilfully thematizes the very pursuit of national characteristics itself by having Aurelle read a book he chanced to pick up at Poperinghe — 'a description of England and Scotland by the Frenchman, Etienne Perlin, Paris, 1558' (38). This volume actually exists, and the hilarious use made of it in the novel represents an early instance of what one might call a meta-imagological strain. A comparison between Maurois' four books on the subject and the Major Thompson books by Pierre Daninos, written around thirty years later, would be fascinating and hilariously demonstrate once again, in the main, the constancy of stereotypic notions. Here, however, we must turn our attention elsewhere.[9]

As we have seen, *The Silence* encompasses the British as a whole, while distinguishing at times (rather less often than might have been indicated) between her various nations. My second example, A. G. Macdonnell's *England, Their England* (1933) is based on the differences among the nations living on the British Isles. The title obviously alludes to the famous poem by Henley.[10] And the thematization of imagology, incidental in *The Silence*, is the very foundation as well as the basso continuo of A. G. Macdonnell's *England, Their England.* The Great War, always at the background of the novel by Maurois, here forms a prelude only. Just before Donald Cameron, a gunnery lieutenant hailing from Buchan in Aberdeenshire, is nearly killed by a shell at Passchendaele, invaliding him out of the War, he had discussed, with another foreigner, the Welsh gunnery lieutenant Evan Davies, a publisher in civilian life, the 'general characteristics of the [English] nation' (Macdonnell 1933:7), whom Davies finds 'extraordinarily difficult to understand' — and so does Donald Cameron. They toss about instances of the Englishmen's incomprehensible behaviour, then Donald comes up with the idea of writing 'a book about them one day' (11). When chance throws them together again after the war, Davies does in fact commission this volume, and all of Donald's adventures provide material for it. The writing of the book becomes in its turn one of the themes. Both feel themselves to be foreigners in England — and this is a general view.

Whereas the Swiss are a nation using four different languages, and present-day Indians form a nation of very many languages — if I remember rightly, twenty-two of them (including English) having each a national literature prize awarded annually by the Sahitya Academy in New Delhi, Britain around 1930 was, and remains to this day, made up of several nations sharing, to all intents and purposes, one language: English. There is some Gaelic spoken in remote parts of Scotland, and a strong Welsh-speaking minority exists (which has enormously increased over the last three decades), and a few people speak Irish in Northern Ireland (not very many more, actually, speak it habitually in the Irish Republic), but English is the major medium in Britain. Donald Cameron has, therefore, an access much more direct to the thinking and the ways of his neighbours south of the border than another foreigner could have.

Again, as in Maurois, the basic tenor is one of sympathy. Particularly in the later chapters the satire recedes. In the last chapter we have the apotheosis of Winchester (Macdonnell's old school). Earlier there is the celebration of the rural communities as represented by the Fielding family and the humble villagers around them in Buckinghamshire (in contrast to farming and life in Scotland). Indeed, earlier on, one already came across a statement about the countryside: 'Donald was enchanted at his first sight of rural England. And rural England is the real England, unspoilt by factories and financiers and tourists and hustle' (84). This closely echoes a key sentence in H. G. Wells's *Mr. Britling Sees it Through* (1916). Taking into consideration demographic distribution and other social, economic and political factors, what sounded surprising in 1916 must have sounded even more so in 1933 — but there is a grain of truth in it. The sentiment, well-known from the past, is still being shared by many English people today. It is not stereotypical, but a real element in the feelings of a fairly large part of the population: further one cannot and need not go.

The party at the Hôtel Joséphine in the penultimate chapter unites, for the last time, all the characters Donald has come across and continues the earlier satirical vein, yet the behaviour of people during the fire towards the end, with the retired major-general quickly taking charge and everyone following and efficiently obeying his orders, is admirable in a way (obliquely recalling the behaviour of the vast majority in the Titanic disaster of 1912), though none the less grotesque for all that.

Early on, the satire ranges freely and bites deep. Highlights include the weekend at Ormerode Towers which is fully as funnily awful as the famous weekend in Saki's 'Tobermory', though of course without the cat; or Wodehouse's 'The Fiery Wooing of Mordred', though without the fire, but heightened into sublime absurdity by the machinations of Hougins alias Huggins, the fantastic person who is not to be outdone in running England down. Also there is the hilarious cricket match of Hodge's firm against a village in Surrey — probably the best-known cricket match in English literature apart from the one in L. P. Hartley's novel, *The Go-Between* (1953). Donald's spell in Geneva as private secretary to the British delegate at a session of the League of Nations provides the occasion for attacks on Britain's muddled stance of having no policy. This is seemingly balanced at a first glance, but the sting is not long in coming:

> For the English, whatever may be said against their home politics, or their climate, or their cooking, or their love-making, or their art, or their sport, have proved themselves over and over again throughout the centuries masters of international diplomacy and foreign affairs. A glance at the history of the world shows how the enemies of England have always collapsed unexpectedly, and mysteriously, whether owing to the sudden uprising of a southerly gale to drive invading galleons from Gravelines to the Pentland Firth, or owing to a trivial miscalculation which isolated the wing of an army in the obscure Danubian village of Blindheim, or owing to a Spanish ulcer, or to the sinking of a *Lusitania*... (123)

The futility of this whole international body — which, alas, evokes lamentable parallels today — is also attacked; and, incidentally, there is a wide panoply of humorously stereotyped national representatives along the lines of 'Chinese and Japanese and Siamese and Cochinese and Cingalese and Tonkinese and Annamese moved inscrutably hither and thither. Frenchmen chattered. Australians in big hats strode. Sinn Fein ex-gunmen, now Ministers of State, sat in cafés and told witty stories' (124–5).

Among Donald's many other experiences there is one that in its grim humour balances the perhaps too idyllic presentation of life in the English countryside. During his stay in Buckinghamshire Donald witnesses a fox-hunt and sees its inevitable end — the fox, having gone to ground, is dug out and killed and devoured by the terriers. Shortly afterwards, the Meet see a gypsy kicking his horse, and are scandalized, nay truly revolted, at this cruelty to animals one young red-coated gentleman even dismounts and starts a fight with the vile offender.

❖

Maurois and Macdonnell offer their image of Britain and England respectively in the form of fiction. Mikes, who arrived in the country from Hungary in 1938, has cast his impressions in the form of a fanciful manual with an admixture of autobiography, although the 'I' figuring on the page need not be taken literally to correspond with the author. More systematically than Capek's travel book (1947), *How To Be an Alien* (1946) operates throughout on Bleicher's main contrast scheme (1980) of 'familiar and regarded as normal'/'unfamiliar and regarded as curious to nefarious', in this case Continental versus English, but the dislike is more ostensible than real. The principal method of achieving comic effects is absurd exaggeration, an impression enhanced still further by

Nicholas Bentley's ingenious illustrations.

In the 'Preface to the 24th Impression' Mikes (as he was to do again with *Switzerland for Beginners*) pretends to be disappointed that his book caused no storm of indignation. While the Rumanian Radio, he asserts, broadcast it 'as an anti-British tract', the Foreign Office asked for his permission to have it translated into Polish for the guidance of the many Polish refugees. And, of course, the book has enjoyed not just an instantaneous, but a lasting impact of huge dimensions. The fun already starts with the original Preface, which uses a marriage proposal (in which a young lady asks Mikes whether he would marry her) to illustrate what we have already discussed as the impression of many foreigners that the English are arrogant. It ends with a set of statements and directions to the person from foreign parts:

> It was a shame and bad taste to be an alien, and it is no use pretending otherwise. There is no way out of it.... A foreigner cannot improve. Once a foreigner, always a foreigner.... He may become British; he can never become English.... How to be an alien? One should not be an alien at all. There are certain rules, however, which have to be followed if you want to make yourself as acceptable and civilized as you possibly can.
>
> Study these rules, and imitate the English. There can be only one result: if you don't succeed in imitating them you become ridiculous; if you do, you become even more ridiculous. (12)

Then follow the irreverently carried points, one by one, including the misery of Sundays (14). Mikes' famous one-liner, 'Continental people have sex life; the English have hot-water bottles' (29) can be matched, approximately, by some documentation assembled in Christopher Hibbert's volume of social history (1987).[11] And one is reminded of the prudish Christmas pecks given to some girls by the officers in Maurois' *Le Silence du Colonel Bramble*. However, this is a marvellous example of stereotyping. Documentation or no documentation, the notion of sexual abstinence as a national characteristic is, of course, a myth, as becomes clear from another page in Mikes. Talking about the art of understatement (introduced by two more classic one liners: 'Foreigners have souls; the English haven't' and 'The English have no soul; they have the understatement instead') he observes that if a boy 'wants to marry a girl, he says: "I say... would you?..." If he wants to make an indecent proposal: "I say... what about..."' (1973:24*f*).

On the face of it, the criticism in Mikes is far more incisive than in Macdonnell and Maurois; the absurdity of many facets of English life is brought sharply into focus. One wonders, if one took all this seriously, what made the man stay not just eight years but the rest of his life among those strange creatures, the English. The thing is, of course, that it should not be taken seriously, but with a ton of salt; the grains of truth remain. The general atmosphere created in Maurois conveys a sense of amicable co-existence, that in Macdonnell more or less a sense of symbiosis. In Mikes, the general effect created is one of alienation, it really looks as if for Central Europeans the indigenous population of the British Isles was at least as incomprehensible as those of the Far East, except that the alienation effect highlights things we have always known, risibly confirming all prejucides, giving profile to what we realise are stereotypical notions as opposed to what we know, are — roughly — the facts. That is the particular charm of this book.

In one of his sermons, John Donne coined the famous phrase 'No man is an island'. Frischeisen-Köhler, on the other hand, asserts: 'The British Isles are to the English a continent of their own' (1915:55). Landauer argues that the English took their culture with them wherever they went on the whole globe (1915:15). Capek, as is to be expected, is not just funnier than both, but miles better and more incisive when he remarks: 'Wherever an Englishman stops, a British Isle comes into being. Travelling Englishmen are migrating British Isles' (1947:174). And — within the limits to which I referred at the beginning of this paper — Capek's is the most sane and humane basic attitude, too: 'I am inclined to think all national peculiarities a constructive enrichment of this world' (168). There is no better phrase to finish with than this.[12]

University of Salzburg

Notes

1 His first (more trenchant and less philosophical) book on Japan was *East is East* Deutsch, London, 1958.

2 See especially pp. iv–vi, where the mutual disregard, distrust and contempt are vividly regretted, p. viii, where the general process of rapprochement is compared to the lowering of the Chinese Wall [sic!] and where the book itself is explicitly put into the service of this process; also p. 7, where the author, invited to spend some time in England and proposing to report about this stay, compares herself to a 'vieux diplomate' recalled to service.

3 Johann Wolfgang von Goethe, *Werke* (Hamburger Ausgabe), Vol. XIV, Naturwissenschaftliche Schriften, II, ed. Dorothea Kuhn (Hamburg: Wegner, 1960), pp. 193–4. Cf. also the study by John Alexander Kelly 1921 *England and the Englishman in German Literature of the Eighteenth Century*, Columbia University Press, repr. Ams Press, 1966. Kelly summarizes: '...eighteenth-century Germans in general had marked admiration for everything English.' (p. 144) — an admiration, he notes with great emphasis, that was not reciprocated. See also for example Franz K. Stanzel, 'National Character as Literary Stereotype: An Analysis of the Image of the German in English Literature before 1800', *London German Studies* 1 (1980), pp. 101–15, with selected references to earlier studies. A good deal of insight into the transition from love to aversion in Germany, together with remarkably balanced views on national stereotypes and a conciliatory attitude, is offered by Richard M. Meyer in his very brief but weighty article, 'Der Engländer in der deutschen Literatur', *Die Nation* 13 (1895/96), pp. 419–20, 433–5.

4 See the discussion and translated version of excerpts in Walter L. Arnstein, 'A German View of English Society: 1851' in *Victorian Studies*, 16 (1972/73), pp. 183–203. Of much larger scope than this brief section on manners and customs in what is, essentially, a Baedeker-type of book (the first Baedeker on England appeared in 1878) is the survey offered, with a high degree of balance and fairness by Bernhard Ellis in *Aus England: Aphoristische Skizzen über Land und Leute*, Hahn, Hannover, 1885.

5 See especially pp. 147–8 for Bleibtreu's bitter complaints of the negative stereotyping of

Germans to be found in contemporary English novels. To a large extent he is right, but there are numerous exceptions.

6 See for example Oskar Ullrich's ugly presentation, enhanced — if that is the word — by a number of nasty caricatures from the brush of H. E. Köhler, in *England und die fünf Erdteile*, Orbis, Prag, 1940.

7 Albers, who entered Britain as a Prisoner-of-War, stayed so long that he felt utterly at home there, speaking, thinking, acting and dreaming in English, as he says (p. 124) — though not perhaps to the extent of Mikes, who not only became a British subject, a wise move for any Hungarian of his generation, but really became as English as it is possible for any foreigner to become.

8 As opposed to *Le Silence du Colonel Bramble* (1918) and *Le Général Bramble* (1920), both of which were almost immediately published in English (tr. Thurfrida Wake, by John Lane at the Bodley Head Press, 1920) the last volume, *Les Discours du Docteur O'Grady* (1922, repr. 1927) does not appear to have been translated into English. There was another sequel, *Nouveaux discours du Docteur O'Grady* (1950), which I do not consider as a proper part of the sequence; it is an afterthought dating from quite a different era. In order to show the similarities more easily, I shall be using Wake's translated version of *Le Silence* here; as the originals of Aurelle's poems are appended, one loses little in this translation — indeed, nothing save the wonderful little anglicisms in the French. They are, however, not central to my purpose here.

9 I am grateful to Milan Dimic (Edmonton, Alberta) for reminding me of this in the discussion following my paper. See in particular Daninos, *Les Carnets du major W. Marmaduke Thompson*, Hachette, Paris 1954, and *Les Nouveaux Carnets du major W. Marmaduke Thompson*, Hachette, Paris, 1973. I have also seen the translation of the first-mentioned book as *Major W. Marmaduke Thompson Lives in France*, tr. Robin Farn, Cape, London, 1955, repr. Penguin, Harmondsworth, 1959. There is also *Un Certain Monsieur Blot*, Hachette, Paris, 1960, but that book I have not yet read. It, too, is available in English: *A Certain Monsieur Blot*, tr. R. Chancellor, Weidenfeld & Nicolson, London, 1961.

10 William Ernest Henley (1849–1903), 'England, my England'. This connection, though obvious once pointed out, had escaped me. I am grateful to Amiya Dev (Vidyasagar University, West Bengal) for drawing my attention to it in the course of the discussion.

11 Chapter 56, p. 633*ff.*, starting: '"Sexual indulgence before the age of twenty-five", a widely-read medical textbook of the 1830s advised, "not only retards the development of the genital organs, but of the whole body, impairs the strength, injures the constitution and shortens life."'

12 I wish to record my gratitude to my wife, Dr Dorothea Klein, to whom I owe a great many references used in this article.

Works Cited

Albers, Karl H. 1982 *England und englisch: England wie es wirklich ist. Land und Leute, Sprache und Sprichwörter, Eigenheiten und Gewohnheiten, Sitten und Gebräuche*. Bock & Herrchen, Bad Honnef.

Bleibtreu, Karl 1909 *Deutschland und England*, 2nd ed. Curtius, Berlin.

Capek, Karel 1947 (1926) *Seltsames England: Erlebnisse einer Reise*, tr. Vincy Schwarz, Heidrich, Cassirer; Wien.

Coulevain, Pierre de 1906 *L'Ile Inconnue*, Calman-Lévi, Paris.

Firchow, Peter 1986 *The Death of the German Cousin: Variations on a Literary Stereotype, 1890–1920*. Bucknell University Press, Lewisburg and Associated University Presses, London.

Fontane, Theodor 1944 (1899) *Der Stechlin* in *Ausgewählte Werke*, ed. Willy Brandl. Kohlhammer, Stuttgart: Cf. ch. XXIII.

Guyard, Marius-François 1954 *La Grande-Bretagne dans le roman français 1914–1940*. Didier, Paris.

Hibbert, Christopher 1987 *The English: A Social History, 1066–1945*. Grafton Books, London, Glasgow.

Kennedy, Paul 1980 *The Rise of the Anglo-German Antagonism 1860–1914*. Allen & Unwin, London.

Mikes, George 1973 (1970) *The Land of the Rising Yen*. Penguin, Harmondsworth.

Müllenbrock, Heinz-Joachim 1967 *Literatur und Zeitgeschichte in England zwischen dem Ende des 19. Jahrhunderts und dem Ausbruch des Ersten Weltkriegs*. Cram, De Gruyter, Hamburg.

Perlin, Etienne 1558 *Description des royaumes d'Angleterre et d'Ecosse*. Trepau, Paris.

Peters, Carl 1904 *England und die Engländer*. Schwetschke, Berlin.

Priestley J. B. 1956 (1926) 'American Notes' in *All About Ourselves and Other Essays*. Heinemann, London.

Sylvie André

La Littérature Exotique en France: Un Moment et une Forme du Dialogue des Cultures

Généralement on insiste beaucoup sur les déterminismes de la pensée et de la sensibilité que constituent la langue maternelle et la culture originelle. Sans doute ne tient-on pas assez compte qu'une langue, une culture, une littérature, sont des structures ouvertes, c'est à dire ayant la capacité d'accueillir ce qui jusqu'ici était inédit, indicible donc impensable, la capacité d'inventer de nouvelles façons de dire et de peindre qui ouvrent à la connaissance humaine de nouveaux domaines.

Si le plus souvent les changements de mentalité, de vision, s'effectuent insensiblement au niveau de la conscience collective, le grand devoir des écrivains est de proposer à la société dans laquelle ils vivent de nouvelles façons de structurer et de percevoir l'expérience vécue par l'intermédiaire d'un travail d'invention, par l'exercice sur le matériau linguistique d'une liberté créatrice. La littérature est 'La forme saisie dans son intention humaine et liée aux grandes crises de L'Histoire…, elle est donc essentiellement "la morale de la forme"', comme le dit excellemment Roland Barthes (1953:5).

❖

De manière plus évidente que tout autre forme littéraire, la fiction narrative exotique s'est trouvée confrontée à une exigence: exprimer dans des formes fixées et inadéquates l'irréductible nouveauté de civilisations qui avaient pensé l'homme et le monde de façon radicalement autre. Inventer une nouvelle manière, une nouvelle écriture, était la condition nécessaire d'expression authentique de la différence, ainsi que le signe non falsifiable que, d'une certaine façon, la vision du monde de l'écrivain et celle de la société pour laquelle il écrivait s'étaient modifiées pour prendre en compte cette même différence.

On insiste beaucoup sur l'échec de la littérature exotique, sur son incapacité à sortir du cercle étroit des mots et des idées convenus. Si l'on en croit les critiques littéraires, les voyageurs occidentaux ne ramènent des tropiques que ce qu'ils y ont apporté. Le mythe de Tahiti dans la littérature peut être une excellente démonstration de ce point de vue. Bougainville n'a-t-il pas projeté sur la société tahitienne qu'il découvrait les couleurs idylliques d'une société primitive, telles que pouvait les concevoir un homme cultivé du dix-huitième siècle? Diderot, sans connaître Tahiti, mais après avoir lu Bougainville et le Baron de La Hontan, a imaginé une société régie selon les lois de la Nature. Et l'on devine en filigrane, dans cette fable apparemment si attrayante, les dangereux excès auxquels peuvent conduire l'idée d'une morale uniquement déduite des réalités biologiques. La réalité tahitienne n'a que fort peu de place, avouons-le, dans cette thématique socio-philosophique. Faut-il en conclure que le discours exotique développe 'des problématiques qui ne concernent en fait que la société de l'observateur' (Mouralis 1975:102)? Ce serait croire à l'impossibilité désespérante de la rencontre.

Or, selon moi, la littérature exotique est l'exemple le plus abouti, à une époque donnée, mais aussi en général, de ce que peut être le dialogue fragile des cultures et non le monologue de l'une ou de l'autre. Pour expliciter mon point de vue, je souhaiterais la distinguer de formes voisines telles que la littérature de voyage, ou plus exactement d'escales ou de bref séjour d'une part, ou à l'inverse de ce que l'on pourrait appeler une littérature coloniale.

Entre les voyages de découverte donnant lieu à une littérature le plus souvent à finalité pédagogique (si elle choisit l'exploration rationnelle) ou fantastique (si elle privilégie l'expression subjective) et la colonisation qui a échoué selon moi à se donner une existence littéraire pour des raisons que je tenterai d'expliciter, la littérature exotique correspond à une situation historique ainsi qu'à un moment de la pensée occidentale.

Ainsi, ne qualifierais-je pas d'exotique le récit de voyage où, la plupart du temps, la vision demeure à la surface des choses mais surtout des êtres: récits où les relevés topographiques, les observations botaniques et géologiques tiennent une place majeure. La communication interculturelle se limite à une quête d'information et à des demandes d'explications par truchements interposés. L'information ainsi recueillie est souvent retranscrite dans sa littéralité, avec une suspension de jugement du narrateur clairement affirmée, mettant en évidence une absolue incompréhension. A l'autre bout de la 'Forme littéraire' qu'a suscitée l'impérialisme occidental on pourrait parler d'une littérature coloniale. J'emprunterai à Segalen sa définition du colon:

> Les colons ne sont rien moins que des exotes. Le premier surgit avec le désir du commerce indigène le plus commercial. Pour lui le divers n'existe qu'en tant qu'il

servira de moyen de gruger. Quant à l'Autre (fonctionnaire colonial), la notion même d'une administration centralisée, de lois bonnes à tous et qu'il doit appliquer lui fausse d'emblée tout jugement. (1986:52)

Il s'empresse d'ajouter, 'La littérature coloniale n'est pas notre fait'. Sa vision du colon correspond tout à fait à la description que donne Tzvetan Todorov des deux grandes idéologies de légitimation de la colonisation. La première, au nom du relativisme et du scientisme, prétend associer les populations colonisées à la grandeur nationale au niveau où elles le peuvent, c'est à dire essentiellement à un niveau de citoyenneté inférieur mais par une participation économique grâce à leur travail, leur consommation et leurs matières premières. La seconde, au nom de l'universalisme, manifeste une volonté assimilationniste. Dans le premier cas de figure, il s'agit de maintenir une rigoureuse séparation des cultures; dans le second de détruire la culture colonisée. Là encore, il n'est nullement question de communication interculturelle.

Par contre les écrivains 'exotes', aventuriers de l'âme autant qu'aventuriers dans l'espace, ont cru à la possibilité d'une communication interculturelle, aussi précaire, fugace et pleine de contresens soit-elle. En contact avec les populations autochtones, peu impliqués dans les rapports sociaux coloniaux, ils ont recherché le dialogue. Sans que l'on puisse, bien sûr, déterminer la priorité de la réalité socio-économique sur le mouvement des idées ou inversement, ce moment de l'histoire, en l'occurrence de l'essor de l'impérialisme occidental, correspond à un moment de la philosophie occidentale.

Il est certes banal de dire qu'il y a la philosophie avant Hégel et la philosophie après Hégel, dont je rappelle qu'il est mort en 1831. Avant Hégel on tente de trouver les critères éternels qui pourraient déterminer le champ du savoir de l'homme. Malgré la première entorse à l'essentialisme qu'a opérée Kant en séparant 'la chose en soi' de la 'chose en moi', on tente de décrire des catégories éternelles, la nature des choses. La perception du Moi est un bon exemple du fait que 'la nature des choses' est à cette époque une réalité intellectuelle structurant une vision collective du monde. Ainsi Loti, si farouchement décrié par Victor Segalen, promène-t-il sur la terre son moi mélancolique et fin de siècle. Il tente de sortir de lui-même par la 'sympathie', en sentant avec et comme l'Autre, mais il demeure infiniment persuadé que son moi est une donnée stable et définitive, aussi évidente que l'eau ou le feu. Il ne 'se mélange' aux sensations exotiques pour reprendre une expression de Segalen, que parce qu'il est intimement persuadé qu'il peut revenir à lui, comme on s'éveille d'un rêve. Il éprouve bien de temps en temps la tentation fugace de se perdre, mais c'est pour mieux savourer le plaisir de se retrouver, toujours le même. Pour lui, son 'moi' appartient à la nature des choses.

Pierre Loti est un pré-hégélien, au sens philosophique si ce n'est chronologique. Mais après Hegel la philosophie s'oriente dans une toute nouvelle direction. Au lieu de grands systèmes spéculatifs se met en place une 'philosophie de l'existence' ou une 'philosophie de l'action'. La vérité est désormais transitoire, contingente. Elle est façonnée par les 'forces objectives', que sont la famille, l'Etat, l'histoire. Aussi le moi n'est-il plus analysé de la même façon. Il se fait et se défait constamment en se définissant toujours par rapport au monde. Le processus dialectique lui enlève toute certitude et il est toujours à construire. Victor Segalen illustre assez bien cette vision post-hégélienne de la personne qui tente de se conquérir par rapport à ce qui n'est pas elle. Pourtant, de toute évidence, il flotte dans la vision des choses de Segalen des relents d'essentialisme car cet écrivain semble tout entier tendu vers la recherche du moment où se révèle l'identité du moi face à la radicale étrangeté de l'Autre. En 1908, ne définit-il pas la sensation du divers comme 'le choc d'une individualité forte contre une objectivité dont elle perçoit et déguste la distance' (38)? Il croit donc encore, d'une certaine façon, à la nature des choses, même si la vanité de cette quête lui apparaît bientôt, comme le démontre le récit de *René Leys*.

Le dialogue avec l'Autre, pour se définir soi-même, c'est peut-être là le rêve philosophique de l'exote, mais il est menacé par le sentiment envahissant de l'évanescence de la nature des choses. Les exotes désormais feront l'expérience de l'inexistence de frontières nettes dans l'échange: c'est toujours moi que je trouve lorsque je crois appréhender l'Autre. Je trouve de l'Autre en moi et du moi en l'Autre. La quête exotique d'un dialogue conçu comme la rencontre de deux identités opposées n'a plus de sens au niveau philosophique. Au même moment le triomphe de l'impérialisme occidental ôte à l'identité culturelle des peuples son évidence: tout le monde devient métis culturel ou pire, acculturé.

Moment du dialogue des cultures, la littérature exotique est pour moi, comme je l'ai déjà dit, une sorte d'équilibre momentané entre la littérature de voyage — où la différence entre moi et l'Autre est figée — et la littérature coloniale — où cette différence n'a plus suffisamment de consistance pour permettre le dialogue, soit que le colonial se sente fils de la terre au même titre que l'autochtone, soit qu'il soit partisan d'une assimiliation totale, persuadé de la supériorité de sa culture, obéissant ainsi à une réaction psychosociologique archaïque.

Cette situation historique confère à la littérature exotique des traits formels spécifiques, qui la différencient de la littérature de voyage ou de la littérature coloniale. L'analyse qu'a faite Edward Saïd dans le troisième chapitre de son livre désormais classique *Orientalism* (1978), peut servir de point de départ à la différenciation récit de voyage/littérature exotique. Il distingue deux structures mentales en particulier qui servent à appréhender la réalité asiatique, d'un côté ce qu'il appelle 'vision' et qu'il qualifie d'''essentialisme synchronique' (240), figeant les Orientaux dans une catégorie définitive et intemporelle, de l'Autre 'narrative story' qui, selon lui, réintroduit la perspective de la complexité mouvante dans l'espace et dans le temps de la réalité asiatique, de sa définition à partir de ses contacts par opposition, par similitude ou par complémentarité avec l'Autre, c'est à dire avec l'Occident. Il associe donc très nettement le procédé de narrativisation à une nouvelle conception d'un phénomène. A partir de là, je me suis posée la question de savoir ce qu'apportait la narrativisation, me faisant une dernière remarque: que seule la fiction narrative était qualifiée sans réticence d'exotique par le sens commun. Pour les autres formes, le vocable 'exotique' est en effet en concurrence avec d'autres que j'ai pour ma part préféré utiliser, tels que littérature de voyage. Donc, en ultime analyse, le passage du récit à la fiction narrative, en tant que procédé littéraire, pourrait être une dimension fondamentale de la définition du texte exotique, différent du roman colonial et des textes du vingtième siècle qui refusent cette qualification.

Il devient nécessaire d'introduire ici les définitions de la fiction narrative de A. J. Greimas. Ce sémioticien définit la structure élémentaire de la signification, bien connue sous le nom de carré sémiotique:

> ...le développement logique d'une catégorie sémique binaire, du type blanc vs noir, dont les termes sont, entre eux, dans une relation de contrariété, chacun étant en même temps susceptible de projeter un nouveau terme qui serait son contradictoire pouvant, à leur tour, contracter une relation de présupposition à l'égard du terme contraire opposé. (1970:160)

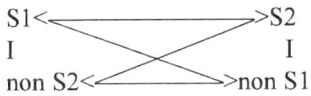

$$S1 \longleftrightarrow S2$$
$$| \quad \times \quad |$$
$$\text{non } S2 \longleftrightarrow \text{non } S1$$

A cette morphologie élémentaire de la signification, susceptible de décrire le sens de n'importe quel univers sémantique, s'ajoute dans la fiction narrative une syntaxe bien précise qui 'consiste en opérations effectuées sur les termes susceptibles d'être investis de valeurs de contenus; de ce fait, elle les transforme et les manipule, en les niant et en les affirmant, ou, ce qui revient au même, en les disjoignant et conjoignant' (166). Il est bien évident que cette syntaxe d'énoncés, de programmes narratifs et de séquences du même ordre n'est pas à situer au niveau de la manifestation discursive elle-même, mais au niveau des structures profondes de la signification.

Ces définitions m'amènent, quant à moi, à concevoir le récit de fiction comme l'expérimentation, plus ou moins consciente, grâce à une syntaxe normative, de la possible conjonction ou non de valeurs contraires ou contradictoires: la fiction exotique ou comment intégrer l'altérité à un univers axiologique qui lui préexiste et qu'elle met en situation de rupture ou d'incohérence. Il ne s'agit pas, bien sûr, d'une intégration purement intellectuelle ou rationnelle, mais bien plus d'une intériorisation, d'un investissement au niveau de structures mythiques, de visions du monde personnelle et/ou collective. La véritable découverte, c'est à dire la prise en compte de la différence dans la représentation du monde d'un individu et/ou d'une communauté, voilà quelle serait la fonction de la fiction narrative exotique.

Le récit de voyage, l'article de journal, l'essai, apportent, dans le meilleur des cas, la délicieuse et fugace émotion que procure la possibilité d'existence d'autres dimensions de la vie, la satisfaction, d'ordre esthétique ou intellectuel, d'une nouvelle connaissance du monde, rien qui ait une chance d'intégrer nos 'mythologies', au sens où Barthes entend le vocable. Si, parfois, cette connaissance superficielle, pittoresque, ou même rationnelle, constitue l'essentiel de la dimension exotique d'une fiction narrative, nous sommes ramenés à cet exotisme de pacotille que refuse si violemment Victor Segalen: 'il ne peut y être question de tropiques et de cocotiers, ni de colonies ou d'âmes nègres, ni de chameaux, ni de vaisseaux, ni de grandes houles ..., ni d'aucune des saugrenuités (sic) que le mot exotisme enferme' (1908:63).

Toujours selon Victor Segalen, le 'pouvoir de sentir le divers', seul garant de la véritable découverte, contient:

> ...deux phases, dont l'une est réductible: l'un des éléments divergents est nous. Dans l'Autre, nous constatons une différence entre deux parties de l'objet. Cette seconde doit se ramener à la première si l'on veut en faire une sensation d'exotisme: alors, le sujet épouse et se confond pour un temps avec l'une des parties de l'objet, et le Divers éclate entre lui et l'autre partie. (66)

Nous retrouvons les catégories binaires de Greimas et les conditions de leur conjonction. Tentons une définition de la fiction exotique dans ce sens: une fiction où la catégorie de l'Autre et du Même est investie de la valeur de contenu essentielle, sur laquelle s'effectuent, au niveau profond, toutes les opérations de syntaxe narrative du texte afin d'envisager les conjonctions ou les disjonctions possibles. Répétons encore que ce qui différencie la fiction est que le jeu des investissements axiologiques s'effectue au niveau des affects et non entièrement au niveau de la réflexion consciente, ou pour employer un langage sémiotique, au niveau des isotopies cachées et non à celui des isotopies évidentes.

Prenons par exemple les *Nouvelles asiatiques* d'A. de Gobineau. Le recueil contient six nouvelles, dans l'ordre: 'La Danseuse de Shamakha', 'L'Illustre magicien', 'L'Histoire de Gamber-Aly' 'La Guerre des Turcomans', 'Les Amants de Kandahar', 'La Vie de voyage'. Si nous appliquons notre lecture aux textes, nous pouvons établir un partage assez net entre deux types de nouvelles: celles où la découverte de l'Autre culturel est une isotopie omniprésente mais non investie de valeur au niveau des opérations syntaxiques; les autres, où cette isotopie, même peu évidente a priori, est à la base des opérations narratives.

Au premier type se rattachent incontestablement 'L'Illustre magicien' et les 'Amants de Kandahar'. Au second 'La Danseuse de Shamakha'. Dans cette catégorie, les parcours narratifs ont comme finalité, chez Gobineau et chez bien d'autres écrivains exotiques, la contestation d'un ordre posé au départ qui est l'irréductible incommunicabilité des cultures, par la recherche d'un dialogue.

Ces fictions miment les oppositions et s'interrogent sur les conditions d'une possible conjonction des contraires que sont l'identité et l'altérité.

Toutefois, dans la littérature exotique la conjonction est toujours sans lendemain, ou bien elle connaît un dénouement tragique. Dans la fiction exotique, l'écrivain tente d'intégrer la découverte d'une réalité autre à son propre univers de valeurs inconscientes, et comme telles fondamentales, en même temps que ces valeurs sont proposées à la communauté destinataire de l'ouvrage. Mais cette tentative butte invariablement sur la destructuration de la personnalité métisse ou sur la dysphorie irréductible des cultures.

❖

Par la littérature exotique, la fiction narrative occidentale dit sa tentative et son échec à faire dialoguer des cultures dans une forme préexistante et codifiée: la fiction romanesque. Pourtant, parfois, une forme s'invente et la différence exotique est à la portée de notre compréhension d'occidental. L'action sur la forme littéraire est action sur l'axiologie d'une société qui comprend et fait sienne la différence. Je citerai deux exemples probants à mes yeux: *Le Mariage de Loti* et *Les Immémoriaux* de Segalen. Ces deux récits romanesques à travers lesquels les Polynésiens eux-mêmes ont bien voulu se reconnaître brisent la forme traditionnelle du roman. Pierre Loti qualifie lui-même son oeuvre de 'Récit sauvage' et il ne fait pas seulement référence à sa thématique. Sauvage il l'est aussi parce qu'il mélange les notes ethnologiques, la fiction romanesque, les légendes tahitiennes, l'observation sociologique, les passages en langue polynésienne, le journal et le récit, réalisant en fin de compte une cohérence miraculeuse.

Les Immémoriaux pour leur part sont qualifiés, sans que l'on perçoive toujours la contradiction de 'roman ethnologique', un roman où l'épaisseur temporelle est traduite par la distance spatiale, où l'écriture se plie aux grandes lois de la culture orale, où les néologismes abondent, où la fiction s'appuie sur la science historique et ethnologique la plus précise. Ces deux oeuvres échappent à leurs auteurs pour devenir le miroir dans lequel chacune des deux cultures concernées accepte de reconnaître son reflet.

Mais très vite après Segalen la littérature exotique va s'anémier. La littérature coloniale tentera de s'imposer. Je l'appelle coloniale et non pas colonialiste car elle n'est pas au service d'une idéologie. Elle est simplement cette tentative des colons pour trouver leur place dans la culture occidentale selon la définition qu'en donne J. Cl. Marimotou (1988). Je ne suivrai pas la définition de Todorov qui distingue dans l'oeuvre de Loti les oeuvres exotiques et les oeuvres colonialistes. Je préfère les distinguer selon les critères que j'ai employés chez Gobineau quant à l'importance de l'enjeu Même/Autre pour la syntaxe profonde.

Au début du siècle Marius-Ary Leblond, colon réunionnais, se propose de définir, par réaction contre l'exotisme à la Loti, une nouvelle catégorie littéraire qui serait le roman colonial. Il publie d'ailleurs une *Anthologie coloniale, morceaux choisis d'écrivains français* (1943) pour laquelle il sollicite le concours de Victor Segalen qui ne donnera pas suite. Le destinataire du discours colonial est a priori le même que celui du discours exotique; il s'agit toujours d'un discours interne à la communauté nationale, puisque la première page de l'anthologie dont je viens de parler définit clairement son but en ces termes: 'Pour faire aimer nos colonies'. Toutefois si le colon, comme le montre l'adjectif possessif, se définit toujours comme appartenant à la communauté nationale, il veut pourtant y intégrer une réalité 'autre', qu'il connaît en elle-même et qui pour lui n'est plus exotique, mais quotidienne, intériorisée. Comme le démontre Jean-Claude Marimoutou, dans son article sur le roman réunionnais du début du siècle, ou comme le dit clairement l'exergue de Leblond, le colon se veut seul dépositaire d'une vérité méconnue et qu'il doit s'employer à faire reconnaître par la communauté d'origine: 'pour faire aimer', en réaction contre le texte exotique, qui présente souvent une vision superficielle et déformée du vécu exotique. La littérature coloniale se veut donc une littérature réaliste, relatant le vécu des colons en contact permanent avec le milieu et les autochtones. Le locuteur souligne ainsi avec insistance sa propre compétence discursive. Comme le remarque très justement Jean-Claude Marimoutou, il s'agit de refuser la compétence de gens de passage, voyageurs et explorateurs qui ne peuvent décrire valablement 'les conditions réelles d'existence à peine entrevues' (1988:224). Il s'agit aussi d'ériger le colon, de par sa connaissance du milieu, en producteur autorisé de la représentation discursive de la réalité.

Dans le carré sémiotique de base de l'exotisme, le colon n'est plus le même, c'est à dire le métropolitain, il n'est pas l'Autre non plus, même s'il partage avec l'autochtone la terre et les sensations primordiales. Dans le carré sémiotique, le colon occupe toutes les positions de la contradiction: il est à la fois non-même et non-autre et ce sont ces contradictions qui empêchent la littérature coloniale de trouver un destinataire. En effet, il semblerait que, si, dans le texte exotique, le contrat idéologique entre le locuteur et son destinataire métropolitain ou co-énonciateur ne fasse pas problème, le principe fondamental de coopération entre les deux producteurs du discours dans le texte colonial soit remis en question. La compétence du colon semble niée par son destinataire ou en tout cas considérée comme non pertinente: en termes simples, le destinataire métropolitain, introduit dans le texte avec le statut de narrataire, semble ne pas accorder de crédit au discours colonial.

Quant à l'Autre par excellence, pourtant si fraternel à certains égards, l'autochtone, il est sommé dans le meilleur des cas de devenir Même et doit renoncer à faire entendre sa différence autrement que dans les limites autorisées par le miroir inversé de l'exotisme. Ainsi sa nonchalance peut-elle exalter ou accuser le goût immodéré du travail des occidentaux, comme son désintéressement sert de repoussoir ou de faire valoir à leur goût du profit. Autant de remises en question que la société blanche a déjà intégrées dans son schéma idéologique. L'Autre est un poncif, une menace, un décor, jamais une valeur intervenant dans les opérations sur la syntaxe profonde.

Dans le texte colonial, la personnalité métisse, celle du colon, ne peut qu'échouer à trouver son expression et donc son identité. En effet, réduit à parler à ses semblables, les colons, l'auteur colonial se prive en réalité de public car il faut du temps pour qu'une culture coloniale apparaisse. Fortes individualités, les colons perdent certes en partie les codes socio-idéologiques implicites qui rendent possible la communication intra-communautaire dans la communauté d'origine. Mais ils échouent très longtemps à reconstituer un lieu psychique d'entente et d'échange dans la communauté qu'ils ont créée.

Par ailleurs, pour qu'une littérature coloniale soit vivace, qu'elle soit reconnue hors de ses frontières, elle doit contribuer à intégrer dans la vision du monde proposée à la communauté, le frère différent: l'autochtone. Je pense notamment aux écrivains d'Afrique du Sud tels que Nadine Gordimer ou Doris Lessing. A ce moment-là elle tend vers sa disparition pour devenir littérature nationale.

Comment intégrer dans ce schéma la littérature en langue de l'ex colonisateur: littératures anglophones, hispanophones, lusophones ou francophones? On peut se contenter de créer deux catégories en fonction de l'identité du locuteur: colonisateur ou son descendant, comme pour tous les mouvements littéraires d'Amérique du Sud jusqu'à une date relativement récente, colonisé ou ses descendants comme pour la littérature d'Afrique noire. La première catégorie relèverait de la littérature coloniale, la deuxième de sa totale inversion.

Mais la relation n'est pas si simple, plutôt qu'une opposition tranchée et confortable, cette littérature est un dialogue de cultures, conflictuel et déchiré. En particulier, la littérature des colonisés n'est pas seulement dans ses débuts l'inverse de la littérature coloniale. N'oublions pas qu'elle a alors très largement un destinataire occidental, très marginalement un destinataire colonisé lui-même, parmi ces peaux noires et masques blancs que fustige Frantz Fanon. Sans destinataire, ou plus exactement avec plusieurs communautés destinataires contradictoires, elle ressemble à la littérature coloniale. Mais plus lucide sur le traumatisme culturel de la colonisation, elle oppose plutôt deux univers antagonistes, à travers l'opposition passé/présent, qu'elle ne tente d'accréditer l'existence de la contradiction (non-même, non-autre) par rapport à la contrariété (même/autre). Le passé idéalisé représente en effet l'identité perdue, alors que le présent dénonce l'altérité (c'est à dire les valeurs occidentales) comme dangereuse et même mortelle. Toutefois cette littérature, avec le postcolonialisme, trouvera son authenticité en acceptant qu'un dialogue des cultures ait eu lieu, quoiqu'on veuille, et que ce soit lui désormais qui conditionne les identités nationales des nouveaux pays américains ou africains.

❖

Nous aimerions donc terminer sur l'évocation d'une catégorie littéraire qui n'a pas vraiment de nom, catégorie où le métissage culturel est intégré favorablement, où il n'est plus l'enjeu idéologique majeur, fictions narratives que l'on a vu naître en Amérique du Sud, en Afrique noire, et pourquoi pas dans le Pacifique. Ainsi, selon Elsa Dehennin, les écrivains sud-américains ont intégré 'les contenus du "réel merveilleux" américain et des techniques appropriées ... à une vision particulière du monde. Qualifions-la de "mestiza", faute de mieux' (1981:74–5).

Les romanciers africains, après avoir tenté de fonder l'expression de l'identité sur la race (la négritude) ou sur un déterminisme historique spécifique (l'aliénation coloniale), tentent de dire une identité 'néo-africaine', en s'inspirant davantage des réussites du réalisme magique latino-américain que du métissage culturel cher à Senghor.

Par exemple, pour Michel Vincent, l'oeuvre romanesque de Tchicaya U Tam'Si est, dans sa matérialité, le lieu de l'identité conquise sur le chaos et, dit-il, 'Si l'auteur ... parvient à faire fonctionner en un ensemble cohérent les éléments disparates dont le brouet grumeleux tient maintenant lieu de culture à tout un peuple, pourquoi celui-ci ne pourrait-il en forger les matériaux d'une société nouvelle?' (1994:75).

Nous revoilà à la fonction de l'écrivain telle que je l'évoquais au début. Désormais, l'univers romanesque dit ce qui est un fait: les cultures ne vivent que de se rencontrer, et les écrivains sont là afin de mimer cette rencontre de telle sorte que leur communauté puisse se la représenter et l'assumer comme elle l'entend.

Université française du Pacifique

Oeuvres Citées

Barthes, Roland 1953 *Le degré zéro de l'écriture*. Seuil, Paris.

Dehennin, Elsa 1981 *Langues néo-latines* (no. 236).

Greimas, A. J. 1970 *Du Sens*. Seuil, Paris.

Leblond, Marius-Ary 1943 *Anthologie coloniale, morceaux choisis d'écrivains français*. Peyronnet, Paris.

Marimoutou, Jean-Claude 1988 *Cahiers CRLH*, CIRA 1, no. 5.

Mouralis, Bernard 1975 *Les Contre littératures*. P.U.F.

Saïd, Edward W. 1978 *Orientalism*. Pantheon Books, New York.

Segalen, Victor 1986 *Essai sur l'exotisme*. Fata Morgana, Paris.

Vincent, Michel 1994 *Le Monde romanesque de Tchicaya U Tam'si*. Ed. nouvelles du Sud.

STEVEN TÖTÖSY DE ZEPETNEK

The Importance of Cultural Dialogue: A Case Study of Ethnic Minority and Cultural Participation in Canada

INTRODUCTION
Understanding cultural diversity through dialogue — between different ethnic minority groups, and between these groups and the mainstream — has led to the formation of multiculturalism as a paradigm. Cultural misreadings — whose negative results can be observed in many walks of life, from personal relationships to social and political situations and business including the marketing of goods — are reduced and mediated through dialogue with the 'Other'. In the case of Canada, a country with a long and continuing history of immigration, both cultural dialogue and cultural misreading play an important part in socialization processes formalized in the government policy of multiculturalism. It is therefore important to know how widespread cultural participation is, as the basis for dialogue between mainstream and minority groups.

In this paper, a case study of the reading of literature and related cultural activities as main factors of cultural participation will be presented.[1] After the presentation of the survey data, I will offer a selected analysis. I will also compare this survey data with the data of my readership survey of urban English-Canadian readers (see Tötösy and Kreisel 1992). The comparison will offer insight into several aspects of our knowledge about the relationship of mainstream and minority to culture and reading.

In the last few years some limited attention has been paid to the question of cultural participation of Canadian ethnic minority groups. In my opinion, the lack of both readership and audience research and research into the situation of cultural participation with regards to both the general Canadian population and to that of ethnic minority groups is a serious knowledge gap in Canadian scholarship. But, in addition to a blind spot with regards to literary, media, and audience research of ethnic minority groups in Canada, there is also an apparent ideological dimension which I can only understand as resulting from some sort of cultural relativism or from lack of information. For instance, John Metcalf, a noted Canadian author and critic, wrote the following curious paragraph in 1987: 'we *are* a nation of immigrants ... the federal government admits that one in five Canadians is illiterate. No one expects a mass or even a large audience for the arts [that is, including literature]' (21). The results of both my English-Canadian and Canadian-Hungarian readership surveys — even though they are pilot projects — contradict this statement and until empirical evidence on a larger scale is gathered about reading habits and cultural participation in general, and of Canadian ethnic minority groups in particular, the impressionistic approach such as Metcalf's remains highly questionable.[2]

The following presentation of data and analysis is based on a survey conducted in Edmonton in late 1994 and early 1995.[3] A questionnaire was mailed out twice, in two different formats in the bilingual Hungarian-English cultural magazine *Toborzó* published by the Edmonton Hungarian Cultural Society. In number 14.3 (1994) a loose-leaf, two-page questionnaire was inserted and in number 15.1 (1995) the questionnaire was printed in the magazine. There was no follow-up strategy either to gain more completed questionnaires or to complete questionnaires only partially completed. The magazine was mailed to 300 households in Edmonton. In both instances the questionnaire was presented in Hungarian. In response, fifteen completed questionnaires were received in total from the two mail-outs.

❖

THE DATA OF THE COMPLETED QUESTIONNAIRES
Demographic profile. The respondents, all Edmonton residents, indicated the following professions: mechanical engineer (1), high school student (1), clerical (2), retired (5), architect (1), stay-home (1), technician (1), dental technologist (1). Two respondents did not indicate a profession or occupation. Of the respondents there were 8 women and 7 men. Incomes were indicated under CAN$10,000 per year in 3 instances, all others between 30,000 and 40,000 per year. The educational levels were as follows: 4 respondents had elementary schooling only, 2 respondents had high school education, 5 respondents had technical college education, and 4 respondents had university education. As per numbers of individuals living in each household, an average of 2.5 family members was reported.

Money spent on books by the respondents; soft- or hard-cover. The average amount of money spent per month on books indicated was $21.00; 8 respondents indicated that they usually purchase soft-cover books and 11 reported that they prefer to buy hard-cover books while several respondents indicated that they buy both hard-cover and soft-cover books.

Time spent on reading per week. An average of 8 hours per week was reported by the respondents. As to the question of whether the respondents re-read texts, the responses indicated that 4 respondents never re-read a text, while 11 more than once re-read a text. 14 respondents revealed that they would read more if they had more time while one male respondent indicated he would not.

Reasons indicated for reading. The following categories were included on the questionnaire and the respondents were asked to indicate several categories if applicable: entertainment (12); knowledge accumulation (7); loves to read (12); necessity (education) (1; there was one student among the respondents, all others had completed their education); loves to speak about books with friends and/or family (3). Types of communication about books indicated: with family members (11) friends (14) colleagues at work (1) neighbours (0) in letters (4).

Data indicating various genres of texts read. Question 1 was, 'What type of texts did you read in the last six months and how many in each category?' This category of the questionnaire included the following genres: short fiction, novel, children's/juvenile literature, travel literature, religious texts, autobiography, historical novel, contemporary literature other than Hungarian, contemporary Hungarian literature, poetry, romance, science fiction, popular magazines, classical Hungarian prose, emigré(e) Hungarian literature, emigré(e) Hungarian poetry, classical non-Hungarian literature, scientific magazine, scientific literature, and detective/crime fiction.

In Hungarian, the respondents indicated in total 65 magazines read (an average of 4.3), in English 86 (an average of 6). Novel reading indicated: in Hungarian 14, in English 12; historical novel: in Hungarian 11, in English 7; scientific journal in Hungarian 10, in English 27; children's literature in Hungarian 6, in English 14; scientific literature in Hungarian 6, in English 7; contemporary Hungarian fiction 4; emigré(e) Hungarian fiction 1; emigré(e) Hungarian poetry 3; poetry in Hungarian 7, in English 2; juvenile literature in Hungarian 6, in English 14. Literature read in languages other than Hungarian and English was indicated in two instances: Russian (novel 5, popular magazines 10, scientific journals 10, and scientific literature 10) and German (novel 2).

Specific titles of texts reported read in the last six months prior to the date of the questionnaire. (In this category, 11 respondents completed the questionnaire.) *Hungarian*: Ferenc Temesvári *Vadászfegyverek*; Vilmos Csernohorszky *Erkölcs és politika*; Béla Ispánki *Az évszázad pere*; *A Trianon forrásai*; Elemér Mályusz *Zsigmond király uralma Magyarországon*; István Csonka *Mi újság*

Pesten?; László Kopcsányi *Jeruzsálem*; László Németh's novels; Róbert Zsolt *Sportolók, sporterkölcsök*; András Sütö *A lött lábú madár nyomában*; László Götz *Keleten kél a nap*; Lajos Zilahy *Két fogoly*; Lajos Zilahy *A Dukay család* (3 vols); Eric Knight *Légy hü magadhoz*; Claire Cenneth 5 novels; Emily Brontë *Üvöltö szelek*; Imre Trencsényi-Waldapfel *Görög regék*; Rózsa Ignácz *Urak, úrfiak*; Miklós Vámos *New York-Budapest*; Katalin Karády *Hogyan lettem szinésznö*; Anna Jókai *Tartozik és követel*; Erich Maria Remarque *Diadalív árnyékában*; James Clavell *A Tajpán*; Danielle Steel *Erösebb a szerelemnél*; Rachel Field *Az életújra szép*; Michael H. Brown *Az útólsó óra*; István Nemeskürty *Mi magyarok*; György Faludy *Jegyzetek a kor margójára*; Sándor Csoóri *A Világ emlékmüvei* and *Breviárium*; György Konrád *Az újjászületés melankóliája*; Antal Fuchs *Dicsértessék a Bakony*.

English: John Ralston Saul *Voltaire's Bastards*; James Clavell *Gai-Jin*; Peter Newman *Merchant Princess*; Loren McIntyre *The Incredible Incas*; John Beaty *The Iron Curtain over America*; Joseph Pungur *An Eastern European Liberation Theology*; Harold Coyle *The Ten Thousand*; Jack Higgins *Thunder Point*; Mordecai Richler *St Urban's Horseman*; James Redfield *The Celestine Prophecy*; Richard A. Berman *Robert Louis Stevenson in Samoa*.

Data with regards to perceived characteristics of classical and modern literature. The respondents were asked to indicate their opinion about characteristics which in their opinion describe classical and modern literature. Classical literature was described by the respondents including the following categories (more than one category could be indicated by the respondent). Classical literature: relaxing (9), easy to read (6), serious (8), morally acceptable (3), requires the reader's full attention (4), entertaining (5). With regards to modern literature the following categories were indicated: interesting (8), relaxing (5), unusual (5), requires the reader's full attention (5), entertaining (6).

Book inventory of the respondents' households, including patterns of origins/acquisition[4]. The following genres were listed in the questionnaire and the respondents indicated in total the following numbers of books in their households: classical non-Hungarian prose: 793 = an average of 53 books per household; juvenile literature: 111 = an average of 7.4 books; science fiction: 50 = an average of 3 books; lexica: 103 = an average of 7; detective/crime novels: 155, indicated by 3 respondents = an average of 10 volumes; classical Hungarian prose: 735 = an average of 49 books; travel literature: 148 = an average of 10 volumes; biographies: 243 = an average of 16 books; poetry: 289 = an average of 19 volumes; romance (Harlequin, Hungarian and non-Hungarian combined): none; contemporary Hungarian prose: 240 = an average of 16 volumes; historical novels: 319 = an average of 21 volumes; religious literature: 59 = an average of 4 volumes. One respondent added a category to the list, 'books on art': 25.

The following categories of the origins of the reading material were given in responses (multiple choices could be indicated). 10 respondents reported book purchase in book stores (Canadian and Canadian-Hungarian [Toronto or Montréal]), 3 respondents reported purchase in used book stores (Canadian), 10 respondents reported the import of books from Hungary, 9 respondents reported that the books they read are in his/her own library, 9 respondents reported that they received books they read as a gift, 4 respondents reported that they borrow from libraries, and 3 respondents reported that they borrow books from friends. 6 respondents indicated that they borrow books from Canadian English-language public libraries, on the average once or twice per month, 9 indicated that they do not borrow. 3 respondents indicated that they borrow books from the Hungarian-language library of the Edmonton Hungarian Cultural Society, on the average once or twice per month, 12 indicated that they do not.

Indicators of related cultural activity. Regarding the question of television viewing per week, the responses indicated 0 hour/week (1 respondent) minimum and 42 hours/week (1 respondent) maximum. The average weekly viewing time of the 15 respondents was 10.5 hours/week television viewing. Regarding the question of frequenting cinema per week, the responses indicated 0 times/week (8 respondents), 1 times/week (3 respondents), and 1-2 times/week (4 respondents), thus cinema viewing averaging to 0.6 times/week. Regarding the question of frequenting theatre per year, the responses indicated an average of theatre 1.7 times per year. Regarding the question of video rental, the responses indicated an average of 1.2 times per week of video viewing.

❖

SELECTED ANALYSIS OF THE SURVEY DATA
As the data suggests, the level of education of the respondents is mid-range. Thus, the relatively high level of time spent reading, the types of texts read, and the inventory of books in the households surveyed is of some significance. Generally speaking, these results suggest a high level of cultural participation of the Canadian Hungarian population of Edmonton. This is the more interesting as the Canadian-Hungarian population of the city (and of the province in general) is historically of a composition more working class to mid-level educated while larger urban centres such as Toronto, Montréal, and Vancouver attracted the larger numbers of the higher-level educated Hungarians during and after the two waves of Hungarian immigration to Canada, the period after the Second World War and the period after the 1956 revolution.[5] Further, the fact that the Canadian-Hungarian population of Edmonton is established (that is, the immigrants arrived in Canada several decades ago), explains the high level of bi-lingual reading, Hungarian and English, including all text types.

The statistical numbers reflecting text types read indicate an overwhelming dominance of the reading of popular magazines, followed by the reading of novels. The statistical dominance of the reading of popular magazines in both Hungarian and in English is of some note as the large number of Hungarian popular magazines read indicates the purchase and importation of such from abroad, most likely directly from Hungary. With regards to prose in general, the data indicate the reading of most genres, evenly distributed between novel, historical and other, travel literature, and adventure. Of some significance is the reading of translated English-language texts into Hungarian. Similarly, it is of note that some same text types are read in both Hungarian and in English. However, there were no indications that the respondents read texts translated from Hungarian into English.

The data about reasons for reading — a most important area for gauging cultural participation — resulted in some interesting findings. Love of reading and interest in entertainment dominate, followed at a distance by interest in knowledge accumulation. The parallel data of entertainment and love of reading most likely explain the high level of non-classical reading material. In the case of the English-Canadian survey data, the response was similar in the sense that 'the pleasure factor in reading appears to be more important than the knowledge factor' but to an insignificant level (Tötösy and Kreisel 1992:223). This led to my suggestion, based on the data, that 'it appears that the knowledge factor for reading is roughly equal to the pleasure factor' (223). Consequently, the Canadian-Hungarian data yielded a different result with reference to the factors of pleasure and knowledge accumulation which suggests that further research would be necessary.

In the case of Canadian-Hungarian subjects, the level of communication about books — with family, friends, and in letters — is relatively high. This is significant because it is an indication of transfer of cultural material and thus suggests a relatively high level of cultural participation in an extended context.

With regards to the respondents' perception of classical and modern literature, a comparison of these categories suggests that classical literature was gauged more relaxing than modern literature, that classical literature engages the reader's full attention less than that of modern literature. However, the characteristic of entertainment was rated slightly higher for modern literature than for classical. These data suggest that 'relaxation' is not gauged analogous to 'entertainment' by the respondents. Of some significance is the finding that the respondents read a moderate amount of emigré(e) literature, prose and poetry. This finding is significant in the context of an existing or at least potential readership of Canadian ethnic minority writing. With reference to the reading of texts written by English-Canadian authors, only two such authors, Richler and Newman, were listed among the fiction titles. These data diverge from my findings in the English-Canadian survey where there was a high level of the reading of English-Canadian authors indicated (see Tötösy 1994).

Interestingly, the data indicate a lack of classical literature read and a dominance of the reading of contemporary popular literature. As mentioned above, this aspect is explained by the respondents' very high level of focus on entertainment as the reason for reading. This aspect of reading is consistent with my findings from a survey of urban English-Canadian readership (see Tötösy and Kreisel 1992:220). The frequent re-reading of literature is also consistent with the data of English-Canadian readers (224).

The data about money spent on books supports my preliminary suggestion that cultural participation is fairly high in the case of this particular ethnic minority group in its economic dimension as well. The responses indicated preferences for soft or hard-cover books is, when compared with the data of the English-Canadian survey, interesting in the sense that in the case of English-Canadian readers 'the size of the book and the cost were not factors that influenced one's decision to read' (221).

With regards to household book inventories, one socio-cultural aspect is noteworthy. The number of juvenile books read, based on the over 40 years average age of the respondents, indicates a high level of retention of either their own books of youth and/or a retention of juvenile literature for their children. A comparison of the average inventory of books per household here with those of my English-Canadian survey reveals that the numbers are comparable. However, in a few instances there are differences. For example, in the category of poetry the Canadian-Hungarian respondents own an average of 19 while the English-Canadian households own an average of 5. Conversely, English-Canadian households own an average of 14 volumes of religious texts while Canadian-Hungarian households own an average of 4 volumes. This latter discrepancy may be explained by the strong appeal of religion to the native English-Canadian population of Edmonton and Alberta. Another category, that of romance, shows that English-Canadian households own an average of 10 volumes while Canadian-Hungarian households of the survey own none; and books of science fiction are owned by English-Canadian households at an average of 85 while Canadian-Hungarian households in the present survey own an average of 3. The latter difference may be explained by the older average age of the Canadian-Hungarian respondents as compared with that of the English-Canadian respondents and/or by cultural identity parameters such as an orientation by the Canadian-Hungarian respondents more towards reading texts re-inforcing aspects of belonging and knowledge and/or the availability of science fiction texts in Hungarian.[6]

Data about the sources of acquisition of books suggest a high level of purchase in bookstores and the import of books from abroad and again this implies cultural participation on the economic level, an indication of some importance. Another aspect of cultural participation is the low level of library book borrowing. Obviously, readers prefer to own. The English-Canadian data differ somewhat: while the highest percentage there too is of books purchased in a bookstore, the next highest score is of books borrowed from the public library

(Tötösy and Kreisel 1992:221). The reason for this difference may be the obvious limit imposed on Canadian-Hungarian readers in their borrowing of Hungarian-language books from Canadian public libraries, owing to the limited holdings of such books in the libraries. The reason why Canadian-Hungarians in Edmonton do not borrow more books from the library of the Edmonton Hungarian Cultural Society may be the limited number and the limited amount of certain genres in that library, as well as the distance to the library from the readers' residences.

With regards to cultural participation in its general context, the data indicate a dominance of television viewing over reading but not significantly: 10.5 hours/week of television viewing versus 8 hours/week of reading (averages). Other cultural activities such as video and cinema viewing and theatre were markedly less than the two former categories of activity.

❖

The most important finding of the survey, I suggest, is that Canadian-Hungarians manifest a high level of cultural participation in general and in the reading of literature in particular. This finding is the more important when we take into consideration the general assumption that immigrants manifest, in general, low levels of literary reading and cultural participation. Significantly, my data support the recent findings of Elrud Ibsch and Rita Ghesquiere about the levels and mechanisms of literary reading of immigrants in The Netherlands: the cultural parameters with regards to immigrants in Canada and in The Netherlands are comparable. Thus my hypothesis that the overall and most important finding of my survey — and those of Ibsch and Ghesquiere — is with reference to the perception of ethnic minority groups in general and by the respective mainstream societies in particular. While the economic importance of ethnic minority groups as consumers and therefore targets has been, in the last few years, increasingly recognised in Canada, the same attention should be applied to the problematics of cultural participation, including the reading of literature.

University of Alberta

Notes

1 Financial support for this research project was provided by the Hungarian Cultural Society of Edmonton and the University of Alberta Research Institute for Comparative Literature. The Academic Relations Division of the Department of Foreign Affairs and International Trade Canada / Direction des Relations académiques du ministère des Affaires étrangères et du Commerce international Canada, within its Cultural Personalities Exchange Program provided funding for my participation in the International Conference on Cultural Dialogue and Cultural Misreading (Peking University, October 1995), where I presented a shorter version of this paper.

2 Taking it from the recent *Statistics Canada* findings that in the period of 1981 to 1991 a higher

percentage of immigrants had university education than the Canadian-born population, one can infer that the levels of cultural participation by ethnic minority groups are probably high (see Badets and Chui 1994:41). This information alone would contradict the suggestion that immigrants to Canada 'do not read'. And Badets and Chui conclude: 'All in all, immigrants comprised an important segment of Canada's population and economy, and have played a major role in creating a socio-cultural mosaic' (71). These implications, I argue, would also be valid for older groups of immigrants and my survey data substantiate my hypothesis.

3 My theoretical and methodological framework for the design of the questionnaire and the analysis of its results is based on the Systemic and Empirical Approach to Literature. For this approach see, for example, Andringa 1994; Schmidt 1982; Tötösy 1992, including my argument that this theoretical framework and methodology would be an innovative and promising approach specifically for the study of ethnic minority writing (1992:31–2 and 1996a).

4 The assumption that household book holdings may be skewed owing to the possibility of book inheritance — thus books being on the shelf but not read — does not, in general, apply either to English-Canadian or to Hungarian-Canadian households. In the case of English-Canadian households it does not apply owing to the general North American situation that books are — again, generally speaking — not passed down. In the case of Hungarian-Canadian households the assumption is impossible as Hungarian-Canadians are a priori refugees or immigrants.

5 For a history of the Alberta and Edmonton Hungarian immigrant population see Tötösy (1993).

6 While the genre of science fiction is a dominant text type in English, in Hungary only recently — that is, after the political changes in 1989 — have such texts become available on a large scale, mostly in translation from English.

Works Cited

Andringa, Els (1994) 'Literature: Empirical Studies' in R. A. Asher (ed.) *The Encyclopedia of Language and Linguistics.* Pergamon Press, Oxford: pp. 2266–71.

Badets, Jane and Tina W. L. Chui (1994) *Focus on Canada: Canada's Changing Immigrant Population.* Ottawa: Statistics Canada. Catalogue No. 96–311E.

Ghesquiere, Rita (forthcoming) 'How Differently Do Ethnic Minority Children Read? The Reading Behaviour of Moroccan, Turkish, and Italian Children in Flanders' in *Reader: Essays in Reader-Oriented Theory, Criticism, and Pedagogy.* Special Issue of *Literary Reading and Readership*, no. 36, ed. Steven Tötösy de Zepetnek.

Ibsch, Elrud 1996 (forthcoming) 'How Different is the Other? A Case Study of Literary Reading in a Multicultural Society' in Steven Tötösy de Zepetnek (ed.) *Literatura Comparada: Novos Paradigmas/Comparative Literature: New Paradigms.* Aframento, Oporto.

Metcalf, John (1994) *Freedom from Culture: Selected Essays 1982–92.* ECW, Toronto.

Miska, John (1990) *Ethnic and Native Canadian Literature: A Bibliography.* University of Toronto Press.

Schmidt, Siegfried J. (1980–2) *Grundriss der Empirischen Literaturwissenschaft.* 2 Vols NIKOL Series 1. Friedr. Vieweg & Sohn, Braunschweig-Wiesbaden (Reprint of Vol. 1, 1991, Suhrkamp, Frankfurt.)

Schmidt, Siegfried J. (1982) *Foundation for the Empirical Study of Literature: The Components of a Basic Theory,* tr. Robert de Beaugrande. Buske, Hamburg.

Tötösy de Zepetnek, Steven (1992) 'Systemic Approaches to Literature: An Introduction with Selected Bibliographies' in *Canadian Review of Comparative Literature/Revue Canadienne de Littérature Comparée* 19.1–2 (March-June), pp. 21–93.

—— (1993) 'A History of the Hungarian Cultural Society of Edmonton, 1946-1986' in *Canadian Ethnic Studies / Etudes ethniques au Canada* 25.2, pp.100–17.

—— (1994) 'Toward a Theory of Cumulative Canon Formation: Readership in English Canada' in *Mosaic: A Journal for the Interdisciplinary Study of Literature* 27.3 (September), pp. 107–19.

—— (1996a forthcoming) 'Literary Theory, Ethnic Minority Writing, and the Systemic Approach' in *Canadian Ethnic Studies / Etudes ethniques au Canada.* Special Issue of *Literary Theory and Ethnic Minority Writing* 28.1, Joseph Pivato.

—— (1996b forthcoming) 'Applied Cultural Studies and Readership Research in Canada: Results and Problems' in *Reader: Essays in Reader-Oriented Theory, Criticism, and Pedagogy*. Special issue of *Literary Reading and Readership*, ed. Steven Tötösy de Zepetnek.

—— (1996c forthcoming) 'A Selected Bibliography of Theoretical and Critical Texts about Canadian Ethnic Minority Writing' in *Canadian Ethnic Studies / Etudes ethniques au Canada*, Special Issue of *Literary Theory and Ethnic Minority Writing*, 28.1, Joseph Pivato.

——, Steven and Philip Kreisel 1992 'Urban English-Speaking Canadian Literary Readership: the Results of a Pilot Study' in *Poetics: Journal of Empirical Research on Literature, the Media and the Arts* 21.3: pp. 211–38.

Theresa Hyun

Translation and Cultural Identity: Geographical Images in Early Modern Korean Newspapers and Journals

INTRODUCTION

Traditionally, Korea developed under the strong influence of China, and in the seventeenth century Korean scholars started to import Western material in translation through China. At this time the scholars of the *Silhak* (practical learning movement) demonstrated a strong interest in Western civilization and began to import both religious and scientific texts dealing with Catholicism, astronomy, medicine, geography and other topics.[1] This early introduction of selected fields of Western knowledge formed the background for the widespread importation of texts through translation which took place during the *Kaehwa* (opening or enlightenment) period at the end of the nineteenth and beginning of the twentieth century.

The *Silhak* scholars who visited China in the seventeenth century were deeply impressed by the Western works which had already been translated into Chinese and they made a concerted effort to introduce them into their own country. These translations undermined Korea's traditionally Sinocentric worldview. After the invention of the Korean phonetic script *hangul* in the fifteenth century, many Chinese texts were translated into the vernacular, including those dealing with Confucianism and ethics. One of the main purposes of these translation efforts was to propagate Chinese thought and to Confucianize the country. In comparison, the translation of Western works into the vernacular had the effect of spreading Western thought and thereby weakening the importance of the Sinocentric worldview.

This paper is part of a larger project to examine translation phenomena during the early modern period in Korea when Western materials flooded into the country. I briefly consider first the translation of Chinese works and traditional values in Korea, followed by translation of Western texts and the transition to modern values. Then I focus on geographical images in translated material appearing in some early modern Korean newspapers and journals. New concepts of geography imported through translation offer an image of the shift from a China-centred to a West-oriented worldview, which contributed to the changing of cultural identity in early twentieth-century Korea.

TRANSLATION AND CULTURAL VALUES IN THE EARLY CHOSON PERIOD[2]

Traditionally Korea's foreign relations were characterized by *Sadae Jueui* or worship of the powerful. China was recognized as a powerful culture and Koreans paid tribute to the Chinese in return for protection from surrounding peoples. Korea remained isolated under the dominant influence of China until the late nineteenth century. Until 1876, when Korea signed her first modern treaty with Japan, Korean foreign relations were centred on China in the traditional Asian style which involved paying tribute in order to maintain peaceful relations.

Various aspects of Chinese civilization were imported into Korea such as the writing system, philosophy, literature and religion. Already in the Three Kingdoms Period (first to seventh century AD) Buddhism, Confucianism, and Chinese characters had been introduced. These aspects of Chinese civilization were at first directed at the elite, and gradually spread to the people; Korea became a little China, accepting the concept that the world could be divided into Chinese and barbarians.

After the creation of *hangul* many Chinese texts were translated into the vernacular, which served to deepen Sinocentric values. Some of the representative works translated were commentaries on the Chinese classics and other Confucian texts with a pedagogical aim, Buddhist scriptures, and literary works. *Hangul* was invented during the reign of King Sejong (1418–50) and at this time, in addition to works on Confucian ethics and the life of Buddha, a collection of Du Fu's works was also translated. During the later part of the fifteenth century translation emphasized Buddhist scriptures, Confucian works and medical texts. The works of Du Fu were considered by Koreans to represent the virtues of Confucianism and they were repeatedly translated throughout the period. At the end of the sixteenth century a collection of fifty-four Confucian classics was translated. The translations of this period from Chinese into Korean retained a Chinese style which was difficult for those without a knowledge of Chinese characters to comprehend.

TRANSLATION AND CULTURAL VALUES IN THE LATER CHOSON PERIOD

The seventeenth century was the transition from the Ming to the Qing dynasty in China. Although at first the Koreans hesitated to recognize the new rulers because they were not ethnic Han Chinese, Korea was later greatly influenced by the technical advances of the Qing in fields such as mathematics, medicine, architecture and agriculture. At that time certain aspects of Western civilization had been introduced to China and the Korean scholars who visited came into contact with new forms of knowledge through Chinese translations. The *Silhak* scholars took an interest in Western science as a possible means of combating the deterioration of agriculture and the impoverished economic conditions of Choson society.

Catholicism attracted the attention of Korean scholars as an aspect of the new Western knowledge and was introduced through texts translated into Chinese along with geography, medicine, astronomy and physics. Eventually Catholicism came into conflict with the traditional Korean way of life and the persecution of this religion began. Along with the official order forbidding Catholicism, Western texts were also banned and Korea entered a period of conflict between Eastern and Western civilization.[3] On the one hand the Sinocentric view continued to hold sway, and on the other *Silhak* scholars remained convinced of the value of Western science.

Geography offers an example of this conflict in values. At the time that Matteo Ricci introduced Western maps in China,[4] the *Ch'onha do* placing China at the centre of the world continued to be used in Korea. One of the early *Silhak* scholars, Yi Ik (1681–1763), recognized the correctness of the geographical knowledge contained in the Western maps introduced in China. In other words he recognized that the earth has two poles with the equator in the middle, and that China occupies one segment of the globe. However, in spite of this Western geographical knowledge, he did not escape from the Sinocentric world view. According to his explanation China occupies the heart of the world's surface.

Hong Tae-Yong, one of the Korean scholars who followed Yi Ik, went beyond the traditional way of dichotomizing the world into Chinese and barbarians. Hong visited China six times and had many discussions with Chinese scholars and Western missionaries about astronomy, geography and medicine. Through these encounters he realized the falseness of the idea that China was at the centre of the globe, and he understood that the earth rotates on its own axis. For the *Silhak* scholars this was a step towards a modern scientific world view because they went beyond the traditional Confucian view that the earth is flat with China at the centre. Pak Jae-ga (1750–1805) was one of these thinkers. His work *Bukhakeui*, written after a visit to China, emphasized that Korea could overcome her backwardness by following the example of Qing China and inviting Western scholars to help with transferring production technology and various cultural systems. He recommended that the technology of advanced civilizations be introduced to overcome the stagnation of Korean culture, to reform society and to promote commerce and industry. Pak felt that these changes would contribute to the well-being of the common people.

However this openness to Western civilization did not occur in Korea until the late nineteenth century, and most of the *Silhak* scholars remained caught in the dilemma of science vs religion. Choson dynasty Korea never adopted the approach used in China where Western civilization was introduced by Matteo Ricci and other European missionaries as a stage in the development of structured scientific knowledge. Although the Korean scholars were greatly impressed by Western science, their approach to religion was limited by their strict neo-Confucian ideology. This attitude of rejection of everything foreign was transmitted to the nineteenth-century Korean scholars who formulated the *Tongdo Sogi Ron* (Theory of Eastern Ethics and Western Technology).[5]

During the late Choson period, as well as works on Western science being translated into Chinese, many Chinese novels were translated into Korean. Chinese literature continued to exert a strong influence on Korean writing. Well-known works such as *T'aep'yong Kwanggi* (Records of the Ancient Chinese Dynasties), and *Samguk Jiyoneui* (Tales of the Three Kingdoms), as well as lesser-known works, were widely distributed in translation and attracted a considerable readership. Unlike the translations into Korean of the earlier period, those of the later period tended towards acceptability with the target audience rather than adequacy in terms of the source text. Thus the translation of Chinese novels contributed to the development of a vernacular writing style.

TRANSLATION, GEOGRAPHY AND CULTURAL IDENTITY IN EARLY MODERN KOREA
Around 1880 many translations appeared which aimed to impart a knowledge of world geography. Before Western maps were introduced Korea used a world map which showed only a part of the globe and reflected the Chinese worldview. The map of the European missionaries in China introduced a new approach to geography which was suppressed by conservative members of the government who feared the new ideas would subvert the authority of the ruling neo-Confucian philosophy. However, the first modern Korean newspapers, which appeared in the late nineteenth century, were quite innovative in introducing facts about geography. One of these publications, the *Hansong Jubo*, printed a series of articles which gave detailed explanations about the continents, the location of various countries, the racial characteristics of the population of each area, and the traditional customs of the people of a region. The appendix to the article included separate maps of the Eastern and Western hemisphere. These early modern newspapers were crucial in going beyond the traditional view which placed China at the centre of the universe, and in educating Koreans about their relation to the rest of the world.

Articles were mostly translated from a Western text into Japanese and then into Korean. During this transitional phase from traditional to modern values the process of cultural importation was indirect, with most translated material coming into Korea by way of Japan. Therefore Japan was replacing China as the mediator in the importation of Western knowledge. The fact that submission in the face of the superiority of Chinese culture had become an anachronism was reflected in the replacement of the old China-centred maps by new ones which relegated China to one section of the globe.

In addition to newspapers, educational texts of the early modern period also focused on geography. One of the best-known texts of this period, *Samin P'ilji* (Essential Knowledge for Scholars and Common People), was written in pure *hangul* in 1895 by an American educator, Hulbert, who had been invited to Korea during the first period of educational reform. In his introduction Hulbert emphasized the importance of knowledge about geography for contemporary citizens and gave an overview of world civilization. This work relied heavily on translations and gave a survey which helped Koreans of the time to broaden their knowledge of the world; there were chapters on the continents with details for each region concerning topography, climate, production, population, language, trade, customs, military affairs, religion, language, and colonial conditions. After 1895 Western-style schools began to appear, and Korea's place in world geography was taught. These educational institutions used newly published geography texts which were based on translations.

❖

At the beginning of the twentieth century one of Korea's first modern literary translators, Ch'oe Namson, displayed a deep interest in geography. His work is instructive for an understanding of the connection between translation and the development of modern cultural identity in early modern Korea. Ch'oe was born in 1890 of a middle-class family and was educated in the Chinese classics. While still in his early teens, he made two brief trips to Japan, first in 1904 to attend a Tokyo middle school, and then in 1906 to attend Waseda University. During these trips Ch'oe was exposed to foreign literary and cultural trends in the already Westernized Japan. These early encounters with the Japanese version of Western culture were to leave their mark on Ch'oe's work.

When Ch'oe returned to Korea, he felt he had a mission to enlighten the young men of his country. He set up his own printing press and published a journal, *Sonyon* (Youth), from 1908 to 1911, for the purpose of educating patriotic, liberal youths who would build a new nation. The works of authors such as Tolstoy, Victor Hugo, Byron and Tennyson were translated with the intent of awakening young people to the world outside the narrow confines of their own nation. Non-literary works dealing with geography, history, mathematics and science were included in an attempt to arouse curiosity and instil what was considered useful in Western knowledge. In particular there were many prose and verse translations focusing on geography in this publication.

The image of the ocean which appears in *Sonyon* indicates one of the ways in which translation was contributing to a new cultural identity in Korea. The ocean is not a common theme in traditional East-Asian poetics. In contrast to much Western epic poetry which features descriptions of sea adventures, one of the common themes in many East-Asian literatures is that of the poet who seeks refuge from the strife of everyday life in the deep mountains. Traditional East-Asian poetics tended to oppose mundane worldliness and promoted retreat into the mountains which represented harmony with nature. Within this tradition the blending of ego and non-ego, of self and nature, was part of the process of producing true poetry.

Ch'oe Namson translated Western poetry dealing with the sea, with the intention of bringing in a new image of purity and absolute freedom. When he wrote the first modern Korean poem, 'From the Sea to the Boys', in praise of the ocean, he was breaking with Korean poetic traditions. In this poem the young gain strength to break with old customs from the sea, and this process brings in new ways of thinking. In Ch'oe's early work the sea symbolized modernization, as well as the endless hope of creating a new world and of heading toward a new era. Later, sea imagery was gradually replaced in Ch'oe's work by mountain imagery, perhaps because he realised that modernization was not without pitfalls. At the turn of the century, however, through the influence of Western works translated into Korean, the sea provided an image of cultural renewal.

York University

Notes

This research was made possible by a grant from the Daesan Foundation.

1 The *Silhak* movement comprised a group of Korean neo-Confucian scholars who attempted to go beyond the abstract metaphysical approaches of neo-Confucianism in order to find practical solutions to the agricultural, economic and social problems facing Korea.

2 The Choson period lasted from 1392 to 1910.

3 Starting in the seventeenth century Western texts were imported into Korea by emissaries who visited Beijing. Among these texts was Matteo Ricci's *True Principles of Catholicism*. Some of the *Silhak* scholars were interested in the new religion and a few were converted. The religion began to spread but it came into conflict with the ruling neo-Confucian ideology and Catholics were accused of being anti-society. The first official persecution began in 1791 followed by others in 1801, 1839, 1846 and 1866 during which many believers were martyred.

4 In 1602 Matteo Ricci introduced a map of the world to China. The map, known in Korean as *Konyo Manguk Jido*, gave details of the five continents and was introduced into Korea the following year by Yi Ik. It greatly influenced the geographical concepts of *Silhak* scholars.

5 *Tongdo Sogi Ron* was proposed by a reformer, Kim Yun-Sik, in 1880. According to this theory Western technology should be accepted while maintaining the superiority of Confucian ethics.

Works cited

Bang, Dong 1975 *Hangukeui Jido* (Korean Maps). Kyoyangguksa Ch'ongso, Seoul.

Catholic Kyori Sinhakwon 1985 *Ch'odae Padun Tangsin*. Catholic Publishing Company, Seoul.

Cho, Dong-Il 1994 *Hanguk Munhak T'ongsa* (History of Korean Literature). Jisik Sanop Sa, Seoul.

Hanguk Jongch'i Oegyo Sa Hyophoe 1993 *Hanguk Oegyo Sa I* (Korean Diplomatic History). Jipmun Dang, Seoul.

Hyun, Theresa 1992 *Translation and Early Modern Korean Literature.* Siwa Sihak Sa, Seoul.

Jo Yun-Jae 1984 *Hanguk Munhak Sa* (History of Korean Literature). T'amgu Dang, Seoul.

Kang Jae-Un 1990 *Chosoneiu Sohak Sa* (History of Catholicism in Choson). Daewoo Haksul Ch'ongso, Seoul.

Kim, Yol-Gyu and Dong-Uk Shin (eds) *Ch'oe Namsongwa Lee Kwangsueui Munhak* (The Literature of Ch'oe Namson and Lee Kwangsu). Seamun Sa, Seoul.

Lee, Ch'an 1970 *Hanguk Jirihak Sa* (History of Korean Geography). Hanguk Munhwa Sa Taegye 3, Koryo Taehakkyo Minjok Munhwa Yongu So, Seoul.

Lee, Kyong-Son 1988 *Hanguk Munhakgwa Jont'ong Munhwa* (Korean Literature and Traditional Culture). Singu Munhwa Sa, Seoul.

Pak, Ch'ung-Suk and Gun-Ho Yu 1980 *Choson Joeui Jongch'i Sasang* (Political Thought of the Choson Period). P'yonghwa Ch'ulp'an Sa, Seoul.

María Elena de Valdés

Latin American Testimonial Literature as a Postcolonial Paradigm

The issues of cultural relations, whether a matter of contestation or not, are never straightforward since they involve the full spectrum of social interaction ranging from alterity to xenophobia. In the case of Mesoamerica —a term by which we designate Mexico, Central America and the Caribbean — the only valid generalization is that the concept of race and, henceforth, of cultural relations has a history of more than five hundred years. The Aztecs certainly had a sense of different peoples, especially of their many conquered neighbours, but this did not extend to a biological generalization of difference. The European idea of race or a biologically different people came to Mesoamerica clothed in notions of racial superiority that have remained a regional social foundation. The history of race relations in this part of Latin America has been markedly brutal, comparable to the European domination of the African majority in South Africa but with the difference that in Mesoamerica it has been reality for five hundred years and is still social, if not political, law in Guatemala and in Chiapas — the southern state of the Mexican republic that borders on Guatemala. This history of exploitation and cultural genocide has been rationalized as religious or paternalistic protection of an inferior, child-like people by a superior and informed one — the Spanish-speaking *mestizo* or *ladino* dominant class. *Ladino* is the term used to designate Spanish-speaking people of mixed race who reject their Indian heritage.

The specific variation of racial superiority imposed by Spain was based on the Spanish obsession with purity of blood, used so effectively by the church to expropriate and expel the Jewish and Moorish population of southern Spain. The extent of the ethnic expulsion and persecution of Jews and Moors during the fifteenth and sixteenth centuries has been examined by numerous historians; what interests us here is the legacy that this Spanish self-destruction gave to the colonial empire which emerged concomitantly with the racial and religious purge in the peninsula.

The representation of race relations in a community has the double function of reflecting upon experience and creating ideological images. And so it has been from the account of Alvar Núñez Cabeza de Vaca (1490–1560) to the testimonial of Rigoberta Menchu (1959). Part of the representation of race relations has also been realized by the creative enactment of these ties through narrative fiction, both the short story and the novel. The Indianist novels primarily imbued with the 'naturalist' descriptive modes of Emile Zola presented the Indian as the abused victim, the unknowable other. My interest here is not to trace the history of the representation of alterity in Mesoamerica but to focus on the testimonial mode of representation wherein the personal experience of the subject is translated into a symbiotic representation of oneself from the point of view of the other. My text is *I, Rigoberta Menchu, An Indian Woman in Guatemala* (1983).

The narration in Rigoberta Menchu's testimonial is mediated first person. This singular distinguishing feature cannot be stressed enough, for it is through this mode of narration that the symbolic representation of the other and the self become a hermeneutic disclosure and retention of identity between languages and ethnic designations. The constant reference to 'our people' is a sign enunciated by a symbiotic source made up of the Quiche informant, Rigoberta Menchu, and the anthropologist-editor-transcriber Elizabeth Burgos-Debray. Certainly it is Rigoberta's experience that is being presented but it is Burgos-Debray who listens, questions, records, edits and structures the story. There is no direct dialogical tie between the narrator and the reader; there is one between the editor and the informant, but we are only allowed to hear part of it.

Rigoberta's text describes a reflective search for an explanation of xenophobia and racial tensions. Who is friend and who is foe, who is to be feared and why would a complete stranger hate someone because they are different in language, race, class or tradition? Of course, there are no rational answers to an irrational alterity, but there does emerge a reflective search for understanding of race relations. Rigoberta narrates:

> All these things were jumbled up in my mind, I couldn't separate my ideas. That's when I began making friends with other villagers in Uspantan. I asked them: 'What do you eat? How do you make your breakfast? What do you eat for supper?' And, yes, they said the same: 'Well, in the morning we eat tortillas with salt and a little pinole [grilled corn flour mixed with water, sugar and cocoa]. At midday our mother brings tortillas and any plants she finds in the fields. At night, we eat tortillas with chile ... and then we go to sleep.'

Rigoberta's conclusion was: 'So everything was the same.' The people from the other villages live the same way; she does find commonality but they still considered her to be different although the difference is not explained. She continues:

> It gave me a lot to think about. I have to tell you that I did not learn my politics at school. I just tried to turn my own experience into something which was common to a whole people.

But what about relations with the others that are not her people, the Spanish-speaking *ladinos*? The political awakening of Rigoberta is about race relations:

> We began to understand that the root of all our problems was exploitation. That there were rich and poor and that the rich exploited the poor — our sweat, our labor. That's how they got richer and richer. The fact that we were always waiting in offices, always bowing to the authorities, was part of the discrimination we Indians suffered. So was the cultural oppression which tries to divide us by taking away our traditions and prevents unity among our people.... And I started wondering: Could it be that not all *ladinos* are bad?... I said to one poor *ladino*: 'You're a poor *ladino*, aren't you?' And he nearly hit me. He said: 'What do you know about it, Indian?' I wondered, why is it that when I say poor *ladinos* are like us, I am insulted. I didn't know then that the same system which tries to isolate us Indians also puts up barriers between Indians and *ladinos*. I knew that all *ladinos* rejected us but I did not know why. I was more confused.

Close analysis of Rigoberta's text reveals three distinguishing features: a marked sensibility to the language of representation and the language of the community; a reflective search for understanding race relations; and a narrative voice that speaks for a commonality and not the singular subjective 'I'.

Rigoberta's awareness of language both as a force for commonality and a barrier that excludes is made evident throughout the text, not only because of the information given about her late acquisition of Spanish but also because of her strong sense that this was the language of the other, of the *ladino* exploiter. She does not entirely overcome a sense of guilt at her decision to learn the language of the oppressor even if it is to fight for her Quiche-speaking people. This heightened sensibility to language and linguistic acculturation gives her an acute awareness of the social meaning of names. We must also remember that the traces of Rigoberta's Quiche, which are in the Spanish text we read, are also a choice, for it is evident that Burgos-Debray chose to leave them in as she also had chosen to use certain narrative patterns rather than the multidirectional speech of conversation. This highly structured story is mediated; I shall return to this feature when I discuss the narrator.

Rigoberta's story is ostensibly *her* story of *her* people, their way of life and their exploitation, but the hermeneutic direction of the text is not a mere descriptive narrative of peoples and places that are exotic to the reader; the direction here is an intellectually shaped dialectic of an explanation of who we are in a quest for who the other is in order to gain an understanding of difference.

The hermeneutic process of explanation and understanding is well developed in Rigoberta's text and can be demonstrated in the cited passages. She begins confronting the irrational nature of race relations and looking for a way out of confusion. She could not make sense of the contradictory experiences and ideas she had received. Why should one exploited group despise another similarly abused group instead of their common enemy?

The reflective process is clearly enunciated: 'It gave me a lot to think about ... I just tried to turn our experience into something which was common to a whole people.' The task of inductive reasoning which lies behind the dialectic of explanation and understanding does not have to be identified to be used effectively. Rigoberta reasons from the contradictory evidence of established xenophobia and the empirical evidence of economic exploitation to general concepts of socio-political domination. The more she works at the explanation of why things are the way they are, the more she approaches an understanding that will not be final but will be a platform from which to build a greater understanding, for there are always more variables, more evidence, more facts to consider as she meets more and more peoples from other native groups and more *ladinos*. Some of these generalizations are already evident in the cited passage: 'I didn't know then that the same system which tries to isolate us Indians also puts up barriers between Indians and *ladinos*.' The dialectic does not end with the generalization but only widens in the continued search for greater understanding: 'I knew that all *ladinos* rejected us, but I didn't know why. I was more confused.' Every time she says that she is confused she signals another push toward a greater understanding since what has been achieved is evidently not enough.

Rigoberta's narrator recognizes economic exploitation as a primary cause of the poverty of her people. She can understand that the existing sociopolitical system is one that promotes division and hatred among the exploited. The text puts it plainly before us:

> It was painful for me to accept [the *ladino* prejudice] that an Indian was inferior to a *ladino*. I kept on worrying about it. It's a big barrier between us, between Indian and *ladino*. I didn't understand it.

The understanding she seeks is a knowledge of the other. The narrative construct that has made this hermeneutic dialectic possible is a unique creation of contemporary Latin American testimonial: the symbiotic voice which constitutes the embodiment of the community. The critic Doris Sommer has recognized this characteristic:

> 'The testimonial I' in these books neither presumes nor even invites us to identify with it. We are too foreign, and there is no pretence here of universal or essential human experience. That is why, at the end of a long narrative in which Rigoberta has told us so much, she reminds us that she has set limits which we must respect. The claim that she is representative helps to explain why, like autobiographers, she uses a singular pronoun, 'I', not 'we'. That is, at the same time that she refuses intimacy with the reader — because intimacy invites identification and perhaps our

imperializing substitution of her as the protagonist of the story — she also takes care not to substitute her community in a totalizing gesture. Instead, her singularity achieves its identity as an extension of the collective. The singular represents the plural, not because it replaces or subsumes the group, but because the speaker is a distinguishable part of the whole.... This is where we come in as readers, invited to be with the speaker rather than to be her. (1991:39)

Earlier in this article, Sommer reminds us that Rigoberta's narrative first person is a mediated composite based on a number of pre-configurative events such as interviews, compilation, editing and narrative structuring. We must also put on the table the basic phenomena of all writing that no memoir or testimonial can ever be fully personal, subjective, confessional or individual since language itself is a mediated symbolic system that functions best as communication when it is intersubjective, that is, when it moves from the idiosyncratic to commonality of the language-speaking community. Thirdly, there is no true collective prose, even when there is extensive collaboration, since someone must make the appropriation of the other's expression into the text. There can be successive hands at work on a text which would make it supra-individual or there can be an intimate symbiotic relationship between two individuals as we have in this text but when they narrate they narrate as one. Fourthly, we must not overstate the conflict of languages in the case of Rigoberta's text. It is true that her native language is Quiche and that her Spanish has been learned only a few years before the composition of the text, but Burgos-Debray is not translating from the Quiche, she is editing an oral transcript into a written one. Few commentators have taken cognizance of this salient factor. The composite narrator created by Burgos-Debray and Rigoberta Menchu is struggling to rescue a form of life that is threatened by the dominant political and economic power of the state through military and cultural warfare. To rescue her people she cannot symbolically represent them textually. The textual embodiment of a community is not unique to Rigoberta's text, but this mode of representation has never been realized better than in her text.

The significance of testimonial as a literary genre in Latin America cannot be overstated. This new genre of the postmodern artistic revolution has become a part of contemporary culture in at least three ways.

Because testimonials raise the voice of people who have been marginalized, they oppose the centrism of a master text which in Latin America has been predominantly Eurocentric, but the testimonials coming from Bolivia, Chile, Cuba, El Salvador, Guatemala and Mexico, do not displace the previous centre with a new one by inverting center and margin. Testimonial writing challenges the paradigm of the master text from a vantage point of plurality.

Secondly, testimonials, as we have said before, use the first person narrative voice in a unique way. Because it is a mediated narrative first person it is an 'I' that does not stand for the individual but rather for the collective embodiment. It is an 'I' that is 'us'.

And thirdly, testimonials are revolutionary in the sense that they have already begun the deconstruction of ideological national hegemony moving toward a multiplicity of cultures sharing the same nation.

University of Toronto

Works Cited

Menchu, Rigoberta with Elizabeth Burgos-Debray 1984 *I, Rigoberta Menchu, An Indian Woman in Guatemala,* tr. Ann Wright. Verso, London and New York.

Sommer, Doris 1991 'Rigoberta's Secrets' in *Latin American Perspectives* 18.3: pp. 32–50.

Tania Franco Carvalhal

Latin America: Cultural Dialogue from the Periphery

When Jorge Luís Borges made a study of Kafka's precursors, in his book entitled *Otras Inquisiciones* (1952), he considered him 'to be as singular as the phoenix of rhetorical praise' and, after frequenting his pages a bit, he came to think he could 'recognize his voice, or his practices, in texts from diverse literatures and periods'. The first was Zeno's paradox against movement. In the second text, the affinity was not one of form but one of tone. It was an apologue by Han Yu, a prose writer of the ninth century, reproduced in Margouliès' admirable *Anthologie raisonnée de la littérature chinoise* (1948). The third text derived from a more easily predictable source: the writings of Kierkegaard. For Borges, it was not only a spiritual affinity between both writers but the fact that Kierkegaard, like Kafka, wrote 'many religious parables on contemporary and bourgeois themes'. The fourth of these prefigurations found by Borges was Browning's poem 'Fears and Scruples', published in 1876.

Borges' series of Kafka's precursors is heterogeneous. For him, the fact that 'not all of them resemble each other' was more significant because in each of these texts he found Kafka's idiosyncrasy to a greater or lesser degree, but 'if Kafka had never written a line, we would not perceive this quality, in other words, it would not exist'. As he says: 'The poem "Fears and Scruples" by Browning foretells Kafka's work, but our reading of Kafka perceptibly sharpens and deflects our reading of the poem. Browning did not read it as we do now'(1952: 201).

The enumeration created by Borges explains his fundamental thesis in this essay, that is, 'that every writer *creates* his own precursors. His work modifies our conception of the past, as it will modify the future'. T. S. Eliot's thinking in *Points of View* (1941) is behind Borges' thought, as the author says. Nevertheless, the concept of 'tradition' in Borges gains an unexpected formulation: the 'individual talent' not only breaks the continuity but also acts as an element that lightens what comes before it, giving it another meaning. Chronology is inverted: the model does not necessarily come before the great work, but it is this work that creates its predecessors. Therefore, the notion of the model becomes poorer: it is not important what comes before the great text — it matters what such a text brings from the past. Thus, the transforming role of a particular text goes in two directions simultaneously: the one of the past, that it enlightens, and the one of the future, that it changes.

From the essay by Jorge Luís Borges we can learn two other lessons: literature is a totality in which traditions interconnect, for a text of a given literature can find its predecessors in other literatures; and the reader's role is to bring back, from a given work, the ones that can be read as its predecessors, constituting, in this wide whole, a tradition that is not exclusively the Western one.

It is not surprising that such ideas are developed by a Latin-American writer. His position of being apart from the established cultural centres as a producer of theoretical concepts offers the Latin American an advantage: that of critical distance. On the one hand he finds a varied and multiform local tradition, resulting from contextual insertion and from external intellectual origin (usually European); on the other hand, he may critically consider not only the Western tradition to which he belongs, but also those from which he is apart.

The Latin American writer is able to dialogue simultaneously with all literatures, since he does not strictly adhere to one tradition: the Western one. Nevertheless, the wide movement permitted to a writer such as Borges does not occur within the limits of his own continent. The biggest affinity is still for what corresponds to far territories, while the close reality remains obscure.

The notion of Latin America suggests a certain unity. In fact, it is not so. It comprises a group of very different countries, where cultural discrepancies and diversities are continuously emerging. As Alfred J. MacAdam says in *Modern Latin American Narratives: The Dreams of Reason*:

> ...there is no unified body of writing from any single Latin American country during any historical period (and this would include the so-called novel of the Mexican Revolution) which would recapitulate all the concerns of the entire continent. There is no single national literature in Latin America that captures the 'spirit of the age' for the rest of Latin America. (1977:2)

Despite this, those who watch it from outside imagine a situation of wholeness in which complete dialogue flows. It is not so. For example, discussion of Brazilian fiction is often absent from studies of Latin American writing. A book such as *On Modern Latin American Fiction* edited by John King (1987) is almost an exception. In fact, as an island where people speak Portuguese, Brazil is a stranger in the middle of the Spanish world, so different is it and with its own peculiar literature. The axis of the cultural dialogue has historically been Europe and Latin America. Common points are due to the regular contacts with European countries. In spite of their geographical proximity, Latin

American literatures are quite unknown to each other.

As a consequence of conquest, of colonizations and of the various immigrations, Latin America is marked in its origin by a cultural bereavement, during which many forms of indigenous language disappeared. As is well known, they were replaced by a new physical and cultural resettlement based on which various nationalities would emerge under the stigma of historical dependence. Therefore, the relation with history in the large sense of the term is crucial in the analysis of the heterogeneous Latin American literary context.

Octavio Paz tells us that 'Latin America is a historical, social and political concept: it indicates a group of countries, not a literature'. Therefore, to study Latin American literature is to think about the building process of Latin America as well as about the aesthetic expression of this process.

If literature and history are interlinked in Latin America, they must go together in this context. It is only by a comparative approach that we can understand, for instance, that the literary evolution in Brazil and in Spanish America was parallel but independent. As a simple example, the term 'modernism' doesn't signify the same in this heterogeneous context. There is no correspondence between Brazilian and Spanish American movements both called 'modernism'. Both looked to Europe and found inspiration there but at different times and with radically different results. For Spanish America, modernism corresponds to the poetry of Ruben Dario and his group, to a kind of symbolism; for Brazilian literature this is a movement which dates from 1922, an avant-garde movement, which implies the possibility of an experimental literature.

Only one thing ties this large literary context together: the search for identity. On the long road from colonization to independence, all forms of Latin American literatures try to 'dress' themselves in the colours of their countries and, no doubt, such a preoccupation seemed at the beginning a sign of vitality and a guarantee of a future.

In searching for 'the nature of America', nineteenth-century writers found an overflowing source of inspiration and they gave their own form to a national way of thinking. In 1873, one of the great Brazilian authors, Machado de Assis, wrote:

> This independence has no 'Sete de Setembro' [7 September, Brazilian Independence Day]; it has no 'Campo de Ipiranga' [locale where the Independence of Brazil was declared], it will not occur in one day, but methodically will grow more durable, become lasting. It won't be the work of one or two generations; many will work for it until it is perfected.

In fact, Latin American writers had to invent their past. They had to reinvent what was lost. All the greatest Latin American historic novels such as *One Hundred Years of Solitude* by Gabriel Garcia Márquez and *Time and Wind* by Erico Verissimo are the story of Latin American foundation, a rewriting of the origins. We can say then that the literatures of these countries represent a search for national identity, for national consciousness.

The Latin American author considered himself at once as a 'latecomer' and a 'newborn', as Geoffrey Hartmann wrote in the preface of *The Fate of Reading* (1975). In front of him he has the 'future' of this new land but behind him he has very little or nothing. Even authors such as Machado de Assis, Jorge Luís Borges or Lautréamont, whose works seem very cosmopolitan, cannot be studied as 'men without a country'. Their nationalities must be taken into account if their works are to be appreciated; no matter how cosmopolitan they seem, there is Latin American sensibility present in all of them.

As Latin American writing is the product of a colonial society influenced by metropolitan centres, it must be analysed in a double perspective. The rich Latin American literary context was marked by two opposite forces: the 'local colour' and the appeal of cosmopolitan ideas. We can read these literatures as an alternation of these two forces and we have to take into consideration the lacerating situation faced by the intellectuals of a peripheral continent hesitant between embracing a Europeanizing internationalism and the nationality instinct that turned them to local aspects and subjects.

In this context, by reassessing historical data Comparative Literature must analyse these tensions, and reproduce this variation through its own performance. Thus, it becomes an abstraction of the relations established by the continent's literatures, examining their ties with Europe and the connections that they maintain among themselves.

At the same time, we have to consider that if European heritage was transplanted it was also transformed. Out of their native context the cultural models changed because *transplantation implies transformation*. In Latin America this notion is very important because we must have in mind that this *transformation* is the sum of Latin American literatures today. They have come a very long way from copying and importing models to original creations; from literary indebtedness to originality.

When I emphasize the importance of these changes, I want to suggest a new dimension to the cultural dialogue in Latin America: it can no longer go in one direction only (from Europe to the peripheral literatures) but it can turn back upon itself, from the periphery to the traditional centres. Intertextuality becomes an important notion that calls to the reader's attention its own deliberate allusiveness as a way to affirm its own historicity and its involvement in historical process.

A DIALOGICAL RELATIONSHIP

The Brazilian poet, Haroldo de Campos, has developed the notion of a new dialogical relationship. As he says, 'today, in both Europe and Latin America, to write means, more and more, to rewrite, to re-chew'. And he adds:

> At a certain moment, with Borges, at least, the European discovered he could no longer write his world prose without the increasingly devastating contribution made

by the voracious Alexandrian barbarians. The book he read could no longer remain the same, after being chewed and digested by the blind Homerian of Buenos Aires, who even dared to rewrite the *Quixote* under the pseudonym of Pierre Ménard. Without Borges, what would be new in Robbe-Grillet's *nouveau roman*? Who could now read Proust without admitting Lezama Lima? Read Mallarmé, today, without taking into consideration the intertextual hypothesis of Vallejo's *Trilce* and Paz's *Blanco*?

In Haroldo de Campos's perspective the intersection of discourses is considered as a necessary dialogue that neutralizes any xenophobic monologue. And we might do well to mind Goethe's very relevant warning: 'Any literature, closed upon itself, finally lapses into tediousness, when it is not renewed and revivified by means of a contribution from without.'

This interaction in the literary world between Europe and Latin America can also be illustrated by the relation between Ruben Dario's works and modernism in Spain or by the works of Jorge Amado, José Lins do Rego and Graciliano Ramos in relation to the new-realism in Portugal. Spanish American modernism could be a good example of how a peripheral literature can contribute to the renovation of European literature much more than the well-known Latin American 'boom'. In fact, this renovation does not imply an original invention but a transformation of some established literary process in a particular way. We can say that Spain received French influence transmuted by Spanish American modernism which acted as an active intermediary of the new tendencies.

In the Brazilian case, modernism arose as a response to European avant-garde artistic movements, as a reaction to the literary codes that had dominated Brazilian letters since the end of the nineteenth century. The 'Week of Modern Art', a series of exhibitions of the visual arts, concerts, poetry and prose readings held in São Paulo in February 1922, marks the official beginning of the movement. This movement was a response to the tension of Latin American intellectuals whose education and inclination was European but who wanted to free themselves from the bond of European hegemony and create an art faithful to national reality.

Oswald de Andrade, with his 'Manifesto Antropófago' (Cannibal Manifesto) in 1928, wanted to 'see with open eyes', to reverse the historically imitative stance of Brazilian literature and the one-directional flow of artistic influence.

I believe that in Brazil, with Oswald de Andrade's 'Antropofagia' (Anthropophagy), we get a strong sense of the need to consider the national element in a dialogical (in the sense intended by Bakhtin) and dialectical relationship with the universal. Brazilian modernism helps us to understand why in Borges' short story 'Pierre Ménard, el auctor del *Quixote*' he decided 'to continue being Pierre Ménard and to arrive at *Don Quixote* through the experiences of Pierre Ménard'. In this case, the author is the reader: this anonymous Pierre Ménard becomes the reader himself whose active interference launches the text in his own time and in its suitable context. Ménard's reproduction gains new interpretive meanings, thanks to the new context in which it appears. The anachronism deliberately inserted in the short story, as the narrator states at the end, illustrates the possibility of a chronological inversion which literary history does not normally consider.

In a Latin American approach we cannot forget Borges' statement mentioned at the beginning that writers invent their predecessors. So, the new text, the one that subverts the established order, the one which stimulates tradition and obliges re-reading of previous works, is the one that functions as a fundamental point of reference, regardless of its localization in literary systems.

In this context, to understand Latin American literature we can consider cultural dialogue as a kind of misreading in which the notion of creative transformation is essential. Parody is central in this process. In a new dialogical relationship, we can handle all European themes. As Borges says, 'handle them without superstition, with an irreverence which can have, and already does have, fortunate consequences' (1952:184). These 'fortunate consequences' are Latin American literature.

Universidade Federal do Rio Grande do Sul

Works Cited

Andrade, Oswald 1928 'Manifesto Antropófago' in *Revista de Antropofagia*. Instinto de Nacionalidade, São Paulo.

Assis, Machado de 1873 *Literatura Brasileira*. Instinto de Nacionalidade, São Paulo.

Borges, Jorge Luis 1952 *Labyrinths: Selected Stories & Other Writings*. New Directions, New York.

Campos, Haroldo de 1981 'Da razão antropofágica: a Europa sob o signo da devoração' in *Colóquio Letras* 65. Fund. C. Gulbenkian, Lisboa.

Hartmann, Geoffrey 1975 *The Fate of Reading and Other Essays*. University of Chicago Press.

King, John (ed.) 1987 *On Modern Latin American Fiction*. Noonday Press, New York.

MacAdam, Alfred J. 1977 *Modern Latin American Narratives: The Dreams of Reason*. University of Chicago Press.

WADE KELSON

Primo Levi and the Humaneness of Cultural Understanding

Human beings generally regard the 'humane' individual as benevolent, compassionate, and understanding. This kind of person typically gratifies another person's need for companionship, communication, or nourishment, by an expression of personal partiality. Consequently, the recipient of this goodwill is sustained. The humane stands in binary opposition to the inhumane, which is characterized by barbarity, savagery, and cruelty. The inhumane person seeks to undermine the individual human being through an expression of explicit disregard. Thus, the victim of this ill-will is negated.

These two poles of humaneness and inhumaneness characterize the duality of humankind. Their struggle against each other appears continuous; however, the cultural mainstream of Western Europe during Nazi domination seemed to have increased the polarization of humankind as the inhumane launched an attack against the humane of an intensity the world had never known. The genocide of European Jews was not a burnt offering as a sacrificial rite to God as the general term Holocaust implies, but rather a programmatic destruction in the name of pseudo-science and religious minorities. No term appropriately titles the extermination of millions, but the word Holocaust has come to signify the offensive. Accordingly, I will refer to the event as Holocaust for the purpose of this article and not as Shoah, although I remain conscious of the victims not as offerings of a sacrificial religious rite, but rather as innocent individuals destroyed by senseless savagery. Their victimization finds poignant expression in the words of the Holocaust survivor Primo Levi, who writes in his autobiographical *Se questo è un uomo*, 'di che cosa avremmo dovuto pentirci, e di cosa venir perdonati? (1958:14). ['What had we to repent, for what crime did we need pardon?' (Woolf 1959:5)]

In his work, Levi immediately draws the reader's attention to the tension tearing his sense of cultural identity apart: he is both Italian and Jewish. During the early 1940s in Italy, this mixed background could only be seen as an intolerable dissonance. Levi was a rebel against the Fascist Party of Italy and was arrested because of that involvement, not because he was a Jew. At the time of his arrest Levi disclosed to his captors his Jewishness as a way of evading immediate death, a death which he thought came certainly to rebels. His admitting being Jewish caused his captors to regard him only as 'Jew' with no consideration of his *Italianitá*. Consequently he moved quickly into the cultural margins of Italy: a holding pen surrounded by guards and barbed wire located near Modena.

Levi's fellow prisoners included families who, although removed from homelands and cultural centres, carried with them a sense of cultural identity which forbade them to enter the savagery of the dominant culture. Even within the inhumane conditions of the detention camp they responded to sustain the fellow human being, particularly the mothers:

> But the mothers stayed up to prepare the food for the journey with tender care, and washed their children and packed the luggage; and at dawn the barbed wire was full of children's washing hung out in the wind to dry. Nor did they forget the diapers, the toys, the cushions and the hundred other small things which mothers remember and which children always need. (Woolf:6)

At Auschwitz, Levi encountered individuals from Hungary, Czechoslovakia, Greece, Poland, Germany, Austria, and Italy. Each person entered the Lager with an identity beyond being Jews: their nationality, their language, their folkways, their physical appearance, and their names. Cultural differences notwithstanding, Levi entered a deeply marginalized world characterized by the vacuity of cultural centring. The following passage expresses the Lager's harsh attempt to eradicate difference among the Jews:

> In a moment, with almost prophetic intuition, the reality was revealed to us: we had reached the bottom. It is not possible to sink lower than this; no human condition is more miserable than this, nor could it conceivably be so. Nothing belongs to us anymore; they have taken away our clothes, our shoes, even our hair; if we speak, they will not listen to us, and if they listen, they will not understand. (Woolf:21)

This paragraph appears near the beginning of *Sul fondo* (On the bottom). The chapter describes extreme debasement, although subsequent chapters reveal worse conditions. That Levi asserts the impossibility of further descending into the dark regions of the inhumane so early on in the book, 'It is not possible to sink lower than this', suggests his sense of the humane: a sense similarly shared by the mothers in the Italian detention camp which discourages him from completely surrendering to the savagery of the Lager.

The author's particular regard for humankind finds its roots outside the cultural mainstream of inhumanity. His homeland which serves as his cultural centre affords him an idea of the humane that seeks to sustain and not negate mankind, characteristic of his affiliation with the Resistance movement, justice and liberty.

The centre exists because of a metaphysics of presence, not because of sign; the culture of Levi's homeland ultimately subjects itself to the arbitrary nature of the present. Therefore, upon being forced to leave his homeland and cross the geographical and cultural boundaries into the Lager, Levi distances himself from the dynamic culture of his homeland present, but carries with him a permanent sense of his homeland past. The centre is fixed only in the present and cannot transcend time in an unmanipulated fixedness, 'that is to say', as Derrida has written, 'a system in which the central signified, the original or transcendental signified, is never absolutely present outside a system of differences' (1978:280).

Displaced from his cultural centre and forced into the Lager, Levi's precious sense of the humane which seeks to sustain humankind undergoes severe scrutiny. The Lager eradicates any sense of being human which the prisoners have brought with them. The prisoners must ignore the laws of humanity to which they had been well accustomed prior to their victimization, and steal from one another food and clothing for their survival. Levi recalls, 'To he that has, will be given; to he that has not, will be taken away' (Woolf:101). The Lager also obliterates intimate conversation among the prisoners.

When the prisoners began to think about a world beyond the Lager, they were tormented by sweet memories of their native homeland. Each prisoner, unable to share the memories, bore alone the unbearable pain of longing for home. Due also to obvious linguistic barriers, Jews in Auschwitz entered into yet another deep isolation within the extreme margins of Nazi Europe. The pain demoralized and defeated the human being, as Levi expresses: 'Here we are, docile under your gaze; from our side you have nothing more to fear; no acts of violence, no words of defiance, not even a look of judgement' (Woolf:177).

Within this vacuum of the Lager, Levi examined, analysed, and probed his personal sense of cultural disjunction. During the months of slavery, Levi came into contact with a vast array of people from extremely disparate backgrounds, cultures, and ethnic origins. Under the great pressure of the concentration camp, cultural difference persisted but became penetrable. The stress of being compelled to the very margins of human existence forced a kind of intercultural exchange that would not have been thinkable in less threatening circumstances. Misunderstandings and misreadings, which had been harboured — often unwittingly — for various reasons related to inauthentic self or group definition, gave way.

Levi describes seeing through the levels of culture to expressions of humane acts that transcend divergent cultural norms and offers a common foundation for the comprehension of all human experience. He encounters ex-sergeant Steinlauf of the Austro-Hungarian army whose ritual of regular bathing awakens Levi's sense of civility and dignity which signifies the power to refuse his consent to die. He meets Jean the Pikolo of his Kommando whose perceptive inquiry of literature momentarily removes the Lager from the foreground. His attempt to recall lines of Dante provides a weak conduit into a world which seeks to sustain the individual. His attempt to communicate Dante to Pikolo encourages a particular sensitivity that he and Pikolo must share to understand one another.

Finally, Levi encounters Lorenzo the civilian bricklayer whose daily gift of bread sustains Levi, not simply because of the nourishment from the bread itself, but because of the nourishment from Lorenzo's simple and gentle gesture of humanity. Consequently, Levi reveals, 'I believe that it was really due to Lorenzo that I am alive today.... Thanks to Lorenzo, I managed not to forget that I myself was a man' (Woolf:142).

With the sanctity of a sacramental rite, Lorenzo, who remains outside of the Lager, shared bread with Levi and Levi in turn shared the bread with his companion Alberto. The dividing and sharing of the bread invokes the etymology of the word 'companionship' implying a nourishing of both body and soul. This act of humaneness gratifies and sustains Levi in the world of the Lager, which 'is hunger and the prisoners are hunger personified' (Patruno 1995:15).

Brigham Young University

Works Cited

Derrida, Jacques 1978 *Writing and Difference*. University of Chicago Press.

Garber, Zev 1992 *Shoah: The Paradigmatic Genocide: Essays in Exegesis and Eisegesis*. University Press of America, Lanham.

Levi, Primo 1958 *Se questo è un uomo*. Giulio Einaudi editore, Torino.

—— 1959 *If This Is a Man*, tr. Stuart Woolf. Orion Press, New York

Patruno, Nicholas 1995 *Understanding Primo Levi*. University of South Carolina Press.

STEVEN P. SONDRUP

Hanyu at the Joy Luck Club

Immigration as a social phenomenon presents a complex array of divided loyalties, hierarchies, and systems of reference. In the case of immigrants themselves, marginalization of many different kinds is a complicated and often deeply disorienting experience. On the one hand, the immigrant feels varying degrees of alienation in the new culture: unfamiliar customs, habits, laws, and language exert a powerful centrifugal force toward the outer edges of society. On the other hand, the immigrant also experiences an alienation from the home culture as well. The forces that combined to occasion emigration — a departure from the familiar, the including, and the defining —often come more clearly and painfully into focus. Not only do the motives and forces that prompted the original emigration loom large, but the distance between the old and the new culture grows ever greater. While the emigrant is living away from the natal culture, that culture continues to change, transform itself, and develop in ways that the emigrant may not have been able to anticipate or even understand. Local and regional dialects often give way to a nationally standardized language in which the emigrant may feel deracinated after an absence. The bind is, thus, double: the emigrant will typically experience at least a degree of marginalization in the new culture but will constantly become ever more alienated from the changing native culture. For the children of immigrants born in the new culture, the tension between assimilation on the one hand and retention of some kind of link to the values, traditions, and language of their parents on the other can be considerable. Many factors play a role in heightening or narrowing, in complicating or resolving, or in exacerbating or relieving the tension. The archetypal generation gap in such families is complicated by one additional and often very complex factor.

The expansion of the canon of American literature begun in the 1960s and continuing into the present has brought the literature and criticism of many minority groups within the United States of America to the attention of much larger audiences. Asian American literature is a strategically constructed term stressing a unitary if not monolithic identity but coined to counter marginalization or complete exclusion.[1] In the late 1970s Elaine H. Kim attempted to define Asian American literature as 'work published in English by writers of Chinese, Japanese, Korean, and Filipino ancestry about the experiences of Asians in America' (1982:xi). By any standard, Asian American literature has thrived in a most remarkable way over the last twenty-five years and achieved extraordinary prominence during the early 1990s. The popular, commercial and critical success of Maxine Hong Kingston's *The Woman Warrior*, Henry Hwang's *M. Butterfly*, and Amy Tan's *The Joy Luck Club* and *The Kitchen God's Wife* are indicative of this new pre-eminence. Notably, the new prominence of Asian American novels, poetry, and drama is well balanced by the numerous articles and books by scholars specializing in Asian American literature.

In presuming to discuss Asian American literature and more specifically one aspect of *The Joy Luck Club*, I am acutely aware of the precariousness of my critical stance. As a Danish American male, I have no access to distinctly insider Chinese cultural knowledge, no facility with a methodology that might be group-specific, and no first-hand experience with mother-daughter relationships that are certainly an extremely important matrix of the novel.[2] Although sensitive, I hope, to the uniqueness and particularity of each of these foci of understanding, I am persuaded, along with those adhering to the approach frequently known as the ethnicity school, that more is to be gained than lost by allowing broad critical entrée to minority literatures.[3]

The issue I wish to raise, albeit as an outsider, is that of the status of the Chinese language in a narratological sense in *The Joy Luck Club*.[4] By definition the Chinese American novel — a specific species of the Asian American novel — is written in English, but Chinese, usually either Yue (or Cantonese as it is more typically known in the United States) or Mandarin, is part of the texture of the novel, a texture that conspicuously plays a role in the narrative strategy in some cases or in others is so smooth it almost vanishes. *The Joy Luck Club* is decidedly of the former type. The question of language is problematized in the opening lines of the novel.

> In America I will have a daughter just like me. But over there nobody will say her worth is measured by the loudness of her husband's belch. Over there nobody will look down on her, because I will make her speak only perfect American English.... Now the woman was old. And she had a daughter who grew up speaking only English and swallowing more Coca-Cola than sorrow. (3)

The speaking of perfect American English is initially a token of full assimilation into American society, a society that is naively thought to be free of social injustices and prejudices. But disappointingly, the mastery of American English at the expense of Mandarin is no warrant of happiness, but rather a source of misunderstanding and at least transitory alienation. To learn perfect

American English is to rebel against traditional Chinese cultural expectations and to resist, forget, or suppress the official language in which they are embedded.

The Joy Luck Club narrates the maturation of four second-generation Chinese women and their eventual bonding with their mothers, all of whom had left China in the hope of finding a better life. Each of these four mothers who played mah-jong together for decades tries in the course of many years to tell her daughter about her past and especially her relationship with her mother in a way in which the values of traditional China, the Chinese diaspora, and male Eurocentrism are engaged. The nature and dynamics of storytelling which create an alternative space and a different history distinct from the official accounts of war and political strife in China during the 1930s and 1940s are foregrounded and become one of the principle axes of the novel.

The linguistic competence of the major characters in the novel is clearly presented. The mothers are all native speakers of Mandarin and are thus a distinct minority in the Chinese American community which is made up of about eighty-six per cent speakers of Cantonese (Ramsey 1987:98). This marginalization within a marginalized community, however, is an issue that is touched upon only in passing. The daughters grow up hearing varying amounts of Mandarin spoken at home and understand their mothers when they speak Mandarin but do not achieve any significant degree of oral fluency themselves. Notably, none can read Chinese, a fact which is a difficulty in that spoken Chinese is much more strongly linked to writing than Western languages are to their respective written forms. The attempt to clarify which meaning of a particular homophone is intended by reference to the appropriate character is incomprehensible and alien to the second generation. The daughters' inability to read Chinese characters, however, stresses the importance of the spoken language and immediate interpersonal relationships as opposed to depersonalized abstractions. The value of the intimacy of an oral tradition that strongly contrasts with the official and public tradition and in many ways subverts it is forcefully adduced.

Oliver Stone's film adaptation of the novel heightens the linguistic contrast in competence between the first and second generation. Early in the film, Jing-mei cautions her aunties not to speak Chinese at the mah-jong table lest she, not being able to understand them, think they are cheating. Yet, when at the end she finally meets her two sisters in China, she is able to speak remarkably fluent Mandarin. The stressing of the difference between the Chinese culture of the mothers and the basically American culture of the daughters takes place very forcefully in linguistic terms in other ways as well. In the film, none of the daughters is ever portrayed speaking Mandarin or giving any evidence of understanding it at all, whereas the novel clearly indicates that they have at least rudimentary control of the language. Moreover, in the film all of the episodes that take place in China are performed in Mandarin accompanied by

English subtitles. The novel, of course, contains no extended passages in Mandarin, and the descriptions of life in China prior to emigration are entirely in English. This cinematic innovation changes one of the fundamental structural aspects of the novel. Whereas the mothers in the novel illustrate the proposition that subalterns can never speak for themselves, that they can only find a voice through others — in this case their daughters who have been brought up to speak perfect American English — in the film they are given their own very distinctive voice which is not only not mediated by their daughters but completely alien to their daughters.[5] The powerful sense of cultural otherness created by Mandarin dialogue is only enhanced by the mothers' gaining of the power of narrative in their own right that is not dependent on the perfect American English of their daughters. Because the cinematic gap between self and other is so much more pronounced in that the other has its own contrasting voice that is not subsumed within the voice of the self, the ultimate resolution of the painful separation of self and (m)other at the end is even more poignant.

Some of the most obvious misunderstandings between the immigrant mothers and those around them have to do with their less than complete mastery of English. Language difficulties have long been part of the caricature of Chinese Americans in American popular culture and take place on many levels. Direct quotations of the mothers' speech are often unidiomatic in English but fully reveal the Chinese syntax lying just below the surface. After a heated description on the difference between Taiyuan and Taiwan, Lindo Jong triumphantly proclaims, 'Now you understand my meaning' (203). Although the intent is perfectly clear, the statement seems peculiar in English but can easily be recognized as a word for word translation of *xianzai ni mingbai wode yisi*. The phonological struggles with English in *The Joy Luck Club*, however, are often witty and provide a telling commentary on contemporary American culture. When Ying-ying St. Clair refers to her social security (the government mandated system of retirement payments) as 'so-so security' (275), the contemporary American will easily understand how such a misunderstanding on the phonetic level could take place but also that 'so-so' in the sense of mediocre and barely adequate is not an altogether inappropriate description of the current state of the system. On another occasion, Suyuan Woo misunderstands a vulgar insult directed toward her in a neighbourhood disagreement in a wonderfully ironic manner. Reporting on the verbal exchange, she says:

> 'And that man, he raise his hand like this, show me his ugly fist and call me worst Fukien landlady. I not from Fukien. Huuh! He know nothing!' she said satisfied she had put him in his place. (224)

Her inability or refusal to understand the single most vulgar and socially unacceptable word in American English is a misprision that rejects the common and base (albeit in the new culture), insists literally on social legitimacy, and reaffirms her insistence on things of only the best quality, the explicit theme of the chapter in which the exchange takes place but more generally the novel as a whole.

The misunderstanding, though, is doing something more. The reader who is also familiar with Chinese will recognize in the word *Fukien* not a standard place name but rather a variation of *Fujian*, that is, Fujian province. To interpret and make sense of her angry neighbour's vulgar appellation which she does not understand or refuses to understand in English requires recourse to Chinese and specifically a dialectical form. Although Suyuan Woo is not in fact from Fujian province, the interpretive process legitimizes Chinese, dialectical Chinese, and English in a complex referential system. This incident is but one example of the rich polyvalence resulting from the interplay of Chinese and English.

Many pages of the novel have several romanized Chinese words or phrases printed in italics so they will stand out from the body text. Often the literal English translation follows immediately, but the syntax of the sentences is so carefully crafted that the non-Chinese-speaking reader may not realize that the translation is a translation. The Chinese thus functions on one level to create the feeling of a situation where cultures overlap and languages are freely mixed; that is, the effect of the real. But in creating the effect of the real, the novel is also less than fully candid with the non-Chinese-speaking reader. Words like *taitai* and *popo* are treated as proper names rather than titles or relationships and the translations that are given are, to say the least, somewhat idiosyncratic. More striking, however, is the romanization of the Chinese. The romanization does not adhere to any one of the major systems but appears to be principally a combination of the Pinyin and Yale systems, with occasional forms that belong to neither.[6] The unsystematic and non-standard romanization probably has no impact on the reader unfamiliar with the various systems of romanization, but for the reader able to take part at least to a degree on both the Chinese as well as the American side of the cultural dialogue, the effect is arresting. In its effort to recreate in presumably the American ear the sound of what was said, it stresses the underlying orality of the experiences being related. These experiences are not typically chronicled in official histories, but rather histories of a different kind, histories that are told by mothers to their daughters. But perhaps even more significantly, when these fundamentally oral experiences are written, their writing subverts and disrupts the established norms of official written discourse to create a special mode of discourse — an alternative narrative space — adequate to the narration of the histories of four women. Just as the official accounts of the civil wars, the Japanese invasion, and the great upheavals of the period are recorded in officially sanctioned and correct forms of the language, the suffering, disappointments, hopes, and joy — the history that is uniquely the women's and not a part of public record — requires a commensurate mode of expression that diverges from publicly accredited norms.[7]

This intersection of generations, cultures, and languages — both official and unsanctioned — constitutes a particularly rich signifying system and complex narrative architecture. One of the most arresting examples is the use of the Chinese word *bing*. It first occurs in the account of the childhood of Rose Hsu Jordan as the name of one of her four brothers: Matthew, Mark, Luke, and Bing. Particularly in the context of a chapter that begins with a description of An-Mei Hsu's Christian faith, the appearance of the name Bing at the end of a list of the New Testament evangelists is particularly disarming. Neither Christian tradition nor mainstream American culture seems to offer any obvious explanation for this curious series of names. Seeking an explanation in terms of what could be a Chinese name is, moreover, problematic because no Chinese tone is marked so the precise reading and meaning is indeterminable. The range of possible meanings is broad. If one assumes the first tone, among the possibilities are: a soldier or a pawn; or ice, icicles, or frost. Assuming the third tone: bright, luminous; to grasp or to hold; or cakes, biscuits, or pastry. Assuming the fourth tone: sickness, disease, a fault or defect, or to be distressed about; together with, incorporate, merge, combine, united; even or equal; or to drive off, to expel, or to arrange. Although this array would not present itself in a Chinese text because each sense would be represented by a different character, this specially forged narrative language — part English, part Chinese, part standardized, part free invention, and part a hybrid combination — offers wide-ranging interpretive possibilities. The immediate narrative situation helps isolate some meanings that may be heuristically helpful. Bing is the youngest of four brothers. On a family excursion to the beach, he wanders off and is drowned in the ocean never to be seen again. In this context, the cluster of meanings associated with sickness, disease, defect and distress certainly suggest themselves. Bing's tragic death would certainly justify an epithet suggesting defect and distress. Although the information that one of the possible readings of Bing provides adds to the character and power of the situation, it does not go very far in accounting for his presence among Matthew, Mark, and Luke.

The word, however, appears in another context. When Waverly Jong becomes very angry with her mother's manipulation and condescending insults, she angrily goes to her parents' home. In a discussion that begins with Waverly's confusing Taiyuan, her mother's home, with Taiwan, her mother in exasperation explains that another name for Taiyuan is Bing and writes the character, though to no avail. The character, however, is very important. The ancient form has been interpreted as two people walking down the same road together, and indeed that chapter of the novel ends with an image of Waverly and Lindo Jong perhaps being able to set aside differences and walk the same path. Although in modern usage, *bing* means side by side, united, together, simultaneously, or merged (as with a small state and a large state), in classical Chinese, particularly during the Zhou dynasty, the more abstract sense of united, or two people or things closely associated, was more pronounced.[8] To the extent that the ancient conflation in one character of a city name and the sense of being side by side or united resonates in the chaotic cultural space of the narrated immigrant community, it enriches, strengthens, and broadens the force of the narrative.

What connection, though, is there between Bing as the alternative name of Taiyuan and the child named Bing who drowned? What interpretive strategy suggests that the two are anything but unrelated homophones? The only response is that the novel seems to invite the juxtaposition. In its portrayal of immigrant life on the fragmented margins of both Chinese and American culture, *The Joy Luck Club* is so conspicuously structured to disrupt any sense of the linear flow of time, conventional narrative practice, or normative language usage in order to make connections that otherwise would not be made that the tentative conjunction of the two seems almost required.

If the little boy's name is interpreted in terms of the idea of being side by side or united, his name is a deeply ironic and tragic contrast to his fate. Being held by the Coiled Dragon (138) beneath the sea, he is completely separated from his family and particularly his mother. The poignancy of the loss is staggering. What, though, of Bing's relationship to his brothers, Matthew, Mark, and Luke in the biblical framework these names suggest? The Apostle John, whose place Bing has taken in the catalogue of the evangelists, has a very rich tradition associated with him: the beloved Apostle, the Apostle who elected to remain on earth until the second coming of Jesus, and the Apostle who beheld the apocalyptic end of the earth and recorded his vision. The element of the Johanine tradition most relevant here, though, is the emphasis throughout his gospel and to a lesser degree in the epistles on unity, on the community of believers, and on the mystical union of the trinity.[9] What links Bing to the evangelist John is, thus, the theme of unity deriving on the one hand from a major theme in the Gospel of John and on the other from one of the earliest senses of the Chinese word *bing*. In the episode dealing with the boy named Bing, he represents the tragically ironic reversal of what his name suggests and, unlike the Apostle John, he is precisely the one who is not permitted to linger.

Chinese at the Joy Luck Club obviously fulfills all of the immediate expectations. It provides the effect of the real by creating the ambience and linguistic color expected in a Chinese immigrant community. It also serves as a reliable index of assimilation: the poorer the mastery of Chinese, the greater the assimilation into American society. But beyond these rather obvious and predictable roles, Chinese significantly enhances the narrative power of the novel. The disruption of its norms by the first generation of immigrants parallels their distortions of English as non-native speakers and creates an alternative narrative space and a special mode of discourse that challenges official conventions but is exactly what is required for the telling of their stories. A medium of communication arises in which the seemingly most disparate of elements can find common ground and walk together just as the novel as a whole can be seen to hinge on the arduous, alienating and almost life-threatening challenge of finding common ground on which different generations, different cultures, different hopes, as well as the self and the other, can meet and walk together.

Brigham Young University

Notes

1 See Lemuel Ignacio's *Asian Americans and Pacific Islanders: Is There Such an Ethnic Group?* for historical background on the term. See also Kim, pp. xi–xii. Lynn Pan's *Sons of the Yellow Emperor: A History of the Chinese Diaspora* provides a useful survey of Chinese emigration to the United States.

2 See Xiaomei Chen's 'Reading Mother's Tale — Reconstructing Women's Space in Amy Tan and Zhang Jie'. See also the 'Introduction' and 'Occidentalism as Counterdiscourse' in *Occidentalism*. See also Susan Cahill's *Mother's Memories, Dreams, and Reflections by Literary Daughters*.

3 Sau-ling Cynthia Wong's *Reading Asian American Literature: From Necessity to Extravagance* deals specifically with reading strategies appropriate for Asian American Literature. See especially pp. 3–5 for a cogent formulation of the issue. See also Werner Sollors *Beyond Ethnicity: Consent and Descent in American Culture*, especially pp. 3–19.

4 For a general introduction to the issues centring on language and ethnicity, see Harald Haarmann *Language in Ethnicity: A View of Basic Ecological Relations*.

5 Although subaltern studies originated with Indian scholars their theoretical implications are finding fruitful application in other areas. See Gail Hershatter 'The Subaltern Talks Back: Reflections on Subaltern Theory and Chinese History'. The richest sources of information on subaltern studies is Oxford University Press's *Subaltern Studies*. See also Spivak's two essays in *In Other Worlds*, 'Subaltern Studies: Deconstructing Historiography' (pp. 197–221) and 'A Literary Representation of the Subaltern: A Woman's Text from the Third World' (pp. 241–68).

6 Notably, the Wade-Giles system does not seem to have played any role at all in any of the romanization except in personal names, for example, An-mei Hsu. Although it may have some advantages in terms of phonetic precision, the complex combination of consonants would probably not be helpful to most readers.

7 The broader question of the extent to which *The Joy Luck Club* fractures normative, patriarchal narrative conventions in creating a distinctly feminist mode of discourse invites further investigation.

8 For example, *Zheng zhong xing yin yi zhong he da zi dian* (Comprehensive Large Dictionary of Forms, Pronunciations, and Definitions, 2nd revised edition) under the entry for *bing* quotes Lin Yi-guang in pointing out that in Zhou Dynasty bronze script the word signified two people standing side by side united as one. And Couvreur's *Dictionnaire classique de la langue chinoise* (1963) offers the straightforward definition: 'deux personnes ou deux choses associées ensemble, associer ensemble deux personnes ou deux choses.'

9 The point is nowhere clearer than in John 17: 21–3: 'Jesus prays, that they all may be one; as thou, Father, art in me, and I in thee, that they also may be one in us: that the world may believe that thou hast sent me. And the glory which thou gavest me I have give them; that they may be one, even as we are one: I in them, and thou in me, that they may be made perfect in one; and that the world may know that thou hast sent me, and hast loved them, as thou hast loved me.' The view represented in the *Anchor Bible Dictionary* (Doubleday 1992) is typical: 'Oneness is the key to proper interpretation of the gospel of John. The key to unity in John is christological unity, specifically the unity of the Son with the Father. Jesus is the one shepherd, the one who is the exclusive shepherd of God s people (10:16). In 10:30 the christological oneness is stated most clearly: I and the Father are one (4:752).'

Works Cited

Cahill, Susan (ed.) 1988 *Mothers: Memories, Dreams, and Reflections by Literary Daughters.* Menton, New York.

Chen, Xiaomei 1994 'Reading Mother's Tale — Reconstructing Women's Space' in Amy Tan and Zhang Jie *Chinese Literature, Essay, Articles, Reviews* 16: pp. 111–32.

—— 1995 *Occidentalism: A Theory of Counterdiscourse in Post-Mao China.* Oxford University Press.

Haarmann, Harald 1986 *Language and Ethnicity: A View of Basic Ecological Relations.* Mouton de Gruyter, Berlin.

Hershatter, Gail 1993 'The Subaltern Talks Back: Reflections on Subaltern Theory and Chinese History' in *Positions* 1,1: pp. 103–30.

Ignacio, Lemuel 1976 *Asian Americans and Pacific Islanders (Is There Such an Ethnic Group?).* Philipino Development Association, San Jose, CA.

Kim, Elaine H. 1982 *Asian American Literature: An Introduction to the Writings and their Social Context.* Temple University Press, Philadelphia.

—— 1992 'Foreword' in Shirley Geok-lin Lim and Amy Ling (eds) *Reading Literatures of Asian Americans.* Temple University Press, Philadelphia.

Pan, Lynn 1990 *Sons of the Yellow Emperor: The History of the Chinese Diaspora.* Kodansha, New York.

Ramsey, S. Robert 1987 *The Languages of China.* Princeton University Press.

Sollors, Werner 1986 *Beyond Ethnicity: Consent and Descent in American Culture.* Oxford University Press.

Spivak, Gayatri Chakravorty 1988 *In Other Worlds: Essay in Cultural Politics.* Routledge, London.

Tan, Amy 1989 *The Joy Luck Club.* Ivy Books, New York.

Wong, Sau-ling Cynthia 1993 *Reading Asian American Literature: From Necessity to Extravagance.* Princeton University Press.

Song Weijie

Local or Global: Cultural Identity in Multicultural Contexts

In his inaugural lecture at University Center for Human Value, Princeton University, Professor Charles Taylor said, 'The crucial feature of human life that I want to evoke is its fundamental dialogical character.... My discovering my own identity doesn't mean that I work it out in isolation, but that I negotiate it through dialogue, partly overt, partly internalized, with others' (1992: 5–6).

Taylor's 'others' may be similar to what George Herbert Mead terms 'significant others'. Although face-to-face contacts with the *other* have been changed into communication through the mass media, the dialogical relations among different individuals and cultures are still necessary for the creation of meanings in transcultural negotiation and understanding.

I would like briefly to discuss the predicaments of dialogue in monoculturalism, cultural relativism and, most importantly, multiculturalism. There is neither actual dialogue nor normal identities in the hegemony of monoculturalism; the relationship between the self and the other, whether at the individual or the cultural level, is that between repression and submission, master and slave, colonizer and colonized (their specific histories and languages have been repressed). The arbitrary monologue and universalization of the dominant cultures and ideologies imply the control of marginalized and oppositional voices, and confine the 'subaltern' others in the 'prison house' of silence. Many negative images and stereotypes have been forced upon minority groups and cultures which are still resisting the distorting pressures with different strategies.

It seems that communication through dialogue is possible within the context of cultural relativism but, in fact, this is only a kind of bogus dialogue, because the socio-cultural hierarchy cannot be revised or deconstructed.

Notwithstanding the barriers of monoculturalism, cultural relativism also sets up its own new boundaries which make profound conversations and communication impossible among different cultures and nations. In other words, it restricts a single culture by unconscious prejudices and adherence to old rules. Cultural relativism constitutes the closed identities within a limited imagination.

Today, multiculturalism has become a new focus. But is this multiculturalism local or global? Professor Amy Gutmann points out that multiculturalism is a challenge, particularly in the United States:

> What does it mean for citizens with different identities, often based on ethnicity, race, gender, religion, to recognize ourselves as equals in the way we are treated in politics? In the way our children are educated in public schools? In the curricular and social policy of liberal arts colleges and universities? (Gutmann and Taylor 1994:3)

Is multiculturalism also a keyword for Chinese cultural contexts? How do we think about cultural identities in local or particular Chinese and Third World contexts?

China is an independent and complicated political society, where the problems of ethnicity and race are not as prominent as those of culture, religion and gender. In the context of contemporary Chinese literature and language, we find rising conflicts between indigenous and foreign cultures, traditional and (post)modern ideas, the elite and the mass, the left and the right, the radical and the conservative, and so on. This does not mean that multiple binary oppositions should or could be solved by dichotomous methods. The controversy of multiculturalism as perceived by the West may have been transposed into the cultural pluralism within the Chinese language and cultural spheres. There may therefore be some urgent need to rethink cultural identities.

Cultural identities may be constructed in the inter-Chinese public space[1], which is shared at the same time by elite and popular utterances and dominated by the prevailing orthodox ideologies[2]. 'Public space' cannot simply be equated with 'public sphere'. After his extremely concrete historical-sociological clarification of the concept, Jürgen Habermas goes on to say:

> *The fully developed bourgeois public sphere was based on the fictitious identity of the two roles assumed by the privatized individuals who came together to form a public: the role of property owners and the role of human beings pure and simple.* (1989:56; emphasis in original)

Contemporary China lacks the theoretical background, political systems and 'the privatized individuals' described by Habermas. It has little public sphere in the strict sense of that word because the coffee houses, reading clubs, intellectual salons and underground journals are restricted by the political authorities. And something resembling a 'public sphere' in China is not autonomous: it exists only in the sense of discourse. It is therefore transposed to the shared 'public space', where the official, elite and popular discourses are juxtaposed without clear divisions.

The 'public sphere' has a close relationship with 'civil society' in the Western tradition. However a relatively crystallized 'civil society' is still absent in China. Charles Taylor suggests that civil society is 'a web of autonomous associations, independent of the state, which bound citizens together in matters of common concern, and by their mere existence of action could have an effect on public policy' (1990:1). As China does not possess a mature civil society and culture, it is problematic whether the term can be used at all. However, considering the larger area — mainland China, Taiwan, Hong Kong, Singapore and the Chinese communities in the United States, United Kingdom, Canada, France, Germany and many other countries — we find that scholars and others do communicate with each other in a bilingual context, and also negotiate with other communities. This is the 'inter-Chinese public space', a relatively autonomous intermediate and buffer zone. Although there is not much difference between Chinese intellectuals within China and those abroad, especially in America, the former mainly deal with the problems of cultural pluralism, and the latter with multiculturalism; both the former and the latter can exchange their experiences and thoughts to complement each other.

Having defined the concrete cultural contexts, we can talk about the issues of identities. Benedict Anderson points out that identity cannot be 'remembered', but must be 'narrated' (1991:204). In other words, identities are constructed by some form of narrative and language. The identities of individuals, groups, nations and states are products of the imagination. This provides an insight into cultural identities in globalized contexts. The possibility of applying the idea to China still needs to be scrutinized, but the problems of identity are important in inter-Chinese contexts.

Describing it simplistically we can say that in the 1980s, radical mainland Chinese intellectuals set off an upsurge of 'cultural frenzy' which highlighted the importance and necessity of Western civilization. Following the traumas of the Cultural Revolution, individuals and the collective longed for 'readjustment and reorientations': 'they must *forge* for themselves a new speech, a new history or life story that would give it some rational or coherent form' (Deane 1990:14). There is the resolve in China that if the 'form' could not be 'forged' or found in China's civilization immediately, then it would be borrowed from other (Western) countries to solve the urgent needs of cultural integration. As Rey Chow says, 'China, perhaps because it is an exception to the rule of imperialist domination by race, land, and language involving a foreign power, in fact highlights the effects of the imperialistic *transformation of value and value-production* more sharply than in other 'third world' culture' (1993:8). Rather than the xenophobic mentality, the appropriations of modern Western theory by some Chinese intellectuals became a kind of new fashion for pursuing freshness, change, and openness. In the 1990s, this tendency has been replaced by the frenzied pursuit of Chinese national culture.

Some intellectuals are trying to return to academic inquiries, searching for the origins of Chinese culture and attempting to rebuild great traditions of the past in contemporary society. Extremists hope to construct a unique and pure Chinese culture and to resist foreign hybrid influences. This skein of nationalist narratives or fables implies a politics of imagination which can be used as a weapon or pharmakon to protect the injured self of a culture. It is the 'nostalgia of some ultimate moment of cure' (Jameson 1981:283), but the cure in this sense is a myth. Third World peoples try to be actively lucid about themselves and the determinations of their desire and their behaviour, however, the cure and integration becomes a kind of hallucination. 'National culture studies', as the symptom of the metaphysics of nationalism, obscures the present reality that China is still oppressed. Nationalism is like metaphysics: 'all nationalisms have a metaphysical dimension, for they are all driven by an ambition to realize their intrinsic essence in some specific and tangible form. The form may be a political structure or a literary tradition' (Deane 1990:8).

It is characteristic of the new nationalist 'frenzy' to reestablish some literary canons and to highlight the 'authenticity' of Chinese indigenous culture. But is there an integrated and unitary 'tradition' or just an amalgam of 'traditions'? The answer is that, on the one hand, Confucianism, Taoism and Buddhism (in fact, a 'foreign' culture introduced into China since the Han dynasty) are diverse and cannot be generalized as a universal Chinese culture. On the other hand, since the May Fourth Movement, foreign (mainly Western) influences cannot be erased from modern Chinese writing.

'Habermas delimits nationalism as a 'specifically modern phenomena of cultural integration', a problem that emerges 'at a time when people are at once both mobilized and isolated as individuals'. Nationalism is, then, a historical construct that fashions from devalued traditions and via mass communication an artificially integrated identity' (Matuštík 1993:4). This 'artificially integrated identity' can also be regarded as the 'true' one, restoring the energy of traditional cultures, and reconstructing positive images to resist the various kinds of false stereotypes imposed on the Orient. In the defence of indigenous cultures, however, the 'naming and renaming' of Chineseness designates a weakening and loss of unique nationality. Even though nationalism may serve a useful function in certain exigencies, along with fundamentalism and totalitarism it should be resisted. Evaluations of the 'frenzy of Chinese national culture studies' have discovered its potential conspiracy with the official ideology which must be exposed in order not to stifle intellectual discourse.

Terry Eagleton once pointed out the key irony of Western bourgeois Enlightenment: on the one hand, it highlights 'the abstract universal right of all to be free, the shared essence of identity of all human subjects to be autonomous'; on the other hand, 'the *telos* of the entire process is not, as the Enlightenment believed, universal truth, right and identity, but concrete particularity ... bourgeois ideology ... has never really been able to reconcile difference and identity, the particular and the universal' (Eagleton, Jameson and Said 1990:30–1). This kind of dilemma has become a globalized tendency in the contemporary world. The common problems of and the concrete differences between Chinese in the inter-Chinese space and larger spheres should not be simplistically juxtaposed with local and global contexts.

There are four kinds of cultural identities in the multicultural context. First, the divided identity, in which culture is selective, not comprehensive. It is not easy to find a perfect culture which we can fully identify with in the multicultural context. Meanwhile, pure culture or pure cultural identities are impossible.

Second, the globalization of cultures is producing saturated identities, because individuals have been endowed with multiple selves and indigenous cultures have been confused with many foreign cultural elements in many hybrid communities. To some extent, we can say that individual or cultural selves are exhausted in those multiple choices.

The third is the situation of fake identities, which exists especially in the discourses of minorities in which the subaltern cultures surrender to mainstream ideologies. The distorted imagination (for example, some stereotypes of the images of China and the Chinese people in American fiction, drama and film) has influenced the construction of self-imagery in inter-Chinese cultural productions. Some inter-Chinese authors wear Westernized clothes to self-dramatize the Oriental world.

The fourth is the reconstruction of identities. Perhaps the idea of universal identity should be abandoned and relatively suitable identities sought in multicultural contexts. That is to say, we should reflect local and global transformations and communications and reject old assumptions based on pre-multicultural contexts, and we should not use one kind of 'pride and prejudice' to resist another.

Cornel West defines a heuristic orientation for cultural identities in multicultural contexts. He calls it a 'new cultural politics of difference':

> ...the distinctive features of the new cultural politics of difference are to trash the monolithic and homogeneous in the name of diversity, multiplicity, and heterogeneity; to reject the abstract, general, and universal in light of the concrete, specific and particular; and to historicize, contextualize, and pluralize by highlighting the contingent, provisional, variable, tentative, shifting, and changing. (1993:203–4)

Peking University

Notes

1 See Benjamin Lee's essay 'Going Public'. Its different versions and reviews of it have appeared in *Public Culture* and the *Working Papers and Proceedings of the Center for Psychosocial Studies*, University of Chicago.

2 For a detailed discussion, refer to Li Tuo, Dai Jihhua, Song Weijie and He Li 1996 'Cultural

Criticism Confronting Challenges: Close Reading of the Texts of Several TV Play Series' in *Beijing Literature* 7.

Works Cited

Anderson, Benedict 1991 *Imagined Communities: Reflections on the Origin and Spread of Nationalism*. Verso, London & New York.

Chow, Rey 1993 *Writing Diaspora: Tactics of Intervention in Contemporary Cultural Studies*. Indiana University Press.

Deane, Seamus 1990 'Introduction' in Terry Eagleton et al. *Nationalism, Colonialism and Literature*.

Eagleton, Terry, Fredric Jameson, and Edward W. Said, *Nationalism, Colonialism and Literature*. University of Minnesota Press.

Gutmann, Amy and Charles Taylor (eds) 1994 *Multiculturalism: Examining the Politics of Recognition*. Princeton University Press.

Habermas, Jürgen 1989 *The Structural Transformation of the Public Sphere: An Inquiry into a Category of Bourgeois Society*, tr. Thomas Burger and Frederick Lawrence. M. I. T. Press.

Jameson, Fredric 1981 *The Political Unconscious: Narrative as a Socially Symbolic Act*. Cornell University Press.

Matuštik, Martin J. 1993 *Postnational Identity: Critical Theory and Existential Philosophy in Habermas, Kierkegaard, and Havel*. The Guilford Press, New York & London.

Taylor, Charles 1990 'Invoking Civil Society' in *Working Papers and Proceedings of the Center for Psychosocial Studies*, no. 31. University of Chicago.

—— 1992 'The Politics of Recognition' in *Working Papers and Proceedings of the Center for Psychosocial Studies*, no. 50. University of Chicago.

West, Cornel 1993 'The New Cultural Politics of Difference' in Simon During (ed.) *The Cultural Studies Reader*. Routledge, London & New York.

Guo Hongan

Le Paradoxe de l'Homme de Lettres

Tout au long de l'histoire chinoise, l'homme de lettres se présente toujours comme un Janus qui a récolté à la fois gloire et mépris. Mais hors de Chine, l'homme de lettres n'a pas eu, me semble-t-il, un sort meilleur. Déjà, dans l'Athènes des quatrième et cinquième siècles avant notre ère, les 'sages' sont souvent ridiculisés par les comédies. Jusqu'au début du dix-neuvième siècle, en France, le métier d'écrivain est plus ou moins méprisable aux yeux de la grande bourgeoisie. Charles Baudelaire en a donné un exemple.

A la sortie de la Seconde Guerre mondiale, les écrivains ont connu une période glorieuse. Mais bientôt le temps des maîtres à penser est révolu pour céder la place à l'âge médiatique. Aujourd'hui, en Chine comme dans le reste du monde, les écrivains se voient écartés de plus en plus du centre de la vie de la cité, du moins leur rôle de guide et de mentor de la société est sérieusement mis en question. Beaucoup d'intellectuels se croient amèrement substitués par les média, même par les stars dans leur fonction de directeur de conscience. La montée de la culture des masses a beaucoup contribué à cet état de choses. Mais en même temps, cela vient probablement aussi de la démarcation entre l'écriture et celui qui écrit. Ce n'est pourtant pas quelque chose de neuf. Si l'on jette un coup d'oeil rétrospectif dans l'histoire, cette démarcation existait depuis la haute antiquité, d'où venait cette querelle sur la méthode de la critique littéraire.

En Chine, l'écriture, la littérature comprise, est toujours hautement appréciée pour ses fonctions morale, politique et éducative. L'idée que la littérature, la poésie par exemple, est une manière de se divertir et, pour cela, est nuisible à la compréhension du Dao (raison, morale) et à la société n'a jamais été une idée dominante. Cao Pi (187–226), un empereur au début du troisième siècle, a dit dans une lettre: 'La littérature est une grande entreprise pour le gouvernement et une cause immortelle pour l'homme' (1979: 195). Pourtant, c'est encore lui qui a dit dans une autre lettre: 'Les gens de lettres anciens comme modernes ne se préoccupent guère de leur conduite. Très peu nombreux se sont établis par leurs bons comportements' (165). Peu après lui, plus d'un homme de lettres a dénoncé les vices et les tares de leurs confrères anciens et contemporains, par exemple, Liu Xie (465–532) dans *La sculpture du dragon et l'âme de l'écriture* et Yan Zhitui (531–590) dans *Les règles familiales*. Depuis lors, 'les gens de lettres sont sans vertu' est devenu une expression toute faite qui court de génération en génération. Cette opinion auparavant largement partagée parmi toutes les couches sociales tend aujourd'hui à regagner des suffrages. Mais d'autre part, l'écriture jouissait toujours d'un grand prestige dans toute la société, parce qu'elle était considérée comme une parole de saints et des sages: 'Comme la vertu de la littérature est grande!' Voilà la première phrase de *La sculpture du dragon et l'âme de l'écriture*.

Cette haute idée que certains hommes de lettres ont faite de l'écriture a conduit les anciens Chinois à prendre tout ce qui est écrit comme quelque chose de sacré et, par conséquent, digne de confiance. Tout papier noirci de caractères reçoit un respect particulier de la part des gens ordinaires. Ainsi l'homme qui sait composer de belles pages jouit d'une grande admiration parmi le peuple. D'où vient la question: l'écriture et celui qui écrit sont-ils identiques?

Selon Confucius lui-même, l'homme de vertu est sûrement l'homme du verbe, mais pas nécessairement vice versa. Donc, l'homme du verbe, c'est l'homme de lettres. Malheureusement, la sagesse de Confucius n'est pas toujours suivie. Le mot 'vertu' possède plusieurs sens chez les anciens Chinois, dont deux: d'une part l'éthique et la morale, d'autre part les rites confucéens. Or, un homme de lettres sans vertu peut quelquefois désigner quelqu'un qui veut simplement se libérer des contraintes imposées par le confucianisme, ou aussi bien quelqu'un qui se conduit malhonnêtement à l'égard des autres, étant vraiment lâche, et homme méprisable. Sauf cas particulier, l'homme de lettres sans vertu désigne plutôt le dernier.

Les gens sans vertu se trouvent parmi toutes les couches sociales et dans tous les métiers. Pourquoi dit-on toujours que les gens de lettres sont sans vertu, jamais les hommes d'Etat, les fonctionnaires, les militaires, les paysans? C'est parce que l'homme de lettres se voit attribuer une fonction spéciale: en haut, il sera le conseiller auprès des empereurs; en bas, l'éducateur du peuple. En un mot, il joue ou prétend jouer avec une autorité morale, le rôle de guide et de mentor de la société en disant aux autres comment se comporter et comment traiter leurs affaires. Pour que cette fonction soit bien remplie, il faut que l'écriture et celui qui écrit soient identiques, c'est-à-dire qu'un livre de bien doit sortir de la main d'un homme de bien. Mais comme tout le monde le sait, ils ne le sont pas en réalité, en Chine comme dans le reste du monde, hier comme aujourd'hui.

Les Chinois ont eu très tôt une idée de la poésie, selon laquelle le verbe est la voix du coeur, la poésie exprime la volonté et le sentiment du poète. A partir de là, les anciens Chinois avaient un principe, selon lequel l'écrit s'identifie à celui qui écrit, ou inversement. De là est née une méthode pour expliquer la poésie, puis une méthode de la critique pour tous les genres littéraires, même pour la peinture et la calligraphie. Cette méthode consiste à connaître l'homme pour connaître l'oeuvre et vice versa. C'est la même méthode que Sainte-Beuve a développée et schématisé en France au dix-neuvième siècle. On connaît les vicissitudes de cette fameuse méthode dite 'la critique biographique'.

Au début du vingtième siècle, Marcel Proust a lancé un défi à cette méthode en partant de la séparation entre l'homme et l'écriture:

> Un livre est le produit d'un autre moi que celui que nous manifestons dans nos habitudes, dans la société, dans nos vices. Ce moi-là, si nous voulons essayer de le comprendre, c'est au fond de nous mêmes, en essayant de le recréer en nous, que nous pouvons y parvenir. (1954:137)

Il en résulte que l'écrivain est un homme exceptionnel, un homme qui a une identité double, c'est dire qu'un homme devient un autre quand il prend la plume. Peu après, Qian Zhongshu, un grand écrivain chinois contemporain, a exprimé une opinion semblable:

> Ecrire pour la création littéraire d'une part, se conduire dans la société de l'autre, voilà deux choses qui sont corrélatives, mais différentes. Elles se touchent ou se séparent selon l'homme qui écrit. L'écriture d'un même auteur peut être différente avec un changement de l'espace et du temps; les pages écrites au même lieu et au même moment peuvent être différentes selon le genre littéraire; l'écriture d'un même genre peut aussi être différente en vertu du sujet et du contenu. (1979:1389)

D'où le fait qu'un grand traître peut écrire des articles très patriotique, qu'un arriviste peut composer des textes fort désintéréssés. Pour conclure, Qian Zhongshu dit qu'on ne peut pas connaître l'homme par ses oeuvres, ni inversement.

Il est intéressant de comparer l'idée de Proust sur la relation entre l'écriture et l'homme avec ce qu'a dit Qian Zhongshu au même sujet. Les deux sont semblables en ce qui concerne la démarcation entre l'oeuvre et l'homme. Ils sont tous deux d'accord sur le point que la vie privée d'un écrivain ne peut pas expliquer son oeuvre, ni inversement. Mais Proust et Qian Zhongshu ont un point de divergence de fond sur ce qui est au-delà de cette démarcation de fait. Proust a insisté sur l'oeuvre et l'homme en tant qu'auteur sans se préoccuper de la conduite réelle de l'écrivain, c'est-à-dire, de l'homme social dont les vices dans la vie privée n'étaient pour lui qu'un fait à constater sans le faire entrer dans la compréhension et l'interprétation de l'oeuvre. En revanche, Qian Zhongshu a reconnu cette démarcation entre l'oeuvre et l'homme, tout en faisant un pas de plus, c'est dire qu'il s'intéresse à celui qui écrit dans le but de critiquer cette démarcation. Il plaint toujours un écrivain sans vertu qui a composé de belles oeuvres.

Bien que Marcel Proust ait mis, en principe, une fin à la méthode biographique de Sainte-Beuve, les critiques n'en ont pas pour autant abandonné définitivement cette tentative de chercher une identité entre l'homme et l'oeuvre. Ils y arrivent quelquefois pourtant. Et Qian Zhongshu cherche, pour sa part, à établir une relation de sincérité entre les deux. Il a donc exprimé une exigence morale à l'égard de l'auteur en tant qu'homme sociale, ce qui montre qu'il a rompu avec la tradition tout en essayant de sauver ce qui mérite d'être sauvé. Cela veut dire que, quand il lit un texte littéraire, il n'écartera jamais purement et simplement l'auteur en tant qu'homme sociale, parce qu'il reconnaît une relation qui existe entre les deux, une relation tantôt d'identité, tantôt de contraire. A ses yeux, si l'on ne peut pas connaître l'homme par l'oeuvre ou inversement, c'est parce qu'on ne peut pas le faire de façon directe. Il n'y a pas de droit chemin entre les deux. Mais cela n'empêche pas qu'il se trouve une voie de biais qui servira de fil d'Ariane aux critiques afin qu'ils ne s'égarent pas dans le labyrinthe des relations entre l'homme et l'oeuvre.

Vers cette fin du siècle, dans tous les pays du monde, un doute se répand sérieusement sur le rôle de gardiens des valeurs et de directeur de conscience que beaucoup d'intellectuels, y compris les gens de lettres, ont prétendu jouer. Il provient, dans une large mesure, de ce relâchement des moeurs parmi les intellectuels, manifestant en Chine notamment depuis l'établissement de l'économie de marché. D'une part, leurs propositions pour guérir la société de ses maux ne sont pas nécessairement valables; de l'autre, ils n'ont pas pu eux-mêmes les pratiquer honorablement, notamment sur le plan éthique. Ce n'est pas que l'intelligentsia chinoise comme étrangère a voulu se désister de son rôle de directeur de conscience, mais le fait est que l'une et l'autre sont en train de perdre du terrain.

Une société civilisée a besoin de mythes et d'utopies et, créer des mythes et des utopies, voilà une des fonctions essentielles des gens de lettres. Pour remplir cette fonction, il faut que les gens de lettres se dotent d'une autorité morale, le talent et le savoir seuls n'étant pas suffisants. Les gens de lettres sans vertu continueront à écrire et même à gagner la notoriété, mais la démarcation entre l'écriture et l'homme a déjà mis les intellectuels dans un embarras indicible. Pessimiste ou optimiste, l'intelligentsia a toujours son rôle à jouer, même si elle avait une nouvelle identité à retrouver. Personne ne pourra se dérober à ces ennuis causés par la démarcation entre l'homme et l'oeuvre.

Académie des Sciences Sociales de Chine

Oeuvres Citées

Cao Pi 1979 'Dianlun. Lunwen' dans *Zhongguo lidai lunwen xuan*, t.1. Shanghaï Guji Chubanshe.
Proust, Marcel 1954 *Contre Sainte-Beuve*. Gallimard, Paris.
Qian Zhongshu 1979 *Guanzhui bian*, t.4. Zhonghua shuju, Beijing.

CAO SHUNQING

Reconstructing Chinese Literary Discourse

In the long history of Chinese civilization, there have been conflicts and collusion between the Southern and Northern cultures, and also confrontation and blending between the East and the West (Sino-India and Sino-Japan). Nevertheless Chinese culture has deep roots, and it occupies the mainstream position with broad acceptability. Toward the end of the nineteenth century, Chinese culture was, for the first time, challenged by the West. Not only did the Western powers literally blast open the iron door of the Empire, they also cleared the way for infiltration of Western culture into China. At this crucial time, China had to 'seek new voices from the foreign lands'. It was a painful process, and one which had to be undertaken at the expense of traditional culture.

But the advocacy of the new at the expense of the old since the May 4th Movement has led to a dilemma. Occidentalization insulted the Chinese people. Signs which stated that 'Chinese and dogs are prohibited' filled thinking Chinese with righteous indignation. When Wen Yiduo went to the United States of America to study the culture of the West, he was shocked by anti-Chinese insults. 'We are people with our own country', he wrote. 'Ours is the one with a history and culture of five thousand years. Why aren't we the equal of the Americans. Is it because we can't make powerful guns that we are not as fair-minded as foreigners? It is hard to describe how our people are looked down upon.' In Yu Dafu's novel, *Sinking*, the hero commits suicide because of the Japanese insults directed at his motherland.

These insults injured national pride. Lu Xun's *True Story of A Q* portrays the result on the Chinese soul. But the disturbed mind of A Q as an artistic model for national consciousness has long been disputed by Chinese academics who have based their interpretations on class. In fact, national consciousness is poorly analysed in China. What Lu Xun portrays is an abnormal mind, an attempt to give expresson to 'an absence of soul' which he sees in his countrymen.

This 'absence of soul' is one of the consequences of cultural discontinuity. A nation without a soul would gradually lose its cohesive force. And yet, the root of Chinese culture has not been lost, although it has been shaken. Many of the intellectuals who promoted occidentalization during the May 4th Movement were deeply attached to Chinese culture, and it is because of this attachment that we can understand why so many intellectuals were self-contradictory. Hu Shi, for example, was among the first to advocate both vernacular writing and occidentalization, but he also encouraged national cultural heritage. Lu Xun is recognized as the standard-bearer of the push to overthrow Confucian thinking, and the strongest critic of the repressive force of traditional culture. He called upon the younger generation to stop reading classical literature, but he himself was an expert in it.

The relationship between traditional Chinese culture and Western culture became a source of anxiety. Discussions revolved around how to solve the difficulties of the relationship, with the most extreme responses advocating total and uncritical acceptance. Some scholars identified an untenable dichotomy between self-importance and self-inferiority, caused by the difficulty of finding a balance. To examine the painful abnormality of the national consciousness is to discover the heavy losses caused by these two extremes of self-importance and self-inferiority. The question now is whether the Chinese people can confront this loss. If a powerful China is to emerge in the next century, as is predicted, there must be not only a healthy economic situation, but a flourishing cultural one as well.

❖

As the world becomes more pluralistic, China is poised to enter the arena. Professor Yu Daiyun (1992) has pointed out that signs of such a transformation have appeared since the Second World War. Economic pluralism, computer technology, the disintegration of the colonial system and the advancement of science have all shown that 'no system of centre is absolute or unchangeable'. In the next century, it is possible that different cultures will find their own strength, and that dialogue and mutual cooperation among pluralistic cultures will occur, and that this environment will make it possible for new systems and cultures to emerge.

For China, this is an opportunity not simply to follow the West, nor to return to tradition. By concentrating on mutual understanding and exchange, both Chinese and Western cultures can move forward, concentrating on difference as a method of mutual replenishment. Through dialogue, new cultures can benefit from cross-fertilization. Drawing on the particularities of cultural discourse, and using contemporary discourse analysis theory, these dialogues can advance the cause of cultural hybridity.

It is a pity that modern Chinese culture is reliant on Western theoretical discourse. The lack of a theory and methodology particular to Chinese cultural analysis means that, according to Sun Jin (1989:290), the concepts are occidentalized. In seeking 'new voices from foreign lands', we negate traditional culture and traditional literary discourse. For younger scholars, it seems that 'we have everything, but at the same time nothing' (Cao 1988:19). The current situation for modern literature has parallels in the study of ancient literature. Western discourse theory is frequently used to interpret ancient Chinese literature, causing certain problems. The lack of a Chinese theoretical discourse has been responsible for asphyxia in Chinese culture. If this is so, how can a culture suffering from asphyxia enter into dialogue with others?

It is essential, therefore, to establish this discourse, and on this question we may be enlightened by Afro-American efforts to construct a discourse of their own. In *The Future of Literary Theory*, Ralph Cohen (1993:12) suggests that feminist and black theoretical discourses are vital forces in the construction of new cultural and political movements. Henry Louis Gates Jr, an Afro-American literary theorist, points out the need to turn to 'peculiarly black structures of thought and feeling to develop our own language of criticism (Cohen 1993:230). Literary theorists lay stress on the reconstruction of black discourse by Gates and others because they predict a trend towards cultural pluralism, and towards dialogue between different cultures.

If it is possible for Afro-Americans, might it be possible for the Chinese? China has a cultural tradition of five thousand years, and has a history of systematic, rational formation of literary theory. Western literary theory dates from classical Greece to modern times and this forms a theoretical set. Classical Chinese literary theory also has its own discourse; for example, the remarkable achievements of traditional Chinese literature reflect the solid foundation and great vitality of Chinese poetic discourse. However, since the May 4th Movement, interpretative approaches have been mainly borrowed from foreign discourses. There is a solid historical basis for a new theoretical discourse to grow from ancient Chinese traditions, and it is necessary to understand these traditions in order to construct new ones. The particular patterns and characteristics of Chinese traditions must be understood. It must not be treated as a dead theory. Secondly, the new discourse should be able to serve all literatures, past and present, Chinese and foreign. And thirdly, while restoring Chinese literary discourse, and making it vital and active, a dialogue between the Chinese discourse and that of the West must be promoted. Within such exchange lies the opportunity for mutual understanding and replenishment, and for the coexistence of new systems of theoretical discourse.

Sichuan Union University

Works Cited

Cao Shunqing 1988 'The Discontinuity and Continuity of Chinese Literary Theory' in *Literary Circle Today*, no. 6.

Cohen, Ralph (ed.) 1993 *The Future of Literary Theory*, tr. Chen Xilin and Wang Xiaolu. China Social Sciences Publishing House, Beijing.

Sun Jin 1989 'The Philosophical Background of Chinese and Western Literary Theory' in *The Study of Cross-disciplinary Comparative Literature*. China Social Sciences Publishing House, Beijing.

Yu Daiyun 1992 'Cultural Transformation and the Dialogues between East and West' in *The Wind of the Century*, no. 2.

WILD PEONY PTY LTD BOOK PUBLISHERS A.C.N. 002 714 276
PO BOX 636 BROADWAY NSW 2007 AUSTRALIA
Fax: 61 2 9566 1052

International Distribution: University of Hawaii Press, 2840 Kolowalu Street, Honolulu Hawaii 96822. Fax: 1 808 988-6052.

- *Shijin: Autobiography of the Poet Kaneko Mitsuharu, 1895–1975*. Introduction and T5ranslations by A. R. Davis; edited by A. D. Syrokomla-Stefanowska. University of Sydney East Asian Series, No. 1; ISBN: 0 9590735 3 1; 1988; 324 pp.; hardcover:AUS $40.00

- Tanizaki Jun'ichiro, *A Cat, Shozo and Two Women*. Translated by Matsui Sakuko. University of Sydney East Asian Series, No. 2; ISBN: 0 9590735 5 8; 150 pp.; 1988; hardcover: AUS $27.95; softcover: AUS $12.95. NOT FOR SALE IN THE USA, CANADA AND UK.

- Yang Lian, *Masks and Crocodile: A Contemporary Chinese Poet and His Poetry*. Introduction and Translations by Mabel Lee; 12 coloured illustrations by Li Liang. University of Sydney East Asian Series, No. 3; ISBN: 0 9590735 7 4; 1990; 146 pp.; softcover: AUS $25.00

- *Gen'ei: Selected Poems of Nishiwaki Junzaburo, 1894–1982*. Translations by Yasuko Claremont. University of Sydney East Asian Series, No. 4; ISBN: 0 9590735 8 2; 1991; 120 pp.; softcover: AUS $19.95

- *Seven Stories of Modern Japan*. Edited by Leith Morton. Translations by H. Clarke, S. Matsui and L. Morton. University of Sydney East Asian Series, No. 5; ISBN: 0 9590735 9 0; 1991; $19.95

- *Kyunyŏ-jön: The Life, Times and Songs of a Tenth Century Korean Buddhist Monk*. Translated and annotated by Adrian Buzo and Tony Prince. University of Sydney East Asian Series, No. 6; ISBN: 0 646 14772 2; 1993; 142 pp.; softcover: AUS $25.00

- *Modernity in Asian Art*. Edited by John Clark. University of Sydney East Asian Series, No. 7; ISBN: 0 646 14773 0; 1993 350 pp.; softcover: AUS $37.50

- *The Chinese Femme Fatale: Short Stories of the Ming Period*. Translations by Anne McLaren. University of Sydney East Asian Series, No. 8; ISBN: 0 646 14924 5; 1994; 102pp.; softcover: AUS $22.95

- *Visiting the Mino Kilns*. Translation and Introduction by Janet Barriskill. University of Sydney East Asian Series, No. 9; ISBN: 0 646 20424 6; 1995; 90 pp. + colour plates 56 pp.; hardcover: AUS $65.00

- Mark Elvin, *Another History: Essays on China from a European Perspective*. University of Sydney East Asian Series, No. 10; ISBN: 0 646 20413 0; 1996; 389 pp.; softcover: AUS $47.50

- Mabel Lee and Meng Hua, *Cultural Dialogue and Misreading*. University of Sydney World Literature Series, No. 1; ISBN: 0 9586526 1 9; 1996; 422 pp.; softcover: AUS $45.00

- Mabel Lee and A. D. Syrokomla-Stefanowska (eds), *Modernization of the Chinese Past*. University of Sydney School of Asian Studies Series, No. 1; ISBN: 0 867 58658 3; 1993; 208 pp.; softcover: AUS $25.00

- Kam Louie, *Between Fact and Fiction: Essays on Post-Mao Literature and Society*; ISBN: 0 9590735 6 6; 1989; 149 pp.; softcover: AUS $22.75

- Lily Xiao Hong Lee, *The Virtue of Yin: Studies on Chinese Women*; ISBN: 0 646 14925 3; 1994; 117 pp.; softcover: AUS $18.95

- A. D. Syrokomla-Stefanowska, *A Classical Chinese Reader*, ISBN: 0 9586526 0 0; 192 pp.; softcover: AUS $40.00

- Mabel Lee and Zhang Wu-ai, *Putonghua: A Practical Course in Spoken Chinese*; ISBN: 0 9590735 0 7; 1984, 1989, 1992; 101 pp.; softcover: AUS $16.99. [Cassettes available from The Language Centre, University of Sydney NSW 2006, Australia.]

- A. D. Syrokomla-Stefanowska and Mabel Lee, *Basic Chinese Grammar and Sentence Patterns*; ISBN: 0 9590735 1 5; 1986, 1989, 1992; 99 pp.; softcover: AUS $16.99. [Cassettes available from The Language Centre, University of Sydney NSW 2006, Australia.]

- *Readings in Modern Chinese*. Compiled by Liu Wei-ping, Mabel Lee, A. J. Prince, Lily Shaw Lee and R. S. W. Hsu; ISBN: 0 9590735 4 X; 161 pp.; 1988, 1990, 1992; softcover: AUS $30.00. [Cassettes available from The Language Centre, University of Sydney NSW 2006, Australia.]

- Mabel Lee and Meng Hua, *Cultural Dialogue and Misreading*. University of Sydney World Literature Series, No. 1; ISBN: 0 9586526 1 9; 1996; 422 pp.; softcover: AUS $45.00

- Mabel Lee and A. D. Syrokomla-Stefanowska (eds), *Modernization of the Chinese Past*. University of Sydney School of Asian Studies Series, No. 1; ISBN: 0 867 58658 3; 1993; 208 pp.; softcover: AUS $25.00

- Kam Louie, *Between Fact and Fiction: Essays on Post-Mao Literature and Society*; ISBN: 0 9590735 6 6; 1989; 149 pp.; softcover: AUS $22.75

- Lily Xiao Hong Lee, *The Virtue of Yin: Studies on Chinese Women*; ISBN: 0 646 14925 3; 1994; 117 pp.; softcover: AUS $18.95

- A. D. Syrokomla-Stefanowska, *A Classical Chinese Reader*, ISBN: 0 9586526 0 0; 192 pp.; softcover: AUS $40.00

- Mabel Lee and Zhang Wu-ai, *Putonghua: A Practical Course in Spoken Chinese*; ISBN: 0 9590735 0 7; 1984, 1989, 1992; 101 pp.; softcover. AUS $16.99. [Cassettes available from The Language Centre, University of Sydney NSW 2006, Australia.]

- A. D. Syrokomla-Stefanowska and Mabel Lee, *Basic Chinese Grammar and Sentence Patterns*; ISBN: 0 9590735 1 5; 1986, 1989, 1992; 99 pp.; softcover: AUS $16.99. [Cassettes available from The Language Centre, University of Sydney NSW 2006, Australia.]

- *Readings in Modern Chinese*. Compiled by Liu Wei-ping, Mabel Lee, A. J. Prince, Lily Shaw Lee and R. S. W. Hsu; ISBN: 0 9590735 4 X; 161 pp.; 1988, 1990, 1992; softcover: AUS $30.00. [Cassettes available from The Language Centre, University of Sydney NSW 2006, Australia.]